Toward

a

General

Theory

of

Action

Toward

a

General

Theory

of

Action

TALCOTT PARSONS

EDWARD A. SHILS

EDITORS

EDWARD C. TOLMAN

GORDON W. ALLPORT

CLYDE KLUCKHOHN

HENRY A. MURRAY

ROBERT R. SEARS

RICHARD C. SHELDON

SAMUEL A. STOUFFER

HARPER TORCHBOOKS · THE ACADEMY LIBRARY

HARPER & ROW, PUBLISHERS, NEW YORK AND EVANSTON

Toward a General Theory of Action

Preface

In the fall of 1948 some members of the Department of Social Relations of Harvard University had an informal discussion with the officers of the Carnegie Corporation of New York about the possibility of a "stocktaking" of the theoretical resources of the field of Social Relations. It seemed to both groups that a careful analysis of the theoretical foundations underlying the synthesis which had been worked out on the organizational level through the foundation of the Department of Social Relations two years before might be useful not only in the Department itself but for the development of the social sciences generally. Within the Department it seemed likely to help greatly in clarifying the problems we faced individually in our teaching and research as well as in our corporate capacity as a department.

After some exploration of the feasibility of the project, the Carnegie Corporation kindly placed a grant at the disposal of the Department. This grant was supplemented by funds from the Laboratory of Social Relations at Harvard. Through the coöperation of Provost Paul H. Buck of Harvard, I was relieved of teaching and administrative duties for the fall term of 1949–50, and two distinguished scholars, Professor Edward C. Tolman of the University of California and Professor Edward A. Shils of the University of Chicago, were invited to come to Harvard for the term to collaborate in the project. In addition, the services of Richard C. Sheldon, Fellow of the Russian Research Center and a social anthropologist, were made available on a full-time basis. The four of us constituted the staff of the project.

In addition to the direct work of the staff, we decided to hold a series of discussions with each of two groups, out of which it was hoped that clear lines of thinking would emerge. Because of the great advantages of discussion in a small group, especially when such subtle questions are at issue, one such group was organized. This, besides the four staff members, consisted in the five who have collaborated with the staff in the present volume. However, this policy, if adhered to alone, would have meant going without the extremely valuable contributions of many other, especially the younger, members of the Department. Hence all interested members of the Department were invited to participate with the staff in a second discussion group on theoretical problems. Many of the more important ideas published here owe much to this larger, and younger, group.

Both of these groups met weekly from late September 1949 through January 1950. A highly informal procedure was followed. There had previously been circulated within the Department some three versions of a document

entitled "Assumptions of Basic Social Science," which had been formulated
in connection with the departmental proseminar on Problems and Concepts
of Social Relations.* This document was taken as the point of departure, and
various attempts to begin a revision of it were made. Some members of the
group also drafted memoranda on particular theoretical problem areas.
In November we reached agreement that the general theoretical scheme in
which we were interested could be couched within what we agreed (in the
smaller group) to call the "action" frame of reference. Shortly after that, stimulated especially by Clyde Kluckhohn's presentation, before the smaller group,
of his approach to the analysis of values, the staff evolved a number of new
theoretical insights and developments. All of the subsequent meetings were devoted to discussion of various aspects of these developments and their possible
implications.

Work was not, however, limited to the weekly meetings; we had many personal discussions and applied ourselves to writing as well. After many long
discussions with Edward Shils, I undertook the first draft of what appears in
this volume as Part II, "Values, Motives, and Systems of Action"; Professor
Shils took the lead in the draft's extensive revision. Professor Tolman began
work on his "Psychological Model," which forms Part III of this book. Mr.
Sheldon's contribution, "Some Observations on Theory in Social Science,"
appears as Chapter II of Part I.†

The question of exactly what the material outcome of the project would be
had to be left in abeyance until we could explore the implications of some of
the new developments. It finally was agreed to prepare the present volume for
publication and to include contributions from the staff and also papers from
the other participants in the smaller discussion group. It was decided that
the non-staff collaborators would write on a subject of particular personal interest which would be relevant to the general theoretical field of the project.
These papers make up Part IV of this volume. This made such a large book
that, unfortunately, contributions from members of the larger discussion
group were precluded; hence, as noted, the book fails to do justice to their
important part in the project.

It gradually became clear that what originally had been drafted as an
introductory chapter of Part II contained the basis of an agreed statement
of general principle. Though this draft, which in turn was based on many
discussions, provided the starting point, it was subjected to several severe
— indeed radical — revisions before it emerged as the "General Statement"
which forms the first chapter of Part I. All members of the group contributed
careful and detailed critical comments on several of the drafts, so that as far

---

* The principal authors were Professors Kluckhohn and Murray.

† Mr. Sheldon also carried the heavy burden of supervising the production of a record
of the weekly meetings; this unfortunately limited the time he could devote to theoretical
work as such.

as humanly possible, the statement represents both a carefully considered and a collaborative product. To be sure that no member of the group was having views attributed to him which he did not really share, we agreed that each one should have the privilege of including over his own initials notes of explication or dissent on particular points. The fact that only two members have availed themselves of this privilege, one of them mainly for clarification, is, we feel, an index of the fullness of the measure of agreement we have been able to attain.

This volume thus is the product of nine individual social scientists. The whole character of the enterprise, however, and the constitution of the group, which included four psychologists, three sociologists, and two anthropologists, make its relation to current movements of thought in the field of some interest. Many influences and sources are discernible in the material here set forth. Perhaps the two most important sources in the field of psychology are the study of human personality and the study of animal behavior. The former involves Freud, and the movements stemming from his work, perhaps more than any other influence, but this stream has flowed through several channels — and in its course has influenced the sociologists and anthropologists in the group as well as the psychologists. Other influences have also been important in their effect on personality theory, particularly those documented in Gordon Allport's book on that subject. The study of animal behavior is, we believe, relatively catholic in its influence upon us.

Sociologically, we have been strongly influenced, especially through two of the group, by the work of the Europeans, Durkheim and Max Weber. Professor Stouffer, however, can be said to represent an almost wholly American influence, with the ideas of W. I. Thomas and Park especially prominent in his theoretical thinking. Finally, on the anthropological side, we also have a variety of sources: Boas, Kroeber, and Sapir stand out, but there are many others as well.

Another significant feature of the background of the group is that quite clearly the major trend of thinking of each member has been notably influenced by more than one "school" and more than one discipline. It might perhaps be said that the very fact that we do embody so many different influences has made it all the more urgent for us to attempt to synthesize our thinking. The process has not been altogether easy. Some of us have been closely associated over a considerable span of years. But when we tried to drive mutuality of understanding to deeper theoretical levels than was usual in our discourse, we frequently found unexpected and apparently serious differences — some of which, of course, were attributable to our having been educated in different academic disciplines, each with its sensitivities and blind spots. However, with patience and persistence, we have found it possible to make what, to us, is substantial progress toward agreement.

This fact, combined with the very diversity of the influences which, through their importance to us, have gone into this product, seems to us to bring out with peculiar vividness the fact that these many streams of thought are in the process of flowing together. We feel that the present effort belongs in the context of a major movement, whose significance to the future of social science far transcends the contributions of any one particular group. If we have helped to deepen the channel of the river and remove some obstacles to its flow, we are content.

Finally, those of us on the regular Harvard staff must acknowledge our special debt to our two visiting collaborators. They contributed not only their great knowledge, acute understanding, and fresh points of view, but through unfailing tact were able to serve as most effective catalytic agents. Their value to the project has been incalculable.

Talcott Parsons

Contents

PART 3 A Psychological Model

Edward C. Tolman

PART 4 The Theory of Action and Its Application

1

The General Theory of Action

1

Some Fundamental Categories of the Theory
of Action: A General Statement

1. INTRODUCTION

The present statement and the volume which it introduces are intended to contribute to the establishment of a general theory in the social sciences. Theory in the social sciences should have three major functions. First, it should aid in the codification of our existing concrete knowledge. It can do so by providing generalized hypotheses for the systematic reformulation of existing facts and insights, by extending the range of implication of particular hypotheses, and by unifying discrete observations under general concepts. Through codification, general theory in the social sciences will help to promote the process of cumulative growth of our knowledge. In making us more aware of the interconnections among items of existing knowledge which are now available in a scattered, fragmentary form, it will help us fix our attention on the points where further work must be done.

Second, general theory in the social sciences should be a guide to research. By codification it enables us to locate and define more precisely the boundaries of our knowledge and of our ignorance. Codification facilitates the selection of problems, although it is not, of course, the only useful technique for the selection of problems for fruitful research. Further than this, general theory should provide hypotheses to be applied and tested by the investigation of these problems. If research problems are formulated in terms of systematically derived theoretical hypotheses, the resulting propositions will in turn contribute toward both the validation and revision of the theory.

Third, general theory as a point of departure for specialized work in the social sciences will facilitate the control of the biases of observation and interpretation which are at present fostered by the departmentalization of education and research in the social sciences.

This statement does not itself purport to be the general theory which will adequately fulfill these three functions. It is rather a formulation of certain fundamental categories which will have to enter into the formulation of this general theory, which for many years has been developing through the convergence of anthropological studies of culture, the theory of learning, the psychoanalytic theory of personality, economic theory,[1] and the study of modern social structure.

2. THE FRAME OF REFERENCE OF THE THEORY OF ACTION

The present discussion will begin with an exposition of the fundamental concepts from which it is intended to develop a unified conceptual scheme for theory and research in the social sciences. In accordance with already widespread usage, we shall call these concepts the *frame of reference of the theory of action*. In order to make the rest of the exposition comprehensible, we shall define a considerable number of the concepts [2] and state their more general bearing on our problem.

ORIENTATION AND SITUATION

In the theory of action the point of reference of all terms is the action of an individual actor or of a collectivity of actors. Of course, all individual actors are, in one aspect, physiological organisms; collectivities of actors are made up of individual actors, who are similarly physiological organisms. The interest of the theory of action, however, is directed not to the physiological processes internal to the organism but rather to the organization of the actor's orientations to a situation. When the terms refer to a collectivity as the acting unit, it is understood that it does not refer to all of the actions of the individuals who are its members, but only to the actions which they perform in their capacity as members. Whether the acting unit is an individual or a collectivity, we shall speak of the actor's *orientation of action* when we describe the action. The concept *motivation* in a strict sense applies only to individual actors. The motivational components of the action of collectivities are organized systems of the motivation of the relevant individual actors. Action has an orientation when it is guided by the meaning which the actor attaches to it in its relationship to his goals and interests.

Each orientation of action in turn involves a set [3] of *objects of orientation*. These are objects which are relevant in the situation because they afford alternative possibilities and impose limitations on the modes of gratifying the

---

[1] See note at end of chapter.

[2] The authors are fully aware of the difficulty of standardizing terminology in the present state of social science. The difficulty is great particularly in view of the heterogeneity of the sources from which the terms here used have been drawn and the new emphasis we have often given them. We are not all equally satisfied with every term, and we do not regard ourselves as bound to use exactly this terminology each in his own work. We have merely endeavored to be as clear as possible, to avoid violent neologisms, and to use terms which would be as nearly acceptable to all members of the group as possible.

[3] The word *set* is used to designate a plurality of entities determinately limited in number and range of variation but not necessarily conceived as interdependent so as to constitute a system.

needs and achieving the goals of the actor or actors.[4] A situation provides two major classes of objects to which the actor who is the point of reference may be oriented. These are either (1) nonsocial, that is, physical objects or accumulated cultural resources, or (2) social objects, that is, individual actors and collectivities. Social objects include the subject's own personality as well as the personalities of other individuals. Where collectivities are objects, sectors of the action systems of a plurality of individual actors form a system which is an object for the actor or actors who are our point of reference. A specific combination of selections relative to such objects, made from among the possibilities of selection which were available in a specific situation, constitutes an orientation of action for a particular actor. The organized plurality of such orientations of action constitutes a system of action.[5]

The orientation of action to objects entails selection, and possibly choice. Selection is made possible by *cognitive* discriminations, the location and characterization of the objects, which are simultaneously or successively experienced as having positive or negative value to the actor, in terms of their relevance to satisfaction of drives [6] and their organization in motivation. This tendency to react positively or negatively to objects we shall call the *cathectic mode of orientation.* Cathexis, the attachment to objects which are gratifying and rejection of those which are noxious, lies at the root of the selective nature of action.[7] Furthermore, since selection must be made among alternative objects and gratifications at a single point of time or through time, there must be some evaluative criteria. The tendency of the organism toward integration requires the assessment and comparison of immediate cognized objects and cathectic interests in terms of their remoter consequences for the larger unit of evaluation. *Evaluation* rests on standards which may be either cognitive standards of truthfulness, appreciative standards of appropriateness, or moral standards of rightness. Both the motivational orientations and the value-orientations are modes of distinguishing, testing, sorting, and selecting. They are, in short, the categories for the description,

[4] The establishment of a definite relationship with objects (e.g., their possession or modification) or the creation of objects may be among the goals sought by actors. Objects once created may in turn become objects of orientation in ensuing actions.

[5] The word *system* is used in the sense that determinate relations of interdependence exist within the complex of empirical phenomena. The antithesis of the concept of system is random variability. However, no implication of rigidity is intended.

[6] By *drive* we mean the *organic energy* component of motivation with whatever elements of organization and directionality may be given with the *genetic constitution* of the organism.

[7] Human beings do much which is inhibiting or destructive of their interests in its consequences; hence the naïve hedonism which maintains that the gratification of a wish explains every overt act is clearly untenable. However, to deny that even self-destructive acts are motivated equally fails to make sense. The postulate that the course of behavior, at least at certain points where alternatives were open, has had motivational significance to the actor, that in some sense he "wanted" to do it, is essential to any logical theory of behavior.

on the most elementary level, of the orientation of action, which is a constellation of selections from alternatives.

It is essential to point out that a description of a system of action must refer not only to the particular constellation of orientations and sets of objects actually selected, but also to the alternative sets from which the selections might have been made but were not. In other words, we are concerned not only with how an actor actually views a situation, but also with how he might view it. This inclusiveness is required for the purposes of a dynamic theory of action which would attempt to explain why one alternative rather than another was selected.

The range of the alternatives of action orientation is determinate; it is inherent in the relation of the actor to the situation and derives ultimately from certain general properties of the organism and the nature of objects in their relation to such organisms. This determinate range of the alternatives which are available for selection marks the limits within which variability is possible.

DESCRIPTIVE AND DYNAMIC ANALYSIS

The complete analysis of a system of action would comprise description both of the state of the system at the given moment and of the changes in the system through time, involving changes in the relations of the constituent variables. This dynamic analysis would treat the *processes* of action and is the proper goal of conceptualization and theory construction. But we feel that it is uneconomical to describe changes in systems of variables before the variables themselves have been isolated and described; therefore, we have chosen to begin by studying particular combinations of variables and to move toward a description of how these combinations change only when a firm foundation for such analysis has been laid. Hence, it should be understood that when we describe the orientations of action in a given system, we are describing the state of the system at a given moment. The variables to which we refer in the analysis of given orientations are also those referred to in the analysis of the processes which maintain one system of orientation rather than another; these same variables are also dealt with in the analysis of the processes in which, through change in the values of the variables, one orientation changes into another. There is, thus, no difference between the variables involved in description of the state of a system and analysis of its processes. The difference lies in how the same variables are used.

PERSONALITY, SOCIAL SYSTEM, AND CULTURE

The frame of reference of the theory of action applies in principle to any segment of the total round of action or to any process of action of any complex organism. The elaboration of behavior to which this conceptual scheme is especially appropriate, however, occurs above all in human action.

In the formation of systems made up of human actions or the components of human action, this elaboration occurs in three configurations. First, the orientation of action of *any one* given actor and its attendant motivational processes becomes a differentiated and integrated system. This system will be called the *personality*, and we will define it as the organized system of the orientation and motivation of action of one individual *actor*.[8] Secondly, the action of a plurality of actors in a common situation is a process of interaction, the properties of which are to a definite but limited extent independent of any prior common culture. This interaction also becomes differentiated and integrated and as such forms a social system. The social system is, to be sure, made up of the relationships of individuals, but it is a system which is organized around the problems inherent in or arising from social interaction of a plurality of individual actors rather than around the problems which arise in connection with the integration of the actions of an individual actor, who is also a physiological organism. Personality and social system are very intimately interrelated, but they are neither identical with one another nor explicable by one another; the social system is not a plurality of personalities. Finally, systems of culture have their own forms and problems of integration which are not reducible to those of either personality or social systems or both together. The cultural tradition in its significance both as an *object* of orientation and as an *element* in the orientation of action must be articulated both conceptually and empirically with personalities and social systems. Apart from embodiment in the orientation systems of concrete actors, culture, though existing as a body of artifacts and as systems of symbols, is not in itself organized as a system of action. Therefore, culture as a system is on a different plane from personalities and social systems.[9]

Concrete systems of action — that is, personalities and social systems — have psychological, social, and cultural aspects. For one thing, the state of the system must be characterized in terms of certain of the motivational properties of the individual actors. The description of a system of action must employ the categories of motivational orientation: cognition, cathexis, and evaluation. Likewise, the description of an action system must deal with the properties of the system of interaction of two or more individuals or collective actors — this is the social aspect — and it must note the conditions which interaction imposes on the participating actors. It must also take into account the cultural tradition as an object of orientation as well as culture patterns as internalized patterns of cognitive expectations and of cathectic-evaluative selection among possible orientations that are of crucial significance in the personality system and in the social system.

[8] The physiological aspect of the human organism is relevant to action theory only as it impinges on the orientation system. However, phantasies and imaginative productions, though they may not refer directly to any realistic situational objects, are unequivocally part of the orientation of personality as a system of action.

[9] Mr. Sheldon dissents from this view. His grounds are stated in Chapter II.

Cultural elements as constituents of systems of action may be classified in two ways. First, they may be differentiated according to the predominance of types of interests corresponding to the predominance of each of the modes of motivational orientation. Second, culture patterns as objects of the situation may be distinguished from culture patterns as internalized components of the orientation system of the actor. These two classifications cut across each other.

In the first method of classification it is convenient to distinguish the following three major classes of culture patterns. (1) Systems of ideas or beliefs. Although cathexis and evaluation are always present as orientational components, these cultural systems are characterized by a primacy of cognitive interests. (2) Systems of expressive symbols; for instance, art forms and styles. These systems are characterized by a primacy of cathectic interests. (3) Systems of value-orientations. Here the primary interest is in the evaluation of alternatives from the viewpoint of their consequences or implications for a system of action or one of its subsystems.

With respect to the second classification, it is quite clear that culture patterns are frequently objects of orientation in the same sense as other types of objects.[10] The actor knows their properties (for example, he understands an idea); he "responds" to them (that is, he is attracted or repelled by them); and he evaluates them. Under certain circumstances, however, the manner of his involvement with a cultural pattern as an object is altered, and what was once an object becomes a constitutive part of the actor. When, for example, he cannot violate a moral rule without intense feelings of guilt, the rule is functioning as a constitutive part of his system of orientation; it is part of his personality. Where this occurs a culture pattern has been internalized.

Before we continue with an elaboration of each of the above three major types of system into which the components of action become organized and differentiated — personality, cultural systems, and social systems — it is essential to review briefly certain other categories of action in general, particularly those that have been developed in behavior psychology.

3. Some Fundamentals of Behavior Psychology

NEEDS AND THE ORGANIZATION OF BEHAVIOR

Certain trends in psychological theory have placed the primary sources of the organization of behavior into the constitution of the organism. They

---

[10] A special position is occupied by physical artifacts which are the products of action. Like the objects of the natural environment they do not *interact* with the actor. They are situational objects which cannot be internalized into the orientation system of the actor. They might serve as instrumental objects in action systems or they might have "meaning" conferred on them by value-orientation systems, in the same way that meaning is conferred on objects of the natural environment.

have done this through some version of the "instinct" theory. This tendency
has continually been challenged by demonstrations of the range of plasticity
of the organism and the corresponding importance of "learning" — a chal-
lenge which has been greatly accentuated by the cultural relativity disclosed
through the work of social anthropology and sociology.

The present analysis will observe a rule of parsimony with regard to assumptions about the constitutional organization of the tendencies of behavior.
There is certainly a system of viscerogenic needs which are grounded in the
interchange of the organism as a physiological system with its environment.
Some of them are highly specific: the need for food is relatively specific;
the needs for sleep and for breathing are much more so. The object which
is constitutionally most appropriate for the cathexis of a viscerogenic need
is, however, seldom absolutely specific. But, on the other hand, the range
of variability open to action and cultural definition always has some limits.
Among these needs which come to be of primary importance for action,
however, the degree of specificity usually tends to be slight, particularly in
the mode as distinct from the fact of gratification. In general, there is a
wide range of variability of the objects and modes of gratification of any
constitutionally given need. In addition to the viscerogenic needs there seem
to be certain needs for "social relationships." These might be constitutionally
given or they might, by being indirectly necessary for the gratification of
viscerogenic needs, be derivative in their origin and come subsequently to
acquire autonomy.

We assume then a set of needs which, although initially organized through
physiological processes, do not possess the properties that permit these physiological processes to be exclusively determinative in the organization of action.
In other words, the direction and modes in which these needs can determine
action is modifiable by influence emanating from the situation of action.
Moreover, the needs themselves can be modified, or at least their effect on
action is modifiable, by the process of becoming embedded into need-
dispositions.

However, even though the set of viscerogenic needs has initially a physiological organization, it possesses one persistent property which plays a
central role as the set of needs evolves into the system of need-dispositions.
It is incipiently organized with respect to a positive-negative discrimination;
that is, it discriminates between need-gratifying and need-blocking or need-
depriving aspects [11] of the situational object system. This discrimination is

[11] *Deprivation* is to be understood here as subsuming: (1) the withdrawal of gratifying objects already possessed by the actor; (2) the obstruction of access to gratifying
objects which the actor does not possess and for which he is striving; (3) the enforced
relationship with objects which are not gratifying, e.g., physical or psychological suffering
of positive pain or injury (this category includes both actively encountering and passively
receiving pain, etc.); (4) the threat of any of the foregoing. Responses by the actors to
each of these types of deprivation might vary considerably.

the point of departure of a complex process of further differentiation into need-dispositions [12] which might possess varying degrees of specificity. In addition to the specific viscerogenic needs and the wider discrimination between gratification and deprivation, the human organism has a constitutional capacity to react to objects, especially other human beings, without the specific content or form of the reaction being in any way physiologically given. This reactive capacity or potentiality may be likened to the capacity to learn language, which is certainly not constitutionally specific to any particular language, and if the individual is not exposed to speech of other human beings, may not be activated at all. The human organism has a "sensitivity" to other objects, a potentiality of cathecting them as objects in various ways, depending on the context of orientation and situation.

This sensitivity extends to nonsocial objects but it is especially significant where *inter*action is involved. Moreover, this sensitivity is, like the discriminatory tendency to which we have already referred, inherently responsive to experience in interactive relationships. On the one hand, gratifying experience with an object engenders a positive attachment-seeking and -forming tendency; on the other, deprivation from an object predisposes the actor to a reaction of flight, escape, or aggression, a tendency to avoid or injure the object in order to control or forestall the deprivational effect of its action.

COGNITIVE AND CATHECTIC ORIENTATION IN THE ORGANIZATION OF ACTION

Impelled by its drives and needs, the acting organism is oriented to social and nonsocial objects in two essential, simultaneous, and inseparable modes. First, it "cathects" particular objects or classes of objects through attributing to them significance for direct gratification or deprivation of impulse-needs.[13] It may become attached to an object as a source of gratification [14] or

---

[12] The term *need-disposition* has been chosen to emphasize that in action the unit of motivation faces two ways. On the one hand, it is involved in the equilibrium of the actor as a personality (and organism), and on the other, it is a disposition to act in relation to one or more objects. Both references are essential. It is to be distinguished from *need* by its higher degree of organization and by its inclusion of motivational and evaluative elements which are not given by viscerogenic needs.

[13] A distinction between *affect* and *cathexis* is desirable for present purposes. *Affect* refers to a state of the organism — a state of euphoria or dysphoria or qualitative variants thereof. *Cathexis* refers to a state of the organism — a state of euphoria or dysphoria — *in relationship to some object*. Thus the term *cathexis* is broader in its reference than the term *affect*; it is *affect plus object*. It is *object-oriented affect*. It involves attaching affective significance to an object; although it involves attachment to one or more properties of the object, as used here it does not itself refer to a property of the object, but to a *relation* between actor and object. Furthermore, there is no connotation either of activity or passivity in the actor's relation to the object implied in the concept.

[14] The content of the gratifications need not be specified here. Gratifications may of course include those experiences or states which are normally viewed as pleasures, such as love, physical comfort; they may also under certain conditions include certain experiences ordinarily conceived as deprivational, such as pain, horror, disgust, but which because of the organization of a given personality system may have gratifying consequences.

repelled by it as a source of deprivation. Second, it cognizes the object field, discriminating any particular object from others and otherwise assessing its properties. Only when the actor knows the relations of objects to one another and to his own needs can his behavior become organized with reference to cathectic-cognitive discriminations.

The essential phenomena in motivational orientation are thus cognitive and cathectic discriminations among objects. When these discriminations become organized in a stable way, they form a system of orientation. The actor *selects* or is *committed* to culturally imposed selections among accessible objects with respect to their potentialities for gratification; he also selects from among the modes of their possible significance to him. The most primitive forms of this selectivity are perhaps acceptance — for instance, incorporation of food, remaining in a comfortable place, etc. — and rejection — spitting out, withdrawal from, or avoidance.

Cathectic-cognitive orientation toward the object world, in any system of behavior extending through time, always entails *expectations* concerning gratifications or deprivations receivable or attainable from certain objects and classes of objects. Action involves not merely discrimination and selection between immediately present objects, and the directly ensuing striving, acceptance, or rejection, but it involves also an orientation to *future* events with respect to their significance for gratification or deprivation. A discrimination between immediately available and future gratifications and the assessment of their relative value is an essential aspect of action.

EXPECTATIONS AND EVALUATIONS

Where there are alternative opportunities for gratification in a present situation and alternatives distributed among present and expected situations, the actor must have some means of deciding which of the alternatives or combinations of alternatives he should follow. The process of deciding among alternatives, of assessing them in the light of their ramified consequences, is called *evaluation*. Evaluation is the more complex process of selection built upon the discriminations which make up the cognitive-cathectic orientation.

There is a variety of possible ways in which action can be organized with respect to expected events. One of the most important categories of reaction to expectations is that of activity-passivity. On the one hand, the actor may *actively* seek out objects and manipulate them in the interest of his goals,[15] or he may explore the situation seeking previously unrecognized opportunities. Alternatively, he may passively *await* the impact of expected situations

---

[15] The cognitive-cathectic and evaluative orientations are connected by the "effort" of the actor. In accordance with a value standard and/or an expectation, the actor through effort manipulates his own resources, including his own body, voice, etc., in order to facilitate the direct or indirect approximation to a certain cathected goal — object or state.

and renounce interest in positive but still unattained goals. (There are various possible combinations of active and passive elements, such as the positive effort to escape from a situation expected to be threatening or enlisting the aid of others to cope with a threat.)

LEARNING

Learning [16] becomes relevant at this point in the development of the frame of reference of the theory of action. Learning is not merely the acquisition of "information" (that is, specific items of cognitive orientation) about the properties of the object world; it is also the acquisition of new "patterns of orientation." That is, it involves acquiring new ways of seeing, wanting, and evaluating; these are predispositions to approach or avoid, to seek actively in certain types of situation or to "lie low" and wait, to keep away from noxious objects or to control them.

Of fundamental importance in learning is the degree and incidence of generalization [17] which is introduced into the actor's orientations to his object world. Generalizations are modes of defining the actor's orientations to particular objects of which he has not yet had experience. This entails the categorization of the particular, concrete objects of his situation into general classes. In the acquisition of systems of cultural symbols, generalization is perhaps the most important of the learning mechanisms. As frames of reference, as the content of communication, and as the foci of common orientations, cultural patterns must possess content with a degree of generality which transcends the particularity of all concrete situations and experiences. Generalization through a cognitive process has consequences for the cathectic aspect of orientation. For example, through generalization it is possible to cathect categories of objects as well as particular objects.

Generalization as a cognitive mechanism orders the object world and thereby defines the structure of alternatives open to the orientation of action. The world in the actor's expectations comes to be composed of classes of objects, as well as particular objects, defined and differentiated by properties significant to the actor. Furthermore, the experiences of gratification or deprivation from particular objects may be generalized to other objects which are, in the actor's definition of the situation, classified with the original objects.

---

[16] Learning is the acquisition of changed modes of orientation to the object world, including in the latter the actor's personality, ideas, culture, social objects, etc.

[17] It is recognized that the term "generalization" has two principal current meanings: (1) the discrimination of the objects in what had previously been a single undifferentiated category to constitute two or more classes still possessing certain common features, and (2) the discernment of common properties in a group of events previously discriminated as different. The common element of the two meanings is the organization of the object world into categories. If it is important to distinguish the two meanings, the applicable meaning will be made clear.

CONSTITUTIONAL AND LEARNED COMPONENTS OF
GENERALIZED NEED-DISPOSITIONS

Anxiety is one type of generalized expectation of deprivation from a class of objects to which the actor is also simultaneously attached. There is a constitutional basis for the reaction to danger which is usually called fear. We speak of anxiety when this reaction to danger is generalized and organized as a need-disposition to anticipate a large class of deprivations. Anxiety exists where the actor "cries before he is hurt"; whether the anticipated deprivation is attributed to his inadequacy, to others, or to "circumstances" is a further distinction which we need not consider here. An anxiety, which might have originated in the fear of a specific class of objects, might become so highly generalized as to permeate virtually the whole system of orientation of a personality. Corresponding to anxiety and fear is the obverse generalized expectation of gratification in what is commonly referred to as optimism or a sense of security.

Some psychologists have tended to treat "aggressiveness" as a set of impulses constitutionally given in the organism.[18] It seems probable that a disposition to "strike back" if attacked or under certain types of intense strain is at least latent in normal human organisms. This disposition will be activated under certain conditions and if it is not overlaid by conflicting motives. However, such an innate disposition does not in any simple way determine responses to an experience or expectation of deprivation. Such responses, when organized as part of the actor's orientation, and if they include a disposition to injure or destroy the object felt to be the source of the deprivation, may be called *aggressiveness*. Aggressiveness, powerful and fundamental as it is, may take many forms; by itself it is one among a set of alternative responses to threats of deprivation. The other responses include withdrawal and avoidance or simply waiting passively for deprivations to occur. Furthermore, aggressiveness as a need-disposition may well be associated with actions which overtly are not aggressive. Which of these alternatives is chosen seems to depend on the prevalence of integrative predispositions [19] in the actor's personality system, which may suppress the expression of aggressive impulses in favor of alternative actions, such as a general tendency to "mastery" over situations as against a tendency to "passivity." Aggressiveness, then, is here treated as the manifestation in the organized orientation of action of the need-disposition to remove, injure, or destroy an object; the constitutional capacity for anger is a part of the organized need-disposition of aggressiveness.

[18] The capacity to experience anger may be different from the disposition to strike back if attacked. Both, of course, may be learned; but they seem to have some innate foundation.

[19] Including internalized cultural norms and the influence of the particular situation.

The individual actor possesses a large set of need-dispositions, some of which are active at the same time that others are quiescent. The gratification and quiescence of one need-disposition may be the signal for the activation of another and vice versa. Two or more need-dispositions are often concurrently activated, pressing the actor toward the performance of conflicting actions which are incompatible in the sense that gratifying one of the need-dispositions entails the deprivation of others. The actor seeking to achieve gratification and avoid deprivation is seldom, within a short time, capable of extirpating or extinguishing a well-established need-disposition even though its overt gratification may entail serious consequences for him. Through the process of evaluation, which operates unconsciously as well as deliberately, he will very often strike some sort of compromise among his conflicting need-dispositions, both simultaneously and over a period of time. Since deprivation is to be avoided or minimized, and since the situation makes some deprivation unavoidable, the compromise represents in some sense the best available in the circumstances, given both the exigencies of the situation and the actor's own personality structure. He will often perform actions which, taken alone, are self-deprivational but which, when seen in the wider constellation of his need-disposition system, represent the most gratifying total balance of action possibilities which could be performed under the circumstances.

So far, little has been said of the internal differentiation of the actor's object world except that it is differentiated along the axis of potentialities for gratification or deprivation. But even on this elementary level it has been possible to show the roles in action of the fundamental categories of orientation and their derivatives, of cognition and need, of evaluative and instrumental orientation, of discrimination and choice, of learning and generalization. When all of these elements are organized into a relatively coherent system of action, then a stable balance between the interest in increasing gratification and in the minimization of deprivation is made possible. This organization would consist of a relatively stable, interrelated set of discriminations or choices which has as a necessary counterpart a relatively stable set of expectations.

INTERACTION AND THE COMPLEMENTARITY OF EXPECTATIONS

Before entering into further discussion of the organization of systems of action, it is necessary to discuss one of the differentiations in the structure of the object world which is very crucial in relation to the actor's gratification interests. Only the potentiality of gratification or deprivation from objects is more crucial. We refer here to the distinction between objects which interact [20] with the acting subject and those objects which do not. These

[20] This is a technical usage of the term *interaction*. It implies a relationship both parties to which are actors in the technical sense. It is thus distinguished from the sense in which *interaction* is synonymous with *interdependence*.

interacting objects are themselves actors or egos [21] with their own systems of action. They will be referred to as *social objects* or *alters*. A potential food-object, at least as it approaches the state of edibility, is not an alter, because it does not respond to ego's expectations and because it has no expectations of ego's action; another person, a mother or a friend, would be an alter to ego. The treatment of another actor, an alter, as an interacting object has very great consequences for the development and organization of the system of action.

When we analyze the interaction of ego and alter, we shift from the analysis of the orientation of a single given actor to the consideration of two or more interacting actors as a system. In this case, the expectations of ego are oriented both to the range of alternatives for alter's actions (i.e., the alternatives open to alter in the situation) and to alter's selection, which is intentionally contingent on what ego himself does, within the range of alternatives. The obverse is true for alter. Ego does not expect the behavior of a nonsocial object to be influenced by expectations regarding his own behavior, although, of course, ego's behavior is influenced by his expectations concerning the behavior of the nonsocial object. It is the fact that expectations operate on *both* sides of the relation between a given actor and the object of his orientation which distinguishes social interaction from orientation to nonsocial objects.

This fundamental phenomenon may be called the *complementarity of expectations*, not in the sense that the expectations of the two actors with regard to each other's action are identical, but in the sense that the action of each is oriented to the expectations of the other. Hence the system of interaction may be analyzed in terms of the extent of *conformity* of ego's action with alter's expectations and vice versa. We have seen that an actor's system of action is oriented to the polarity of gratification and deprivation. Social interaction introduces a further complication in that the motivational significance is no longer attributed only to the properties of the immediate object alone, but also to alter's expectations with regard to ego. The contingent reactions of alter to ego's action may be called *sanctions*. Their efficacy derives precisely from the gratificational significance to ego of alter's positive reactions and the deprivational significance of his negative reactions. The significance of these secondary gratifications and deprivations to ego rests on two bases: (1) Any need-disposition can be directly or indirectly gratified or deprived through the consequences of alter's reactions to ego's actions. (2) Personalities certainly develop need-dispositions directly for certain types of response from actors who are significant objects to them, whatever the

---

[21] This usage of the term *ego* is different from that current in psychology. Here it refers only to an actor taken as a point of reference in his relation to another actor referred to as *alter*. The term as here used is parallel to anthropological usage in the description of kinship systems.

constitutional basis of this fact. In other words, they develop social-relational needs.

Thus, sanctions have two kinds of significance to ego. First, alter's intentional and overt action, which can change ego's objective situation, may have direct significance to ego by increasing his opportunities for gratification or limiting them, insofar as alter controls important aspects of ego's situation of action. But ego through generalization also becomes sensitive to alter's attitudes toward him and his action, so that even where alter has no specific intentions in the situation, it will still matter to ego whether alter approves or disapproves of his action — whether he shows love, hostility, or some other attitude toward him.

Thus consideration of the place of complementarity of expectations in the processes of human interaction has implications for certain categories which are central in the analysis of the origins and functions of cultural patterns. There is a *double contingency* inherent in interaction. On the one hand, ego's gratifications are contingent on his selection among available alternatives. But in turn, alter's reaction will be contingent on ego's selection and will result from a complementary selection on alter's part. Because of this double contingency, communication, which is the precondition of cultural patterns, could not exist without both generalization from the particularity of the specific situations (which are never identical for ego and alter) and *stability* of meaning which can only be assured by "conventions" observed by both parties.

Furthermore, the double contingency implies the normative orientation of action, since alter's reaction of punishment or reward is superadded to alter's "intrinsic" or direct behavioral reaction to ego's original selection. If punishment or reward by alter is repeatedly manifested under certain conditions, this reaction acquires for ego the meaning of an appropriate consequence of ego's conformity with or deviation from the norms of a *shared symbolic system*. A shared symbolic system is a system of "ways of orienting," plus those "external symbols" which control these ways of orienting, the system being so geared into the action systems of both ego and alter that the external symbols bring forth the same or a complementary pattern of orientation in both of them. Such a system, with its mutuality of normative orientation, is logically the most elementary form of culture. In this elementary social relationship, as well as in a large-scale social system, culture provides the standards (value-orientations) which are applied in evaluative processes. Without culture neither human personalities nor human social systems would be possible.

4. Interaction and the Development of Personality

The *inter*active element in the system of action, when joined with the fundamental variables of the organization of behavior discussed above, accounts for the enormously complicated differentiation and organization of the social and personality systems. In interaction we find the basic process which, in its various elaborations and adaptations, provides the seed of what on the human level we call personality and the social system. Interaction makes possible the development of culture on the human level and gives culture its significance in the determination of action.

SOCIALIZATION

Before we begin our analysis of the personality system, we shall examine briefly the significance of interaction in the socialization process. We have referred above to the social-relational needs [22] of the infant. The importance of these needs centers on the infant's state of initial dependency. As a result of this dependency, the social-relational context in which viscerogenic needs are gratified or deprived becomes perhaps just as important as the intrinsic gratification or deprivation of the viscerogenic needs themselves. The child's overwhelming sensitivity to the reactions of the significant adult objects, particularly to the reactions of the mother, opens the door to new possibilities of frustration and even trauma. The child develops needs for appropriate attitudes on the part of these adults. It is on the basis of these new needs that the human attains levels of organization beyond those open to animals.

The learning of the behavior patterns characteristic of the adult culture requires new kinds of generalization, including symbols which abstract from particular situations and which refer to classes of objects by means of language. In order to learn such generalizations, particularized attachments which are essential in the earliest stages must be superseded. This substitution takes place through a mechanism like the following: the child forms a social attachment which transcends any particular viscerogenic gratification which the object confers. This attachment makes it possible for the child to accept the necessary deprivations which are involved in renouncing earlier types of gratification and to acquire the new attachment in that although continuance of the old gratifications is made more difficult still favorable reactions from the significant social object are received. The newly learned generalization is acceptable if the child feels that the adult wants it to do the things in question and that it is loved.

Although the problem is still obscure, there is approximate agreement that the development of identification [23] with adult objects is an essential mechanism of the socialization process. For present purposes the most significant

---

[22] When subsequently we use the term *relational needs* it should be understood to refer to what we are here calling *social-relational needs*.

[23] It is well known that use of this term is by no means consistent. It seems essential to distinguish (1) the internalization of the values but not the role of the model from (2) internalization of his specific role. Though there are still other meanings of the term, these two seem to be the most important for present purposes. In both cases, what is taken over is a value pattern and not an action.

characteristic of identification in this sense is the child's acceptance of the adult's values in the relevant contexts; in other words, what the adult wants for the child, the child comes to want for itself. The extent to which this necessarily involves the child's formation of an ideal image of itself as similar to the adult in all respects (for example, with respect to sex, even though the adult is of the opposite sex) remains an open question.

The value-orientations and other components of the culture, as well as the specific accumulated objects which make up the cultural tradition in the form of skills, knowledge, and the like, are transmitted to the on-coming generation. Through the process of socialization, however, expectation systems become organized into patterns of selection in which the effective criterion is the differential significance of the various alternatives for the gratification-deprivation balance of the actor. To say then that a system of action has a degree of stability as a system is to say that there is a certain stability and consistency in its choice patterns. Such stability and consistency are prerequisites of the development of the higher levels of cultural behavior.

Because the child is dependent on the adult, the latter's reaction patterns become crucially important factors in the organization of the child's choice patterns. The child becomes oriented to the wishes which embody for him the values of the adult, and his viscerogenic needs become culturally organized needs, which are shaped so that their gratification is sought in directions compatible with his integration into this system of interaction.

PERSONALITY AS A SYSTEM

The child's development of a "personality" (or an "ego structure") is to be viewed as the establishment of a relatively specific, definite, and consistent system of need-dispositions operating as selective reactions to the alternatives which are presented to him by his object situation or which he organizes for himself by seeking out new object situations and formulating new goals. What will be needed, therefore, for the coherent description and analysis of human personality *as a system* will be the categories and hypotheses bearing on four main sets of variables.

1. Fundamentals of behavior psychology of the sort discussed above: motivation, the gratification-deprivation balance, primary viscerogenic and possibly social-relational needs, cognition and learning, as well as the basic mechanisms of cognitive and cathectic-evaluative learning and adjustment. The latter involves the examination of such learning mechanisms as differentiation and generalization, where cognitive interests have primacy, and reinforcement, extinction, inhibition, substitution, identification, and imitation, where cathectic or evaluative interests have primacy.

2. The allocative processes,[24] by which the strivings toward gratification

---

[24] By *allocation* we mean the distribution of significant components *within* a system in such a way as to be compatible with the functioning of the system in a given state. The term is borrowed from economics.

are distributed among the different available objects and occasions and gratification opportunities are distributed among the different need-dispositions.
These processes keep conflict and anxiety within the limits necessary for the
working of the personality system; the failure of their smooth operation calls
the special mechanisms of defense and adjustment into play.

3. The mechanisms, classifiable as those of defense and adjustment,[25] by
which the different components of need-dispositions are integrated internally
as a system and directed toward objects.

4. The integration of the various need-dispositions into an "on-going"
personality capable of some degree of self-control and purposeful action.
The character of the on-going personality cannot be understood without reference to the relatively independent subintegrations within the personality
structure and the adjustive mechanisms which relate them to each other.

The constitutional foundations of the need-disposition structure of personality continue to function throughout life. But because of the plasticity of the
human organism they directly determine the behavior of the human adult far
less than in many other species. Through learning and interactive experience
they become integrated with the symbolic structures of the cultural tradition
to form an interdependent system of acquired need-dispositions, many of the
latter being closely fused into specific object attachments and systems of role-
expectations. In comparison with its physiological base, the structure of human
personality is highly autonomous and socialized. In addition, the personality
usually has a high degree of autonomy vis-à-vis the social situation at any
particular moment, in the sense that the variations in the social situation do
not bring about completely corresponding variations in the personality
systems.

PERSONALITY AND SOCIAL ROLE

One particular crucial aspect of the articulation of personality with the
social system should be mentioned briefly. Once an organized system of interaction between ego and alter becomes stabilized, they build up reciprocal
expectations of each other's action and attitudes which are the nucleus of
what may be called *role-expectations*. Alter expects ego to behave in given
situational conditions in certain relatively specific ways, or at least within
relatively specific limits. Alter's reaction will then, contingent on the fulfillment
or nonfulfillment of his expectations, be different; with fulfillment leading
to rewards and/or favorable attitudes, and nonfulfillment leading to the
reverse. Alter's reaction is in turn meaningfully interpreted (not necessarily
correctly — distortion is of course possible and frequent) by ego and this

---

[25] By *mechanisms of defense* we mean the motivational processes by which conflicts
internal to the need-disposition system of a personality are resolved or the severity of
their consequences mitigated. *Mechanisms of adjustment*, on the other hand, are the processes by which *strains* on the actor's relations to objects are coped with. Complete resolution may occur through normal learning, but short of this special mechanisms operate.

interpretation plays a part in shaping the next stage in the process of his action toward alter (all this, of course, takes place in reverse too). The pattern of expectations of many alters, often generalized to include all of those in the status of ego, constitutes in a social system the institutionalized [26] definition of ego's roles in specified interactive situations.

Ego's system of need-dispositions may or may not predispose him to conform with these expectations. There are, of course, many complex possibilities of variation between dispositions to complete conformity and to drastic alienation — that is, predispositions to avoid conformity, to withdraw, or to rebel. There are also many complex possibilities of accommodation between dispositions not to conform, in varying modes and degrees, and interests in avoiding the sanctions which nonconformity might incur.

Moreover, alienative and conformist responses to institutional role-expectations do not exhaust the possibilities. Some actors possess, to a high degree, the potentialities of elaborating their own goals and standards, accepting the content of institutional role-expectations but simultaneously modifying and adding something new to them. These are the creative personalities whose conformity or alienation is not motivated mainly by a need-disposition to accept or reject the given institutional role-expectations, but rather by the need to discover, elaborate, and conform with their own ego-ideal.

The group of problems centering around conformity, alienation, and creativity are among the most crucial in the whole theory of action because of their relevance to problems of social stability and change. It is essential, in order to make progress in this area, to have conceptualized both the personality and social system adequately so that the points of empirical articulation where integration and unintegratedness are in balance can be analyzed.[27]

5. Cultural Aspects of Action Systems

INTERNALIZED ORIENTATIONS AND CULTURAL OBJECTS

We have already stated that the organization of the basic alternatives of selective orientation is fundamental to any system of action. Without this organization, the stable system of expectations which are essential to any sys-

---

[26] By *institutionalization* we mean the integration of the expectations of the actors in a relevant interactive system of roles with a shared normative pattern of values. The integration is such that each is predisposed to reward the conformity of the others with the value pattern and conversely to disapprove and punish deviance. Institutionalization is a matter of degree, not of absolute presence or absence.

[27] Although many schemes will allow the *ad hoc* analyses of some of the points of articulation, the scheme presented here seems to have the advantage of proceeding systematically from the elements of orientation. This permits the formulation of concepts which reveal the points of conceptual correspondence among the different types of systems — and this in turn offers a basis for a more comprehensive and more rigorous analysis of the points of empirical articulation.

tem of action could not exist. Not only does the child receive the major organization of his own selective orientations from adults through the socialization process, but consensus with respect to the same fundamental selections among alternatives is vital to a stable social system. In all societies the stabler and more effective patterns of culture are those which are shared in common — though in varying interpretations with varying degrees of conformity, idiosyncrasy, creativity, and persistence — by the members of societies and by groups of societies. The pattern of "commitment" to a particular set of such selections among the potentially open alternatives represents the point of empirical articulation of systems of actions.

Once the analysis of the organization of systems of action is pursued to the levels of elaboration which are necessary for the analysis of the structure of personalities, it also becomes necessary to examine the direct articulation with the patterns of cultural orientation, which have come to be one of the principal objects of anthropological study. The same basic set of categories of the selective alternatives which is relevant for the analysis of personality structures will also be involved in the macroscopic differentiation and classification of the cultural orientations or traditions of social systems.

THE ORGANIZATION OF CULTURE PATTERNS IN SYSTEMS

A cultural system is a highly complex constellation of elements. We may refer here to the two parallel classifications of the actor's modes of motivational orientation as cognitive, cathectic, and evaluative, and of the basic cultural orientations as systems of ideas or beliefs, systems of expressive symbols, and systems of value-orientation (as set forth above). Each type of culture pattern might then be regarded as a solution of a type of orientation problem — systems of ideas are solutions of cognitive problems, systems of expressive symbols are solutions of problems of how "appropriately" to express feelings, and systems of value-orientations are solutions of problems of evaluation, particularly but not exclusively in social interaction.

Value-orientation patterns are of particularly decisive significance in the organization of systems of action since one class of them defines the patterns of reciprocal rights and obligations which become constitutive of role-expectations and sanctions. (Other classes of value-orientation define the *standards* of cognitive and appreciative judgments.)

Cultural patterns tend to become organized into systems. The peculiar feature of this systematization is a type of integration which we may call *consistency of pattern.* Whether it be the logical consistency of belief system, the stylistic harmony of an art form, or the rational compatibility of a body of moral rules, the internal coherence of a body of cultural patterns is always a crucial problem for the student of culture.

The determination of the extent of the consistency of pattern and devia-

tions from it in a given culture presents serious difficulties to the analyst. The
overt or explicit culture almost always appears fragmentary at first, and its
parts seem disconnected. Only under special conditions — for example, in
highly sophisticated systems of ideas or legal systems — is explicit systematization carried out by the creators and bearers of the culture themselves. In
order therefore to determine the existence of systematic coherence where there
has not been explicit systematization, it is necessary for the student of culture
to uncover the implicit culture and to detect whatever common premises may
underlie apparently diverse and unconnected items of orientation. Very close
approximations to complete consistency in the patterns of culture are practically never to be found in large complex social systems. The nature and
sources of the mal-integration of cultural patterns are as important to the
theory of action as the integration itself.

THE INTERNALIZATION OF CULTURE PATTERNS

It has already been made clear that, whatever its systematic form, a cultural pattern may be involved in action either as an object of the actor's
situation or it may be internalized to become part of the structure of his
personality. All types of cultural patterns may be internalized, but particular
importance is to be attributed to the internalization of value-orientations, some
of which become part of the superego structure of the personality and, with
corresponding frequency, of institutionalized role-expectations.[28]

Cultural patterns when internalized become constitutive elements of personalities and of social systems. *All concrete systems of action, at the same
time, have a system of culture and are a set of personalities* (or sectors of
them) *and a social system or subsystem.* Yet all three are conceptually independent organizations of the elements of action.

Because of this empirical interrelatedness, there is a dynamic theory of
culture which corresponds to that of the dynamic theory of personality and
social systems. It is concerned with the conditions under which certain types
of systems of culture can exist in certain types of personalities or societies.
It analyzes the processes of cultural innovation and change in terms of their
motivational determinants, as these operate in the mechanisms of the social
system and in the mechanisms of personality. It is concerned with the imperfections in the integration of cultural patterns and accounts for them in
terms of the empirical interdependence of culture orientations with the
strains and processes of the social and personality systems.

---

[28] This fact of the internalization of values was independently and from different points
of view discovered by Freud in his theory of the superego and by Durkheim in his
theory of the institutionalization of moral norms. The fact that the two men, working
from different premises, arrived at the same conclusion is one of the landmarks of development of modern social science.

6. The Social System

When, in the above discussion of action, we reached the point at which interaction of an actor with other persons or social objects became crucial, we disclosed the nucleus of the development of social systems. Personality as a system has a fundamental and stable point of reference, the acting organism. It is organized around the one organism and its life processes. But ego and alter in interaction with each other also constitute a system. This is a system of a new order, which, however intimately dependent on them, does not simply consist of the personalities of the two members.

ROLE AS THE UNIT OF SOCIAL SYSTEMS: SOCIAL SYSTEM AND PERSONALITIES

In the present terms a social system is a system of the interaction of a plurality of persons analyzed within the frame of reference of the theory of action. It is, of course, composed of relationships of individual actors and only of such relationships. The relationships themselves are constellations of the actions of the parties to the relationship oriented toward one another. For most analytical purposes, the most significant unit of social structures is not the person but the role. The role is that organized sector of an actor's orientation which constitutes and defines his participation in an interactive process. It involves a set of complementary expectations concerning his own actions and those of others with whom he interacts. Both the actor and those with whom he interacts possess these expectations. Roles are institutionalized when they are fully congruous with the prevailing culture patterns and are organized around expectations of conformity with morally sanctioned patterns of value-orientation shared by the members of the collectivity in which the role functions.

The abstraction of an actor's role from the total system of his personality makes it possible to analyze the articulation of personality with the organization of social systems. The structure of a social system and the functional imperatives for its operation and survival or orderly change as a system are moreover different from those of personality.[29] The problems of personality and social structure can be properly treated only if these differences are recognized. Only then can the points of articulation and mutual interdependence be studied.

When we recognize that roles rather than personalities are the units of social structure, we can perceive the necessity of an element of "looseness" in the relation between personality structure and the performance of a role. Role situations are situations with potentially all the possible significances to

[29] A further distinction between social and personality systems lies in the fact that a social system is not tied to any one *particular* aggregate of organisms. Furthermore, there is no reason to believe that when, having undergone a change of personnel, the social system remains the same, the new actors who have replaced those which were lost are necessarily identical in all the details of their personality with their predecessors.

an actor that situations can have. Their significance and the resultant effect on the motivation of behavior will be different with different personalities. But, in the organization of the latter's reactions where the stability of the sector of the social system in question is maintained, there are certain "control mechanisms" which serve to keep the potential dispersion of the actor's reactions within limits narrower than would be produced by the combination of the total situation and the actor's personality without this specificity of role expectations.

An important feature of a large proportion of social roles is that the actions which make them up are not minutely prescribed and that a certain range of variability is regarded as legitimate. Sanctions are not invoked against deviance within certain limits. This range of freedom makes it possible for actors with different personalities to fulfill within considerable limits the expectations associated with roughly the same roles without undue strain. It should also be noted that role-expectations and sanctions do exert "pressures" on individual actors which may well generate types of strain which have important repercussions in various parts of the personality. These will be manifested in types of action which in turn have a variety of social consequences and often result in either the development of further mechanisms of social control or the generation of pressures toward change, or in both. In this manner, personality and role structure constitute closely interdependent systems.

ROLE TYPES AND THE DIFFERENTIATION AND INTEGRATION OF SOCIAL SYSTEMS

The structural roles of the social system, like the structure of need-dispositions of the personality system, must be oriented to value alternatives. Selections are of course always actions of individuals, but these selections cannot be inter-individually random in a social system. Indeed, one of the most important functional imperatives of the maintenance of social systems is that the value-orientations of the different actors in the same social system must be integrated in some measure in a *common* system. All on-going social systems do actually show a tendency toward a general system of common cultural orientations. The sharing of value-orientations is especially crucial, although consensus with respect to systems of ideas and expressive symbols are also very important determinants of stability in the social system.

The range of variation and the shape of the distribution of the types of roles in a social system is neither parallel to nor fully congruous with the range of variation and the distribution of the personality types of the actors filling those roles. The actual operation of this structure of roles as an on-going system is, of course, possible in the last analysis only because the component personalities are motivated to act in the requisite ways and sufficient gratification is provided to enough individuals within the immediate system of roles itself or in the more embracing system of roles. There are functional imperatives limiting the degree of incompatibility of the possible kinds of roles in the same action system; these imperatives are ultimately related to the conditions of maintenance of a total on-going social system of the type in which the more constitutive of these roles are found. A social system, like a personality, must be coherently organized and not merely a random assortment of its components.

As in the case of personality, the functional problem of social systems may be summarized as the problems of allocation and integration. There is always a differentiation of functions within any action system. There must accordingly be an allocation of such functions to different classes of roles; the roles must be articulated for the performance of collaborative and complementary tasks. The life span of the individual being limited, there must be a continual process of replacement of personnel within the system of roles if the system is to endure. Furthermore, both the facilities necessary to perform functions and the rewards which are important to the motivation of individual actors are inherently scarce. Hence their allocation cannot be left to an unregulated competitive process without great frustration and conflict ensuing. The regulation of all these allocative processes and the performance of the functions which keep the system or the subsystem going in a sufficiently integrated manner is impossible without a system of definitions of roles and sanctions for conformity or deviation. With the development of a considerable complexity of differentiation there emerge roles and subsystems of roles with specifically integrative functions in the social system.

This determination of functions and allocation and integration of roles, personnel, facilities, and rewards in a social system implies a process of selection in accordance with standards of evaluation applied to characteristics of the objects (individual and collective). This does not mean that anyone ever deliberately works out the "plan" of most social systems. But as in the other types of action systems it is not possible for the choices of the actors to fall at random and still form a coherently organized and functioning social system. The structure of the social system in this respect may be regarded as the cumulative and balanced resultant of many selections of many individuals, stabilized and reinforced by the institutionalization of value patterns, which legitimize commitment to certain directions of selection and mobilize sanctions in the support of the resultant orientations.

The patterns of commitment which, in their function as institutional role-expectations, are incorporated into the structure of social systems are, in at least one fundamental aspect of their content (that is, in the commitments which define rights and obligations) identical with the cultural value-orientation discussed above. The latter, in the form of the general moral consensus regarding rights and obligations, constitutes therefore one fundamental component of the structure of the social system. The structural differences between different social systems will often be found to reside in differences in the content and range of this consensus.

Although the moral consensus of the pattern of value-orientation provides the standards and sets the limits which regulate the allocations, there must also be special institutional mechanisms through which the allocative decisions are made and implemented. The institutional roles to which power and prestige are attached play a preponderant part in this process. The reason for this lies in the fact that power and prestige possess a highly general significance for the distribution of other facilities and rewards. The distribution of power and prestige and the institutional mechanisms which regulate that distribution are therefore especially influential in the working of a social system.

The general requirement for integration, therefore, demands that the control of allocative and integrative processes be associated with the same, or with closely interacting, roles; and that the mechanisms regulating the distribution of power and prestige apportion sufficient power and prestige to these allocative and integrative roles. And finally, it is essential that the occupants of these roles perform their allocative and integrative functions with a view to conforming with the value consensus of the society. These allocative and integrative roles (whether they be roles filled by individuals or by subcollectivities) may be considered to be important integrative mechanisms of the society. Their absence or defectiveness causes conflicts and frustrations.

It must be recognized that no social system is ever completely integrated just as none is ever completely disintegrated. From the sectors of unintegratedness — where expectations cannot be fulfilled in institutional roles or where need-dispositions are frustrated by institutionalized expectations or where the strain is not absorbed in safety-valve mechanisms — from these sectors some of the most important sources of change and growth are to be found.

Any system of interactive relationships of a plurality of individual actors is a *social system*. A *society* [30] is the type of social system which contains within itself all the essential prerequisites for its maintenance as a self-subsistent system. Among the more essential of these prerequisites are (1) organization around the foci of territorial location and kinship, (2) a system for determining functions and allocating facilities and rewards, and (3) integrative structures controlling these allocations and regulating conflicts and competitive processes.

With the institutionalization of culture patterns, especially value-orientation patterns, in the social structure, the threefold reciprocal integration of personality, social system, and culture comes full circle.[31] Such value pat-

---

[30] Partial social systems, so long as their relation to the society of which they are parts is made clear, are certainly legitimate objects of empirical investigation.

[31] Although — as must almost inevitably be the case with each individual signer — there are some things I should prefer to see said somewhat differently, there is only one point on which I remain slightly uncomfortable. This is the relation of social structure,

terns, institutionalized in the social structure, through the operation of role mechanisms, and in combination with other elements, organize the behavior of adult members of society. Through the socialization process, they are in turn constitutive in establishment of the personality structure of the new adult from the plasticity of early childhood. The process of socialization, it is clear from the above, is dependent upon social interaction. Adults in their orientation to the child are certainly acting in roles, very largely institutionalized, and almost from the beginning the child himself develops expectations which rapidly become role-expectations. Then within the framework of the personality structures thus formed, adults act both to maintain and to modify the social system and the value patterns in which and by which they live, and to modify or keep within the pattern the personality structures of their living descendants.

The reader should bear in mind that what we have presented in the foregoing pages is a highly general and abstract scheme. We are fully aware that *by itself* it cannot do justice to the immense richness and particularity of the human scene. But it can help us to analyze that scene and organize our knowledge of it.

The general outlines of the nature of action systems sketched here, the interrelations of the various components and the interdependence of the system levels of organization of those components, seems to be quite clearly implied in much contemporary theory and research. But the empirical complexity is immense, and the unexplored areas are, in the light of present knowledge, Stygian in their darkness. To us, progress toward unraveling that complexity and illuminating some of the obscurity depends, along with empirical investigation, on more precise and explicit conceptualization of the components of action and of the ways in which they are interrelated.

Talcott Parsons   Henry A. Murray, Jr.
Edward A. Shils   Robert R. Sears
Gordon W. Allport   Richard C. Sheldon
Clyde Kluckhohn   Samuel A. Stouffer
Edward C. Tolman

---

social system, role, and culture. Many anthropologists (and certainly the undersigned) will agree today that there is an element in the social (i.e., interactive) process which is not culturally patterned, which is in some sense autonomous from culture. Nevertheless, one whose training, experiences, and prejudices are anthropological tends to feel that the present statement does not give full weight to the extent to which roles are culturally defined, social structure is part of the cultural map, the social system is built upon girders supplied by explicit and implicit culture. On the other hand, whatever my reservations, I welcome the publication of the statement in its present form because I am convinced that in the present stage of social science it is highly useful to behave experimentally with reference to conceptual schemes — Clyde Kluckhohn.

A NOTE ON THE PLACE OF ECONOMIC THEORY AND POLITICAL THEORY IN THE
GENERAL THEORY OF ACTION

The general preoccupations and terminology of the foregoing statement are those current in the disciplines of psychology, sociology, and social anthropology. It is reasonable to ask about the relevance of the theoretical interests of the well-established social science disciplines of economics and political science.

Economics is today, in a theoretical sense, probably the most highly elaborated, sophisticated, and refined of the disciplines dealing with action. It was by far the earliest to conceive of the relevant phenomena in terms of a system of interdependent variables and thus to interpret particular phenomena in the light of their interrelations with others in a system. It has also achieved a high level of technical refinement of its concepts and analytical methods.

Most certainly economic theory is a part of the theory of action in the present technical sense. It has not, however, been explicitly dealt with above because most of its problems arise only at points of elaboration and differentiation in the development of social systems beyond those to which we have carried our analysis.

It is true that there is an "economic" aspect of *all* empirical action systems — that aspect which we have designated as the "allocative," by borrowing a term from economics. But this concept of economics is so general as to preclude its being used as the basis of a technical theoretical development. This latter occurs only with the emergence of specially differentiated types of orientation of action within a correspondingly differentiated social system. Only with the development of money, of markets, and of the price mechanism or other differentiated mechanisms of allocation of resources do the phenomena of special technical interest to the economist appear on a substantial scale.

Economic theory is the conceptual scheme for analyzing such phenomena as production — as oriented to a set of market conditions or allocative policies — exchange, and determination of particular prices and of price levels. As such its technical basis rests on the fundamentals of action theory as here set forth — particularly instrumental orientation as an action type and the conditions of mutuality of such orientation. Its empirical relevance, on the other hand, rests on certain types of development of social systems. Just as the economic variant of instrumental orientation must be placed relative to other types and the particular combinations of action components they involve, so must the empirical processes of special interest to the economist be placed in terms of their relations to those other aspects of the total social system which are not susceptible of analysis in terms of economic theory.

Economic theory, then, is the theory of a particular set of processes or of a subsystem within a class of highly differentiated social systems. This subsystem is of very great strategic significance in these societies. Economic theory has its conceptual foundations in the categories of action theory here set forth, but only becomes a distinctive subtheory of the general theory on a considerably more elaborate level of differentiation than that reached here.

The case of political science is somewhat different. Its historical focus has been much more on a class of concrete phenomena, those of government, than on a disctinctive conceptual scheme. What has traditionally been called political theory has contained more of philosophical and ethical explication of the problems of government than of empirical analysis of its processes and determinants. In the sense of a distinctive *empirical conceptual scheme*, political theory has clearly not been in the same category with economic theory.

Since government constitutes one of the most strategically important processes and foci of differentiated structures within social systems, its study is clearly a legitimate basis for the specialization of a discipline within the social sciences. But, like economics, its special relevance does not emerge until degrees of differentiation on both theoretical and empirical levels beyond those reached in the present general statement have appeared.

It appears, furthermore, that the processes and structures of government necessarily have highly diffuse functions in social systems. It seems likely, therefore, that if the empirical focus of political science is to remain on the phenomena of government, it will not as a discipline be able to attain a sharpness of theoretical focus comparable to that of economics. It is more likely to draw from a much wider range of the components of the general theory of action and to find its distinctiveness in the way it combines these components in relation to its special empirical interests, rather than in the technical elaboration of a narrow and sharply focused segment of the theory of action, as is the case with economics.

2

RICHARD C. SHELDON

Some Observations on Theory

in Social Science[1]

Social science deals with one sector of the activity of human beings. Basically, activity can be considered to be any expenditure of energy of any part of the organism. It includes the biochemical processes which go on in the body. But social science does not deal with biochemical processes as such; they are in the domain of physiology. Social science is concerned with activity as related in some manner to things outside the organism itself — activity in terms of *principles of relationship* — and its basic task is to discover such principles and develop them into a coherent body of science.

By "things outside the organism itself" I do not necessarily mean material entities with independent existence. Such things as beliefs and images of the self and its capacities of course do not exist independently except insofar as they may be written down on paper; but it is true that they are developed in the course of contact with independent entities, usually other people. A relatively small number of things such as bodily pains may have no apparent external connections, and parts of the body are not outside the organism, but they can be behaved toward as though they were separate entities. In general, "things outside the organism itself" includes those things which can be behaved toward and which may exist in the past, present, or future, in material or nonmaterial form. Their designation is an integral part of the principles expressing the relationship between them and the organism which manifests activity; hence we need be concerned with their existence or location only as a part of the theoretical structure which we erect.

Since social science does not deal with activity in all its forms, abstraction is necessary. The sector of activity which is abstracted for study can be called by any convenient term. *Behavior* is one possible term, but it generally connotes observable bodily movements and does not include thoughts, and it often

[1] I am grateful for discussions and criticisms to Professor Clyde Kluckhohn and Edward C. Tolman and to Drs. Florence Kluckhohn, Gardner Lindzey, and Ivan D. London. I have incorporated many of their suggestions in this article, but the final form of the article is my own development, and the responsibility for any possible misuses of their suggestions is of course mine.

refers to individual styles of movements which may or may not be relevant to the study at hand. A more neutral term and one which has gained some currency in social-scientific thought is *action*, the term which has been adopted for this book. Action is activity which is related in some manner, by principles of relationship (or one may prefer the term *interrelationship*), to things outside the organism. It is the basic unit with which social science deals.

This basic unit may be broken down into certain components. *Environment* refers to all those things "outside" the organism to which action may be related. *Situation* refers to the organism and the environment in theoretical relationship but without action of the organism having taken place. Both terms, *environment* and *situation*, involve abstraction, but of different types. In describing environment one must abstract because one cannot describe everything. In describing situation one abstracts because the principles of relationship which are involved select features of the environment and of the organism for study, and the abstraction is done in terms of the theory which designates the principles of relationship. The features of the environment which are abstracted in the study of situations are *objects*; the abstraction from the organism is the *actor*. Although the situation consists of both actors and objects, it is convenient to speak of actors and situations as though the two were to some extent independent concepts: one speaks of actors in situations. If more precision is necessary for certain purposes, one can use the term *object situation* as differentiated from the *total situation*, which includes both objects and actors. It is *actors* in *situations* who *act* (manifest *action*); *organisms* in *environments* have *activity*. In other words, that which impinges upon our senses and which our measuring instruments record is the activities of organisms in environments; what we deal with on the scientific level are the actions of actors in situations, which are abstractions in terms of principles of relationship.

The crucial problem of social science is to develop these principles — to develop, in other words, the principles of action. The major portion of this book represents an attempt toward a solution of this problem. The principles of action, the operational ways in which they are connected to sense data, and the logical modes of their relationship to one another form the *theoretical structure of social science*. Because of the importance of the problem, it is useful to discuss at some length some of the characteristics of such a theoretical structure.

Possibly the most fundamental statement which can be made about the general principles that make up a body of science is that these principles are the free creations of the human intellect, as Poincaré has shown:[2] they do not necessarily reflect something inherently "given" in the phenomena observed, nor do they come from the inherent makeup of the human mind.

[2] Henri Poincaré, "Science and Hypothesis," *The Foundations of Science* (New York: The Science Press, 1929).

Therefore they are not imposed by the material dealt with. They are useful in a practical sense, however, only insofar as they can be identified in some manner with sense data, so that they can be used to predict occurrences which can be observed. Thus, although there is an infinite range of possibilities open in forming principles, experiment can indicate which are most useful for present purposes. To take a simple example, it is well recognized now that Euclidean geometry is based on a set of postulates which are not self-evident truths but are a set of conventions regarding the use of such terms as *line* and *point*. Because operations can be found to connect these terms with sense data, and because Euclidean geometry in connection with these operations produces predictable results for a certain range of phenomena, Euclidean geometry is useful. But assumptions of postulates other than Euclidean ones produce geometries which are consistent and do not lead to contradictions, and for certain purposes these non-Euclidean geometries have proved to be more useful than Euclidean geometry. One cannot, however, say which geometry is true, for the geometries are products of the intellect and are not imposed by nature. Likewise statements involved in such general principles as the law of inertia are not descriptions of pure facts which can be observed as such; they are conventions regarding the use of certain terms — definitions of expressions such as *uniform motion along a straight line*. We cannot be sure whether we are observing uniform motion or a straight line in any absolute terms, terms imposed by the data themselves. Instead we develop operations which if they produce certain results are said to indicate that uniform motion along a straight line has taken place. By doing this we have made an operational definition of a general principle. The principle itself is the free creation of the human intellect; the operations are necessary to connect it with sense data. Only after it has been so connected can we subject it to experimental test to see whether or not it is useful.

It can be seen from the above that for a system of propositions to have scientific meaning it must involve at least two sets of definitions. One set is a series of conventions about how to use certain terms; the other is a series of conventions about how to attach these terms to observable events. If the second set is not present, propositions involving only the first set of definitions are not susceptible to observational test and might be factually meaningless although they may be logically perfect. This does not mean that propositions involving only the first set of definitions — the free creations of the human intellect — should not be developed. Operational uses of such sets of propositions may be discovered later, as the history of non-Euclidean geometry shows. But in order for such propositions to become useful, they should be stated in terms which can be subjected to operational test when the time comes. Let us consider a common proposition of social science: "Human beings act as if they seek goals," or briefly, "Human beings have goals." This proposition has a certain observational base: we observe that organisms engage in activity and then cease activity; we say that they have achieved a goal. Such observation may be called an operational definition of a goal; the idea *goal* itself is a theoretical construction. But if we let the matter rest at this, the proposition, "Human beings have goals," does not have scientific meaning because the operations used to connect it with observable events are the same operations used to establish the convention about how the term *goal* is to be used. The proposition is analogous to one such as "Bodies move when force is applied." It is a principle which relates the organism to the environment, but it is not useful because it is not stated in terms subject to empirical test. It is merely a statement that *goal* is one of the concepts that will be used in whatever discussion follows.

In order, therefore, that a proposition be empirically testable it must be stated in such a way that the concepts involved may be attached to empirical data by operations other than those which merely restate the proposition. Usually this is done by expressing a relationship between two or more concepts, each of which can be defined by independent operations. Then what is tested is whether this relationship is stated correctly or not. The concepts and postulates of a theoretical system are by their nature untestable, but if from them logical conclusions are drawn and stated in terms of a relationship, it can be shown whether this stated relationship is correct or wrong, provided the relationship is stated precisely enough. The logical system which enables conclusions to be drawn and stated in terms of relationships is the third ingredient of a scientific theoretical structure; the first ingredient is the concepts and postulates, the free creations of the mind, and the second is the operational ways in which these concepts are attached to sense data. Because it is the relationships and not the other ingredients that are tested, this third ingredient is of enormous importance. This is why mathematics is such a powerful tool, because in mathematics one has at hand a magnificently developed system for drawing logical conclusions and because relationships can be stated with great precision by the use of that simple symbol, the equals sign. I do not propose here to enter the controversy as to whether the social sciences should be mathematized or can be mathematized. My purpose is to point out the necessity for very careful examination of the processes by which logical conclusions are drawn in the social sciences and of the terms in which relationships are stated, for it is only with these processes and terms that we can test the usefulness of our concepts.

In the social sciences relationships are usually stated in terms of the language of the person who describes them. The implications of this should be carefully examined. Let us take a purely hypothetical example. Suppose that in a given society it is observed that infants are brought up to their mothers' breasts but have to spend some time seeking the nipple before they get nourishment. It is also observed that there is a high amount of creative intellectual effort among the adults of this community: they seek new ideas. One might relate the one set of these seeking actions to the other. I have no doubt over-drawn this example to get the point across, but the point is this: there is an implicit assumption here that whenever the term *seeking*, as commonly understood, can be applied to two sets of data, these data are equatable. Modern linguistics has shown that the implicit categories embedded in language are such that one should subject such a procedure to careful analysis before placing too much reliance in it.[3] The use of language in this manner is often felt to be justified because there is a common feeling that "the social sciences have not advanced far enough yet to use more exact methods of the natural sciences." The result is that investigators often go on developing more and more observational categories without worrying much about how these categories can be related to one another.

But if a consistent body of social scientific theory is to be developed, one must give considerable thought to the relationship of categories. One of our most prominent theorists of science, Philipp Frank, has this to say about the nature of theory:

> The traditional presentation of physical theories frequently consists of a system of statements in which descriptions of observations are mixed with mathematical considerations in such a way that sometimes one cannot distinguish clearly which is which. It is Poincaré's great merit to have stressed that one part of every physical theory is a set of arbitrary axioms and logical conclusions drawn from these axioms. These axioms are relations between signs, which may be words or algebraic symbols; the important point is that the conclusions that we draw from these axioms are not dependent upon the meanings of these symbols. Hence this part of a theory is purely conventional in the sense of Poincaré. It does not say anything about observable facts, but only leads to hypothetical statements of the following type: "If the axioms of this system are true, then the following propositions are also true," or still more exactly speaking: "If there is a group of relations between these symbols, there are also some other relations between the same symbols." This state of affairs is often described by saying that the system of principles and conclusions describes not a content but a structure.[4]

If the system of principles and conclusions that make up a scientific theory describe not a content but a structure, then an adequate theory for the social sciences must take into cognizance the means whereby by structural relationships are established. A multiplication of observational categories which are related more or less intuitively by the structure of the language of the observer is not sufficient for really rigorous theory; it produces what one may call metaphorical theory.

It is important to remember that the relationship between the symbols in the theory is contained in the theory itself and not in nature. Gravity, for

[3] See, for example, B. L. Whorf, *Four Articles on Metalinguistics* (Washington: Department of State, Foreign Service Institute), 1949.

[4] Philipp Frank, *Modern Science and Its Philosophy* (Cambridge: Harvard University Press, 1949), p. 12.

example, is a relationship between symbols in Newtonian mechanics, not in nature, and it disappears in relativity mechanics. The conclusions we draw from it are not dependent upon the meanings of the symbols. Lack of the realization of this fundamental fact of the construction of theory can lead to difficulties. Such difficulties are at the bottom of the dissatisfaction that many social scientists feel with the functional approach in social science, which assumes that every action has the function of promoting the maintainance of a system, either a multipersonal, sociocultural system or a stable personality. "Function" is a principle relating action to object, but it is dependent upon the meaning of the symbols related; the relationship is assumed to be in nature. We can say that eating is functional because it promotes maintenance of the life of the actor, but it serves no end to say that A is functional because it promotes B. Such a statement has no meaning apart from specific meanings of A and B, which means that it contains nothing that enables us to draw logical conclusions about other relationships, and hence the axioms of the theory are not testable. The relationships are assumed to be in nature, and the theory has content but not structure. All one can do with such a theory is to fill in the content, and the end result can be statements such as, "Suicide is functional because it promotes peace of mind." [5]

Let us consider an example from social science in which there is a structure apart from the meanings of the symbols. One of the things anthropologists are concerned with is the degree of behavioral fit to ideal patterns. Given a tribe with a certain culture, the anthropologist can determine what per cent of the tribe's members do a certain thing which is ideally prescribed; then if the anthropologist is confronted by another settlement or tribe with an identical culture, he can predict what per cent of its members will do the same thing. Stated very briefly, the reasoning process involved is something like this:

1. Given A, B, C (usually actions or products of action), we say that X (a cultural pattern) is present.

2. Having determined X in a situation P (a tribe), we observe that such and such a percentage of R's (actors) do S (an action or group of actions). (S is usually connected in some way with A, B, or C, but for the purposes of this example, the connection is irrelevant.)

3. We then set up the hypothesis that given X, such and such a percentage of R's do S.

4. In situation Q (another tribe), we observe A, B, and C.

5. Therefore X is present and we predict that in situation Q such and such a percentage of R's will do S.

---

[5] The above discussion has been confined to the narrow functional concept that all actions must be functional. However, if it is considered that some actions may be disfunctional, or functional in one context but disfunctional in another, the basic point of the discussion nevertheless remains unchanged.

6. This prediction is then subjected to experimental test.

Such a line of reasoning is structural; it arrives at the expression of a relationship which by its nature can be shown to be true or false, and operations can be designed to connect the categories used with sense data. But although neutral symbols without meaning can be used to show the reasoning process — that is, although the relationships can be *stated* independently of the meaning of the symbols used — and although the categories used can be called operational, let us not say that the meaning of the symbols is irrelevant or that the formulation is operational to the extent of being merely a sum of defined operations. Any set of propositions such as the above is rooted in a great deal of observation and intuitional hunch that derives directly from the content of the things observed. Such a simple distinction as that between situation P and situation Q is made because situations P and Q originally had meaning, and the distinction is far from purely operational: although operations can be devised to distinguish the two situations, the fact that the distinction is made or is thought to be possible involves a reasoning process that comes before the operations and is quite distinct from them. Thus, although the system of principles and conclusions that makes up a theory indeed describes not a content but a structure, the devising of the theory involves far more than mere formal manipulations of symbols with meanings which are purely "operational": it involves immersing oneself first in the facts as known and then getting some good intuitions.

I emphasize this point because I have noticed that it is often thought that the facts follow the theory, on the grounds that all observation is in terms of a conceptual scheme. While it is true that all observation is in terms of a conceptual scheme and that a fact is a sense datum in terms of a conceptual scheme,[6] this does not mean that one must have a fully worked out theory in order to do any observation at all. The history of science indicates that the most fruitful theories have been those developed to explain known facts: the motions of the planets were fully known before Newton provided laws from which to derive these motions. From the original theories are then deduced additional facts to be discovered in nature, but the starting point has been the setting up of principles from which already known facts could be derived, and these known facts have usually been quite limited in range. Theories which encompass many facts start from a few. An example of this sort of thing is given in the reasoning process outlined above: the culture pattern X. Why, it may be asked, does one need this culture pattern? Why not merely say, given A, B, and C, such and such a percentage of R's do S? Such a statement would be analogous to one such as: given day, night follows. The culture pattern relates S to A, B, and C and tells us why S should be expected. For the purposes of the reasoning process, I said that the relation-

[6] See Talcott Parsons, *The Structure of Social Action* (New York: McGraw-Hill, 1937), p. 41.

ship of S to A, B, and C, was irrelevant, but it was irrelevant only because of the intent of the example. For the purposes of building a theory of action, it is very relevant, for then the same principles evolved to relate A, B, and C also extend to S; and the more S's that can be subsumed under one or a few principles, the more adequate the theory is. The aim of the theory is generality. But the theory begins with the relating of A, B, and C — known facts — and then is gradually extended to other facts.

How has the development of general theories — theories which fit a wide range of facts — proceeded? I am speaking here of those theories which produce statements that can be shown empirically to be true or false, not of theories which are general systems of knowledge. Usually they have begun by fitting a small range of facts, and as they were extended to fit more facts, they have been changed and have become more and more complicated and cumbersome. There may also have been a number of disparate theories which fitted the same or similar facts. Finally a fundamental revision of the theory has been made which has restored simplicity, and then the process has begun all over again. Such at least has been the course of development in physics. I do not by any means maintain that the same kinds of theories which are used in physics must be used in the social sciences, but the spectacular successes of the theories in physics at least suggest that the procedure followed in devising these theories might be fruitful for the social sciences. If something like this procedure is not followed, the theories of social science are in danger of being too far removed from the observational facts of activity; and while such theories may be useful as means of organizing thoughts, it is difficult to produce from them statements the affirmation and denial of which imply a difference capable of empirical test, which is the only way the theory may be given practical meaning. In general, the most fruitful all-embracing theories are developed from relatively small beginnings, and although they are free creations of the human intellect, they are rooted in observational fact (some of the theories of mathematics are exceptions, but these theories were developed as logical systems and not as models for events of physical existence).

Let us sum up the argument to this point. The crucial problem of the social sciences is to develop the principles of action into a theoretical structure or structures. Such structures, like all theories, consist of certain categories and axioms which are free creations of the human intellect; in the case of social science these are abstractions from organisms and environments and the relational principles which deal with these abstractions. By means of various operations the free creations can be attached to sense data. The structural aspect of the theory is produced by means of some system of logical derivations whereby there are stated relationships other than those originally stated in the categories and axioms. These derived relationships are the statements that are put to empirical test, and such derivations must be made if the theory is to have factual meaning. The categories and axioms are devised through familiarity with the data and with the help of intuition, and through refinement of already existing theories. Their starting point is the setting up of principles from which we can derive already known facts of rather limited range, and the use of the principles is then extended to encompass new facts, which may be discovered through logical derivation from the theory or may become known through other sources.

The setting up of a theory or theories of action, or indeed the setting up of any scientific theory, involves the assumption that action is *ordered*, that there is a certain regularity which permits of systematic study. Strictly speaking, the statement that there is order in action means this: that there can be set up a set of principles of such a nature that a very large number of actions can be derived from the principles. In other words, we do not need a different set of principles to explain each individual action, and hence action, or at least large segments of it, can be predicted. In speaking of individual actions, we must recognize the possibility that there may be large numbers of individual actions that are not predictable, just as in physics single subatomic events are not predictable, but that in the aggregate many such actions average out or converge,[7] which makes the application of general principles possible. It must be remembered that the order is in the principles and that different kinds of order will emerge with the use of different kinds of principles; as long as this is remembered, it is acceptable to say, for simplicity's sake, that action is ordered. On a simple level, we know that much action is ordered — we know when neckties will be worn, that the language which is comprehensible today will be comprehensible tomorrow, and so forth. On a more complex level, certain aspects of the ordered features of action have crystallized into foci of study.

One such focus has been the actor *qua* actor, or the actor as distinguished from other actors in similar situations. Actors exhibit certain regularities of action over a period of time and also exhibit what might appear to be certain inconsistencies. Insofar as principles can be set up from which these inconsistencies can be derived, the inconsistencies are ordered as much as the regularities. In social science it has become common to impute to the actor certain drives, needs, habits, traits, attitudes, beliefs, cognitions, etc., by which, in the proper admixture, to account for his actions. The study of these concepts, their content, their mechanisms, their interrelations in the actor, and their positions in the situation constitutes the discipline of psychology. The relatively ordered system of resultant actions in one actor is called his *personality*. One of the main foci of interest in psychology is the degree and manner of such ordering. (Remember that action is an abstract concept, that the ac-

[7] See Ivan D. London, "Some Consequences for History and Psychology of Langmuir's Concept of Convergence and Divergence of Phenomena," *Psych. Review*, LIII (May 1946), 170–188.

tivities from which it is abstracted are not just simple bodily movements, and that it always implies a relationship. This is not a Watsonian behaviorism or an oversimplified stimulus-response psychology, although both of these types of psychology would fit in.)

A second focus of the study of order in action has been around groups of actors. There is order in groups of actors — i.e., there are ordered systems of different personalities — of such a nature that it does not become apparent in the study of single individuals and which develops in various lines as more and more actors become encompassed in a study. This is the field of sociology and social or cultural anthropology. It is futile to try to draw a fine line of distinction between the disciplines of sociology and anthropology, but it may be said that in their common field the principles of order fall into two relatively distinct although interrelated types. The first type of principles derive from the fact that in a given situation there are a certain number of interacting actors with certain characteristics. The simplest example of this sort of thing is probably the peck order of chickens. The second type of principles of order are those that deal with learned, historically transmitted types or patterns of action which do not derive directly from the actors them- selves or from the situations as such. These patterns are part of the body of *culture*, which also includes the products of action. Of course, culture ulti- mately derives from actors in situations, but it is transmitted beyond the or- iginal actors and situations, and at a given moment only relatively few of its components will be new. Leaving out psychological considerations for the moment, in any given situation action is partly determined by situational exigencies — that is, it can be treated by principles of order of the first type — but most of the action is determined to a greater or lesser degree by trans- mitted culture.

To say that action is determined by culture is, of course, merely a con- venient way of speaking. Culture is a theoretical model, and the abstractions and principles from which it is made up are free creations of the mind. Some of these abstractions and principles deal with matters that are close to the minds of the individual culture bearers, who can tell you, for example, that certain actions are prescribed at certain occasions. This aspect of culture is usually called *explicit culture* or some similar term. Other aspects of culture, the *implicit culture*, are so generalized that in many cases the culture bearers are unable to formulate them — these are the "ways of life," tacit premises about how things are. All aspects of culture, however, are abstractions from activity, and the abstractions are put together by ordering principles. These principles refer chiefly to patterned action, the patterns of which are trans- missible, and hence one can deal with culture itself alone, without having to refer in each instance to the actions of specific actors in specific situations. As the structure of cultural theory becomes more highly developed, one is able to treat more and more adequately the makeup of the patterns and the interrelations of patterns among themselves. It is at present possible, for example, to make statements about the probability of the coexistence of certain types of kinship terminology and residence and about the developmental direction that such complexes can take.[8] Similar theoretical formulations are needed on the level of implicit culture. But whatever the nature of the formulation, we must remember that culture is a set of such formulations, a theoretical model, a system of categories and principles set up in such a fashion as to give order to action; or, more loosely speaking, we may say that culture is a system, or structure, of ordered action.

When dealing with groups of actors, a somewhat different, although related, approach puts more emphasis on particular actors in particular situations. Situations are grouped, according to regularities of action in them, into *institutions*; an institution is thus a concept which states that many separate situations have features in common, in terms of principles of abstraction or order, and in which, in the same terms, actors exhibit the same or closely similar actions. These similar actions are said to be *institutionalized* if the actors expect them to occur and there are cultural sanctions opposing nonconformity with expectations. In the formal description of institutions the position of the actor is described by saying that he occupies a *status*. When he acts in this status he is said to be acting out a *role*. Thus institutions are in another sense systems of roles. Institutions, or systems of roles, are grouped into larger systems called *social systems*. There are other meanings of social system in current usage, but the above is the one adopted in the theory which forms the major portion of this book.

We turn now to a brief examination of this theory from the point of view of the considerations contained in the preceding paragraphs. The theory, which is presented in Part II, "Values, Motives, and Systems of Action," is an attempt to provide a general basis on which subordinate theories of personality, culture, and social system can be worked out, all using the same or similar categories and concepts, thus providing opportunity for cross-disciplinary fertilization and coöperation and, in the end, for a more or less unified body of social scientific theory. In the theory of Part II the concepts personality and social system are used much as they have been presented in the preceding paragraphs, but the concept of culture is given a somewhat different meaning from what has been stated above. Most action which the anthropologist would call cultural is put in the social system (and to some extent into personality) as institutionalized norms, role behaviors, and so forth. For the category of culture proper is left only systems of ideas and beliefs, systems of expressional symbols (for example, art forms), and systems of value-orientations. And in the working out of the theory by far the major attention is paid to value-orientations, because much of the theory is concerned with the selection by actors of objects and gratifications in terms

[8] G. P. Murdock, *Social Structure* (New York: Macmillan, 1949).

of normative prescriptions, in which "should" and "ought" statements —
values — play a large role. This procedure produces a dichotomy in the use
of the concept of culture. That part of what, in ordinary anthropological usage,
is generally called culture which is put into the social system and into personality is considered to be an element in the orientation of action; the part of
culture that remains as a system in itself is considered to be an object of
orientation.

What are the implications of this procedure? The implications are stated
above in the General Statement: "Apart from embodiment in the orientation
systems of concrete actors, culture though existing as a body of artifacts and
as systems of symbols is not in itself organized as a system of action. Therefore culture as a system is on a different plane from personalities and social
systems." Culture as a system is thus considered to be a body of artifacts and
symbols, not a set of theoretical principles for ordering action as such.
Action is considered to be confined to specific actors in specific situations. It would be foolish to worry about whether a certain item of action should be put into a category labeled "culture" or "social structure,"
but one may legitimately inquire whether something may not be lost by
confining the application of theoretical principles to specific actors in specific
situations, particularly when one is dealing with implicit culture. In the past
there has been demonstrated the utility of dealing with basic action configurations in terms that are not specifically situational; in fact, aspects of action
patterns in specific situations can only be derived from the more general
configurations. Such a category as Benedict's "Dionysian," for example, is
not action in a specific situation, nor is it a system of ideas, expressional symbols, or values considered as objects toward which action can be oriented,
although it colors all of these things. It is an ordering principle, a free creation of the intellect. It is a principle which orders action just as the principles
involved in the conceptions of personality and social system order action.

Culture, personality, and social system — all three — are theoretical
models, systems of free concepts and principles. All are abstractions from
activity and relate activity to things outside the organism. If this fact is accepted, one can by definition restrict culture to objects and put the ordering
principles of culture all in personality and social system if one wants to;
but one does this by definition and not because of the inherent nature of
action or of the concepts personality, social system, and culture. In its opposition of "action" systems (personality and social systems) to culture,
which "is not organized as a system of action," the proposal for a theory of
action contained in Part II of this book seems to be making a classification
along the lines of what is conceived to be the inherent nature of the concepts.
And by doing so it rules out some of the demonstrated benefits of the use of
the concept of culture and also rules out future developments of this concept along lines which have been shown to have been fruitful. Of course, if

such a ruling out is done from purely logical considerations, one should not object to it for *a priori* reasons but must await empirical demonstrations that it constitutes an advance in our conceptual treatment of action. Such a demonstration is always possible, and in any event a demonstration of usefulness is the final criterion no matter how the theory is arrived at. But if the ruling out is done from what appears to be a misconstrual of the theory at hand, and if it appears that the ruling out restricts the usefulness of conceptual advances already made, then a reëxamination of the theory is in order.

As the title of this book indicates, the theory of action which will be presented in the following pages does not purport to be a final, fully worked out theory. In large measure it is a statement of the categories, or variables, which are to make up a complete general theory for the social sciences. In the General Statement which introduces the book it is stated that "the present statement . . . is a formulation of certain fundamental categories which will have to enter into the formulation of this general theory." These categories are designed so as to codify and provide a common language for existing knowledge in all branches of social science and to facilitate common effort in increasing knowledge. Such categories are needed and are highly useful. But I believe that one should make with considerable caution statements that such and such a set of categories *have* to be used. Considering the nature of theory in general, one can never be sure that one's categories are the best possible for handling the data at hand; and as I have pointed out, the experience of science has shown that a set of data does not impose theoretical categories which have to be used. This is a matter of fundamental importance and is not hairsplitting. Mechanistic physics got into a cul-de-sac in the later nineteenth century by assuming that observations had to be presented in terms of what Frank has called "a certain preferred analogy" [9] — the laws of Newtonian mechanics — and it was not until it had been shown that there was nothing in nature which imposed such a theoretical framework that physics was able to progress into fields which had hitherto been thought to be inaccessible. In social science it should always be recognized that no matter how fruitful a theory or approach has been, it may be possible to make a great advance by completely revising the categories of that theory. A fruitful approach should be followed through as thoroughly as possible, but it should not be taken as gospel.

The basic assumption of Professor Parsons and Shils's proposal for a theory of action (see Part II) is that the actor strives to achieve goals. In his goal-seeking the actor is oriented to objects, and the orientation is assumed to be in three modes: cognitive, cathectic, and evaluative. These modes are the basic principles which relate actors to objects and are thus the basic principles by which activity is conceptualized as action. Objects of orientation

---

[9] Philipp Frank, *Einstein, His Life and Times* (New York: Knopf, 1947), p. 47.

are assumed to be relevant in the situation because they afford alternative possibilities and impose limitations on the ways of gratifying the needs and achieving the goals of the actor. Orientation of action toward these objects hence entails selection. Actors, objects, and modes of orientation (principles relating actors to objects) being the basic conceptual material of personality, culture, and social systems, it should be possible to provide a unified basis for the development of these latter three categories in terms of the basic conceptual material. A very complicated classification and cross-classification of modes, objects, and alternative possibilities of selection among them is developed which crosscuts and intermingles with the concepts of personality, culture, and social system and allows the categorization of a tremendous number of kinds of action. The theory is indeed an all-embracing one, and the potentialities for developing a unified social science theory are high, provided one can give factual meaning to the categories in terms of operations and provided one can derive from these categories relationships subject to empirical test.

It is on these two "provideds" that the theory will stand or fall, and for the present we must await their full testing. The theory of action as it now stands does not purport, as I have said, to be developed to the state of being a complete general theory for the social sciences. It is a system of categories, which belong — speaking in terms of abstract theory — to the type of concepts which have been called here free creations of the intellect (this does not mean, of course, that the categories have been created out of thin air; they are based on years of empirical work by social scientists). The other two major ingredients of a general theory are not specifically contained in the theory of action as presented in Part II: the operations whereby the categories are to be connected to sense data, and the principles independent of the original assumptions whereby relationships subject to empirical test can be derived. The theory of action in its present form is propounded to be used for "describing the state of the system at a given moment" (see General Statement) rather than for "dynamic" analysis — describing changes in the system through time. But a description of the system at a given moment here means classifying action according to the categories of the theory, and such a classification remains in the realm of the untestable assumptions of the theory. Testable relationships can be derived from categories regardless of whether the system is considered to be changing or not, and it is the derivation of these relationships which is the immediate problem; dynamism refers merely to a certain type of derived relationships. The theory of action is not used in this general derivational manner in its present state of development. It can be used to say, "Given the present state of the system, certain variables must be present in certain situations," but such a statement is a definition of what the state of the system is assumed to be and of what the variables are, not an independent derivational statement. If it is recognized that such a statement is not imposed by the nature of the data treated but is a freely created theoretical supposition, then the way is cleared for developing the necessary theoretical and operational procedures for deriving from it relational statements susceptible to empirical test. When this is done, we shall have a complete theory.

In the body of social science as it now exists there is much to aid in the development of this complete theory. In particular, there are many operations already developed to connect hypothesis with sense data. If these operations can be coördinated with a set of general categories such as are contained in the present theory of action, much will be gained in generalizing the present departmentalized categories of social science. It is not the purpose of this chapter to outline specific ways in which this should be done. The history of science indicates that such a procedure should be closely coördinated with experiment and applied first to the explanation of relatively restricted areas of already known facts, and each step in the procedure could in itself be the subject of a complete article. My purpose here has been merely to indicate the kind of statements and assumptions which the experience of science has shown to be nontestable and what it has shown to be testable, and how inherently nontestable but necessary assumptions are utilized in developing fruitful theories. If the various components of a theory are recognized for what they are, one can stay out of blind alleys and one can most efficiently direct his energies toward developing ways for predicting action, which is the final goal. The theory of action presented in Part II is not complete as it stands, nor is it supposed to be complete, but if its development produces results, it provides promise, because of its wide range, of being an important step toward that goal.

2

Values, Motives, and Systems of Action

TALCOTT PARSONS

EDWARD A. SHILS

**With the assistance of
JAMES OLDS**

Introduction

This section is, in a sense, a continuation of the enterprise started in the General Statement of Part I. That statement sets forth a conceptual scheme concerning the nature of action. It holds that the elements of action can be organized into three different interdependent and interpenetrating, but not mutually reducible, kinds of systems. These three kinds of systems — personalities, social systems, and cultural systems — are all important in social theory.

The conceptual scheme set forth in the General Statement is the framework we share with our collaborators. It underlies our work and it will be taken for granted here. Our aim in the present section is to develop, from these starting points, a more technical and more highly differentiated conceptual scheme.

The body of Part II falls into four chapters. The first chapter defines more completely than has been done heretofore certain elements of the orientation of action and certain elements of the structure of the situation. These elements of orientation and structure are important in all three kinds of systems. In the same chapter, a further analysis of the interrelations of these elements is carried out. Specifically, the scheme of five "pattern variables" of value-orientation will be developed as a tool for analysis of such interrelations. The pattern-variable scheme presents a systematization of one of the crucial points of articulation of the three kinds of systems.

The second chapter is concerned with the way the action of the individual is organized into a personality system. The chapter attempts to organize certain motivational variables with those of the theory of action so as to form the two into one coherent system. Particularly, it points up relationships that obtain between motivational and value-orientation variables. And, it tries to show the relationship of the latter to the defensive and adjustive mechanisms by which the individual personality system copes with the exigencies of its situation.

The third chapter is concerned with culture. It takes up the systematic analysis of value patterns themselves and their organization into systems. It places them in the context of larger culture systems and analyzes their articulation with social systems and personalities. Sources of imperfect integration of certain value systems are also discussed; these are such as expose the systems to processes of change.

The fourth chapter takes up the social system, analyzing its bases of organization and its functional problems. It shows how value-orientation patterns enter into the institutionalization of roles and of the allocative and integrative structures of the social system and how the motivation of individual actors is channeled into role behavior. There is also consideration of the problem of the bases of structural variability and change of social systems. The final chapter briefly summarizes the main analysis and suggests certain lines of promising work for further development.

The most important thread of continuity running through Part II is the "pattern variable" scheme. It might be well to familiarize the reader with this scheme here at the outset so that he will be prepared for some of the complex material that will precede its technical introduction into the text of this work. The following paragraph, therefore, will show the reader something of what is to come.

The pattern-variable scheme defines a set of five dichotomies. Any course of action by any actor involves (according to theory) a pattern of choices with respect to these five sets of alternatives.[1] Ignoring technical terminology, we may define the five dichotomies as follows. The first is that between accepting an opportunity for gratification without regard for its consequences, on the one hand, and evaluating it with regard to its consequences, on the other. The second is that between considering an act solely with respect to its personal significance, on the one hand, and considering it with respect to its significance for a collectivity or a moral code, on the other. The third is that between evaluating the object of an action in terms of its relations to a generalized frame of reference, on the one hand, and evaluating it in terms of its relations to the actor and his own specific relations to objects, on the other. The fourth is that between seeing the social object with respect to which an action is oriented as a composite of performances (actions), on the one hand, and seeing it as a composite of ascribed qualities, on the other. The fifth is that between conceding to the social object with respect to which action is oriented an undefined set of rights (to be delimited only by feasibility in the light of other demands), on the one hand, and conceding to that social object only a clearly specified set of rights on the other.

The pattern-variable scheme to be presented below will attempt to formulate the way each and every social action, long- or short-term, proposed or concrete, prescribed or carried out, can be analyzed into five choices (conscious or unconscious, implicit or explicit) formulated by these five dichotomies.

We should perhaps give a brief résumé of the problems which gave rise to this method of analysis. Certain elements of this scheme were developed some years ago in an attempt by one of the authors to systematize the analysis of

---

[1] Actions may be long-term or short-term; they may be planned or concrete; they may be prescribed or carried out. A long-term action may be comprised by a sequence of shorter-term actions. A planned action may or may not eventuate in a concrete action; similarly, a prescribed course of action may or may not be carried out. Nevertheless, any specifiable course of action, short- or long-term, proposed or concrete, prescribed or carried out, is by theory analyzable into a pattern of choices with respect to these five dichotomies.

social role-patterns.[2] This attempt in turn grew out of dissatisfaction with then current dichotomous classifications of types of social relationships, of which Toennies' *Gemeinschaft* and *Gesellschaft* was the most prominent. Though applied to the analysis of professional roles and elsewhere, the pattern-variable scheme remained incomplete and its grounding in general theory obscure. This line of thought converged with ideas derived by the other author largely from critical consideration of Max Weber's four types of action and the difficulties in Weber's scheme.[3]

The problems posed by these concepts have proved to open up one of the main paths to the higher level of systematic integration of theory presented here. It appeared above all that these variables were not peculiar to social structure but were grounded in the general structure of action — they were hence involved in personalities as well as in social systems. It further appeared that they were patterns of value-orientation and as such were part of culture. This insight contributed greatly to the understanding of culture and of the ways in which it became integrated in personalities and social systems. The pattern variables have proved to form, indeed, a peculiarly strategic focus of the whole theory of action.

Several questions may arise about whether the substance of this monograph constitutes a "system" in the theoretical sense.[4] In one sense every carefully defined and logically integrated conceptual scheme constitutes a "system," and in this sense scientific theory of any kind consists of systems. Beyond this, however, there are three questions relevant to the "systematic" nature of a theoretical work. The first has to do with the generality and complexity of the scheme. The second is concerned with the degree to which it may claim "closure"; here the problem is whether the implications of its assertions in some parts are systematically supported or contradicted by assertions in other parts. The third is concerned with the level of systematization; that is, with how far the theory is advanced toward the ultimate goals of science.

Let us propose, in advance, some answers to these questions about the systematic nature of our work. Since we carry deductive procedures further than is common in the social sciences (excluding, perhaps, economic theory), we may justly be called system-builders on the first count. In default of formal, logical, or mathematical tests of completeness or closure, however, we are unable to judge how far the present scheme approaches such a standard; it seems almost certain that it is relatively incomplete in this sense. We do feel

---

[2] Cf. Talcott Parsons, *Essays in Sociological Theory*, esp. chap. viii.

[3] E. A. Shils, "Some Remarks on the Theory of Social and Economic Organization," *Economica*, 1948.

[4] Here the notion of a "theoretical system" should be kept separate from the notion of an "empirical system." The latter notion will be defined and discussed at the end of Chapter I. In the present section we are concerned with whether or not our conceptual scheme constitutes a theoretical system. Thus we are asking about the coherence and utility of our scheme. The other question (about an empirical system) has to do with criteria for coherence and harmony to be applied to some specific body of subject matter.

that we have carried the implications of our assumptions somewhat further than others have carried theirs; yet we do not feel that the fruitful implications of our assumptions have been even nearly exhausted. We believe that there is much more to be done.

So far as the "level" of systematization is concerned, it seems useful to distinguish four different levels of systematization of conceptual schemes, in order of their "primitiveness" relative to the final goals of scientific endeavor: (1) *ad hoc* classificatory systems, (2) categorial systems, (3) theoretical systems, and (4) empirical-theoretical systems.

The first type involves the use of more or less arbitrary classes for the sake of making summary statements about the subject matter. No attempt is made to fit the classes to the subject matter in such a way that the relations among the classes will be patterned upon the relations among the items of the subject matter summarized by these classes. The classes are quite independent of one another and any relations which may be discovered must come from *ad hoc* researches. Such common-sense classifications as that of "fish, flesh, or fowl" are illustrative of this type of classificatory system.

The second, the categorial type, involves a system of classes which is formed to fit the subject matter, so that there are intrinsic relations among the classes, and these are in accord with the relations among the items of the subject matter. Thus, in these systems, the principles of classification,[5] themselves, include statements of certain relationships among classes. The elements are so defined as to constitute an interdependent system. And the system has sufficient complexity and articulation to duplicate, in some sense, the interdependence of the empirical systems which are the subject matter. A categorial system, thus, is constituted by the definition of a set of interrelated elements, their interrelatedness being intrinsic to their definition. Thus in classical mechanics such concepts as space, time, particle, mass, motion, location, velocity, acceleration and their logical interrelations constitute a categorial system. A categorial system in this sense is always logically prior to the laws which state further relations between its elements. The laws state generalized relationships of interdependence between variables in the system. The laws presuppose the definitions of the variables, and they presuppose those relations which are logically implied by the definitions and by the kind of system in question. Insofar as specific laws can be formulated and verified, a categorial system evolves into a theoretical system. Thus a categorial system whose laws relating elements have been formulated is a theoretical system. But it is quite possible to have a categorial system or many parts of one before we have more than a rudimentary knowledge of laws.

In the field of action, our knowledge of laws is both vague and fragmentary. We know, for instance, that there is a positive relationship between reward and learning, but we cannot say in any specific situation how reward

[5] The principles of classification *are* the definitions of the elements of the system.

or its absence will interact with other variables; we do not know, that is, what effect will be produced by a concrete interaction of many variables even when reward is one of the ingredients of the situation. We do know, of course, that certain variables are highly significant, and we know certain things about the direction of their influence and how they combine with other variables. Knowing that a variable is significant, having a definite conception of it and its logical distinctions from other variables and other aspects of the empirical system is categorial knowledge; and that is where most of our theoretical knowledge of action stands today.

We have already said that a theoretical system is a categorial system whose laws relating elements have been formulated. The classical mechanics is the commonest example of what we mean here by a theoretical system. By logical manipulation of this system it is possible to make detailed predictions about the consequences of specific changes in the values of specific variables; this is because the general laws of the system are known. It should be noted, however, that the classical mechanics does not tell us how empirical systems will actually behave; it tells us rather how they might behave if an ideal set of scientific or "standard" conditions were to exist. Insofar as an empirical system can be subjected to such standard conditions in a laboratory, or insofar as it exists in some "pure" medium, so far is the theoretical system an adequate tool for the prediction of the changes which actually occur in the empirical system. Thus, in certain empirical fields, such as the astronomy of the solar system, the theoretical system of classical mechanics is, to a close approximation, empirically adequate. But in other fields, such as ballistics, or practical mechanics, the classical system by itself gives only much rougher approximations. This is because of the intervention of such variables as air-resistance and friction. The latter variables, insofar as they have no place in the system itself, bring about "error" in prediction, that is, error in the fit between the theoretical and the empirical systems.

This gives us the basis for our definition of empirical-theoretical systems. We speak of an empirical-theoretical system whenever a sufficient number of relevant variables can be brought together in a single (theoretical) system of interdependence adequate for a high level of precision in predicting changes in empirical systems outside special experimental conditions. This is the long-term goal of scientific endeavor.

It has often been said that in our field we have a "structural-functional" theory. This refers to the fact that we have achieved in our field the stage where the categorial requirements are relatively well met; the knowledge of laws has not yet reached far enough to justify calling ours a theoretical system in the sense of the classical mechanics. The progress of knowledge will, however, move it steadily in that direction.

The present monograph is a straightforward exposition of a conceptual scheme. We deliberately decided to forego documentation by references to the relevant literature. This would have been a heavy task, would have greatly increased the already considerable bulk of the monograph, and would have substantially delayed publication. We would like this monograph to be received as an essay in theory construction as such, not as a work of scholarship in the traditional sense.

It is always difficult to acknowledge adequately indebtedness for others' contributions to such a work. In the deepest sense our debt is to the work of the great founders of modern social science theory, among whom we may single out Durkheim, Freud, and Max Weber; but in addition to these many other psychologists and anthropologists have influenced us greatly. More directly, our collaborators in the present project have stimulated us profoundly through many discussions, formal and informal; by their criticisms; and, of course, by their writings. Among them Professor Tolman and Mr. Sheldon, with whom we shared the privilege of release from normal academic obligations, stand out. Members of the Harvard Department of Social Relations also played a very important part. The debts to our Harvard colleagues are relatively immediate because of the discussions in which we have jointly participated. These acknowledgements should not obscure the great indebtedness we feel to many colleagues and writers outside Harvard.

The final draft of this manuscript was turned over to Mr. James Olds for careful editing in the interest of clarity and readability. Mr. Olds's services were on a level far above that normally expected of an editor. He has contributed substantially to the content of the monograph at a number of important points as well as to the improvement of the presentation. We are most happy to acknowledge his contribution and to have him associated with us in the authorship of the monograph.

Finally, because of their close relationship to this work, we should mention two publications. *The Social System,* by Talcott Parsons, will be published in 1951 by the Free Press of Glencoe, Illinois. This book could be regarded as a second volume to the present monograph; it takes essentially the subject matter of Chapter IV and elaborates it into a full volume. The general foundations in the theory of action on which it builds are those developed in the General Statement of Part I and the present monograph. *The Primary Group in the Social Structure* by Edward A. Shils, will also be published by the Free Press. In a somewhat more special field, it analyzes the interrelations of personality systems, primary groups, and larger social systems, using much of the conceptual scheme presented here in Part II.

T. P.
E. A. S.

1

Categories of the Orientation and
Organization of Action

ACTION AND ITS ORIENTATION

The theory of action [1] is a conceptual scheme for the analysis of the behavior of living organisms. It conceives of this behavior as oriented to the attainment of ends in situations, by means of the normatively regulated expenditure of energy. There are four points to be noted in this conceptualization of behavior: (1) Behavior is oriented to the attainment of ends or goals or other anticipated states of affairs. (2) It takes place in situations. (3) It is normatively regulated. (4) It involves expenditure of energy or effort or "motivation" (which may be more or less organized independently of its involvement in action). Thus, for example, *a man driving his automobile to a lake to go fishing* might be the behavior to be analyzed. In this case, (1) *to be fishing* is the "end" toward which our man's behavior is oriented; (2) his situation is the road and the car and the place where he is; (3) his energy expenditures are normatively regulated — for example, this driving behavior is an *intelligent* [2] means of getting to the lake; (4) but he does spend energy to get there; he holds the wheel, presses the accelerator, pays attention, and adapts his action to changing road and traffic conditions. When behavior can be and is so analyzed, it is called "action." This means that any behavior of a living organism might be called action; but to be so called, it must be analyzed in terms of the anticipated states of affairs toward which it is directed, the situation in which it occurs, the normative regulation (e.g., the intelligence) of the behavior, and the expenditure of energy or "motivation" involved. Behavior which is reducible to these terms, then, is action.

[1] The present exposition of the theory of action represents in one major respect a revision and extension of the position stated in Parsons, *The Structure of Social Action* (pp. 43–51, 732–733), particularly in the light of psychoanalytic theory, of developments in behavior psychology, and of developments in the anthropological analysis of culture. It has become possible to incorporate these elements effectively, largely because of the conception of a system of action in both the social and psychological spheres and their integration with systems of cultural patterns has been considerably extended and refined in the intervening years.

[2] Norms of intelligence are one set among several possible sets of norms that function in the regulation of energy expenditure.

Each action is the action of an actor, and it takes place in a situation consisting of objects. The objects may be other actors or physical or cultural objects. Each actor has a system of relations-to-objects; this is called his "system of orientations." The objects may be goal objects, resources, means, conditions, obstacles, or symbols. They may become cathected (wanted or not wanted), and they may have different significances attached to them (that is, they may mean different things to different people). Objects, by the significances and cathexes attached to them, become organized into the actor's system of orientations.

The actor's system of orientations is constituted by a great number of specific orientations. Each of these "orientations of action" is a "conception" (explicit or implicit, conscious or unconscious) which the actor has of the situation in terms of what he wants (his ends), what he sees (how the situation looks to him), and how he intends to get from the objects he sees the things he wants (his explicit or implicit, normatively regulated "plan" of action).

Next, let us speak briefly about the sources of energy or motivation. These presumably lie ultimately in the energy potential of the physiological organisms. However, the manner in which the energy is expended is a problem which requires the explicit analysis of the orientation of action, that is, analysis of the normatively regulated relations of the actor to the situation. For, it is the system of orientations which establishes the modes in which this energy becomes attached and distributed among specific goals and objects; it is the system of orientations which regulates its flow and which integrates its many channels of expression into a system.

We have introduced the terms *action* and *actor*. We have said something about the goals of action, the situation of action, the orientation of action, and the motivation of action. Let us now say something about the *organization* of action into systems.

Actions are not empirically discrete but occur in constellations which we call systems. We are concerned with three systems, three modes of organization of the elements of action; these elements are organized as social systems, as personalities, and as cultural systems. Though all three modes are conceptually abstracted from concrete social behavior, the empirical referents of the three abstractions are not on the same plane. Social systems and personalities are conceived as modes of organization of *motivated* action (social systems are systems of motivated action organized about the relations of actors to each other; personalities are systems of motivated action organized about the living organism). Cultural systems, on the other hand, are systems of symbolic patterns (these patterns are created or manifested by individual actors and are transmitted among social systems by diffusion and among personalities by learning).

A *social system* is a system of action which has the following characteristics: (1) It involves a process of interaction between two or more actors; the interaction process as such is a focus of the observer's attention. (2) The situation toward which the actors are oriented includes other actors. These other actors (alters) are objects of cathexis. Alter's actions are taken cognitively into account as data. Alter's various orientations may be either *goals* to be pursued or *means* for the accomplishment of goals. Alter's orientations may thus be objects for evaluative judgment. (3) There is (in a social system) interdependent and, in part, concerted action in which the concert is a function of collective goal orientation or common values,[3] and of a consensus of normative and cognitive expectations.

A *personality system* is a system of action which has the following characteristics: (1) It is the system comprising the interconnections of the actions of an individual actor. (2) The actor's actions are organized by a structure of need-dispositions. (3) Just as the actions of a plurality of actors cannot be randomly assorted but must have a determinate organization of compatibility or integration, so the actions of the single actor have a determinate organization of compatibility or integration with one another. Just as the goals or norms which an actor in a social system will pursue or accept will be affected and limited by those pursued or accepted by the other actors, so the goals or norms involved in a single action of one actor will be affected and limited by one another and by other goals and norms of the same actor.

A *cultural system* is a system which has the following characteristics: (1) The system is constituted neither by the organization of interactions nor by the organization of the actions of a single actor (as such), but rather by the organization of the values, norms, and symbols which guide the choices made by actors and which limit the types of interaction which may occur among actors. (2) Thus a cultural system is not an empirical system in the same sense as a personality or social system, because it represents a special kind of abstraction of elements from these systems. These elements, however, may exist separately as physical symbols and be transmitted from one empirical action system to another. (3) In a cultural system the patterns of regulatory norms (and the other cultural elements which guide choices of concrete actors) cannot be made up of random or unrelated elements. If, that is, a system of culture is to be manifest in the organization of an empirical action system it must have a certain degree of consistency. (4) Thus a cultural system is a pattern of culture whose different parts are interrelated to form value systems, belief systems, and systems of expressive symbols.

Social systems, personality systems, and cultural systems are critical subject matter for the theory of action. In the first two cases, the systems themselves are conceived to be actors whose action is conceived as oriented to

---

[3] A person is said to have "common values" with another when either (1) he wants the group in which he and the other belong to achieve a certain group goal which the other also wants, or (2) he intrinsically values conformity with the requirements laid down by the other.

goals and the gratification of need-dispositions, as occurring in situations, using energy, and as being normatively regulated. Analysis of the third kind of system is essential to the theory of action because systems of value standards (criteria of selection) and other patterns of culture, when *institutionalized* in social systems and *internalized* in personality systems, guide the actor with respect to both the *orientation to ends* and the *normative regulation* of means and of expressive activities, whenever the need-dispositions of the actor allow choices in these matters.

COMPONENTS OF THE FRAME OF REFERENCE OF THE THEORY OF ACTION

1. *The frame of reference of the theory of action* involves actors, a situation of action, and the orientation of the actor to that situation.

a. One or more *actors* is involved. An actor is an empirical system of action. The actor is an individual or a collectivity which may be taken as a point of reference for the analysis of the modes of its orientation and of its processes of action in relation to objects. Action itself is a process of change of state in such empirical systems of action.

b. A *situation* of action is involved. It is that part of the external world which means something to the actor whose behavior is being analyzed. It is only part of the whole realm of objects that might be seen. Specifically, it is that part to which the actor is oriented and in which the actor acts. The situation thus consists of objects of orientation.

c. The *orientation of the actor to the situation* is involved. It is the set of cognitions, cathexes, plans, and relevant standards which relates the actor to the situation.

2. The *actor* is both a system of action and a point of reference. As a system of action the actor may be either an individual or a collectivity. As a point of reference the actor may be either an actor-subject (sometimes called simply *actor*) or a social object.

a. The *individual-collectivity* distinction is made on the basis of whether the actor in question is a personality system or a social system (a society or subsystem).

b. The *subject-object distinction* is made on the basis of whether the actor in question occupies a central position (as a point of reference) within a frame of reference or a peripheral position (as an object of orientation for an actor taken as the point of reference. When an actor is taken as the central point of reference, he is an actor-subject. (In an interaction situation, this actor is called *ego*.) When he is taken as an object of orientation for an actor-subject, he is a social object. (In an interaction situation, this actor is called *alter*.) Thus, the actor-subject (*the* actor) is an orienting subject; the social object is the actor who is oriented to. This distinction cross-cuts the individual-collectivity distinction. Thus an individual or a collectivity may be either actor-subject or social object in a given analysis.

3. The situation of action may be divided into a class of social objects (individuals and collectivities) and a class of nonsocial (physical and cultural) objects.

a. Social objects include actors as persons and as collectivities (i.e., systems of action composed of a plurality of individual actors in determinate relations to one another). The actor-subject may be oriented to himself as an object as well as to other social objects. A collectivity, when it is considered as a social object, is never constituted by all the action of the participating individual actors; it may, however, be constituted by anything from a specified segment of their actions — for example, their actions in a specific system of roles — to a very inclusive grouping of their actions — for example, all of their many roles in a society. Social objects, whether individuals or collectivities, may be subjected to two further types of classification which cross-cut each other: they may be divided on the basis of whether they are significant to the actor-subject as "quality" or "performance" complexes; and they may be divided on the basis of the "scope of their significance" to the actor-subject.

i. The *quality-performance* distinction: In the first place, social objects may be significant to the actor-subject as *complexes of qualities*. When the actor-subject sees another actor solely in terms of what that actor *is* and irrespective of what that actor *does*, then we say that actor-object is significant to the subject as a complex of qualities. In other words, whenever the actor-subject considers another actor only in terms of that actor's *attributes*, and whenever the actor-subject is not, in the specific context, concerned with how the actor will perform, then the actor being oriented to is a *complex of qualities*. The qualities are those attributes of the other actor which are for the nonce divorced from any immediate connection with the actor's performances. The significant question about the object is what it *is* at the relevant time and in the relevant context, regardless of actual or expected activities. For our purposes, qualities in this sense shall include *memberships* in collectivities and *possessions*, whenever the possession of an acknowledged claim to property is considered as one of the actor's attributes.

In the second place, social objects may be significant to the actor-subject as *complexes of performances*. When the actor-subject sees another actor solely in terms of what that actor *does* and irrespective of what that actor *is*, then we say that the actor-object is significant to ego as a complex of performances. In other words, whenever the actor-subject considers another actor only in terms of that actor's capacity to accomplish things (what that actor has done in the past, what he is doing, what he may be expected to do) then the other actor is a complex of performances.

ii. The *scope of significance* distinction: In the first place, social objects may have such a broad and undefined significance for the actor-subject that he feels obliged to grant them any demand they make of him, so long as the granting of the demand does not force him to fail in other obligations higher on a priority scale of values. In this case we may say the object has for the actor-subject a broad scope of significance. Its significance is *diffuse*.

In the second place, social objects may have such a narrow and clearly defined significance for the actor-subject that the actor-subject does not feel obliged to grant them anything that is not clearly called for in the definition of the relationship which obtains between them. In this case we say the scope of significance of the object for the actor-subject is *specific*.

b. Nonsocial objects are any objects which are not actors. Nonsocial objects may be classified on the basis of whether they are physical objects or cultural objects.

i. *Physical objects* are those objects which are located in space and time; which do not "interact" with the actor-subject, as other actors do; and which constitute only objects, not subjects, of cognitive, cathectic, and evaluative orientation. Thus they can constitute instrumentally significant means, conditions, goal objects, obstacles or significant symbols.

ii. *Cultural objects* are elements of the cultural tradition or heritage (for example, laws, ideas, recipes) when these are taken as *objects* of orientation. These too may be objects of cognitive, cathectic, and evaluative orientation in the sense that one may understand the meaning of a law, want a law, decide what to do about a law. Also, these may serve as normative rules, as instrumentally significant means, and as conditions or obstacles of action, or as systems of significant symbols.

These cultural objects are the laws, ideas, and so forth, as the actor-subject sees these things existing outside of himself. The same laws and ideas may eventually become internalized elements of culture for the actor-subject; *as such* they will not be cultural objects but components of the actor-subject's system of action. Cultural objects as norms may be divided into classes (cognitive, appreciative, and moral) exactly parallel to the three classes into which the value standards of the motivational orientation of the actor will be divided in the next section of this outline. Since these three classes will be defined at that point, we need not define them here.

4. The *orientation of the actor to the situation* may be broken down into a set of analytic elements. These elements are not separate within the orientation process; they might be conceived as different aspects or different ingredients of that process. They may be divided into two analytically independent categories: a category of elements of *motivational orientation* (appearances, wants, plans), and a category of elements of *value*-orientation (cognitive standards, aesthetic standards, moral standards).

a. Motivational orientation refers to those aspects of the actor's orientation to his situation which are related to actual or potential gratification or deprivation of the actor's need-dispositions. We will speak of three *modes* of motivational orientation.

i. The *cognitive* mode involves the various processes by which an actor *sees* an object in relation to his system of need-dispositions. Thus it would include the "location" of an object in the actor's total object-world, the determination of its properties and actual and potential functions, its differentiations from other objects, and its relations to certain general classes.[4]

ii. The *cathectic* [5] mode involves the various processes by which an actor invests an object with affective significance. Thus it would include the positive or negative cathexes implanted upon objects by their gratificational or deprivational significance with respect to the actor's need-dispositions or drives.

iii. The *evaluative mode* involves the various processes by which an actor allocates his energy among the various actions with respect to various cathected objects in an attempt to optimize gratification. Thus it would include the processes by which an actor organizes his cognitive and cathectic orientations into intelligent plans. These processes make use of cognitive norms (bits of knowledge) in order to distribute attention and action with respect to various objects and their possible modalities, with respect to various occasions for gratification, and with respect to the demands of different need-dispositions. Evaluation is functionally necessary for the resolution of conflicts among interests and among cognitive interpretations which are not resolved automatically; and which thus necessitate *choice*, or at least specific selective mechanisms.

b. *Value-orientation* [6] refers to those aspects of the actor's orientation which commit him to the observance of certain norms, standards, criteria of selection, whenever he is in a contingent situation which allows (and requires) him to make a choice. Whenever an actor is forced to choose among various means objects, whenever he is forced to choose among various goal objects, whenever he is forced to choose which need-disposition he will gratify, or how much he will gratify a need-disposition — whenever he is forced to make any choice whatever — his *value-orientations* may commit him to certain norms that will guide him in his choices. The value-orientations which commit a man to the observance of certain rules in making selections from available alternatives are not random but tend to form a system of value-orientations which commit the individual to some organized set of rules (so that the rules themselves do not contradict one another). On a cultural level we view the or-

[4] Tolman's concept "cognitive mapping" well describes this mode. The extent to which this involves instrumental orientation will be taken up below, pp. 75–76.

[5] It is through the cathexis of objects that energy or motivation, in the technical sense, enters the system of the *orientation of action*. The propositions about drive in the General Statement are here taken for granted. Their implications for action will be further elaborated in Chapter II.

[6] Standards of value-orientation are of course not the whole of a system of cultural orientation. This has been made clear in the General Statement. They are however *strategically* the most important parts of culture for the organization of systems of action. Their relation to the other parts will be more fully analyzed in Chapter III, below.

ganized set of rules or standards as such, abstracted, so to speak, from the actor who is committed to them by his own value-orientations and in whom they exist as need-dispositions to observe these rules. Thus a culture includes a set of *standards*. An individual's value-orientation is his commitment to these standards. In either case our analysis of these standards of value-orientation commitment may be the same.

We shall speak of three modes of value-orientation, which parallel the modes of motivational orientation.

i. The *cognitive* mode of value-orientation involves the various commitments to standards by which the validity of cognitive judgments is established. These standards include those concerning the relevance of data and those concerning the importance of various problems. They also include those categories (often implicit in the structure of a language) by which observations and problems are, often unconsciously, assessed as valid.

ii. The *appreciative* mode of value-orientation involves the various commitments to standards by which the appropriateness or consistency of the cathexis of an object or class of objects is assessed. These standards sometimes lay down a pattern for a particular kind of gratification; for example, standards of taste in music. The criterion in formulating such appreciative standards is not what consequences the pursuit of these patterns will have upon a system of action (a person or a collectivity). Rather, these standards purport to give us rules for judging whether or not a given object, sequence, or pattern will have immediate gratificatory significance.

iii. The *moral* mode of value-orientation involves the various commitments to standards by which certain consequences of particular actions and types of action may be assessed with respect to their effects upon systems of action. These standards define the actor's responsibility for these consequences. Specifically, they guide the actor's choices with a view to how the consequences of these choices will affect (a) the integration of his own personality system and (b) the integration of the social systems in which he is a participant.

Fig. 1 is an attempt to summarize this outline. It shows that the frame of reference of the theory of action includes subjects and objects. Only actors are subjects; objects include actors and nonsocial objects. The box in the center shows how social systems and personalities interpenetrate one another whether they are subjects or objects: a role is the segment of a personality's actions (or orientations) which goes into the constitution of any particular group (the concept will be discussed in detail later). At the bottom of the diagram is a section that indicates how cultural systems are abstracted from the action frame of reference. (All figures referred to in Part II are grouped, in sequence, following page 245.)

COMMENTARY ON THE FRAME OF REFERENCE

The frame of reference of the theory of action is a set of categories for the analysis of the relations of one or more actors to and in a situation. It is not directly concerned with the internal constitution or physiological processes of the organisms which are in one respect the units of the concrete system of action; its essential concern is with the structure and processes involved in the actor's *relations* to his situation, which includes *other actors* (alters) as persons and as members of collectivities. There is an inherent relativity in this frame of reference. The determination of which is actor and which is object in a situation will depend on the point of reference required by the problems under consideration. In the course of an analysis this point of reference may shift from one actor to another and it is always important to make such a shift explicit. It is also fundamental that a *collectivity* may be chosen as a point of reference, in which case the relevant segments of the action of its members do not belong to the situation, but to the collectivity as actor.[7] By the same token the actor himself, as either an organism or personality or as both, may be treated as an *object* of his own orientation. It is very important to understand that the distinction between actor and situation is *not* that between *concrete* entities distinguished in common-sense terms. It is an *analytical* distinction, the concrete referents of which will shift according to the analytical uses to which it is put.

The frame of reference of the theory of action differs in two ways from the biological frame of reference which has, explicitly and implicitly, in-

[7] The collectivity as an action system, whether it be subject or object in a given analysis, is not the simple sum of the actions of the individual actors involved. It is rather composed of the segments of their action; specifically, those segments of their action which are oriented to and in this collectivity. To the individual actors the collectivity is an object of orientation, that is, a social object (thus an alter), and the actions of the collectivity may themselves be more specific objects of orientation for the individual actor. But when the collectivity is taken as the actor-subject, the actions of these individuals (the members of the collectivity) insofar as they are oriented to the collectivity, are the *actions of the collectivity*. Thus, when the collectivity is the actor, then the collectivity-oriented actions of its members are not objects of orientation for the collectivity; they are the actions of the collectivity. A collectivity may be viewed as an actor in either of the following senses: (1) as a social system in relation to a situation outside itself. In the most important case, the collective actor is a subsystem of the larger social system interacting as a unit with other subsystems and/or individual actors (which are taken as objects of *its* situation). Viewed internally the collective actor must be interpreted as a concert of actions and reactions of individual actors, and the conceptual scheme for its analysis will thus be that used for the analysis of *social systems*. The conceptual scheme used in the analysis of personality systems is hence inappropriate for the description of a collective actor, especially in the imputation of motivation. The *mechanisms* which explain the action of the collective actor are those of the social system, *not* of the personality. (2) A collectivity may be viewed as an actor when it is the point of reference for the orientation of an individual actor in a *representative role*. In this usage, a member of a collectivity acts on behalf of his collectivity, his role as representative being accepted by fellow members and by those who are the situational context of the collective actor. (Collectivities as systems of action may of course be treated as objects by the actors in a situation.)

fluenced much current thought about behavior. In the first place, the theory of action is not concerned with the internal physiological processes of the organism. It is concerned instead with the organization of the actor's processes of interaction with objects in a situation; in this sense it is *relational*. The course of a stream may be said in the same sense to be a *relational* matter; it is no property of water to flow in one direction rather than another, nor is it the contour of the land alone which determines the direction of the flow. The stream's course is determined by a relationship between the properties of the water and the contour of the land; however, the map-maker can chart the flow of a stream by means of *relational* concepts without recourse to any but a few of the intrinsic properties of land or water. The map-maker is not interested in the principles of moisture-absorption, condensation, and gravitation, which, in a sense, account for the direction of the stream's flow; he is satisfied merely to plot the structure of the channel which actually guides the water's flow. The structure of the river system, thus, is not the structure of the water, but it is a structure — in this case, of the water's relationships to the earth's undulations. Similarly, the structure of action is *not* the structure of the organism. It is the structure of the organism's relationships to the objects in the organism's situation.

One of the apparent paradoxes of the theory of action stems from this lack of concern for internal structure. The paradox is that with all its emphasis on structure, the theory of action describes an actor who sometimes does not seem to have any internal structure at all. This paradox arises only on one level of conceptualization; [8] that level in which the actor is treated as the unit of interaction within a larger system of action. On the level dealing with the dynamic analysis of social interaction, however, the actor does indeed have very much of a structure. When we go beyond the description of an orientation and seek to *explain* what has occurred, the actor is not only a *point* of reference, but also definitely a system of action which we call personality. Even at this level, however, the internal, physiological process of the organism, although highly relevant to the concrete phenomena of action, is

---

[8] When the individual actor is seen as the interacting unit within a larger scale structure (for example, within a social system, or within the total action frame of reference which comprehends both actors and objects) the actor does not seem to have a structure. This is similar to the notion that any molecule of water in the stream is simply an unstructured unit of flow to the man charting the river. But this is true only on one level of conceptualization: both the molecule and the actor may be analyzed as systems in themselves if one seeks explanation on a deeper level. When we treat the actor as a unit in the system of interaction with the object world, our abstraction ignores the internal structure and processes of that unit and considers *only* its relations with the situation. Nevertheless, any particular act of this unit may in fact be a very complex resultant of internal personality factors. When these internal complications are an object of study the personality is not treated merely as an actor but as a system of action. It will be recalled that there is just as much *interaction* between elements within the personality as a system as there is between persons in the social system.

only relevant insofar as it affects the system of orientations. The physiological process will enter the picture as the source of the viscerogenic drive or energy of action and in various ways as part of the object system, as a system of qualities and of capacities for performance. We emphasize, however, that only the empirical *consequences* of this aspect of the organism, formulated in terms of their *relevance* to the system of action, interest us here.

In the second place, the frame of reference of the theory of action differs from common biologically oriented approaches in the categories used to analyze the interaction of organism and environment. The most obvious difference is the *explicit* concern of our theory with *selection* among alternative possibilities and hence with the evaluative process and ultimately with value standards. Thus, our primary concern in analyzing systems of action with respect to their aims is this: to what consequences has this actor been committed by his selections or choices? [9] This contrasts with the primary concern of biological theorists, who, in a motivational analysis, would ask a parallel but quite different question: what does this person have to do in order to survive? In the system of action the question is what does this actor strive for, not what does he *have* to strive for in order to survive as an organism. Further, we ask: on what bases does the actor make his selections? Implicit is the notion that survival is *not* the sole ground of these selections; on the contrary, we hold that internalized cultural values are the main grounds of such selective orientations.

The role of choice may be implicit in much biological analysis of behavior, but in the frame of reference of the theory of action it becomes explicit and central.[10]

The *empirical* significance of selective or value standards as determinants of concrete action may be considered problematical and should not be prejudged. But the theory of action analyzes action in such a way as to leave the door open for attributing a major significance to these standards (and their patterning). The older type of biological frame of reference did not leave this door open and thus prejudged the question.

The theory of action formulates the components of the action frame of

[9] The terms *selection* and *choice* are used more or less interchangeably in this context. Where alternatives exist which cannot all be realized, a selection must result. The mechanisms by which this occurs are not at issue at this stage of the analysis. The present problem is, then, analysis of the structure of the system of alternatives, not the determinants of selection between them.

[10] The notion of selection or choice in the present discussion is closely connected with the notion of expectations and normative orientations in the General Statement of Part I. These concepts all underline and define the voluntaristic or purposive aspects of systems of action as conceived by the present analytical scheme. Without this purposive aspect, most of the elements of the orientation of action under consideration here — and above all the patterns of value-orientation — would become analytically superfluous epiphenomena.

reference in terms of their direct relevance to *choice orientation*.[11] The situation is treated as a constellation of objects among which selections must be made.[12] Action itself is the resolution of an unending series of problems of selection which confront actors.

It is against the background of these observations that the subjective viewpoint of our frame of reference should be considered. We do *not* postulate a substantive entity, a mind which is somehow dissociated from the organism and the object world. The organization of observational data in terms of the theory of action is quite possible and fruitful in modified behavioristic terms, and such formulation avoids many of the difficult questions of introspection or empathy.[13] In Tolman's psychology, it is postulated that the rat is oriented to the goal of hunger gratification and that he cognizes the situation in which he pursues that goal. Tolman's concepts of orientation and cognition are ways of generalizing the facts of observation about the rat's behavior. The concept of expectation is also essential to this mode of organizing data. By broadening this notion to include the "complementarity of expectations" involved in the action of an ego and the *reaction* of an alter, we have all the essential components of the analysis of action defined in Tolman's manner without raising further difficulties. What the actor thinks or feels can be treated as a system of *intervening variables*. The actor and his cognitive, cathectic, and evaluative processes are neither more nor less real than the "particle" of classical mechanics and its composition.

CLASSIFICATION OF OBJECTS

The foregoing discussion constitutes a commentary on items one and two of our outline. We have tried to give the reader a general familiarity with the significant features of the action frame of reference, and in the course of the discussion we have sought to clarify the relation of the actor-subject to the frame of reference. We shall proceed now to a discussion of the objects of the situation, item three of our outline. Specifically, we shall discuss the classification of objects in terms of the *object modalities*. A *modality* is a property of an object; it is one of the aspects of an object in terms of which the object may be significant to an actor. Some (if not most) objects have several modalities in terms of which they may have meaning to an actor. A given actor may "choose" to see the object only in terms of one, or a specific set, of these modalities. The relevant action of the actor will be a function of the modalities he chooses.

[11] The terms *choice orientation, selective orientation,* and so forth, refer to the actor's acts of choosing. That is, they refer to the subjective processes involved while the actor is making a choice.

[12] Actually choices are not made so much with respect to the objects themselves as among possible relations to these objects.

[13] This procedure does not necessarily commit one to any specific position on the more ultimate epistemological problem of the nature of our knowledge of other minds.

The most fundamental distinction bearing on the object system is that between the *social* and the *nonsocial* modalities of objects. By *social* in this context, we mean interactive. A social object is an actor or system of action, whose reactions and attitudes are significant to the actor who is the point of reference. The social object, the alter, is seen by ego to have expectations which are complementary to ego's own. The distinction between those objects which do and those objects which do not have expectations complementary to ego's is fundamental to the theory of action. It should, however, be clear that the same *concrete* object may be social or nonsocial in different contexts. Thus, on the one hand, a human being may be treated *only* as a physical object and no account taken of his possible reactions to ego's action, and, on the other, an animal may be a social object.

Within the category of social objects a further discrimination has been made between complexes of qualities and complexes of performances. In one sense, of course, all action is performance and all social objects are "performers"; yet it is possible to orient objects either (1) in terms of characteristics they possess regardless of their performances, or (2) in terms of characteristics they possess by virtue of their performances.

A social object is a complex of qualities when the actor, in the orientation of action to the objects, overlooks actual or possible performances and *focuses* on "attributes" [14] as such. These attributes may in the further developments of interaction be related to performances in many ways, but in the immediate situation, it is the attribute which is the basis of discrimination. Thus, to take a very obvious example, for the normal heterosexual person, the sex of an object rather than its "capacity for giving erotic gratification" may be the *first* criterion of object-choice. Only within the category of those possessing the quality of *belonging to the opposite sex* from ego do performance criteria become relevant.[15]

A social object is a complex of performances when the actor, in the orientation of action to the object, *focuses* on its processes of action and *their outcomes* rather than its qualities or attributes. The significant focus is not a *given state*. It may be remarked that orientation to performance has become so central in Western society that there has been a tendency to assimilate all social objects to this modality. A comparative perspective will dissolve this illusion.

Certainly the most obvious reason for emphasis on the distinction is the very great importance in the organization of social relations of ascriptive

[14] Confusion is very easy here because logically *anything* predicated of an object may be considered an attribute. Here we have a special definition of the term in mind. An attribute of a social object is some quality or descriptive term which would characterize the object irrespective of any action that object might perform.

[15] Of course the two aspects are so fully integrated in the actual system of our cultural orientations that it never occurs to most of us to make such a distinction, and in daily life, there is no reason why it should be done.

qualifications for status. But the distinction will be seen to permeate systems of action very generally. It should be emphasized here that this distinction, like the distinction between social and nonsocial objects, refers to aspects of objects, not to discrete concrete entities. The same object may, in different contexts of the same system of action, be significant for its qualities or for its performances.[16]

In addition to the quality-performance distinction, a scope-of-significance distinction can also be applied to social objects. An object's scope of significance is not really a modality of the object; it is rather a special relationship which obtains between the actor and the object. Thus a social object, whatever the content of an actor's concern for it, may be significant to him in terms of one, several, or numerous of its aspects. The range or scope over which the object is significant to the actor cannot be deduced from, and is thus analytically independent of, the modalities of the object. It is likewise analytically independent of motivational orientations and value-orientations, and it might thus be regarded as an additional category of orientation.

The category of nonsocial objects comprises both physical and cultural objects. They have in common the fact that they do not, in the technical sense, *interact* with actors. They do not and cannot constitute alters to an ego; they do not have *attitudes* or *expectations* concerning ego. Both may, however, be immediately cathected as objects; they may constitute conditions or means of instrumental action, and as symbols they may become endowed with meaning.

Although physical and cultural objects have these features in common, there is a crucial set of differences which centers on the fact that cultural objects can be internalized and thereby transmitted from one actor to another, while only *possession* of claims to physical objects can be transmitted. This difference rests on the fact that the cultural object is a pattern which is reproducible in the action of another person while it leaves the original actor unaffected. Only in a figurative sense does an actor *have* patterns of value-orientation. In a strict sense he *is*, among other things, a system of such patterns. Of course, another actor, an alter, cannot be internalized either. Only his cultural patterns — for instance, his values — can be "taken over" by orientation or identification.[17]

The distinction between cultural patterns as objects, on the one hand, and as components of the actor's system of orientation, on the other, must be held separate from the classification of *types* of culture patterns themselves — that is, from the classification in terms of belief systems, systems of expressive symbols, and systems of value-orientations. The first distinction is not a differentiation among the parts of a cultural system; it distinguishes

---

[16] The term *performance* has been chosen to avoid confusion with the general meaning of the term *action*. Orientation to an object in terms of its qualities is action.

[17] See Chapter II, pp. 116, 130.

modes of the relationship of cultural patterns to action, regardless of the type of the pattern. In principle *every* kind of cultural object is capable of internalization. It is this "transferability" from the status of object to the internalized status and vice versa which is the most distinctive property of culture and which is *the fundamental reason why culture cannot be identified with the concrete systems of action.*

The Freudian hypothesis concerning the formation of the superego has made the internalization of patterns of value-orientation widely known. It is also strategically the most important case for us. But the internalization of instrumental and expressive patterns such as skills and tastes is also of the highest importance in the analysis of action.

Before leaving the problem of objects, we should speak briefly about the problem of the "phenomenological" approach to the object world which we use. We are interested in the object world not as an abstract scientific entity but as something which significantly affects the action of an actor. Thus we are only interested in those aspects of that world which do affect, which are relevant to, ego's action. But, to become relevant to ego's action, all classes of objects must be known or cognized in some way or other. Thus our tendency is to pattern our abstraction of the object world after ego's cognition of that world. There is always a distinction between the actually and the potentially known. Only the hypothetical mind of God is omniscient. An observer may, however, know many things about another actor's situation and his personality which the other actor himself does not know. The observer might thus well know much more than ego about those properties of the objects in ego's situation which affect ego's behavior indirectly.

We should therefore recognize the implicit if not always explicit distinction between the situation as known to or knowable by an observer and as known to the actor in question. Of course, ego's knowledge may be increased by processes of investigation; and through the search for knowledge, as well as by other processes arising from the properties of the object situation, new objects not previously part of the situation of action may enter. The most usual condition is for relatively few of the knowable properties of the object situation to be known to the actor. He will seldom know the systemic interconnections of the objects of his situation which the scientific observer might know and would have to know in order to account for their behavior.

Let us turn now now from item three of our outline, the situation, to item four, the orientation of the actor to that situation, and discuss the categories for analysis of the actor's system of relations to the object world.

ORIENTATION TO THE SITUATION

What can we say about the actor's orientation to a situation? At the outset we must mention two general features which characterize and perhaps define all such orientations, but which are of such a general nature that they are not treated as separate modes of orientation. These are (1) the choice aspect and (2) the expectancy aspect of the orientation. The first implies that every orientation is explicitly or implicitly an orientation to alternatives; the orientation involves a scanning of several possible courses of action and a choice from them. The second implies that every orientation is an "expectancy" in the sense that it is an orientation to the future state of the situation as well as to the present. We mention these two points at the outset as they pervade the following discussion of the modes or orientation.

Besides the aspects mentioned above, the salient features of an actor's orientation are these: (1) There is orientation to discriminated and related objects; various things are seen or expected, and they are seen or expected in relational contexts. (2) There is orientation to goals; various things are wanted. (3) There is orientation to the gratification-deprivation significance of the various courses of action suggested by the situation, and there is comparison of the gratification-deprivation balance presented by each of the alternative courses. (4) There is orientation to standards of acceptability which (*a*) narrow the range of cognitions, sorting "veridical" from "nonveridical" object-orientation; (*b*) narrow the range of objects wanted, sorting "appropriate" from "inappropriate" goal objects; and (*c*) narrow the number of alternatives, sorting "moral" from "immoral" courses of action.

Points one, two, and three make up the three modes of the motivational orientation in our classificatory scheme. Point four is the value-orientation. We will discuss first the three modes of motivational orientation and then the three modes of value-orientation.

The first two modes of motivational orientation, the cognitive and cathectic modes, are the minimal components of any act of orientation. Similarly they are the minimal components of any act of selection or choice (this is redundant in the sense that any orientation involves an explicit or implicit choice, but it serves to emphasize another aspect of the problem). One cannot "orient" without discriminating objects, one cannot discriminate an object without its arousing some interest either by virtue of its intrinsic gratificatory significance, or by virtue of its relationships to other objects. Similarly, one cannot make a choice without "cognizing" the alternatives; and also one cannot select except on the basis of the cathectic interest aroused by the alternatives. The discrimination of objects is the cognitive mode of motivational orientation. The having of interest in an object is the cathectic mode of motivational orientation. The "expectancy" aspect of the orientation enters into both modes; both modes, that is, have a future reference: the cognitive discrimination of an object includes a cognitive prediction regarding a future state of the situation; the cathectic interest in an object includes a readiness to receive gratification and avoid deprivation.

Let us dwell for a moment on the notion, implicit in the paragraph above, that cognition and cathexis are simultaneously given and only analytically separable. In the first place, there can be no *orientation* to the cathectic or gratificatory significance of objects without discrimination, without location of the relevant object or objects in relation to others, without discrimination between objects which produce gratification and those which are noxious. Thus the cognitive mapping of the situation, or relevant parts of it, is one essential aspect of any actor's orientation to it. Nor can there be cognition without an associated cathexis. Each object of cognition is cathected in some degree either by virtue of its intrinsic gratificatory significance or by virtue of its relationships to other objects of intrinsic gratificatory significance. The limiting case is the object of "pure knowledge," and even this is cathected in the limited sense implied by the existence of a cognitive interest in it. Furthermore, the standards of cognitive judgment must certainly be objects of cathexis and the act of cognition might also be cathected.

Of these two modes of orientation, the cathectic mode is most specifically *relational* in the sense that we have already said the orientation itself is relational. That is, a cathexis relates an actor and an object. Specifically it refers on the one side to a motivation — that is, a drive, need, wish, impulse, or need-disposition — and on the other side to an object. It is only when the motivation is attached to a determinate object or objects through the cathectic mode of motivational orientation that an organized system of behavior [18] exists.

We have just said that a cathexis relates a motive to an object, and in the section of the General Statement on behavior psychology, quite a bit is said about the motivation that makes up one side of this picture. Hitherto, however, we have said nothing about the kinds of objects that become cathected — that is, the kinds of objects which gratify need-dispositions — and it is not possible to do more than indicate them briefly here. Except for the objects which gratify specific organically engendered need-dispositions, the most pervasive cathected object is a positive affective response or attitude on the part of alter and the corresponding positive affective attitude on the part of ego toward alter or toward himself as object (e.g., love, approval, esteem). The sensitivity to which we alluded in the General Statement is primarily a sensitivity to these positive affective attitudes. This sensitivity enters as an ingredient into many need-dispositions with complex institutional objects, such as the need-dispositions for achievement, charity, and so forth. The sensitivity is learned through a series of processes in which generalization, substitution, and identification play preëminent parts.

---

[18] The degree to which this organized system of behavior is an active pursuit of gratification or merely a state of passive receptive gratification may of course vary. In either case we have action in the sense that the active pursuit or passive reception is selected from alternatives by the actor. Both activity and passivity share elements of "expectancy." Activity involves the expectation of gratification in consequence of performance. Both are directed toward future developments in the situation in both cognitive and cathectic modes.

When an object is sufficiently gratifying to the need-dispositions or set of need-dispositions which are directed toward it over time, we may speak of an object-attachment. The actor will recurrently seek out the object when the need-disposition is reactivated or he will seek to maintain (or possess) at all times a given relation to it. This possession of objects, or maintenance of relationships to them, serves to stabilize the availability of objects and thus to stabilize the orientation system of the individual actor (that is, he knows where to find things; his little world is not a chaos). Finally, it should be remembered that through the mechanisms of generalization, *categories* of objects may be themselves objects of attachment.

The third of the three basic modes of motivational orientation is evaluation. The evaluative mode is essentially the organizational or integrative aspect of a given actor's system of action and hence it is directly relevant to the act of choice. It operates wherever a selection problem is presented to the actor, where he wants or could want two or more gratifications, both of which cannot be attained — where, in other words, there is actually or potentially a situation in which one "wants to eat one's cake and have it too." [19] That this situation exists on the level of animal behavior is amply attested by Tolman's work. It becomes particularly significant on the human level with the involvement of culture and cultural standards in the act of choice.

Several things are to be said about this evaluative mode. The first is that it cannot be understood properly except as an aspect of the cognitive-cathectic orientation process; the evaluative mode tends to be inextricably related to the cognitive mode whenever cognition is at all complex. The second is that it is our organizational concept which parallels the system of instincts in biological analysis of behavior. The third is that it is to be sharply distinguished from the value standards of the value-orientation. The fourth is, on the other hand, that it designates the point in the system of motivation at which these value or cultural standards of the value-orientation become effective in guiding behavior.

Let us return to our first point, the relation between the evaluative and cognitive modes. The evaluative process in some sense transforms the function of the cognitive mode of motivational orientation. Abstracted from the evaluative mode, cognition is simply in the service of specific motivations

---

[19] The emphasis on choice, choice alternatives, patterns of choice, etc., which is central to this scheme of analyses, should not be interpreted to mean that the actor always deliberately and consciously contemplates alternatives and then chooses among them in the light of a value standard. The decision regarding which of the realistic alternatives he should choose is often made for him through his acceptance of a certain value-orientation. (In a figurative sense, it might be said that the value-orientations which are part of the cultural value system by being institutionalized come to make the choice rather than the actor.) From one point of view, the function of the institutionalization of value standards is to narrow the range of effective choice to manageable proportions.

or need-dispositions, being instrumental to their gratification. In conjunction with the evaluative process, cognition begins to serve not only the specific motives one at a time, but the functional harmony of the whole. The actor learns to take account of the *consequences* of immediate gratification; in the absence of evaluation, he only takes account of how to arrive at that gratification. Thus, whenever cognition is involved in the solution of any sort of conflict problem, it is inextricably related to the evaluative mode.

Second, let us point out what we mean by saying that evaluation is our organizing principle. In any complex system, some mediating mechanism is required to accomplish the discipline of the parts with a view to the organization of the whole. Biologically oriented theorists have been wont to postulate "instincts" or "systems of instincts" as the mechanisms which mediate this discipline. Instincts were innate organizers, or innate systems of discipline. In our theory, instincts thus defined account for little of the over-all organization. That is, we believe that such innate organization as may exist leaves a wide area of freedom; there is a certain plasticity in the relation of the organism to the situation. Having given up instinct as the over-all organizing principle, we require some compensative element of organization. For us, that element is the evaluative mode of motivational orientation. It regulates selection among alternatives when several courses of action are open to the actor (owing to the plasticity of his relationship to the situation).

Third, let us distinguish clearly between the evaluative mode of motivational orientation and the value standards of value-orientation. The evaluative mode involves the cognitive act of balancing out the gratification-deprivation significances of various alternative courses of action with a view to maximizing gratification in the long run. The value standards are various recipes or rules (usually passed from person to person and from generation to generation) which may be observed by the actor in the course of this balancing-out procedure. They are rules which may help the actor to make his choice either by narrowing the range of acceptable alternatives, or by helping the actor foresee the long-run consequences of the various alternatives.

Fourth, we say that the evaluative mode designates the point in the system of motivation at which these value or cultural standards of the value-orientation become effective. The way is *cleared* for the orientation of value standards to have a decisive effect upon behavior whenever there is a significant degree of behavioral plasticity of the organism, that is, whenever the motivational orientation allows two or more alternative courses of behavior. But it is precisely at this point that the evaluative mode becomes relevant. The evaluative mode itself concerns the weighing of alternatives and the act of choosing. When this evaluation is made with an eye to any standards for guiding choice, then the evaluative mode has brought in some aspect of the value-orientation. It should be remembered that the *act of choosing* is essentially the aspect of orientation implied by the term *evaluative mode*; the *standards on which choices are based* are the aspects of the orientation implied by the term *value-orientations.*

At this point, we shall proceed to a discussion of the value-orientation as such, and its various modes.[20] We have already said that the way is cleared for value standards to be effective whenever the plasticity of the organism leaves a realm of freedom in the relation between the situation and the organism and we said that value standards are involved in the *evaluative mode* of the motivational orientation as rules and recipes for guiding selections. We have said too that the value standards themselves constitute what we call the value-orientation and we have mentioned in passing that these standards guide selection (*a*) by narrowing the range of alternatives open and (*b*) by amplifying the consequences of the various alternatives. In much the same vein, we have said these are standards of acceptability and that they (i) narrow the range of cognitions, (ii) narrow the range of objects wanted, and (iii) narrow the number of alternatives.

We have also pointed out that cultural values are effective in two main ways. On the one hand, through interaction, they become built into the structure of personality through the learning process; on the other hand, they are objects in the situation which become particularly significant through their involvement in the sanction system which is associated with roles in the social structure. It is only *through* these channels that value standards enter the motivational process and play a part in the determination of action.[21] By the same token a cathexis must be involved before action is affected. If not the standard itself in an abstract sense, then at least the objects which are chosen in accord with it, must be cathected for value standards to influence behavior.

Value standards are classified on the basis of their relationship to the three modes of motivational orientation. Action is organized by cognitive, cathectic, and evaluative modes of motivational orientation. There are regulatory standards applicable to all three aspects of orientation; thus there are cognitive, appreciative, and moral standards. Classification of standards along these lines offers great convenience for the analysis of action. In the following paragraphs we take up the three categories or modes of value-orientation formulated by this method of classification.

[20] Let us emphasize that we are not turning our attention from one kind of orientation to another kind. The three elementary modes of motivational orientation do not define any type of concrete act even when they are all taken together. The motivational orientation is inherently involved in every act, but so also are the modes of value-orientation, and the objects of the situation. It is only when the three sets of components — objects, motivational orientations, and value-orientations — combine that we even begin to be able to discuss concrete actions and types of actions.

[21] It may again be noted that value-orientation standards are only *part* of culture. We do not mean, moreover, to imply that a person's values are entirely "internalized culture" or mere adherence to rules and laws. The person makes creative modifications as he internalizes culture; but the novel aspect is not the cultural aspect.

Every concrete action involving a cognitive component (by definition, this is true of every action) entails the operation, usually only below the level of deliberation, of standards of cognitive validity. The standards of cognitive validity enter into the construction of expectations (predictions), the testing of observations. The category of cognitive value-orientation is present in all cultural value systems, although there may be variations in the content of the standard with regard to different types of knowledge; for example, the standards of validity of empirical knowledge might vary from those applied in the demonstration of religious beliefs.[22] It is desirable to distinguish between the standards of cognitive validity and the *organization* of cognitive content and perception; [23] cognitive content comes more properly under the cognitive mode of motivational orientation.

The appreciative mode of value-orientation corresponds to the cathectic mode of motivational orientation. It is particularly important here to bear in mind that we are discussing *standards*, not motivational content. The standards applied in the evaluation of the alternatives involved in cathectic choices [24] are at issue here. As in all evaluation, there is a disciplinary aspect of appreciative standards. The choice always involves at least an implicit sacrifice, in that an actor cannot have *all* of what are in one sense potential gratifications, and choosing one involves a "cost" in that it excludes alternatives. The payment of this cost is the disciplinary element.[25]

The use of the term *appreciative* diverges from common usage. In its literal sense, *aesthetic* as connoting desirability would be preferable, but it has come to be used so largely with regard to the fine arts, and so forth, that it is too narrow for our purposes. The term *expressive* has been suggested. If the choices governed by these standards were simply choices with respect to which need-disposition should be expressed, this term would suffice; but choices between objects, modalities, and occasions also come under this head. Thus a broader term is needed. The term *expressive* will be reserved for the *type* of action in which cathectic interests and appreciative standards have primacy.

The category of *moral* value standards extends and makes more explicit the common meaning of the term *moral*. Moral value standards are the most comprehensive integrative standards for assessing and regulating the *entire system of action under consideration*, whether it be a personality or a society

---

[22] But whatever the range of criteria of validity which may be represented as clustering about a mode, no fundamental epistemological question is raised here concerning the validity of the criteria of empirical truth.

[23] The organization of cognitive content might involve the selection of foci of attention, or the organization of knowledge.

[24] Cathectic choices may be among objects, object modalities, need-dispositions, or occasions.

[25] Freud's conception of the "economic" aspect of libido theory, which is the allocation of gratifications within a feasible system, is the psychoanalytic equivalent of the disciplinary element.

or a subsystem of either. They are the "court of last appeal" in any large-scale integrative problem within the system.

Any specific system of morals is adapted to the specific integrative problems confronted by the action system which it, in one sense, controls. Morals, in this sense, are relative. It is the relativity of moral standards to the social system which may be an unfamiliar element in the present definition of moral standards. We live in a culture where the standards are mainly "universalistic," and we therefore tend to think of a moral standard as transcending the particular system of action of the society in which it is exercised. The student of society is concerned with the comparative analysis of different systems of action. He needs a category of value integration which is relative to the system of action in question. The category of moral value standards [26] serves such a purpose for us. The significant criterion for definition of the moral concept is concern for the broader consequences for a system of action.[27]

The concluding paragraphs of this discussion will be concerned with various *kinds* of orientations or actions. It has been stressed throughout our discussion of the *modes* of orientation that these various modes are not different kinds of orientation but simply different aspects that might be abstracted from any orientation. Now we are going to be concerned explicitly with the problem of different kinds or types of action.

It is certanly fair at times to speak of an intellectual activity, an expressive activity, and a responsible or moral activity. Since these are types of concrete action, all of them entail all modes of motivational orientation and some value standards. How, then, are the various kinds of action differentiated? Two problems of emphasis are involved.

In the first place, motivation attaches to activity as well as to objects; that is, certain activities are cathected in their own right as means or goal objects; even cer.ain modes of activity may be cathected. When we speak of a cognitive interest, a cathectic interest, or an evaluative interest, we refer to the fact that these modes of the action process are, to some small or large degree, cathected in their own right.

In the second place, when there is orientation to standards, and these standards are guiding choices, then. if several kinds of standards are oriented at once, there is always the possibility of a conflict. When there is a conflict among standards, theve is a problem of primacy. One standard or set of standards must be emphasized, given primacy; it must dominate, the other must give way. In any specific action, primacy may be given to cognitive, appreciative, or moral standards.

---

[26] The moral value standards might be universalistic, that is, concerned with the consequences for a class of phenomena wherever found; or they might be particularistic, that is, concerned with the consequences for a collectivity of which the actor is a member.

[27] It may be noted that this is in accord with the usage of Sumner, Durkheim, and the French anthropologists.

In order to make a basic classification of *types of action*, we will conjoin the problems of interest (in the modes of motivational orientation) and of primacy (among the modes of value-orientation). Thus the three basic types are: (*a*) *intellectual activity*, where cognitive interests prevail and cognitive value standards have primacy (i.e., investigation or the "search for knowledge"); (*b*) *expressive action*, where cathectic interests and appreciative standards have primacy (i.e., the search for direct gratification); and (*c*) *responsible* or *moral action*, where evaluative interests and moral standards have primacy (i.e., the attempt to integrate actions in the interest of a larger system of action).

A special position is occupied by another derivative but very prominent type: *instrumental action*. Here, the goal of action is in the *future*. Cathectic interests and appreciative standards have primacy with respect to the goal, yet cognitive standards [28] have primacy with respect to the process of its attainment.[29] The primacy of cognitive considerations therefore bifurcates into the purely cognitive type, here called "intellectual activity" or investigation, and the instrumental type in the interest of a cathected goal.

Before leaving our discussion of the frame of reference, we should give some brief treatment to the allocative and integrative foci for the organization of empirical systems. When we begin to treat this problem, we find we must first differentiate the distinctive types of action systems from each other. Then we must give the two types separate treatment. The point is that when action occurs (when something is wanted or chosen and thus brings forth action) it is simultaneously embraced in two types of action systems: personality systems and social systems.

As we said in the General Statement, these two systems are distinguished by the differences in the foci around which they are organized. The personality of the individual is organized around the biological unity of the organism. This is its integrative focus. The allocative mechanisms within the system are the need-disposition (and other motivational) systems which serve to relate orientations to one another. The social system is organized around the unity of the interacting group. This is the integrative focus. The allocative mechanisms within this system are the roles which serve to relate various orientations to one another.

The system of interaction among individuals, however, cannot be organized in the same way as the system of action of the individual actor; they each face different functional problems. Personality and social systems, thus, are constituted by the same actions and they are in continuous causal interdependence, but as systems they are not reducible to one another.

---

[28] Where an orientation is only to immediate gratification, only cathectic-appreciative (and possibly moral) interests and standards apply.

[29] Evaluation is, of course, also involved; it places both the particular goal and the processes of attaining it within the larger system of action.

Neither systems of value-orientation nor systems of culture as a whole are action systems in the same sense as are personalities and social systems. This is because neither motivation nor action is directly attributable to them. They may conjoin with motivation to evoke action in social systems or personalities, but they themselves cannot act, nor are they motivated. It seems desirable to treat them, however, because of the great importance of the particular ways in which they are involved in action systems.

With the transition to the analysis of systems of action — personalities and social systems — the descriptive structural analysis with which we are particularly concerned here begins to shade into dynamic analysis. Dynamic problems emerge as soon as we begin to deal with the functional problems of allocation and integration. Our knowledge of the fundamentals of motivation, as it will be analyzed in the next chapter, is of course crucial for the analysis of dynamic processes. Much empirical insight into dynamic problems on *ad hoc* levels has already been achieved. But without further analysis of the structure of action, we could not have the coördinates which would raise empirical insight to a higher level of systematic generality.

Dilemmas of Orientation and the Pattern Variables

Those who have followed our exposition thus far have acquired a familiarity with the definitions of the basic elements of the theory of action. There are further important conceptual entities and classificatory systems to be defined, but these, in a sense, derive from the basic terms that have already been defined. The point is that the further entities can be defined largely in terms of the entities and relationships already defined, with the introduction of a minimum of additional material.

The next section of the present chapter will be devoted to the highly important, derived, classificatory system, the pattern-variable scheme. If one were to look back over the sections of this chapter devoted to the objects of the situation and to the orientation of the actor to the situation (items three and four in our outline), he would see that an actor in a situation is confronted by a series of major dilemmas of orientation, a series of choices that the actor must make before the situation has a determinate meaning for him. The objects of the situation do not interact with the cognizing and cathecting organism in such a fashion as to determine automatically the meaning of the situation. Rather, the actor must make a series of choices before the situation will have a determinate meaning. Specifically, we maintain, the actor must make five specific dichotomous choices before any situation will have a determinate meaning. The five dichotomies which formulate these choice alternatives are called the *pattern variables* because any specific orientation (and consequently any action) is characterized by a pattern of the five choices.

Three of the pattern variables derive from the absence of any biologically given hierarchy of primacies among the various modes of orientation. In the first place, the actor must choose whether to accept gratification from the immediately cognized and cathected object or to evaluate such gratification in terms of its consequences for other aspects of the action system. (That is, one must decide whether or not the evaluative mode is to be operative at all in a situation.) [30] In the second place, if the actor decides to evaluate, he must choose whether or not to give primacy to the moral standards of the social system or subsystem. In the third place, whether or not he decides to grant primacy to such moral standards, he must choose whether cognitive or appreciative standards are to be dominant, the one set with relation to the other. If cognitive standards are dominant over appreciative standards, the actor will tend to locate objects in terms of their relation to some generalized frame of reference; if appreciative standards are dominant over cognitive, the actor will tend to locate objects in terms of their relation to himself, or to his motives.

The other pattern variables emerge from indeterminacies intrinsic to the object situation: social objects as relevant to a given choice situation are either quality complexes or performance complexes, depending on how the actor chooses to see them; social objects are either functionally diffuse (so that the actor grants them every feasible demand) or functionally specific (so that the actor grants them only specifically defined demands), depending on how the actor chooses to see them or how he is culturally expected to see them.

It will be noted now that the three pattern variables which derive from the problems of primacy among the modes of orientation are the first three of the pattern variables as these were listed in our introduction; the two pattern variables which derive from the indeterminacies in the object situation are the last two in that list.

At the risk of being repititious, let us restate our definition: a *pattern variable* is a dichotomy, one side of which must be chosen by an actor before the meaning of a situation is determinate for him, and thus before he can act with respect to that situation. We maintain that there are only five *basic* pattern variables (i.e., pattern variables deriving directly from the frame of reference of the theory of action) and that, in the sense that they are *all* of the pattern variables which so derive, they constitute a system. Let us list them and give them names and numbers so that we can more easily refer to them in the future. They are:

1. Affectivity–Affective neutrality.
2. Self-orientation–Collectivity-orientation.
3. Universalism–Particularism.
4. Ascription–Achievement.
5. Specificity–Diffuseness.

[30] In a limited sense the evaluative mode is operative, even when no thought is given to the consequences of immediate gratification; this in the sense that aesthetic (apprecia-

The first concerns the problem of whether or not evaluation is to take place in a given situation. The second concerns the primacy of moral standards in an evaluative procedure. The third concerns the relative primacy of cognitive and cathectic standards. The fourth concerns the seeing of objects as quality or performance complexes. The fifth concerns the scope of significance of the object.

These pattern variables enter the action frame of reference at four different levels. In the first place, they enter at the concrete level as five discrete choices (explicit or implicit) which every actor makes before he can act. In the second place, they enter on the personality level as habits of choice; the person has a set of habits of choosing, ordinarily or relative to certain types of situations, one horn or the other of each of these dilemmas. Since this set of habits is usually a bit of internalized culture, we will list it as a component of the actor's value-orientation standards. In the third place, the pattern variables enter on the collectivity level as aspects of role definition: the definitions of rights and duties of the members of a collectivity which specify the actions of incumbents of roles, and which often specify that the performer shall exhibit a habit of choosing one side or the other of each of these dilemmas. In the fourth place, the variables enter on the cultural level as aspects of value standards; this is because most value standards are rules or recipes for concrete action and thus specify, among other things, that the actor abiding by the standard shall exhibit a habit of choosing one horn or the other of each of the dilemmas.

From the foregoing paragraph, it should be obvious that, except for their integration in concrete acts as discrete choices, the pattern variables are most important as characteristics of value standards (whether these be the value standards of a personality, or the value standards defining the roles of a society, or just value standards in the abstract). In the sense that each concrete act is made up on the basis of a patterning of the choices formulated by the scheme, the pattern variables are not necessarily attributes of value standards, because any specific concrete choice may be a rather discrete and accidental thing. But as soon as a certain consistency of choosing can be inferred from a series of concrete acts, then we can begin to make statements about the value standards involved and the formulation of these standards in terms of the variables of the pattern-variable scheme.

What is the bearing of the pattern variables on our analysis of systems of action and cultural orientation? Basically, the pattern variables are the categories for the description of value-orientations which of course are in various forms integral to all three systems. A given value-orientation or some particular aspect of it may be interpreted as imposing a preference or giving

---

tive) standards may be invoked to determine the "appropriateness" of the form of gratification chosen. Only in this limited sense, however, does evaluation enter the immediate gratification picture.

a primacy to one alternative over the other *in a particular type of situation.* The pattern variables therefore delineate the alternative preferences, predispositions, or expectations; in all these forms the common element is the direction of selection in defined situations. In the personality system, the pattern variables describe essentially the predispositions or expectations as evaluatively defined in terms of what will below be called ego-organization [31] and superego-organization. In the case of the social system they are the crucial components in the definition of role-expectations. Culturally, they define patterns of value-orientation.

The pattern variables apply to the *normative* or ideal aspect of the structure of systems of action; they apply to one part of its culture. They are equally useful in the empirical description of the degree of conformity with or divergence of concrete action from the patterns of expectation or aspiration. When they are used to characterize differences of empirical structure of personalities or social systems, they contain an elliptical element. This element appears in such statements as, "The American occupational system is universalistic and achievement-oriented and specific." The more adequate, though still sketchy, statement would be: "Compared to other possible ways of organizing the division of labor, the predominant norms which are institutionalized in the American society and which embody the predominant value-orientation of the culture give rise to expectations that occupational roles will be treated by their incumbents and those who are associated with them universalistically and specifically and with regard to proficiency of performance."

These categories could equally be employed to describe actual behavior as well as normative expectations and are of sufficient exactitude for first approximations in comparative analysis. For more detailed work, however, much more precise analysis of the degrees and incidence of deviance, with special reference to the magnitude, location, and forms of the tendencies to particularism, to ascriptiveness, and to diffuseness would have to be carried out.

We will now proceed to define the five pattern variables and the problems of alternative selection to which they apply. They are inherently patterns of cultural value-orientation, but they become integrated both in personalities and in social systems. Hence the general definitions will in each case be followed by definitions specific to each of the three types of systems. These definitions will be followed by an analysis of the places of the variables in the frame of reference of the theory of action, the reasons why this list seems to be logically complete on its own level of generality, and certain problems of their systematic interrelations and use in structural analysis.

---

[31] The term *ego* is here used in the sense current in the theory of personality, not as a point of reference.

THE DEFINITIONS OF PATTERN VARIABLES

1. *The dilemma of gratification of impulse versus discipline.* When confronted with situations in which particular impulses press for gratification, an actor faces the problem of whether the impulses should be released or restrained. He can solve the problem by giving primacy, at the relevant selection points, to evaluative considerations, at the cost of interests in the possibility of immediate gratification; or by giving primacy to such interests in immediate gratification, irrespective of evaluative considerations.

a. Cultural aspect. (1) *Affectivity*: the normative pattern which grants the permission for an actor, in a given type of situation, to take advantage of a given opportunity for immediate gratification without regard to evaluative considerations. (2) *Affective neutrality*: the normative pattern which prescribes for actors in a given type of situation renunciation of certain types of immediate gratification for which opportunity exists, in the interest of evaluative considerations regardless of the content of the latter.

b. Personality aspect. (1) *Affectivity*: a need-disposition on the part of the actor to permit himself, in a certain situation, to take advantage of an opportunity for a given type of immediate gratification and not to renounce this gratification for evaluative reasons. (2) *Affective neutrality*: a need-disposition on the part of the actor in a certain situation to be guided by evaluative considerations which prohibit his taking advantage of the given opportunity for immediate gratification; in this situation the gratification in question is to be renounced, regardless of the grounds adduced for the renunciation.

c. Social system aspect. (1) *Affectivity*: the role-expectation [32] that the incumbent of the role may freely express certain affective reactions to objects in the situation and need not attempt to control them in the interest of discipline. (2) *Affective neutrality*: the role-expectation that the incumbent of the role in question should restrain any impulses to certain affective expressions and subordinate them to considerations of discipline. In both cases the affect may be positive or negative, and the discipline (or permissiveness) may apply only to certain qualitative types of affective expression (e.g., sexual).

2. *The dilemma of private versus collective interests,* or the distribution between private permissiveness and collective obligation. The high frequency of situations in which there is a disharmony of interests creates the problem of choosing between action for private goals or on behalf of collective goals. This dilemma may be resolved by the actor either by giving primacy to interests, goals, and values shared with the other members of a given collective

---

[32] A role-expectation is, in an institutionally integrated social system (or part of it), an expectation *both* on the part of ego and of the alters with whom he interacts. The same sentiments are shared by both. In a less than perfectly integrated social system, the concept is still useful for describing the expectations of each of the actors, even though they diverge.

unit of which he is a member or by giving primacy to his personal or private interests without considering their bearing on collective interests.

a. Cultural aspect. (1) *Self-orientation*: the normative pattern which prescribes a range of permission for an actor, in a given type of situation, to take advantage of a given opportunity for pursuing a private interest, regardless of the content of the interest or its direct bearing on the interests of other actors. (2) *Collectivity-orientation*: a normative pattern which prescribes the area within which an actor, in a given type of situation, is obliged to take directly into account a given selection of values which he shares with the other members of the collectivity in question. It defines his *responsibility* to this collectivity.

b. Personality aspect. (1) *Self-orientation*: a need-disposition on the part of the actor to permit himself to pursue a given goal or interest of his own — regardless whether from his standpoint it is only cognitive-cathectic or involves evaluative considerations — but without regard to its bearing one way or another on the interests of a collectivity of which he is a member. (2) *Collectivity-orientation*: a need-disposition on the part of the actor to be guided by the obligation to take directly into account, in the given situation, values which he shares with the other members of the collectivity in question; therefore the actor must accept responsibility for attempting to realize those values in his action. This includes the expectation by ego that in the particular choice in question he will subordinate his private interests, whether cognitive-cathectic or evaluative, and that he will be motivated in superego terms.

c. Social system aspect. (1) *Self-orientation*: the role-expectation by the relevant actors that it is *permissible* for the incumbent of the role in question to give priority in the given situation to his own private interests, whatever their motivational content or quality, independently of their bearing on the interests or values of a given collectivity of which he is a member, or the interests of other actors. (2) *Collectivity-orientation*: the role-expectation by the relevant actors that the actor is *obliged*, as an incumbent of the role in question, to take directly into account the values and interests of the collectivity of which, in this role, he is a member. When there is a potential conflict with his private interests, he is expected in the particular choice to give priority to the collective interest. This also applies to his action in representative roles on behalf of the collectivity.

3. *The dilemma of transcendence versus immanence.* In confronting any situation, the actor faces the dilemma whether to treat the objects in the situation in accordance with a general norm covering *all* objects in that class or whether to treat them in accordance with their standing in some particular relationship to him or his collectivity, independently of the objects' subsumibility under a general norm. This dilemma can be resolved by giving primacy to norms or value standards which are maximally generalized and which have a basis of validity transcending *any* specific system of relation-

ships in which ego is involved, or by giving primacy to value standards which allot priority to standards *integral* to the *particular* relationship system in which the actor is involved with the object.

   a. Cultural aspect. (1) *Universalism*: the normative pattern which obliges an actor in a given situation to be oriented toward objects in the light of general standards rather than in the light of the objects' possession of properties (qualities or performances, classificatory or relational) which have a particular relation to the actor's own properties (traits or statuses). (2) *Particularism*: the normative pattern which obliges an actor in a given type of situation to give priority to criteria of the object's particular relations to the actor's own properties (qualities or performances, classificatory or relational) over generalized attributes, capacities, or performance standards.

   b. Personality aspect. (1) *Universalism*: a need-disposition on the part of the actor in a given situation to respond toward objects in conformity with a general standard rather than in the light of their possession of properties (qualities or performances, classificatory or relational) which have a particular relation to the actor's own. (2) *Particularism*: a need-disposition on the part of the actor to be guided by criteria of choice particular to his own and the object's position in an object-relationship system rather than by criteria defined in generalized terms.

   c. Social system aspect. (1) *Universalism*: the role-expectation that, in qualifications for memberships and decisions for differential treatment, priority will be given to standards defined in completely generalized terms, independent of the particular relationship of the actor's own statuses (qualities or performances, classificatory or relational) to those of the object. (2) *Particularism*: the role-expectation that, in qualifications for memberships and decisions for differential treatment, priority will be given to standards which assert the primacy of the values attached to objects by their particular relations to the actor's properties (qualities or performances, classificatory or relational) as over against their general universally applicable class properties.

   4. *The dilemma of object modalities.* When confronting an object in a situation, the actor faces the dilemma of deciding how to treat it. Is he to treat it in the light of what it is in itself or in the light of what it does or what might flow from its *actions*? This dilemma can be resolved by giving primacy, at the relevant selection points, to the "qualities" aspect of *social objects* as a focus of orientation, or by giving primacy to the objects' performances and their outcomes.

   a. Cultural aspect. (1) *Ascription*: the normative pattern which prescribes that an actor in a given type of situation should, in his selections for differential treatment of social objects, give priority to certain attributes that they possess (including collectivity memberships and possessions) over any specific performances (past, present, or prospective) of the objects. (2) *Achievement*:

the normative pattern which prescribes that an actor in a given type of situation should, in his selection and differential treatment of social objects, give priority to their specific performances (past, present, or prospective) over their given attributes (including memberships and possessions), insofar as the latter are not significant as direct conditions of the relevant performances.

b. Personality aspect. (1) *Ascription*: the need-disposition on the part of the actor, at a given selection point, to respond to specific given attributes of the social object, rather than to their past, present, or prospective performances. (2) *Achievement*: a need-disposition on the part of the actor to respond, at a given selection point, to specific performances (past present, or prospective) of a social object, rather than to its attributes which are not directly involved in the relevant performances as "capacities," "skills," and so forth.

c. Social system aspect. (1) *Ascription*: the role-expectation that the role incumbent, in orienting himself to social objects in the relevant choice situation, will accord priority to the objects' given attributes (whether universalistically or particularistically defined) over their actual or potential performances. (2) *Achievement*: the role-expectation that the role incumbent, in orienting to social objects in the relevant choice situation, will give priority to the objects' actual or expected performances, and to their attributes only as directly relevant to these performances, over attributes which are essentially independent of the specific performances in question.

5. *The dilemma of the scope of significance of the object.* In confronting an object, an actor must choose among the various possible ranges in which he will respond to the object. The dilemma consists in whether he should respond to many aspects of the object or to a restricted range of them — how broadly is he to allow himself to be involved with the object? The dilemma may be resolved by accepting no inherent or prior limitation of the scope of the actor's "concern" with the object, either as an object of interest or of obligations, or by according only a limited and specific type of significance to the object in his system of orientation.

a. Cultural aspect. (1) *Diffuseness*: the normative pattern which prescribes that in a given situation the orientation of an actor to an object should contain no prior specification of the actor's interest in or concern with or for the object, but that the scope should vary with the exigencies of the situation as they arise. (2) *Specificity*: the normative pattern which prescribes that in a given type of situation an actor should confine his concern with a given type of object to a specific sphere and not permit other empirically possible concerns to enter.

b. Personality aspect. (1) *Diffuseness*: the need-disposition to respond to an object in any way which the nature of the actor and the nature of the object and its actual relation to ego require, actual significances varying as occasions arise. (2) *Specificity*: the need-disposition of the actor to respond to a given object in a manner limited to a specific mode or context of significance of a social object, including obligation to it, which is compatible with exclusion of other potential modes of significance of the object.

   c. Social system aspect. (1) *Diffuseness*: the role-expectation that the role incumbent, at the relevant choice point, will accept any potential significance of a social object, including obligation to it, which is compatible with his other interests and obligations, and that he will give priority to this expectation over any disposition to confine the role-orientation to a specific range of significance of the object. (2) *Specificity*: the role-expectation that the role incumbent, at the relevant choice point, will be oriented to a social object only within a specific range of its relevance as a cathectic object or as an instrumental means or condition and that he will give priority to this expectation over any disposition to include potential aspects of significance of the object not specifically defined in the expectation pattern.

Of the five pattern variables defined above, the first three are determined by primacies among the interests inherently differentiated within the system of value-orientation itself and in the definition of the limits of its applicability; the other two are determined by the application of value-orientations to the alternatives which are inherent in the structure of the object system, and in the actor's relation to it. The derivation of the pattern variables from the basic categories of the action scheme is presented in diagrammatic form in Fig. 2. (Figures follow page 245.)

The first of the pattern variables, affectivity versus affective neutrality, represents the problem of whether any evaluative considerations at all should have priority. It is thus the marginal choice between complete *permissiveness*, without reference to value standards of any kind, and *discipline* in the interests of any one of the various kinds of value standards.

This dilemma is inherent in any system of action. There can in principle be no such dilemma involving cognitive and cathectic modes of orientation, since both modes are inherently operative in any action whatever. But as soon as *consequences* for the functioning of a system come into the picture, a problem of evaluation arises and it becomes necessary to impose some discipline in order to restrict damaging consequences and facilitate favorable ones. This is, therefore, in a sense, the most elementary dilemma of systems of action.

The second pattern variable essentially reproduces the same basic dilemma in a somewhat different perspective and with an additional complication deriving from a difference of level. In the pattern variable of affectivity–affective neutrality there is no reference to the beneficiary on whose behalf discipline is exercised. This problem becomes preëminent in the pattern variable of self-orientation versus collectivity-orientation. The same basic distinction between permissiveness and discipline is repeated, but permissiveness is no longer solely for immediate gratification in the psychological sense; it now includes action in terms of "ego-organization," with all the discipline associated with that. The occurrence of this problem in the personality system is dealt with in a very similar way in Freud's later writings about ego and superego organization.[33]

When the actor accepts discipline, the problem of the standards and the objects in behalf of which discipline is to be exercised requires solution. Collectivity-orientation is the resolution of one of these problems through the primacy of the moral value standards, either over other types of value standards or over nonevaluative modes of orientation. In this connection it is important to refer to the earlier definition of moral values (pp. 60, 73–74). What is at issue here is *not* the concrete *content* of the relevant moral standards but — whatever this may be — their primacy over other nonmoral standards. Moral standards were specifically defined as those which refer to consequences for the system of relation in question, whether it be the society as a whole, a subcollectivity, or even a deviant "subculture." Sometimes moral standards are, as is usual in our culture, universalistically defined, in which case they do in fact transcend the particular relational system. But this is a matter of the concrete content of moral values, not of the definition of what moral values themselves are.

Cognitive and appreciative values may be more or less fully integrated with moral values in the total value system. The area in which they are allowed primacy of a permissive or deviant nature may vary in scope. These problems must be reserved for the discussion of the patterns of value-orientation. Here we are merely concerned with defining the variable elements which go into them.

Even when the actor has selected the moral value standards as his guiding star, he still must make a decision about how he is to judge the object. Is he to respond to it in the light of cognitive or appreciative standards? Is he to judge objects by the class categories which he can apply to all of them, or is he to judge them by what they mean to him in their particular relationship to him? Cognitive standards are by their very nature universalistic. They are assessments of events, the demonstration of the existence of which does not depend for validity on any *particular* actor's need-dispositions, value patterns, or role-expectations. The criteria of whether a proposition is true or false are not bound to a particular time or place or object-relationship.[34] If a proposition is true, it is, for the conditions (explicit or implicit) to which it applies,

[33] The distinction between *id* and *ego* in Freud's later theory is essentially the same as our distinction between affectivity and discipline. Indeed the first two pattern variables form the major axis of Freud's conception of the organization of personality or what psychoanalysts sometimes call the structural point of view.

[34] Ideas, to the contrary, are, to be sure, current, especially among proponents of the "sociology of knowledge," but they rest on epistemological confusions, failing to distinguish between the qualifications and adaptations in the *content* of knowledge which are indeed relative to and necessitated by the "perspective" of the actor, and the *criteria of validity*, which are not.

true. It is not true for one person and false for somebody else. Its *significance* for or *relevance* to action may, of course, vary in different relational contexts, but not its validity. A value standard, then, in which cognitive propositions have primacy — and which may be put into the form, "this is valid for me as a standard guiding my action because such-and-such a proposition is cognitively true" — is universalistic, and its applicability transcends any particular relational context.

On the other hand, insofar as purely appreciative criteria are given primacy in the determination of a standard, the values concerned have their validity *in their relationship to the actor* who is judging. The ultimate basis of validity of the appreciative standard comes to be that the actor (or actors) admires or enjoys the object, which is thought or felt to be in a suitable or appropriate relationship with him; "suitability" or "appropriateness" means here harmony with a pattern which may have already been internalized. Thus the standard itself is *particularistic*; that is, it is *immanent* in the particular relationship complex or system of action of which it is a part. There is a possible source of confusion here, similar to that involved in the concept of moral standards. In a culture where universalistic values are prominent, many *concrete* appreciative values are also universalistically defined. This is not the result of the primacy of appreciative criteria in their definition; it happens rather because the *particular* appreciative standards are part of a general system of value-orientation in which cognitive standards have primacy, and the cognitive standards therefore shape appreciative values as well as others.[35]

These first three pattern variables exhaust the possibilities of relative primacies within the system of modes of orientation. The fourth and fifth pattern variables derive from choices that must be made with respect to the modalities and scope of significance of the object system. The distinction between the modalities of qualities and performances as foci for action orientation [36] has already been discussed and does not need to be elaborated upon here, except to note that it presents an authentic selection alternative involved in all systems of interaction.

[35] Here as elsewhere a clear distinction must be made between the analytical and the concrete. In a concrete standard contained in judgments in the appreciative field, it is possible for cognitive, appreciative, or moral criteria to have primacy. This is true also of the concrete standards governing cognitive or moral judgments. But the present concern is not with this concrete level. It is with the classification of types of *criteria* of value judgments and the consequences of differences of relative primacies among such types of criteria.

[36] This distinction, in its obverse form, is related to that frequently made in psychological analysis in the distinction between *activity* and *passivity*. Achievement criteria require activity, as a qualification of the actor not the object, while ascriptive criteria do not. See below, Chapter II. This distinction has become known in Anglo-American anthropological and sociological literature through Linton's *The Study of Man*, in which it is applied to the analysis of social structure.

The fifth pattern variable presents the alternative modes of delimiting the actor's relationship to a social object. It also is distinctly a *relational* category, specifying neither a general characteristic of the actor nor an intrinsic property of the object, but rather one aspect of the way a given actor is related to a specific object. A social object either has "defined" rights with respect to ego, or it has the rights of "residual legatee." Let us be more explicit. In the first place, if a social object is related to ego at all, then it has some "rights," in the sense that it has some significance. Ego, that is, is granting alter some rights as soon as alter becomes a social object for him. This happens because alter's action has consequences within ego's orientation of action and thus functions among the determinants of ego's action.[37] The rights of a social object with respect to ego are either defined (so that ego and alter know the limits of ego's obligations) or they are undefined (so that ego must render to alter such of his efforts as are left over when all of his other obligations are met). The social object, that is, either has specific (segmental) significance for ego (in which case obligations are clearly defined); or it has diffuse significance (in which case obligations are only limited by other obligations).

The segmental significance of an object may, in a concrete orientation, coincide with the primacy of one mode of motivational orientation, such as the cognitive-cathectic. But analytically these ranges of variation are independent of one another.

The most feasible empirical criterion of the difference between the two alternatives is the "burden of proof." If a question arises concerning the determination of the range of responsibility, in the case of specificity, the burden of proof rests on the side that claims a certain responsibility to exist (to be included in the contract, so to speak). A possible right of alter which is not included in the mutual expectations which defines the relation between ego and alter is *prima facie* to be excluded as irrelevant, unless specific argument for its inclusion can be adduced. In the case of diffuseness, the burden of proof is on the opposite side, on the side that claims a responsibility does not exist. Any possible right of alter is *prima facie* to be regarded as valid, even though neither ego nor alter has heretofore given the right in question any thought, unless ego can adduce specific other and more important obligations which make it impossible for him to grant alter this right.

Thus, even if an object's significance is defined in diffuse terms, the range of obligation is not unlimited, because the allocation of orientation interests among objects is a basic functional imperative of all action systems. Therefore, the range of diffuseness can never be unlimited, because this would lead directly to encroachment on the interests in, and obligations to, other objects. In the case of diffuseness, it is always the potential conflict with the relations

---

[37] To grant an object "rights" in the last analysis is nothing else than to allow it to affect one's action. Alter's rights over ego, that is, refer to those things which ego "has to do" because of alter's relations to ego's motives and ego's system of values.

to other objects which limits the orientation to the first object; whereas it is the set of expectations concerning the particular object which brings about the limitation in the case of specificity. When, therefore, a question of evaluation arises, the justification for rejecting a claim, in the case of specificity, is simply the denial of an obligation (e.g., "it wasn't in the contract"). In the case of diffuseness, the rejection of a claim can be justified only by the invocation of other obligations which are ranked higher on some scale of priority.

As with the other pattern variables, the dilemma presented in the specificity-diffuseness pattern variable is inherent in any orientation of one actor to another. Almost invariably an explicit choice has to be made. If the contact between two people is fleeting and casual, the significance of one for the other may be highly specific without any explicit choice occurring. But if the relationship continues, the problem of its scope becomes explicit. The possibility of diffuse attachments will then become more pressing and a decision will have to be made.

THE INTERRELATIONS OF THE PATTERN VARIABLES

We hold that the five pattern variables constitute a *system* covering all the fundamental alternatives which can arise directly out of the frame of reference for the theory of action. It should be remembered that the five pattern variables formulate five fundamental choices which must be made by an actor when he is confronted with a situation before that situation can have definitive (unambiguous) meaning for him. We have said that objects do not automatically determine the actors "orientation of action"; rather, a number of choices must be made before the meaning of the objects becomes definite. Now, we maintain that when the situation is social (when one actor is orienting to another), there are but five choices which are completely general (that is, which must always be made) and which derive directly from the action frame of reference; these choices must always be made to give the situation specific defined meaning. Other choices are often necessary to determine the meaning of a situation, but these may be considered accidents of content, rather than genuine alternatives intrinsic to the structure of *all* action. To be a pattern variable, a set of alternatives must derive directly from the problems of dominance among the modes of orientation, or from the problems arising from the ambiguities of the object world which require choice on the part of ego for their resolution. In order to show that our five pattern variables constitute a system, we must show that they exhaust these problems. Let us take up first the problems of dominance among modes of orientation, and second, problems arising from the ambiguities of relation to the object world.

There are only three completely general problems of dominance arising directly from the modes of orientation. Since the cognitive and cathectic modes of motivational orientation are so inseparable as to abnegate any problem of primacy, we do not find any conflict between them. Thus, the first pattern variable is between them acting alone, on the one hand, and an evaluative orientation, on the other. The problem is: Will evaluation enter into the determination of this course of action? A decision must always be made (explicitly or implicitly, consciously or unconsciously).

The other two pattern variables arising from primacy problems with respect to orientation modes are not on the same level as the first in terms of generality within the concrete act, because if affectivity is selected in the concrete situation instead of affective neutrality, the problems presented by pattern variables two and three never arise. (If an actor does not evaluate, he does not have to decide which standards will get primacy within the evaluative process.) However, in discussing the orientation *habits* which make up a value, a role-expectancy, or a need-disposition, we can see that the second two pattern variables have just as much generality as the first. Although an actor may be regarded in affective terms in some concrete situations, and even though ego may have the habit of affectivity with respect to alter, this still does not mean that the "affectivity attitude" will apply to alter all of the time. (The habit implies that in perhaps a majority of the situations an attitude of affectivity will apply, but no relationship between human beings can remain always on the affectivity level — this, perhaps, is what we mean by saying "we are not beasts".) When on rare or frequent occasions the affectively neutral attitude is assumed, when evaluation of the relationship evokes value standards, the problems formulated in pattern variables two and three immediately become relevant, and choices must be made.

Thus, one must choose, if one evaluates, whether or not to give primacy to collectivity-integrating moral standards. If moral standards are invoked at all, they will have primacy owing to their status as the "final court of appeal" on any problem of integration. Cognitive and appreciative standards, on the contrary, are always invoked in any evaluative problem; thus, the problem of their relative primacy with respect to one another always arises, whether or not moral standards are invoked. Hence, the problem of the relative primacy of appreciative and cognitive standards must always be resolved. If cognitive standards are to dominate appreciative ones, then the objects will be judged primarily in terms of their relationship to some generalized frame of reference; if appreciative standards are to dominate cognitive ones, then objects will be judged primarily in terms of ego as the center of the frame of reference. Thus, these three problems of choice and only these three, derive directly from problems of dominance among the modes of orientation.

Similarly, there are only two completely general ambiguities with respect to social objects as these are defined in our frame of reference. These are (1) the quality-performance ambiguity and (2) the diffuseness-specificity ambiguity. In every social situation, anywhere, ego either implicitly or explicitly has to resolve these two ambiguities by choosing one side or the other of both dichotomies before the social object can have determinate meaning for him. Thus, we complete our case for the exhaustiveness of our list of pattern variables.

Certain other pairs of concepts, representative and autonomous roles for instance, are derivatives from pattern variables. The pair in this example are derivatives of the second pattern variable — self versus collectivity-orientation — on a more concrete level. Let us show how this derivation is made. First, a distinction must be made, in dealing with a collectivity, between the internal relations of its members, and their relations outside of the collectivity. In analyzing their relations outside of the collectivity, the bearing of their membership on the external relations must be taken into account. Now, a representative role is characterized as follows: in external relations a member is oriented primarily to the role-expectations which govern his conduct as a member of the collectivity; this primacy of collectivity-orientation over self-orientation defines the representative role. Correspondingly, an autonomous role is one in which the actor is free (oriented independently) of his roles as a member of the collectivity in external relations; the primacy of self-orientation defines the autonomous role.

Similarly, rational as opposed to traditional action has been suggested as a pattern variable. This seems to be a complex derivative from the pattern variables. It has a special relation to the universalism-particularism dichotomy, because cognitive standards are inherently rational. But the reference in the rational-traditional dichotomy is not to the generality of the frame of reference (as it is in universalism) but to the stability of patterns over time. Thus the rational-traditional dichotomy is a way of formulating alternative ways of adapting primary (pattern variable) value-orientation patterns over a period of time in an empirical action system.

In another sense, the rational-traditional dichotomy may be seen as a way of characterizing any long-run sequence of pattern-variable choices. In choosing the various sides of the pattern-variable dichotomies, a person may choose in a rational or traditional fashion. That is, he may shift his choices in accord with the pragmatic exigencies of the situation (in which case the choices would be considered rational), or he may select in accord with his life-long idea of the way his group, or his family, has always made selections in a given matter (in which case his whole set of pattern-variable choices would be considered traditional). Thus, the rational-traditional variable is in some sense a characteristic of the content of a person's patterned choices over a period of time. The more consistent a person's selections, independent of varying situations, the more traditional we say he is; the more his choices vary with the situations, the more rational we say he is. This distinction, however, is certainly not on the same level as the pattern variables; it is not a choice which must be made in addition to other pattern-variable choices before the situation has determinate meaning. Rather it is a characteristic of the pattern-variable choices themselves; or if it is a choice alternative at all, it stands on a level antecedent to the pattern variables, being perhaps a choice which ego will make in deciding what will be the basis for his pattern-variable choices.[38]

There are three assumptions in our contention that the five pattern-variable dilemmas are an exhaustive set. These assumptions are: (1) acceptance of the basic frame of reference as we have defined it; (2) acceptance of the level of generality on which we are proceeding, which is the *first* level of derivation from the basic frame of reference; (3) acceptance of our method of derivation through the establishment of primacies among types of interest and the resolution of ambiguities intrinsic to the world of social objects.

Finally, it should be emphasized that the variables as we have stated them are dichotomies and not continua. In a series of concrete actions, a person may be partly "affective" and partly "neutral." But this series would be composed of dichotomous choices; no specific choice can be half affective, half neutral. The same is true of the other pattern variables. One who has carefully read the definitions and discussions will see that each concept sets up a polarity, a true dilemma.

CLASSIFICATION OF NEED-DISPOSITIONS AND ROLE-EXPECTATIONS

The pattern variables are tools for the classification of need-dispositions and role-expectations, which, as has been pointed out, represent allocative foci for both personality and social systems. Before we go into the classification of these units, it might be wise to recapitulate briefly the way the allocative and integrative foci fit into the frame of reference of the theory of action. We have said that action systems, as either actors or social objects, may be personalities or collectivities, both of which are abstracted from the same concrete action. The different principles of abstraction used in locating the two systems derive directly from the notion that personalities and collectivities have different kinds of allocative and integrative foci. The integrative foci are, in some sense, the principles of abstraction used in locating or delimiting the system: thus, the individual organism is the integrative focus of a personality system and the interacting social group is the integrative focus of a social system. The integrative foci are therefore used for abstracting social systems themselves from the total realm of possible subject matter.

The allocative foci, on the other hand, are the primary units used for analyzing the action system into elements or parts. The allocative foci of personality systems are need-dispositions. The personality system is in a sense

---

[38] Other pairs of concepts, such as dominance-submission and autonomy-heteronomy should similarly be regarded as being on a different level of complexity. Some of these will be considered in more detail in later chapters.

composed of a variety of need-dispositions; each of these assures that some need of the personality system will be met. The referent of a need-disposition is, in a sense, a set of concrete orientations. That is, a need-disposition is an inferred entity; it is inferred on the basis of a certain consistency of choosing and cathecting in a wide variety of orientations. Thus, when we speak of a need-disposition, we will sometimes seem to be talking about a real entity, causally controlling a wide variety of orientations and rendering them consistent; other times we will seem to be talking about the consistent set of orientations (abstracted on the basis of the postulated entity) themselves. Logicians have shown that it is usually fair to use interchangeably the inferred entity postulated on the basis of a set of data and the whole set of data itself. The postulated entity is, in some sense, a shorthand for the set of data from which it is inferred.

The allocative foci of social systems are roles or role-expectations. The social system is in a sense composed of a variety of roles or role-expectations; each of these assures that some need of the social system will be met. The referent of a role, like that of a need-disposition, is a set of concrete orientations; the role or role-expectation is an inferred entity in exactly the same fashion as is the need-disposition. Each orientation, according to postulate, is a joint function of a role (which partly controls it), a need-disposition (which also partly controls it), and probably of other factors not mentioned here.[39] When orientations are grouped (or abstracted) according to the need-dispositions that control them, and according to the individual organisms who have these need-dispositions, we are dealing with personality systems. When orientations are grouped (or abstracted) according to the roles or roles-expectations that control them, and according to the interacting groups to which they belong, we are dealing with social systems.

Now, since none of the depth variables (allocative foci, etc.) are effective except as they influence the orientation of action (which is not necessarily either conscious or rational), and since all orientations tend to have not only the allocative foci of both social and personality systems as ingredients but also value standards (which, when internalized, are depth variables similar to need-dispositions and role-expectations), no need-disposition, nor any role-expectation, is effective except in conjunction with certain value-orientations with which it is systematically related (at least in the sense that both control the same orientation for the moment). Hence, in discussing personalities or social systems, using as the primary units of abstraction need-dispositions or role-expectations, we may regard the value-orientation components of the orientations so grouped to be the value-orientation components of the need-dispositions or role-expectations themselves. Thus we

---

[39] As will be seen in a moment, each orientation is in some sense a function of the value standards which partly control it. Furthermore, each orientation is certainly partly a function of the present object situation.

can classify the need-dispositions and role-expectations in terms of the value-orientations with which they tend to be linked.

In principle, therefore, *every* concrete need-disposition [40] of personality, or every role-expectation of social structure, involves a combination of values of the five pattern variables. The cross-classification of each of the five against each of the others, yielding a table of thirty-two cells, will, on the assumption that the list of pattern variables is exhaustive, produce a classification of the basic value patterns. Internalized in the personality system, these value patterns serve as a starting point for a classification of the possible types of need-dispositions; as institutionalized in the system of social action, they are a classification of components of role-expectation definitions.[41]

It should be clear that the classification of the value components of need-dispositions and of role-expectations in terms of the pattern variables is a *first step* toward the construction of a dynamic theory of systems of action. To advance toward empirical significance, these classifications will have to be related to the functional problems of on-going systems of action.[42]

As a last word before taking up the problem of classification itself, we should mention that of the logically possible combinations of the pattern variables, not all are likely to be of equal empirical significance. Careful analysis of their involvement in a wide variety of phenomena shows that they are all in fact independently variable in some contexts and that there is no tautology in the scheme. Nonetheless there are certainly tendencies for certain combinations to cluster together. The uneven distribution of combinations and the empirical difficulty, or even perhaps impossibility, of the

[40] A need-disposition as the term is used here always involves a set of dispositions toward objects. In abstraction from objects the concept becomes elliptical. Only for reasons of avoiding even greater terminological cumbersomeness is the more complex term "need-disposition toward objects" usually avoided. However, such a need-disposition and the *particular* objects of its gratification are independently variable. The mechanism of *substitution* links the need-disposition to various objects that are not its "proper" gratifiers.

[41] The classification of role-expectations and need-dispositions according to value patterns is only a part of the larger problem of classifying concrete need-dispositions and role-expectations. Other components of action must enter the picture before a classification relevant and adequate to the problem of the analysis of systems is attainable. For example, one set of factors entering into need-dispositions, the constitutionally determined components, has been quite explicitly and deliberately excluded from the present analysis. So far as these are essential to an adequate classification of the need-disposition elements of personality, the classification in terms of pattern variables obviously requires adjustment.

[42] This means above all that the motivational *processes* of action must be analyzed as processes in terms of the laws governing them, and as mechanisms in terms of the significance of their outcomes for the functioning of the systems of which they are parts. In due course the attempt to do this will be made. Also, it should be noted that the necessary constitutional factors which are treated as residual in this conceptual scheme will find their place among the functional necessities of systems.

realization of some combinations in systems of action will raise important dynamic problems.

To classify need-dispositions and role-expectations, we must begin by making the cross-classification tables mentioned above. In constructing such tables we find that certain of the pattern-variable dichotomies are of major importance with respect to need-dispositions (and hence personality systems). Similarly, certain pattern-variable dichotomies are of major importance with respect to role-expectations (and hence social systems). Furthermore, the pattern variables of major importance for classification of need-dispositions are not the same as those of major importance for classification of role-expectations. In fact, the two sets are more or less complementary; those of major importance for need-dispositions are the ones of minor importance for role-expectations, and vice versa.

The only one of the pattern variables equally applicable to both need-dispositions and role-expectations is the self-collectivity variable (number two). Of the other four, the first, affectivity-neutrality, and the fifth, specificity-diffuseness, are chiefly important with respect to need-dispositions. The third, universalism-particularism, and the fourth, ascription-achievement, are chiefly important with respect to role-expectations.

Figs. 3 and 4 present the formal classifications of types of need-disposition orientation and of role-expectation orientation, respectively. In each case, for the sake of simplicity, the pattern variable concerning the distribution between private and collective values and interests is omitted. This variable seems to occupy, as we shall see presently, a special place in the comprehensive integration of systems of action and is the only one which has a fully symmetrical relation to both diagrams. It is therefore possible to omit it here and introduce it when personality systems and social systems are discussed in more detail subsequently.

The characterizations of each of the types in the cells of the main diagrams and the illustrations in the supplementary ones indicate that each of the cells makes sense empirically. Concrete phenomena can be adduced as illustrations without distortion. The two figures do not have an identical arrangement. Figure 3 is divided into four major "blocks" by the cross-classification of the first and the fifth pattern variables while the further subdivision within each of the blocks is the product of cross-classification of the other two variables, universalism-particularism and ascription-achievement. In Fig. 4 the four main blocks are the result of the cross-classification of universalism-particularism and ascription-achievement, while the subdivisions within the major types are produced by cross-classifying affectivity-neutrality and specificity-diffuseness. The pattern variable, self- versus collectivity-orientation, is not involved in the symmetrical asymmetry of these fundamental classificatory tables and is omitted.

Let us discuss for a moment the reasons why the pair of pattern variables primary for personality is the obverse of the pair primary for social systems. Personality systems, as we have said, are primary constellations of need-dispositions. The primary problems regarding need-dispositions and the orientations they control are these: (1) On the orientation side of the orientation-object division, the primary question is whether or not the need-disposition allows evaluation. Metaphorically, we might ask whether the need-disposition interacts peacefully with the other need-dispositions in the system. If it allows evaluation, it interacts peacefully, if it disallows evaluation, it competes for all or no affective control of the organism. (2) On the object side, the question is whether the need-disposition which mediates attachment to any given object is segmental (being perhaps an uncomplex residue of the biological drive system, or some very segmental learned motivational system), or whether it is a complex integration of many drives and motives into one diffuse and complex need-disposition that can be aroused by many different situations and conditions. These two problems are primary because they concern the most basic aspects of the relations which obtain between need-dispositions; thus, the selections of the various need-dispositions on these questions are in a sense constitutive of the nature of the personality system in question.

Social systems, we have said, are primarily constellations of roles or role-expectations. The primary problems relative to role-expectations and the orientations they control are these: (1) On the orientation side, the question is whether or not the role's mutual relationships to other roles (or to the role-expectations which define the role) are based on cognitive or appreciative standards. (If this role is related to other roles on the basis of cognitive standards, then, its chief characteristics do not derive from its specific relations to other social objects; and its characteristics do not change so much depending on the alter with which it is interacting.) (2) On the object side, the question is whether this role (qua object) is related to other roles on the basis of the performance or the quality characteristics of its incumbents. These two problems are primary because they concern the most basic aspects of the relations which obtain between roles; thus, the selections of roles (or occupants of roles) on these questions are in a sense constitutive of the nature of the social system in question.

At this point, it would be wise to turn to Figs. 3, 3a, 4, and 4a (pp. 249–252). Fig .3 presents the major classification of need-dispositions; that is, according to the affectivity-neutrality variable and the specificity-diffuseness variable. Fig. 3a presents the further cross-classification of Fig. 3 by the two pattern variables of secondary importance for personalities, universalism-particularism and quality-performance. Fig. 4, similarly, presents the major classification of roles; that is, according to the universalism-particularism variable and the quality-performance variable. Fig. 4a presents the further cross-classification of Fig. 4 by the two pattern variables of secondary importance for social systems, affectivity-neutrality and specificity-diffuseness.

Fig. 5 illustrates the "symmetrical asymmetry" pointed out above. It shows that affectivity-neutrality and diffuseness-specificity apply most directly to problems of motivational orientation and thus to systems composed of motivational units and that universalism-particularism and ascription-achievement apply most directly to problems of value-orientation and thus to systems composed of units established by social values and norms (that is, systems of roles and role-expectations). Finally, it shows that the self-orientation — collectivity-orientation variable applies equally to problems of motivational and value-orientation, and thus equally to personality and social systems.

For those who already comprehend the diagrams, the following explanation is unnecessary. A new topic begins on page 98. Similarly, those who are interested in the outline but not the finer details of our theory may proceed to that page. For those who wish it, however, we give a brief discussion of these diagrams.

The four main types of need-dispositions (given in Fig. 3) are variants of the actor's attitudinal attachments to any object, further differentiated by the scope of the attachment to the object. Two of them (Cells I and III) represent the actor's needs for direct gratification through specific or diffuse attachments. In the former there are *specific* relations to objects (e.g., objects for the gratification of hunger or erotic needs). In the latter, the attachment is diffuse and involves a large portion of ego's action system in the relation to the object. The attachment to the object comprises both the reception of the attitudes of the object and the possession of the reciprocally corresponding attitudes toward the object. A lack of reciprocity in this responsiveness-receptiveness structure of a need-disposition (which mediates an attachment) is, however, extremely frequent empirically. Thus it presents a major problem in the dynamic analysis of personalities and social systems. It must be analyzed by the introduction of other variables in addition to those so far considered (see below, Chapter II).

The other two main types of need-disposition (Cells II and IV) are directed toward less immediate, less intensely positive affective gratification. The value standards figure more prominently in them. In the *specific* variant of this more disciplined need-disposition, the needed attachment is to a specific quality or performance. Again there is receptive-responsive reciprocality — the need-disposition is to approve of the qualities or performances of other persons and to be approved by others for one's own qualities or performances in conformity with some specific value standards (which have been internalized in the personality). In the diffuse variant the needed attachment is to a whole person; the need is to be esteemed by others on the basis of conformity to a set of standards applying to the whole person, and to esteem others on the basis of their conformity to similar standards. It should be stressed that the cathexis which is fundamental here covers both phases of the attachment, to loved and loving objects, to esteemed and esteeming objects, and so on.

In commenting on this simplified systematic classification of need-dispositions, we ought to point back and show whence it is derived; then point to examples and show that the different kinds of need-dispositions do exist; then, perhaps, show how these need-dispositions are generated within the personality. However, in such an essay as this we cannot spell out all steps completely. Suffice it to say that the categories are derived from our basic categories of action through the pattern variables. We have tried to make the steps of this derivation explicit. As for pointing to examples, we will not here go into all of the specific kinds of need-dispositions that fill our various categories, but we can point out that there are these needs to receive certain attitudes from others and to respond with certain attitudes to others. If it is asked how ego comes to be so concerned about the attitudes of approval, love, esteem, and so forth, which alter directs toward ego (and which ego directs toward alter) we must point to the cathectic *sensitivity* to the attitudes of others which is developed in the course of socialization. The child learns to need the love or approval or esteem of others and in the same sense he learns to need to love or approve or esteem others through identification. In somewhat different form, the same is true of the need for specific attachments to objects as immediate sources of gratification. There are perhaps physical components of all these need-dispositions, according to which they also might also be classified. And ultimately, of course, they are genetically derived from organic sources in the infant's dependency — his needs as a biological organism — but in their operation as parts of a system of need-dispositions they acquire a very far-reaching functional autonomy in the form of the personality system.

The fundamental reason why Fig. 4 is constructed from pattern variables omitted from Fig. 3 has already been given. We may expand it briefly. Personality systems are primarily systems of need-dispositions; the primary questions about need-dispositions (which always govern orientations of actors to objects), when we are concerned with a system of them, are: (1) Does the need-disposition in question integrate harmoniously with other need-dispositions in the system? (2) Is the need-disposition in question diffusely related with many other sectors of the system, or is it more or less segmental and cut off with respect to the other aspects of the system of which it is a part? Hence in the description of the fundamental need-dispositions, the primarily relevant pattern variables are (1) that derived from the problem whether or not evaluation is called for (whether the need-disposition has to be integrated with others) and (2) that derived from the problem of whether the object shall be endowed with diffuse or specific significance (whether the need-disposition which mediates the object attachment involves much or little of the action system of ego).

A social system is primarily a system of roles. The primary questions about roles (which govern mutual orientations of individuals within a social system) when we are concerned with a system of these roles, are: (1) Does the role in question integrate with other roles on the basis of universalistic or particularistic principles of organization? (2) Are the roles in question defined and thus related in terms of the quality or performance characteristics of their occupants? It should be remembered that the determination of how roles are related in this respect is largely a function of the value standards institutionalized in the social system. Consequently, the pattern variables most relevant to the description of the normative patterns governing roles (i.e., role-expectations) are achievement-ascription and universalism-particularism. The four main types of role-expectations are presented in the four cells of Fig. 4. Fig. 4a is constructed by further cross-classifying each main type of role-expectation. What are classified in Fig. 4 are only the primary value-orientation components of the role-expectations and most emphatically *not* the concrete roles themselves.

These two diagrams in a slightly different formulation also constitute classifications of constellations of the alternatives of choice which make up systems of value-orientations themselves. They are components of "patterns of culture." Again it should be emphasized that they are classifications of constellations of *components* of systems of value-orientation, not of *types* of such systems. Types of systems are formed from such constellations when they are related to the more concrete "problems" presented by the situation of action. These and related questions will be taken up in the analysis of systems of value-orientation in Chapter III.[43]

CLASSIFICATION OF COMPONENTS OF THE OBJECT SITUATION

Here we shall recapitulate briefly what has been said above about the structure of the object world and elaborate further on the classification of the components of that structure.[44] The structure of the object world in the most

---

[43] There is one implication of the above discussion which may be noted now for further analysis. The symmetrical asymmetry which has been discussed implies a difference between the systematic focus of a value-orientation system for personality, and the corresponding one for the social system (see Fig. 5). A system of personal values will be organized primarily around the actor's motivational problems, such as permission and restraint, and the scope of the significance of objects. The patterns of relationship between persons beyond these bases of interest will be conceptually secondary, although of course they will have to be integrated with the primary foci. A system of *social values*, on the other hand, will be organized more about the problems of choice between the types of normative patterns which govern the relations among individuals and the aspects of those individuals which are to be constitutive of their social statuses and roles. This asymmetry may be of considerable importance in defining the relations between the study of culture and personality, on the one hand, and culture and society, on the other. Fig. 5 presents in schematic form the relationship of the pattern variables of motivational orientation on the one hand, and role-expectation on the other. The second pattern variable, self- or collectivity-orientation, belongs equally to both and is central to neither.

[44] Every action system has, in one sense, three components: a pattern of value-orientation, a structural object world, and a set of allocative and integrative foci. Of these three sets of components, the value patterns and the object world are common, without essential differences, to personality and social systems and even to cultural systems. The

general terms takes form from the distinction between social and nonsocial objects, the further differentiation of the former into the categories of qualities and performances, and the further differentiation of the latter into the categories of physical and cultural objects. Nonsocial objects, it will be remembered, are distinguished by the fact that ego does not see them as having expectations about ego's behavior. Ego knows that social objects "expect" him to do certain things; he does not see nonsocial objects as having such expectations. Cultural objects, it will be remembered, are distinguished from physical objects in that the former are subject to "internalization," the latter are not.

Taking these distinctions as our starting point we will now further differentiate objects along lines which are of maximal significance in the orientation of action.

Social objects may be distiguished as individual actors and collectivities, which are systems of action involving a plurality of individual actors but which are treated as units. Among physical objects one subclass in particular has such importance for action that it must be singled out. This is the organism of the individual actor, whether it be ego's own body or that of alter. Within the class of individual social objects it is desirable to distinguish the personality of alter from that of ego himself as an object. Internalized cultural objects are no longer distinct objects but parts of the personalities of ego and alter and of the structure of collectivities.

Finally, we must divide objects in accordance with whether the properties on the basis of which actors are oriented toward them are attributes of a class (of qualities or performances) or whether they are possessed by virtue of a relationship. This distinction is not identical with the quality-performance distinction; in fact, it cuts across it. Nor is it derived from the distinction between universalism and particularism, though it is closely related to it. It is derived from the distinction between the actor as such and the system of action which involves status and role in relationships. The actor *in abstracto* is simply a set of properties by which he can be classified; in action he is involved in a system of relationships. Hence social objects can be distinguished by certain properties which they have independently of their relationships as well as by those which they have in their capacities of participants in a relationship which may be social, biological, or spatial.

Fig. 6 presents in schematic form the structure of the object world. Each of the "units" listed at the left may be integrated into action in several (or many) different ways. It is, of course, a different kind of object, depending on how it is integrated into action. The columns which make up the body

differences between personality, social, and cultural systems lie (1) in the different allocative and integrative foci, and (2) in the empirical organization and integration of these elements in the concrete control of action. Thus the components of the object situation, like the patterns of value orientation, can be analyzed once and for all, and the categories so developed should be applicable to all three kinds of systems.

of the chart show the various ways each of the units may be integrated as an object. (Fig. 6 is on page 254.)

The distinction of modalities applies chiefly to social objects and only these form interactive relationships; the first two columns therefore present this distinction for social objects. The nonsocial objects appear separately in the right-hand column, since the quality-performance distinction is inapplicable to them.[45] The latter are relevant to action as empirical and symbolic means, conditions, and obstacles of the gratification of need-disposition.

The classification of social objects within each of the modalities follows the distinctions employed in our analysis of actor and situation: the actor as an individual as an object, alter as an individual as an object, and a collectivity as an object.

We have already remarked that the actor is a special sort of methodological abstraction, a point of reference. The particular actor who is performing the particular action at a particular moment cannot be an object of an orientation which has a future reference. Only the empirical system of action which has duration and which is referable to that point of reference (i.e., the personality) can be an object. From the point of view of any given actor, ego, *his own* personality (i.e., his system of action or any part of it which is larger and more extensive in time than the action which he is performing at the moment) may be an object and is, as a specific, concrete object, differentiated from the personality of any other actor. The inclusion of the personality of ego, expressly *as an object* and not only as the actor, is fundamental to the theory of action. It is only through the employment of this device that many of the most crucial analytical operations of the theory of action, such as the use of the mechanism of identification and the corresponding concept of the "internalization" of cultural norms, become possible. Common sense, we may say, lays *all* the stress on the *difference* between ego and alter as two separate entities. The theory of action accepts this difference as fundamental and embodies it in *one* of its major classifications. But it also employs a classification according to which certain analytical distinctions, such as that between the object modalities, apply equally to ego and to alter because, both being objects precisely to ego, the categories which are significant for the orientation to objects apply to both of them. It then becomes possible to relate ego's own personality as an object to the rest of the object world in a way which would not be possible so long as a rigid qualitative distinction is maintained between the self as a concrete entity and all objects which are classified as belonging to the "outside" world. In essence we are *analytically* splitting the concrete self into two components, the self as actor and the self as object.

---

[45] There seems to be one exception to this rule. Organisms, as physical objects, seem amenable to the quality-performance distinction; thus the nonsocial column is placed at the bottom of the diagram.

These distinctions are indispensable for the analysis of the interaction of social objects and make possible the basic structural homology [46] between various personalities (on other than constitutional, biological bases) and between personalities and social systems, which is fundamental to our analysis of the interdependences between the two systems.

The second basic distinction within the category of social objects is that between the individual actor and the collectivity as action systems. It should be remembered that the individual actor (as a personality or a subsystem of it) is here defined as a system of action. A collective system of action, of which the actor may or may not be a member, can be an object of orientation just as an individual can. The collectivity in this case may be either a whole society (a self-subsistent social system) or a partial social system.

In a collectivity as a system of action no one actor or his personality is the point of reference, and indeed, strictly speaking, the individual personality as such is not a relevant point of reference at all when we speak of a social system from an analytical standpoint. (Empirically, of course, the personality system of the members will be very relevant to our understanding of the working of a collectivity as a social system.) When ego and alter are oriented toward one another, the question whether they are or are not members of the same collectivity will be important in their orientation; it will determine the relational qualities of alter and ego. They will not in these terms be orienting themselves toward collectivities as objects but toward alters as objects having relational or membership qualities. For this reason memberships are classified in Fig. 6 as the qualities of individuals as objects and not as the qualities of collectivities. Its membership composition (i.e., the number and kinds of members) *is*, on the other hand, a quality of the collectivity.

It is nonetheless important to bear in mind that collectivities as such, past, present, and future, may well be objects of orientation. The actions of individuals in membership, representative, or executive roles are oriented toward collectivities (other collectivities and their own) as *systems* of actions, and not merely toward individuals with membership qualities. The maintenance by an executive of a given system of relationships within a corporate body or collectivity, as well as the discontinuance or prohibition of certain corporate practices, is an orientation toward a collectivity. It is not just an orientation to a single alter as an object, but toward a system of relationships among a plurality of alters who form a system.

It is particularly important to realize that the collective object is usually a *partial* social system. The individual actor, on the other hand, is typically a member not of one but of many collectivities. He is a member of all the subsystems in which he has distinguishable roles. The concept of the collectiv-

---

[46] The term *homology* refers to certain formal identities. It will be discussed at the end of this chapter.

ity of which the actor is himself a member *as an object of orientation* by others is fundamental to the concept of role, which is crucial to the analysis of social systems. From this point of view, the actor's role in a particular collectivity is an organized subsystem of his total system of action. It is a normatively regulated orientation to a collectivity as an object, i.e., to an organized plurality of alters in terms of the reciprocal interlocking of ego's role-expectations concerning his own action, with his expectations of *their* interindividually organized or concerted contingent reactions to the various possibilities of his behavior.

Within the category of nonsocial objects as units, a further distinction appears which is not directly relevant to the classification of modalities: the distinction between organisms and other nonsocial objects.[47] In its conceptualization, the theory of action does not treat the *actor* as an organism — the common, though usually implicit, assumption that he is, is a basic biological fallacy in the analysis of behavior. The concrete *individual* who behaves is, however, also *in one aspect* always an organism. He must be distinguished from other objects since in his personality aspect he is "tied" to a particular organism. This is of course equally true both for ego and for alter. The qualities and the propensities for performance of the organism provide criteria which may become fundamentally important foci for action orientation, again both ego's own organism and alter's. For instance, the significance of ego's own sex for his personality structure, as in his "acceptance" of his sex role, is to be analyzed in terms of the role of this particular "trait" of his body *as an object* in his orientation, by virtue of which he "classifies himself" with fellow persons of the same sex as distinguished from those of opposite sex. The same holds, of course, for performance capacities or propensities, such as physical strength or agility.

It should be quite clear that we are here speaking of the organism or the body *as an object*. This excludes the organism as a source of motivation, or in its significance as the id.[48] The energy which the physiological organism supplies for action, according to the paradigm of the theory of action, is in-

---

[47] It will be noted in the diagram that this is a very particular class of nonsocial objects, as the quality-performance distinction does apply to it, whereas it does not apply to other nonsocial objects. This is because concretely the actor's personality and the organism are not separate.

[48] In relation to the action schema, the psychoanalytic conception of the id fails to differentiate between two things: (1) the organic energy which enters into action as motivation, and thus is prerequisite to personality; (2) certain aspects of dispositions which are organized within the personality in relation to the object world. The latter component in present terms is definitely part of, not prerequisite to, personality as a system of action. In recent psychoanalytic theory the tendency seems to have been to include most of the latter in the unconscious parts of the ego. The distinction between points 1 and 2 is vital in the theory of action. Whether and at exactly which point a line corresponding to that drawn by Freud between Id and Ego should be drawn *within* the personality as a system of action, rather than *between* it and the organic need-motivation system, is a question which may be deferred until Chapter II.

corporated into the *modes of motivational orientation. It does not go into but only toward the constellation of objects.* The distinctions among ego's body, ego as personality, and ego as actor underlies much that is specific to action theory. This is essential to avoid the confusions involved in much of the traditional biological way of looking at human action. But, however fundamental these distinctions, it is also equally fundamental clearly to distinguish the organism, whether of ego or of alter, as an object from other physical objects in the situation.

The rest of the nonsocial object system is classified into physical objects and cultural objects. However important the distinction between physical and cultural objects for many purposes, *relative* to social objects they have much in common: on the one hand, they constitute objects of immediate cognitive-cathectic significance; on the other, they are instrumentally significant means — that is, "resources" — conditions, and obstacles. In the present context, it is as *units* of the object system, as distinguished from other units, that the first lines of distinction are drawn. A house, an automobile, a tree, or a book are different objects of orientation in the sense that they are distinguishable — one house as a unit from another house, and a house from an automobile — but they are also all distinguishable from actors as units and from the bodies of actors. However within the class of nonsocial objects the distinction between cultural and physical objects remains as of very marked conceptual and empirical significance.

A particularly important class of such nonsocial units are, however, concretely both physical and cultural. Of those mentioned, only a tree is a purely "natural" object. But a house or an automobile is primarily significant as a *humanly shaped and adapted* physical object; whereas a book is primarily a cultural or symbolic object, which has a "physical embodiment." It is the "content" of the book, not the paper, ink, and covers, which primarily makes the book into an object of orientation.

Just as the motivation of ego is not an object of orientation, neither are his *internalized* culture patterns. We have already remarked that for analytical purposes internationalized value standards are treated as an independent category of the system of action, *not* as part of the object world.

We should also repeat here a point which has rather general bearing. The system of objects is known to the actor(s) in question. It is only when known (i.e., cognized) [49] that it is a set of objects of orientation. We must therefore distinguish the known situation from those features of the situation "as it really is" which may be known, or are intrinsically knowable, to an observer, but are not at the moment known to the actor(s). The interrelations between the actor's situation as he is oriented toward it and the situation as discerned by a contemporary or later observer raises some of the

---

[49] Cognition need not be explicit or conscious.

most important problems of empirical analysis. In principle, the same is true of new elements which may come into the situation and which may be predictable to an observer. Hence the distinction between what is known to the actor and what is not is always potentially important. For a standard by which to assess this, it is necessary to have an appraisal of the situation as it is known to or knowable by an observer.

The cognitive orientation of the actor may not only pass over an object completely so that the actor is ignorant of it, but it may also be distorted. It may involve errors of perception and interpretation. This is of first importance to the analysis of action, and again can only be assessed with reference to a conception of the situation "as it really is," which is the equivalent of its being known by an observer. The observer's knowledge need not and cannot be absolute; it is only necessary that it should be adequate to the problem in hand.

Another source of complexity and possible misunderstanding is the question of whether ego's orientation to an object must, in whole or in part, be conscious. The answer is quite clear; it is not necessary. The criterion is whether ego acts toward the object in a meaningful way so that it is reasonable to interpret his action as based on his orientation to what the object is, has been, or is expected to be. This means of course that a given "situation" will often be the object of several cognitions by the actor: he will perceive it in accordance with the current canons of valid perception, and he will also perceive it as possessing the properties imputed to it by his unconscious need-dispositions to attribute certain probably empirically invalid properties to objects that he has already perceived to possess certain other properties. For example, an action by a person in an authoritative role will be interpreted (i.e., perceived) unconsciously as also having certain properties of aggressiveness. The *unconscious* in the psychoanalytic sense can be analyzed in terms of the theory of action, and its actual formulation in present-day psychoanalytic theory is not very far removed from the terms of the theory of action. In other words, the line between conscious and unconscious has nothing to do with the limits of analysis in terms of the frame of reference of the theory of action, including, of course, cognitive orientation.

Neither of these two problems creates any difficulties for our classification of objects — although they add greatly to the complexities of empirical analysis. The "real" situation (of the observer) and the "cognized" situation (of the actor) can both be described in terms of our classification of objects. The consciously perceived situation of the mildly neurotic adult, and the distortedly perceived situation of his unconscious reinterpretation, are likewise subject to description in the same categories. Indeed, this possibility of describing discrepancies contributes to the formulation of many important problems in the study of personality and social systems.

In conclusion, it may again be pointed out that the scheme of the pattern variables as the variable components of value-orientations and the classification of the structural components of the object system are *common to all three* types of system in which action elements become organized: personalities, social systems, and systems of cultural orientation. It is this which gives unity to the theory being developed here. This conceptual unity and its consequent advantages for systematic empirical analysis will be indicated in the three chapters which follow, in which we will attempt to present a systematic account of each of the three types of system and certain of their conceptual and empirical interrelations. No effort will be made to demonstrate the empirical hypotheses derived here, since our aim will be to show only that they can be derived from this conceptual scheme. It should not be forgotten, however, that applicability to the study of the real behavior of human beings is the ultimate test of *any* theoretical scheme.

THE BASIC STRUCTURE OF THE INTERACTIVE RELATIONSHIP

The interaction of ego and alter is the most elementary form of a social system. The features of this interaction are present in more complex form in all social systems.

In interaction ego and alter are each objects of orientation for the other. The basic differences from orientations to nonsocial objects are two. First, since the outcome of ego's action (e.g., success in the attainment of a goal) is contingent on alter's reaction to what ego does, ego becomes oriented not only to alter's probable *overt* behavior but also to what ego interprets to be alter's expectations relative to ego's behavior, since ego expects that alter's expectations will influence alter's behavior. Second, in an integrated system, this orientation to the expectations of the other is reciprocal or complementary.

Communication through a common system of symbols is the precondition of this reciprocity or complementarity of expectations. The alternatives which are open to alter must have some measure of stability in two respects: first, as realistic possibilities for alter, and second, in their meaning to ego. This stability presupposes generalization from the particularity of the given situations of ego and alter, both of which are continually changing and are never concretely identical over any two moments in time. When such generalization occurs, and actions, gestures, or symbols have more or less the *same* meaning for both ego and alter, we may speak of a common culture existing between them, through which their interaction is mediated.

Furthermore, this common culture, or symbol system, inevitably possesses in certain aspects a normative significance for the actors. Once it is in existence, observance of its conventions is a necessary condition for ego to be "understood" by alter, in the sense of allowing ego to elicit the type of reaction from alter which ego expects. This common set of cultural symbols becomes the medium in which is formed a constellation of the contingent actions of both parties, in such a way that there will simultaneously emerge a definition of a range of *appropriate* reactions on alter's part to each of a range of possible actions ego has taken and vice versa. It will then be a condition of the stabilization of such a system of complementary expectations, not only that ego and alter should *communicate*, but that they should *react appropriately* to each other's action.

A tendency toward consistent appropriateness of reaction is also a tendency toward conformity with a normative pattern. The culture is not only a set of symbols of communication but a *set of norms* for action.

The motivation of ego and alter become integrated with the normative patterns through interaction. The polarity of gratification and deprivation is crucial here. An appropriate reaction on alter's part is a gratifying one to ego. If ego conforms with the norm, this gratification is in one aspect a reward for his conformity with it; the converse holds for the case of deprivation and deviance. The reactions of alter toward ego's conformity with or deviance from the normative pattern thus become sanctions to ego. Ego's expectations vis-à-vis alter are expectations concerning the roles of ego and of alter; and sanctions reinforce ego's motivation to conform with these role-expectations. Thus the complementarity of expectations brings with it the reciprocal reinforcement of ego's and alter's motivation to conformity with the normative pattern which defines their expectations.

The interactive system also involves the process of generalization, not only in the common culture by which ego and alter communicate but in the interpretation of alter's discrete actions vis-à-vis ego as expressions of alter's *intentions* (that is, as indices of the cathectic-evaluative aspects of alter's motivational orientations toward ego). This "generalization" implies that ego and alter agree that certain actions of alter are indices of the *attitudes* which alter has acquired toward ego (and reciprocally, ego toward alter). Since these attitudes are, in the present paradigm, integrated with the common culture and the latter is internalized in ego's need-dispositions, ego is sensitive not only to alter's overt acts, but to his *attitudes*. He acquires a need not only to obtain specific *rewards* and avoid specific *punishments* but to enjoy the favorable attitudes and avoid the unfavorable ones of alter. Indeed, since he is integrated with the same norms, these are the same as his attitudes toward himself as an object. Thus violation of the norm causes him to feel shame toward alter, guilt toward himself.

It should be clear that as an ideal type this interaction paradigm implies *mutuality* of gratification in a certain sense, though not necessarily equal distribution of gratification. As we shall see in the next chapter, this is also the paradigm of the process of the learning of generalized orientations. Even where special mechanisms of adjustment such as dominance and submission or alienation from normative expectations enter in, the process still must be described and analyzed in relation to the categories of this paradigm. It is thus useful both for the analysis of systems of normative expectations and for that of the actual conformity or deviation regarding these expectations in concrete action.

In summary we may say that this is the basic paradigm for the structure of a solidary interactive relationship. It contains all the fundamental elements of the role structure of the social system and the attachment and security system of the personality. It involves culture in both its communicative and its value-orientation functions. It is the nodal point of the organization of all systems of action.

The Concept of System and the Classification of Types of Systems

With our discussion of interaction we have entered upon the analysis of systems. Before we discuss more fully personality and social systems, it is desirable to state explicitly the principal properties of empirical systems which are relevant for the present analysis. The most general and fundamental property of a system is the interdependence of parts or variables. Interdependence consists in the existence of determinate relationships among the parts or variables as contrasted with randomness of variability. In other words, interdependence is *order* in the relationship among the components which enter into a system. This order must have a tendency to self-maintenance, which is very generally expressed in the concept of equilibrium.[50] It need not, however, be a static self-maintenance or a stable equilibrium. It may be an ordered process of change — a process following a determinate pattern rather than random variability relative to the starting point. This is called a moving equilibrium and is well exemplified by growth. Furthermore, equilibrium, even when stable, by no means implies that process is not going on; process is continual even in stable systems, the stabilities residing in the interrelations involved in the process.

A particularly important feature of all systems is the inherent limitation on the compatibility of certain parts or events within the same system. This is indeed simply another way of saying that the relations within the system are determinate and that not just anything can happen. Thus, to take an example from the solar system, if the orbit of one of the planets, such as Jupiter, is given, it is no longer possible for the orbits of the other planets to be distributed at random relative to this given orbit. Certain limitations are imposed by the fact that the value of one of the variables is given. This limitation may in turn be looked at from either a negative or a positive point of view. On the one hand, again using the solar system as example, if one of the planets should simply disappear, the fact that no mass was present in that particular orbit would necessitate a change in the equilibrium of the system. It would make necessary a readjustment of the orbits of the other

---

[50] That is, if the system is to be permanent enough to be worth study, there must be a tendency to maintenance of order except under exceptional circumstances.

planets in order to bring the system into equilibrium. This may also be expressed in the statement that there is a change in the structure of the system. On the other hand, the same problem may be treated from the standpoint of what would happen in the case of the coexistence of "incompatible" elements or processes within the same system. Incompatibility is always relative to a *given* state of the system. If, for example, the orbits of two of the planets should move closer to each other than is compatible for the maintenance of the current state of the system, one of two things would have to happen. Either processes would be set up which would tend to restore the previous relation by the elimination of the incompatibility; or if the new relation were maintained, there would have to be adjustments in *other* parts of the system, bringing the system into a new state of equilibrium.

These properties are inherent in all systems. A special additional property, however, is of primary significance for the theory of action. This is the tendency to maintain equilibrium, in the most general sense stated above, within certain boundaries relative to an environment — boundaries which are not imposed from outside but which are self-maintained by the properties of the constituent variables as they operate within the system. The most familiar example is the living organism, which is a physicochemical system that is not assimilated to the physicochemical conditions of the environment, but maintains certain distinct properties in relation to the environment. For example, the maintenance of the constant body temperature of the mammal necessitates processes which mediate the interdependence between the internal and the external systems in respect to temperature; these processes maintain constancy over a wide range of variability in environmental temperatures.

The two fundamental types of processes necessary for the maintenance of a given state of equilibrium of a system we call, in the theory of action, *allocation* [51] and *integration*. By *allocation* we mean processes which maintain a distribution of the components or parts of the system which is compatible with the maintenance of a given state of equilibrium. By *integration*, we mean the processes by which relations to the environment are mediated in such a way that the distinctive internal properties and boundaries of the system as an entity are maintained in the face of variability in the external situation. It must be realized that self-maintenance of such a system is not only maintenance of boundaries but also maintenance of distinctive relationships of the parts of the system *within* the boundary. The system is in some sense a unity relative to its environment. Also, self-maintenance implies not only control of the environmental variations, but also control of tendencies to change — that is, to alteration of the distinctive state — coming from within the system.

---

[51] The term *allocation* is borrowed from the usage of economics, where it has the general meaning here defined. Specifically, economists speak of the allocation of resources in the economy.

The two types of empirical systems which will be analyzed in the subsequent chapters are personalities and social systems. These systems are, as will be repeatedly pointed out, *different* systems which are not reducible to each other. However, there are certain conceptual continuities or identities between them which derive from two sources. (1) They are both systems built out of the fundamental components of action as these have been discussed in the General Statement and in the present chapter. These components are differently organized to constitute systems in the two cases; nevertheless, they remain the same components. (2) They are both not only systems, but both are systems of the boundary-maintaining, self-maintenance type; therefore, they both have properties which are common to systems in general and the more special properties which are characteristic of this particular type of system. (3) A third basis of their intimate relation to each other is the fact that they *interpenetrate* in the sense that no personality system can exist without *participation* in a social system, by which we mean the integration of *part* of the actor's system of action as *part* of the social system. Conversely, there is no social system which is not from one point of view a mode of the integration of parts of the systems of action which constitute the personalities of the members. When we use the term *homology* to refer to certain formal identities between personalities and social systems which are to be understood in terms of the above considerations, it should be clear that we in no way intend to convey the impression that a personality is a microcosm of a social system, or that a social system is a kind of macrocosmic personality.

In spite of the formal similarities and the continuous empirical interdependencies and interpenetrations, both of which are of the greatest importance, personalities and social systems remain two distinct classes of systems.

2

Personality as a System of Action

The preceding chapter dealt with certain common features of systems of action. Besides their common properties as systems, systems of action have certain common substantive features. In *both* social systems and personalities, the actions which make up the systems are oriented to the same classes of objects and entail selections from and commitments to the same system of alternatives of value-orientation. Having stated the general properties of systems, we will show how these substantive components are organized to form personalities. We will accordingly turn to a further discussion of motivation as it was treated in the General Statement of Part I and develop some of the categories and hypotheses presented there in order to lay the groundwork for showing systematic relationships of (1) the patterns of value-orientation and (2) the organization of objects to (3) the components of motivation (which are the allocative foci of personality systems). This will require a certain amount of recapitulation of our earlier argument. At the end of the chapter we shall analyze certain aspects of the interrelation of this system with the social system in which the actor lives.

MOTIVATIONAL CONCEPTS

Since this chapter will be concerned largely with the relation between the motivation of action and the orientation of action, we shall start out by defining carefully the important terms, chiefly the term *motivation* itself. We must define also the other motivational terms *drive*, *drives*, and *need-dispositions*.

The term *motivation* has at least two accepted meanings; the use of the word without distinguishing these two meanings serves only to confuse the reader. When we speak of an animal or a human being as having "a lot of motivation," we refer to the amount of energy being released in the course of the animal's behavior. In this sense, motivation is the organically generated energy manifested in action. It is sometimes called *drive*. When, on the other hand, we say "the motivation of an organism," referring to the organism's "motives" or "drives," [1] we refer to a set of tendencies on the part of the organism to acquire certain goal objects (or really, certain relationships to goal objects).

Motivation (or motives) in this last sense may be conceived as denoting certain more or less innate systems of *orientations* involving cognition of and cathectic attachment to certain means and goal objects and certain more or less implicit and unconscious "plans" of action aimed at the acquisition of cathected relationships to goal objects. Motivation in the former sense (as energy) supplies the energy with which such plans of action are conceived and carried out.

When *motivation* refers to the tendency to acquire these relationships to goal objects, then it is (as the paragraph above implies) also a tendency to "orient" in a certain fashion (that is, to see certain things, to want certain things, and to do certain things). Thus its referent may be either the group of orientations which follow the pattern marked out by the "tendency," or a postulated entity which, by hypothesis, controls or brings about orientations of this kind.

From now on, we will use the term *drive* [2] to refer to the physiological energy that makes action possible. We will use the term *drives*, or such terms as *a drive* or *sex drive*, to refer to the *innate* tendencies to orient and act in such a fashion as to acquire cathected relationships to goal objects. The term *need-dispositions* will be used to refer to these same tendencies when they are not innate but acquired through the process of action itself. Need-dispositions may integrate one or several drives, together with certain acquired elements, into very complex tendencies of this nature. We will avoid *ad hoc* hypotheses about the amount of biologically determined structuring of drives which would beg the empirical and conceptual questions of the extent and ways in which structuring is a need-disposition problem. That is, we will not try to decide in advance how much the structuring of tendencies is innate and how much it is a function of the structure and situation of action.[3]

The term *motivation* itself will be reserved as a general term to refer to all the phenomena discussed above. Thus action may be said to be motivated by "drive," or by "drives," or by "need-dispositions," depending on what is meant by *motivation*, and depending on the stage of development of the personality involved, and the type of action being discussed. Some actions are perhaps jointly motivated by drives and need-dispositions, in an organism where some drives are organized into need-dispositions and others are not.

---

[1] For example, the organism's hunger-drive or sex-drive.

[2] This term is only singular (an animal's drive, an amount of drive, and so forth) when it refers to energy; when we speak of "a drive," the animal's "drives," the term refers to a tendency.

[3] A statement of the general problem of the relation of constitutional elements in behavior to action elements was made in the General Statement of Part I and need not be repeated here.

All actions are in one sense motivated by the physiological "drive" of the organism insofar as the ultimate energy of behavior comes from the organism as a physiological system. Nevertheless, the important question of how this energy expenditure will take place, what behavior will result, what will be accomplished, requires analysis of *drive* and *need-dispositions* in the categories of action, rather than an analysis of where the energy or drive comes from. Therefore, our chief concern with motivation in this chapter will be with the orientation and action tendencies which are denoted by the terms *drive* and *need-disposition*. Moreover, since we are most concerned with the analysis of the action of human beings (and usually human beings with some degree of maturity), we will usually be more concerned with need-dispositions than with drives.

For our purposes, the drives may be regarded as action tendencies in which the chief objects are the actor's own organism and those physical objects which are necessary to achieve some state of the organism. (We include under physical objects the physiological organisms of other persons.) We need not for the time being go in detail into the degree of specificity of the physical objects or the content of the states of the actor's own organism as an object which is required for activating the drive or bringing it to quiescence. All we need say is that there are varying degrees of specificity in the two classes of objects and that there is always some plasticity in the organization of the orientation toward the objects. *All* concrete drives and need-dispositions (in relation to objects) on the personality level — that is, above the most elementary organic level — have a structure which can be analyzed in the categories of the theory of action. They can be analyzed only in terms of orientation to an object world, which varies of course through time, and in terms of the organization of value-alternative selections and commitments into patterns of need-dispositions and value-orientations which make up the personality.

One significant difference between drives on the most elementary organic level [4] and drives and need-dispositions as these are formulated in terms of the theory of action is that the former are conceived as "automatic" regulatory devices. The animal orients to the object; the object orientation automatically engages a drive; the drive implants a cathexis on the oriented object; action and consummation automatically ensue. No selection or choice is involved. There is no orientation to anything beyond the present and immediately given aspect of the situation of action. We might say the system of orientation seems to have no time dimension. No orientation to the future may take place; thus the animal is *driven* by the situation of the moment, he cannot choose on the basis of the long-run integration of his action system.

[4] The notion of drives on the most elementary organic level may, of course, be simply a limiting case not existing in either animals or human beings; there may be no such things.

Whatever may be the case on purely organic levels, when drives and their modes of gratification become organized into and with symbolic systems on the cultural level, the system of orientation necessarily *acquires* a temporal dimension. The orientation of action is not directed merely to the situation at the moment but also to future states of the system and to the potentialities for future occurrence or change of the objects in the situation. The future therefore is cognitively differentiated and its probabilities evaluated above all as differing alternatives of action. Gratification then is not merely associated with responses to a current situation; it is *distributed in time* in connection with *expectations* concerning the future development of the situation. The conception of the orientation of action by selection from a set of alternatives thus includes future as well as present alternatives and attendant consequences. A need-disposition therefore has as one of its essential properties an orientation of expectancy relative to future possibilities.[5]

We proceed on the postulate that drives tend toward gratification through the cathexis of objects. The interruption of any established process of gratification is a disturbance of equilibrium. The possible sources of interruption are twofold: first, changes in the situation which make maintenance of an unchanged relation to the cathected object impossible; second, internal processes which motivate the actor to change his relations to objects. Thus our conception of the actor's drives is that they are organized in an equilibrated system of relationships to an object world and that this system, if disturbed, will set in motion forces tending either to restore a previous state of equilibrium or to make stable a new state. This conception will underlie all our analysis of learning processes and of the operation of the personality as an on-going system.

In action, therefore, drives do not ordinarily operate simply to gratify organic needs in a pure form. They are integrated into need-dispositions,[6] which are for us the most significant units of motivation of action. A need-disposition represents the organization of one or more drive elements, elaborated into an *orientation* tendency to a more differentiated object situation than is the case with elementary drives. The drive component of a need-disposition is *organized* with cognitive and evaluative elements. Cognitively, objects of the situation are more finely discriminated and more extensively generalized in need-dispositions than in the simpler cognitive organization of drives. At the same time the selection from value alternatives is not so "automatic" but entails relatively complex and stable orientations to selective standards.

The equilibrium of drive gratification thus operates within the context of

---

[5] Without the property of "future-orientedness" in need-dispositions it would be difficult to understand the nature of such phenomena as anxiety.

[6] See p. 10, n. 12, of the General Statement of Part I.

an equilibrium of need-dispositions and their systems. It is not a direct gratification of elementary drives.

A common formula describing the relations of drive to action is the "tension reduction" hypothesis. For our purposes this theory is inadequate for three reasons. First, it fails to take explicit account of the organization of the drive element into the system of need-dispositions. Second, "tension" tends to be merely a name for an unknown; hence an explanation of action by tension reduction tends to be a tautology to the effect that tension is reduced because it is the nature of tension to seek reduction. Third, explanation of action by tension reduction tends to translate action into an oversimplified, relatively undifferentiated rhythm of tension activation and quiescence, so that specific differentiation in relation to elements of the situation and of orientation of action are obscured.

However, whether formulated in terms of tension reduction or otherwise, the careful study of the process of gratification of particular drives has made important contributions to our understanding. It has produced a first approximation to an analysis of the motivation of behavior. Our concern here, however, is to consider the problems on more complex levels of organization of motivation involved in human action.

To make this advance from the simplifying hypothesis of need reduction, we must remember that a need-disposition does not operate in isolation in the sense that it may become activated, impel action, culminate and come to rest independently of a whole constellation of other need-dispositions, some of which work in opposition to (or even as defenses against) the originally activated need-disposition.

This brings to a close our general discussion of motivational concepts. Our next major step will be to show how need-dispositions (as the elements of the personality system) are related to one another, to the personality system as a whole, and to the world of objects, by means of certain processes which mediate these relationships. Then we must show how these processes, when classified in terms of the ways they serve to solve the various major problems of personality systems, comprise the *mechanisms* of personality. Before we do this, however, it seems wise to give some special discussion to the specific kind of motivational variable with which we will be most concerned, that is, the need-disposition.

NEED-DISPOSITIONS

Need-dispositions, we have said, are tendencies to orient and act with respect to objects in certain manners and to expect certain consequences [7] from

---

[7] The expectations of consequences is nothing more than the cognition of a certain object as leading to a certain set of consequences and the cathexis of an object in the light of its antecedent relationship to a more cathected set of consequences. In other words, the expectation is nothing more than the cognition and cathexis of a means object qua means to an end.

these actions. The conjoined word *need-disposition* itself has a double connotation; on the one hand, it refers to a tendency to fulfill some requirement of the organism, a tendency to accomplish some end state; on the other hand, it refers to a disposition to do something with an object designed to accomplish this end state. We have already said that its denotation is a group of orientations (or the postulated variable which controls that set of orientations), all following a pattern involving the discrimination of an object or a group of objects, the cathecting of an object or group of objects, and the tendency to behave in the fashion designed to get the cathected relationship with the object. In the last analysis, the identifying index of a need-disposition is a tendency on the part of the organism to "strive" for certain relationships with objects, or for certain relationships between objects. And the tendency to "strive" is nothing more than the tendency to cognize and cathect in certain ways and to act in a fashion guided by those cognitions and cathexes. The differences between a need-disposition and a drive, we have said, lies in the fact that it is not innate, that it is formed or learned in action, and in the fact that it is a tendency to orient and select with an eye to the future, as well as with an eye to immediate gratification.

Three different types of need-dispositions are chiefly important in the theory of action: (1) Need-dispositions vis-à-vis the attitudes of and relationships with social objects (these need-dispositions mediate person-to-person relationships); (2) need-dispositions vis-à-vis the observance of cultural standards (these need-dispositions are the internalized social values); and (3) role-expectations, which are on a somewhat different level from the other two.[8] Other types of need-dispositions enter as variables into personality systems, but none has nearly the importance of these as determinants of action, particularly when (as is always the case) the various aspects of the per-

---

[8] Here we are classifying need-dispositions in terms of their foci; that is, in terms of objects and relationships at which they direct the actor's attention and toward which they direct his strivings. Chiefly important for our system are *two* fundamental foci of need-dispositions — *social objects* and *value patterns*. Thus, the first two classes of need-dispositions are listed. Role-expectations, although they incorporate components of both of the first two, are not a special subclass of either but a special way of organizing them together. A role *always* involves both. It is defined by the *complementarity* of expectations (such that ego and alter must, in some sense, both have need-dispositions which require one set of actions and attitudes by ego and another set by alter; and ego must require of himself what alter requires of him; conversely, alter must require of himself what ego requires of him). The complementary expectations are both cognitive and cathectic in their relevance to both personalities. And the expectations (in order to have this complementary "fit" with one another) must be subject to (or governed by) common value patterns, as was pointed out in the General Statement. There can be need-dispositions to cathect objects or (object relationships) without this complementarity. And there can be value patterns which do not help mediate the complementarity of role-expectations. Nevertheless, a role-expectation itself may legitimately be called a need-disposition within the personality, but it tends to be a slightly different sort of abstraction (from the concrete orientation of the actor), since it gets some of its components from those elements which make up values and some from those elements which make up need-dispositions vis-à-vis social objects.

sonality system are also integrated into social systems and cultural systems. Note that these three types of need-disposition variables in the personality system correspond to the three types of system which we are considering: the first subsume pure personality-personality relations, the second subsume personality–cultural system relationships, the third subsume personality–social system relationships. Let us discuss briefly the way in which all of these three types of variables are in fact need-dispositions on the personality level and the way they are all classifiable in terms of the pattern variables, and thus the manifold ways the pattern variables may enter as characterizations of personality systems or of their subsystems.

In the first place, need-dispositions vis-à-vis social objects are exemplified by the need-dispositions for esteem, love, approval, and response, when these are directed toward specific human beings or classes of human beings, or toward collectivities of them. In their broadest sense, these need-dispositions include more than role-expectations. In a sense, they constitute the foundations for the internalization of role-expectations and values. They are dispositions to discriminate and group social objects in certain fashions, to cathect some social objects or groups of them (or, specifically, certain relationships with social objects), and thus to behave in certain ways vis-à-vis these classes of social objects.

Values or internalized value standards are, as we have repeated several times, need-dispositions. That is, they are, on the one hand, *needs* to realize certain functional prerequisities of the system. (Specifically, they aim at those end states which are not in conflict with and which are demanded by such cultural value standards as have been internalized and have come to define, in part, the system.) On the other hand, they are dispositions to handle objects in certain fashions in order to bring about the cathected relationships.

Role-expectations are "needs" to get "proper" responses and attitudes from alter and "dispositions" to give "proper" attitudes and responses to alter. In another sense, they are needs to cognize a set of cathected complementary relationships between ego and alter and dispositions to manipulate the self and the objects in order to bring about the set of cathected relationships. Note how the role expectation organizes a need-disposition vis-à-vis a social object with a value in terms of which the attitudes, and so forth, are judged "proper."

In the personality system, all of these variables, as we have said, are need-dispositions. Now, we add that all have value-standard components, and thus all three types of need dispositions are classifiable in terms of the pattern variables. Need-dispositions vis-à-vis social objects tend to have value-standard components, in the sense that (as was said in the last chapter) any relationship between ego and a social object tends in the long run to be controlled by value standards, and these long-run relationships are the ones mediated by need-dispositions. Role-expectancies are internalized values as integrated with object relationships, thus they obviously involve value standards. And finally the *value* need-dispositions are themselves the internalized cultural standards which are above all classifiable in terms of the pattern variables. Let us show how the pattern variables enter the picture at this level of the organization of personality. (We point out, however, before we start, that the pattern variables enter the personality picture at several other levels: they may be used to characterize the personality as a whole, or the *mechanisms* which integrate the variables which we are discussing here.) At this level they constitute a method for classifying need-dispositions, which are the basic variable of personality systems.

With respect to any particular need-disposition, the most elementary alternative is whether or not it is to be released in action in the particular situation. The alternative which we have called *affectivity* refers to the inability of the need-disposition to present any internal barrier to direct release or gratification. The opposite alternative is for the need-disposition to respect inhibition from immediate gratification when this is demanded for the good of the system. Where the need-disposition can be held in check — that is, where the mechanism of inhibition may operate — we shall speak of *affective neutrality*.

The second pair of alternatives refers to the scope of significance of the object. In the one case the orientation is defined by the specificity of that significance, in the other, by its diffuseness in the form of an attachment.

The third pair of alternatives defines the basis on which the relation between actor and object rests. In the one case the significance of the object rests on its membership in a general category, so that any object conforming with the relevant general criteria would be equally appropriate as an object for cathexis and evaluation in relation to this particular need-disposition or combination of them. This is the universalistic alternative. In the other case the significance of the object may rest on its standing in a particular relationship to ego. Regardless of its general attributes, no other object is appropriate unless the particular relationship to ego exists or can be established. This is the particularistic alternative.

Ego is an object to himself. As such all the other categories of object-orientation apply to him, but in particular he must categorize himself as an object in value-orientation terms. The most fundamental basis of categorization, since it defines the characteristics peculiar to social objects, is the distinction between an object as a complex of *given qualities* and an object as an *actor*, striving toward goals. In his self-image or ego-ideal (i.e., the set of need-dispositions which relate him to himself as a social object), the actor may emphasize either the given qualities of his personality, by which he *ascribes* himself to categories, or he may emphasize his *achievement*, past or potential. Similarly, the need-dispositions which relate him to social objects may emphasize *their* qualities or their achievements. Thus the fourth of these pairs of alternatives is *ascription-achievement*.

Finally, any specific gratification may be sought in isolation from any potential significance of the object other than that of its power to gratify the need-dispositions of ego. This alternative, since it disregards any significance of the object other than its capacity to gratify ego, we call self-orientation. On the other hand, the gratification may take place in the framework of an attachment to the particular object from which the gratification is being sought or to some other object which will be affected by the change in the relationship between ego and the former object. In this case, the object as an entity acquires significance to ego. Its "welfare" is therefore a value for ego independently of the specific gratifications he receives from it directly. Since by such an attachment, when the object is a social object, ego and alter constitute a collectivity, we call this *collectivity-orientation.*[9]

When we take the step from the consideration of the particular need-disposition to the description of a system of need-dispositions, we must examine the basis on which the different need-dispositions in the system are differentiated from each other. The starting point for this analysis is provided by the pattern variables in their relevance to the constituents of motivation. These five variables when cross-classified provide thirty-two possible types of orientations. These, however, as we have seen, are not all equally relevant to personality. The problems of which need-dispositions are to be gratified in a given situation and of whether the object has a specific or a diffuse significance are the primary problems because of their direct impingement on motivation. The variable of affectivity-neutrality comprehends the alternative possibilities of direct gratification and inhibition in relation to objects and occasions, while that of specificity-diffuseness refers to the breadth of the cathexis of the object.

How affectivity can characterize a need-disposition is immediately obvious. The case of neutrality is more complex. Affective neutrality in itself does not contain a gratification interest, the term referring simply to the fact of inhibition relative to certain immediate objects or occasions. But it does mean that the gratification interest is focused on a future goal, or on some other aspect of the object or situation or relation, to which the inhibition, including the attitude of alter applies. Neutrality therefore characterizes the state of a need-disposition system in which potential immediate gratifications may be renounced because of their incompatibility with other gratification interests of the system. A need-disposition system is *never* affectively neutral in its entirety but only vis-à-vis certain *specific* opportunities for gratification.

Accepting the predominance of these two pattern variables for personality, we can construct a classification of four major types of need-dispositions as presented in the four main sections of Fig. 3 in Chapter I. The concurrence of affectivity and specificity has been called the *specific gratification* need-

---

[9] The element of collectivity-orientation is the core of what Freud called the *superego.* Its source in the processes of identification will be evident from the above.

disposition. Such a need is gratified in specific object cathexis, or attachments, and not in diffuse attachments (e.g., foods, appreciation of specific qualities or acts). In relation to a social object it is the need for receptiveness and/or response in a specific context on the part of the object.

When affectivity occurs together with diffuseness, however, the specific gratification is no longer possible in isolation, since the other components of the object of diffuse attachment cannot be disregarded. Such an attachment entails the reorganization of specific gratification interests into a system focused on the object as a totality, and in the case of social objects, inherently connected with expectations of reciprocation. In such a case we may speak of a need for a diffuse attachment, or in current terminology, a need for love objects. The need to be loved is its reciprocal in relation to a social object; it is derived conceptually from the complementarity of expectations.

The combination of specificity and affective neutrality in orientation toward a social object represents one of the variants of the basic sensitivity toward positive response which, as we have already indicated, is the basic substantive need-disposition of the human being in relation to social objects. It involves the postponement of gratification pending the attainment of a goal or the occurrence of an anticipated situation. There may also be direct gratification through alter's and ego's own attitudes of approval. Such an orientation toward a person toward whom there is an attachment, and toward whose responsiveness one is sensitive, will be called approval. It is a response to a specific type of action or quality, and it is restrained or disciplined. The need for this kind of response from social objects to whom we are attached is to be called the need for approval.

It is, however, also possible for affective neutrality to be combined with a diffuse attachment as well. In this case the relation of the postponed or otherwise renounced gratification interests to each other and to the object is essentially the same as in the case of the need for love, with the difference that there is a less immediate affectual content. This we shall designate as the need for esteem. In the present conceptual form, this is complementary and covers both the need to grant esteem and the need to be esteemed. Here again we have the need for positive responsiveness, but in this particular case, the response is given to the attachment without reference to specific qualities or actions.

Within these four basic orientations there is the possibility of a further differentiation through subclassifying each orientation according to the values of the other three. There is space here for only a brief consideration of a few of these possibilities. For example, achievement-ascription differentiates the basic orientations on the dimension of whether a need-disposition is a tendency to orient to alter on the basis of his active strivings or given qualities.[10]

Universalism-particularism presents still another possible range of varia-

[10] If ego orients himself in terms of qualities, he is more apt to be passive.

tion. In this case, the object of the basic need-dispositions may be chosen by either of two criteria. On the one hand, the object may be chosen from a plurality of objects on the basis of its universalistically defined capacities or qualities independently of a particular relation to ego except that established by the selection. On the other hand, an alter who stands in a given particular relation to ego may, by virtue of the fact, be selected as the object of one of the basic need-dispositions. Thus, in the case of an object of attachment, the basis of cathexis may be the fact that the object stands in a given particular relation to ego (e.g., *his* mother or *his* friend). The basis of the attachment may be instead the possession by the object of universalistically defined qualities or performance capacities independently of any particular relationship (e.g., the possession of certain traits of beauty or character).

Finally, any one of the four major types may be subdivided according to whether the orientation is or is not in terms of obligation toward a collectivity-orientation. Thus in the need-disposition for approval (neutrality-specificity) the goal may be shared with alter which means that the actor seeks the approval not only for himself but also for the collectivity of which he is a member. However, ego's orientation may be independent of the bearing of his actions on alter's values or gratifications. In the need-disposition for love, normal reciprocity is collectivity-oriented since sensitivity to alter's needs and gratifications is an essential part of the relationship. This sensitivity, however, may be subordinated to an interest of ego which motivates him to disregard the bearing of his action on alter's need-disposition.

The need-disposition system of different personalities will contain different proportions of these basic types of need-dispositions and their differences in their distribution in a society. There will, however, be certain clusters where the range of variability is narrower than chance would produce because of the particular significance of certain types of need-dispositions in the relevant areas.

FUNCTIONAL PREREQUISITES OF THE PERSONALITY SYSTEM

In any system we may discuss the conditions of equilibrium which are in the last analysis the conditions of the system's being a system. Here, we shall discuss these problems as they affect the personality system. When viewed from the outside, the conditions which must be met in order that the system shall persist are the functional prerequisites of the system. When viewed from the inside (from the actor's point of view rather than the observer's), these are the functional foci of action organization. The over-all problem of personality systems thus may be viewed in two ways: (1) from the outside, or from the scientific observer's viewpoint, it is the problem of maintaining a bounded system; in other words, it is the personality's problem of continuing to be the kind of system it is. (2) From the inside, or from the actor's viewpoint, it is the problem of optimization of gratification. We have already discussed to some extent the external aspect of this problem, and we will take up in a moment its specific meaning for personality systems. Let us discuss briefly here, however, the way this problem looks from the actor's point of view.

To the actor, all problems may be generalized in terms of the aim to obtain *an optimum of gratification.* The term *optimum* has been deliberately chosen as an alternative to *maximum.* The latter is too involved in the traditional hedonistic fallacy which rests on the tautology that gratification is held to be both the result and the motive of every action, even that which appears to be deprivational in its immediate consequences. It ignores the consequences of the interrelations of need-dispositions in systems, which in cases of conflict often entail the inhibition and hence deprivation of many particular need-dispositions. In this sense self-deprivation is a common phenomenon. The term *optimum* avoids this difficulty by emphasizing that the level of gratification toward which the personality system tends is the optimum relative to the existing set of particular need-dispositions in the particular situation. Out of their conflicts within the system often come commitments to particular self-deprivations. The optimum of gratification is the best that can be obtained from the existing conditions, given the existing set of need-dispositions and the available set of objects. The personality may thus be conceived as a system with a persistent tendency toward the *optimum* level of gratification. This proposition involves no judgment about the absolute level of gratification or the specific gratifications sought or the trend of development of the personality toward higher or lower levels. It simply asserts that at any given time, and with a given set of need-dispositions, mechanisms will be in operation which will adjudicate among conflicting need-dispositions and will tend to reduce the state of dysphoria (the subjective experience of deprivation) to tolerable limits.

Our classification of the problems of personality systems is the same whether we are looking at the problems from the outside or from the inside. Nevertheless, the problems will be stated primarily in terms of the *ways they appear to the actor.* Therefore, they may be construed as the various modes in which the problem of optimization of gratification appears to him. The following classification is in terms of the kinds of problems to be solved. After this classification has been discussed, we will take up the way the problems break down again depending on the kinds of processes which solve them.

Problems can be classified first on the basis of where the actor sees the problem to lie, that is, in terms of the phenomenological place of the problem. On the one hand, problems may be seen to lie in the external [11] world: these are cognitive and cathectic problems involving perceived and cathected facts (or objects) which may be seen to conflict with need-dispositions (in the sense

---

[11] It should be noted that the term *external* when applied to the phenomenological place of a problem is quite different from the term *outside* which is used to distinguish the way the system looks to an observer.

that those need-dispositions implant negative cathexes upon the perceived facts). On the other hand, problems may be seen to lie within the personality system: these are evaluative problems involving the allocation of functions or time and effort to different need-dispositions, or the adjudication of conflicts between need-dispositions.

Problems can also be classified in terms of the kind of problem presented: (1) problems of allocation and (2) problems of integration. This classification crosscuts the external-internal distinction. Problems of allocation are primarily problems of seeing that the system gets done all of the things that need to be done. Thus, in the personality system, it breaks down into two kinds of problems: (a) allocating *functions* to the various units of the system or subsystems, (b) allocating time or action among the various units so that they may accomplish their functions. External allocation problems involve chiefly the allocation of cathexes (and thus attention) among different possible goal and means objects (so that all the demands of the situation will be met). Internal allocation problems involve chiefly the allocation of functions and time to the various need-dispositions so that all of the requirements of the system will be met.

Problems of integration are primarily problems of adjudicating conflicts between various elements of the system. External integration problems involve chiefly the problems posed when cognized facts conflict with one another or when these facts "conflict" with need-dispositions. A fact is in conflict with a need-disposition whenever it is negatively cathected (since all cathexes arise out of need-dispositions). These problems are all solved by actions which change the perception or cognition of the situation: these may be overt operations which change the situation, and thus change the perception of it, or they may be operations of reorganization of the perceived facts so they no longer conflict, or they may be merely operations which change the perceptions without either changing the situation (as the observer sees it) or getting a new organization of the facts. These are all primarily cognitive problems.[12] Internal integration problems involve chiefly the resolution of conflicts between need-dispositions.

From the foregoing it can be seen that the external-internal distinction when crosscut by the allocative-integrative distinction provides in some sense a parallel structure to the cognitive-cathectic evaluative analysis which runs through our whole work. This is because the cognitive and cathectic aspects of an orientation (or an orientation group, that is, a need-disposition) are those aspects which relate the actor to the external world. The actor cognizes and

---

[12] Role conflicts may be either internal or external integrative problems, depending on whether or not the roles in question have been internalized. If they are not internalized, the actor cognizes a fact (to wit, that he must do two incompatible things or incur sanctions), which fact is negatively cathected by the need-dispositions to avoid the sanction involved. If they are internalized, the actor wants to do two incompatible things at the same time and he has a conflict between need-dispositions.

cathects objects. Here, also, the cognitive is the integrative aspect; it relates objects to one another as all in one class, associated in time, associated in space (being context to one another), or associated as cause and effect. And the cathectic is the allocative aspect; it serves to distribute attention and interest among the objects.

The evaluative aspects of an orientation or system of orientations, on the other hand, are those aspects which relate one internal variable to other internal variables. The evaluative aspects handle both allocative and integrative problems at the internal level. That is, they relate variables in the system to one another (which is the integrative function) and they relate variables to the system as a whole (which is the allocative function).

We turn now to the kinds of processes or changes in the personality system which can function to solve the problems we have presented.

LEARNING PROCESSES AND PERFORMANCE PROCESSES

There are two kinds of systematic changes that occur within the personality system; these changes are always governed by the systematic requirements set forth above. First, there are changes determined by the structure of the personality system itself; these we may call the changes of normal performance, or the performance processes. These processes transmit changes from variable to variable without changing the structure of the system. They are like the processes whereby the energy of the automobile motor is transmitted to the wheels without changing the structure of the machine involved. Second, changes in the structure or pattern of the system itself are occurring all of the time along side of (and partly determined by) the performance processes of the system. These we may call the changes of learning, or the learning processes. It is as if the structure of the automobile's transmission system were being constantly changed while the engine is driving the car.

When the performance and learning processes of a system are interpreted (or categorized) in terms of the ways they solve the functional problems outlined in the previous section, they constitute the *mechanisms* of the personality system. The next sections will deal with these mechanisms as such and with their various classifications. There is, however, an important superordinate problem concerning mechanisms which depend entirely on the learning-performance distinction (when this is taken as relevant to the over-all problem of the system — the optimization of gratification). It is the controversial problem of the law of effect. Since all changes in personality systems are governed by the general prerequisite of maintaining the system (that is, of optimization of gratification), it is possible to interpret the effects of any of these processes in terms of the way it serves to solve or help solve this problem. This means that all processes are governed by what psychologists have termed the "law of effect." This says nothing more than has already been said; namely, that all processes can be interpreted in terms of what they do for the maintenance of the boundaries of the system (or, again, in terms of their contribution to the optimization of gratification).

The problem of the law of effect, however, breaks down into two problems based on the learning-versus-performance distinction. The "law of effect as a law of learning" is prominent in the psychology of the Yale school. The "law of effect as a law of performance" is prominent in the psychology of Tolman. The standard argument in psychology is whether the former is simply a derivative consequence of the latter (as is maintained by Tolman); or whether the latter is a derivative consequence of the former (as "law of effect" psychology maintains).[13] This question (even if the truth is all on one side, as may not be the case) need not concern us here; for in either case, we do have a "law of effect" in action and it crosscuts the distinction between learning changes and performance changes in systems of action. It is simply another way of saying that the system is a system in both its learning and performance processes.

There are still many controversial questions concerning the nature of the processes by which the outcome of action motivated by a given need-disposition serves to strengthen or weaken the disposition to repeat the action in future situations. There can, however, be no doubt that in a broad sense an orientation or action which has repeatedly led to more gratification than deprivation of drives and need-dispositions in a given type of situation is more likely to be repeated or strengthened than if the experience has been one of repeated deprivation. For our purposes this is the essential point about the law of effect. This point is particularly crucial to the theory of action because of its bearing on the significance of sanctions in interactive relations. It seems probable that many of the complications of the reinforcement problem relate to the interrelations of many need-dispositions in a system rather than to the conditions of strengthening or weakening a particular orientation tendency by virtue of its gratificatory significance to one need-disposition taken in abstraction from the operations of other need-dispositions. Our main reservations about some current learning theory are concerned with the implications of this hypothesis.

A particularly important case in point is the significance to ego of alter's attitudes as distinguished from alter's particular overt acts. The attitude of an alter is rarely a specific reward or punishment in the sense in which that term is used in learning theory. It usually constitutes an organized and generalized pattern under which many particular sanctions are subsumed. The generality of such an attitude as love or esteem renders it impossible for its relevance to

---

[13] Hull's statement would be that, since those actions which foster the maintenance of the system are *learned* at the expense of those which don't, performances which foster maintenance of the system tend to occur. Tolman would say that since the animal tends to do those things which he knows will foster the maintenance of the system, and since frequency of performance fosters learning, the animal therefore learns the things that foster the system better than those that don't.

be confined to a single need-disposition. Alter's attitude therefore affects a broad sector of ego's system of need-dispositions.

THE MECHANISMS

All of the processes we have discussed above can be categorized in terms of the way they serve to meet the problems of the system. When the processes of learning and performance are classified on the basis of the way they serve to meet the requirements of the system, they are termed mechanisms. That is, a process is a mechanism, insofar as it is viewed in terms of its relevance to the problems of the system.

Fig. 7 gives us a classification of the mechanisms of personality systems. We have three kinds of distinctions relevant to the classification of the mechanisms: (1) the distinction between the types of process that may be involved — thus mechanisms may be learning or performance mechanisms; (2) the distinction based on the phenomenological place of the problems involved — thus mechanisms may be relevant to external or internal problems; (3) the distinction based on the type of problem involved — thus mechanisms may be mechanisms of allocation or mechanisms of integration. It should be noted that each of these bases for classification cuts across the other two; thus there should be eight different types of mechanisms. We will take up below those portions of Fig. 7 (page 255) most relevant to the psychological problems of action.

The mechanisms of learning. Learning is perhaps best defined as the acquisition and extinction of orientation and action tendencies. Thus, for our purposes, the important learning mechanisms deal with acquisition or extinction or any other changes in habits of cognition, cathection, and evaluation (including changes in internalized value standards). We have already said that our term *mechanisms* of learning implies that there is a "law of effect" in the field of learning — that is, all mechanisms are in some sense functional with respect to the maintenance of the systems. Thus the learning mechanism must involve the acquisition of those tendencies which better maintain the system at the expense of those which are detrimental to the system.

The learning mechanisms may be analyzed into categories on the basis of whether they are chiefly cognitive, cathectic, or evaluative; or they may be classified as external, internal, allocative, integrative. The two methods of classification will in general accomplish the same thing, as external-integrative is almost equivalent to cathectic. Internal, integrative, and allocative is almost equivalent to evaluative. Actually, all learning occurs within the whole cognitive-cathectic-evaluative matrix; thus all of it involves some changes in all these aspects of motivational orientation. Similarly, all learning has ramifications for internal and external, allocative and integrative problems. The question of the primacy of one of the modes or categories has to do simply with which aspect of the orientation must undergo greatest change in order to solve the problem. The terms *cognitive, cathectic,*[14] *evaluative* define the aspects of orientation process which can be more or less independently varied. The terms *external, internal, integrative, allocative* define types of problems. The parallelism derives from the fact that the changes required to solve these different types of problems ordinarily take place mainly in the parallel aspect of the orientation. Thus external-integrative problems are always solved by a series of changes of orientation; *ordinarily* this series of changes (which will involve changes in all aspects of orientation) will involve most change in the cognitive aspect. We will discuss three different kinds of learning, (1) cognitive, (2) cathectic, and (3) evaluative: these will be different learning processes each of which involves changes in all aspects of orientation, but each of which involves most changes in that aspect after which it is named. And, owing to the considerations above, these three kinds of learning can be seen as also comprising (1) the external-integrative, (2) external-allocative, and (3) internal, integrative, and allocative mechanisms of learning.

First, let us take up the mechanisms of cognitive learning. We shall confine our consideration here to two, discrimination and generalization. The first concerns the cognition of differences between different objects and different attributes of the same objects in terms of the significance of these differences for the actor. Generalization is the process by which different objects and groups of them are classed together with respect to those properties which they have in common and which are significant to the orientation of action. These are both aspects of the "cognitive mapping" of the situation.

The cognitive mechanisms enter into all systems of action oriented toward objects because knowledge or cognitive orientation is inseparably associated with cathexis and evaluation, and the latter cannot occur without it. As we go on to discuss the other mechanisms of the personality system, we will see that generalization is a necessary condition for substitution and for many of the mechanisms of defense. It is a prerequisite for the emancipation from particular object attachments, as well as of any extensive capacity for instrumental manipulation of the situation.

Because of both the continual changes in the situation and the equally continual process of reorganization of the actor's own personality (need-disposition) system, nothing like a stable system of orientations would be possible without some capacity for flexibility in the transfer of orientations from one object to another. Thus, the learning process by which different objects are rendered functionally equivalent is essential to the establishment of systematic stability and equilibrium.

Similarly, because of the very different consequences which may ensue upon very slightly different situations, the personality system becomes sensitized to the very slight differences between objects which are indices of im-

---

[14] In learning, cognitive and cathectic are more independently variable than in performance. This is because an actor may retain his principles of grouping but learn to give the objects involved different cathexes (or their value as means or goals changes).

portant and big differences in consequences. Thus the learning process by which similar objects become discriminated on the basis of their radically different consequences is very important to the adjustment of the personality system to its environment.

Next, we take up the mechanisms of cathectic learning. Here we are faced with the problem of the choice of concrete objects (or classes of objects). A given need-disposition or combination of them has the alternative at any given time of remaining attached to the same objects or transferring cathexis to new objects. The process of transfer is called *substitution*. Substitution is the process of replacing one particular object of a given need-disposition by another, which may be in the same class or another class but which in terms of gratification of the need-disposition is to some degree the equivalent of the relinquished object. Particularly, of course, in the developmental process, object attachments which may be essential at one stage must be given up if a higher stage of personality organization is to be attained. Substitution is the mechanism by which this giving up and transfer to another object takes place. As in the case of other mechanisms, the concept substitution refers to the outcome in the working of the system of a class of processes. Even though certain regularities in such outcomes are known, much about the processes is obscure and can only be understood after much further research. In very general terms, however, we may say that there usually must be some combination of barriers to access or retention of the old object (which may be inhibitions or situational barriers) and, as well, positive incentives to cathect the new object. (All of which is to say that there is a law of effect operating here as there is everywhere in the mechanisms.)

Now let us turn to the mechanisms of evaluative learning. The expression of a need-disposition is not dependent on its own strength alone but also on its compatibility with other need-dispositions in the same system. Learning theory hitherto has rightly tended to treat the unimpeded carrying out of a motivational pattern as unproblematical. Where it has been impeded as a result of conflict with other need-dispositions, the term *inhibition* has been employed. The basic problem here is, of course, that of choice of need-dispositions to be satisfied. *Inhibition* refers to a very generalized aspect of this highly complex set of choice phenomena. The chief features of the concept are two: first, the checking of the impulse to release a need-disposition into action; second, the fact that the source of the inhibition is internal to the personality. The enormous significance of this mechanism comes directly from the nature of personality as a system which maintains distinctive patterns and boundaries. Incompatible motivational tendencies are inherently operative; unless the system had modes of protection against the potentially disruptive consequences of the conflicts involved, it could not function as a system.

This concludes our classification of the mechanisms of learning insofar as that classification is based upon the phenomenological place of problems, the type of problems, and the kind of learning processes chiefly responsible for solution of the problems. It should be noted, however, that the cognitive learning processes, generalization and discrimination, which taken together constitute the learning how to perceive and how to construct an integrated cognitive map of the situation, are the normal *learning* processes used in the solution of external-integrative problems. (Thus, whether the problem be one of conflict between two facts, between a fact and a need-disposition, or between two different role-expectations, if the problem is solved as an external problem,[15] and if it is solved by learning, its solution consists in learning new ways to perceive and thus new ways to manipulate the situation.) It should be noted too that the cathectic learning process, substitution, is the normal learning process used in the solution of external-allocative problems. (Thus, whenever there is a problem of how to distribute attention between different objects or events in the external world, if the problem is solved by learning, it constitutes the learning of a new cathexis, that is, the substitution of a new object of interest for an old.) Finally, it should be noted that the evaluative learning process (the learning of inhibition) is the normal learning process used in the solution of internal, allocative, and integrative problems, insofar as the problems require that one or several need-dispositions be held in check while others are being allowed gratification. (Thus, whenever there is a problem of conflict between two need-dispositions or a conflict over which need-dispositions should get most time and effort for the good of the organism, if the problem is solved by learning, its solution constitutes the learning of an order of inhibition whereby various need-dispositions may be inhibited by others.)

At this point we are going to take up a different method for classification of learning processes, which again cuts across all the classifications made above. We shall classify the learning processes on the basis of the kind of relationship which obtains between the learning actor and the environmental objects while the learning is going on. When classified on this basis, learning turns out to be "invention," "imitation," or "identification." The learning of cognitive, cathectic, and evaluative patterns can, any of them, be either invention, imitation, or identification. A need-disposition, as we have seen, is organized in terms of patterns of orientation. A personality confronts the problem of acquiring these patterns for itself by creating new ones, or by acquiring them from some existing pattern which serves as a model. In the former case we have invention. In the latter case, we have either imitation or identification (which are both ways that patterns may be acquired from social objects).

---

[15] Such problems can become internal problems, as we have said elsewhere, when the fact which conflicts with a need-disposition (which is negatively cathected in terms of that need disposition) arouses that need-disposition into active conflict with other need-dispositions active at the same time. When this happens, the problem is internal, and if it is solved by a learning process, the process is an evaluative learning process.

In the case of invention, the actor has no specific "learning-relevant" relationship with another social object during learning. That is, he has no model for either imitation or identification. He has run into a problem which requires a new pattern (because the old pattern has got the system into some sort of problem), so he simply tries different patterns until one of them solves the problem. Invention may be either trial-and-error learning, in which the actor tries new patterns at random until one of them works; or it may be "insight" learning in which the actor constructs a new pattern systematically on the basis of several old ones.

The two major mechanisms for the learning of patterns from social objects are *imitation*, which assumes only that alter provides a model for the specific pattern learned without being an object of a generalized cathectic attachment; and *identification*, which implies that alter is the object of such an attachment and therefore serves as a model not only with respect to a specific pattern in a specific context of learning but also as model in a generalized sense. Alter becomes, that is, a model for general orientations, not merely for specific patterns.

With imitation and identification we come to the distinctive part played by social objects in learning. Knowledge and other patterns *may* be acquired through independent discovery by the actor himself. But more frequently knowledge is taken over from other actors.[16] (This is the type of learning that forms the basis of the cultural accumulation of knowledge — and of other cultural orientations as well.) The acquisition of patterns in such a fashion (like all learning), is instrumental to fulfilling certain requirements of the personality system (or of the need-dispositions which are subsystems). Thus, we may say that all such learning must be motivated in the sense that it must result from some need-disposition tendency of the personality (or from some tendency generated by a problem of the system as a whole).

It is possible and common for ego to be motivated to acquire a specific pattern from alter without any attachment to alter extending beyond this particular process of acquisition. Alter thus is significant only as an object from which the pattern is acquired. It is the pattern not the attitudes of alter as a person which is the object of cathexis. Alter is only its bearer. This is the meaning of the term *imitation*. Imitation is very prominent in the acquisition of various specific elements of culture, such as specific knowledge, technical skills, and so forth. It is much less important in the acquisition of more general patterns of orientation, such as standards of taste, fundamental philosophical or ethical outlooks, and above all, patterns of value-orientation.

---

[16] The relation of ego to the alter from whom he learns a cultural pattern need not involve direct personal contact. He may for example read a book which alter has written. This mediation by independent physical embodiments of culture adds only a further elaboration of the same fundamental elements which enter into learning through direct personal contact and need not be analyzed here.

By *identification,* on the other hand, we mean the acquisition of *generalized* patterns of orientation motivated by an attachment to a social object. An attachment, as we noted in the last chapter, develops at the point where not only alter's specific acts are significant to ego as sanctions but where by generalization ego has become sensitive to alter's attitudes toward him as a person, to his responsiveness when it takes the form of granting or withholding his approval, love, or esteem. In this case the object is not the cultural *possessions* of alter — what he *has* — but alter himself as a person — what he *is.* The cultural patterns acquired by ego are in fact, as we have seen, part of alter's personality. They are patterns that alter has internalized. It is, however, the characteristic feature of cultural patterns as objects that, being systems of symbols, they are transmissible. Ego cannot himself become alter, nor can any part of alter's personality so become part of ego's personality that it is lost to alter — in the way, for example, in which a particular article of clothing once worn by alter cannot, if worn by ego, simultaneously be worn by alter. An orientation *pattern,* however, can be adopted without necessitating a change in alter's personality.

When alter is cathected *as a person,* as distinguished from specific attributes, possessions, or actions, we speak of an *attachment.* (Alter as a person is a complex constellation of attributes, possessions, and actions, significant in a multiplicity of aspects which focus on the significance of his attitudes.) An attachment thus exists when alter possesses a general significance as an object for ego, when not merely his specific acts, qualities, and possessions are significant to ego. This generalized significance for ego focuses on ego's concern with alter's attitudes toward him, and it underlies the development of a need-disposition to attain and maintain certain types of such attitudes. For example, instead of the specific gratification of a hunger need being the focus of the significance of the mother, her provision of food becomes generalized into an appropriate expression of her love or approval. Once the retention of such a favorable attitude has become important for ego, it is possible for other actors to impose frustrations of particular needs and to have them accepted as long as they can gratify the need to retain the favorable attitude.

Because of the element of generality in attachments, the patterns of value-orientation taken over through identification are necessarily *generalized* patterns of orientation. They are not *specific* skills or perceptions or appreciative judgments. The patterns of cultural value-orientation, because of their generality, are acquired for the most part through identification. Specific skills, appreciative judgments, and cognitive propositions, however, are often acquired *by imitation* within the framework of an identification. The imitative process may be greatly facilitated by its coincidence with identification.[17]

---

[17] It should be borne in mind that because our knowledge of the mechanisms consists of empirical generalizations, no definitive list can be drawn up. The number of such mechanisms into which it is convenient to divide the empirical problems involved is a conse-

The patterns acquired through identification are general patterns of orientation which vary as a function of variations in the character of the underlying attachments. These variations we shall analyze in terms of the two basic pattern variables for motivational orientation: specificity-diffuseness and affectivity-neutrality. The four combinations of the values of these two variables define the major types of attitude on alter's part, the security of which can become the primary focus of ego's attachment to alter.

This concludes our discussion of the mechanisms of learning. The mechanisms of allocation and integration will be discussed below. This discussion may have relevance to some of the mechanisms of learning, when these are taken in their broader context as mechanisms of allocation and integration (including learning and performance processes) rather than merely as learning mechanisms. Nevertheless, since learning has been covered here, the ensuing discussion will tend to emphasize the performance mechanisms of allocation and integration.

The mechanisms of allocation. The structure of personality is the result of a cumulative process of commitments between the alternatives of orientation and their consequences for defense or resolution within the system, and *adjustment* to the situation. Each possible alternative selection point confronts the actor with a situation in which he cannot perform two conflicting actions simultaneously. There are inherent limitations on what is possible, arising from the nature of alternatives and the consequences attending commitment to them. The choice of one of a pair of alternatives not only excludes the other alternative but it also affects the direction of choice in other categories as well.

The result of these limitations is the necessity for an *allocative distribution* among the possibilities which are logically open. By allocation we mean the processes by which the action of a system is distributed among its different parts in such a way that the conditions necessary for the maintenance of the system, or an orderly pattern of change, are met. Allocative distribution in the personality system may be analyzed into two constituent distributions, the importance of each of which is inherent in the structure of the action system. The first is external allocation — the distribution of object-selections or event-selections relative to any *particular* need-disposition. (The distribution of time and effort to different need-dispositions is primarily an internal problem; thus the choice of one event or occasion over another may be an internal rather than an external allocative problem, unless both events are cathected by

---

quence of the structure of the system and the functional "problems" of the system. But it is also a function of the state of theoretical knowledge at the time. An advance in the latter may well make it necessary to make a distinction which had not previously been current, or make it possible to consolidate two mechanisms which it had previously been necessary to treat separately. As an illustration of the former change, the mechanism of identification seems to have entered the picture as a result of Freud's discoveries of the ways in which the significant object-relations of childhood lay at the foundation of an individual's unconscious "self-image." Before Freud the empirically crucial problem covered by the concept of identification was not in the field of psychological attention.

the same need-disposition and are mutually exclusive for some nontemporal reason. The distribution of cathexis in terms of place and context is simply a subhead of distribution among objects; since objects, in the last analysis, are constituted by their place or context.) The second is internal allocation — the distribution of gratification opportunities among *different* need-dispositions.

We will take up internal allocation first, because it constitutes the more important of the two allocative mechanisms for personality systems. Need-dispositions relative to the object world become organized into a differentiated structure. A variety of specific need-dispositions (for gratifications, for love from particular types of objects, for approval for particular qualities or performances, etc.) develop from the original drives and energy of the organism in interaction with the situation. It is inherent to motivational phenomena that there is a drive for more gratification than is realistically possible, on any level or in any type of personality organization. Likewise it is inherent to the world of objects that not all potentially desirable opportunities can be realized within a human life span. Therefore, any personality must involve an organization that allocates opportunities for gratification, that systematizes precedence relative to the limited possibilities. The possibilities of gratification, simultaneously or sequentially, of all need-dispositions are severely limited by the structure of the object system and by the intra-systemic incompatibility of the consequences of gratifying them all. The gratification of one need-disposition beyond a certain point is only possible at the cost of other need-dispositions which are important in the same personality.[18]

Next, we turn to external allocation. Each particular need-disposition generally involves a more or less definite set of cathexes to particular objects or classes of objects. Hence the allocation of objects is very closely associated with the allocation of gratifications. Nevertheless, it is desirable to distinguish the allocation of object choices relative to a need-disposition as another of the functional problems of a personality system. Certain types of commitments to one object preclude assignment of the same significance to another object. For example, if there is to be a plurality of objects of sexual attachment, certain features of an exclusive attachment to one object become impossible. Even though a need-disposition for a certain *type* of object relationship has been granted precedence, the allocation of the relevant cathexes between appropriate particular objects is still a problem which requires solution if the system is to operate.[19]

The allocative aspect [20] of the organization of the total need-disposition system (i.e., of the personality system) is in a sense the "negative" aspect of

---

[18] Therefore, the allocation of opportunities for gratification between different need-dispositions is as fundamental to personalities as the allocation of wealth-getting or power-getting opportunities between persons, or classes of persons, is to social systems.

[19] The fact that ego is in competition with other actors for objects, especially the response of social objects, is of course fundamental to this aspect of the allocative problem.

[20] It is this allocative aspect which Freud called the "economic."

its selectivity. It designates the structure arising in consequence of the necessity of being committed to only one of each of a number of pairs of intrinsically desirable alternatives and thus rejecting, or relegating to a lesser place, the other alternative of the pair. The second major aspect of the systemic structure is the integration (into a system) of the various elements which have been allocated. The allocative and integrative aspects of the personality system are complementary. The allocative commitments distribute time and attention among various need-dispositions, objects, and so forth. This distribution is regulated by the over-all requirements of the personality system; once the distribution of functions has been made, each of the need-dispositions constitutes a subsystem with its own systemic requirements. This introduces the possibility of conflict; integrative mechanisms prevent or alleviate conflict. We next turn our attention to them.

The mechanisms of integration. As we have said, integration is a function peculiar to the class of systems which maintain distinctive internal properties within boundaries. In such a system certain processes become differentiated as mechanisms which solve actual conflicts and prevent threatened conflicts by integrating the internal variables with one another and by integrating the whole system with the situation outside of it. In relation to personality, therefore, integrative mechanisms have two main classes of functions. The first is the integration of the subsystems created by the allocation of functions into one over-all system. This involves the forestalling of potential conflicts and minimizing their disruptive consequences for the system when they arise. This class of functions is handled by what we have called the *internal integrative mechanisms.* They are also sometimes called the mechanisms of *defense.* The second class of functions is the adjustment of the system as a whole to threatened (or actual) conflicts between it and the external environment. This class of functions is handled by what we have called the *external integrative mechanisms.* They are also sometimes called the mechanisms of *adjustment.*

We will discuss first the *mechanisms of defense.* These, as we have said, handle conflicts between different need-dispositions. Though many features of conflict between need-dispositions are specific to the particular need-dispositions concerned and the particular situation, there are certainly general properties of conflict and the response to it which we can analyze here.

Before we can give a complete discussion of these general properties of conflict and the responses to it, however, we must introduce the problem of fear. Although fear is in fact out of place here, as it is one of the chief problems of *external* integration, we must nevertheless discuss it briefly because it is the genetic antecedent of several important problems of internal integration. (It will be discussed further when we take up the external-integrative mechanisms.) Fear is the cognition and cathexis of a negatively cathected fact in the external world. Since all cognition-cathexes have a temporal dimension (that is, they are expectancies) we can say that fear is the cognition of an expected deprivation. The negatively cathected object (that is, the expected deprivation) is placed phenomenologically in the external world. Thus fear is an important antecedent to the mechanisms of external integration; it may be seen as a superordinate situational antecedent for a whole set of mechanisms of adjustment. For our present purposes, we must show the relationships of fear to pain and anxiety, both of which are relevant to mechanisms of internal integration. Anxiety is internalized fear. That is, when a fear of deprivation has been experienced often, the organism develops a need-disposition to avoid the objects involved and to avoid the situations in which the fear arises. The arousal of these internalized fears constitutes anxiety.

Pain is the actual deprivation of need-dispositions (fear is only an expectancy of that deprivation; anxiety is a specific need-disposition aimed at avoiding even the fear of deprivation). Both anxiety and pain are problems of internal integration.[21] An aroused anxiety need-disposition conflicts with other need-dispositions; it constitutes an internal threat to the system. Similarly, any deprived need-disposition conflicts with the requirements for the functioning of the system and constitutes an internal threat to the system. Finally, any internal conflict, whether generated by a specific anxiety, a specific deprivation, or simply a recurrent conflict between need-dispositions, generates its own "anxiety" need-disposition which constitutes, now, a need to avoid the conflict. In this last sense anxiety may be interpreted as a warning signal within the system for the personality to mobilize its resources in order to meet any threatened conflict and minimize disruptive consequences. It is a universal correlate and condition of activation of the mechanisms of defense.

Complete resolution of a threatened conflict would necessitate modification of either one or both of the relevant need-dispositions so that in relation to the exigencies of the situation no deprivation would be imposed. *Resolution* in this sense is continually going on in normal personalities and should authentically be called the first mechanism of defense. It may well be that cognitive generalization plays a particularly important part in the process. A variety of other processes may be involved in resolution. The strength of one or both of the need-dispositions may be altered so one gives way. Their structure may be changed to eliminate the particular strains. Objects or occasions may be reallocated.

The resolution is always accomplished by giving primacy to one or the other (or to some superordinate value) of the conflicting need-dispositions. Thus normal resolution may be seen as always involving choice, which, as we have shown, is based on values and the pattern variables. Therefore, evaluation itself might be seen as the normal mechanism of defense.

Frequently, however, the strength and rigidity of either or both sides are too great for much or full resolution to take place. Then special mechanisms

---

[21] Pain may also be a problem of external integration, as will be seen.

of defense are resorted to. Before we continue, we must introduce a digression to explain the nature of our list of these special mechanisms. The reader will remember that we held the distinction between external and internal integrative problems to be roughly parallel to the distinction between the cognitive and evaluative aspects of orientation. This parallelism, we said, was due to the fact that external integrative problems were usually solved by changes in the cognitive aspect of orientation and internal integrative problems by changes in the evaluative aspects of orientation. This parallelism held up fairly well in discussion of the learning mechanisms. Also, in our discussion of the allocative mechanisms, the external allocative mechanisms involved chiefly changes in evaluative procedures. Finally, the normal performance aspect of the internal integrative mechanisms (that is, the resolution of conflicts between need-dispositions by application of standards of primacy relations based on pattern-variable choices) were evaluative, as they should be according to our parallelism. As we will see later, the normal external integrative mechanisms will involve chiefly cognitive changes, as they should according to the parallelism. The abnormal or rigid internal mechanisms, however, apparently are not open to interpretation in these parallelistic terms. This seems to be owing to the fact that the problems of conflict, which are actually internal conflicts between need-dispositions and are thus internal problems, are often not recognized by the actor as internal problems at all. On the contrary, they are often localized by him in the external world, and thus solved as though they were external problems of integration. We are forced to make a choice: we see that phenomenologically they seem to be problems of adjustment for the subject involved; yet we know that there is behavior which indicates a real (although perhaps subconscious) subjective awareness that these are internal problems.

Thus we list all of the mechanisms aimed at the resolution of internal problems as mechanisms of defense, even though we know that the actor-subject is not always aware that these are mechanisms for the resolution of internal problems. It will be remembered that external integrative problems are resolved primarily by cognitive changes; this will be seen to hold true when we take up the mechanisms of adjustment. It was said that internal integrative problems are solved largely by evaluative changes; it will be seen in the following paragraphs that many if not most internal integrative problems are so distorted as to constitute seemingly external integrative problems for the actor. Therefore, most of the mechanisms which solve them will involve primarily changes in the cognitive sphere.

Here we will simply list and define briefly each of the special mechanisms of defense.

First is *rationalization*. This involves a distorted perception by the actor of the relation which obtains between his need-dispositions and the goal of an action. The goal is "seen" to be relevant to (and cathected by) one set of need-dispositions (need-dispositions of which the person is proud — often his values). Actually the goal is cathected by another set of need-dispositions, which are not even seen to be operative in this situation. Usually the need-dispositions which are kept out of the picture would come into conflict with some value need-dispositions of the actor if they were allowed in the picture. Thus a conflict is averted by the technique of rationalization. Although this mechanism is primarily a method for handling problems generated by internal conflicts, the problem often appears to the actor as one of adjustment. Ego is threatened by the negatively cathected perception of himself (if he sees himself as possessing a characteristic which he does not like, he will be constantly uncomfortable in the presence of the perceived trait, which, by definition, constitutes a deprivation). Therefore, ego chooses to distort the facts so that he may perceive himself as a cathected object. The problem can be perceived as an external problem by ego, because of the fact that ego as actor can perceive himself as an object. Rationalization occasionally arises as a purely *adjustive* mechanism (i.e., dealing with really external problems) when it is used as a method of distorting a negatively cathected fact that really arises out of the external world (as when one justifies something which he wants to believe with sophistic arguments).

Second is *isolation*. This is the refusal to cognize and cathect an object in terms of one need-disposition, A, while it is being cognized and cathected in terms of another conflicting need-disposition, B. Thus an overt conflict between A and B is avoided. This involves a distorted perception of the object which will obscure its relevance to A.

Third is *displacement*. This is the removal of the positive cathexis implanted by need-disposition A from an object which is negatively cathected by need-disposition B; and the attachment of that positive cathexis to a new object which is not negatively cathected. This is nothing more than substitution, which has already been discussed, under conditions of conflict and for the purpose of resolving conflict.

Fourth is *fixation*. This is the obverse of displacement. It is the compulsive retention of a cathexis on the least threatening object in order to avoid some conflict that would be engendered by the substitution that would normally occur in the development of the personality.

Fifth is *repression*. Repression involves the destroying of internal systematic interconnections between some threatening need-disposition and the rest of the system; this is accompanied by radical repression of the offending need-disposition. The threatening need-disposition is cut off from normal internal interdependence with the rest of the personality system and at the same time it is denied direct gratification.

Sixth is *reaction formation*. This is a special case of repression. When the threat is originally engendered by a conflict between two need-dispositions, the more threatening of the two is repressed, and the one with which it conflicted is reinforced.

Seventh is *projection*. This is a combination of repression, reaction formation, and rationalization, in a special fashion. Ego represses a threatening motive and reinforces the motive which did not allow tolerance for the repressed motive, just as in the case of reaction formation. Then ego refuses to see himself as possessing the repressed motive, and he explains the anxiety generated by the repression by seeing alter as possessing the motive which he cannot tolerate. Thus, the "reaction" need-disposition (the one that does not allow tolerance) can negatively cathect alter instead of implanting a negative cathexis on ego himself, which would involve continual deprivation and pain.

These are the principal classical mechanisms of defense.[22] In each case normal learning mechanisms are operative with the addition of special features imposed by the situation of conflict, in consequence of which modifications of both intensity and direction occur. If full resolution of conflicts fails, the other mechanisms of defense reduce conscious anxiety and otherwise minimize the disruptive potentialities of conflict. But at the same time, this is possible only at the cost of impairment of potential activities, which will be severe according to the degree of failure of full resolution. The overt manifestations of these impairments of function are the symptoms of psychopathological disorders.

The consequences of the mechanisms of defense, which are operative to some degree in every personality, are the introduction of a set of modifications of the need-dispositions.

The *mechanisms of adjustment* solve external integrative problems. Here we are confronted with problems of two types: there may be conflicts between facts, or there may be conflicts between facts and need-dispositions. In the first case (which is less important for the whole personality system) we have a conflict between two possible ways of perceiving (i.e. cognizing) the external world; and since the actions of the actor are determined by his orientations, these conflicting facts bring about impulses to conflicting actions.

The latter case, which is of prime importance for personality systems, involves what we called the conflict between a fact and a need-disposition. How, one may ask, can a fact conflict with a need-disposition? For our purposes, a fact is nothing more than the cognition of an object or an event. It has simply the status of any phenomenological object. An object can be said to conflict with a need-disposition whenever it is negatively cathected. Any need-disposition which implants negative cathexes on anything (and it seems that all need-dispositions negatively cathect some deprivational objects) constitutes a tendency to withdraw from or to abolish the deprivational phenomenological object. In the case of a negatively cathected fact, the tendency of the need-disposition is to change those facts which conflict with it. Facts can

---

[22] Sublimation is not a special mechanism of defense in this sense but a special case of the normal learning mechanism of substitution. It may, of course, play a highly important part in resolution of conflicts.

be changed by means of actions that change the actual relations between objects and thus change the perception of those relations (the perceptions being the facts); or facts can be changed by merely distorting the perceptions of the relations between objects without really altering the relations at all. In either case the problem is solved by constructing a new set of perceptions in which the "facts" cognized are no longer in conflict with the need-dispositions; that is, by bringing about a situation where the negatively cathected facts are not cognized. Insofar as there is a personality problem here, it is chiefly a problem of altering the cognitive aspect of the orientation.

Every personality problem, of course, involves need-dispositions, and thus it involves cognitions and cathexes and (usually) evaluations too. The question in classifying the problems, however, is this: which aspects of the orientation (and the system too, since every change in the orientation is at least a superficial change in the system) is chiefly important in the changes which must be made to solve the problem.

Usually conflicts between need-dispositions and facts are of a rather superficial nature, in that the fact is not an actual deprivation of the need-disposition but rather simply a threat of deprivation — something instrumental to deprivation which, if allowed to continue, might result in actual deprivation. Such problems can be solved by changing the facts before the negatively-cathected threat of deprivation brings about the deprivation itself. If the threatened deprivation is not counteracted, actual deprivation may ensue, bringing about actual pain. In this case the deprived need-disposition comes into conflict with other need-dispositions and with the system as a whole by blocking normal process. At this point, the problem is no longer external but internal, and the mechanisms of defense come into operation to defend the system against the perseveration of the injured need-disposition (better amputate the diseased element than give up the whole system).

It can be seen that the entire discussion above may be interpreted as a discussion of fear. Whenever a perceived fact constitutes the threat of deprivation of one of the need-dispositions, then we have what we called fear. Thus, we can say that the mechanisms of adjustment are ways of doing away with fears, or with actual deprivations, by changing the relationships which are seen to obtain between the personality and the world of objects (chiefly, for our purposes, social objects). Also, referring back to the beginning of this section, we may say they are ways of solving conflicts between facts themselves.

Let us discuss briefly the method for adjudicating conflicts between two factual propositions, before we go on to discuss the methods for solving conflicts between facts and need-dispositions. The normal method for adjudicating conflicts between dissonant cognitive elements within one orientation is "reality testing." This has to do with allowing the law of effect to operate, insofar as it applies to the acceptance or rejection of cognitions in both learning and performance. It is the external equivalent of the internal tendency toward optimum gratification in the sense that it represents an adjudication of the various possibilities of cognition. It is the descriptive term for the process of selecting objects of attention, focusing on some and avoiding others as possibilities for gratification and dangers of deprivation. Like other functions this cognitive system is oriented to the future as well as the present. What it does is to adjudicate conflicts between different possible cognitions by looking into the future to see which actually serves to guide action in a fashion which is most gratifying and least deprivational in the long run.

Reality-testing is functionally crucial to the personality system as a link between the system and the situation. It imposes limits on the variability of action. It allows the actor to group objects in terms of their expected outcomes, and thus to stabilize, in some sense, the outcomes he gets from interaction with objects.

When we come to problems of conflict between facts and need-dispositions, a learning process similar to reality-testing provides the normal method for their resolution. The actor must learn to perceive new relationships which will guide action in such a fashion as to avoid the deprivation. This is the problem of inventing and learning new patterns of perception. For example, when ego is in some immediate danger, he must find some relationship — usually causal — between some event he knows how to produce by his own action and the event that he wants, that is, the averting of the calamity. He does this by reality-testing his invented patterns until one of them succeeds in avoiding the deprivation.

The normal techniques of adjustment are parallel to the normal mechanisms of defense (which involve simple evaluative choices based upon the pattern variables). As was true in that case, so it is true here that there are certain cases where rigidity prevents normal resolution of conflicts and thus gives rise to special mechanisms of adjustment. The cases where rigidity prevents normal external integration arise chiefly when the actor suffers real or threatened deprivation of cathected relationships with social objects. Four major types of problems are possible here. At this point the pattern variables enter the picture in a new way. They define certain typical problems of adjustment to which the personality is exposed in its relations to the social objects of the situation. These problems derive from the conditions required for the fulfillment of the four main types of need-dispositions arrived at in the table which cross-classified affectivity-neutrality with specificity-diffuseness. Each of these kinds of need-disposition presents the personality with a special kind of problem of adjustment. We will discuss these main types of need-dispositions only in terms of their relevance in mediating attachments to social objects.

First is the need-disposition that results from the combination of specificity and affectivity. This constitutes the case where the actor is striving for immediate specific gratification vis-à-vis an object. If there is no internal barrier to gratification, the primary factor on which gratification depends is the availability of the appropriate specific objects. A problem is occasioned by absence, or threatened deprivation, of the specific objects. Anxiety focuses on this possibility.[23] The need-disposition may, of course, cope with such a threat actively or passively.

Second is the need-disposition that derives from the combination of diffuseness and affectivity. This constitutes the case where the actor strives for love or affection. Here the problem is that of maintaining the security of the attachment, including the dependability of alter's attitude of diffuse love or affection.

Third is the need-disposition that derives from the combination of neutrality with specificity. This constitutes the case where the actor strives for approval by alter. Here again the problem is that of the availability of the appropriate object, which this time is the attitude of approval of alter. These attitudes may be actively sought, or they may be passively "hoped for."

Fourth is the need-disposition that derives from the combination of neutrality with diffuseness. This constitutes the case where the actor strives for esteem by alter. Here the problem is that of possible loss of esteem by alteration of ego's relationship to the object. It is not ego's immediate gratification opportunities which are threatened; rather, the danger is that ego will not fulfill his obligations to alter, these obligations being the conditions of future gratifications. Alter's attitudes, again, are of paramount significance. This time it is not a question of alter's approval of specific acts or qualities but of his esteem for ego as a person.

In all of these problems, the threat on which anxiety is focused is the possible disturbance of ego's cathected relationship to alter as an object. To resolve these problems, to cope with these threats, there are two fundamentally opposite directions in which ego's need-dispositions can be modified. Ego may intensify his motivation to retain and consolidate the relationship or he may accept the possibility of its relinquishment. The intensification of the need to retain the attachment to alter as an object results in *dependency*. If, on the other hand, the path of relinquishment is taken, we may speak of *compulsive independence*, which may concretely involve a reaction formation to dependency needs. When selections have been made from these alternatives, the question whether the search for security by retention or relinquishment is to be sought by active or passive devices still remains.

With this introductory discussion complete, we may now proceed to classify the special mechanisms of adjustment, which are all applicable to the four major types of problems of adjustment to social objects.

When ego chooses to cope with the threat by striving to retain the relationship with alter, we may speak of *dominance* as the active alternative and

---

[23] It is lack of receptiveness and/or responsiveness on which anxiety focuses.

submission as the passive alternative. Dominance thus means mitigation of the danger of loss or deprivation engendered by ego's attempting actively to control the object on which he is dependent or with whose expectation he must conform. Submission, on the other hand, seeks to forestall unfavorable reactions of alter by ego's ingratiating himself with alter and fulfilling his wishes. This presumably must be correlated with the renunciation of one set of ego's conflicting needs, a renunciation which may be possible only through the operation of the mechanisms of defense. Indeed, from one point of view the mechanisms of adjustment as ways of coping with threats or relations to objects must always have their counterparts in mechanisms of defense as ways of coping with threats arising within ego's own personality. This complementary relationship is inherent in the kind of significance and importance which object attachments have for the whole personality. It follows from this that the most strategic need-dispositions are those which mediate the reciprocal attachments.

Turning to the case of willingness to relinquish the attachment to alter, we again find the corresponding possibilities. *Aggressiveness* is the active alternative and *withdrawal* the passive. Aggressiveness is basically the need-disposition to get rid of a noxious object — to take active steps to render the object's noxious activities impossible. This may or may not entail what is ordinarily considered injury to or destruction of the object; it may be limited to the prevention of certain activities. The case where injury to the object is positively cathected is a further complication of aggressiveness; it may be called *sadism*. Withdrawal scarcely needs comment. It is renunciation of the object, accompanied either by inhibition of the need-disposition (which may require repression) or substitution of a new object (which may involve displacement). The logical relations of these four primary mechanisms of adjustment are shown in Fig. 8 (page 256).

As in the case of sadism, dynamic relations between the mechanisms of defense and of adjustment may be established from which many of the clinically familiar patterns of motivation may be derived. For example, masochism may be treated as involving the combination of submission as a primary pattern of adjustment with strong elements of guilt-feeling and hence a need-disposition to accept suffering. This combination may in turn favor a positive cathexis (e.g., in erotic terms) of certain states of suffering at the hands of an object of attachment. Or, to take another example, compulsive independence taking the passive form of withdrawal from love attachments may be combined with expression of a dependency need in the affectively neutral form of a compulsive need for approval.

The outcome of such motivational combinations may be a selective orientation as between the different types of attachment as formulated in terms of the basic pattern-variable combinations of Fig. 3. Thus a need to secure specific approval through dominance will pose quite different problems of execution from those entailed in a need to ensure an attitude of diffuse love on alter's part. To carry out all these possibilities would involve us in far too much classificatory detail for present purposes.

Before leaving these questions it is important to emphasize again that there are processes of *resolution* in this area as there were in the sphere of internal integration. The actor's relation to his world of objects is, in fact, continually changing, and adjustments to these changes must continually be made. So far as this adjustment is carried out without manifestation of strain or conflict, it is to be regarded *as a process of learning* and the normal mechanisms of learning will operate. There will be not only in the developmental period but throughout life a continual succession of new reinforcements and extinctions, inhibitions, substitutions, imitations, and identifications. The *special* mechanisms of adjustment come into operation only when the normal learning mechanisms fail to operate without strain, when the resolution is incomplete or absent.

The process of internal integration and situational adjustment are, as noted, interdependent with each other. A new adjustment problem which cannot be resolved by normal learning processes creates a strain that reacts not merely on one or two need-dispositions but has repercussions in the system of need-dispositions. If in turn these repercussions, which will always create some conflicts, cannot be adequately resolved, mechanisms of defense will come into operation. Conversely, the operation of a defense mechanism arising out of an internal conflict will create in the need-dispositions concerned needs either to intensify some of their cathexes or to withdraw them. Unless these needs can be fully inhibited, the result will be the intensification or creation of a problem of adjustment, which in turn may activate or intensify a mechanism of defense. Thus the processes of resolution, of defense, and of adjustment are all mutually interdependent.

Anxiety, as we have seen, is the danger signal given by anticipations of danger to the equilibrium of the personality from within. There are other dimensions of a diffuse feeling of dysphoria. One type of special significance to our study is that manifested in relation to ego's own violation (actual or anticipated as possible) of value standards which he has internalized. Here the relation to the internal integration of personality, on the one hand, and to situational objects, on the other, is significant. Such a dysphoric feeling directed toward ego's own internalized standards, in such a way that he himself is the judge, may be called *guilt*. If, on the other hand, the orientation is toward alter's reaction, according to what are interpreted to be his standards of approval or esteem, it may be called *shame*. If finally it is concerned *only* with *overt* consequences which will be injurious to ego, it is *fear*.

SUBINTEGRATIONS IN THE PERSONALITY SYSTEM

In the preceding section we have been discussing certain complex need-dispositions engendered by the problem of maintaining the level of gratification in the face of threats from within the personality and outside it. We have said nothing about the possibility of these need-dispositions becoming dominant features in the integration of the personality system. It is to this that we wish to give our attention at this point.

The personality system is an organized set of primary and complex need-dispositions which are related to one another in a hierarchical way. Certain of the need-dispositions are generalized and fused with more specific need-dispositions. Thus, such need-dispositions as aggressiveness, dominance, submissiveness, and so on, might find release simultaneously with more specific need-dispositions; for example need-dispositions for love, achievement, erotic gratification. This simultaneous gratification of several need-dispositions gives unity to the personality system. It provides what Murray has called the "unity thema"; but it does more than provide a unified pattern of orientation. It is also an allocative and integrative factor.

Integration, however, is not a homogeneous phenomenon. We may speak of total integration and subintegration. Subintegrations are groupings of need-dispositions around certain objects or classes of objects or around object or occasion modalities.[24] Particular sets of need-dispositions will be activated and gratified by certain objects; that is, they will press for release and will be released without disruptive conflict with their "co-operative" need-dispositions in connection with certain objects. Insofar as several need-dispositions (whatever their level of complexity) are simultaneously gratified in a stable recurrent manner about particular objects, object classes, or modalities, we shall speak of subintegrations (regardless of whether the simultaneous gratification is accompanied by resolution or by some mechanism of defense or adjustment).

These partial integrations within the personality structure are built up in the course of particular sequences of experience (experiences of action and interaction in a situation). They acquire a kind of relative independence in their functioning, a "functional autonomy." The situation which provokes one of the constituent need-dispositions of the integration system also provokes the others. Each subsystem, so far as it has become an integrated system, becomes a unitary need-disposition, itself, with its appropriate gratifications, more complex in structure and with wider systemic connections and ramifications than more elementary need-dispositions (e.g., for love, esteem, etc.). Through their repercussions in the personality system these subsystems may either indirectly or directly produce real conflicts with other subintegrations.

---

[24] A compulsive fixation on time-allocation is a familiar phenomenon. Special significance of particular places, such as a home, is also an example.

A subintegration such as a need-disposition for passively received love might come into conflict with some other need-disposition, primary or complex, or with another subintegration such as the compulsive need for independence from authority. Thus conflict might be dealt with by allocative resolution, as by the selection of love objects and sources which neither exercise nor symbolize authority; or it might be dealt with by some defense mechanism such as repression or reaction formation. With the mastery of conflicts between subintegrations of need-dispositions, we return to the phenomenon of the total integration of the personality system.

Again the hierarchical organization of need-dispositions plays a central part. One generalized complex need-disposition is especially significant here: namely, that built around the self-collectivity orientation alternative.

There are two primary aspects of this integration about collectively shared values. In the first place the values of the collectivity themselves define areas of control and areas of permissiveness. That is, there are areas in which ego is expected to be guided by considerations constitutive of his membership in the collectivity, and other areas of permissiveness, within which he is free to act and choose independently of obligations of membership. This distinction will exist with respect to every institutionalized role definition and normally will become incorporated into personality structure in the form of a generalized need-disposition, usually called a "sense of obligation." It will be a need-disposition to conform with institutional expectations. Insofar as ego's personality structure is integrated with and by such collective value-expectations which impose obligations upon him, we will speak of "superego-integration." When, in addition to the integration with collective values the area of permission to pursue his own interests and/or values irrespective of (*not* in conflict with) role-obligations in collectivities is included, we will speak of "ego-integration."

This distinction between modes of personality integration relative to collectivity membership obligations should be clearly distinguished from another set which is also important in the analysis of such obligations: "conformative" and "alienative" need-dispositions. The latter, exceedingly crucial distinction concerns in the first instance the articulation of the personality system with the role structure of the social system; it stresses the involvement of role structure (in one crucial respect) in the structure of personality. The value patterns institutionalized in the role-expectations of ego's roles may become an integrated part of his own personality structure, in which case he will have a need-disposition to conform with the expectations of the role in question. On the other hand, this integration may be absent, and he may have one of a number of possible types of need-disposition to avoid, or to rebel against, conformity with such expectations. A need-disposition to conformity or alienation acquires a special compulsive force when in addition to or in place of the general need-disposition there develops a specific anxiety about the attitudes of the object.

It should be clear from the whole foregoing analysis that a personality does not have in a simple sense *one* homogeneous "superego," but precisely because he is involved in a multiplicity of roles in as many collectivities, he has several superego-integrations in his personality. Very frequently the most important internal as well as external conflicts are not between obligations imposed by a general collective value system and "self-interest" but between the obligations of different roles, that is, between the constituent, more or less specific, need-dispositions in the superego. The actor is put in the position of having to sacrifice one or the other or some part of each. This is an authentically internal personality conflict, and not merely a conflict over the possible "external" consequences of sanctions; as such it is extremely important.

A certain trend of thought tends to treat personality simply as a cluster of what in the present terms would be called superego-integrations. The importance of this aspect of personality is indeed great, but it alone is not adequate and would introduce serious biases unless related to other aspects. Not only does there seem to be much evidence for the importance of areas of sheer gratificatory autonomy without reference to any role obligation, but also it is within the area of autonomy vis-à-vis defined role obligations that individual "creativity" [25] and personal morality occur. This autonomous area of individual action may occur within a zone of permissiveness provided by the institutional structure of the society; it might also exist in zones which are institutionally regulated, but in accordance with standards which are contrary to the predominant institutional expectations.

Another basic element in the comprehensive integration of the personality system is a "personal value system." This problem will be taken up in the following chapter. At this point it should be emphasized that the integration of a personality as a concrete empirical action system can never be a simple "reflection" or "realization" of a value system. It must involve the adjustment of such a value system to the exigencies of the object situation and to the exigencies of organic needs. There is, therefore, a presumption that the integration of the value system into action will be less than perfect. There will be necessary elements of compromise, evasion, and more or less open conflict. This is particularly true because of the "historical" character of both personal and social value systems. The personal value system is built up in the course of a career, the different components of which, especially in a complex society, may not articulate very well with each other. In general it can be said that the nonintegration of the personal value system is "veiled" by the mechanisms of defense. This means that the actor is usually only

---

[25] If individual "creativity" is required by a set of role-expectations, then, of course, it does not occur in the area of autonomy. Thus the scientist is expected to create theory.

partially aware of the structure and importance of many of his conflicting elements — unless, of course, he has been very thoroughly psychoanalyzed, and even then much will remain obscure.

But although the integration of personality in terms of the value system is always less than perfect — and is, in fact, usually considerably so — it does not follow that the degrees or modes of integration are unimportant. They are of primary significance.

For example, the characterization of *total* personalities, in terms of what Murray calls their "unity thema," clearly presupposes an analysis of the degree and nature of the integration of the personal value system. But because of its applicability to both personality and social system levels, it has seemed best to treat the general problem of the structure of value systems separately in the following chapter. It is clear that the results of this treatment should be incorporated into the analysis of personality as a system and are not to be thought of separately as relevant only to problems of "culture." Similarly, in the formulation of an over-all characterization of a personality, the manner and degree of its integration in the social structure presents a critical problem. The following discussion presents a first approximation to the solution of this problem.

The Articulation of Personality and Social Systems

In the analysis of the empirical interdependence of personality and social systems, the best point of departure would be an examination of the points of contact between the two types of system. This procedure has been rendered much more feasible from a theoretical standpoint by virtue of our derivation of all major concepts from a few basic categories of the theory of action. The use of the same set of basic categories for the description of discrete actions and for the description of systems allows us to study not the identities of the two types of system but the points of their integration and mal-integration which is the central empirical problem of this field of social science.

In Fig. 9 we have schematically summarized the component elements of the two systems with a view to showing the areas in each system which correspond to the other. In what follows we shall present some brief considerations on these points of empirical articulation or correspondence between the concrete structures in the two systems.

In the left-hand column Fig. 9 presents a minimum list of structural elements of a social system, all of which must be present in any empirical case. These are first the two primary classes of unit elements of the social system: (1) the ways in which actors are categorized as objects of orientation, that is, by qualities (age, sex, territorial location, collectivity memberships) and performance capacities, and (2) the ways in which the roles in which they act are defined, the types of pattern and their distribution. The two together define the role structure of the system; the first defines the actors' characteristics on the basis of which they are assigned to roles, and the second defines those roles (in terms of who shall occupy them and of the requirements the occupants must meet) and the relations of roles to one another within the system. Next, every social system must have an organized allocation of orientations vis-à-vis the two fundamental types of interests in objects, the instrumental and the expressive. This includes the distribution of transferrable objects of interest, facilities and rewards, and therefore it includes the structure of the systems of power and of prestige. Finally, every social system has structures of primarily integrative (or in the social sense, moral) significance — on both the cultural and the institutional levels. In the latter case the most important phenomenon is the presence of roles which carry special institutionalized responsibility and with it both authority and prestige greater than those of most actors in the system.

We may now begin to examine the implications of the existence of these fundamentals of the social system for the personality organization of its component actors. In the first place, it is quite clear that there must be a fundamental correspondence between the actor's own self-categorization or "self-image" and the place he occupies in the category system of the society of which he is a part. Many aspects of this categorization, such as sex, age, ethnic adherence, seem too obvious to consider explicitly. But even where there is such an obvious biological point of reference as in the case of sex, it is clear that self-categorization must be learned in the course of the socialization process, and the process is often very complex, and to some degree the individual must learn to "see himself as others see him" (that is, to accept the socially given definition of his status). Even in the case of sex, certainly among children, fantasies of belonging to the opposite sex are very common, and there is reason to believe that on deeper levels these fantasies may reflect c serious difficulty in accepting the membership in the sex group to which the individual has been biologically ascribed. Such pathological phenomena indicate that categorization even by sex is not simply given with the anatomical structure of the organism but has to be built into the personality. Failure for it to work out fully is very probably an important component in at least some types of homosexuality. What is true of sex is much more obviously so in such a case as ethnic membership. For a person of light skin color to categorize himself as a Negro is obviously something which must be learned. It should be remembered that the criterion of social ascription to the Negro group is not physical characteristics as such, but parentage. *Any* child of a Negro is in social terms a Negro, even if his physical characteristics are such that he would have no difficulty in "passing."

Another important type of such categorization concerns performance capacities and character traits. What the individual believes about himself — with respect to his intelligence, his abilities to do various things, whether he is honest or attractive and so forth — becomes constitutive of his person-ality itself. This is, of course, not merely a matter of cognitive belief alone but of internalization as part of the need-disposition system.

Of course, in this as in so many other respects, the correspondence between the personality structure and the social system is not exact. But the elements of looseness and the frequency of discrepancies between self-image and actual social role should not obscure the fundamental importance of a broad correspondence.

In the second place, as we have so often pointed out, the social system places every individual in a series of roles where he is expected to conform with certain expectations of behavior. The need-disposition structure which controls one's responses to the expectations defining one's various roles is therefore one of the most fundamental aspects of any personality, for the simple reason that social objects constitute the most important part of the situation in which he acts. Therefore, in the performance as well as the qual-ity modality of his involvement in the social system, the individual person-ality inevitably must be shaped around the definition of role-expectations. There are, of course, the two primary aspects of this. Within the range per-mitted by biological plasticity, there is the possibility that, through the so-cialization process, the constitution of the need-disposition system itself will be organized in terms of the motivation to fulfill role-expectations. Perhaps the most important single instance of this is the internalization of value-or-ientation patterns through the processes of identification.

The second aspect is that, however the need-disposition system may come to have been constituted, at every point in the life processes the individual is confronted with the actions and attitudes of others as part of his situation of action. Because he is a social being participating in processes of social interaction, he can never escape being oriented to the reactions of others, to their attitudes and the contingencies of their overt behavior. In this connec-tion, then, the meaning of these role-expectations as expressed in the attitudes and actions of his interaction partners is always a fundamental point of ref-erence for his own motivations. Role-expectations are so fundamental to the social system that all human social motivation closely involves the problem of conformity with them. Hence one of the most important dimensions of any need-disposition system of a personality must be what we have called the conformity-alienation dimension. There may, of course, be widely varying degrees to which a need-disposition for either conformity or alienation is generalized in the personality, but whether it applies only to a narrow sec-tor of the role-system or is highly generalized, it is always present.

The next two major aspects of the social system constitute in a sense a further specification of the implications of these first two fundamental ones. Each, however, has certain special features of its own which may be com-mented upon briefly. As an essential part of every social system there is, as has been noted, an allocation of (mutually oriented) instrumental activities to the various roles and a corresponding allocation of sanctions and rewards. As we shall see in discussing the social system later, there is a variety of possible ways in which these activities can be organized relative to other components of the social system. But whatever this organization may be, it has to have its counterpart in the motivational organization of the individual personalities involved.

This becomes particularly evident in two more or less antithetical contexts. First, it is clear that the more complex and sophisticated types of instrumental activity require high levels of self-discipline on the part of the individual. The person who is unduly responsive to every passing opportunity for immediate gratification is incapable of the sustained effort and implementation of planning which is necessary — the capacity for sustained work is essential. A wide development of the instrumental aspects of a social system therefore presupposes the development of personalities capable of the requisite levels of disciplined application — as well as other capacities, of course, such as that for handling abstract generalizations. Not least among these capacities is that for a certain *flexibility* of orientation. The personality which is too highly dependent on highly detailed "ritualistic" routines of life is not ordinarily capable of the higher levels of instrumental achievement.

At the same time, a stable system of action requires other elements than instrumental disciplines, and this leads us to the second aspect. A stable system requires above all the internalization of value-orientations to a degree which will sufficiently integrate the goals of the person with the goals of the collectivity. In the economy of instrumental orientations one of the principal points at which this problem arises is with respect to the control of "self-interest." In popular terms we are likely to say that in addition to instrumental capacities people must have certain levels of "moral integrity" and of "responsibility" to be satisfactory members of a society. The prerequisites for such qualities in the structure of personality are somewhat different from the prerequisites of instrumental efficiency or adaptiveness.

Each social system at the same time has an "economy" of rewards and of the expressive orientations and interests connected with them. In motivationally significant terms this comes down to the question of what are the most important immediate and ultimate gratifications, and how they are organized and distributed within the social system. It is here that perhaps the most important single inference from the paradigm of interaction needs to be drawn. Human society, we may say, is only possible at all because, within the limits of plasticity and sensitivity, sufficient basic human gratifications come to be bound up with conformity with role-expectations and with eliciting the favorable attitudes of others. Both the immediate presocial gratification needs and the individualistic type of instrumental reciprocity provide too brittle and unstable a basis for social order. The phenomena of attachment and of identification are altogether fundamental here.

There seem to be two primary dimensions to this significance. First, through the diffuseness of what has been called the love type of attachment, the mutuality of dependency is extended to the social object as a whole, which precludes his being "used" as a facility for specific immediate gratifications without regard to the totality of the attachment relationship. Second, the mechanism of identification in the context of role-orientation provides a motivation for the acceptance of still further disciplines by leading to the development of the needs for approval and esteem; that is, for favorable attitudes relatively independent of the provision of other immediate gratifications. This need to be approved and esteemed is sometimes a source of social strains, but it is a fundamental motivational basis for the acceptance of socially necessary disciplines. There is a sense in which, paradoxical as it may seem, the core of the reward systems of societies is to be found in the relevance of this element of the motivation of individuals. What people want most is to be responded to, loved, approved, and esteemed. If, subject, of course, to an adequate level of physiological need-gratification, these needs can be adequately gratified, the most important single condition of stability of a social system will have been met. Hence the study in personality of the conditions both of building up and of gratifying the need-dispositions in this area is crucial for the study of social systems. Conversely, the understanding of the social situation, both in the course of socialization and in adult interaction, is crucial to this phase of personality study.

It will be made clear in Chapter IV that institutionalization itself must be regarded as the fundamental integrative mechanism of social systems. It is through the internalization of common patterns of value-orientation that a system of social interaction can be stabilized. Put in personality terms this means that there is an element of superego organization correlative with every role-orientation pattern of the individual in question. In every case the internalization of a superego element means motivation to accept the priority of collective over personal interests, within the appropriate limits and on the appropriate occasions.

Certain aspects of this larger class of superego elements, however, are particularly significant in the articulation of personality with the social system. Of these two may be singled out. First is the organization of attitudes toward authority, which is of crucial significance, since, however great its variability, authority is always a functionally essential element of social systems. The significance of this dimension in personality development, with its close connections with the structure of the parent-child relationship, is well known, of course. Perhaps because we live in a society with an anti-authoritarian orientation, a converse problem has, however, received less attention: the problem of motivation to the acceptance of responsibility. This, like the problem of authority, of course, is closely involved with the general conformity-alienation problem. But there seems to be much evidence in our society of the great importance of deviance in the direction of withdrawal from responsibilities; the use of illness in this connection is a familiar example. This problem, in its significance to the social system, poses extremely important questions of the articulation of social systems with personality.

Up to this point we have been treating the points of articulation between personality and social systems in a manner which assumed, on the whole, a far-reaching integration of the personality into the social system. It was for the sake of convenience and emphasis in exposition that this integration was portrayed first. The articulation which we have presented does not depend, however, for its validity on any particular degree of empirical "closeness of fit" between personality and social system.

The validity of the conceptual scheme which we used in analyzing the articulation of highly integrated personality and social systems is thus not affected by cases in which the integration is far from perfect. In fact, the imperfections of integration can be described only by careful observance of the same conceptual scheme which analyzes the positive integration. To illustrate the equal relevance of the conceptual scheme to situations of mal-integration, we may enumerate some of the possibilities.

First, with respect to categorization: alienation of the actor from his collectivity will exist where the various categories of qualities and performance-relevant qualities are differently assessed; that is, where the expectations of the actor concerning himself do not correspond to the expectations which others have formed concerning him. The actor, identifying himself, for instance, with respect to certain categories of qualities or performance capacities on which he places a high evaluation, will have expectations regarding the obligations of others to him which will not be acknowledged by those whose image of him diverges from his own — unlike the situation where the general value-orientation of the actor and his fellows are similar. In such situations, the non-integration of the actor's personality with the social system with respect to categorization may become associated with ambivalences in the actor's own categorization of himself. When this happens, the unifying regulation of need-dispositions by a harmonious allocative scheme gives way to contradictory allocative standards and consequent instabilities of behavior and internal conflict, as well as conflict between the actor and the members of his collectivities.

Second, with respect to role systems and role orientations: an individual whose capacity for diffuse object-attachment is impaired so that he is, for example, unable to make object-attachments of certain types (e.g., with persons of the opposite sex) will very likely become isolated. He will be unable to conform with expectations in a way which will enable him to fulfill certain roles in certain types of solidary relationships (e.g., marriage). He will perhaps find his way into some subsystem populated by the types of persons with whom he can establish attachments but his performance in roles in relation to other members of the society will be impaired. Similarly, fear of diffuse attachments to members of his own sex may hamper his collaboration in some specific roles where there is a "danger" of the emergence of diffuse "homosexual" attachments.

Third, with respect to the allocation of instrumental functions of the roles in which a person performs: in most cases, individuals perform role functions in the division of labor which do not, as such, completely and directly gratify any specific need-disposition or any set of the need-dispositions of their personality system. It is the nature of instrumental action that it should be this way. Conformity with the role-expectations is possible, however, either through a generalized need-disposition to conformity or through instrumental orientations. The latter, while making possible conformity with role-expectations, do involve (as we have just said) the renunciation of certain gratifications and therewith the generation of strains in the personality system. In the extreme case, which is relatively infrequent because of prior allocative processes, the primary or derivative need-dispositions are so pressing that no adaptation is possible and the expectations (of alters) concerning the actor's behavior in a particular role in the division of labor are completely frustrated.

The disjunction between role-expectations (of alters) and need-dispositions (of ego) may in some instances be a product of an alienative adjustive mechanism, a derivative need-disposition to avoid conformity. The disjunction might in its turn, by virtue of the negative sanctions which it incurs, produce anxieties which have to be coped with by defensive mechanisms and which modify the functioning of both the personality and the social system. Another possibility is that the role expectations may be so general that they allow persons with diverse sets of need-dispositions to perform the role in accordance with their spontaneous tendencies. The gap between prestige allocation and need-dispositions for approval and esteem can likewise be viewed with respect to its effects on the social system and on the personality system. Under certain conditions, the gap might activate certain learning mechanisms, for example, inhibition of the approval and esteem need-dispositions or the substitution of other social objects; in either case the gap might reduce motivation for conformity with role-expectations and weaken the aspiration to approximate certain role models. Within the personality system, the irritated state of certain ungratified, rigid need-dispositions might cause a reorganization of the personality as an adaptation or defense against this deprivation.

Finally, with respect to the mechanisms of social control and the internalization of shared values, we have already indicated that the superego need not consist only of the more generally shared values. Insofar as this is true, the integration of the personality into the social system will be less than complete. Where this divergence among the superego contents of the members of the society becomes relatively widespread, it might result also in the modification of the position of the superego in the personality system. In some instances the integrative-controlling function of the superego is weakened through the withdrawal of the reinforcement which is provided by the perception of numerous other individuals whose action seems to show conformity with the same internalized value-orientations. As a reaction to this threat, in some personalities, the superego functions more repressively and this strengthens its position within the personality system.

It is clear that the development of the need-disposition system is a function of the interaction of the actor with the situation throughout life. The types of mal-integration discussed above are therefore markedly influenced and irritated by the actor's exposure to conflicting expectations from different significant objects or inconsistencies in the expectations which are directly toward him by significant social objects concerning the same type of situation at various times. But the way in which these strains are coped with and their consequences for the personality cannot be deduced from the behavior of the objects alone. They must be referred to his personality as a functioning system.

Thus the problems of the pathology of personality must be understood in terms of a complex balance between the internal conflicts and strains of the personality as a system and the difficulties of adjustment to the situation, the latter in turn having repercussions on the personality. It is both a "psychological" and a "sociological" problem.

From the foregoing it has become clear that the contact surface of the personality and social systems lies between need-dispositions of ego and role-expectations of various alters. We shall therefore undertake a somewhat more elaborate examination of this crucial zone of action theory.

NEED-DISPOSITIONS AND ROLE-EXPECTATIONS

The starting point is the *interaction* of persons or, to put it in other words, of ego with a system of social objects. From the beginning of the actor's life, the significant social objects in his situation act in roles, of which presumably the major elements are institutionalized. In consequence of his dependence on these social objects, the actor as an infant builds up a set of roles of his own response to his treatment by adults. Only by doing so is he able to survive.

This process takes the form of his establishment of expectations regarding the social objects in his situation — in the first instance, his mother — and of the formation of attachments to them. The social object is not, however, an inert source of gratification, but *reacts* toward him, so that there enters a *conditional* element into the fulfillment of expectations. Alter has expectations of ego and vice versa; this is what we have already called a "complementarity of expectations." At the very beginning the infant is perhaps almost an environmental object to the adult. But this aspect changes quickly, a reciprocity of responsiveness builds up, the infant's smile calls forth responses, and organization along the axis of gratification and renunciation becomes more differentiated. As all this happens, he begins to *play a role* in the social system; that is, he acts in accordance with expectations, just as the adult does.

The essential element in the role is the complementarity of expectations. The outcome of ego's action, in terms of its significance to him, is *contingent* on *alter's* reaction to what he does. This reaction in turn is not random but is organized relative to alter's expectation concerning what is "proper" behavior on ego's part. The reaction, then, is organized about the problem of whether, and to what degree, ego "conforms" with alter's expectations of what he should do. At the very beginning the expectations may be purely predictive, but very soon they acquire a normative content. (This normative aspect has indeed been included in the concept of expectation from the start.)

Ego, then, is oriented, not only to alter as an object in the immediate environment, but to alter's contingent behavior. His orientation follows the paradigm "If I do this, he will probably do (or feel) such and such; if, on the other hand, I do that, he will feel (and act) differently." These reaction patterns of alter, which are contingent on what ego does, we have called *sanctions*. Role-expectations, on the other hand, are the definitions by *both* ego and alter of what behavior is proper for each in the relationship and in the situation in question. *Both* role-expectations and sanctions are essential to the total concept of a "role" in the concrete sense of a segment of the action of the individual. Sanctions are the "appropriate" behavioral consequences of alter's role-expectations in response to the actual behavior of ego.

Both role-expectations and sanctions may be institutionalized to a greater or lesser degree. They are institutionalized when they are integrated with or "express" value-orientations *common* to the members of the collectivity to which both ego and alter belong, which in the limiting case may consist only of ego and alter. (Of course, for the newly born infant, role-expectations cannot be institutionalized.) But so far as he "internalizes" the evaluations of the social objects around him, his own expectations may become institutionalized, at least within his family circle. Only as this happens, as he develops a "superego," can he be said to be "integrated" in the collectivity in the sense of sharing its values.

Sanctions, being responses interpreted as gratifications or deprivations, are organized about a positive-negative axis. Ego's fulfillment of alter's expectations generally brings forth in some form positive sanctions; for example, the "granting" of gratifications such as love and approval and the performance of actions which gratify ego. Failure to fulfill expectations, on the other hand, generally brings forth negative sanctions; for example, the withholding of gratification, love, or approval, and "doing things" which are dis-advantageous or unwelcome to ego, such as imposing further deprivations or "punishments."

It is in the *polarity* of sanctions and their *contingency* that their special relevance to the learning process is to be found. By virtue of their efficacy in relation to the learning mechanisms, ego is forced into the path of conformity with alter's expectations. Thus is established the relationship with social objects that becomes so directly constitutive of personality structure. Early childhood is selected for illustration only because of the dramatic character of the influence of this interaction system on a highly fluid and unorganized personality. In principle, however, the same basic processes go on throughout life. It is through the mechanisms of the system of sanctions operating on the learning, adjustive, and defensive mechanisms of the individual that a social system is able to operate and especially to control the action of its component individuals.

INDIVIDUALITY

Because of the paramount significance to any personality of its system of relations to other persons, the institutionalized organization of roles (in relation to significant social objects and through them to cultural and physical objects) is central to the organization of personality itself. The pattern of expectations governing one's system of relations to other persons comes to be internalized into the structure of one's personality. But this system of internalized roles is not the only constituent of personality, for a variety of reasons, which may be briefly reviewed. In the first place, those concrete role-expectations which become internalized are themselves only partly the ones which are institutionalized. That is, not *only* the institutionalized role-expectation patterns become incorporated into the personality but also other elements, which are important in particular interactive relationships. In relation to the social structure in question, these may be deviant elements or merely variations within the limits of permissiveness. In either case, the institutionalized definitions of role-expectation will account for only part of the interaction.

Second, even to the extent that the component role-expectations in a given institution might be classed together as uniform, the sets of such expectations will probably vary for the different actors who participate in the institution. The degree to which this is true will vary for different types and parts of the social structure, but generally, and especially in our type of society, there will be considerable variations. Although there is some measure of uniformity, for example, in the mother-child relationship regardless of the sex of the child, there is also a difference of expectation on the mother's part regarding her male and her female children. The matter is further complicated by differences of sex in relation to birth order — a boy who follows two girls will necessarily be treated differently from a first-born son. In school and in play groups too the treatment will vary according to the individual characteristics of the actor so that variations in expectations will offset uniformities. Hence there is, in the combinations of the role-expectation elements which affect different personalities, a basis for *differentiation* between personalities which have been exposed to the "same" experiences as other persons in the "same" category.

Third, it must be recalled that the organization of a personality occurs in a *particular* organism. This has two aspects. On the one hand, ego's own organism as an *object* has features which differentiate it, and therefore him, from others who may be in similar status-positions in the social structure. Ego, in this sense, may be tall or short, fat or thin, black-haired or blonde, strong or weak. All this creates an influential source of differentiation. There might, furthermore, be variations of energy and of the strength of organic needs and capacities, such as hunger-needs, erotic needs, and motor-activity capacities.

The upshot of these considerations is that, though in a fundamental sense personality is a function of the institutionally organized role-expectations of the social system in which ego is involved, in an equally fundamental sense, it cannot be even approximately fully determined by this aspect of its structure. In confrontation with a given pattern of role-expectations in any given situation, there is therefore every reason to believe that there will be a dispersed distribution of personality types which are faced with approximately the same specific role-expectations.

These observations imply that there can be no neatly schematic relation between the *role-expectations* (of ego and alter) and the *specific* organization of behavior and sanctions. The same reactive sanction behavior cannot be guaranteed to have a completely standardized impact on the personality of any ego. In the learning process relative to role behavior there are many possibilities of divergent development from essentially similar starting points, the divergences being a cumulative function of the aspects of the personality in question *other than* the specific role-expectation confronting the actor in the particular situation.

DEVIANCE

Just as sanctions are contingent upon the fulfillment or nonfulfillment of alter's expectations, so the significance of the sanctions to ego will also vary in accordance with whether he is motivated by a predominantly conformative or alienative set of need-dispositions. Internalization of patterns of value is crucial in the integration of an actor in a role system. Insofar as internalization occurs without exceptionally great unmastered conflict, ego will develop need-dispositions to conform with expectations;[26] while faulty internalization

---

[26] It does not follow that this necessarily makes him a "conformist" in the popular sense of the term. Many of the values which are institutionalized in role systems enjoin

(internalization attended by ineffective defense mechanisms or incomplete resolution of conflicts) may produce alienative need-dispositions, which are derivative need-dispositions to refuse to fulfill expectations. According to the
structure of his personality in other respects, ego, if alienatively disposed, will
tend (1) toward withdrawal, or (2) to evade the fulfillment of expectations,
or (3) to rebel by openly refusing to conform. The alternative which he selects
will be dependent on the activity-passivity need-dispositions of his personality.

An alienative need-disposition in this sense does not by itself necessarily
produce deviant behavior. Normally the operation of the sanction system will
lead ego to have an interest in the avoidance of the negative sanctions which
would be attached to overtly deviant behavior. He may thus control his
deviant tendencies and conform overtly, but the alienative need-dispositions
may still be highly important in his personality structure, and the failure to
gratify them might engender strains. There is an almost endless range of
possibilities of compromise.

Alienative need-dispositions may become unconscious through repression. This often takes place through defense mechanisms (such as reaction
formation, displacement or projection of the associated aggressiveness) which
serve to reduce the anxiety engendered by (1) the infringements on the
superego and (2) the prospective thwarting of authority.

Furthermore, ego is an object to himself. And, although the ultimate
sources of the role-expectations which become internalized in the personality
must be sought in relations to external objects, once expectations are internalized their aspect as internal objects of orientation may become of crucial
importance. Guilt and shame are indeed negative sanctions applied to ego by
himself, as punishment for his failure to live up to his own and others' expectations respectively.

The balance within ego's personality between conformative and alienative
need-dispositions is perhaps the primary source *in personality* of the dynamic
problems and processes of the social system. There are, of course, sources
of deviation from alter's role-expectations other than ego's alienative predisposition; for example, ego's exposure to conflicting role-expectations
from one or more alters, or an instrumental orientation which leads ego
to deviate from the immediate expectation because the expected result is
more highly valued than alter's positive response. But alienative tendencies
are ordinarily operative in deviant orientations when they occur on any
considerable scale.

The absence of a simple correspondence between the structure of any
given personality and the role-expectation structure of the roles he occupies

independence and initiative, as is true of many in our own society. The person who refuses
to stand on his own feet or take initiative, because he is anxious about others' reactions.
is not "conforming" to the role-expectation, though in another sense he may be conforming
to what he *thinks* others want him to do.

means that conformity and deviance in overt action (any overt action, for that matter) can be understood neither as an "acting out" of ego's own need-dispositions alone nor as determined solely by the expectations of immediate and remote alters with their various powers to impose sanctions. The sanction system [27] interposes a set of intermediate determining factors into the operation of the various need-disposition constellations. Thus, there are *mechanisms* of social control other than the internalization of value-orientations as parts of the personality system.

Nonetheless, a stable social system does depend upon the stable recurrence of the mechanisms which render more probable those patterns of action essential to the make-up of the social system. The "same" patterns may have widely different functions in different personalities; the social problem is to get the patterns whatever their functional significance to the person. One example will suffice. A disposition in the direction of "economically rational behavior," (that is, methodical organization of resources and work habits, prudence, careful consideration of the future, an orientation toward specific rewards) may have quite different functional significances for different personality structures. In a large-scale industrialized social system, economically rational behavior has a very important, relatively definite, and uniform function. The effectiveness with which such a system operates will depend to a high degree on the presence of such complex need-dispositions on the part of a sufficiently large proportion of the population. It does not matter whether there are important differences among types of personality possessing this need-disposition as long as it exists. Moreover, it does not even matter greatly whether the dominant subintegrations of need-dispositions are not directly gratified by economically rational behavior as long as the personality systems allow them to carry out the action without more than a certain amount of strain, and as long as there are noneconomic institutions capable of absorbing and tolerating the repercussions of the strain. Furthermore, the sanction system provides a secondary "line of defense" for the social system, in that it is possible to secure conformity even though the need-disposition is relatively weak or even within limits, definitely alienative. What does matter is that there should be sufficient personalities capable of producing "economically rational behavior" either directly in response to the pressure of their own subintegrates of need-dispositions or the anticipated rewards or punishments.

[27] This includes both the impact of actual sanctions on ego and the influence of their anticipation on his behavior.

3

Systems of Value - Orientation

Patterns of value-orientation have been singled out as the most crucial cultural elements in the organization of systems of action. It has, however, been made clear at a number of points above that value-orientation is only part of what has been defined as culture. Before entering into a more detailed consideration of the nature of value systems and their articulation with the other elements of action, it will be useful to attempt a somewhat more complete delineation of culture than has yet been set forth.

The Place of Value-Orientation Patterns in the Organization of Culture

Culture has been distinguished from the other elements of action by the fact that it is intrinsically transmissible from one action system to another — from personality to personality by learning and from social system to social system by diffusion. This is because culture is constituted by "ways of orienting and acting," these ways being "embodied in" meaningful symbols. Concrete orientations and concrete interactions are events in time and space. Within the personality these orientations and interactions are grouped according to the need-dispositions denoting tendencies which the concrete orientations and interactions exhibit. Within the society they are grouped according to roles and role-expectancies denoting requirements which the concrete orientations and interactions both stipulate and fulfill. Both *need-dispositions* and *role-expectancies* are, in another sense, postulated entities, internal to personalities, and internal to social systems, controlling the orientations which constitute their concrete referents. As such, they cannot either of them be separated from the concrete actions systems which have and exhibit them. A need-disposition in this sense is an entity internal to a personality system which controls a system of concrete orientations and actions aimed at securing for the personality certain relationships with objects. A system of role-expectations is a system of need-dispositions in various personalities which controls a system of concrete mutual orientations and interactions aimed by each actor at gaining certain relationships with other social objects, and functioning for the collectivity in which it is institutionalized to bring about integrated interaction. In either case, the postulated entity is internal to and inseparable from the system of action which it helps to regulate. Cultural objects are similar to need-dispositions and role-expectations in two senses: (1) since they are ways of orienting and acting, their concrete referent consists in a set of orientations and interactions, a set which follows a certain pattern. (2) In another sense cultural objects are postulated entities controlling the orientations which constitute their concrete referents. However, unlike need-dispositions and role-expectations, the *symbols* which are the postulated controlling entities in this case are not internal to the systems whose orientations they control. Symbols control systems of orientations, just as do need-dispositions and role-expectations, but they exist not as postulated internal factors but as objects of orientation (seen as existing in the external world along side of the other objects oriented by a system of action).

Because of the internal character of need-dispositions and role-expectations, they cannot exist, except insofar as they represent actual internal (structural) factors in some concrete action system. This holds both for elemental need-dispositions and role-expectations and for complex patterned need-dispositions and role-expectations (these being complex structures of the simpler ones). Elemental symbols are similarly tied to concrete systems of action, in the sense that no external embodiment is a symbol unless it is capable of controlling certain concrete orientations in some action systems. (This means that each elemental symbol must have its counterpart in terms of a need-disposition on the part of an actor to orient to this object as a symbol, and thus to orient in a certain way wherever this symbol is given.) On the other hand, a complex "manner of orienting" (which can be termed either a complex cultural object or a complex symbol, the two terms meaning the same thing) can be preserved in an external symbol structure even though, for a time, it may have no counterpart in any concrete system of action. That is, symbols, being objectifiable in writing and in graphic and plastic representation, can be separated from the action systems in which they originally occurred and yet preserve intact the "way of orienting" which they represent; for, when they do happen to be oriented by an actor (to whom each element is meaningful) they will arouse in him the original complex manner of orientation.

By the same token, a complex external symbol structure (each element of which has a counterpart in terms of need-dispositions on the parts of the several actors who participate in a collectivity) can bring about roughly the *same* type of orientation in any or all of the actors who happen to orient to it. And since the concrete referent of the symbol is not the external object but rather the "way of orienting" which it controls, we may say that complex symbols are transmissible from actor to actor (i.e., from action system to action system). That is, by becoming a symbol, a way of orienting can be transmitted from one actor to another. This is because the physical embodiment of the symbol is a first or second order [1] derivative from the orientation of the actor who produces the symbol, and it controls (because it is a symbol) roughly the same orientations in the other actors who orient to it. Thus symbols differ from need-dispositions and role expectations in that they are separable from the action systems in which they arise, and in that they are transmissible from one action system to another.[2] Both of these differences derive from the fact that they have external "objective" embodiments, rather than internal "unobservable" embodiments. On the other hand, insofar as they are "ways or patterns of orienting and acting" and insofar as their concrete referent is a set of orientations (which follow a pattern, or better, of which the pattern is an ingredient), they have exactly the same status as role-expectancies and need-dispositions.

To show what symbolization does for action systems, we may point out that symbols or cultural objects involve "interpersonalizing" the kind of "abstraction" or "generalization" which characterizes all stable systems of orientation (which, by the same token, characterizes the organization of concrete orientations into the subsystems, here called need-dispositions). This calls for some digression to show how the word "generalization" (which was originally introduced in the General Statement in the section on behavior psychology) can be rendered equivalent to the term "abstraction" and used in this context. Action is said to be generalized when the *same* form of action (according to a set of criteria formulated either by ego or by an observer) is given in different situations or in different states of the same situation or by different persons, as we will show shortly. This is what is meant by the term when it is used in behavior psychology. In terms of the theory of action, this occurs whenever a need-disposition is constructed. For every need-disposition groups situations on the basis of selected criteria (thus constituting for the actor a generalized object) and causes them all to be oriented to in the same fashion (or as one object). Thus every need-disposition, when it is formed, constitutes a generalization of orientation, and by the same token "creates" an object (the object being created in terms of the criteria whereby the generalized orientation is rendered relevant). But here, it may be noted, we have the process called *abstraction*, which is nothing more than the creation of objects from the field of experience by grouping situations according to

---

[1] We say a first or second order derivative because action itself is the first order derivative from the orientation; that is, it is caused by the orientation. Sometimes the action itself is the symbol. Other times the symbol derives from (is caused by) the action.

[2] It can be noted here that role-expectations, insofar as they have a status at all different from complex need-dispositions (for social-object relationships), have that status by virtue of the fact that they are complex (internalized) need-dispositions which have symbolic counterparts, and which thus can be the same for both ego and alter. Thus role-expectations are a specific interpersonal class of need-dispositions controlling complementary expectations because they are symbols as well as need-dispositions.

selected criteria. Every need-disposition within a personality system is therefore a generalized orientation (or an abstraction, in one manner of speaking)
which allows the actor to orient different concrete events as all of one class,
and thus brings about roughly similar action with respect to all these events.
Within a personality, therefore, the term *generalization* refers to "orienting in
the same way" at several different times (and places). Or at least, such similarity of orientations is generalization when it occurs by virtue of some systematic internal controlling factor and not by chance.

We have already suggested that a "way of orienting" may be exemplified
not only at different times within the same personality system, but also within
different personality systems, and this may be a systematic and not a random
occurrence if the various persons within whom the way of orienting occurs
are controlled by the same complex symbol system.[3] Thus, we say, symbolization allows "interpersonalized" generalization. It is this very capacity for
"interpersonal-generalization" which is the essence of culture. And, in turn,
this capacity is the prerequisite of its crucially important role in systems of
action; for it implies the transmissibility of ways of orienting from person to
person, and hence a dimension of development which is known only rudi-
mentarily among nonhuman species of the biological universe. In other words,
communication, culture, and systems of human action are inherently linked
together.

The Classification of the Elements of Culture

The various elements of culture have different types of significance. The
criteria of classification for these elements are to be sought in the categories
of the fundamental paradigm of action. Every concrete act, as we have seen,
involves cognitive, cathectic, and evaluative components organized together.
These categories provide the major points of reference for analyzing the
differentiations of the symbol systems (just as they do for need-dispositions).
Hence the content of clture may be classified in accordance with the primacies [4] of the three fundamental components of the orientation of action.

The classification of symbol systems based on these primacies runs as
follows. Symbol systems in which the cognitive function has primacy may be
called "beliefs" or ideas.[5] Symbol systems in which the cathectic function has

---

[3] This may of course involve broadening the criteria of "sameness" so that the various
orientations of different actors to one system of symbols may all be classified as following
one "manner of orientation."

[4] We have said that symbols are ways of orienting controlled by external physical
objects. Now, just as a single orientation may be primarily cathectic, evaluative, or
cognitive (as in the case where a person is "merely considering a fact" which has very
little motivational importance), so also may a *way* of orienting (a cultural object) be
characterized by the primacy of such modes.

[5] Beliefs, since they are primarily cognitive, always relate the individual to his environment. Thus they are all existential (even mathematics and logic provide concepts and rules
for assertion of existential propositions). On the other hand, existential beliefs may be

primacy may be called "expressive" symbols. As compared with cognitive symbols the primary reference of the orientations involved in cathectic symbols is more inward toward the affective state which accompanies the orientation than outward toward the properties of the object oriented to.[6] The object is significant as the occasion of the affective state in question and cognition of its properties is subordinated in this context. Symbol systems in which the evaluative function has primacy may be called "normative ideas" or "regulatory symbols." They are the standards of value-orientation or the value-orientation modes about which we have said so much. In a moment, we will see that these evaluative standards themselves can be subclassified into cognitive, appreciative, and moral standards. First, we must clarify briefly the distinction between the classification of symbols into cognitive symbols, expressive symbols, and value standards; and the classification of the standards themselves into cognitive, appreciative and moral standards.

We have already said that symbols are ways of orienting which are embodied in or controlled by the external symbolic objects. It is roughly true, now, to state the following equivalencies: (1) Systems of cognitive symbols (beliefs) are ways of cognizing, these ways being controlled by the external symbolic objects. (2) Systems of expressive symbols are ways of cathecting (similarly controlled by symbolic objects). (3) Systems of value-orientation standards are ways of evaluating (also controlled by symbolic objects); that is, ways of solving conflicts between various units. Thus they can be ways for solving conflicts between various beliefs, between various cathexes (or wants), and between various evaluative mechanisms.

It is immediately apparent, therefore, that the third type of symbols (the evaluative ones), which have been called the value-orientation standards, *can* be subclassified again on the basis of the cognitive-cathectic-evaluative distinction. Thus, the evaluative symbols which outline ways of solving cognitive problems are cognitive standards; those which outline ways of solving cathectic problems are appreciative standards; and those which outline ways of handling purely evaluative problems are moral standards.

The three types of systems of value standards, it must be noted, are all systems of evaluative *symbols*. And thus they are to be distinguished from systems of cognitive symbols and of expressive symbols. For example, a single belief may be a part of a system of cognitive symbols, but it is not necessarily part of a system of cognitive standards. A criterion of truth, on the other hand, on the basis of which the belief may be judged true or false, is a *cognitive standard* (and thus an evaluative symbol).

---

empirical or nonempirical, depending on whether or not they are amenable to the verification procedures of modern science.

[6] Systems of expressive symbols will often be fused with elaborate systems of ideas, so that as a result aesthetic experience and criticism will often have a very profound outward tendency. The ultimate criterion remains, however, the actor's sense of fitness, appropriateness, or beauty.

It seems to us that these standards, which we have variously called patterns of *value-orientation, normative ideas,* and *evaluative symbols,* are symbols of a somewhat different type from the cognitive and expressive symbols. This is perhaps because they are ways the actor has of orienting to (and acting with respect to) his own orientations, rather than ways of orienting to objects outside alone.

Let us discuss for a moment the complex (and still poorly understood) differences between the standards and the other classes of symbols. In the first place, they all seem to represent in some fashion a synthesis of cognitive and cathectic elements. Objects *cognized* are *evaluated* in terms of whether or not they will help the actor get what he *wants.* Thus, in this sense, a cognition cannot be evaluated except insofar as its long-run cathectic consequences are taken into account. Similarly, a cathexis cannot be evaluated except insofar as the object cathected is cognized in its patterned relationships to other cathected objects.

In other words, when a particular cathectic component is *evaluated,* its implications must first be developed. It must be synthesized into a wider cognitive structure, and then the balance of cathectic attachment to the whole set or system of implications may be discovered. This is cathectic evaluation. Similarly, when a particular cognized object or fact is to be evaluated, its cathectic implications must be developed. One must, in a certain sense, find out whether a *fact* may be *cathected* as a truly instrumental means to some ulterior goal, before one can evaluate it as true or false.

In both of these cases of evaluation, therefore, the actor has a commitment to orient himself in terms of *a balance* of consequences and implications rather than being free to orient himself to the particular cultural symbol on its immediate and intrinsic merits. Thus his orientation to a particular complex of symbols must conform with the imperatives of the larger system of normative orientation of which it is a part. Otherwise, the normative system becomes disorganized.

It is, indeed, in the evaluative synthesis of cognitive and cathectic modes of orientation that the major lines of the patterns of value-orientation of a system of action emerge. This source of patterns of value-orientation helps to explain their particularly strategic significance in action. But it also helps to explain their relative lack of functional independence. The cognitive reference connects the orientation with the object world, particularly with respect to the anticipation of consequences, which flow from actual commitments to action and which might flow from hypothetical courses, which, because of these anticipated consequences, may indeed be rejected as alternatives in the situation of choice. The cognitive orientation provides one of the bases of the range of freedom which we have called choice, and of which one of the most important aspects is the choice among alternatives in time. There is also the cathectic dimension, which has its meaning in terms of gratification-deprivation. Alternatives are selected with respect to their different consequences for the actor on this level. Value-orientations become organized into systems of generalized, normative patterns which require consistency of cognitive-cathectic and consequently evaluative orientation from one particular situation to another.

Value-orientations elaborated into cultural patterns possess (in their categorial organizations) the potentiality of becoming the common values of the members of a collectivity. Concretely, value-orientations are overwhelmingly involved in processes of social interaction. For this reason consistency of normative orientation cannot be confined to one actor in his action in different situations and at different times; there must also be integration on an interindividual level. Rules, that is, must be generalized in a manner to apply to all actors in the relevant situations in the interaction system. This is an elementary prerequisite of social order. On a psychological level, systems of symbols may have cognitive or cathectic primacy in their relation to particular actions of individuals. Where they are constitutive of the role-expectation systems of a social system, however, they *must* necessarily involve an evaluative primacy, since roles must be organized relative to alternatives of time and situation. It does not follow that systems of cognitive symbols and of expressive symbols do not have functional significance. But there is a sense in which ideas and expressive symbols branch off from the trunk of the ramifying tree of action lower down than do the modes of value-orientation themselves.

Ideas, evaluative standards, and expressive symbols, respectively, can become the primary foci of orientation of certain types of *concrete action.* Action where cognitive beliefs have primacy in relation to the attainment of a given goal may be called *instrumental action.* Action where expressive symbols have primacy will be called *expressive action.* Where evaluative standards have primacy (and where there is usually a concern for the gratification of other actors) the action will be called *moral action.* Instrumental actions are subsidiary in the sense that the desirability of the goal is given by patterns of value-orientation, as is the assessment of cost which is felt to be worth while to pay for its realization (i.e., the sacrifice of potential, alternative goals). But *given* the goal and the assessment of the permissible sacrifice, the problem of action is instrumental, and is to be solved in accordance with given standards of efficiency. It becomes a question of what the situation *is*, and this is answerable in cognitive terms. Thus the cultural element in instrumental action consists solely of beliefs, or ideas. *Skills* constitute the integration of these ideas with the motivational and physiological capacities of individual actors. The ideas which enter into the skill have been internalized.

The category of instrumental actions is a very broad one indeed. It includes the cultural aspects not only of the skills ordinarily used in a utilitarian context but at least a large component of those employed in the expressive field, as in ritual and art. It also applies in such basic general activities as the use of language, which is, of course, not exhausted by it. The essential criterion is subordination of action in a particular situation to a *given* goal.

Expressive orientations of action are concerned not with goals beyond the immediate action context but with organized gratifications in relation to cathected objects. The element of normative ordering to which this gratification process is subjected in a culture is the manifestation of appreciative standards of value-orientation. These appreciative standards have the same function of furthering the generalized consistency of behavior in this field as cognitive standards perform in the instrumental field. The normative regulation of religious ritual or of artistic style are familiar examples.

The focus of moral value standards is, as we have asserted previously, on the integration of a larger system of action. Moral standards set the limits of the permissible costs of an expressive gratification or an instrumental achievement — by referring to the consequences of such action for the other parts of the system and for the system as a whole.

The basic components of the structure of culture may be classified as follows. (This analysis is based on the modes of orientation as these were given in Chapter I.)

(1) *Types of Cultural Symbol Systems.*[7] (*a*) Systems of ideas (cognitive primacy). (*b*) Systems of expressive symbols (cathectic primacy). (*c*) Systems of standards of value-orientation (evaluative primacy).

(2) *Types of Standards of Value-Orientation.* (*a*) Cognitive. (*b*) Appreciative. (*c*) Moral. .

(3) *Types of Orientation of Action.* (*a*) Instrumental: here, expressive and moral problems are treated by the actor as solved, and the primary focus of attention is on cognitive problems which must be solved by reference to cognitive standards. Thus the problem is one of discovering the most efficient means vis-à-vis a *given* goal, subject to *given* moral rules. (*b*) Expressive: here, cognitive and moral problems are treated as solved (the actor knows what the situation is, and he knows which actions are "good" in this situation), and the primary focus of attention is on cathectic problems which must be solved by reference to appreciative standards. Thus the problem is one of discovering whether or not it is appropriate for the actor to want or "like" a given cognized object, after it has already been determined that there is no moral reason why the object should be either liked or disliked. (*c*) Moral: here, cognitive and cathectic problems are treated as solved (the actor knows what he sees, and he knows what he wants), and the primary focus of attention is on evaluative problems which must be solved by reference to moral standards. Thus the problem is one of discovering whether or nor it is *right* (in the light of the norms expressing the values of the system of action as a

---

[7] A good deal of confusion in the analysis of culture has arisen from failure to distinguish these three major aspects of culture.

whole) for an actor to adopt a certain course of action whose outcome is both known and wanted.

This is an *analytical* classification. In concrete cultural phenomena, many combinations and nuances are possible. The fact that by no means every empirical case can be put neatly into one and only one category of an analytical classification will not be a valid objection to the classification itself.

From the point of view of comparative cultural analysis, which is our primary interest here, an especially great significance rests with the category of cognitive orientation or, more specifically, existential beliefs. This is because systems of beliefs constitute in the nature of the case a generalizing, systematizing, organizing component of systems of action.

COGNITIVE SYMBOLS

Existential ideas are an integral part of the *system* of culture which in turn is an integral part of action systems. They are therefore in principle interdependent with all the other elements of action. A concrete system of ideas, therefore, is a *resultant* of this interdependence. Even science is not simply a reflection of reality,[8] but is a selective system of cognitive orientations to reality — to parts or aspects of the situation of action.

The cognitive element has special significance for the integration and consistency of a cultural system as well as for the adaptation of action to the exigencies of the situation. This is perhaps particularly true of the nonempirical aspects (those aspects not testable by modern, scientific methods of verification) of the system of existential ideas. As compared with empirical ideas, the nonempirical ones are less controlled by the process of verification. Choices among the cognitive possibilities are therefore less subject to control by the immediate consequence of action in the situation. They enjoy therefore a greater range of freedom. The question, "Is it a fact?" cannot so readily be given a definite answer. The larger measure of freedom permits more flexible adaptation and therefore a more harmonious relationship with other elements in the cultural system.

There are many reasons why noncognitive interests are often particularly pressing in many spheres in which empirical cognitive orientations cannot operate. In the areas which Max Weber called the "problems of meaning," [9] cognitive answers are required which cannot be conclusively demonstrated by empirical means. Thus, why rewards and deprivations should be so unevenly distributed among men, and what the relation of this distribution to their "deserts" may be, are not questions satisfactorily answerable in scientific terms. Whatever the ultimate state of knowledge may turn out to be, at any

[8] It is worth noting here that "facts" are not "realities" but *statements* about reality. They may be "true" and yet highly selective in relation to any conception of the "total reality."

[9] The word "meaning" here has a somewhat teleological import. It refers to the desire on the part of human beings to know why things ought to be one way or another.

given stage of the advancement of knowledge, there is always a range of cognitive problems which are vital to human beings but which cannot be authoritatively answered by science. Hence, because of their great importance in reconciling normative expectations and actual responses (rewards and allocations) *common* orientation through nonempirical ideas has great significance for the social system.

Various possibilities of disequilibrium arise from the fact that these nonempirical ideas are not always common to all the members of a collectivity (as they need to be in order to maintain stability). It is, in fact, more difficult to get common acceptance in this area owing to the relatively greater indeterminacy of the answers to nonempirical cognitive problems. However, these possibilities of disequilibrium are reduced by the intervention of noncognitive mechanisms in the "enforcement" of uniformity and stability in beliefs. These mechanisms are of two major types, "traditionalism" and authoritative or administrative enforcement. At the same time the functional necessity of resort to such mechanisms of control creates strains since in a system of cognitive values it is inherent that the ultimate criteria of truth should be cognitive, not traditional or authoritarian.

Systems of beliefs, or cognitive orientations relate the actor to his situation. Hence the classification of the elements of the situation, of the different types of object, should provide a set of invariant points of reference for the classification of the most important ranges of variation of systems of ideas. The classification set forth in Fig. 6 (page 254) may be used for this purpose. We have recurrently emphasized that the most important distinction is that between social and nonsocial objects. Here, however, the distinction between physical and cultural objects within the category of the nonsocial objects is also highly important. Hence the invariant points of reference of the cognitive orientations may be classified in four categories as follows: (1) *Persons* constitute one invariant point of reference. Although it is essential, in the analysis of action, to discriminate between ego as actor and alter as actor, in the analysis of systems of belief this distinction may be disregarded. A unified cultural tradition will not maintain fundamentally different sets of beliefs about the ways in which human beings act and hence they will not need to distinguish between ego and alter. They must accordingly be classed together in the cognitive orientation system as persons or human beings. Otherwise, without these common beliefs about human action, complementarity of orientation would not be possible. This sector of the cognitive orientation system of a culture may be called its *conception of human nature*. (2) The *collectivity* as an object is another invariant point of reference, whether or not ego is one of its members. The collectivity figures as an object of central importance in political and economic ideologies; for example, "capitalism" or "socialism." (3) From this we must distinguish cognitive orientations toward physical objects (including organisms) and their connections in systems and subsystems. In the Western world we ordinarily call this *nature*. (4) Finally the cultural tradition itself, the tradition of the society in question and of others of which knowledge is current,[10] will be the object of cultural orientations.

The question of the ranges of variation of cognitive orientations with respect to each of these classes of situational objects is complex and cannot be systematically explored here. Only a few suggestions may be made. First, the primacy of cognitive interests in relation to systems of belief means that the grounds of validity of beliefs are always a crucially important problem. Hence the "epistemology" which is always implicit, if not explicit, in a cultural tradition constitutes a highly significant set of problems with respect to which variant beliefs may be held. Second, the problem of the "meaning" of the phenomena in each of these categories, as they are cognized in the culture in question, will always be crucial. We refer here to the conceptions of their bearing on human interests and goals, and specifically the interests and goals of the actors in the society which incorporates the culture. The problem of meaning, as can be seen, is inevitably and intricately bound up with the gratification-deprivation balance. Hence it contains a judgment of objects on the basis of their relative favorableness or unfavorableness to what are conceived as the worth-while human goals and interests. Nature, for instance, may be thought of as compliant or resistant in its relation to human goals.

Finally, there must be an over-all integration of a culture's system of ideas or beliefs which may be more or less explicitly worked out in cognitive terms. This will include, so far as it is explicit, a set of beliefs about man's relation to time and the ordering of his actions in time and to the nonempirical grounds of the world in general. This is essentially the cosmology of the culture, its way of looking at the universe and life, which is the primary cognitive foundation of the "ethos" of the culture. It is not possible to go further at present. But the next step would be to attempt to approach the problem of working out a typology of cognitive orientation systems.

Expressive Symbols

Systems of expressive symbols also may be differentiated according to the classes of objects in relation to which they organize the actors' cathexes. Following the above classification of objects, we may distinguish (1) the appreciative symbolization of responses to nature, such as landscape art and appreciation; (2) the appreciative organization of responses to human personalities, for example the conception of the admirable or beautiful person; (3) the appreciative organization of responses to collectivities, for instance

[10] This classification of the principal foci of cognitive orientation resembles in some respects and is indebted to Dr. Florence Kluckhohn's, in her "Dominant and Substitute Profiles of Cultural Orientations: Their Significance for the Analysis of Social Stratification," *Social Forces*, May 1950.

a conception of "good company"; (4) the appreciative orientation to cultural objects, for example, a poem or a mathematical demonstration.[11]

EVALUATIVE SYMBOLS

A system of evaluative symbols comprises: (1) a subsystem of standards for solving cognitive problems, (2) a subsystem of standards for solving cathectic or appreciative problems, and (3) a subsystem of "moral" standards for the over-all integration of the various units of the system, the various processes of the system, and the various other standards involved into a single unified system. These are collectivity-oriented or self-oriented moral values, depending on whether the system to which they have reference is a collectivity or a personality. Thus, the evaluative symbols, which are the value standards, can be subclassified, as we have said, as cognitive, appreciative, and moral. The moral standards may be considered to represent the superordinate integrative techniques of a system of action (whether they are collectivity-oriented or self-oriented). In another sense, they are ways of combining all the other ingredients of action, or recipes for the arrangement of the elements or aspects that make up concrete orientations.

The moral value standards, as we can see, are diffuse patterns of value-orientation. They are organizers which define and integrate whole systems of action (and also many subsystems). These patterns are, above all else, classifiable in terms of the pattern variables. Thus, we might say, we have thirty-two cells for the subclassification (or categorization) of the moral standards, the number of cells deriving from the cross-classification of the five pattern variables. The strategic place of the pattern variables in the analysis of action derives from the fact that they present a very general set of categories which comprise all the possible ways of relating the personality processes of cognizing, cathecting, and evaluating, with cultural standards on the one hand and social objects on the other. Thus they give us a typology, in some sense, of the moral value possibilities.[12]

---

[11] These classes of objects are likewise subject, in all cultural traditions, to evaluations which are elaborated systems of value-orientation. Thus there will be (1) normative or moral judgments which organize responses toward environmental objects (e.g., judgments of the benevolence or hostility of nature towards the realization of human ends). There will be (2) normative or moral judgments which govern responses toward personalities as systems or toward segments of personalities; these are expressed in the value-orientations which define and prescribe the good or virtuous man, or the good or virtuous action. There will be (3) normative or moral judgments governing responses toward collectivities; these judgments are expressed in conceptions of the good society or the ideal commonwealth and in prescriptions of the right social policy. Finally (4) normative or moral judgments will organize our responses toward cultural objects. Among these judgments will be found those which evaluate the goodness of the pursuit of truth in the economy of human life, or which judge the moral status of aesthetic or expressive activities.

[12] The pattern variables do seem to define, above all, ways of integrating all the ingredients of action into systems. Thus they present a classification of the moral value standards of persons and collectivities. On the other hand, the moral standards of a culture,

We shall begin the analysis of the systems of moral standards by calling attention to a certain congruence with the functional problems of systems of action. This congruence resides in the fact that there is a certain range of *problems* of orientation which are inherent in the structure of systems of action and that an orientation to each of the problems is a functional imperative of action. These are problems which are produced by the very nature of action — by the very nature of orientations to objects — and particular moral values may be regarded as pragmatic solutions of these problems. Since the problems have a determinate form arising from the nature of action, the number and logical relations of the types of alternative solutions is also determinate. Each of the pattern variables states a set of possibilities of selective response to the alternatives presented by the situation of action. We have enumerated five such pattern variables and we have given reasons for believing that it is legitimate to consider them an exhaustive set. The exhaustive character of the classification of pattern variables has far-reaching implications for the analysis of systems of moral standards; it provides a determinate range of variability and it allows only a number of combinations of alternatives which — on this level of generality at least — is sufficiently small to permit analysis with the resources we possess at present. There has been a tendency, under the impact of insight into the wider range of differences among cultures to think, implicitly at least, of a limitlessly pluralistic value-universe. In its extreme form, the proponents of this view have even asserted that every moral standard is necessarily unique. There is much aesthetic sensibility underlying and justifying this contention, but it is neither convincing logically nor fruitful scientifically. If carried to its logical conclusions, it denies the possibility of systematic analysis of cultural values.

In fact, of course, all patterns of moral standards are interdependent with all the other factors which operate in the determination of action. They will, as systems, inevitably fall short of "perfect integration" *which in the case of cultural pattern systems must be interpreted to mean consistency of pattern.* At the same time the imperative of approximating consistency of pattern arising from the need to minimize the strain of conflict within a system of action is so strong that it is improbable that the actual ranges of variation of systems of moral standards will coincide with the range of possible combinations of orientations to different classes of objects.

Moral standards are not logical deductions from systems of beliefs or manifestations of systems of expressive symbols, nor do they derive from

---

which govern the integration of the other standards (and particular moral standards themselves) into action systems, color the other standards (and the other symbols and need-dispositions, too, for that matter). That is, cognitive and cathectic standards tend to differ depending on the kind of moral standards which control their integration into action. Therefore, the pattern variables can be seen as presenting a typology of all evaluative symbols (of all value-orientation patterns) owing to the fact that they primarily present a classification of various types of moral standards.

cognitive or appreciative standards. They depend in part on such systems, but they draw on all the elements of cognitive, cathectic, and evaluative selection from the alternatives of action. The important alternatives (which define the problems of action) emerge for the actor only when he, armed with his cognitive and cathectic symbols and standards, directly confronts the relevant situation with all its functional exigencies. As he develops general methods for making choices among these alternatives, he thereby gains a new set of superordinate standards. These are moral value standards.

The pattern variables are crucial here because they *are* the alternatives of action and provide the problems of the actor, the problems which are solved by reference to moral standards. These problems of action are (1) the basis of choice (or treatment) of the object to which an orientation applies (ascription-achievement), (2) the appropriateness or inappropriateness of immediate gratification through expressive action in the particular context (effectivity-neutrality), (3) the scope of interest in and obligation toward the object (specificity-diffuseness), (4) the type of norm governing the orientation toward it (universalism-particularism) and (5) the relevance or irrelevance of collective obligations in the immediate context (self-collective orientation).

Whatever may prove to be the most useful way of classifying the elements and types of systems of moral standards the resultant classification will enumerate those choices among pattern-variable alternatives to which, in the context of commitments to action, they predispose the actor.

A concrete orientation of action cannot be confronted just by any one or two of these pairs of alternatives; it must explicitly or implicitly confront all five and accept commitments in all five directions. If the pattern variables are to be used to characterize concrete systems of moral standards, rather than specially abstracted aspects of them, all five variables must be explicitly included. The consistency of pattern of such a system will exist to the extent to which the same combination of value judgments formulated in these terms runs consistently throughout the actors' responses to different situations; that is, to different classes of objects, different objects in the same class, and the same objects on different occasions. A type of moral system then will be characterized by the *dominance* in all major types of situation of a particular pattern-variable combination, that is, the content of a cell or group of cells in, for instance, Figs. 3 and 4 (Chapter I), or a particular *integration* of two or more such combinations of the values of pattern variables.

PATTERN CONSISTENCY AND SOURCES OF STRAIN

Complete consistency of pattern is an ideal type. The moral standards which are actually held and acted upon by a concrete personality or social system cannot possess complete consistency of pattern; it is indeed probable that complete empirical pattern consistency is impossible. The inconsistency of pattern which we frequently observe is engendered by the adjustive problems which arise from the difficulties of articulation of value-orientation systems with personality or social systems. It is an empirical problem, growing up from the relation between cultural systems and systems of action and from the coexistence of a plurality of cultural subsystems in the same society or personality.

The evaluation of all the strategically significant categories of the object world is a *functional imperative* of a system of moral standards. It is imposed by the nature of human action. Another principal imperative, which is not necessarily harmonious with the first, is the maximization of the consistency of pattern.[13]

Evaluative orientation confronts situational events which may be both "reinterpreted" and creatively transformed, but only within limits. The recalcitrance of events, particularly the foci of man's organic nature and the scarcity of means or resources, imposes certain functional imperatives on action. There is no necessity, and certainly little likelihood, that all the facts of a situation which in a pragmatic sense must be faced can be dealt with by the actor in accordance with all the canons of a given value system. The various value systems will be differentially selective as to which facts fit and which do not, and how well or how badly, but there will always be some facts [14] that will be *problematical* for every value system. They can be dealt with only on the basis of standards that will be inconsistent with the principal standards of the actor, whatever these may be.

In one sense the *facts* of the system of social objects are more malleable than the other classes. They are, to an important degree, themselves a product of the cultural system prevailing in the action system. Thus both a man and a society *are* in some measure what they believe. A favorable response from alter never strains ego's own values; the interacting plurality of individuals which share common values therefore stands in a sense united in defense against threats to those values. However, there are definite limits to the effectiveness of such common defense if the values in question conflict seriously with functional imperatives of systems of action, which must be dealt

---

[13] Systems of action are functional systems; cultural systems are symbolic systems in which the components have logical or meaningful rather than functional relationships with one another. Hence the imperatives which are characteristic of the two classes of systems are different. In systems of action the imperatives which impose certain adaptations on the components result from the empirical possibilities or necessities of coexistence which we designate *as scarcity*, and from the properties of the actor as an organism; in cultural systems the internal imperatives are independent of the compatibilities or incompatibilities of coexistence. In cultural systems the systemic feature is *coherence*; the components of the cultural system are either *logically consistent* or meaningfully *congruous*.

[14] *Problematical* facts in the present sense are those which it is functionally imperative to face and which necessitate reactions with value implications incompatible with the actor's paramount value system.

with. *Some* of these functional imperatives make it most improbable that the actual concrete structure of *any* concrete action system will permit the realization of full consistency of the various parts of *any* value system. There must therefore be some sort of adjustment or accommodation between them. One mode of adjustment is the tendency to "force" the structure of the system of social objects into conformity with the value system, at the cost of increased strain. Another mode of adjustment is to tolerate and in varying degrees to institutionalize into the social system or to internalize in the personality system value patterns which are not in harmony with the major emphases of the dominant value system. The inconsistencies of value patterns are intra-individually adjusted through the mechanisms of defense, and interindividually adjusted through such social control mechanisms as isolation and segregation.

It is impossible for a functionally important sector of the social system to be organized and stabilized without some degree of institutionalization, and for a correspondingly important sector of the personality to be organized and stabilized without internalization of values. In those sectors of the system of action which are out of harmony with the dominant value-system, "adaptive institutionalization" will tend to occur. There will be a special mode of integration into the action system of that sector of the value-orientation system which is more or less in conflict with the main value-orientation system and its related institutions. There will consequently exist more or less fully institutionalized value-patterns, at variance with the paramount value system; these are "endemic" in the social system, and on occasion may become important foci for structural change.

An example may be drawn from American social structure. In our value system the "individualistic achievement complex" is dominant. It is most fully institutionalized in the occupational system, but penetrates very far into the rest of society. One of the systems, however, in which it is most difficult to institutionalize is kinship, since occupation is predominantly universalistic, specific, and oriented toward achievement, while kinship is much more particularistic, diffuse, and necessarily contains elements of ascription. Although our kinship system is less incompatible with the complex of individualistic achievement than are most, there still remains a significant amount of strain between the dominant value-orientations and that contained in the kinship system. The balance between them is consequently not always stable. Occasionally, the type of value-orientation characteristic of kinship may become dominant; for example, in situations in which kinship or ethnic group membership becomes the decisive criterion in allocation of roles and rewards.

Where this order of strain exists, the accommodation will often be facilitated by "rationalization" or ideological "masking" of the conflict. This reduces awareness of the existence of a conflict and its extent and ramifications. Mechanisms of defense in the personality and mechanism of social control in the social system operate in these areas of strain to bring the system into equilibrium. Their inadequacy to reëstablish such an equilibrium constitutes a source of change.

Inconsistencies within the value system result in strain in the system of action, personal and social. Such inconsistencies often originate through historical circumstances which resulted in exposure to inconsistent value-orientation patterns so that two or more sets may have been internalized or institutionalized in some sector of the system. This source of strain, however, can only add to the original sources of strain inherent in the nature of systems of action. This original source of strain lies in the fact that *no* fully integrated internally consistent system of value-orientation can be adequate to the functional needs of any concrete system of action. Given the inevitability of strain, there must therefore be adaptive value-integrations in the sectors in which the dominant value-integration is least adequate and which compensate for these inadequacies. Were it not for this basis of malintegration in the nature of action in a system, historical malintegrations would certainly not be either severe or persistent.

Alongside the tendency for inconsistencies in the value system to engender strains in the system of action and vice versa, there is a tendency of systems of action to build up and maintain levels of consistency as high as the exigencies of action will permit. The basis of this tendency rests in the functional need for order which underlies *any* action system, and which entails the need for integration of its cultural components. The need for order is seen in its simplest and most elementary form in the complementarity of role expectations. Without stability and consequently predictability, which is the essence of order, ego and alter could not respond to one another's expectations in a mutually gratifying way. Correspondingly the need-dispositions within a personality system must be organized into a stable pattern as a condition of avoiding frustration and holding down anxiety. The recognition of this need for order in systems of action is the central reason for our introduction of evaluation as one of the few most fundamental categories. The fundamental need for order in a system is the root of the strain which appears when an inconsistent value system is translated into action.

In relatively stable systems of action there are then the two tendencies to build consistent systems of value-orientation and the contrary tendency to generate and to tolerate inconsistent subsystems with the strain which they produce. There will be a delicate dynamic equilibrium between the two maintained by a wide variety of accommodating mechanisms. Empirically the value-orientation is not autonomous except in the sense that it may be treated as an independent variable, interdependent with other variables in a system. Among the basic components of an action system, there is no causal priority of any factor as the initiator of change. Change may come from any source in the system. The outcome will depend on the balance of forces in the system at the time.

THE INTEGRATION OF SYSTEMS OF VALUE-ORIENTATIONS
IN THE SOCIAL SYSTEM

Although a set of *dominant themes* or an *ethos* may be preëminent in the concrete value system prevailing in a given society, still there will in addition be many lesser themes representing some or all of the possible pattern-variable combinations to be found in it. They will have functions homologous to the adjustive mechanisms of the personality (see Chapter II). For this reason, the "emanationist" hypothesis which asserts that action is simply a consequence of the prevailing value system cannot be accepted. A further deficiency of this view is its assertion that all sectors of the value system are explicable by logical derivation from the central themes or premises. It is on this account that it is necessary to conceive of both a *functional integration* of value-orientations and a *pattern integration*. The latter refers to the extent to which a given pattern or theme of orientation is *consistently* manifested in the specific evaluative attitudes of the actors throughout the social system. Functional integration refers to the integration of values with systems of action and it therefore involves priorities and allocations of diverse value components among proper occasions and relationships. This is one of the principal aspects of the structure of social systems, and it is by these mechanisms that standards which are not integrated with respect to their patterns are brought into a measure of functional integration sufficient to allow the social system to operate.

If we examine the list of pattern variables and the list of components of a society described in Chapter II and Fig. 9, we will see that each possible variant of the value patterns will find a situation in which it has primacy. In general, without some affective expression no personality and hence no society could function, but neither could it function without the institutionalization of discipline over otherwise spontaneous affective expression. Conversely, the complete absorption of personality, or of subgroup interest into the larger collectivity, would involve a rigidity of social control incompatible with the functional conditions of a society as well as with the inevitable need of human beings for some expressive spontaneity. Some amount of subordination of private interests or expression remains, however, indispensable for the operation of a society. Particularistic ties and solidarities, such as those of kinship, are found in every society, but at the same time universalistic criteria of skill, efficiency, and classificatory qualities are never entirely ignored by any of these societies. Certain ascriptive qualities of social objects are given and are not and cannot be subordinated in all situations to performances, but performance is so crucial in some situations for all societies that ascriptive qualities do not and cannot always take precedence. The segregation of certain significance-contexts of objects such as the instrumental seems to be essential at times, but many social relationships are of such a character that the diffuse type of significance — for instance, in a parent-child relation — also inevitably develops.

The functional imperatives (which arise from the nature of the organism and the pressures of scarcity of time, opportunity and resources in the object situation) are unevenly distributed within any given social system. The kinship cluster imposes a strong tendency toward particularistic, diffuse, and ascriptive commitments. The nature of the personality system and the nature of the roles of the child-parent relationship make affective expression more likely in the kinship situation than elsewhere. Hence there is an irreducible minimum of commitments to that combination of pattern variables within the kinship sphere. At the same time, however, beyond this irreducible minimum, values institutionalized in the actual role structure of kinship systems may vary very considerably, in accordance with the value-orientations dominant throughout the society. Thus classical Chinese kinship has a strong preponderance of particularistic emphasis, placing kinship loyalties very high in the general priority scale of social values. The American kinship system, on the other hand, while granting a place to particularistic commitments, tends to restrict them even within kinship. It tends, as far as possible, to accept a commitment to reward universalistically judged classificatory qualities, such as intelligence and the kinds of performances which are assessed by universalistic criteria rather than particularistically judged qualities such as blood ties. Even obligation to a parent comes to be measured to a considerable degree by the extent to which the parent is considered "worthy" in universalistic terms. For example, the definition of a son's gratitude and hence his obligation toward his mother, is based less on the biological *fact* of the relationship than on her services and attitudes on his behalf.

Integration, both within an individual's value system and within the value system prevailing in a society is a compromise between the functional imperatives of the situation and the dominant value-orientation patterns of the society. Every society is of necessity shot through with such compromises. Therefore it may be well briefly to review the main elements of such a value system insofar as they are relevant to integration of different value patterns within the social system.

The leading element in the real interindividual or systemic integration is the major value-orientation pattern dominant in the system (*ethos*). The basic standards of the social system are, as we have seen, characterized by the two variables of universalism-particularism and ascription-achievement. Each of the four basic types will be further differentiated by admixtures of elements from the other three types. The second element is the suborientations, which are described by the combinations of the two basic pattern variables with the other three. Thirdly, there are adaptive value-orientations such as authoritarianism, traditionalism, and so forth, which often come to play a part in the concrete value system.

The ethos will tend to be relatively fully institutionalized in some sectors of the social system, less fully in others, and not at all in still others. The main mechanism of accommodation is the *priority scale* which is implicit in the existence of a *dominant* value-orientation. This may vary in character from the prescription of a rather loose hierarchy to the virtual exclusion of any alternative values; in extremely authoritarian cultures, for example, evaluations which are in any way critical of authority are suppressed. Short of this extreme there will be various degrees of tolerance toward alternative value patterns.

Allocation of conflicting standards between different sectors of the social system is another of the mechanisms of accommodation. Values which are not consistent with the dominant ethos may be confined to special contexts and roles. Thus even in a highly universalistic system, particularism may still be sanctioned in kinship and friendship. Affective expression will be allowed a place even though the general trend toward discipline is dominant. Such allocated subvalues are usually integrated in a certain way with the main system. Their position is not merely permitted; conformity with them is often enjoined upon those in the relevant roles.

Freedom is another of the mechanisms of accommodation of unintegrated patterns of moral standards. Varying widely in scope and distribution within different societies, spheres exist within which persons or collectivities may act freely within limits. The area of freedom in this sense is not necessarily identical with the area of self-orientation in the *institutionalized* pattern-variable sense. In the area of self-orientation there may be, apart from direct obligations to a collectivity or to several collectivities including the society as a whole, an obligation to act autonomously, which may entail an obligation to pursue certain types of private self-interest. The particular content of the actions in such cases is not institutionally prescribed, but some important elements of the choice may be; for example, self-interest and universalism. Even there however the specific content of the goals to be pursued by self-interest might be limited by expectations of pecuniary gain and the procedures will be limited too by the prohibition of violence. Freedom, however, need not entail so much prescription, and may accordingly allow more tolerance. There is, for example, no approval in the current American ethos for certain ethnic value patterns, such as the immanent-perfection ideal of the Spanish Americans. Within limits, however, tolerance is institutionalized in America so that usually there is felt to be an obligation to allow a minority to live its own life, although its principal value patterns do not conform with those of the dominant sector of the society. Similarly, some of the values held among the intelligentsia in Western society since the French Revolution have deviated widely from the prevailing ethos, but the mechanism of toleration has held in check what under other conditions would have been severe conflict and repression.

Openly tolerated patterns of divergence from the ethos shade into those which are not tolerated and which, if they exist at all, have to be protected by a mechanism of withdrawal or isolation. There are certain activities and their associated values which manage to exist alongside the prevailing ethos by the operation of the mechanisms of withdrawal or isolation which separate the bearers of the divergent value-orientations from one another, thus reducing the possibility of conflict. In most social systems considerable sections of the borderline between conformity and deviance are indistinct. This has great functional significance. The ambiguity of the standards or expectations and the legitimately divergent interpretability may also allow diverse value patterns to coexist by holding frustration and conflict in restraint.

The functional inevitability of imperfections of value integration in the social system does not, as we have seen, necessarily destroy the social system, because a set of mechanisms, which are homologous with the mechanisms of defense in the personality, limit the disintegratedness and confine its repercussions. These mechanisms render possible the continued operation of the social system; that is, the interdependent coexistence of the various parts of the system. These mechanisms moreover may even render possible a measure of limited collaboration between the sectors of the society committed in other respects to incompatible values. Just as in the personality certain defense mechanisms keep dangerous impulses below the level of consciousness, thus keeping down the level of anxiety and conflict, so in the social system certain accommodative mechanisms permit contradictory patterns to coexist by allocating them to different situations and groups within the society. The extreme rationalist or the doctrinaire who takes a system of institutionalized values as something to be rigorously and consistently applied in all situations can for this reason be a seriously disturbing influence in a social system.

Social systems and especially large-scale societies are inescapably caught in a very fundamental dilemma. On the one hand they can only live by a system of institutionalized values, to which the members must be seriously committed and to which they must adhere in their actions. On the other hand, they must be able to accept compromises and accommodations, tolerating many actions which from the point of view of their own dominant values are wrong. Their failure to do so precipitates rebellion and withdrawal and endangers the continuation of the system even at the level of integration which it has hitherto achieved. In this paradox lies a principal source of strain and instability in social systems, and many of the most important seeds of social change.[15]

[15] At the same time this situation is, from the theoretical point of view, the main reason for refusing to regard the problems of the integration of systems of cultural value-orientations and of social systems as homologous. It is also the predominant reason why the type of analysis of value-orientation associated particularly with the name of the late Ruth Benedict cannot serve as the sole or even primary basis for an analysis of the dynamic processes of the social system.

Systems of Personal Values

We have been considering largely the integration of moral standards into social systems. It is equally relevant to examine some of the problems arising in connection with the integration of these standards into the personality system. In certain respects, the considerations which were relevant above are equally valid here. It is in the combinations of the values of the pattern variables that variability of moral values is to be sought. The system of moral standards of the individual actor will have its elements of consistency and inconsistency, developing from the history of the individual personality, from its genetic processes of development, and from the various influences to which it has been exposed in its course. Where there is imperfect integration of pattern, as to some degree there always must be, there will also be strain, which can within the limits imposed by the nature of the inconsistency be ameliorated by the mechanisms of defense.

The relation between social and personal systems of values cannot, however, be wholly symmetrical. We have seen that culture as a system of symbolic meanings inherently embodies the generalized or interpersonalized aspects of the organization of action. What is commonly referred to as a culture cannot therefore be limited to the sector incorporated in a single personality. The latter is in some sense a particularized variant of emphases and selections from the major combination of themes which in the social system is generalized for many personalities. The culture of a personality, so far as it is more than a microcosm of a set of generalized patterns, is a particularized version, selected from a more comprehensive total pattern. Adding usually something of its own through interpretation and adaptation, it consists of the elements which are relevant and congenial to the particular actor in the light of his particular situations.

Order — peaceful coexistence under conditions of scarcity — is one of the very first of the functional imperatives of *social systems*. A social system has no independent source of motivation of its own; this comes only from the component individuals. The personality is in a sense a motivational "engine"; the structure and direction of its motives are derived from the modifications imposed on the innate structure by social interaction and culture. Gratification — the most general concept for the fulfillment of its motives — is the primary functional need of personality.

The personality has been treated as an organized complex of need-dispositions. The combinations of the pattern variables, as we have shown in Chapter I, describe in one sense the fundamental types of need-disposition organizations. From the exigencies confronting the need-dispositions in the external situation and in relations to each other, the further elements which we have called mechanisms of defense and adjustment are developed. The problems of the appropriate occasions for gratification or its renunciation, of diffuse attachment to an object or the specific limitation of its cathectic significance are the primary orientational dilemmas. Problems of the character of norms and of the modalities of objects are less immediately crucial and hence their solutions are more likely to be imposed by situational factors.

The generality of the values of the larger culture which are institutionalized in the social system gives them a greater share in the creation of this framework of imposed order. The range of variability available to the values of particular personalities is fixed primarily by the limits which are part of this framework.

From these considerations it becomes evident that there are *two* primary ranges of variability of personal moral patterns. First, like social value systems, personal value systems are constituted by the choices from the alternatives represented in the pattern variables. In addition, however, the existing institutionalized value system of the society must always be an independent point of reference. Regardless of its content, by virtue of his membership in the society, the individual is confronted with the problem of the degrees and modes of his acceptance or rejection of these values. Unless the social system approaches a state of extreme disorganization, the personal consequences of radical deviance are always serious.

Some of the most subtle problems of the relations of personality and culture arise in this context. Personalities as systems are thoroughly permeated by culture — the very composition of the need-dispositions which are constitutive of personality is a fusion of organic energy into a framework made up of commitments to the alternatives of value-orientation. Even after the personality has become a relatively stabilized system of need-dispositions allocated among various occasions for gratification and integrated into some approximation to a working unity, it is still continuously confronting the cultural patterns as situational objects of orientation. Even in a simple society, the cultural pattern presented as a situational object will be richer in content, more varied in scope, and of course, more contradictory than a single personality system, with its functional imperative of integration as a basic gratification, can incorporate.

The personality system will therefore tend to select particular elements from the available cultural pattern which will then become parts of the orientation system of the actor. It is certainly not permissible to assert that the actor chooses only those elements of the pattern (as a situational object) which are identical with his existing need-dispositions. If that were so, there could be no changes in the behavior of actors through their exposure to different culture patterns in the course of their lifetime. Nor is the selection a random one. There must therefore be some correspondence in general orientation between the need-disposition system of the personality and the elements selected from the available cultural patterns; that is, the pattern elements which become incorporated into the actor's orientation must still permit an adequate balance of the gratification of the various need-dispositions. The cognitive orientations accepted must have some congruity or consistency with the cognitive orientations already operative in the personality system. But it certainly need not be and is extremely unlikely to be a very detailed identity.

The reasons for this relative looseness of fit between personality systems and the selection of cultural orientations from situational cultural patterns are numerous. There seem to be two main reasons. First, need-dispositions are relatively generalized orientations in the personality system and the cultural object system is also relatively generalized, but they cannot exactly coincide. Hence in confrontation with concrete situations, the need-dispositions must become particularized and integrated with a correspondingly particularized interpretation of the relevant sector of the culture. Their balance undergoes a momentary change in accordance with the pressure of the circumstances, and the capacity of the generalized orientation to guide behavior gratifyingly is inadequate. Hence some more differentiated or particularized orientation pattern must be added to the actor's orientation system to increase his ability to maintain the level of gratification. The second reason lies on a different plane. In the first instance we spoke of the substantive content of culture patterns and their potency in providing gratifying orientations; but there is another selective factor at work: the conformity-alienation need-disposition, which in some magnitude or direction is operative in every personality. Hence there is a factor at work in the selection of cultural patterns which is independent of their content and which is determined primarily by the strength and direction of the conformity-alienation need-disposition. Cultural patterns which in their general content are quite contradictory to the value-orientation of the other need-dispositions in the personality system might well be accepted if their acceptance gratifies the conformity-alienation need-disposition. There need not necessarily be a conflict between these two criteria of selection of elements from the cultural object situation. They might well coincide and often do.

What has been said here about selection is true also of the creation of new value patterns in the personality. This occurs not only through selection but also through integration and adaptation. Here the strength of the need-dispositions and their consequent potentiality for resisting the pressure of expectations — independently of alienative need-dispositions — might be said to be one of the most important factors in determining a creative variant of an available cultural pattern. Creativity here refers to the production of new patterns of personal value-orientation which diverge significantly from any of the available cultural patterns. The newly created pattern will probably stand in closer correspondence substantively or formally to the need-dispositions of the personality than in the case of selection from situationally available patterns. But here too it is not merely a matter of finding a correspondence with the value-orientations implicit in the need-dispositions. It is the creation of a new pattern which adds to the existing body of orientations in the cultural pattern. It extends to new objects or new relations among them; it entails new patterns of cognition, expression, or value-orientation. Some important aspects of the newly created pattern will always reveal its continuity, even though remote and complex, with the elaborated need-disposition system which makes up the personality.

The personal creation of new cultural orientations might itself be a function of the selection of certain specific cultural patterns in the situation. The personal pattern of orientation toward creativity on the part of the scientist or poet, with its high evaluation of new truths and new images, is greatly promoted by the presence in the cultural orientation system of a positive pattern which highly evaluates creativity in the search for truth without requiring the acceptance of any particular substantive truths.

The differentiation of personal value systems with respect to their degree of creativity or its absence must not be confused with that of need-dispositions to conform with or be alienated from institutionalized culture patterns. These two sets of categories cut across each other. The scientist within a culture which highly values scientific creation might be much more creative than the revolutionary or the religious prophet who stands in rebellion against the prevailing patterns of his culture. Creativity is not identical with rebellion; while conformity with existing patterns may be the result of an orientation toward its mere existence or toward its content.

THE PROBLEM OF CLASSIFICATION OF VALUE SYSTEMS

Our previous discussion has assumed the possibility of a systematic classification of types of moral standards. The task however still remains to be done. It should of course be placed in the context of the larger problem of classification of cultural orientations in general. This could not, however, be undertaken within the limits of this monograph.[16]

Variations in the structure of these standards may be described systematically by the various possible combinations of the values of the pattern variables. Of the five pattern variables, it was asserted in Chapter I that one, self- versus collectivity-orientation, can be omitted from the more basic treatment of the structural *variability* of the two kinds of systems of action. The reason for this is that it refers to the integration of action systems which is *equally* a functional problem to *both* types of system. The form and scope of integration depends on the nature of the elements to be integrated, and not the other way around. This should not be understood to imply that there is no significant variation with *respect* to this variable; the variation, however, is primarily a resultant of the problems of the functional integration of the system and it is not constituent of that type of system.

[16] A tentative attempt in this direction has been made in Talcott Parsons, *The Social System*, chaps. viii and ix.

Attention may now again be directed to what was called in Chapter I (pp. 88, ff.) the "symmetrical asymmetry" of the relations among the remaining four pattern variables. Two of them, affectivity-neutrality and specificity-diffuseness, are, as we saw, peculiarly applicable to personality systems; the other two, universalism-particularism and ascription-achievement are primarily applicable to social systems.

The *primary* significance of the two pattern variables more closely related to personality lies in their organization of orientation in relative independence of the type of situation; the two pattern variables more closely related to social systems have their primary significance in the organization of the situation in relative independence of the type of orientation. Both pairs are very important in each type of action system, but their position is not the same in each.

Proceeding from this assumption, the four main types in the four cells in Fig. 4 (page 251), further elaborated in terms of their cultural significance as Fig. 10, provide the basic framework for the classification of systems of values for the social system. This classification will give us the systems of common values which are, in relation to the situational factors, the primary focus of the main institutional structure of the social system. The types in Fig. 3 (page 249) provide the corresponding framework for value systems of the personality. Of the two classifications, however, the social value-orientations (Fig. 4) have greater significance for the analysis of cultures. Cultures, being shared by many actors, comprise the values which define the common elements in the situations in which they act. (Fig. 10 is on page 258.)

The best correspondence between these major types of value patterns and social systems will be found in the more comprehensive or macroscopic kinds of comparative analysis. They will also be found in those sectors of the social system which are freest for variability, as a result of being least determined by certain of the more specific functional imperatives. For example, governmental structures and those centering about the stratification subsystem should show on the whole closer correspondence with dominant value patterns than kinship, which is bound to the relatively more specific functional conditions of man's biological nature. Kinship systems therefore do not vary as widely in terms of pattern variables,[17] and they are also less likely to fit the dominant value-orientation than are the larger governmental and stratification subsystems. Thus an increase in size introduces new functional imperatives which tend to shift the balance in the direction of universalism, specificity, etc.

A complete survey of the variability of social value systems is out of the question here; only a few illustrations can be provided. The universalism-achievement combination (Fig. 10, cell 1) approximates the dominant Amer-

---

[17] They do, of course, vary widely in terms of their composition and relations among the constituent solidary groupings.

ican "achievement complex." The particularism-achievement combination (cell 2) fits the classical Chinese value system rather closely. Universalism-ascription (cell 3) fits the pre-Nazi German value system, and finally, particularism-ascription (cell 4) seems to correspond to the Spanish American pattern.[18]

Fig. 10a further elaborates these four main types of logically possible value systems. Fig. 11 classifies each of the four main types of value patterns by each of the six classes of situational objects distinguished in Fig. 6 (page 254). For the sake of refinement and completeness, three foci of orientation are distinguished within each object class: (1) the significance of the object for the actor's symbol system (i.e., the diagnostic definition of the object with reference to which the actor prepares to act); (2) the types of striving toward a goal which, in terms of the value-orientation, it will be appropriate for the actor to undertake; and (3) the principal locus of strain in relation to the object. The third aspect is particularly important in the analysis of the integration of a system of moral standards into an empirical action system.

If the present approach is consistently adhered to, each subtype of each of the four main types of value-orientation system may be further differentiated by confrontation with each main object class. A sample of such a classification for sixteen subtypes, omitting the self-collectivity variable and confining the elaboration to three selected object classes, is presented in Fig. 12.[19]

The general theory of action points to important determinate interrelations between the cultural standards institutionalized in the social system and the distribution of personal standards among its population. Within any social system, even within any particular status within it, there will tend to be a variety of personality types. (We use the term *personality type* here to refer to a personality system characterized by its dominant complex of need-dispositions.) In principle all of the possible personality types may appear in the same society, but the nature of the relations between personality and social structure is such that their distribution cannot vary at random in any given society. In view of the special pertinence of the variables of affectivity-neutrality and specificity-diffuseness to personality, the cells within the main types of Fig. 11, in addition to defining subtypes of cultural values of the

[18] These assertions would of course have to be justified by more detailed discussion than is possible here, and they are in any case acknowledged to be only first approximations.

[19] For instance, within the transcendent-achievement pattern, the most significant variations lie perhaps between the subtypes distinguished by affectivity and discipline. The commitment to the transcendent-achievement pattern precludes a prominent position for diffuse obligations. The disciplined alternative more nearly characterizes the American value system with its strong emphasis on *instrumental* achievement and the puritanical attitude toward pleasure which prevailed until recently; it might be suggested very tentatively that the affective alternative comes close to certain aspects of the French with their greater emphasis on the style of life with its refined patterns for affective expression in consumption, convivial relations, etc.

social system, may also define the personality types most likely to be produced in, or at least to be necessary for the functioning of, a society with a major value system oriented in terms of one of the main cultural types.

This possibility may be illustrated with respect to the universalistic-achievement orientation which is rather characteristic of important tendencies in American culture. In Fig. 3 the four major need-disposition types are designated as the *segmental gratification* value-orientation (affectivity-specificity), *approval* (neutrality-specificity), *love* (affectivity-diffuseness) and *esteem* (neutrality-diffuseness). The high evaluation of approval is perhaps most peculiarly American. In one direction, this fuses with the hedonistic (*segmental gratification*) value-orientation producing an orientation toward achievement, with an inclination toward immediate gratifications. This is certainly one of the directions of the break-down of Puritan discipline in American society in recent decades. Hence such orientations may be deviant, and thus likely to be in conflict with the predominant value system. A second direction of deviance is from orientation toward *specific* performances assessed by universalistic standards to a *diffuseness* leading to the "esteem" orientation. This too finds its counterpart in American culture in recent years and is enhanced by the growth of mass communications. The personality types that seek to be the center of attention, who are not content with specific achievements and the corresponding approval by themselves and others, and who must be recognized as *generally* superior, would fall into this category. In American culture, this type has tended to be defined as somewhat deviant — although perhaps less so now than a half-century ago — and certain attendant strains have thereby been produced. Perhaps the least common of the four orientations in American society is the "love" pattern. Quite understandably it is more likely to be found among women than men because women have been excluded from the achievement complex and they have a special role in the kinship structure. But it is by no means necessarily confined to women. Even though not frequently found as a dominant orientation among men, it frequently is a very important counterfoil as a partial orientation pattern in such contexts as the romantic-love complex, where it represents a segregated revolt against some of the other tendencies of the culture.

These remarks are at best intended only to be suggestive of the possibilities of analysis through the use of these categories.

Both the major orientations and the subtypes are *ideal types* and there is no reason why any concrete and in particular any dominant value-orientation should conform exactly to any one of them. There are undoubtedly many significant marginal cases. Because of this ideal-typical character, this scheme is highly formal and can be only a first step in the analysis of actual or historical systems of value-orientation. Much more would have to be added before the scheme could be used for detailed concrete analysis. For instance, our treatment of the universalistic-achievement pattern of orientation does not specify which particular classes of achievements are valued. These might be scientific, technological, artistic, military, and so on, and concrete cultural orientations certainly do differ markedly in these respects. Moreover, the pattern-variable scheme, at this stage of the logical construction of the categories of cultural orientations, dos not explicitly formulate the types of value-orientations which are embodied in unequal but complementary social relations such as dominance-submission. The value-orientations implicit in these social relationships are to be analyzed as adaptive mechanisms mediating between major cultural patterns and the exigencies of social situations.[20]

This formal quality, although a limitation, is not in principle a deficiency of the scheme. The enormous empirical complexity of concrete value-orientation systems is not subject to question. *Any* conceptual scheme which attempted to take account of all this complexity at one stroke would be scientifically useless in the present stage of development of social science because it would be far too cumbersome to handle systematically without mathematical techniques, which, for a variety of reasons, cannot yet be applied to the relevant social science concepts. The question is not, therefore, whether the pattern-variable scheme, by being formal, "oversimplifies" empirical reality; any analytical scheme would do so. The question is whether the *selection* of variables incorporated in this scheme is more or less useful than an alternative selection. There are two kinds of criteria of the usefulness of such a selection. One is its fruitfulness in research. This test is still to be made. The other is the relationship of the chosen set of variables to other variables in a highly generalized conceptual scheme, which in its various parts has already proved itself useful in research. From this source the pattern-variable scheme draws strong support. It employs analytical concepts which have been derived from the basic categories of action, which themselves in more concrete versions have been applied with success to the study of cultures as various as ancient Israel, China, India, and modern Christendom.

The derivability of a variety of concepts from the major categories of the definition of action merits further consideration. In Chapter II, principal need-disposition orientations were derived from the general orientation scheme, through the pattern variables by means of certain techniques of conceptual derivation. The same can be done for systems of cultural orientation. A value system which appraises authority very highly is, for instance, conceptually homologous to the need for dominance in the personality and to a high degree of concentration of authority in the social system and it seems, similarly, to derive from combinations of the pattern variables.

Concretely, the type of value-orientation toward authority which will develop will depend on the combination of pattern-variable values which is associated with it. Thus in the universalism-achievement orientation author-

---

[20] A similar limitation in the use of the most elementary pattern-variable combinations in concrete description was observed in our discussion of personality.

ity will be linked to status based on achievement. At the opposite pole, in the particularism-ascription orientation, there will be a tendency to acknowledge the authority exercised by persons with an ascribed status within a particularistic structure.[21]

By similar techniques other aspects of orientations toward authority can be derived from *combinations* of the pattern variables within given cultural and social contexts without making orientation toward authority itself *one* of the basic types of value-orientation. In the present conceptual scheme, orientations toward authority belong on a derivative level of concreteness in the classification of systems of value-orientations. They are not a fundamental type. What is true of the place of the evaluation of authority would also be true of adherence to tradition or of other differentiated concepts such as the evaluation of prudence, or of adventurousness, or even the evaluation of the things of this world as distinguished from those of the "next." [22]

The different pattern-variable combinations, when integrated into action systems, will of course predispose the actors toward those derivative patterns of value-orientation which are consistent with them. Thus the universalism-ascription pattern has a tendency to authoritarianism, because the authoritarian "ideal state" involves *allocation according to qualities* and the implication that this "ideal state" should be *acknowledged by everyone*. Given the likelihood of deviant tendencies in all systems the resort to authoritarian enforcement in universalistic-ascriptively oriented culture is highly probable. Similarly, in a culture with a predominantly particularistic value-orientation, a universalistic orientation is enabled to exist only if it is "projected" into an "other worldly" sphere, thereby reducing the strain which it would otherwise cause. Thus the attainment of Nirvana in Buddhism is very strictly a universalistic-achievement value, which has been enabled to flourish in the particularistically organized social structures of Oriental societies only by virtue of its other-worldliness. Such inferences, however, must be drawn with caution; and the concrete orientations will be a resultant of many factors ranging from the functional imperatives imposed by the organism and the situation and the general value-orientations involved.

This chapter has presented an exceedingly sketchy treatment of a very complicated subject. Its aim has not been to produce a complete analysis but to indicate the main lines along which the general analysis of action presented in Chapter I could be developed in the study of value-orientations. Compared to other current modes of analysis, it possesses two distinctive features which may be regarded as significant. First, by showing the relation between cultural value-orientations and the pattern-variable scheme, it

[21] This is the predominant feature of what Weber called "traditional authority."

[22] It may be noted incidentally that the distinction between transcendence and immanence of *reference*, which is involved in th universalism-particularism variable, is not the same as the distinction between worldly and other-worldly orientations.

relates the former directly to the constitutive structural elements of personality and social systems in a way which is theoretically both generalized and systematic. For purposes of theory construction, it makes the place of cultural orientations in systems of action much clearer, and helps greatly to clear away some of the confusions involved in many current controversies in the field. It gives a general theoretical demonstration of why the analysis of value-orientations on the cultural level is of such crucial importance in the theory of action and in all its special branches. It also shows that the interpretation of concrete action exclusively in categories of value-orientation is not admissible, except as a special case. The second distinctive feature of this analysis is that it provides points of departure for a systematic classification of systems of value-orientation. This leads into the systematic classification of types of systems of action themselves as wholes and of their component parts. In both fields there has been a great need for a better basis of such systematic classification. It is hoped that the present scheme might provide the ground work for a more fundamental solution of the problem.

However, the formidable nature of the task of elaborating in detail the implications of such a scheme in relation to the infinitely various nuances of empirical differentiations should not be underestimated. We are under no illusion that more has been done here than to indicate certain fundamental starting points for such a process of elaboration.

4

The Social System

The social system is made up of the actions of individuals. The actions which constitute the social system are also the same actions which make up the personality systems of the individual actors. The two systems are, however, analytically discrete entitites, despite this identity of their basic components.

The difference lies in their *foci of organization* as systems and hence in the substantive functional problems of their operation as systems. The "individual" actor as a concrete system of action is not usually the most important unit of a social system. For most purposes *the conceptual unit of the social system is the role*. The role is a sector of the individual actor's total system of action. It is the point of contact between the system of action of the individual actor and the social system. The individual then becomes a unity in the sense that he is a composite of various action units which in turn are roles in the relationships in which he is involved. But this composite of roles is *not* the same abstraction as personality as a system. It is a special type of abstraction from the concrete totality of ego's system of action, with a highly selective inclusion of the dynamic processes and mechanisms, the selection being made on the basis of an interest in ego as a composite of action units relevant to various collectivities, no longer on the basis of an interest in ego as an action system *per se*. These distinctions, segregating the individual actor as a system, his unit of action and the role to which it corresponds, and the social system, are a precondition of any fruitful empirical analysis of social order and change, as well as of personality adjustment and cultural change.

The primary ingredient of the role is the role-expectation. Role-expectations are patterns of evaluation; their primary constituents are analytically derivable from the pattern-variable combinations and from derivatives of the pattern variables when these are combined with the specific types of situations. Role-expectations organize (in accordance with general value-orientations) the reciprocities, expectations, and responses to those expectations in the specific interaction systems of ego and one or more alters. This reciprocal aspect must always be borne in mind since the expectations of an ego *always* imply the expectations of one or more alters. It is in this reciprocity or complementarity that sanctions enter and acquire their place in systems of action. What an actor is expected to do in a given situation both by himself and by others constitutes the expectations of that role. What the relevant alters are expected to do, contingent on ego's action, constitute the sanctions.[1] Role expectations and sanctions are, therefore, in terms of the content of action, the *reciprocal of each other*. What are sanctions to ego are also role-expectations to alter, and vice versa. However, the content of ego's and alter's expectations concerning ego's action need not be identical with the content of the expectations of alter and ego regarding alter's action in response to ego's.

It may further be noted that each actor is involved in the interaction process in a dual capacity. On the one hand, he is an actor who as ego is *oriented* to alter as an object. This aspect may be called his *orientation role*. On the other hand he *is* an object of alter's orientation (and in certain circumstances of his own). This is his *object role*. When, for instance, he is *categorized* relative to others, it is as object; but when he imposes on himself the renunciation of an affective orientation in favor of a neutral one, he is acting in his orientation role.

In a social system, roles vary in the degree of their institutionalization. By institutionalization we mean the integration of the complementary role-expectation and sanction patterns with a generalized value system *common* to the members of the more inclusive collectivity, of which the system of complementary role-actions may be a part. Insofar as ego's set of role-expectations is institutionalized, the sanctions which express the role-expectations of the other actors will tend to reinforce his own need-dispositions to conform with these expectations by rewarding it and by punishing deviance.

The sanctions will be rewards when they facilitate the realization of the goals which are part of his action or when they add further gratifications upon the completion of the action at certain levels of proficiency; they will be punishments when they hinder his realization of the goals which are part of his action or when they add further deprivations during or after the execution of the action. Conformity on the part of alter with ego's expectations is a condition of ego's goal realization. In addition to the conformity or divergence of alter's actions with respect to ego's expectations, alter's attitudes of approval or disapproval toward ego's behavior are also positive or negative sanctions. In addition to these two immediate types of reward and punishment, there should be mentioned alter's supplementary granting of gratifications for ego's conformity with expectations or transcendence of them and alter's supplementary infliction of deprivations for deficiencies.

Thus far we have been treating the social system only in its most elemen-

---

[1] *Sanctions* is used here to indicate both positive and negative responses by alter to ego's response; i.e., to ego's conformity with or deviation from alter's expectations.

tary form; namely, as the interaction in which the actions of the incumbents of each role are regulated by the double contingency of expectations. Concrete social sytems are, however, more than the simple interaction of two or more individual actors with a common system of values. Social systems give rise to, and often themselves constitute, collective actors in the sense that the individual members interact with one another and with members of other social systems for the achievement of shared collective goals. By collective goals we mean (1) those which are either prescribed by persons acting in a legitimate position of authority and in which the goal is expected to involve gratifications for members other than but including the particular actor, or (2) those goals which, without being specifically prescribed by authority, have the same content as regards the recipients of their gratifications. Shared collective goals are goals which, having the content described in the preceding sentence, have the further property of being simultaneously pursued by a plurality of persons in the same system of interaction.

A social system having the three properties of collective goals, shared goals, and of being a single system of interaction with boundaries defined by incumbency in the roles constituting the system, will be called a *collectivity*.[2] The action of the collectivity may be viewed as the *action in concert* of a plurality of individual actors. Collectivities may act in concert toward their own members or toward objects outside themselves. In the latter case, complementarity of expectations and the associated shared value system exist among the actors within the collectivity but it will not exist *to the same extent* with the actors who are part of another social system. In the case of the former, complementarity of expectations and the shared value system might well exist among all the actors in the situation, with all reorganization of the action of the members being in accordance with shared general value-orientations and with specifically complementary expectations. Even in this case, there will always be involved some orientation toward social and/or nonsocial objects which are outside the collectivity.

The concept of boundary is of crucial significance in the definition of a collectivity. The boundary of a collectivity is that criterion whereby some persons are included as members and others are excluded as nonmembers. The inclusion or exclusion of a person depends on whether or not he has a membership role in the collectivity. Thus all persons who have such roles are members; they are within the boundary. Thus, the boundary is defined in terms of membership roles.

The location of the boundary of a collectivity will vary from situation to situation. Accordingly, the "concerted action" criterion must be interpreted with regard to a defined system of action; that is, a limited range of action.

---

[2] A collectivity may be defined as the integration of its members with a common value system. This integration implies that the members of the collectivity will, under appropriate circumstances, act in "defense" of the shared values.

It is only in a *given situation* that a specific role-expectation becomes the focus of the orientation of behavior. The solidarity of a collectivity may, therefore, be latent as long as certain types of situation which would activate them fail to arise. In other words, the boundary may be latent or temporarily inoperative. Thus, certain obligations to more distant kin might be activated only if such a kinsman were in danger and the actor knew it. Here the boundary of the kinship collectivity would be activated; otherwise it would not be operative. The solidarity of a collectivity might operate frequently and in a variety of situations, and conversely, the situations in which a given plurality's actions are concerted and thus solidary might be of infrequent occurrence. An aggregate of persons might be continuously solidary; that is, whenever they are in a common situation, they will act in concert, but the types of actions in which they are solidary might change continuously: for example, a military unit which has been solidary from the beginning of basic training, through combat, to the state of demobilized civilian life. To meet the definitional requirement of a collectivity, however, an aggregate of persons need not be continuously solidary; they need be solidary only when they are objects to one another in a common situation and when the situation is one which is defined by the value patterns and more specifically by the system of role-expectations as falling within the range of interest of the collectivity.

The criterion of action in concert, then, is another way of formulating the concept of the primacy of collectivity-orientation over self-orientation or private interest. It may be a purely negative, contingent solidarity, which consists in the avoidance of actions that would, in their consequence, damage the other members of the collectivity. Here, too, there is common value orientation, a conforming response to the expectation of other collectivity members.

A *collectivity*, as the term is used here, should be clearly distinguished from two other types of social aggregates. The first is a *category* of persons who have some attribute or complex of attributes in common, such as age, sex, education, which do not involve "action in concert." It is true, of course, that such categories enter into the definitions of roles and thus affect action in concert. But a number of elements must be added before such a category of persons becomes a collectivity. The second type of social aggregate is a plurality of persons who are merely interdependent with one another ecologically. The participants in an ideally perfect competitive market, as that concept is used in pure economic theory, represent an ecologically interdependent aggregate.

A collectivity differs from both these pluralities in being characterized by the *solidarity* of its members. Solidarity is characterized by the institutionalization of shared value-orientations; the values being, of course, oriented toward collective gratifications. Acceptance of common value patterns permits the more differentiated institutionalization of the action of the members of the collectivity in a wide range of specific situations. The range may be broad or narrow, but in each specific situation institutionalization exists when each actor in the situation does, and believes he should do, what the other actors whom he confronts believe he should do. Thus institutionalization is an articulation or integration of the actions of a plurality of actors in a specific type of situation in which the various actors accept jointly a set of harmonious rules regarding goals and procedures. The concrete content of these rules will differ, in the same situation, from actor to actor and from role to role. But the rules, if followed in such a situation of full institutionalization, will lead to perfectly articulated, conflictless action on the part of the several actors. These rules possess their harmonious character by virtue of their derivation, by deliberation and less conscious processes, from common value-orientations which are the same for all members of the institution or the set of institutions in the collectivity. These value-orientations contain general standards in accordance with which objects of various classes are judged, evaluated, and classified as worthy of various types of response of rewards and punishments. Specific institutional situations are differentiated by the concrete state of the objects which each actor confronts and hence by the specific rules which are appropriate in acting toward those objects. In institutionally highly integrated collectivities, situations in which uncertainty prevails about the appropriate action can in principle be clarified by closer scrutiny of the objects and more careful study of the implications of the common value-orientation. (In reality, however, new situations, because they are not always subject to this treatment and because previous cognitive orientations prove inadequate, are dealt with in a variety of ways.) Those, therefore, who share common value-orientations as commitments to action patterns in roles, constitute a collectivity.

Some additional clarification of this definition is necessary. First, with respect to the relationship of the collectivity to the properties of aggregates (sexual qualities, beauty, etc.): insofar as certain sexual qualities become the foci of roles and thus become institutionalized in a society, the relevant value patterns defining and regulating sexual roles, along with other value patterns, are part of the constitution of a collectivity. But within this larger collectivity, those characterized by the same sexual characteristics do not necessarily act as a collectivity with a preponderant focus on sexual qualities or activities in all or even in any situation. Sex, among many other object characteristics which serve as criteria of admission and which evoke certain role-expectations, plays a constitutive part in many collectivities. An example would be a combat unit in the armed forces; but even though the demonstration of manliness is here an important goal, it is not the chief goal on which the unit is focused. There are few collectivities in which ascription by sex does not figure to some extent in the determination of admission to membership roles and in providing the chief focus of the appropriate expectations. The extent however to which any given object quality, such as sex, ethnic membership, or beauty, will perform these functions varies.

Second, some further remarks on the boundaries of collectivities are in order. Sub-collectivities within a larger inclusive collectivity may be: (1) independent of one another in the sense of having no overlapping members and having either no contact with one another or being in contact with one another only as collectivities; or (2) they may overlap in the sense that they share certain members but not all; or (3) they may be inclusive in the sense that one of the collectivities may be smaller than the other and thus all of its members be in the latter. The inclusive type of collectivity is not, however, distinguished merely by its relative size and the plural memberships of the members of the smaller, included collectivity. The smaller collectivity may be constituted by role-expectations and actions which are specifically differentiated versions of the general value-orientation of the larger inclusive collectivity. They may be oriented toward more specific goals within the general class of goals pursued by the inclusive collectivity. They may be confronted by a special class of objects within the general classes of objects with which the inclusive collectivity is constitutively concerned, including other parts of the inclusive collectivity. The role structure of the members of the smaller collectivity within the inclusive collectivity will, figuratively speaking, be onion-like in shape. One role will fit within another and so on. Thus a particular professor in a university department who is a member of a departmental research group is simultaneously fulfilling, by a given set of actions, three roles: (1) his membership in the research group is part of (2) his role as professor, and his role as professor of a certain subject is part of (3) his role as a member of the university. The latter role may include cognate roles such as service on committees, service in representative roles, and so forth, which have nothing to do with the content of his research role, but all of which fall within the common value system and within the system of solidarity of the university as a collectivity.

The same is true of the market. Common values define general roles for participation in market relations in our society. But it is only when there are common values defining specific rights and obligations vis-à-vis other collective units or persons that, *within* the market system, a collectivity would exist. The members of a cartel are not merely interdependent, they constitute a collectivity, with shared collective goals and concerted action within boundaries which define the types of rights and obligations which are to be effective. The members of the cartel follow a set of expectations vis-à-vis one another which are different from those which they direct toward persons outside the boundaries. But both sets are in the main derived from or subsumable under the general expectations characteristic of the market as a social system.

A social system, then, is a system of interaction of a plurality of actors, in which the action is oriented by rules which are complexes of complementary expectations concerning roles and sanctions. *As a system*, it has determinate internal organization and determinate patterns of structural change. It has, furthermore, as a system, a variety of mechanisms of adaptation to changes in the external environment. Those mechanisms function to create one of the important properties of a system; namely, the tendency to maintain boundaries. A total social system which, for practical purposes, may be treated as self-subsistent — which, in other words, contains within approximately the boundaries defined by membership all the functional mechanisms required for its maintenance as a system — is here called a *society*. Any other is a *subsystem* of a society. It is of the greatest importance in connection with any specific problem to place the subsystem in question explicitly in the context of those parts of the total society which are outside the subsystem for the purposes at hand.[3]

The social system of which roles [4] are the elementary units will of necessity involve the differentiation and allocation of roles. The different individual actors participating in the social sytem will each have different roles, and they will accordingly differ in their specific goals and cognitive orientations. Role-expectations bring into specific focus patterns of generalized orientation. They sharpen the edges of commitments and they impose further disciplines upon the individual. They can do so only as long as the conditions are present in the personality and the social system which enable human beings to *live up to these kinds of expectations*, which diminish or absorb the strains to which people are subjected, including both the "internal strains" connected with difficulty in fulfilling internalized norms and the strains which are associated with divergence from expectation.

Motivational orientations within the personality system might vary among different individuals who conform equally with the same set of expectations. But in the analysis of the social system, particularly in its descriptive analysis, we need be concerned only with the motivational orientation toward the specific set of role-expectations and toward the role itself — and may tentatively disregard the "rootedness" and repercussions of this orientation in the rest of the personality system of the actors involved. Of course, these motivational orientations will not vary at random with respect to the types of personality systems in association with which they are found, but for certain types of important problems, this aspect may be passed over. There will be for each social system, and for social systems in general, certain types of motivational orientations which are preconditions of the working of the system.

The motivational prerequisites of a social system, then, are the patterns

---

[3] It is probable that the sociologist who deals with modern large-scale societies is more frequently called upon to deal with partial systems than is the social anthropologist, who studies smaller societies, or the psychologist, who in his analysis of personality more frequently deals with the system as an integral unit.

[4] Roles are differentiated (1) with respect to value-orientation patterns and (2) with respect to specific functional content. The latter can vary over considerable ranges independently of patterns of value-orientation.

made up of the more elementary components of motivation — those which permit fulfillment to an "adequate" degree of the role-expectations characteristic of the social system in question. These necessary motivational patterns will not be the same for the different parts of the social system, and they must therefore be properly distributed in accordance with the role structure of the social system in question.

THE FOCI OF ORGANIZATION

A social system is a system of the actions of individuals, the principal units of which are roles and constellations of roles. It is a system of differentiated actions, organized into a system of differentiated roles. Internal differentiation, which is a fundamental property of all systems, requires integration. It is a condition of the existence of the system that the differentiated roles must be coördinated either negatively, in the sense of the avoidance of disruptive interference with each other, or positively, in the sense of contributing to the realization of certain shared collective goals through collaborated activity.

When a plurality of individual actors are each oriented in a situation to gratify sets of need-dispositions, certain resultant phenomena are inevitable. By virtue of the primordial fact that the objects — social and nonsocial — which are instrumentally useful or intrinsically valuable are scarce in relation to the amount required for the full gratification of the need-dispositions of every actor, there arises a problem of allocation: the problem of who is to get what, who is to do what, and the manner and conditions under which it is to be done. This is the fundamental problem which arises from the interaction of two or more actors.

As a result of the scarcity of the social and nonsocial objects of need-dispositions, the mutual incompatibility of claims might extend theoretically in the extreme case to the "state of nature." It would be the war of "each against all" in its Hobbesian formulation. The function of allocation of roles, facilities, and rewards does not, however, have to contend with this extreme possibility. The process of socialization in the family, school, and play groups, and in the community focuses need-dispositions in such a way that the degree of incompatibility of the active aspirations and claims for social and nonsocial objects is reduced, in "normal conditions," to the usually executable task of making allocations among sectors of the population, most of whose claims will not too greatly exceed what they are receiving. Without a solution of this problem, there can be no social system. It is indeed one of the functions which makes the social system. It arises in every social system, and though the solutions can vary within limits which from the standpoint of ethical values might be very wide apart, yet every allocative process must have certain properties which are common to all of them. Where the allocative process is not carried out successfully — where the allocative process either interferes with effective collaboration or is not regarded as sufficiently legitimate — the social system in question will tend to disintegrate and to give way to another social system.

The term *allocation* should not be interpreted anthropomorphically. Allocation is a resultant that is only in part a product of deliberate decision; the total allocation in a social system especially may be the product of many processes that culminate in a distribution which no individual or collective actor in the system has sought.

A social system must possess a minimum degree of integration; there must be, that is, a sufficient complementarity of roles and clusters of roles for collective and private goals to be effectively pursued. Although conflict can exist within a social system and, in fact, always does, there are limits beyond which it cannot go and still permit a social system to exist. By definition the complementarity of expectations which is associated with the complementarity of roles is destroyed by conflict. Consequently, when conflict becomes so far reaching as to negate the complementarity of expectations, there the social system has ceased to exist. Hence, for conflict among individuals and groups to be kept within bounds, the roles and role clusters must be brought into appropriately complementary relations with one another.

It is highly important to what follows to distinguish here two functional problems of social systems: (1) *What* roles are to be institutionalized in the social system? (2) *Who* is to perform these roles? Every social system has certain tasks imposed on it by the fact that its members are mortal physiological organisms, with physiological and social needs, existing in a physical environment together with other like organisms. Some variability is possible regarding the tasks which are considered as worthy of being undertaken (in the light of the prevailing value-orientations and the external situation of the social system). This selection of tasks or functions may be phrased as an answer to the question "what should be done with the existing resources of the society?" in the sense of what *jobs* are to be done.

The first allocative function of a social system, therefore, is the allocation of human capacities and human resources among tasks. In addition to a distribution of resources among tasks or functions which can be performed only by a complex of roles, each social system, inasmuch as its members are not born genetically destined to particular functional roles, must allocate its members among those roles. Also, since tasks change, and with them the roles by which they can be met, reallocation is a necessity quite in addition to that imposed by man's birth, plasticity and mortality. One of the ways in which this is done in some social systems is by definition of the criteria of eligibility for incumbency of the role by membership in solidary groups, thus regulating the flow of persons into such roles. In all social systems access to roles is regulated by the possession of qualifications which might be, but are not always necessarily, memberships or qualities.

A closely related allocative problem in the social system concerns the allocation of *facilities* for the performance of roles. The concept of role has been defined as a complementary set of expectations and the actions to be performed in accordance with these expectations. It includes as part of the expectations the rights to certain types of reaction which the actor is entitled to expect from others and the obligations to perform certain types of action which the actor believes others are entitled to expect from him. It is convenient to distinguish *facilities* from the other components in the definition of role. The term refers to those features of the situation, outside the actual actions entailed in the performance of role itself, which are instrumentally important to the actor in the fulfillment of the expectations concerning his role. Thus one cannot be a scholar without the use of books or a farmer without the use of the land for cultivation.

Facilities thus are objects of orientation which are actually or potentially of instrumental significance in the fulfillment of role-expectations. They *may* consist of physical objects, but not necessarily. The physical objects may, to varying degrees, be "natural" objects or manmade objects, such as buildings or tools. They may be the physical embodiments of cultural objects, such as books. The cultural objects may be accessible not through a physical but through a human agent; we may cite as an illustration of such a facility the type of knowledge which must be secured orally from another human being.

In the same sense that we speak of the *rights* to the *action of others* and the *obligations* to perform the *actions expected by others,* the facilities which are necessary roles are likewise the objects of rights and obligations. When the facility is a social object — that is, the action of another person — it becomes identical with the action to which one has a right and concerning which one has certain obligations. It should, however, be stressed that not all the complementary responses of alter are classifiable as facilities. Only those which ego has the right to use in an instrumental manner, without *specific* [5] regulation by a shared and collective value-orientation, are to be designated as facilities. When a social object, either an individual or a collective action system, is a facility, it may be called an opportunity; privileges are unequally distributed opportunities.

The regulation of the relationship between the incumbent of a role or the "possessor" of a facility and actual or potential claimants to displace that possessor is part of the allocation problem. This is of course a major aspect of the institution of "property." The allocation of facilities, as of roles, is made on the basis of the actor's possession of qualities or his manifestation of performances. Rights of access to facilities may, for example, be contingent

---

[5] The specificity with respect to the concrete situation of action is important here. In nearly all cases short of the limits of extreme brutality, instrumental use of the actors of others occurs within the framework of a *generalized* shared collective value-orientation, which, though not necessarily always conscious, sets limits to the right of instrumental use while leaving an area of freedom for the possessor of the right within those limits.

on the possession of a membership "quality" or on certain performances. The peasant may own his own land by virtue of his membership in a family; the factory worker does not himself own his machine, and his access to it is dependent on his fulfillment of certain performances specified in the "contract of employment" with the company in which ownership is vested, and whose claims are protected by the power of the state and the general value-orientation prevailing in the culture.

The allocation of facilities in a social system may be viewed as an aspect of the allocation of power. There are two senses in which this is so. First is the fact that, while the particular facilities appropriate to the attainment of particular goals may have many singular characteristics, the widespread competition for facilities (which are used to reward collaborators) gives an especially high value to those facilities which have the generalized property of enabling more specific facilities to be acquired. A facility is often such that it can be used to pursue quite a wide variety of goals that might themselves be facilities or substantive goals. This generalized potency is enormously enhanced by the development of money, which is a general medium of exchange, so that "having the price" becomes in effect equivalent to having the concrete facility on the more general level. To have the power to command by virtue of the possession of money or any other qualification is equivalent to having the concrete facility, since the latter can be purchased with the former.

Second, the achievement of goals is often possible in a social system only through collaboration in complementary role situations. One of the means of ensuring collaboration in the pursuit of goals is to control the actions of others in the relevant respects — positively by commanding their services or negatively by at least being in a position to prevent their interference. Therefore the degrees to which and the ways in which an actor (individual or collective) is enabled to control the action of others in the same social system is dependent on the facilities which have been allocated to it (or him). Facilities are powers over objects, social and nonsocial. Power, by its very nature, is a relatively scarce object; its possession by one actor in a relationship is a restriction of the other actor's power. Its intrinsic scarcity and its generalized instrumental status make it into one of the most avidly and vigorously competed for of all objects — we pass over here its very great importance as a direct cathectic object for the immediate gratification of a variety of derivative need-dispositions. It is therefore of the greatest urgency for the determinate allocation of power and the derivative allocations of other facilities to be established and generally accepted in a society. Unless this allocation is well integrated internally and with the value system so that its legitimacy is widely acknowledged, the amount of conflict within the social system may very well rise to the point of disintegration.

THE ALLOCATION OF REWARDS

The allocation of rewards is the systematic outcome of the gratification-orientation of action. It is in the nature of action for gratifications to be sought. Here as much as in the preceding categories of allocation, the objects which gratify need-dispositions [6] are scarcer than would be necessary to satisfy the demand — indeed, in the allocation of rewards, it is sometimes its very scarcity which gives an object its function of gratifying a need-disposition, that is, makes it into a reward. In a system of interaction each of the actors will strive for rewards, the attainment of which might not only be reciprocally contingent, but they might indeed actually come from the same source. The amount one actor gets will affect the amounts other actors get. The resultant, in most societies, is a distribution of rewards that is deliberately controlled only to a restricted extent. It is a resultant of the prior distribution of facilities and is effected by allocative mechanisms which work within the framework of a system of value-orientation.

In the social system the allocation of rewards has the dual function of maintaining or modifying motivation and of affecting the allocation of facilities. Where allocations of rewards diverge too widely from what is thought by the aspirant to be his right in the light of his qualifications, his motivation for the performance of his role will be affected. The effects might range from the inhibition of the need-disposition underlying the previous action to fixation and intensification of the attachment to the gratification object, to the point of disregarding the obligations usually associated with the rights to the object. The maintenance or change of object-attachment is influenced not only by the degree of congruity or discrepancy between expected (entitled) and received rewards but also by the actor's beliefs about the prevailing congruities and discrepancies between entitled and received rewards in the social system at large. Hence, as a cognitive and cathectic-evaluative object, the distribution of rewards plays a large independent part in the motivation of action and particularly in the motivation of conformity and alienation vis-à-vis general value-orientations and specific role-expectations.

The distinction between rewards and facilities is by and large not one between the "intrinsic" properties of the relevant objects, but concerns rather their functional relation in sytems of action. A facility has instrumental significance; it is desired for the uses to which it can be put. A reward, on the other hand, is an object desired for its own sake. The same concrete object may be, and indeed often is, *both* facility and reward to an actor. Not only may an object which is useful as a facility be accepted as a reward, but objects which have a high significance as rewards might also be facilities leading to

---

[6] The interdependence of the need-dispositions is one of the factors accounting for this expansiveness of human demands. The gratification of one need-disposition sets other need-dispositions into action, and inhibition of one sets up a tendency to seek alternative gratifications.

further rewards. Also, in the motivational system of the actor, there is a tendency for particular facilities to acquire reward value. Hence an object which is useful as a facility comes to be cathected directly so that its possession is also interpreted by the actor and by others as a reward. Nevertheless, it is proper to distinguish these two phases of the allocative problem of the social system.

Just as the problem of the allocation of facilities raises the problem of the allocation of power, so the allocation of rewards raises the problem of the allocation of *prestige*, and for similar reasons. Specific rewards, like specific facilities, may have highly specific relations with certain actions which they reward. But the very fact that they become the objects of competing claims — which is, of course, the fact from which the "problem" of allocation derives — is in part evidence of their generalizability to cover the claims of different individuals and to reward the different types of performance. This generalizability intensifies the concentrations of reward value on certain classes of valued objects: especially income, power, and prestige. To possess this generalized quality, each class of rewards must, in some sense, constitute a single scale rendering equivalent different qualifications for the reward. There will also tend to be a common evaluative scale cutting across the different classes of rewards; for example, a scale which enables income to be roughly equated to prestige. This evaluative scale, of course, is seldom explicitly invoked.

It should be made somewhat clearer in just what senses income and power are to be treated as rewards and not as facilities. Their *generalized* character is of significance to *both* functions. But the way in which income and power are integrated into systems of instrumental orientation makes it inevitable that they should be valued; the possession of *anything* valued — the more so if comparison with others is, as it must be, involved — is a source of prestige. Their acquisition, then, can become a goal of action and success in acquisition a *measure* of achievement. Finally, the man with money or power is valued not only for what he has done but for what he *can do*, because possession of generalized facilities widens the range of capacity for achievement. Thus the status of money and power as rewards goes back fundamentally to the valuation of achievement and to their acceptance as *symbols* of achievement, whether actual or potential.

The allocation of power in a society is the allocation of access to or control over the means of attaining goals, whatever they may be. The allocation of prestige, correspondingly, is the allocation of one of the most generalized gratifications which is, at the same time, a very generalized qualification for access to facilities and thus to further and other rewards.

THE INTEGRATION OF THE SOCIAL SYSTEM

This brings us to the consideration of the integrative problems of the social system. From the present point of view, the primary integration of the social system is based on an integrated system of generalized patterns of value-orientation. These patterns of value-orientation are to be described in the categories of the pattern variables. The pattern variables and the derivative patterns of value-orientation can, however, never by themselves adequately define the specific role-expectations which govern behavior in particular situations. Orientation to specific features of the situation in particular ways must be developed in any social system. These will be elaborations and concrete specifications of the values derived from the pattern variables.

A system or a subsystem of concerted action which (1) is governed by a *common* value-orientation and in which (2) the common values are motivationally integrated in action is, as we have said, a collectivity. It is this integration by common values, manifested in the action of solidary groups or collectivities, which characterizes the partial or total integrations of social systems.

Social integration, however much it depends on internalized norms, cannot be achieved by these alone. It requires also some supplementary coördination provided by explicit prescriptive or prohibitory role-expectations (e.g., laws) enunciated by actors in specially differentiated roles to which is attached "responsibility" in collective terms. *Responsibility* in this sense may be subdivided into two types: first, responsibility for the allocative functions in the social systems themselves, the definition and enforcement of the norms governing the allocative processes; second, responsibility for the conduct of communal affairs, for the performance of positive functions on behalf of the collectivity, especially vis-à-vis "foreign" social systems or subsystems. Insofar as such roles of responsibility are institutionally defined, they always involve a collective orientation on the part of their incumbents as one of their fundamental components.[7]

The word institutionalization means both the internalization of common values by the members of a collectivity, and also the enunciation of prescriptive or prohibitory role expectations by occupants of responsible roles.

The institutionalization of value-orientation patterns thus constitutes, in the most general sense, the mechanism of integration for social systems. However, social integration does not require a single uniform set of value-orientations equally and universally distributed throughout the social system. Social integration may well include a whole series of subsystems of common value-orientations varying around a basic pattern. Institutionally, this brings us before the integrative problem of partial integrations or collectivities within the larger social system, on the one hand, and the total collectivity as an integrated entity, on the other.

---

[7] It should go without saying that these considerations apply to any collectivity, no matter how small a part of a total society it forms. This fundamental structural homology between the total society and sub-collectivities within it is one of the most important aspects of the structure of social systems.

The role-expectations in all these situations are focused by the pattern variable of self- and collective-orientation. Every social system will have institutionalized definitions of the spheres within which a collective subunit or an individual is legitimately permitted to go its own way without specific reference to the interests of a larger collectivity, or to specific obligations toward it. On the other hand, there will be institutionalized spheres of direct obligation to the larger collectivity. This usually will be latent and will be active only discontinuously when situations arise in which the objects are threatened or in which conflict occurs. In the first case, negative sanctions apply only when the limits of permission are exceeded; in the second, they apply whenever the positive obligations fail to be fulfilled. Social systems, of course, will vary greatly with respect to the points at which this line is drawn. Only the solidary group in which there are positive collective obligations would, in a specific sense, be called an integrated social system.

There is a final point to be made in connection with social integration and nonintegration. No social system can be completely integrated; there will, for many reasons, always be some discrepancies between role-expectations and performances of roles. Similarly, at the other extreme, there is never likely to be a completely disintegrated society. The mere fact that the human beings who live in a social system are socialized to some extent gives them many need-dispositions which can be gratified only by conformity with the expectations of others and which make them responsive to the expectations of others. Even societies ridden with *anomie* (for example, extreme class conflict to the point of civil war) still possess within themselves considerable zones of solidarity. No society ever "disintegrates completely"; the "state of nature" depicted by Hobbes is never reached by any real society. Complete disintegration is a limiting case toward which social systems might sometimes move, especially in cerain sectors of the structure, but they never arrive there. A particular social system might, of course, lose its identity, or it might be transformed into one which is drastically different and can become absorbed into another social system. It might split into several social systems where the main cleavages follow territorial lines. But dissolution into the "state of nature" is impossible.

CLASSIFICATION OF SOCIAL SYSTEMS AND THEIR COMPONENTS: STRUCTURAL TYPES

The foregoing analysis of the foci of organization of social systems is a first step toward the comparative analysis of the structural variations of social systems. The beginning of such an analysis is classification. It is, however, only after the logically requisite and empirically significant invariant points of reference have been defined and the range of variability explored that the problem of classification can be seriously approached.

The construction of a classification of types of social systems is much too large a task to attempt to carry very far within the limits of the present work. A few remarks on the nature of the problem may, however, be made, and a few starting points indicated.

The principal obstacle has been the enormous variety of structural variables. The possible combinations of these are so numerous that anything approaching a determinate and manageable classification has been out of the question. Furthermore, we have hitherto lacked systematic theoretical criteria by which to select the most significant of these variables. Progress therefore depends on the selection of a limted number of criteria of strategic significance. It is the aim of the present analysis, with its point of departure in the most elementary features of the frame of reference of the theory of action and its purpose to build step by step from these features to the conception of a complex social system, to provide the required criteria.

The elements of this conceptual scheme are numerous: three modes of motivational orientation, three of value-orientation, two object modalities, six classes of objects, three allocative foci, five pattern variables, and so forth. It is not, however, necessary to treat all the conceptual elements which enter the scheme as of equal significance, or as completely independent of each other. Selection can be made, in terms of strategic significance, for the purpose. Our conceptual scheme itself yields the criteria of selection which enable us to reduce the degree of complexity.

In the first place, the basic distinctions in the structure of the object world may be eliminated as a source of further complication. They need appear only in the distinction between the modalities of quality and performance, which is, of course, included in the pattern-variable scheme. Since the three modes of motivational orientation and the three modes of value-orientation are already included in the pattern variables, the construction of the basic patterns of orientation in social relationships can proceed from the combinations of the pattern variables. The resultant combinations may then be used for the description of the structures through which the allocative and integrative functions are performed.

We may begin with the allocative problems. It is possible here to treat the three categories of allocation of personnel, facilities, and rewards together. They constitute the process of "circular flow" which may occur within a social system that is in equilibrium, without being accompanied by a change in the essential structure of the system itself. They may therefore be treated independently of the resultant substantive distribution, at least preliminarily. Further analyses will have to relate the properties of the allocative process to the distributions which they bring about.

Social systems will vary, in this range, according to whether these allocative processes are organized and controlled in terms of ascriptive or performance object properties. In different social sytems, different object properties are adjudged relevant in allocative decisions. The evaluative standards which are primarily embodied in allocative decisions, therefore, are those of ascription and achievement. Individual actors may be granted roles, facilities, or rewards in accordance with their possession of certain classificatory qualities, such as sex, age, physique, personality traits (without regard for their value for the prediction of achievement), or in accordance with their possession of certain relational qualities such as biological (kinship or ethnic) relationships, territorial location, memberships in associations, wealth, and status. On the other hand, they might be granted roles, facilities, or rewards in accordance with their past or prospective achievements, such as instances of their physical strength, performance in examinations or past roles, their power in present roles (i.e., their capacity to gratify or deprive) within a collectivity or among collectivities. Naturally it is not always easy to disentangle these various properties on the basis of which allocations are made (and acknowledged), since they often operate jointly. Indeed, a given characteristic might have several functions simultaneously; for example, take the case of proximity to the exercise of power. Individuals whose occupational roles bring them close to those who exercise great power might receive prestige and other valued objects, both because of the relationship itself and because of the potentiality which these individuals possess of influencing the direction and content of the power and thus themselves gratifying or depriving.

It is at this point relevant to recall that a concrete allocation, once made, cannot be expected to be settled indefinitely. The first and basic reason is the finiteness of life and the continual process of change of need-dispositions and situations during its passage. For a social system to function over a period extending beyond the life span of a generation, there must be a continuous recruitment of new personnel into roles, and naturally, the recruiting must be regulated by some standards of evaluation.

In addition to this fundamental source of the need for continuous allocation, many facilities and rewards are not indefinitely durable but are "consumed" or "wear out" in the course of time, and tasks change, of course, with the consequent change in roles to which there must be new allocations. Therefore, there must also be a continuous flow of replacements in these categories. Incumbency in some roles is much longer than in others, and some facilities and rewards are more durable than others; these differences in "life span" are of prime significance for many empirical problems. But here the essential point is the relative impermanence of all three classes of elements of the system; hence the functional necessity of a continuous flow of replacement and of the regulation of the process. Along side of all this, and only analytically separable from it, there are changes in the substantive content of the expectations governing roles and the organization of the roles about tasks. These changes of content are empirically intimately related to the allocative flow. Indeed, strains arising from the working of the allocative mechanisms may constitute some of the most important sources of changes in the content of roles and the mode of their organization.

As a first approximation, we may distinguish three types of mechanism by which the allocative flow can be regulated. The first is allocation by a process of deliberate selective decision by an authoritative agency and according to an established policy in which either qualities or achievements may be the chief criteria. The second is the institutionalization of some automatically applied rules of allocation, in which the chief criteria of allocation are qualities, especially memberships. The third is allocation as a resultant of a process of individual competitive or emulative achievement, or promise of achievement, whereby the "winners" automatically secure the roles, facilities, and rewards which, according to the prevailing systems of values, are the most desirable.[8] Perhaps the emulative aspect is prominent only in some cases; the most essential criterion in the third type is that the outcome is free from determination either by a fixed automatic rule or by the decision of an authority. The first type, as distinguished from the second and third, tends to be more centralized, and the actor who grants the role, facility, or reward is less likely to make his decision on the basis of a formalized examination established primarily as a recruitment device. Of course, different mechanisms may operate in different parts of the social system and in some parts there may be combinations of any two or of all three types. But variability with respect to the incidence and distribution of these types of mechanisms, which are distinguished by (1) the type of criteria (concerning objects) which they employ and (2) the extent to which organized authority makes the selective decisions, constitutes one major range of variability of social structures.

The relation to the pattern variables, and hence to the system of value-orientations, may be treated briefly. It is with special reference to its bearing on these mechanisms that the ascription-achievement variable is of primary significance, especially in the allocation of personnel. In all societies the ascriptive criteria of sex and age at least limit the eligibilities for participation in different roles, and hence memberships in collectivities. Beside these, the ascrption of roles on the basis of the criteria of biological relationship and territorial location of residence plays some significant part in all societies, by virtue of the fact that all have kinship systems and that kinship units are units of residence. But, of course, the range of allocative results determined by these ascriptive criteria varies enormously in different societies. The maximum application of the "hereditary principle" — in, for example an Australian tribe or the Indian caste system — represents one extreme of variation in this respect. Our own society is considerably removed in the opposite direction.

---

[8] Even in the case of a system of allocation by individual competition, much of the allocation will be by virtue of qualities such as membership and particularly membership in a kinship group. The winner in individual competition usually shares the prizes with his family.

However widely complexes of qualities may operate as determinants in a social system in which there is a competitive allocative process, they set limits to, rather than serve as a constitutive part of that process. Such a system therefore accords primacy to criteria of performance and increases the range of roles which can be entered through achievement. It is noteworthy in this connection that ascriptive criteria may, and often do, include memberships in collectivities — for example, by virtue of birth — but criteria of achievement cannot do so, as far as the allocation of personnel is concerned. In this context, therefore, an orientation toward achievement is inherently "individualistic." Of course, the same basic schema may be applied to the relationships of collectivities, such as those of business firms.

With respect to the ascription-achievement variable, allocation by authoritative decision is, as we have said, neutral; it may lean either way or combine both types of criteria. Indeed, it may facilitate the adjustment of the two types of processes to each other. However, the more widely ascriptive criteria are applied in allocation, the less necessary specific authoritative decision becomes for routine cases. There is thus a definite relationship between such a situation and traditionalism. There are, however, almost always small openings left by ascriptively oriented allocative processes, and these tend to be regulated by authoritative decision.

Allocation by authoritative decision quite often serves as a mechanism for the universalistic application of an achievement-oriented system of allocation. In the Chinese bureaucracy the allocation of personnel by appointment, on the basis of achievement in examinations, made access to bureaucratic roles more dependent on achievement than it probably would have been if it had been left to open emulative competition under the conditions then prevailing in Chinese society.

In short, the variability of social structures with respect to the incidence of these various types of allocative mechanisms seems capable of empirical establishment and is, as well, of central theoretical importance.

The Content of Roles

The allocative process does not determine the role structure of the social system or the content of the roles. It is necessary, therefore, to develop categories which make possible the analysis of the variability of the social system with respect to the content and organization of roles. We will take up role contents first, and the structural integration of roles later.

Role contents can be classified according to three sets of invariant points of reference. That is, there are three separate classes of problems that must be solved by all role occupants; if we classify the solutions to these problems generally enough, we will thereby have, in some sense, a classification of role contents. The three sets of problems (or invariant points of reference) are

(1) problems of instrumental interaction, (2) problems of expressive interaction, and (3) integrative problems.[9]

Problems of instrumental interaction concern relationships with alters
which ego engages in, not primarily for their own sake, but for the sake of
goals other than the immediate and direct gratification experienced in contact with the object. The social elaboration of instrumentally significant
activities is what, in economic theory and its utilitarian philosophical background, has come to be called the division of labor. Problems of expressive
interaction concern relationships with alters which ego engages in primarily
for the immediate direct gratification they provide. Integrative problems are
problems of a somewhat different order. They are the problems which arise
when one would maintain proper relationships between roles with an eye to
the structural integration of the social system. We will take up in the following pages, first, problems of instrumental interaction as bases for classification
of role contents, and second, problems of expressive interaction as bases for
classification of role contents. Then we will go on to discuss problems of
structural integration.

A system of instrumentally interdependent roles has a basic structure
which, throughout the variability of the substantive goals which are being
instrumentally sought, may be treated as constant. There are a limited number
of functional problems arising in ego's instrumental relations with others,
problems which have to be solved if the system is to persist. These problems
are constant in all systems of instrumental interaction although some of them
are logically appropriate to higher degrees of differentiation of the instrumental system, and thus need not be considered at the more elementary
levels. These problems provide a set of invariant points of reference or comparative categories for the analysis of the structure and content of roles in
systems of instrumental allocation.

It is inherent in the nature of human action that some goals should be
sought instrumentally. It is consequently inherent in the nature of social
systems that their members should perform certain mutually significant
functions on the instrumental level — functions which require disciplined
activity and in which the actor's interest in direct and immediate expression
of gratification will not have primacy. But it is equally a precondition of the
functioning of social systems that they should provide a minimum of essential
gratifications direct and indirect to their members (i.e., to a sufficient proportion of them a sufficient proportion of the time). These direct gratifications of need-dispositions are so organized into a system of relationships that
the structure of that system is just as vital to the actor's interest in expressive

---

[9] So far as problems of instrumental and affective interaction are concerned, it seems
fair to treat complex societies and smaller units (e.g., the conjugal families) of which it is
composed as homologous. They will differ, of course, with respect to their structural
integration.

gratification as the structure of the instrumental system is to their instrumental interests. Moreover, the systems of gratification and instrumentality are intertwined in the same concrete system of social roles, and many of the factors that cause change emerge from this intertwining.

If we take the instrumental system first, we find there are four fundamental problems. The first derives from the fact that, given the division of labor,[10] one or more alters must be the *beneficiaries* of ego's activities. In the terminology of economics, they must be the consumers of his product. In addition to the *technical* problem, then, of how ego is to organize his own resources, including his actions to produce the service or commodity, there is the further problem of determining the terms on which alter is allowed to become the beneficiary. This is a special case of the problem of the terms of exchange; specifically it is the problem of the terms of disposal. Thus, the problem of disposal is the first problem of instrumental interaction. Secondly, insofar as ego specializes in a particular type of instrumentally significant activity, he becomes dependent on the output of one or more alters for meeting his own needs. These may or may not be the same alters involved in the former relationship of disposal — in a complex economy they usually are not. At any rate there is an exchange problem here, too, growing out of the functional need, as it may be called, for ego to receive *remuneration* for his activities. Thus, the problem of remuneration is the second problem of instrumental interaction.

Problem of access to facilities (alters as *suppliers* of facilities)		Disposal problem (alters as *consumers*)
	Technical instrumental goal-orientation of ego	
Problem of collaboration (alters as *collaborators*)		Remuneration problem (alters as *sources* of income)

Third, only in a limiting case will all the facilities that ego needs to perform his instrumental functions be spontaneously available to him. It will be necessary for him to acquire or secure access to some of them through arrangement with one or more alters, involving still a third set of exchange relations and the associated standard incorporated into the terms of exchange. This third instrumental problem is that of access to facilities. Fourth, the product may not be capable of production by ego through his own unaided efforts. In this case he is dependent on still a fourth set of alters for collaboration in the joint instrumental process. The process requires organization

---

[10] Individual self-sufficiency is of no interest here because it does not entail interdependence.

in which ego and alters collaborate to produce a unitary result which is the object of instrumental significance. Thus, the fourth instrumental problem is the problem of coöperation or collaboration. These relations are set forth in the accompanying diagram.

In each of these relationships of ego and the alters, there is a problem of exchange, the solution of which is the settlement of the terms on which ego enters into mutually acceptable relations with the relevant alters. The settlement of the terms of exchange is a basic functional problem inherent in the allocative process of social systems. It was not directly taken account of in our discussion of the institutionalization of roles, but it must be treated in a more differentiated analysis. In our analysis of institutionalization we treated the evaluative content of the expectations of the actors toward themselves and others as unproblematical. In actuality, however, each expectation contains or is associated with an evaluation of the action of the actor in its relation to the value of the complementary action of the alter.[11] All human interaction contains a scale of evaluative equivalence. In instrumental relationships this scale of evaluative equivalence tends to be determinate, specific, and explicit. In diffuse affective attachments the equivalences are much broader and less determinate and much less explicit, as well. The standards of the terms of exchange not only become imbedded in the expectations of instrumental orientations; they also become institutionalized, as do the processes for establishing them when they are not spontaneously and automatically effective. The institutionalization of the processes and standards by which the terms of exchange come to be settled constitutes one essential component of social structures.

In addition to this, *exchange* implies a thing which changes hands. This entity may be called a *possession* and analysis will show that *possession* is always reducible to *rights*. Physical objects are significant insofar as one actor (individual or collective) has various types of control — acknowledged as legitimate — over them while others do not. The terms on which possessions are held, used, controlled, and disposed of is another focus of the functional problems of allocation: *property*.

We turn now to a somewhat different problem, also derivative from the division of labor. A most important range of variability occurs along the continuum of *fusion* and *segregation* of roles in instrumental relationships. The role allocated to ego may be confined to a technical instrumental content, such as the arrangement of the facililties through his own resources while assigning the "responsibility" for the execution of all four of the essential conditions of that role to the incumbents of the other roles. Such a *technical*

---

[11] The notion here is this: when ego acts with respect to alter, his action is seen as having some ("evaluative") value to alter. That is, it gratifies alter, or helps alter along the road toward gratification. When ego acts in such a fashion, alter is expected to return the favor by acting with respect to ego with an action of similar value.

role would be the extreme of segregation. This is the typical case of the functionally specific (specialized) roles within large-scale organizations in modern society. At the other extreme, is the type of role in which the incumbent has not only the responsibility for the technical performance but for all four associated functions — as in the case of the medieval craftsman, or the ideal type of independent general practitioner in medicine. This may be called the artisan [12] role.

The larger and more differentiated an instrumental system the more essential management or managed coördination becomes to keep the organization going as a functioning concern. With this, there emerge *executive* or managerial roles. In the executive role is centered the responsibility for the specification of roles to be performed, the recruitment of personnel to perform the roles, the organization and regulation of the collaborative relations among the roles, the remuneration of the incumbents for their performances, the provision of facilities for performance of the roles, and the disposal of the product. The organization of an instrumental complex into a corporate body which exists in a context of other individual actors and corporate bodies involves also the management of "foreign relations." Here rearrangements of the internal organization and the use of the power to gratify or deprive which the corporate body has at its disposal are available to the manager (as well as the invocation and interpretation of the common value-orientations which are shared with the "foreign" body).

Thus social systems may be further characterized by the extent to which they are made up of fused or segregated roles in an instrumental context or, more concretely, of technical, of artisan, and of executive roles.[13]

Up to this point, our discussion has entirely passed over that aspect of the system of relationships which is oriented primarily by interests in direct and immediate gratification.[14] Within such a system of relationships oriented toward direct and immediate gratification the basic functional categories are homologous with those of the instrumental complex. In the first place, direct gratification in relation to a cathected social object is a relation to that ob-

---

[12] The independent professional role is then defined as a special subtype in which the technical competence of the incumbent includes the mastery of a generalized intellectual orientation. The professional role, too, is subject to a fairly high degree of segregation of its component elements, although some limits are imposed by the generalized intellectual orientation.

[13] The executive or managerial function itself might be fused or segregated. The more segregated it is, however, the more functionally necessary is some type of integrative mechanism which will perform the function of fusion at this level.

[14] Here gratifications which do not involve social relationships with a cultural component may be ignored. In the context of the present discussion, we are using the terms *gratification interests* and *expressive interests* more or less interchangeably. By expressive orientation we mean a type of action orientation parallel to the instrumental through its inclusion of a cultural component. It is gratification *within* a pattern of appreciative standards.

ject as a "consumer" of the impulse. It is not enough to have the need-disposition. An object must be available which is both "appropriate" for the gratification and "receptive." Alter must allow himself to be an object and not resist or withdraw.

Second, there is also a parallel to remuneration in the dependence of ego, not merely on the receptiveness but on what may be called the *response* of alter. Alter does not merely allow ego to *express* or gratify his need-disposition in the relationship; alter is also expected to act positively in such a way that ego will be the receptive object. These two types of functional preconditions for the gratification of need-dispositions are not always fulfilled by the same objects — where they are we may speak of a symmetrical attachment.

Third, gratification needs not merely an object but is also dependent on the set of circumstances referred to in Chapter II as occasions, which appear, in certain respects, to have functions homologous with those of facilities in the instrumental relationship. Occasions often center around relations to third parties, both because of the necessity of ego's distribution of his expressive orientations among the different objects in a system and be-

Availability of appropriate occasions (depending on third parties)		Social objects as appropriate and receptive
	Specific gratifications of a particular need-disposition	
Diffuse attachments (coördinating particular need-dispositions)		Social objects as responsive

cause the prerequisite of giving gratification to and receiving it from certain actors in a system is a certain relationship with all other actors in the system.

Finally, if we take the need-disposition for gratification and not the object relation as the unit, there is an important functional parallel with coöperation in the instrumental complex. Some need-dispositions, like some technical performances, may be segregated into a separate object relation. But for reasons which have already been discussed, there is a strong tendency for ego to become attached to particular objects for the gratifications of a variety of different need-dispositions. We have called this kind of object relationship a diffuse "attachment." Such an attachment organizes need-disposition gratifications into a "coöperative" system. Putting these various elements together we derive the accompanying homologous paradigm of the structure of the system of relationships of direct and immediate gratifications or expressions. This paradigm analyzes the elementary structure of a social relationship system relevant to the actor's needs for direct gratification or expression. For *n* actors to participate in the same social system, the relationships involved in this paradigm must be organized and controlled, generally through institutionalization. There is in each case a problem of the settlement of the terms on which the gratifications in question can be attained, or in other terms, of the reciprocal rights and obligations to receive and to give various types and degrees of gratification, which is directly homologous with the problem of the settlement of the terms of exchange.

There is, furthermore, in the expressive system an important homologue to possessions in the instrumental system, since there are entities which can "change hands." The actor can acquire them from someone else or grant them to someone else and he can have, acquire, or relinquish rights in them. In the focal case where alter is the cathected object, this must mean the establishment of rights vis-à-vis the *action* of alter, that is, of a situation where ego can *count* on alter's actions. This will include expectations of alter's overt behavior, but for the reasons which have already been discussed, the central interest will be in alter's *attitudes*. Such a right to a given attitude on alter's part may be called a relational possession. Relational possession in this sense constitutes the core of the reward system of a society and thus of its stratification, centering above all on the distribution of rights to response, love, approval, and esteem. (This also means that there will be an equivalent in the expressive system to the "terms of exchange.")

The expressive system of an actor will therefore, to a highly important degree, have to be organized in a system of relationships with other actors in appropriate roles. This system will regulate choice of objects, occasions — and what is primarily at issue in the present discussion — which objects have segmental significance, gratifying only one need-disposition at a time, and which other objects have diffuse significance, gratifying many need-dispositions at the same time. Here the two most obvious types of role would be on the one hand, segregated or specific gratification roles; on the other, diffuse attachment roles. A diffuse attachment then would involve gratification of a plurality of need-dispositions; it would place each object in both receptive and responsive roles and would involve the actor in a more or less continuous complex of appropriate occasions.

The instrumental complex and the complex of direct gratifications or expressions are both aspects of the total allocative mechanism of a concrete social system. The next step in our analysis then, is to see how they both work in a single system. Once again the concepts of fusion and segregation are pertinent. Instrumental and expressive functions may be segregated from each other, each being performed by distinctly separate objects in distinct roles, or they may be fused in the same objects and roles. Where there is segregation of the instrumental and need-gratifying roles and orientations toward objects, it does not necessarily mean that the need-dispositions are always frustrated. It means that the roles and objects which are instrumentally defined may be either neutral or negative as far as their capacity for the gratification of direct need-dispositions is concerned. There certainly can be and very frequently are cases of conflict where segregation is imperfect and positive fusion is impossible. In these cases there must be either frustration of the immediate and direct gratification of need-dispositions or the instrumental complex will be distorted because the instrumentally necessary actions will not be performed in accordance with instrumental role-expectations. In the total economy of the personality, however, adequate motivation of instrumental activities becomes impossible if the performance of instrumental roles imposes too heavy a sacrifice of the larger gratification interests of the personality.

It would be possible to carry out the classification of the possible combinations in this sphere to a high degree of elaboration. For our present purposes, however, it is sufficient to distinguish six major types of combination which are particularly relevant to the broader differentiations of role types. They are the following:

1. The segregation of specific expressive interests from instrumental expectations; for example, the role of a casual spectator at an entertainment.

2. The segregation of a diffuse object attachment from instrumental expectations; for example, the pure type of romantic love role.

3. The fusion of a specific expressive or gratificatory interest with a specific instrumental performance; for example, the spectator at a commercialized entertainment.

4. The fusion of a diffuse attachment with diffuse expectations of instrumental performances; for example, kinship roles.

5. The segregation of specific instrumental performances, both from specific expressive interests and attachments and from other components of the instrumental complex; for example, technical roles.

6. The fusion of a plurality of instrumental functions in a complex which is segregated from immediate expressive interests; for example, "artisan" and "executive" roles.

This classification has been constructed by taking the cases of fusion and segregation of the instrumental and direct gratification complexes and, within each of the segregated role orientations, distinguishing the segregation of role components from the fusion of role complexes. The technical role (5) and the executive role (6) are the two possibilities of segregation and fusion in the instrumental complex when it is segregated from the direct gratification complex. The role of casual spectator (1) and the romantic love role (2) are the two possibilities of segregation and fusion of the direct gratification complex when it has been segregated from the instrumental complex. There is a fusion of the two complexes in roles (3) and (4). In the role of the paying spectator there is segregation both in the direct gratification and in the instrumental orientation; in the role of member of a kinship group there is fusion of all role components in each orientation. (See Fig. 13, p. 273.)

Before proceeding to examine the dynamic implications of this scheme and its closely connected relevance to the comparative analysis of social systems, we shall reformulate it in terms of the pattern-variable scheme in order to show its derivation from the basic categories of the theory of action.[15]

Three pattern variables are involved: affectivity-neutrality, universalism-particularism, and specificity-diffuseness. Primacy of direct and immediate gratification interests implies affectivity. Neutrality is expected in the orientation which is central in the instrumental complex. Where instrumental considerations have primacy, the discipline is institutionalized. Neutrality is not, however, to be found only in institutionalized instrumental orientations.

The pattern variable of specificity underlies the segregation of role components. Specificity consists in this sphere in the segregation of an instrumental performance or of an expressive interest from *responsibility* for its context of preconditions or repercussions so that no evaluative adaptations in this area are required of the actor. Diffuseness unites the particular component with the other components which make up its relational context. From a certain point of view, therefore, the institutionalization of diffuse orientations into fused roles and relationships constitutes a highly important mechanism of social control, in that it binds together empirically the potentially independent elements of a system of relationships. When, on the other hand, diffuseness breaks down and specificity emerges so that roles become segregated into their components and the complexes become segregated too, certain additional problems of control, particularly the promulgation and the regulation of the terms of exchange and of the maintenance of rights to possession and of motivation — emerge with it.

A further subdivision is introduced by the pattern variable particularism-universalism. Whereas affectivity-neutrality refers to an orientation toward objects focused on the mode of their appropriateness for gratification, particularism-universalism refers to an orientation toward objects focused on their membership or quality *in relation to* the actor as a member of a collectivity or an ecological complex. To the extent that the *relationship* (of common membership) to the actor is disregarded we have a universalistic orientation, the object being then judged by its properties in relation to objects other than the actor. Thus, a segregated specific expressive interest is compatible with a universalistic orientation so long as a *class* of objects defined by general properties is appropriate to the gratification and ap-

---

[15] Owing to the rather difficult and technical nature of this derivation, those satisfied of its possibility might be advised to pass over the next four paragraphs.

propriateness is not confined to members of a class already in a special relation to the actor. Therefore, roles 1 and 3 *may* be universally institutionalized. Particularism, on the other hand, though it *may* be involved in specific gratifications, is much more fundamental to diffuse attachments. Therefore, any role in which the element of attachment has primacy is almost necessarily particularistic.[16]

When the possible combinations of these three pattern variables are considered, all of our six types are found, in addition to one other which we did not mention; one which combines universalism, diffuseness, and affectivity.[17] Since a diffuse-affective orientation has been specifically defined as an attachment, we must inquire into the possibility of an attachment without particularity of object. As an empirical phenomenon in a social system, it is a marginal case. It corresponds to "universal love" in a religious sense, which is certainly a value-orientation of great importance. Perhaps it might be desirable to add it as a seventh type. In any case, the difficulties of its institutionalization are obvious.

With respect to their composition in terms of role contents, then, social systems should be susceptible to classification with respect to the functional importance and frequency in different parts of the system of the above enumerated six (or seven) types of role. As far as major societies are concerned, by far the most prominent are the fourth, fifth, and sixth types. The grounds for this lead us into some important dynamic considerations.

In social systems, because of the dependence of ego's gratifications on the responses — actions and attitudes — of alter, there tends to be a primacy of functional interest in performance of roles. The gratifications the actors receive are, therefore, in a sense secondary and instrumental to this interest; the performance of a role in accordance with expectations — i.e., in conformity with standards of obligation and efficiency — becomes established as an intrinsic good. Moreover, in the major role structure of the social system, a particular functional importance tends to fall to those role patterns which perform functions other than gratifying direct expressive interests. When conflict arises between functional role performance in accordance with obligations and direct gratifications, there is always a strong tendency, although not always a successful one, for the former to be given priority. In a secondary sense, however, types one, two, and three are both widespread and functionally very important in most social systems in the reduction of strains created by instrumental roles and sometimes in the disruption of institutions. But only where it is directly integrated with instrumental expectations in the

---

[16] This connection of particularism with diffuse attachments is explicitly limited to the present context. When patterns of value-orientation are taken into consideration, other bases of particularism might be found, notably, the orientation to solidarity based on value-integration.

[17] See Fig. 14

context of diffuse attachment is direct expressive orientation prominently institutionalized in the wider social structure.

Furthermore, these considerations point toward a very important set of dynamic relations between the social system and the personality. All action in roles is motivated and hence must bear some relation to the need-disposition system of the actor. A given need-disposition can be best gratified in certain types of roles, and the balance of the system of need-dispositions in the personality will have much to do with the probable "adjustment" of ego to different types of role. Generally speaking, the need-dispositions for specific gratifications (cell 1, Fig. 14, p. 274) will be best fitted to roles one and three. Since these roles are usually functionally peripheral to the organization and working of the social structure, a person in whom these need-dispositions are especially strong will probably have a difficulty in adjustment in most societies. The need for love, on the other hand, will fit best with roles two and four. There may, however, be a problem engendered by the instrumental expectations and hence the elements of discipline necessitated by adjustment to role four. Finally, roles five and six would seem most effectively to gratify, other things being equal, the need-disposition for approval and esteem, when there is no necessity for either diffuse or specific immediate gratifications or expressions.

The fourth type of role would probably be the stablest, inasmuch as it offers the possibility of directly gratifying the need-dispositions and enhances stability through the effect of diffuseness in both instrumental and expressive systems.

The relative strength of the different classes of need-dispositions will, of course, vary with different personality types and hence with different types of socialization experience. However, there is likely to be a certain minimum strength of each of these need-dispositions although some might undergo pronounced transformations through the mechanisms of defense and adjustment. A society which makes the institutionalization of roles five and six very widespread must have, if it is to continue more or less stable, some compensatory mechanisms for the gratification of need-dispositions for immediate gratification. The emphasis in the American kinship system on affectivity, especially the prominence of romantic love and the emergence of various types of relatively undisciplined hedonism in our society such as commercialized entertainment, drinking, and the literature and films of violence, might be among the adjustive consequences of the institutional emphasis. These might be regarded as a balancing of the "one-sidedness" of roles five and six through compensating outlets allowed by roles two and three. The interrelationships are, however, neither immediate nor direct and many other factors are involved.

INTEGRATION: CONSENSUS AND POWER

The foregoing discussion has been concerned with the allocative organization of social systems. Variability will also be found in structures which are primarily of integrative significance. Of these, two classes are especially important. They are the systems of value-orientation, which are institutionalized in the social system and define the scope and depth of solidarities among its members, and the adaptive structure through which the system achieves sufficient integration to keep going as a system.

We have already discussed systems of value-orientation in general in the last chapter. Systems of value-orientation defined (in the categories of the pattern variables) the main outlines of the expectations governing roles. But even though there is a relatively definite "ethos" in the value system of the culture, the roles in a social system are not uniform. The distribution of the different types of roles within the social system cannot be explained merely by reference to this ethos, for reasons which have been reviewed already. Hence there will not be one internally consistent system of values in a society. Even in a highly integrated society, there will be at best a heterogeneous combination of variants of the main theme of the ethos, with numerous elements of compromise and inhibition of the consistent application of the system of values which is generally acknowledged as legitimate.

The fifth pattern variable, self-orientation–collective-orientation, is especially important in the analysis of solidarity. This pattern variable defines the scope of the obligations to the collectivity and consequently the areas of permissiveness which are left open to private goals, whether they be sought instrumentally or as objects of immediate and direct gratification. The private goals may be those of individuals or of collectivities vis-à-vis other collectivities. Social systems vary greatly in the ways and in the scope which they allow the sphere of permissiveness. Although no society is entirely without a sphere of permissiveness, just as no society is without a high degree of regulation, yet the differences both in magnitude and qualitative incidence may be extremely significant from both an ethical and a scientific standpoint.

Thus the patterns of value-orientation, as defined in pattern variable terms, can be seen to define the scope and depth of solidary groupings in the social system. The functions of all solidary groupings are largely, although by no means entirely, allocative, as we have seen. The value patterns may, like the ascription-achievement variable, be particularly relevant to the regulation of the allocative flow of personnel, facilities, and rewards among roles and incumbents of roles; or, like affectivity-neutrality, universalism-particularism, and specificity-diffuseness, they may describe the roles and systems of roles within which this flow takes place. Or, finally, like self-orientation–collective-orientation, their relevance may lie in defining the boundaries of the obligations of solidarity and the areas of permissiveness which these leave open. In doing this, they have a large share in the settlement of the terms of exchange.

Where the terms of exchange are not arrived at spontaneously and simultaneously by the partners to the exchange relationship, some type of adjudication or settlement becomes necessary. The bargaining or discussion by which they arrive at a settlement might be simply the result of the coercive power [18] of one of the actors over the other. Usually, however, it will not be; for no social system could persist through time and meet most of the functional problems which arise in it if the terms of exchange in its instrumental complex — both economic and political — were exclusively or even predominantly settled by coercion. The threat of coercion certainly has an important place, and actual coercion, too, plays a marginal though very significant part. In periods of extensive disintegration, indeed, actual coercion assumes a more prominent position as a factor both in disintegration and in reintegration. But at almost all times the terms of exchange — the expectations of what will be given him on the basis of which ego acts in a given situation — have their roots in the generalized patterns of value-orientation widely shared in the society. However, there is a gap between the generalized patterns and the specific terms of exchange. Sometimes this gap can be closed by a gradual give-and-take, a trial-and-error process in the course of which a balance satisfactory to the parties immediately involved is gradually worked out. More likely is some sort of adjudication by discussion, in which the generalized patterns are invoked as legitimating specific proposals for settlement. Other forms of settlement include threats of deprivation within the sphere of permissiveness allowed by the generalized patterns and settlement through declaration or legislation by an authority whose powers are regarded as legitimate in the light of the generalized patterns of value-orientation.

Even in a society in which the consensus on the generalized patterns of value-orientation — by their nature, patterns of value-orientation must be generalized — is great, it will still be insufficient for the maintenance of order. Nor can the equally necessary specificity of role-expectation be counted upon to remedy the deficiency. Some sort of institutionalized mechanism is indispensable, and this is the function of authority. We have already mentioned the function of authority in connection with the allocation of facilities and rewards. Here we shall refer briefly to the function of authority in integration. The standard governing the terms of exchange, or the standard by which expectations are made mutual and articulated so that both ego and alter obtain the gratification which they seek in the particular situation, is an evaluative standard. It is the functional link between allocation and integra-

---

[18] Coercive power is the capacity to inflict deprivations despite physical resistance. Short of this extreme, coercive power is the imposition of deprivations which cannot be evaded because attempting to do so would result in other more serious deprivations.

tion. It is the measuring rod of apportionment, and its acceptance by the recipients is the foundation of an integrative social system of social order.

THE ANALYSIS OF SOCIAL STRUCTURE

We may now try to deal more synthetically with the various components
and functional processes of the social system. The object orientations and
processes which we have treated constitute characteristic *trait complexes* of
the social system as a whole. They are found throughout the system, although they are particularly prominent in some section of it; and they may
be regarded as resultants of all the factors hitherto explicitly dealt with,
including the specific situation of the social system and its history.

They may be most conveniently classified in the categories of Fig. 15
(p. 275). First, all social systems will, in these terms, have certain relatively
general patterns of categorization of their units, both individual actors and
collectivities. All societies, for example, evaluate individuals by their age and
sex, although the particular evaluations will vary from society to society.

In the second place, all social systems have characteristic patterns of role
orientation to which both individual and collective actors adhere. The
basic variations are, as we have seen, definable in terms of combinations of the
pattern variables. But in consequence of adaptation to the exigencies of situational and motivational conditions — societies will vary with respect to the
distribution of these patterns throughout their respective structures. Thus
a role exercising authority may, as we saw in the last chapter, be defined
in relatively sharp authoritarian terms; or a role placing emphasis on individual responsibility may receive a strong anti-authoritarian emphasis. The
sources of these adaptive reorganizations of the fundamental role-expectations
(conceptually derived from the pattern variables) are essentially those analyzed in the last chapter in connection with the integration of value-orientation patterns in the social system. With reference to the dominant ethos of
the society, they give rise to such broad traits as are usually called "indvidual-
ism," "collectivism," "traditionalism."

With regard to our third category, we need do no more than refer briefly
to the division of labor, since it has already been dealt with earlier in this
chapter. No attempt was made above to characterize types of the division of
labor as a whole; for example, with respect to the degree of differentiation
of functions or the points at which the fusions and segregations occur. These
tasks still remain. In respect to our fourth category, we have dealt with the
system of social stratification, which is the reward system integrated about
the allocation of prestige. This is a major structural aspect of all social systems, and produces extremely far-reaching functional consequences. Finally,
the fifth category comprises the specifically integrative structures of collectivities, with the society as a whole regarded as the most important of these
collectivities. These integrative structures include the modes of organization

and regulation of the power system and the ways in which orientation to a paramount focus of values, as in religion, are organized. These integrations take the form of state and church, insofar as differentiation has made them distinctive structures. It is here that differentiated roles with integrative functions on behalf of the social system as a whole will be found. The components which enter into them will, however, be those already discussed.

Whatever success we have in the development of categories which will be useful in describing the ranges of variability of social structures will prepare us to approach those really important problems for which classification is not the solution. One of the foremost of these is the problem of the discovery and explanation of certain empirical clusters among the formally possible structural clusters. Thus in kinship, for example, although there is nothing intrinsic to either the socialization of the child or the regulation of sex relations which makes it necessary that these two functions should be handled by the same institution; yet they do both tend to be accomplished by one institution, usually the family. Their thoroughgoing separation, where it has been attempted, has not lasted long. Similarly, the distributions of prestige and power do not vary independently of one another, even though intrinsically the two are quite discrete. A wide discrepancy between the distribution of power and prestige limits the degree of integration and creates a disequilibrium; the discrepancy cannot last long unless special mechanisms reduce the strains and reinforce the capacity of the system to withstand them. Otherwise the system will have to undergo marked modifications before an equilibrium is reëstablished.

The existence of such empirical clusters simplifies the ultimate problem of classification and helps us to formulate more systematically the problems of dynamic analysis. It reduces the variety of types which must be taken into consideration, and it more sharply defines the problem of explanation by presenting for any variable both those categories or series with which it is highly correlated and those with which it has a low correlation. An adequate explanation should account for both. Thus this method of classification enables us to perceive problems in relationships which had previously been regarded as scientifically unproblematical, and it enables us to trace out more sharply the particularly dynamic property of certain of the variables which we use.

It is by no means necessary to suspend all comparative structural analyses pending the emergence of a comprehensive systematic classification of types of society. Work of the highest order can be done in particular areas of social subsystems, and although it might have to be reformulated in the light of general theory, its intrinsic value is indisputable. As the general theory of social systems and particularly of societies develops, the nature of the situation in which subsystems operate can be clarified. Gradually the analysis of such subsystems may be expected to merge into the general theory. At the same time, the development of the general theory of social systems needs to be carried on with special attention to the task of elaboration toward the more specific, more concrete subsystems.

Our own analysis is thus very far from a classification of actual structural types of social systems. But it does present, we feel, a systematic approach to the problem, which is capable of further development into the very heart of substantive theory. It delineates all the principal components — the elements of orientation and the functional problems which it will be necessary to incorporate into such a classification — and works out some of their relations to each other.

MOTIVATION AND THE DYNAMICS OF SOCIAL PROCESS

The preceding section has led us necessarily to the border of the dynamic problems of the stability and change of social systems.[19] It is a measure of the validity of our conceptual scheme that it should have done so since it may be regarded as evidence that our categories even in their most elementary form were defined so as to include dynamic properties. A cursory retrospect of all our categories will show that they were from the very start directed, not just toward classificatory or taxonomic description, but toward the explanation of why various structures endure or change. The employment of motivational categories in our description of action meant that we had made the first preliminary step toward the analysis of the conditions of persistence and change. The categories of cognitive, cathectic, and evaluative orientation carried in them the possibilities of the redirection of action with changes in internal or external conditions. The introduction of the concepts of gratification-deprivation balance and of the optimum of gratification provided a first approximation to the formulation of hypotheses about the direction of modifications where these occur, and of the continuation of a given pattern of

[19] Only in a very specifically qualified sense is the problem here one of "psychology." It is not sufficient to take over the theoretical genralizations held to be established in psychology and apply them without further ado to the analysis of the behavior of many individuals interacting as a social system. "Psychologism" is inadequate for our task because we must study dynamic problems in the context of a social system and the social system and the personality system are of course not identical. The social roles in which the actor is implicated become constituents of the structure of his personality. They become such through identifications and the internalization of the value-orientations of alters, which are thus part of the shared value-orientations of the members of a collectivity. Without categories which permit the analysis of the significance of relations to social objects, and hence of sensitivity to sanctions, "dynamic psychology" (i.e., the study of personality within the action frame of reference) would be impossible.

Likewise, without the basic constituents of personality, without the elements of motivational orientation, the organization of orientations to objects and so on, action in the role structure of the social system could not be successfully analyzed. The dynamic processes involved in the maintenance and change of institutional structures could not be treated without a basic understanding of personalities as well as of culture. But the analysis of the dynamics of social process is *not* simply an application of the theory of personality.

action. The categories of value standards — cognitive, appreciative, and moral — were again constructed with reference to the persistent possibilities of change which are present when alternative paths of action must be discriminated and selected in the light of standards. The object classification had the same function of preparing our scheme for use in dynamic analysis — it was a further step in the delineation of the fundamental alternatives in confrontation with which either persistence or change may result. The pattern variables carried in themselves the same dynamic properties which were present in the more elementary categories from which they were constructed. This could most clearly be seen in our analysis of the personality system where a direct line runs from cathexis through attachment and the dependence on positive attitudinal response to identification, and it could be seen in the concept of need-dispositions as well. When we placed the individual actor in the context of the social system, the dynamic implications became even more apparent. The concept of functionally necessary tasks, the performance of which in certain ways is a condition of the maintenance of social order, and the concept of strain which is a systemic concept, referring to the problems arising from the coexistence of different entities in the same system, brought us into the very midst of the problems of dynamic analysis.

We have argued above that there is no point-for-point articulation between the performance of a role and the personality of its incumbent and that the social structure could not be described from knowledge, however detailed, concerning the personality systems of its members. This should not, however, be interpreted to mean that social process can be analyzed in any other than motivational categories or that the analysis of the processes of its maintenance or change can proceed at any stage without referring to components and mechanisms of personalities.

Thus, although a close correspondence is impossible, it is equally impossible that personality structure and the structure of role-expectations should vary at random with respect to each other. In the first place, the mere existence of an internalized common culture as a component of personality precludes this and so, although in different ways, does the existence of the same basic object system, which is equally a target of evaluation for both personality and social systems.

The core of the personality system may be treated in great measure as a product of socialization, both through learning and by adjustments and defenses against threats introduced in the course of the socialization process. It is also a product of the expressive and instrumental involvement of the individual, in the course of life, in his various statuses within the social system. These connect the personality with the primary patterns of value-orientation. There is no doubt of the influence of these components in the personality and consequently of the great part which the personality system plays in the maintenance of certain generalized orientations.

There has, however, been a strong tendency in some of the recent discussions of "personality and culture" to assume an altogether too simple relationship between personality structure and social action. The proponents of these views have tended to impute too much rigidity to behavior, and they have also overestimated the uniformity of behavior within a given society and even within a subsystem. They have overgeneralized their often penetrating observations of some uniformities into a nearly complete uniformity. They have tended to regard most adult social behavior as little more than the "acting out" of the need-dispositions of a typical character structure, as if the actor were incapable of reality-testing, discipline, and evaluation when confronting particular situations with their own particular tasks.

Of course the individual's character structure has much to do with his response to a situation. It influences his cognition and expectations and the selections which he makes from the various aspects of the situation. Nonetheless, nothing approaching absolute uniformity, even for those individuals who have been socialized in relatively specific and uniform statuses, can be legitimately assumed. Both the constitutional endowment and the concrete practices of child training will vary from individual to individual — though within limits and certainly not randomly. The internal variations of socialization practices within the same society contribute further to the heterogeneity of personality types in a given society.

There is also no reason to believe that all personality structures are equally rigid. They do undergo change, again within limits imposed by pre-existing structures, but the constellation of need-dispositions, reality-testing capacities, and disciplinary capacities can change through action in situations (even in situations which are not specifically therapeutic).[20] In the study of the bearing of personality on social processes, however, the overwhelmingly important point is that behavior is not uniform in different situations. If behavior were merely the acting out of personality qualities, it would be uniform in different types of situations. It would show no adaptability to variations in the situation. Once it is acknowledged that personality systems do have a reality-testing function which explores situations and contributes to the guidance of behavior, then it follows that the situation as a set of opportunities for direct expressive or instrumental gratification and of possible threats of deprivation must be regarded as a co-determinant of behavior in the *here and now*. Only when the structure of opportunities can be treated as constant can interindividual differences of concrete behavior be attributed *exclusively* to the factor of personality structure. And even then such propositions would be methodologically and substantively defective.

[20] This phenomenon has not been sufficiently appreciated in contemporary analysis — partly because of the difficulties of intensive and accurate biographical studies, partly because the source of much of our insight into personality, psychoanalytic theory, has grown up in a context in which the uniformities of the personality system through quite long periods of life of an individual have been selected for concentrated scrutiny.

These strictures on the explanation of social behavior simply by reference to personality are directed only against certain exaggerations. Personality variables *are* obviously in the first rank among the factors which are continuously operating in behavior at all times. The attention given earlier to the importance of the gratification-deprivation balance and the optimum of gratification, the sensitivity of the actor to the approval and disapproval of alter, the need-disposition scheme, and the concept of attachment is an indication of the large place allowed to personality in the working of social systems. Social systems work through their impact on the motivational systems of individuals, and the intra-individual complications and elaborations of motivation into systems lead back into the social system. The destination to which it is led back, however, is determined by the situation. The role in which the individual is expected by others to act, and in which he will act when there is a correspondence between his own expectations and the expectations of the others who surround him, was not the product of his personality. In any concrete situation it is given to his personality as a set of alternatives. His action is limited to the alternatives, and his choice is partly a function of his personality system, partly a function of the repercussions which may be expected by him from each of the alternatives in the way of gratifications and deprivations of various types.

Thus for the social system to continue to function as the same system, the reliable expectations of ego's gratification through the alternatives which the other actors in the situation expect him to follow will be the basis of his conformity with their expectations (regardless of whether he is motivated by a specific substantive need-disposition or by a generalized conformist need-disposition). To the extent that these expected gratifications are not forthcoming at the expected times and places in the system ego will not produce the expected actions, and the system will accordingly undergo some change. The kinds of expectations which ego will have, the selective focus of his cognitive orientation, the kinds of gratifications which he will seek, will, of course, all be integral to his personality system. The same responses of alters will not be equally gratifying to all individuals since all individuals will not all have the same system of need-dispositions.

The social system depends, then, on the extent to which it can keep the equilibrium of the personality systems of its members from varying beyond certain limits. The social system's own equilibrium is itself made up of many subequilibriums within and cutting across one another, with numerous personality systems more or less in internal equilibrium, making up different equilibrated systems such as kinship groups, social strata, churches, sects, economic enterprises, and governmental bodies. All enter into a huge moving equilibrium in which instabilities in one subsystem in the personality or social sphere are communicated simultaneously to both levels, either disequilibrating the larger system, or part of it, until either a reëquilibration takes place or the total equilibrium changes its form.

The equilibrium of social systems is maintained by a variety of processes and mechanisms, and their failure precipitates varying degrees of disequilibrium (or disintegration). The two main classes of mechanisms by which motivation is kept at the level and in the direction necessary for the continuing operation of the social system are the *mechanisms of socialization* and the *mechanisms of social control*.[21] The mechanisms of socialization are those mechanisms which form the need-dispositions making for a generalized readiness to fulfill the major patterns of role-expectation which an individual will encounter. From the personality point of view this is one essential part of the learning process, but *only* one. The mechanisms of socialization, in this sense, must not be conceived too narrowly. They include some which are relevant to the production of relatively specific orientations toward certain roles (e.g., the sex role). But they also include more general traits such as relatively generalized "adaptiveness" to the unforeseen exigencies of different roles. The latter may be particularly important in a complex and changing society.

The process of socialization operates mainly through the mechanisms of learning of which generalization, imitation, and identification are perhaps particularly important. The motivational processes which are involved in the learning mechanisms become organized as part of the mechanisms of socialization through the incorporation of the child into a system of complementary role-expectations. Two main levels may be distinguished. First, mainly in the identifications formed through the attachments of early childhood, the primary patterns of value-orientation in the institutionalized role-system become internalized as part of the child's own personality. Second, at a later stage, on the foundations thus laid, the child acquires orientations to more specific roles and role complexes and learns the definitions of the situation for incumbents of these roles, the goals which are appropriate to them according to the prevailing value-orientations, the procedures which are appropriate according to the same standards, and the symbolic structure of the rewards associated with them.

The first type of process forms what is sometimes called the basic char-

---

[21] This classification of the mechanisms of the social system rests on the fact that all motivational processes of action, hence all mechanisms, are processes *in the individual personality*. It is individuals who are socialized and whose tendencies to deviant behavior are controlled. There is no motivation of a collectivity *as such*. Cutting across this classification of the social mechanisms, however, is a set of distinctions relative to the locus of functional significance for the social system of a given motivational mechanism. This significance may center in (a) its bearing on the adequacy of motivation of individuals to the performance of their social roles, i.e., their gratification-deprivation balances; (b) its bearing on the allocative processes of the social system; or (c) its bearing on the integration of the social system. Mechanisms either of socialization or of social control may have any one or any combination of these types of significance.

acter or personality structure of the individual. But the orientations on this level are too general to constitute adequate motivation for the fulfillment of specific role-expectations. Furthermore, although there are undoubtedly modal types of such character orientation within a given social system, the product cannot be uniform; there will always be considerable variability about such modal types. For both these reasons the second level of the socialization process, which may be called the situational specification of role-orientations, is vital to the development of adequate social motivation. The mechanisms of socialization thus prepare the actor on a fairly broad level of generalization for the various roles in which he is likely to be placed subsequently in his career. Some of these roles may be uniform through time, subsequent to childhood; others might vary according to the various qualities and performance propensities which he possesses. The mechanisms of socialization will not prepare him for these roles in detail, but they will, insofar as they function effectively, give him the general orientations and expectations which will enable him to add the rest by further learning and adjustment. This preparation in advance makes the inevitable occurrence of succession less disruptive of equilibrium than it might otherwise be. Where the socialization mechanisms have not provided the oncoming generation or the native-born or immigrants with the requisite generalized orientation, a disequilibration will be very likely to occur.[22]

Failure of the mechanisms of socialization to motivate conformity with expectations creates tendencies to deviant behavior which, beyond certain critical points, would be disruptive of the social order or equilibrium. It is the function of the mechanisms of social control to maintain the social system in a state of stable or moving equilibrium; and insofar as they fail to do so, as has often happened in history, more drastic disequilibration will take place before equilibrium is reëstablished; that is, there will be changes in the structure of the social system.

It is not possible to draw a rigid line between socialization and social control. But the rough delimitation of the former would be given by the conception of those mechanisms necessary to maintain a stable and institutionally integrated social system through the formation of a given set of appropriate personality systems and the specification of their role-orientation with the assumption that there would be no serious endogenous tendencies to alienation from these institutionalized role-expectations, no serious role-conflict, and a constant measure of institutionalized flexibility. Such a social system is of course the concept of a limiting case like that of a frictionless machine and does not exist in reality. But the function of the mechanisms of social

---

[22] The proportion of the population whose major need-dispositions are left ungratified is less important than the cruciality of their position in the social system and the magnitude of the discrepancy between needs and expectations on the one hand and fulfillments on the other.

control is indicated by the extent to which actual social systems fail to achieve the above order of integration through socialization.

In the first place, the generalized patterns of orientation which are formed through socialization need constantly to be reinforced through the continuing presence of the symbolic equivalents of the expectations, both generalized and specific, which were effective at earlier stages in the socialization process. The orientations which have become the shared collective and private goals must be reinforced against the perpetual pressures toward disruption in the personality system and in the social system. The mechanisms for the maintenance of the consensus on value-orientations will have different functions depending on the type of social system in which they are operating. A social system with a very high degree of consensus covering most spheres of life and most types of activities and allowing little area to freely selected modes of behavior will have different problems of maintaining equilibrium than a system which allows large areas of individual freedom — and their mechanisms of control will also be different.

Even if the strains which come from inadequate socialization and from changes in the situation of the social system in relation to nature or to other social systems were eliminated, the problems of control would still persist. Tendencies toward alienation are endogenous in any social system. The arguments adduced in the preceding chapter concerning the impossibility of the complete cultural value-integration of a social system bear directly on these endogenous alienation tendencies. There cannot be a society in which some of the members are not exposed to a conflict of values; hence personality strains with resultant pressures against the expectation-system of the society are inevitable. Another basic source of conflict is constitutional variability and the consequent difficulties in the socialization of the different constitutional types. It is impossible for the *distribution* of the various constitutional endowments to correspond exactly to the distribution of initial or subsequent roles and statuses in the social system, and the misfits produce strains and possibly alienation. What is more, the allocative process always produces serious strains by denying to some members of the society what they think they are entitled to, sometimes exacerbating their demands so that they overreach themselves and infringe on the rights of others. Sometimes denial deadens the motivation of actors to role fulfillment and causes their apathetic withdrawal from the roles which they occupy. Where the sense of deprivation is associated with an identification with a collectivity or a class of individuals who come to identify themselves as similarly deprived in the allocation of roles, facilities, and rewards, the tasks of the control mechanism, and the strains on the system, become heavy indeed.

We cannot undertake here the construction of a systematic classification of the mechanisms of social control. All that we will offer will be illustrations of some of them.

One of the most prominent and functionally most significant of them is the artificial identification of interests through the manipulation of rewards and deprivations. This is the exercise of authority in its integrative function. When alienation exists because of ineffective socialization, character-determined rebelliousness, conflicting value-orientation, or apathy, the incumbent of a role endowed with the power to manipulate the allocation of facilities, roles, and rewards can redirect the motivational orientation of others by offering them objects which are more readily cathected, or by threatening to take away objects or remove opportunities. Much of the integration in the instrumental institutional complex is achieved through this artificial identification of interests, which usually works in the context of a consensus concerning general value-orientations. The weaker the consensus, however, and the larger the social system, the greater the share borne by these mechanisms in the maintenance of some measure of integration.

Among the other mechanisms of social control, insulation has an important part. Certain types of deviant behavior which do occur are sealed off, and thereby their disruptive potentialities are restricted, since in their isolation they cannot have much direct effect on the behavior of the other members of the society. On the individual level, this mechanism operates with both the criminal and the ill. On the collective level, it operates in the case of deviant and "interstitial" "subcultures" or collectivities which are not positively fully integrated with the main social system, and which are more or less cut off from widespread contact with the dominant sector of the social system — a contact which, if it did occur, would engender conflict. Segregation is the spatial consequence of the operation of the mechanism of insulation.

Another type of mechanism of social control is contingent reintegration; the care of the ill in modern medicine is a good example of this in certain respects. The medical profession exposes the sick person, so far as his illness constitutes "deviant behavior," to a situation where the motivation to his deviance is weakened and the positive motivations to conformity are strengthened. What is, from the viewpoint of the individual personality, conscious or unconscious psychotherapy, is from the viewpoint of the social system a mechanism of social control.

These examples should give the reader a general idea of what is meant by the control mechanisms of the social system which have their efficacy through their effect on motivation.

THE PROBLEM OF SOCIAL CHANGE

The present theory of the social system is, like all theories involving causal or functional explanation, concerned equally with the conditions of stability and the conditions of change. It is equally concerned with slow cumulative change and with sudden or fluctuating change, and the categories and the variables which have been presented are equally applicable to stable or rapidly or slowly changing systems.

The state of a system at a point in time or at a series of points in time is a fundamental referent for the analysis of social systems. It is also the fundamental referent for the analysis of change from that state to other states of the system. The theoretical scheme here presented offers a number of categories and hypotheses by which possibilities of change may be described and analyzed.

We have given prominence in earlier phases of our analysis to the integration of motivational elements into patterns of conformity with role-expectations, to the general category of alienation and the conditions of its emergence, and to the part played by the mechanisms of social control. The entire discussion of motivation and its relation to the mechanisms of socialization and control in the section immediately preceding was directly addressed to the problems of stability *and* change. If analyzed in these terms, the maintenance of any existing status, insofar as it is maintained at all, is clearly a relatively contingent matter. The obverse of the analysis of the mechanisms by which it is maintained is the analysis of the forces which tend to alter it. *It is impossible to study one without the other.* A fundamental potentiality of instability, an endemic possibility of change, is inherent in this approach to the analysis of social systems. Empirically, of course, the degree of instability, and hence the likelihood of actual change, will vary both with the character of the social system and of the situation in which it is placed. But in principle, propositions about the factors making for maintenance of the system are at the same time propositions about those making for change. The difference is only one of concrete descriptive emphasis. There is no difference on the analytical level.

A basic hypothesis in this type of analysis asserts the imperfect integration of all actual social systems. No one system of value-orientation with perfect consistency in its patterns can be fully institutionalized in a concrete society. There will be uneven distributions among the different parts of the society. There will be value conflicts and role conflicts. The consequence of such imperfect integration is in the nature of the case a certain instability, and hence a susceptibility to change if the balance of these forces, which is often extremely delicate, is shifted at some strategic point. Thus, change might result not only from open deviation from unequivocally institutionalized patterns but also from a shift in the balance between two or more positively institutionalized patterns, with an invasion of part of the sphere of one by another. The loopholes in the institutionalized system are one of the main channels through which such shifts often take place. Hence, in the combination of the inherent tendencies to deviation and the imperfections of the integration of value-orientations, there are in every social system inherent possibilities of change.

In addition to these two major sources, positively institutionalized sources of change are particularly prominent in some social systems. The most prominent type of case seems to be the institutionalized commitment to a cultural configuration, in Kroeber's sense, so that there is an endogenous process of development of the possibilities of that configuration. Where the cultural orientation gives a prominent place to achievement and universalistic orientation, this endogenous tendency toward change may be very pronounced. The obvious example is modern science, with its technological applications. Scientific knowledge is by its nature open to development — otherwise the activities concerned could not be called scientific investigation. When made into the object of concern by scientific institutions — universities and research organizations — there is an institutionalized motivation to unfold this possibility. There are, furthermore, powerful tendencies, once the ethos of science is institutionalized in a society sufficiently for an important scientific movement to flourish, to render it impossible to isolate scentific investigation so that it will have no technological application. Such applications in turn will have repercussions on the whole system of social relationships. Hence a society in which science is institutionalized and is also assigned a strategic position cannot be a static society.

What is very conspicuously true of science is also true of the consequences of many religious movements, once certain processes of internal development have started. The value-orientations of modern capitalistic enterprise are similarly endogenously productive of change. Any society in which the value standards, as in a legal code (even though it is not in their formal nature to undergo development), are capable of reinterpretation will also tend toward change. Any society in which the allocations create or maintain dissatisfaction will be open to change; especially when the cultural standards and the allocations combine to intensify need-dispositions, change will be a certainty.

Changes in the external situation of a social system, either in its environmental conditions (as in the case of the depletion or discovery of some natural resource), changes in its technology which are not autonomous, changes in the social situation of the system (as in its foreign relations), may be cited as the chief exogenous factors in change. Inspection of the paradigm for the analysis of social systems will show that these variables can be fully taken into account in this scheme of analysis (see Fig. 15).

There is no suggestion that these sources of social change exhaust the list, but they will suffice for the present. The possibility of doing empirical justice to all of them is certainly present in the treatment of social systems in terms of the theory of action. Furthermore, this type of analysis puts us in possession of important canons for the criticism of other theories of social change. It would seem, for instance, that there is no inherent reason why the "motive force" of social change *in general* has to be sought in any one sector of the social system or its culture. The impetus to a given process of change may come from an evolution of "ideas." It may come from secular changes in climate which profoundly alter the conditions of subsistence. It may center in shifts in the distribution of power or in technological developments which permit some needs to be satisfied in ways that change the conditions and the level of satisfaction of the needs of other actors in the sytsem. The theoretical generalization of change will in all probability not take the form of a "predominant factor theory," such as an economic or an ideological interpretation, but of an analysis of the modes of interdependence of different parts of the social system. From such hypotheses it should be possible to predict that a certain type of change, initiated at any given point, will, given the main facts about the system, have specifiable types of consequences at other points.

To avoid confusion, one final point should be mentioned. The analysis of social change is not to be confused with the analysis of the dynamics of action in the theory of action. There is much dynamic process in action, including change in the structure of personalities, *within a stable social system.* Indeed it is inherent in the frame of reference that *all* action is a dynamic process. The emphasis of this work on the organization of action is not to be taken to imply that organization has some sort of ontological priority over dynamic process. They are the two aspects of the same phenomenon. It has been more convenient to stress the organizational aspect since it provides certain relatively definite and manageable reference points, which make possible a more incisive and rigorous analysis of certain problems in the process of action.[23]

[23] As noted in the Introduction, a greatly expanded treatment of the subject-matter of this chapter will be found in Talcott Parsons, *The Social System* (Glencoe, Illinois: The Free Press, 1951).

5

Conclusion

We have now set forth the main conceptual scheme of the theory of action and its elaboration in each of the three areas of systemic organization. In conclusion we shall summarize briefly, underscore a few specific features of the scheme, and indicate some of the problems toward which future effort might be directed.

Logically the scheme is founded on certain categories of behavior psychology. These contain by implication the main categories of the frame of reference of the theory of action. The implications, however, have not heretofore been drawn in a manner which would be adequate to the study of human personality, cultural, and social systems, although the categories developed previously by Tolman in his study of animal behavior have brought these implications within reaching distance.

The present analysis began with the set of fundamental definitions which constitute the frame of reference for the analysis of the structure of human action. The dynamic properties of this frame of reference have not been treated with the same degree of explicitness as the more descriptive aspects. We have devoted more attention to the derivation of complex concepts descriptive of structure than we have to the formulation of the dynamic hypotheses implicit in some of these concepts. However, it seems to us that a whole system of dynamic hypotheses is implicit in our conceptual scheme and that these hypotheses are susceptible of treatment by the same kind of systematic deductive procedure which has been used in constructing the descriptive side of the scheme. We have regarded it, however, as more urgent to develop the descriptive side first.

The basic frame of reference deals with action as a process of striving for the attainment of states of gratification or goals within a situation. The polarity of gratification and deprivation, and hence of the two fundamental tendencies of action — seeking and avoidance — are inherent in this conception. So also is the reference to the future, which is formulated in the concept of expectations. Finally, the selective nature of the orientations of action, which is formulated in the concept of the pattern variables, is similarly logically inherent in the basic conception of action.

In our construction of the categories of the theory of action, we distinguished three major modal aspects of the frame of reference which have been called motivational orientation, value-orientation, and the structure of the situation. These are *all* elements of the "orientation" of an actor to a situation; *each* of them is involved in *any* action whatever. Only when objects are both cognized and cathected does "drive" or "need" become motivation in action. But the completely isolated elementary "unit action" is an abstraction. Actions occur only in systems which necessitate evaluations of alternative paths of action and commitments to those alternatives which have been chosen. Selection or choice is an essential component of action as we view it. Selectivity is a function both of the goal-orientedness of the actor and the differentiation of the object situation. Selectivity in orientation moreover entails simultaneous orientation toward criteria of the validity of the substantive selections. There thus seems to be no doubt of the fundamental independent significance of value standards, and this justifies the granting to value-orientation a conceptually independent place in the frame of reference.

Moreover, it is of the first importance that the structure of the situation be analyzed not only in terms of the classes of concrete objects, but of the modalities of objects, especially of the quality and performance modalities. The modality classification, already widely applied in more concrete studies, has crucial theoretical significance in the analysis of the role-expectations, cultural orientations, and need-dispositions.

The basic frame of reference is in principle applicable to the hypothetically isolated actor in a nonsocial situation. In a situation in which a plurality of actors are in interaction, the scheme must be further differentiated to take into account the fact of complementarity of expectations — but this involves no modification in the basic frame of reference, merely a more elaborate deductive treatment. It is through the complementarity of expectations in interaction that the symbols essential to human action are built up, that communication on the humanly significant levels, and therefore culture, become possible. It is with analysis of action on these levels of complexity that the scheme is primarily concerned.

Following the delineation of the fundamentals of the frame of reference in terms of the three major aspects of action, the first major *theoretical* step was taken with the derivation from that frame of reference of a systematic scheme for defining and interrelating the choice-alternatives toward which there is evaluative orientation of action. The alternatives toward which the evaluative orientation is focused are called the *pattern variables*. It is clear that the pattern-variable elements could not have been derived if the independent significance of value-orientation had not been established beforehand. But the pattern variables are not a product solely of value-orientations;

they involve relations among the different components of the frame of reference.

The pattern variables had previously been developed in a less systematic fashion in connection with the analysis of certain concrete problems of social structure. They were not originally devised for the analysis of personality and cultural systems. However, in attempting to develop the analysis of personality systems in the framework of the action scheme, it became clear that if personality is to be analyzed in terms of the action schema at all, the pattern variables must also be relevant to the analysis of personality. The further pursuit of that line of inquiry showed that the need-dispositions which had previously been classified largely in an *ad hoc* clinical way, could be defined in terms of the pattern variables with results which showed a remarkable correspondence with the results of clinical observation. Finally, it became apparent that they constituted principal categories for the description of value-orientations, and not only of the empirical action systems in which value-orientations are involved. After all, role-expectations, which are the essential element of institutionalized behavior, are drawn in general from the same general dispositions as cultural value-orientations. The perception of this relationship provides a most important means for clarifying the conceptual relations between cultural orientations on the one hand and personality and social systems on the other, and for preparing the way for the study of their empirical interrelations.

Preliminary consideration of the pattern-variable scheme in relation to these two types of system also revealed the symmetrical asymmetry of its application to personalities and to social systems.

The definition of the main terms of the action frame of reference, and the derivation of the pattern variables from the frame of reference have thus provided a point of departure for the analysis of the three types of system into which the elements of the action scheme are organized. (Of course, the "fundamentals of behavior psychology" are assumed in the definition of the elements of action and the derivations into which they enter.)

But the concepts thus constructed are insufficient in that particular form for the analysis of systems of action. The problem of constructive systemic concepts was first dealt with in connection with personality in Chapter II. It is essentially a matter of the conditions and consequences of the differentiation of action elements and their integration into a system. The types of differentiation which are logically conceivable can, in the nature of the case, be realized only in a highly selective manner. There are definite imperatives imposed by the conditions of empirical coexistence in the same system. The further conceptual differentiation, to be added to the elements considered in Chapter I, is presented in the paradigm of the "functioning system" of a personality. The structure of such a system is constituted by the interrelations of the elements of action (formulated in the categories of the action frame of reference), their elaboration in the pattern-variable scheme. The structure is complicated by the derivation of the origins and place in the system of certain "adjustive" mechanisms (such as needs for dominance or for aggression) and defensive mechanisms.

It is particularly important that motivational factors should be viewed with reference to their functional significance for personality as a system. The concept of mechanism was introduced because it provides a conceptual tool for the analysis of motivational factors in just this light.

In the social system too the concept of mechanism is introduced because of its relevance in dealing with the dynamic aspects of *systemic* problems, particularly the problems of allocation and integration. In consequence of the fundamental difference in the locus of personality systems on the one hand and social systems on the other, the functional mechanisms which operate in both systems may be regarded as homologous only to a limited extent. Only when these differences are clarified is it possible to make progress in the analysis of the nature of the empirical articulations between them. In the persent monograph only a few initial considerations could be presented concerning this very complicated set of problems.

Systems of value-orientation (discussed in Chapter III) do not entail the existence of functional mechanisms because they are not empirical action systems, and hence do not have either motivational processes or the *same kinds* of allocative and integrative problems. After a discussion of their place in the general structure of culture, the problem of the consistency of systems of value-orientation was explored through relating the major combinations of the pattern variables to certain features of the situation.

The model of the system of value-orientation with a fully consistent pattern, however important for theoretical purposes, can serve only as a point of departure for the analysis of empirical value systems, as they operate in personality and in social systems. The pattern-consistent system is both formal and elementary. In systems of action, the system of value-orientation takes rather different directions, but they could not be fully treated here. In particular, the complications arising from orientation to many of the "adaptive" problems, such as authority or freedom from control, have not been included; they must be worked out in relation to the more concrete action structure and situation. A further limitation on the empirical utility of the concept of the completely pattern-consistent system of value-orientation is that concrete systems of action are not oriented toward such pattern-consistent value systems. The exigencies of the empirical action system are such that there will be areas of strain and even of sheer impossibility of full integration of a consistent value-orientation. Where these areas of strain and incompatibility are located and how they are organized and responded to will depend on the dominant value system and on the structure of the particular situation.

This means that the study of concrete systems of value-orientation should be related to the study of empirical systems of action. The purely "cultural" type of analysis, though indispensable as a first step, can only carry us a certain distance. Even when we are concerned with the cultural value orientation, in order to account for its inconsistencies and heterogeneities, we must consider the interdependence of that system with the motivational and situational components of personality and with the functional problems of social systems. Of course, even when the theory of personality is the prime object of our interest, we cannot do without the cultural analysis of value-orientations.

Finally, from the point of view of the general anthropological student of culture, the treatment of cultural problems in this monograph must appear highly selective if not one-sided. We have intentionally placed primary emphasis on value-orientations because they constitute the strategically crucial *point of articulation* between culture and the structure of personalities and of social systems. In the introductory section of Chapter III we attempted to place value-orientations in relation to the other elements of cultural systems as a whole. But this brief treatment did not attempt to do justice to the intricacy of the problems and their implications for action — for example, the role of ideas or belief systems or the role of expressive symbols. Also the complex interdependencies between the internalized culture and culture as an accumulation of objects other than value-orientations have merely been suggested, not analyzed.

Can any general statement be made about the significance of what has been achieved in this monograph? In the first place it should be quite clear that nearly all the concepts which have here been brought together have been current in various forms and on various levels of concreteness in the social sciences in the twentieth century. Whatever originality exists here can be found only in the way in which the concepts have been related to one another.

It may well be that an equally comprehensive or even more comprehensive synthesis could have been made from a different point of view, with different emphases and combinations. But even if this is so, it might be fairly claimed that the present scheme offers the basis of an important advance toward the construction of a unified theory of social science. It perhaps may be said to put together more elements, in a more systematic way, than any other attempt yet made on this level of abstraction. We also think that it has been sufficiently differentiated here to show that it can be useful in the analysis of empirical problems in an open, undogmatic way. It should thus contribute substantially to the development of a common way of looking at the phenomena of human conduct.

Nothing could be more certain than that any such attempt is tentative in its definitions and in their particular derivations and combinations; it is thus destined to all manner of modifications. A critic may well be able to find serious difficulties, or may simply prefer, for good reasons of his own, to use a different scheme. But the whole course of development of work in the social sciences to which this monograph has sought to give a more systematic theoretical formulation is such that it is scarcely conceivable that such a large measure of conceptual ordering which connects with so much empirical knowledge should be completely "off the rails." It seems therefore that however great the modifications which will have to be introduced by empirical application and theoretical refinement and reformulation, the permanently valid precipitate will prove to be substantial.

In very general terms, one of the achievements of this undertaking is the clarification of the relations between what have been called the "levels" of action. The doctrine of "tandem emergence," most recently and fully stated by Kroeber, seems to be definitely untenable. The idea that personality is emergent from the biological level of the organism, social systems are emergent from personality, and culture from social systems, which this view puts forth, has been shown to be wrong. In place of this we have put forward the view that personality, culture, and social system are analytically coequal, that each of the three implies the other two. If there is anything like emergence, it is *action* as the category embracing all three which is emergent from the organic world. One of the general implications of this contention is that the analysis of social systems and of culture is not a derivation of the theory of personality. Nor can there be "sociology" which is precultural or independent of culture, whether it be conceived as "applied psychology" or as a Durkheimian "theory of social facts." Finally, culture cannot stand in isolation, as something self-sufficient and self-developing. Culture is theoretically implicated with action in general, and thus with both personalities and social systems. Indeed the only prerequisites of any essential part of the theory of action are the organic and situational prerequisites of action in general, and not any one subsystem.

This conception of the relations of the three system-levels to each other is not in its most general form original. But in the current discussion of these problems there has been a large amount of uncertainty and vacillation about these matters. There has been a tendency for the proponents of each of the three disciplines concerned to attempt to close their own systems, and to declare their theoretical independence of the others. At the same time, even among those who asserted the interdependence of the three fields, it has tended to be done in an *ad hoc*, fragmentary manner, without regard to the methodological and theoretical bases of such interdependence. The present scheme may claim to have resolved in large part both of these difficulties.

One of the major difficulties in relating culture to social structure has been uncertainty about the meaning of the institutionalization of culture patterns. In the light of the present analysis, this uncertainty can be seen to derive from the fact that the meaning of institutionalization is different for the different parts of a cultural system. A set of beliefs, of expressive symbols, or of instrumental patterns may be institutionalized in the sense that conformity with the standards in question may become a role-expectation for members of certain collectivities, as is the case, for example, when there is a high valuation of abstract art in a certain circle. But only patterns of value-orientation — that is, in our terms, pattern-variable combinations — become directly constitutive of the main structure of alternative types of social relationships which is the central structural focus of social systems. This is the set of primary institutions of a social system. The others are structurally secondary. This differentiated analysis of the relations between culture and systems of action makes it possible to overcome the "emanationist" fallacy which has plagued idealistic social theory. If culture as a system is treated as closed and either conceptually or empirically independent of social structure and personality, then it follows that culture patterns "realize themselves" in personality or social structure without the intervention of motivation. The proponents of one view invoke only a few "obvious" mechanisms connected with child training in order to explain the personality which becomes the recipient and bearer of culture. This theory, although it alleges to show the "human element" in the great impersonal patterns of culture, assumes, quite unjustifiably, that there *is* in concrete reality a cultural orientation system, given separately from the system of action. This is the exact counterpart of the view that there is a human nature independent of society and culture. In both cases, the procedure has been to determine what the system is, and then to analyze how it affects the other systems. The correct procedure is to treat the cultural orientation system as an integral *part* of the real system of action, which can be separated from it *only analytically*. Culture in the anthropological sense is a condition, component, and product of action systems.

Similarly, the pattern variables seem to provide a crucial clue to the relation between personality and culture. The distinction between cultural objects (accumulation) and cultural orientations, which has been followed in the present analysis, turns psychologically on the internalization of values and other elements of culture. Insofar as a value pattern becomes internalized, it ceases to be an object and becomes directly constitutive of the personality. It is "transferred" from one side of the "action equation" to the other. (It is this transferability of cultural factors which in the last analysis makes it necessary to treat them as an independent range of variation in the basic paradigm of action.) Internalization of values in the personality is thus the direct counterpart of their institutionalization in the social system. Indeed, as we have seen, they are really two sides of the same thing. This institutionalization and internalization of value patterns, a connection independently and from different points of view discovered by Freud and by Durkheim, is the focus of many of the central theoretical problems of action theory. Many elements in action, both organic and situational, are causally independent of role-value structure. But only through their *relation* to this problem, can they be systematically analyzed in terms of the theory of action.

A second and closely related accomplishment of the present analysis is the clarification of the functional problems of the theory of action in the analysis of systems. Incompatibilities among the component actions and actors in the several systems result from their coexistence in the same situation or the same personality. Insofar as the system remains a system, some mechanisms must come into play for reducing these incompatibilities to the point where coexistence in the system becomes possible. (These mechanisms do of course change the character of the system but they allow it to function as a system.)

Now these mechanisms cannot be derived simply from the theory of motivation in general. Some conception of *functional imperatives* — that is, constituent conditions and empirically necessary preconditions of on-going systems, set by the facts of scarcity in the object situation, the nature of the organism, and the realities of coexistence — are necessary.

We have stressed that these mechanisms are to be defined by the systemic conditions which give rise to them and the systemic consequences or functions which are effected by their operation. There are, of course, certain dangers in the use of such functional analysis. The overtones of teleology must be guarded against particularly in dealing with the social system. There are dangers of hypostatization of the "system" and its "needs" which can be insured against only by bearing constantly in mind that the system is a system of individual actors and their roles but that needs in the systemic sense are not the same as the need-dispositions of the actors or even homologous with them — although there are complicated empirical interrelations among them. Systemic needs can never be reduced to need-dispositions although systemic needs are the resultant of the coexistence in determinate relationships in a situation of a plurality of actors each of whom has a system of need-dispositions. If it is remembered that the mechanisms which are the systemic modes of responding to the "needs of the system" are empirical generalizations about motivational processes — a sort of shorthand for the description of complex processes which we do not yet fully understand — we may feel free to employ functional analysis without involvement either in metaphysical teleology or in hidden political and ethical preferences. Neither of these is in any way *logically* entailed in the kind of functional analysis which we have presented here.

In addition to the two general directions in which we believe progress has been made, there have been a good many categories and hypotheses of a more specific sort which have emerged or which have been reformulated in the course of this analysis. Rather than attempt a summary of these, however, we will conclude with a brief suggestion of three general lines of development along which it might be fruitful to move in the formulation of general social science theory.

One field which is basic to our work here and development of which is necessary for further progress deals with the nature and role of symbols in action. The present monograph has not specifically dealt with these problems. But symbolism has emerged as almost a kind of counterpoint theme throughout the discussion and requires much more explicit attention than it has received. There are many points at which such an analysis could begin. It should not center so much in the "origins" of symbols as in their actual role in the interactive processes which have been central to this analysis. A central problem will be the relation among the symbolic elements in cognitive and in cathectic orientations. Every one of the psychological mechanisms discussed operates through responses to symbols. For instance, the mechanism of generalization which operates when ego comes to attribute significance to alter's attitudes as distinguished from his "overt acts" is possible only through a process of symbolization. There is probably no problem in the analysis of action systems which would not be greatly clarified by a better understanding of symbolism. Motivation in particular will be better understood as a knowledge of symbolism advances. Indeed, there is much to be said for the view that the importance of culture is almost synonomous with the importance of what in motivational terms are sometimes called "symbolic processes." There is at the very least an intimate connection.

Second, it is important to press forward with systematic structural classification of types and their component elements, in all three types of system. The bearing of this task on the structural-functional character of the theory of action should be clear. Our dynamic generalizations have to be formulated relative to their structural setting. The present state of knowledge does not allow the establishment of dynamic generalizations which both cut across many different social and personality structures and are sufficiently concrete to be very helpful in the solution of concrete problems. Thus we may say that "in the long run only behavior which is adequately rewarded will tend to persist," but if we do not concretely know what the reward structure and its relation to the value and role structure of the requisite social system are, this helps us very little. Indeed it may get us into a great deal of trouble if we tacitly assume that the concrete rewards of our society will exist in another society. Only when we know what the concrete reward system is does the generalization become useful. We cannot rest content with a pure *ad hoc* empiricism in this respect.

We must try to systematize the relations between different types of reward systems which means systematizing the classification of the cultures and social structures within which the rewards are given. This is the most promising path to the extension of the empirical relevance of generalizations from the one structural case to families of structural cases. It is the way to transcend the "structural particularism" of the particular personality, the particular culture, or the particular social structure. We think that some of the procedures we have proposed provide starting points for such classificatory systematization, and that further work in this direction is likely to be productive.

The development of a classification of types of structures is necessary particularly for the elaboration of *middle principles*, that is, propositions of lower ranges of generality (and consequently greater concreteness). The working out of a typology of structures will enable us to know what we are holding constant in our concrete investigations into *middle principles*. And it will also make much more feasible the absolutely indispensable unification of theory of the present level of generality and theory on the level of middle principles.

Finally, the last direction of development has been emphasized so often that it does not need to be extensively discussed again. This is the dynamic analysis of the role or role-constellation where value pattern, social structure, and personality come together. This, without doubt, is the most strategic point at which to attempt to extend dynamic knowledge in such a way that it will promise a maximum of fruitful general results for the theory of action. The establishment of the crucially strategic place of this complex should not, however, lead one to underestimate the difficulty of the theoretical problems surrounding it.

It has repeatedly been pointed out that this difficulty above all derives from the undoubted fact that in spite of the basic structural homology of personalities and social systems, the two are not directly, reciprocally translatable. This translation can be accomplished only through certain "transformation equations," of which unfortunately many constituents are still unknown. The basic grounds of this difficulty have been explored at various points in the course of the foregoing analysis. Among other things this analysis provides canons of criticism of the various oversimplified solutions of the problem which are current. But in addition to attaining critical vantage points, real progress has been made in defining the nature of the problems, and here and there is a glimmer of positive insight. It may confidently be hoped that intensive and competent work toward pushing forward this frontier of our knowledge should yield results of some value. Here, above all, the resources of modern social science can be mobilized for the task of extending and ordering our knowledge of human conduct.

FIGURES 1-15

Accompanying Part II

Fig. 1 COMPONENTS OF THE ACTION FRAME OF REFERENCE

THE SUBJECT	THE OBJECT
1. An actor-subject: the actor whose orientation of action is being analyzed. (In an interaction situation, this actor is called "ego.")	2. Objects: those objects to which the actor-subject is oriented. These are (i) social objects and (ii) nonsocial objects.

The actor-subject is sometimes called simply the "actor" and is always an "action system." Thus the actor-subject is either:

    a. A personality.
    b. A social system.

    i. Social objects are actors (i.e., action systems) but here they are objects rather than subjects in a given analysis. (In an interaction situation, these actors are called "alters.") Social objects are:

        a. Personalities.
        b. Social systems.

Personalities and Social systems fit together in the following fashion whether they are subjects or objects.

	Personality A	Personality B	Personality C
Social system 1	Role 1-A* Motivational aspects Value aspects	Role 1-B Motivational aspects Value aspects	Role 1-C Motivational aspects Value aspects
Social system 2	Role 2-A Motivational aspects Value aspects	Role 2-B Motivational aspects Value aspects	Role 2-C Motivational aspects Value aspects
Social system 3	Role 3-A Motivational aspects Value aspects	Role 3-B Motivational aspects Value aspects	Role 3-C Motivational aspects Value aspects

    ii. Nonsocial objects may be:

        a. Physical objects
        b. Cultural objects (i.e., symbols or symbol systems).

Cultural Systems

Cultural systems are the common values, beliefs, and tastes of the actors (as either subjects or objects) interacting with symbol systems (as objects). Thus the underlined components above show the abstraction of cultural systems from the action frame of reference.

*Each of these roles is a subsystem of orientations. This subsystem can be analyzed with respect to either (i) the personality's motives, of which the orientations are a function, or (ii) the values which the personality respects in this specific social system. Thus roles are divided into motivational aspects and value aspects.

Fig. 2 DERIVATION OF THE PATTERN VARIABLES

SUBJECT

Orientation of the Actor-Subject	Three Pattern Variables Derivable from the Orientation

The actor-subject is analyzed with respect to the modes of his orientation. (These orientations, taken in constellations, make up the "roles" in Fig. 1.)

A. Motivational orientation
  1. Cognitive
  2. Cathectic (Inseparable modes)
  3. Evaluative: brings in thought for consequences and can invoke value standards.

No. 1

Affectivity: cognitive-cathectic modes determine behavior without evaluation.

Affective neutrality: behavior does not occur until after evaluation has occurred (and thus, usually, some of the value-orientation standards invoked). (Cognitive-cathectic modes of course, are also active.)

No. 3

B. Value-orientation
  1. Cognitive standards ————→

  2. Appreciative standards ————→

Universalism: whether or not moral standards have primacy in an evaluative situation, cognitive standards have primacy over appreciative.
Particularism: whether or not moral standards have primacy, appreciative standards have primacy over cognitive ones.

No. 2

  3. Moral standards
    a. ego-integrative

Self-orientation: whether or not evaluation occurs, the actor does not give primacy to collective moral standards, but instead to cognitive or appreciative or ego-integrative moral standards, or no standards are invoked.

    b. collectivity-integrative

Collectivity-orientation: evaluation occurs and the actor gives primacy to collective moral standards.

OBJECT

Alternatives within the Class of Social Objects	Two Pattern Variables from these Alternatives

Only the class of social objects is relevant here, since all pattern variables are in one sense modes of relationship between people. Two distinctions which cross-cut each other can be applied to the category of social objects:

A. The quality-performance distinction
  1. A social object may be a complex of qualities.

  2. A social object may be a complex of performances.

No. 4

Ascription: the actor chooses to see a social object as a complex of qualities.

Achievement: the actor chooses to see a social object as a complex of performances.

B. The scope-of-significance distinction
  1. A social object may have diffuse significance.

  2. A social object may have specific or segmental significance.

No. 5

Diffuseness: the actor chooses to grant a social object all requests that do not interfere with other obligations.
Specificity: the actor grants a social object only such rights as are explicitly defined in the definition of the relationship between them.

Fig. 3 VALUE COMPONENTS OF NEED-DISPOSITIONS

	AFFECTIVITY	AFFECTIVE NEUTRALITY
SPECIFICITY	**I. Segmental Gratification** The need-disposition to find a receptive and/or responsive social object and to be responsive vis-à-vis that object, in a context of direct gratifications and specific qualifications without regard to responsibilities beyond it.	**II. Approval** The need-disposition for such approval and its reciprocation in a relation with a social object with respect to value standards governing specific types of quality or performance and without regard to responsibilities outside the specific context.
DIFFUSENESS	**III. Love** The need-disposition for a relationship with a social object characterized by reciprocal attitudes of diffuse love, without regard to any particular content of specific gratifications or specific qualifications.	**IV. Esteem** The need-disposition to be esteemed and to reciprocate this attitude in a relation to a social object in a diffuse way, without regard to a particular context of specific qualities or performances, but with regard to the standard by which the person as a whole is the object of esteem.

Fig. 3a TYPES OF VALUE COMPONENTS OF NEED-DISPOSITIONS

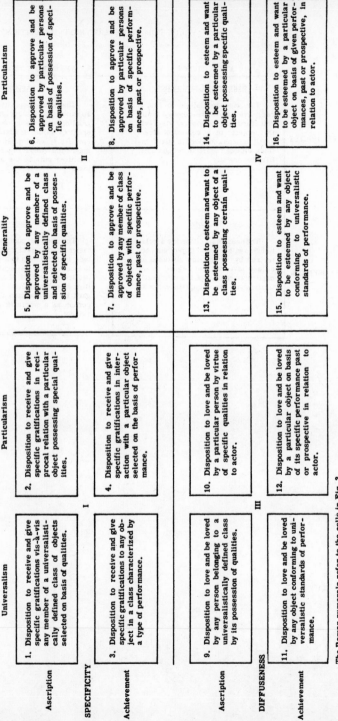

The Roman numerals refer to the cells in Fig. 3.

Fig. 4 VALUE COMPONENTS OF ROLE-EXPECTATIONS

	UNIVERSALISM	PARTICULARISM
ASCRIPTION	I. <u>Expectation of conformity with universal norms.</u> The orientation of action to an expectation of conformity with a universalistic standard governing the conduct of actors possessing certain qualities (classificatory or relational) universalistically assessed.	II. <u>Expectation of orientation by virtue of particular prior relationship.</u> The orientation of action to an expectation of conformity with a standard governing the conduct of actors possessing certain qualities (classificatory or relational) assessed in the light of their particular relationship to the actor.
ACHIEVEMENT	III. <u>Expectation of successful accomplishment.</u> The orientation of action to an expectation of achievement in accordance with a universalistic standard of attainment of a minimum level of satisfactory achievement or a requisite degree of excellence above that minimum.	IV. <u>Expectation of obligations of particular relationship or membership.</u> The orientation of action to the expectation of performance in conformity with a standard of achievement appropriate to a particular membership in a class or relationship independent of universalistically defined standards of performances.

Fig. 4a TYPES OF VALUE COMPONENTS OF ROLE-EXPECTATION

UNIVERSALISM

	Affectivity	Neutrality
Specificity	1. Orientation toward an expectation of specific affective expression on basis of qualities toward class of objects defined by universalistic standards.	2. Orientation toward an expectation of specific disciplined action on basis of qualities toward class of objects defined by universalistic standards.
ASCRIPTION		I
Diffuseness	3. Orientation toward an expectation of diffuse affective expression on basis of qualities toward class of objects defined by universalistic standards.	4. Orientation toward an expectation of generalized disciplined action on basis of qualities toward class of objects defined by universalistic standards.
Specificity	9. Orientation toward an expectation of specific affective expressions toward class of objects designated on basis of achievement defined by universalistic standards.	10. Orientation toward an expectation of specific disciplined action in relation to a class of objects designated on basis of achievement defined by universalistic standards.
ACHIEVEMENT		III
Diffuseness	11. Orientation toward an expectation of diffuse affective expression toward classes of objects on basis of achievement defined by universalistic standards.	12. Orientation toward an expectation of generalized disciplined action toward classes of objects on basis of achievement, defined by universalistic standards.

PARTICULARISM

	Affectivity	Neutrality
Specificity	5. Orientation toward an expectation of specific affective expression toward object on basis of qualities in particularistic relation to actor.	6. Orientation toward an expectation of specific disciplined action toward object on basis of qualities in particularistic relation to ego.
		II
Diffuseness	7. Orientation toward an expectation of diffuse affective expression toward object on basis of qualities in particularistic relation to actor.	8. Orientation toward an expectation of generalized disciplined action toward object on basis of qualities in particularistic relation to actor.
Specificity	13. Expectation of specific affective expression vis-à-vis an object on the basis of its achievements in a particular relation with the actor.	14. Expectation of specific disciplined action toward an object on basis of performances in particularistic relation to actor.
		IV
Diffuseness	15. Orientation toward an expectation of diffuse affective expression toward object on basis of performance in particularistic relation to actor.	16. Orientation toward an expectation of generalized disciplined action toward object on basis of performance in particularistic relation to actor.

The Roman numerals refer to the cells of Fig. 4.

Fig. 5 GROUPING OF CHOICE PATTERN VARIABLES

Value-Orientation

Focus of Social Value Systems

Universalism-Particularism   Ascription-Achievement

Collective-Self-Orientation

Diffuseness-Specificity   Neutrality-Affectivity

Focus of Personal Value Systems

Motivation-Orientation

Fig. 6 ACTION RELEVANT STRUCTURE OF THE OBJECT SYSTEM

Objects as Units	Social Objects		Cultural Objects	Physical Objects	
	QUALITY COMPLEXES	PERFORMANCE COMPLEXES		QUALITY COMPLEXES	PERFORMANCE COMPLEXES
Self (ego as personality)	Classificatory: Personality traits Relational: Memberships, possessions	Classificatory: Performance propensities Relational: Roles in relationship systems	Cognitive and cathectic field and instrumental means, conditions and obstacles, and symbols		
Alter (as personality)	Classificatory: Personality traits Relational: Memberships, possessions	Classificatory: Performance propensities Relational: Roles in relationship systems	Cognitive and cathectic field and instrumental means, conditions and obstacles, and symbols		
Collectivity	Classificatory: Group characteristics plus size, status structure, membership composition. Relational: Memberships, possessions plus membership status, internal and external.	Classificatory: Performance propensities plus scope of collective activity Relational: Roles in relationship systems plus propensities of role in collective relationship systems	Cognitive and cathectic field and instrumental means, conditions and obstacles, and symbols		
Organisms (ego's own and alter's)			Cultural Objects as conditions of organic functioning and survival	Classificatory: Sex, age, physical qualities Relational: Biological relatedness, territorial location	Organic capacities, skills, etc.
Other Environmental Objects			Cognitive and cathectic field and instrumental means, conditions and obstacles as traits of ego's object world	Cognitive and cathectic field and instrumental means, conditions, obstacles, etc.	
Symbols, Belief Systems, Standards, etc.			Cognitive and cathectic field and instrumental means, conditions and obstacles as traits of ego's object world	Cognitive and cathectic field and instrumental means, conditions, obstacles, etc.	

Fig. 7 CLASSIFICATION OF THE MECHANISMS

Type of Problem	Learning Processes *	Performance Processes †
	FOR SOLVING EXTERNAL PROBLEMS ‡	

Integrative §	1. Mechanisms of congnitive learning
	
	2. Reality testing
		1. Reality testing
		2. Dependency
		  a. dominance
		  b. submission
		3. Compulsive independence
		  a. agressiveness
		  b. withdrawal

Allocative	1. Substitution (2. Displacement) (3. Fixation) 4. Mechanisms of cathectic learning	1. Allocation of attention to different objects. 2. Allocation of cathexes to different means and goals
	FOR SOLVING INTERNAL PROBLEMS	
Integrative //	1. Learned inhibition 2. Learned evaluation patterns of functioning with an eye to prevention of conflicts.	1. Rationalization 2. Isolation 3. Displacement 4. Fixation 5. Repression 6. Reaction-formation 7. Projection
Allocative	1. Allocation of functions to various need-dispositions 2. Changes of evaluation patterns with an eye to maintaining the system.	1. Allocation of "action-time" to various need-dispositions.

*Changes in structure.

†Changes without changes in structure.

‡The terms "external" and "internal" refer to the phenomenological place of the problems.

§The mechanisms which solve external integrative problems are the mechanisms of adjustment. Specifically, the "performance" mechanisms here are the ones traditionally attributed to adjustment.

//The mechanisms which solve internal integrative problems—specifically those listed under performance processes—are the mechanisms of defense.

Fig. 8 CLASSIFICATION OF THE PRIMARY MECHANISMS OF ADJUSTMENT

	Retention (Dependency)	Relinquishment (Compulsive independence)
Active Alternative	Dominance	Aggressiveness
Passive Alternative	Submission	Withdrawal

Social Systems	Personality Systems
1. Categorization of object units (individuals and collectivities) in terms of ascriptive qualities and performance capacities.	1. Cognition and cathexis of self and alters in terms of qualities and/or performance (and more or less stable need-dispositions to cognize and cathect in certain ways).
2. Role definitions including: <u>a</u>. Who shall occupy role (in terms of qualities and performance). <u>b</u>. What he shall do. <u>c</u>. The relation of roles to one another.	2. Ego's several roles (which are superordinate need-dispositions within his character structure) and his role-expectancies (which are need-dispositions to get certain responses from alters).
3. The allocation of functions and facilities to roles.	3. Ego's orientation (and need-dispositions which control them) to various alters (and to the specific attitudes and actions of alters) as means to ego's ulterior goals. Alters are seen as consumers, sources of income, collaborators.
4. The allocation of sanctions and rewards (especially prestige and status).	4. Ego's orientation (and the need-dispositions which control it) to various alters as objects of gratification, attachment and identification, and to nonsocial reward objects.
5. Integrative structure of the social system: sub-collectivities, the inclusive collectivity, and internal roles with integrative functions.	5. Ego's superego organization (which has the status of a superordinate need-disposition) including the organization of the adjustive mechanisms.

Fig. 10 MAJOR TYPES OF SOCIAL VALUE-ORIENTATION

	UNIVERSALISM	PARTICULARISM
ACHIEVEMENT	**1. The Transcendent Achievement Ideal** The valuation of directional activity toward the achievement of universalistically defined goals, and the requisite performance propensities.	**2. The Immanent Achievement Ideal** Valuation of a harmonious system achieved by effort and maintained or restored by it. Emphasis on responsibility in this context.
ASCRIPTION	**3. The Transcendent Quality-Perfection Ideal** Valuation of a set of ideal qualities of action system or collectivity and of action oriented to their realization and maintenance. Absolutism of an ideal state and dualism of contrast to the evil state.	**4. The Immanent Quality-Perfection Ideal** Valuation of the harmonious and accepting adaptation to the given situation, "making the most" of it as an expressive opportunity.

Fig. 10a THE TRANSCENDENT-ACHIEVEMENT IDEAL

UNIVERSALISM

ACHIEVEMENT			Affectivity	Neutrality
	SPECIFIC	Self	Valuation of specific affective expression to class of persons designated on basis of achievement (e.g., expectation of respect from others on basis of specific achievement).	Valuation of specific disciplined action in relation to a class of persons designated on basis of achievement (e.g., readiness to collaborate with technically qualified persons).
		Collectivity	Valuation of specific affective expression on behalf of a class of persons designated on basis of achievement (e.g., loyalty to professional group which is recruited on basis of standards of specific performance).	Valuation of specific disciplined action with obligation to a class of persons designated on basis of achievement (e.g., professional relation to client).
	DIFFUSE	Self	Valuation of general affective expression toward classes of persons or groups on basis of achievement (e.g., expectation of esteem on part of the successful).	Valuation of general disciplined action toward classes of persons or groups on basis of achievement (e.g., generalized readiness to collaborate, in equal or subordinate role, with persons who are esteemed on a basis of achievement.
		Collectivity	Valuation of general affective expression and action on behalf of class of persons on basis of their specific or diffuse achievement (e.g., general prestige of achievement group; rationalistic social engineering enthusiasm on part of scientists; general prestige of the versatile person with diffuse achievements).	Valuation of general disciplined action on behalf of a class of persons on basis of their achievement (e.g., obligations of "citizenship" within an achievement collectivity).

PARTICULARISM

		Affectivity	Neutrality
SPECIFIC	Self	Valuation of action constituting self-gratification in accordance with a conception of right and appropriate relations in a specific situation vis-à-vis particularistically designated persons or classes of persons (e.g., expectation of rightfulness of abusing Negroes under certain conditions.)	Valuation of disciplined action, in conforming with a differentiated standard, leading toward self-gratification in a specific situation (e.g., the behavior of the head of a long-established business enterprise).
	Collectivity	Valuation of specific affective action as on behalf of one's particular collectivity (e.g., expectation of devoted defense for one's collectivity in a conflict situation in accordance with a general code of responsibility appropriate to the situation).	Valuation of disciplined action on behalf of one's particular collectivity in conforming with a differentiated standard in a specific situation (e.g., expectation of father as provider for family in a stable family system).
DIFFUSE	Self	Valuation of action constituting self-gratification in a wide variety of situations vis-à-vis particular persons (e.g., in romantic love: selection of partner; friendship selection).	Valuation of disciplined action in conforming with a differentiated standard leading toward self-gratification in a wide variety of situations vis-à-vis particular persons (e.g., status behavior of arrived and parvenu classes in a "status" oriented society).
	Collectivity	Valuation of action involving affective expression in a variety of situations on behalf of a particular collectivity or on behalf of a particular person (e.g., charismatic leadership and followership in a situation in which such behavior is considered to be appropriate).	Valuation of disciplined action in a variety of situations on behalf of a particular collectivity (e.g., traditionalistic authority and responsibility).

ACHIEVEMENT

UNIVERSALISM

		Affectivity	Neutrality
SPECIFIC	Self	Valuation of specific emotional gratifications in specific types of situations or with specific types of ascriptively designated persons (e.g., affective expression permitted under certain convivial conditions).	Valuation of specific style patterns appropriate to specific situations or with specific types of ascriptively selected persons (e.g., modes of dress appropriate to weddings).
	Collectivity	Valuation of certain kinds of affective action in specific types of situations or with specific types of persons; the action is an obligatory one toward ascriptively selected persons (e.g., condolence, congratulations on birthday, etc.) organized deference behavior.	Valuation of certain kinds of disciplined action in specific types of situations or with specific types of persons ascriptively designated (e.g., bureaucratic etiquette in official capacity; organized deference behavior in hierarchies).
DIFFUSE	Self	Valuation of general affective expression (or receptiveness) with classes of persons ascriptively selected (e.g., expectations regarding appropriate types of affectivity in male and female relationships).	Valuation of a general discipline or style of life, either individually of within a group, with action toward classes of persons and objects in accordance with their ascribed qualities (e.g., expectation of behavior in accordance with a differentiated "style of life" which stresses appropriateness of various types of action for various situations).
	Collectivity	Valuation of a general affective obligation toward ascriptively selected classes of persons (e.g., expectation of completely selfless absorption into a community insofar as the process represents some high ethical ideal).	Valuation of a general discipline which imposes obligations toward classes of persons and according to classes of situations (e.g., aristocratic code of honor; Kantian ethics).

ASCRIPTION

PARTICULARISM

		Affectivity	Neutrality
SPECIFIC	Self	Valuation of specific affective expression toward particular (ascriptively designated) persons (e.g., expectation of anxiety or pleasure of a particular sort from presence and activities of certain individuals or groups).	Valuation of disciplined utilization of particular persons or groups in a specific way (e.g., conformity with a specific renunciatory pattern of behavior in relations with a particular group member selected by his qualities).
	Collectivity	Valuation of specific affective expression and action toward particular persons or groups ascriptively designated (e.g., expectation of anxiety or pleasure of a particular sort from participation in collective undertakings such as ceremonials).	Valuation of disciplined action on behalf of particular persons in performance of specific actions (e.g., expectation of conformity with code of behavior in such collective activities as agricultural cooperatives even though conformity involves renunciation of pleasures).
DIFFUSE	Self	Valuation of general affective action in relation to ascriptively designated particular persons or groups (e.g., generalized gratification expectation in connection with individuals or groups having certain qualities and having a particularistic relation to ego).	Valuation of general disciplined action in relation to particular persons ascriptively designated (e.g., hostile or suspicious attitudes and action vis-à-vis ethnic outgroups).
	Collectivity	Valuation of general affective action in relation to an ascriptively designated particular person or group (e.g., expectation of anxiety or pleasure of a general sort from membership in a particular collectivity independently of the actions undertaken).	Valuation of general disciplined action in relation to an ascriptively designated particular person or group (e.g., Chinese kinship system; obligations of citizenship to a particular country or group).

ASCRIPTION

Fig. 11 TYPES OF SOCIAL VALUE-ORIENTATION IN RELATION TO CLASSES OF OBJECTS

Object Focus	ORGANISMS			
	Transcendent Achievement Pattern 1	Immanent Achievement Pattern 2	Transcendent Quality-Perfection Pattern 3	Immanent Quality-Perfection Pattern 4
Problem of object-significance (diagnosis)	Ego's, alter's and collectivity's utilization of bodily qualities and impulse forces so far as possible in a performance context for positive achievements; warding off and controlling threats to the achievement.	Ego's and alter's bodies as capable of being fitted into a harmonious system by requisite control of impulses and cultivation of qualities.	Sharply dualistic problem of whether impulses and bodily qualities do or do not fit the perfection ideal.	Impulses and bodily qualities as "God given" or as possible threats to the perfection of the ideal system.
Type of goal-striving in relation to object	Realization of valued goals without reference to ultimate terminal point; utilization and requisite control of bodily capacities in goal interest, not suppression of them as intrinsically evil.	Attempt to control impulses and to shape them and bodily qualities in interest of a harmony ideal.	Attempt to shape impulses and make the most of bodily uniformity with ideal, but to master or eliminate everything deviant.	Attempt to make the most of the given gratification capacities of the body and appreciate bodily qualities.
Locus of strain	Danger that body will not be adequate or its needs or propensities will interfere with achievement goals.	Those impulse factors and bodily qualities which cannot be made to "fit," or only with difficulty.	The right-wrong duality: what to "do about" impulses and bodily qualities that are not right.	The danger that impulse forces and bodily qualities will not fit—one will be aggressive or lack beauty.

Fig. 11 (Cont.)

EGO AS ROLE PERSONALITY

	1	2	3	4
Problem	Ego's capacities, including "will power," for valued achievements.	The "fitting" of ego, as personality, into the harmonious system. Can he be "educated" to his role?	Suitability of ego as a personality for his perfection destiny.	Personality as "in tune" with the expressive opportunities.
Type of goal-striving	To "try hard" in the right kind and direction of activity, universalistically valued.	To try to "do the right thing" in order to fit oneself into a harmonious order.	To achieve the ideal state without regard to cost.	To take advantage of the situation in accord with an appreciative standard, but avoid disturbing order.
Locus of strain	Problem of adequacy relative to the more particularized achievement contexts: "Can I do it?"	Possibility of discrepancy – a personality which fails to fit the requirements of role-achievement expectations.	Conflict between commitment to the ideal and deviant need-dispositions.	Possible incompatibility with conditions of a given system: "Am I out of tune?"

Fig. 11 (Cont.)

ALTER AS ROLE PERSONALITY

	1	2	3	4
Problem	Alter as the kind of person who can be expected to "pull his oar," or at least not to "gum the works." Respect for his point of view, his interests and commitments.	Definition of alter's complementary role of co-responsibility for the harmonious system: "Where does he fit?"	Do alter and I "belong together" in the ideal company? Is he "worthy" to be a comrade or fellow-disciple?	Does alter "belong" and can I have satisfactory reciprocity with him within the given system? Will he conform or "rock the boat"?
Type of ego's goal-striving	To facilitate securing alter's co-operation — if irrelevant — to respect his "rights."	To "do his part" in specific reciprocation with alter's, properly respecting alter's status (not rights).	To live up to the imperative of comradeship or to bring alter up to it; if hopeless to do so, to "treat him as he deserves."	Reciprocal gratification and appreciation. To take care not to let him step out of line.
Locus of strain	Alter's "reliability," as pulling his oar or respecting ego's rights to "go about his job his own way."	The possibility of the breakdown of reciprocities from either side; failure of responsibility.	Ego's or alter's worthiness with respect to the perfection ideal; danger of either or both "backsliding."	Possibility of alter's "not fitting," "stepping out of line," and becoming a disturbing element.

Fig. 11 (Cont.)

COLLECTIVITY

	1	2	3	4
Problem	Is the collectivity a cooperative system within which ego can play his achievement role — or at least a "free country" where he can count on non-interference?	Does the collectivity measure up to the ideal of a cooperative achievement system? How can this be maintained or restored?	Is the collectivity an embodiment of the ideal or an evil countertype? Which?	Suitability of the collectivity as a stage for expressive activity.
Type of ego's goal-striving	To "do his job" within the system, to take advantage of its opportunities and to combat features threatening to interfere with either.	To "take responsibility" according to his status for his share of maintenance or restoration of the immanent pattern.	To help realize the ideal social order and combat the evil countertypes.	To combat threats to its integrity —otherwise indifference.
Locus of strain	General basis of difficulties of "securing cooperation" or of securing freedoms and opportunities.	Tendencies for the ideal order to "break up" and the collectivity to fall into disharmony; need for continual effort to maintain it.	The precariousness of maintenance of the ideal and imminence of the threat of its subversion; the "lurking enemy."	Instability of the established taken-for-granted order.

Fig. 11 (Cont.)

PHYSICAL ENVIRONMENT

	1	2	3	4
Problem	The environment's utility as a set of resources and conditions relative to achievement goals: What can ego do with it?	How to shape and fit the environment into a harmonious pattern — the cultivated world.	Is nature part of the ideal state or inimical to it?	Discrimination of "God given" nature and its threatening aspects.
Type of ego's goal-striving	To make the most effective use of resources and progressively to overcome obstacles.	Adaptation of nature to man, and vice versa, into a harmonious system.	Enjoyment of idealized aspects and attempts to master inimical aspects.	Enjoyment of good part; warding off of threats.
Locus of strain	Recalcitrance of nature to being used effectively by men.	Threats of disorderliness and disruption of harmonious system.	The struggle against the inimical aspects; transitoriness and instability of the ideal aspects.	Instability of the natural conditions of immanent perfection.

CULTURAL ACCUMULATION OBJECTS

Fig. 11 (Cont.)

	1	2	3	4
Problem	"Knowledge for what?" Cultural tradition as means of achievement.	How actively to fit cultural elements into a harmonious pattern; utility but in an aesthetic setting.	Is cultural element good or bad? Expression of ideal, or of evil.	Discrimination of the elements that belong and those that do not.
Type of ego's goal-striving	Attempts to make the most of available cultural resources; to overcome "ignorance" and other limitations.	Attempts to construct actively harmonized cultural system; active aestheticism.	Attempts to create idealistic art and to attain perfection of knowledge; search for an absolute.	Enjoyment and acceptance of a given culture and aesthetic patterns. Avoidance of what does not fit.
Locus of strain	Problem of adequacy of cultural resources to "do the job."	Elements of cultural disharmony which cannot be organized.	Uncertainty about perfection of cultural possessions.	Threats to the given perfection of the culture.

Fig. 12 TRANSCENDENT ACHIEVEMENT

Types of ego's goal-striving toward classes of objects	Affectivity-Specificity 1	Affectivity-Diffuseness 2	Neutrality-Specificity 3	Neutrality-Diffuseness 4
Ego's body	Striving to achieve specific types of bodily enjoyment or gratifying performances: e.g., food, sex, pleasurable motor activity in sports.	Striving to achieve diffuse bodily well-being and to exercise bodily capacities: cult of "enjoyment of health."	Striving to achieve specific types of bodily efficiency and discipline, such as athletic prowess. Specific instrumental uses of body.	Striving for a diffuse state of bodily efficiency and discipline—be "in training," General instrumental utilization of body.
Alter as personality	Striving to achieve specific gratification from alter, reciprocally or otherwise.	Striving to achieve and utilize a diffuse affective attachment to alter, for mutual gratification: romantic love, "winning" the object.	Striving to win and utilize alter as a cooperator or exchange partner in achieving specific goals, or to "get something out of him" for a specific goal.	Striving to bring alter into a diffuse relation of solidarity in the interest of general achievement orientation.
Physical environment	Striving to secure or control specifically enjoyable resources: foods, beautiful locations, etc.	Striving to secure diffuse gratifications from nature by earning or winning them.	Striving to control requisite resources for specific achievements and to shape them accordingly.	Striving to attain diffuse control over nature to be available for any goal.

Fig. 12 (Cont.)

IMMANENT ACHIEVEMENT

	1	2	3	4
Ego's body	Striving to maintain strict limitation on gratifications through use of body by allotting special times, places to such activities. Constant concern not to allow pattern or harmony to be broken.	Striving to maintain a diffuse state of bodily gratification in accordance with an established pattern of harmony among bodily and other pleasures and among various bodily pleasures.	Striving to maintain specific types of discipline as part of a general pattern in which body is controlled: carriage, physical fortitude, etc.	Striving to maintain a general state of discipline as part of a pattern in which body is controlled but not repressed. Valuing discipline without stressing its repressive function.
Alter as personality	Restricted stylized enjoyment of relations with alter according to an established pattern, with carefully structured expectations as to limits of the relationship.	General stylized enjoyment of relations with alter according to an established pattern covering many relationships with same persons, each of which is regulated by a standard of propriety.	Striving to maintain a restrained disciplined relationship strictly bound by limits of propriety and in right proprotion to other relationships and activities.	Striving to maintain a generally disciplined set of relationships extending to all spheres and not differentiated by context. A generalized respectability.
Physical environment	Enjoyment of specific resources – food, beautiful locations, etc. – within context of an established pattern.	Striving to maintain general enjoyment of nature in its various aspects with concern to keep a proper balance between these enjoyments and other activities.	Striving to maintain natural environment in an ordered differentiated pattern relevant to specific activities; e.g., gardening.	Striving to maintain nature in a generally ordered state conforming to a pattern in which gentle wildness and cultivation might be intermixed.

Fig. 12 (Cont.)

TRANSCENDENT QUALITY-PERFECTION

	1	2	3	4
Ego's body	Striving to conform with an ideal which allows certain bodily gratifications and strictly represses others.	Striving to achieve some state of ideal beauty or euphoria; horror of ugliness.	Striving to conform with an ideal which imposes specific deprivations and repressions which are highly evaluated.	Striving to conform with a generally repressive ideal in which the repressive element is highly evaluated as such.
Alter as personality	Intense specific demands on alter to achieve ideal relationship in a particular activity.	Striving to achieve an ideal of complete fusion of love or comradeship; fear of anything less.	Striving to achieve an ideal of proper fulfillment of specific obligations in relations with others; e.g., bureaucratic fulfillment of obligation (formal justice).	Striving to achieve a repressive relationship in all spheres vis-à-vis others as fulfillment of an ideal of manly or paternal authority.
Physical environment	Striving to achieve some enjoyment in a specific activity; e.g., reaching a particular landscape or mountain peak.	Striving to achieve an ideal state through contact with nature as such or Reality.	Striving to achieve some specific discipline or deprivation by extreme exertion vis-à-vis nature, the end being the performance of the action itself.	Striving to achieve an ideal state in which all of nature is fully under control, with nothing left to nature's own operations (but not for instrumental purposes).

IMMANENT QUALITY-PERFECTION

Fig. 12 (Cont.)

	1	2	3	4
Ego's body	Acceptance of opportunities for specific gratifications along already established channels. No substitutibility of one mode of gratification for another.	Acceptance of opportunities for any gratification as they occur or as need emerges. No attachment to specific objects or modes of gratification.	Acceptance of specific deprivations as imposed by object situation. (Not ethically required to accept them but absence of feasible alternatives renders it necessary.)	Acceptance of deprivations in general on grounds that they are imposed by the situation.
Alter as personality	Acceptance of a specific alter as a satisfactory partner for enjoyment of a specific gratification. No joint exertion with alter to achieve hitherto unrealized goals.	Acceptance of any alter as a satisfactory partner for enjoyment of any gratification as needs arise and as opportunities occur. No joint exertion with alter to achieve hitherto unrealized goals.	Acceptance of a specific alter as imposing deprivations which are not to be avoided since they are part of the situation.	Acceptance of other persons in general as agents of deprivations which are not to be avoided since they are part of the situation.
Physical environment	Acceptance of available opportunities for specific gratifications afforded by environment and some effort to ward off loss of these opportunities without, however, effort to extend range of opportunities for gratification or to guarantee them.	Acceptance of available opportunities for any kind of gratifications as they occur and as need arises. Efforts to ward off losses taken only with respect to most immediately enjoyed gratification opportunity but in view of wide substitutibility of gratification objects.	Acceptance of specific environment deprivations as they occur with little effort to avoid them in the future, looking upon them as given by the situation.	Acceptance of environment as generally deprivational without alternatives and hence with little effort to avoid them.

Fig. 13

INSTRUMENTAL COMPLEX

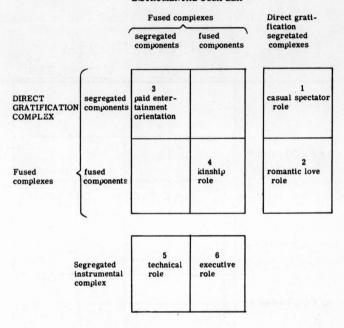

		Fused complexes		Direct gratification segretated complexes
		segregated components	fused components	
DIRECT GRATIFICATION COMPLEX	segregated components	**3** paid entertainment orientation		**1** casual spectator role
Fused complexes	fused components		**4** kinship role	**2** romantic love role
	Segregated instrumental complex	**5** technical role	**6** executive role	

Fig. 14

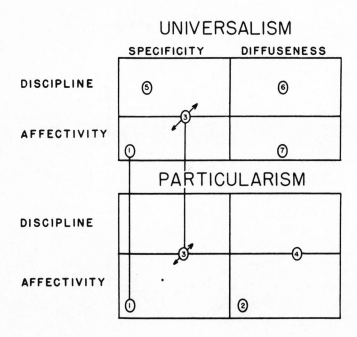

Fig. 15 POINTS OF CORRESPONDENCE BETWEEN SOCIAL SYSTEMS AND PERSONALITY SYSTEMS

Social Systems	Personality Systems
1. Categorization of object units (individual actors and collectivities) in terms of ascriptive qualities and performance capacities.	1. Categorization of self as object in relation to alters—as possessing qualities and performance capacities.
2. Distribution types of role-orientation pattern—of individuals and collectivities—in the social system.	2. Ego's different types of role-orientations as an interdependent system.
3. The economy of instrumental orientations (division of labor) in ecological complexes and in organizations.	3. The relational complex of ego's instrumental orientations to alters as consumers, sources of income, facilities, collaborators.
4. The economy of expressive orientations in attachment patterns and the corresponding symbolic reward system.	4. The relational complex of ego's expressive orientations to alters as objects of gratification, attachment, and identification.
5. Integrative structures of the social system; sub-collectivities, the over-all collectivity, and internal role of differentiation relative to collective responsibility.	5. Ego's integration with social system in terms of superego-integration, including the organization of adjustive mechanisms relative to collective obligations.

3

A Psychological Model

EDWARD C. TOLMAN

1

Introduction

Part III will attempt to place those concepts especially pertinent to psychology, which have been developed in Parts I and II, within a more strictly psychological framework. In other words, a theoretical system of psychology will be presented which contains, it is believed, all the descriptive and theoretical constructs necessary for explaining and predicting the action or behavior [1] of individual persons as this concept has been developed above. And again it will be emphasized that such action or behavior of individual human beings practically always takes place *in*, and is *relative to*, an environment which typically contains not only "mere" physical objects but also other persons, collectivities, culturally presented values, and accumulated cultural resources.

The general theoretical organization to be used in the present analysis is one which today has received relatively wide acceptance among psychologists. This organization distributes all descriptive and explanatory constructs into: (1) independent variables; (2) the dependent variable of behavior or action; (3) postulated intervening variables; and (4) postulated causal connections between the three types of variables. Let us consider each of these four headings.

The Independent Variables

The independent variables are the initiating causes of the individual's action. The main types of independent variable which have been found by psychologists to date are three:

[1] The terms "action" and "behavior" will be used interchangeably in this section. I have previously used the term "behavior" (Tolman [22]) with practically all the connotations which have been given here to the term "action." That is, a behavior, or an action, differs from a mere movement or response in that a behavior or action can be fully identified and described in terms only of the organism-environment rearrangement which it produces. A mere movement or a response can, on the other hand, be identified in purely intra-organism terms, e.g., as consisting of such-and-such muscle contractions or glandular secretions.

(1) *Stimulus situation* (i.e., the environmental entities presented to the individual actor at the given moment). These environmental entities consist of physical, social, and cultural objects and processes. Such environmental objects and processes can, of course, in the last analysis affect the action of an individual only through the mediation of sense perception and memory-trace arousal. But the technical understanding of such neurophysiological processes will not, as such, be our concern. Rather, we shall assume that, for the level of causal determination with which social science is concerned, one can assume, within reasonable limits (without, that is, detailed psychophysiological, "mediational" investigation), what potential "perceptions" [2] are possible and probable as a result of the presence to the individual actor of a certain stimulus situation (i.e., certain physical, social, and cultural objects).[3] Granting this assumption to be valid, one general problem of psychology will be that of discovering why, although certain specific types of social, cultural, and physical objects are presented environmentally, the given actor on a given occasion will react only to certain ones of these objects or will behave to these latter only with certain degrees of distortion as compared with the "normal," "standard," or "usual" ways of behaving.

(2) *States of drive arousal and/or drive satiation.* The physiological entities of drive arousal and drive satiation can today roughly be identified by a physiologist from observations of the recency and/or intensity of just past "consummatory behaviors." [4] (By "consummatory behaviors" are to be understood such types of "terminal behavior" as eating, drinking, copulating, sleeping, dominating, submitting, affiliating, aggressing, avoiding, etc., which terminate spells of activity.) But the real definition of drives, as we are conceiving the term here, lies not in the resultant readinesses or non-readinesses for such types of terminal behavior but in precise statements concerning the states of the underlying organs and tissues themselves. It is these organ and tissue states which ultimately define "drives" as they are discussed here as one of the three main types of independent variables. The resultant readinesses or non-readinesses for types of consummatory behavior will constitute, rather, what we shall define below as the "needs." And such needs, as will also be seen below, are to be considered as a type of intervening variable.

(3) *Such individual-difference-producing variables as heredity, age, sex, and special physiological conditions such as those produced by drugs, endocrine disturbances, and the like.* These variables are assumed to act direct-

---

[2] The term "perception" will be used throughout in a broad sense to cover immediate memories and inferences as well as perceptions in the narrower sense.

[3] This fact of a great consistency between the given environmentally presented entities and the probable perceptions that will be "achieved" (irrespective of tremendous variability in the mediational neurophysiological mechanics from occasion to occasion) is, of course, the problem of "thing constancy." The most fruitful and searching analyses of this problem have, I believe, been made to date by Brunswik [3].

[4] Such observations have sometimes been called "maintenance-schedule" observations.

ly in determining those types of intervening variables which are called traits — either capacity traits or temperamental traits. These trait variables are assumed to interact with the other or "content" variables so as to enhance or depress the magnitudes of the latter. But any final and definitive assumptions as to the nature of the interacting functions between "traits" and "contents" seem to be a problem for the future. And in the present essay the whole problem of traits will be largely ignored or at the most only formally acknowledged.

The Dependent Variable of Behavior (Action)

This dependent variable is conceived as consisting of responses which, from the point of view of a purely physiological analysis, are merely combinations of verbal, skeletal, and visceral reactions; but which from the point of view of the present action schema are identified and defined not in terms of their underlying physiology but in terms of their "action meanings." In other words, a given behavior or action is to be identified and defined, in the last analysis, only in terms of the ways in which it tends to manipulate or rearrange physical, social, or cultural objects relative to the given actor. An actor "goes toward the light," "consumes food," "aggresses against a friend," "avoids the shade," "puts on a coat," and so on. In other words, it appears that the mediational problems of muscle contraction and of gland secretion, like those of sense-perception, can for our purposes be largely ignored because the action meanings tend to remain the same through a wide diversity of alternative, physiological movement-details.[5]

Intervening Variables

Intervening variables are postulated explanatory entities conceived to be connected by one set of causal functions to the independent variables, on the one side, and by another set of functions to the dependent variable of behavior, on the other. A certain misunderstanding as to what may thus be the ultimate definition of such intervening variables must, however, be corrected.

In a recent article MacCorquodale and Meehl [15] have suggested that different schools of psychology have defined intervening variables in two different ways. One school employs what these authors have decided to call the initial, or pure, concept of intervening variables. The pure concept assumes, they say, that the whole character and meaning of an intervening variable is given in and exhausted by its assumed functional (mathematical) relationships to the causal independent variables on the one side, or to the

---

[5] Again we are indebted to Brunswik [3] for having emphasized these facts. Guthrie and Horton [6] have suggested the use of the two terms *act* and *action* for the response defined in terms of the environmental-actor rearrangements which it tends to produce and the term *movement* for the detailed physiological character of the response.

caused dependent behavior on the other. The second type of theory assumes, they say, more full-blooded types of intervening variable, which they designate as "hypothetical constructs." This second type of theory ascribes, they believe, ostensively definable, substantive properties to intervening variables, which properties can, hypothetically at least, eventually be given direct operational measurement. "Hypothetical constructs" thus are defined by substantive properties which are separate from and more than the mere functional relationships of such constructs to the independent variables or to the dependent behavior.

I agree with MacCorquodale and Meehl that this distinction between the functional or mathematical identification of intervening variables and a denotative, ostensive identification of intervening variables is an important one. Further, I would also agree that this is a distinction between two different approaches to the intervening variable which has been slurred over in previous discussions. MacCorquodale and Meehl have done us a service in bringing these two approaches to light. On the other hand, I do not agree with these authors that, corresponding to these two ways of defining, there are really to be found two disparate classes of theory. I shall contend rather that actually all current psychological schools — whatever their explicit (or lack of explicit) statements — define intervening variables *both* by the assumed functional relations of such intervening variables to the independent and/or to dependent variables *and* by the postulated, ostensive properties also attributed to such intervening variables. The differences between different theories seem to me to lie not in whether or not they ascribe constitutive properties to their intervening variables, but rather in the nature of such ascribed properties.

In fact, three major trends in current theories relative to such ascribed properties are to be found. These may be called (1) the neurophysiological trend, (2) the phenomenological trend, and (3) the trend toward a *sui generis* model. Let me briefly summarize each of these.

(1) The theories which adopt the *neurophysiological trend* ascribe primarily (either implicitly or explicitly) neurophysiological constitutive properties to their intervening variables. Most of the stimulus-response theories, whether of Hull [8] and his students or of Guthrie [5] and his, in inventing their intervening variables, rely, I believe, on more or less explicit assumptions to the effect that these intervening variables are in the nature of afferent, efferent, or associative neural connections.[6]

(2) Theories which adopt the *phenomenological trend* ascribe primarily

---

[6] Köhler [12], Krech [9 and 10] and Hebb [7] also belong to the neurophysiological trend, but their neurophysiological constructs involve more in the way of brain fields and less in the way of insulated nerve channels.

Hull [8] tends to deny that he is using neurophysiological constructs in thinking of his intervening variables. Nevertheless, it seems to me that he *is* relying on them, at least implicitly if not explicitly, for his notions about how these intervening variables act.

introspectively derived, experiential characteristics to their intervening variables. Much of Freudian theory would seem to belong in this category. Gestalt psychology also seems to belong here (as well as in the first category) since Gestalt psychologists postulate not only brain-field events but also correlated phenomenological events. In fact, Gestalt theory seems to have begun with phenomenological constructs and then to have moved back to correlated physiological constructs as its more basic explanatory device.

(3) Theories which exhibit the *trend toward a sui generis model* invent a set of explanatory structures and processes (hypothetical constructs) which draw on analogies from whatever other disciplines — mathematics, physics, mechanics, physiology, etc. — as may be deemed useful. Freud's water-reservoir concept of the "libido," Lewin's "topological and vector" psychology, and the theory to be presented in the following pages belong primarily in this third category.[7]

The theory to be presented here will then be quite frankly one which develops (by various analogies drawn from simple physics and mechanics, from Lewin's "topological and vector" psychology, and from common experience) a *sui generis* model. This model has its own (tentatively) ascribed intervening constitutive structures and processes and its own variety of interconnecting causal functions. The justification for such a model is, of course, wholly pragmatic. Such a model can be defended only insofar as it proves helpful in explaining and making understandable already observed behavior and insofar as it also suggests new behaviors to be looked for. And any such model must, of course, be ready to undergo variations and modifications to make it correspond better with new empirical findings. Finally, insofar as such a model holds up and continues to have pragmatic value, it must be assumed that eventually more and more precise and intelligible correlations will be discovered between it and underlying neurophysiological structures and processes — especially as more about the latter comes to be known and verified by physiologists.[8]

[7] A fourth type of theory, of which that of Brunswik [3] and that of Skinner [21] are the most distinguished examples, seeks to do without much in the way of intervening variables (Skinner does postulate a "reflex reserve") and to attempt to develop at once direct empirically establishable functions between the initial independent variables and the final dependent behavior.

[8] It was this assumption that such a model is eventually to be correlated with neurophysiology which led me in another place [25] to describe it as a "pseudo-brain model." It may be noted further that the position I am adopting here is similar to, but slightly different from that proposed by Krech [9 and 10]. He has proposed a much more explicitly neurophysiological model. But the substantive properties which he ascribes to his neurophysiological "dynamic system" draw, I believe, more from the findings concerning behavior or action than from neurophysiology as such. That is, Krech is proposing to remake neurophysiology in the image of psychology, whereas I am proposing merely to make for psychology a pragmatically useful model of its own — leaving it for the future to discover the correlations between it, this pseudo-brain model, and a true neurophysiological model.

POSTULATED CAUSAL CONNECTIONS

Before turning to the model itself we must consider briefly the fourth category listed above — that of the postulated types of causal (functional) relationships between independent variables, intervening variables (hypothetical constructs), and the dependent variable of behavior. It is obvious from the above discussion of types of intervening variables that the types of postulated interconnecting causal functions assumed by the different theories will be intimately connected with the types of assumed intervening variables. To analyze these relationships for each of the three major types of theoretical trends cited above would be too great a task to attempt here. All I shall do is to develop my own model and to indicate the sorts of interconnecting causal functions assumed in it. Let us turn then to the model.

2

The Model

A schematic outline of the model is presented in Fig. 1.
The three groups of independent variables are located at the left. The intervening variables, which in this exact form are, of course, peculiar to the present theory, are presented in the middle. And the dependent variable of behavior has been placed at the right. The nature of the independent variables and of the dependent behavior have already been discussed so that the features of the model which need principal consideration here are the intervening variables.

These intervening variables comprise six main yet closely interconnected items: need system (A); belief-value matrix (B); immediate behavior space (C); locomotion within the immediate behavior space (D); restructured behavior space resulting from locomotions or from learning or from the psychodynamic mechanisms (E); and capacity and temperamental traits (T), which are assumed to interact with the other five and with their functional interconnections.

The arrows in Fig. 1 represent the postulated directions of causal determination (see IV). The solid arrows indicate the initial directions of such causation. These causations are assumed to result from the original values of the independent variables before behavior or restructuring have taken place. The broken-line arrows represent subsequent causations in reverse directions. That is, the changes in the behavior space due to locomotions, learning, and the psychodynamisms may result in changes in the belief-value matrix, which in turn may produce changes in the need system. This matter of causal determination is, however, complex and will become only somewhat cleared up in the course of our further discussion of the intervening variables. Finally, it is to be noted that locomotion (represented by the arrow *D*), which is an intervening variable to be distinguished from the actually observable behavior, is conceived both to cause a restructuring of the behavior space and to produce the externally observable dependent variable of behavior.

Let us turn now to a more full-bodied diagram. In Fig. 2 the picture has

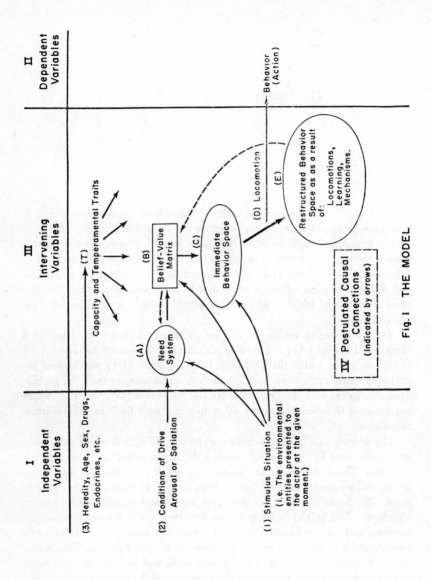

Fig. I THE MODEL

I	III	II
Independent Variables	Intervening Variables	Dependent Variables

(3) Heredity, Age, Sex, Drugs, Endocrines, etc.

(T) Capacity and Temperamental Traits

(B) Belief-Value Matrix

(A) Need System

(2) Conditions of Drive Arousal or Satiation

(1) Stimulus Situation (i.e. The environmental entities presented to the actor at the given moment.)

(C) Immediate Behavior Space

(D) Locomotion

(E) Restructured Behavior Space as as a result of: Locomotions, Learning, Mechanisms.

Behavior (Action)

IV Postulated Causal Connections (Indicated by arrows)

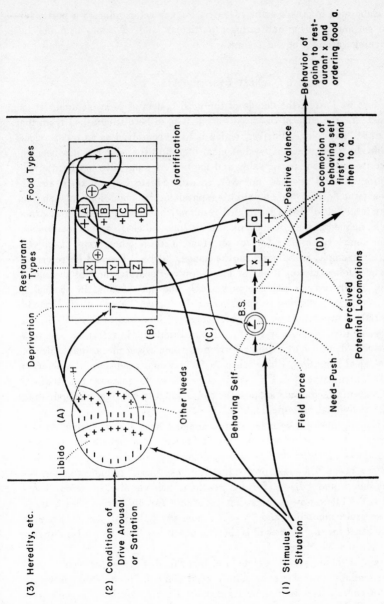

Fig. 2 GOING TO A PARTICULAR RESTAURANT WHEN HUNGRY

been elaborated for the specific case of a hungry actor going to a particular restaurant and ordering and eating a particular food.[1] We may examine the intervening variables one at a time.

NEED SYSTEM (A)

Before we look at the details of the need system as here pictured, let us consider first the concept of "need" itself. It is to be distinguished from the concept of "physiological drive," which is to be conceived as an independent variable. In most previous psychological literature the tendency has been to use the two terms interchangeably and the two concepts have not been clearly distinguished. I propose, however, to differentiate between them and to use the term "drive" for an initiating physiological condition only and to use the term "need" for a postulated resultant, intervening, behavioral process to be defined in the last analysis as a readiness to get to and to manipulate in consummatory fashion (or to get from) certain other types of object. Thus, for example, in referring to the hunger "drive," I would be referring to the physiological conditions of the digestive apparatus and of the blood stream, or whatever, which are presumably the main factors in producing the hunger need; whereas in speaking of the hunger "need" itself, I would refer, rather, to a readiness to go to a standard food and to consume it and at the same time to go away from nonfoods. Similarly, in referring, say, to a dominance "drive," I would be referring to some as yet unspecifiable neurophysiological condition, which when in force would predispose the actor to exhibit a dominance "need"; that is, a readiness to go toward a standard goal situation which would support the consummatory behavior of dominating another individual or individuals.

It should, however, be noted that although I have chosen "drive" to designate the physiological determiner and "need" to designate the resultant psychological or behavioral readiness, some psychologists may prefer just the reverse usage. They may prefer, that is, to use "need" to indicate a physiological defect and "drive" for the resultant behavioral disposition. I am doing it the other way around simply because for me "drive" has a more physiological connotation and "need" a more psychological one. And it may be noted that my use of "need" is the one which has been adopted and given wide currency by Murray [17].

Again, it should also be pointed out that this distinction between "drive" as an essentially physiologically defined condition and "need" (though having itself, of course, its own unique neurophysiological correlate) as an essentially psychologically or behaviorally defined condition allows for the fact that in certain situations the magnitude of a given need may be determined

---

[1] In this diagram the broken-line "back-acting" arrows and the trait variables have, for the sake of simplicity, been omitted.

more by the character of the given stimulus situation than by the strength of any single univocally correlated drive. Thus, for example, the presence of an especially tempting food as part of the stimulus situation may arouse the hunger need even though the hunger drive as a determining physiological condition is, and remains, relatively weak.

Finally, it may be noted that a given need, even when caused primarily by the arousal of physiological drives, may characteristically be activated not by a single drive but rather by some combination of drives. Thus, for example, the hunger need itself (defined as the readiness to go toward and to consume food) may in certain individuals be activated not univocally by the hunger drive but also by the arousal of other drives such as gregariousness, fear, or the like. For by now it is a psychological commonplace that in certain individuals an aroused gregariousness or an aroused fear drive may also express themselves in the hunger need. Individuals so affected will be observed to overeat in loneliness or in stress.

But let us now look at the need system as a whole as depicted in Fig. 2. It is represented by the circle labeled A and is shown as containing a number of interconnected compartments. Each of these compartments is intended to represent a single need and, when the need in question is aroused, the compartment is conceived to contain both positive and negative "electromagnetic" charges. When the need is strong the compartment contains many charges; when the need is weak it contains few charges. In this particular diagram the two main needs depicted are a libido need, so labeled, and a hunger need, labeled H. Two undesignated needs are also indicated. The term "libido" has been used without any preconception as to the nature of this need libido, other than that it seems to be correlated primarily with some physiological energy and that it seems to vary in average magnitude from individual to individual and to go up and down in any one individual with such factors as health, sickness, and time of day. Further, it is postulated that this libido need has no specific goals of its own, but through contact with all the other specific needs (whatever the list of these may eventually turn out to be), it adds magnitudes to the electromagnetic charges in these other specific needs. Thus, it is assumed that when the energy or tension in the libido is great, there will be more tension than there otherwise would be in all the other need compartments. It is assumed, in short, that the energy or tension in the different special compartments of the whole need system maintains some sort of an interactive balance with the tension in the basic libido compartment.

Look now at the hunger need, labeled H. The amount of energy (number of plus and minus charges) in this hunger need is conceived to be determined primarily by the strength of the physiological hunger drive and in some degree by the character of the stimulus situation (i.e., whether or not food objects are present). For it will be assumed that, if food stimulus objects are present, and especially if they are particularly tempting, the strength of the hunger need will be increased over what it otherwise would have been as a result of the mere hunger drive. Also the strength of the hunger need will be affected, other things being equal, by the strength at the moment of the general libido tension.

Before we turn to the next feature of the diagram, let us discuss briefly the positive and negative charges, which are represented by the small plus and minus signs. The introduction of these charges as constituting the nature of need tensions is an electromagnetic analogy which should not at present be taken too seriously. It seems useful, however, as a way of summarizing the fact that needs express themselves both as a readiness to go *to* certain types of objects (positive valuing), and as a concomitant readiness to go away from certain other types of objects (negative valuing). When the specific hunger need is high in tension, the actor may be conceived to have both a strong positive readiness (many plus charges) *for* foods and strong negative readiness *against* nonfoods. An increase in the hunger tension within the hunger compartment is to be represented by an increase in both positive and negative charges. The positive charges are then conveyed — see arrows in the diagram — to one end of a belief-value matrix (or a number of different belief-value matrices) and the complementary negative charges are conveyed to the opposite end, or ends, of such a matrix or matrices. The further usefulness of this introduction of the concept of positive and negative charges will become more obvious when we turn now to a consideration of the belief-value matrix.[2]

BELIEF-VALUE MATRIX (B)

In the situation depicted in Fig. 2, the belief-value matrix chosen for representation is a relatively banal one. It is constituted by the cognitive categorizations, beliefs, and values of an actor (obviously one in our culture) relative to hunger deprivation, hunger gratification, foods, and restaurants.[3] In understanding this matrix it will be helpful if we consider it in successive steps. Let us then turn to Fig. 3, which represents this same matrix but with the value features left out and only the categorizations (differentiations) and beliefs left in.

The small squares or "cells" in Fig. 3 represent "typed" (not concrete) images of objects [4] which the individual possesses by virtue of the differentia-

---

[2] It should be noted that the concept of belief-value matrices is practically identical with that of need-dispositions in the preceding parts of this book.

[3] It will be pointed out below that any such simple single matrix as this will, of course, be only one among a vast number of matrices (i.e., sets of categorizations, beliefs, and values relative to other types of objects and other types of gratification and deprivation) which must be assumed to be "built in" (some with more permanency than others) into any developed personality.

[4] The term "image" is here used in a purely objective (nonphenomenological) sense, to designate a categorized readiness to perceive, which the actor in question is to be

tions and categorizations of the object world (specifically in this case of restaurants and foods) which he has previously acquired. These typed images are conceived to be arranged along functionally defined "generalization dimensions" — in the present example, along a restaurant (or food-providing) generalization dimension and along a food (or hunger-gratification-providing) generalization dimension. The units of these generalization dimensions, if we had them, and the relative locations along these dimensions, stated in

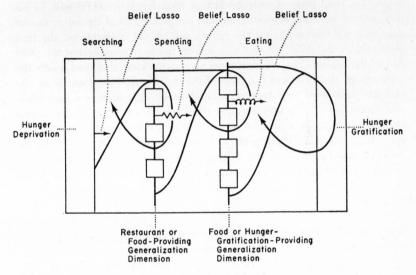

Fig. 3 BELIEF-VALUE MATRIX *re* TYPES OF RESTAURANT
AND TYPES OF FOOD (Values omitted)

terms of such units, of the different typed images would indicate the precise degrees of functional similarity between such images. Our present lack of knowledge concerning the nature of most such dimensions and their units and the relative locations of the specific "typed" images along them is, I believe, one of the reasons why psychology is at present so frustrating. In other words, I would argue that we have to date little theoretical or empirical knowledge as to what and how many such dimensions of generalization can be assumed and what their units are for any given actor or even for most actors in any given culture — save for simple, perceptual dimensions such as colors, shapes, sizes, pitches, loudnesses, tastes, etc.

thought to possess as a result of past experiences with instances of the given type of "object." It has already been indicated in the preceding parts of this book that the term "object" is to be used to cover a number of "modalities," such as the qualities of self and of others; the performances of self and of others; the qualities and performances of collectivities; cultural accumulation objects (physical artifacts, languages, ideologies, industrial techniques, skills, etc.), as well as purely physical, environmental things.

By way of illustration of the sort of further data which we need, I would point to a recent important contribution toward the discovery of a really new and important generalization dimension for children in our culture provided by the work of Sears and his collaborators on doll play [20]. They have discovered by working with nursery-school children that in expressing aggression, the children arrange their dolls in a certain order along a dimension — "things to be aggressed against." If a child is high in need aggression (and there is little conflicting need fear) the child will, in his play, express the most aggression against the parent doll of the same sex, the next most aggression against the parent doll of the opposite sex, the next most against the child doll of the same sex, the next most against the child doll of the opposite sex, the next most against the baby doll, and finally the least against the walls and furniture of the doll house. This, then, is an empirically discovered new type of generalization dimension — a generalization dimension which, with regard to the specific ordering of the objects along it, is obviously a function of our culture. Children raised in other cultures with different family constellations might well order their dolls for the purposes of aggression in a different sequence. But many other such generalization dimensions for all kinds of functional purposes, as well as for aggression, must be discovered and made precise if psychology is finally to achieve wide practical significance.

Look next at the looped arrows of Fig. 3. These arrows (or, we might call them "lassos") represent what I call means-end beliefs [5] and are very important constitutive features in the representation of any matrix. The double tail at the beginning (left) of each arrow, or lasso, represents the generalization spread as regards the kind of initial (*terminus a quo*) typed images. That is, the spread and shape of this forked tail indicate the range of initial types of objects or situations along one dimension which will be accepted (and with what degrees of readinesses) as appropriate means (or instigations) for releasing a given type of behavior-act *in order to get to* such and such a further *terminus ad quem* type of object or situation. The cell or cells caught by the loop (to the right of the fork) of a lasso indicate the specific differentiated types of *terminus ad quem* end-object or situation, which the actor "believes" will be achieved by the type of behavior-act included in the lasso. And the little arrow issuing out of each generalization dimension indicates the particular type of behavior-act which is thus believed to be involved. Specifically, the diagram as a whole represents, then, a hypothetical

---

[5] What I am here calling "beliefs" are essentially what were called "expectations" in the preceding parts of this book. I am using the term "beliefs" to designate the readiness or potentialities for expectations which the actor entertains, and am reserving the term "expectations" to designate the concrete particularized instances of such beliefs which result from the presence of a particular stimulus situation. Thus (see Fig. 2) whereas I would locate "beliefs" in the belief-value matrix, I would locate "expectations" or particularizations of those beliefs in the behavior space.

case in which the actor in question has come to *believe* [6] that, if he is hungry (i.e., if he negatively values hunger deprivation and positively values hunger gratification) and if he should respond by the act of searching for and going to (indicated by the small straight arrow) certain types of restaurants, and if those restaurants were responded to by the act of spending (indicated by the zigzagged arrow) this would get him to certain types of food, and that, if these certain types of food were responded to by the act of eating (indicated by the corkscrew arrow), it would get him finally to hunger gratification.

But Fig. 3 presents, as has been said, only the cognitive (categorization and belief) side of a belief-value matrix. In actuality, the categorizations and beliefs are usually accompanied by value concomitants. Thus, the individual will usually at one and the same time not only believe that certain types of food, if eaten, will lead to hunger gratification but also will have a positive value for hunger gratification and a negative value for hunger deprivation. Similarly, he will have positive value for certain restaurants and certain foods. In other words, a complete diagram of any matrix will tend to contain not only differentiations (categorizations) and beliefs but also values [7] — that is, goodnesses or badnesses deposited on the various cells of the matrix. In Fig. 4, therefore, plus and minus value charges have been added. The magnitudes of the final positive hunger-gratification value and the final negative deprivation value at any given moment are conceived to be largely determined by the plus and minus charges in the hunger-need compartment at that moment (see connecting arrow in Fig. 2, issuing from the hunger-need compartment, bifurcating, and running to both ends of the matrix). But the magnitudes of these values may also be determined in part by the character of the presented stimulus situation. Some stimulus situations will in themselves tend to activate a given matrix.

Next, given types of food are represented as having different degrees of positive values insofar as they are "believed" to lead on successfully to hunger gratification and away from hunger deprivation. The relative successes with which the different foods are thus believed to lead on are represented by a generalization gradient — that is, by the shape of the initial *terminus a quo*, or forked, end of the lasso. The plus value is brought back by the arrow (see the plus sign in the circle at the point of the arrow). Then this value is dis-

---

[6] A "belief" is operationally defined as a connection that makes a readiness to perceive and to behave in a certain way relative to one type of object (as end) give rise to a readiness to perceive and to behave in a certain way relative to certain other types of objects (as means). What I am here calling a belief is thus essentially what I have previously designated [22] as a "means-end readiness."

[7] It should be emphasized that I am using the term "value" here in a more specific and special sense than it is used in the other sections of this book. I am using it to designate what types of object or situation will in the given context of need-activation and belief tend to be approached or to be avoided by the given actor.

tributed to the specific types of food according to the shape of the forked tail of the arrow. Further, in order to make the illustration as general as possible, one type of food is indicated in the diagram as actually having negative value because "it is believed" by the actor actually to lead away from hunger gratification and toward hunger deprivation.[8] Similarly, the different types of restaurants are represented as having different positive values because they are believed to lead on with different degrees of success to a given valued type of food.

    a. Modal matrix for a culture. A further point to be noted, now, is that Fig. 4 may also be used to represent (for a very simple area) a culturally and

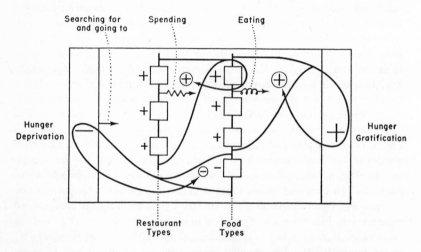

Fig. 4   BELIEF - VALUE MATRIX
(Values added)

sociologically determined belief and value system as shared by a community of individuals. This belief and value system, this matrix, if correctly inferred by the observer for a relatively homogeneous group of individuals, would be stable in verbal propositions such as: (1) If X (the modal individual in this culture) were positively valuing hunger gratification and correspondingly negatively valuing hunger deprivation, he would value certain types of food-to-be-eaten in a certain order by virtue of his beliefs concerning their respective gratification-producing characters. (2) If X values certain types of food, he would be ready to value positively certain types of restaurant because of his

---

    [8] It is to be noted that the concept and term "cathexis" will refer to these relative degrees to which the different foods are believed to lead on to hunger gratification and away from hunger deprivation. The food which through the behavior of eating is believed by the actor to lead most readily to hunger gratification would be the most strongly "cathected" food.

belief that these types of restaurant would lead to the certain types of food through the act of spending.

Further, insofar as questionnaires and verbal reports can be considered reliable forms of data, these propositions about the matrix could be relatively adequately inferred from mere questionnaires or interviews. Thus, for example, one could ask the subjects: (1) "What are you ready to do when you haven't eaten for a considerable length of time?" (2) "What kinds of food do you like? Name six varieties of food in order of preference. What do you like about each of these six?" (3) "For each of these six foods what types of restaurant would you go to and in what order? List all the considerations you would take into account in choosing the one kind of restaurant or the other."

Suppose we now obtain from such questionnaires (of course, far better constructed ones) statistically reliable answers indicating that practically all the individuals of a given social status [9] in a given culture give practically the same answers. We could then use these answers to define the modal belief-value matrix relative to foods and restaurants for individuals of this status in this culture. This would be the statistically average or "modal" matrix relative to a given need and a given type of environmental situation for the given group of similarly placed individuals. Indeed, such a modal matrix, or rather a whole collection of such modal matrices, shared by a whole society and concerned with relatively basic needs and relatively general features of the environment, is, I believe, what anthropologists have sometimes called the *ethos* of a culture. By conceiving such an ethos as a very large and relatively general belief-value matrix system I am, I believe, merely saying in my terms what has already been implied in Chapter III of Part II.

b. A matrix equation or modal matrix for an individual. It must be noted, now, that a matrix for a single individual may also be conceived as a "modal" affair. It may be drawn, that is, to represent not the actual momentary absolute magnitudes of the values, the beliefs, and the categorizations, but rather their average *or modal* magnitudes relative to one another. In other words, a matrix may be drawn to represent merely an equation in which specific absolute magnitudes have not yet been substituted. When a matrix is so drawn, the absolute magnitudes on any specific occasion will be arrived at by the substitution in this matrix equation of the then-and-there absolute magnitudes of the attached need or needs and of the specific stimulus situation. The formal or modal matrix is a "mathematical equation" which states the functional interrelations between the variables within it. The absolute magnitudes to be given to these variables on a given occasion will be determined by the substitution in this equation of specific need-gratification and need-deprivation magnitudes resulting from the then-and-there aroused physiological drives and from the then-and-there presented stimulus situation.

Let us turn now to C — the behavior space.

[9] See Linton [14] for this use of the term *status*.

Behavior Space (C)

Return to Fig. 2 and look at *C*. There are two main types of causal arrows shown as determinative of the contents of *C*: a causal arrow springing directly from the stimulus situation of the moment, and three causal arrows coming down from the belief-value matrix. A behavior space is thus to be defined as a *particularized* complex of perceptions (memories and inferences) as to objects and relations and the "behaving self," evoked by the given environmental stimulus situation and by a controlling and activated belief-value matrix (or perhaps several such matrices). What is perceived (expected) is thus determined by what is presented by the stimulus situation at the moment and by the store of categorizations, beliefs, and values which the actor brings to the presented stimuli. Or, to put it another way, the immediate behavior space is to be defined as an array of particular objects, in such-and-such particular "direction" and "distance" relations to one another, which are perceived by the actor at the given moment. And some of these objects tend to have positive or negative "valences" on them.[10] Among such particular objects a very crucial one is the actor's self (designated as the behaving self) which is also a part of any such perceived array.

The words "perceive" and "perception" have been chosen as the most appropriate ones for summarizing the behavioral character of a behavior space.[11] Several provisos are, however, to be kept in mind in this use of the terms.

The first proviso is that "perception" as here used covers not only perception in its narrow meaning of strict sense-perception, in which physical stimuli for the corersponding objects are all then and there present to the senses, but also includes the perception of objects some of whose parts are, in common-sense terms, merely inferred or remembered. Thus, for example, I myself, as the actor, may often be considered to "perceive" (i.e., to have present in my immediate behavior space) not only the objects on my desk and before my eyes at the moment, but also some of the familiar objects on the wall behind my back or even such an object as the University Campanile outside my window at the left. For I might well be found to be immediately ready to behave toward all these other objects and not merely toward those on my desk.

Further, this broader use of the term "perception" includes whatever

---

[10] A belief-value matrix contains "universals"; a behavior space contains "particulars." Thus a "valence" is a particularization of a value. In other words, whereas a value is deposited on the image of a type of object, a valence is deposited on the perception of an instance of such a type of object.

[11] In other places [23 and 24] I have used the terms "apprehend" and "apprehension" for this immediate character of the behavior space. It is felt now, however, that the good old words "perceive" and "perception" used in a *general* sense more nearly carry the desired meaning.

concrete particularized instances of spatial, temporal, aesthetic, mathematical, or other such relations as may be immediately given along with the objects themselves as ways of getting from one object to another. That is, a behavior space will contain not only particular objects but also their particular spatial and temporal, or other, relations to one another. Or, in other words, the "medium" (i.e., the "directions" and "distances" constitutive of a behavior space) may be not only spatial and temporal, but also mechanical, aesthetic, mathematical, or the like. Thus, for example, when I behave on a specific occasion in terms of the number system, the French language, simple logical principles, simple aesthetic principles, or the like, these particularizations as to how to get from one object to another are to be conceived by the psychologist as at that moment "there" in my behavior space along with the objects which they relate.

A third proviso is that "perception" (and hence the behavior space) may also include entities of which the actor is not then and there consciously aware. Any concrete particular objects or relations which govern the actor's immediate action are to be said to be in the behavior space — that is, to be also "perceived," whether or not (in introspective terms) the actor is then and there consciously aware of them.[12]

But let us look now in more detail at the behavior space presented in Fig. 2. The entity surrounded by the two concentric circles and labeled *B.S.* is the "behaving self." This is the actor's behaving self as perceived by him at the given moment and perceived as located in a certain way with respect to other objects. The symbol a represents a particular food of the type A perceived as within the available environment. And x is a particular restaurant of the type X also perceived as within the available environment. The plus signs on a and x represent positive "valences." [13] These positive valences are represented as determined (see arrows) by the positive values in the belief-value matrix on the corresponding typed objects X and A. It is to be observed next that there is a negative charge within the behaving self. This negative charge is labeled "need-push," which is conceived as evoked in the behaving self by the negative charge in the hunger-deprivation compartment in the belief-value matrix (see connecting arrow). That is, any need deprivation in a matrix arouses in the behaving self a corresponding negative need-push. Fur-

---

[12] Just what the further refinements may be, as far as the governance of behavior is concerned, between those behavior-space contents which are consciously present and those which are unconsciously present is a question which I shall touch upon below but to which no completely adequate answer can, I believe, now be given, because of the present inadequate state of our empirical knowledge.

[13] Plus and minus signs in a belief-value matrix (see above) indicate plus and minus "values" for categorized *types* of objects. Plus and minus signs on objects in the behavior space indicate the resultant concrete pulling or repelling properties of particular, perceived *instances* of such types of object. The term "valence" is used to distinguish these specifically located pullings and repellings from the values. The term "valence" has, of course, been borrowed from Lewin [13].

ther, given a positive valence and a complementary negative need-push, there will result a field force tending to push the behaving self toward the positive valence. Also, if there were a negative valence and a corresponding negative need-push, there would result a field force tending to repel the behaving self away from such a negatively valenced object. In the present case the behaving self is impelled first to the restaurant x and then to the food a. And this will tend to result in the actual locomotion of the behaving self first to x and then to a.

An important point to be emphasized is that some such concept as that of a need-push (perhaps a better term for it could be found) seems to be necessary. Thus the food need-push (corresponding to the activated strength of hunger deprivation) may be relatively great in a given instance, although no strongly valenced food or foods may be present in the immediately perceived behavior space. In such a case, I would make a further assumption: to wit, that such a need-push may evoke, by some process analogous to "electromagnetic induction," positive charges in any regions of the behavior space which the behaving self is not then in. As a result of these "induced" positive charges the behaving self will be attracted to such regions. When, however, the behaving self locomotes to them, no actual food is perceived and hence no discharge takes place. The food need-push remains practically unreduced. I assume further that thereupon some small portion of the negative electric charge of the behaving self need-push spreads by "conduction" to this immediately surrounding region which makes the region then somewhat negative; whereupon the behaving self is propelled away from it to new regions. It would, in short, be by some such assumptions that I would explain some of the restless, exploratory behavior of a hungry animal who does not yet perceive actual food in any region in the behavior space.

Let us now consider still another important feature of the behavior space. This concerns the fact, already noted, that the "directions" and "distances" which are constitutive of a behavior space may be other than spatial; they may be temporal, mechanical, social, mathematical, and so forth. In other words, the "locomotion" of the behaving self which would get it to or from a perceived object, may involve time manipulations, mechanical manipulations, social manipulations, or mathematical manipulations, as well as simple spatial manipulations (i.e., mere spatial "goings-to" or "goings-from"). To what extent these different dimensions of locomotion have to be conceptually separated out in the case of a complex behavior is not yet known. It may turn out that for predicting any save the simplest behavior one will have to draw different behavior spaces lying in different locomotor planes (dimensions) and that the final locomotion must be depicted as some resultant of all these according to some principles analogous to those of descriptive geometry. For the present, however, I shall leave such further complications aside. And actually, I personally tend to believe that an actor himself does not normally have any clear differentiation between such different dimensions of locomotion. A given goal object is "over there" in space and time, mechanics, society, and so on, all at once. The perceptions of the directions in all these dimensions occur simultaneously as some sort of total Gestalt. For the present, then, until further work has shown it necessary to assume otherwise, I shall hold that locomotions, however complicated, can all be represented as occurring in a single behavior-space plane. But let us consider now in more detail the nature and result of such locomotions.

LOCOMOTION AND RESULTANT RESTRUCTURING
OF THE BEHAVIOR SPACE

Any diagram of the behavior space (see C in Figs. 1 and 2) can obviously indicate a state only and not a process. The C's in a diagram depict the assumed behavior space before locomotion (or other restructuring) takes place. And the E's represent the new behavior space after such locomotions or a succession of such locomotions (resulting in learning or in one of the psychodynamic mechanisms) have taken place. What, now, is the nature of locomotion? First of all it must be emphasized again that locomotion is an intervening variable — a hypothetical construct — which is not identical with the overtly measurable dependent variable of behavior to which it gives rise. Locomotion is a passage of the behaving self from one region of the behavior space to another (or through a succession of such regions). It is such passages from region to region that express themselves in overt behaviors; but such passages or locomotions are not identical with these resultant behaviors.

But this raises another important question which we have slid over until now. What is meant by a region in the behavior space? A region in the behavior space is to be defined in the last analysis by the sorts of behaviors which the actor perceives as possible for the behaving self if the behaving self is in that region (i.e., in the presence of such-and-such an object or objects). Such an array of possible behaviors is obviously dependent both upon the types of behavior which the given actor is capable of, as a result of innate endowment and previous sensory-motor learning, and upon the presence of objects which will support such behaviors. Behavior cannot take place in a vacuum. When an actor perceives, say, restaurant x as over there (when, that is, he perceives the behaving self as now in one region and restaurant x as in such-and-such another region) he perceives his behaving self as now presented with such-and-such an array of immediately possible behaviors. He also perceives that one of these behaviors defining the present region will get his behaving self to the region of restaurant x, which latter will be defined by certain further possible behaviors (such as ordering steak, eating, tasting, etc.). Locomotion is thus a *selection* from perceived immediately possible behaviors as the way to get to such-and-such another region — other perceived immediately possible behaviors. And what we call an object in the behavior space is essentially a part of a region and a collocation of perceived "supports" for such-and-such particular behaviors. It must be emphasized further that among such behaviors, which an object will support and which thus define any object or region in the behavior space, are to be included the purely perceptual discriminatory behaviors which such an object makes possible. These discriminatory behaviors constitute a large part of the defining characteristics of any object or behavior-space region. That is, a behavior-space region or object is defined both by qualities — i.e., the discriminatory behaviors — which it will support, and by the types of other more manipulatory behaviors which it will also support.[14]

To summarize, a locomotion is a *selection* from one or more perceived immediately possible behaviors (i.e., the region in which the behaving self is initially located) *as the way to get to* such-and-such other potentially possible behaviors (the region *to* which the behaving self is locomoting). A locomotion in the behavior space is thus not a behavior itself but a selection or a series of selections which *result* in a behavior or in behaviors.

It is to be noted further, however, that locomotion not only causes behavior but the continuance and success of locomotion is, of course, contingent upon the fact that the behaviors to which it gives rise shall actually take place and be successful. Let me illustrate by an example. Assume an actor who perceives his behaving self as in the region of "being in the house" (i.e., as in the presence of supports for such-and-such discriminatory and manipulatory behaviors). Assume that he also perceives another region, that of "being outside in the garden," where such-and-such other discriminatory and manipulatory behaviors would be supported. The garden, let us say, has a positive valence, and we shall assume that there is in the behaving self a need-push complementary to this positive valence. The behaving self will, therefore, be propelled to locomote in the direction of the garden. This locomotion will consist in a successive selection from the perceived immediately possible behaviors of those special behaviors which are perceived as appropriate for getting the actor into the garden. If the original behavior-space perception was veridical, then these successive selections — this locomotion — will give rise to a series of actual sensory-motor acts which will in fact get the actor into the real garden and thus lead to a new behavior space in which the behaving self will be perceived as in the garden. If the original behavior-space perception had, however, been nonveridical, then the locomotion would have consisted in the selection of inappropriate behaviors — ones which would not have got the actor into the real garden or the perceived behaving self into the perceived region of a garden.

The *E*'s in the diagrams (see Fig. 1) represent, then, the new layout or

---

[14] These two types of support are what I have previously distinguished as "discriminanda" and "manipulanda" [22].

restructuring of the behavior space which results when the behaving self has locomoted, let us say successfully, to a new region — a region which was perceived as in a certain direction and at a certain distance in the original behavior space before such locomotion took place. It is to be noted that such restructurings as a result of mere successful locomotion are quite simple. They consist merely in the fact that the behaving self is in a different position relative to objects and regions than it was before. If the actor were to be put back into the same initial objective stimulus situation that he was in before the locomotion and consequent behavior took place, his behavior space might well be, to all intents and purposes, the same as it was on the previous occasion.

Restructurings of another sort, however, do occur. In such cases, if the actor is put back into the original objective stimulus situation, he will perceive a definitely different behavior space from that which he perceived on the original occasion. How do these more permanent restructurings come about? They also originate out of locomotions. But in these cases the locomotions lead not simply to a new position of the behaving self in the behavior space but rather to enlargements or other fundamental restructurings of the behavior space. Further, these enlargements or restructurings may be roughly separated into two main classes: (1) those resulting from learning and (2) those resulting from the psychodynamic mechanisms. Moreover, it will also appear that learning and the psychodynamic mechanisms involve not only such enlargements or restructurings of the behavior space but also correlated changes in the belief-value matrix system.

Before passing on, however, to these questions of learning and the psychodynamisms we must briefly note the other main item among the intervening variables of the model: capacity and temperamental traits.

CAPACITY AND TEMPERAMENTAL TRAITS (T)

At the top of the middle portion of Fig. 1 there is an entity labeled T. This symbol represents a whole collection of individual difference variables or traits. These traits are shown to produce an array of radiating causal arrows which are conceived to impinge (although these impingements are not indicated) upon all the other intervening variables and upon the various interconnecting functions. This feature of the diagram is, of course, no more than a mere formal acknowledgement that there are trait variables. The fact that no terminations for the arrows have been indicated is a confession that no clear hypotheses have been worked out as to the relations between trait variables and the other or "content" variables. The truth seems to be that the methods hitherto used to arrive at trait variables — ratings, test scores, intercorrelations, and factor analyses — have as yet for the most part never been closely integrated with the methods and variables used in the determination of the content variables. Traits are presumably constants or parameters in the equations determining the magnitudes of the content variables, but they have practically never been studied as such.

For example, we do not yet know whether such a trait as the I.Q. (obviously one of the most studied) consists primarily in individual differences in the formation of appropriate belief-value matrices, in the ready perception of adequate behavior spaces, in the rapid learning of specific behavior-space expectations, in the readiness to translate behavior-space locomotions into appropriate muscle responses, in the presence of useful and the absence of handicapping psychodynamic mechanisms, or in some combination of all of these. We must conclude, in short, that the necessary empirical and theoretical work which must be done in order to integrate traits with contents is still largely untouched.

With this very brief and purely formal acknowledgement of the problem of traits, let us return now to a discussion of learning and the psychodynamic mechanisms.

3

Learning and the
Psychodynamic Mechanisms

LEARNING

There seem to be two distinctive types of empirical problems with one or the other of which practically all studies of learning have been concerned. These two problems or setups I shall call the pure association setup and the reward setup. Let us consider them successively.

a. The pure association setup. Here the stimulus situation presented to the actor consists in two (not at the time specifically valued or valenced) objects which are presented in a given temporal and/or manipulative order. For example, a buzzer is sounded and followed after a mere time interval by a light. Or the animal goes from one place in, say, a maze by a certain manipulative running activity of his own to another place in the maze. If we assume that the actor's behavior-space perceptions correspond more or less veridically to the objective stimulus objects, this means that the rat's or the human being's behaving self is first in the region of the one object and then — either through the locomotion of "selecting to wait through time" or else through that of "selecting out a special set of spatial, mechanical, or other manipulatory behaviors" — it comes into the region of the second object. When this succession of the two objects (together with the interconnecting locomotion) has been repeated a number of times, it will be found (if, that is, learning takes place) that on a subsequent occasion the stimulus situation of only the first object will evoke an enlarged behavior space which will contain not only the perception of this first object but also a "perception" of the second object and of the direction and distance of the locomotion which led from the first to the second.

It is my contention that such learning by "seemingly pure association" can and often does take place without either of the two objects being, to any appreciable degree, an immediate goal object for any specific utilitarian need such as hunger, thirst, sex, or the like. Thus, for example, rats in the so-called "latent learning" experiments can apparently often learn "what leads to what" in a maze, even though the final "what" may not be a goal object for any special need which may be operative at the moment. However, it also appears that, if the animal is highly apathetic or has in his behavior some other object or objects with very high valences for specific needs, which are then and there active, the animal is less likely to learn (i.e., acquire this type of associative enlargement of its behavior space).

We have to explain two contrasting facts: first, the fact that such learning tends to take place without either of the two objects being specifically a goal object; and second, the fact that such learning does not tend to take place if the behaving self is either totally lacking in need-pushes or contains a need-push for which some other irrelevant, but strongly valenced, object is present. To explain these contrasting facts I shall have recourse to the notion of a "general exploratory" or "curiosity" or "placing" need. The need compartment corresponding to such an exploratory or placing need is assumed to be in close communication with the compartments for all the other needs so that the arousal of any of these other needs — hunger, thirst, fear, sex, dominance, etc. — will also arouse the general exploratory need. However, the laws by which other needs are to be assumed to arouse this general need are not simple. Thus it would appear that, whereas an increase of a specific need will tend to cause an increase in the general exploratory need up to a certain magnitude of the specific need, beyond that point further increases in the magnitude of the specific need will tend to decrease the magnitude of the exploratory need. In any event, given that the exploratory need is aroused in some degree (whatever the cause), this, by definition, will mean that *all* types of new objects will have positive value in a corresponding exploratory or placing belief-value matrix and that perceived instances of such objects in the behavior space will have positive valences. To reach these valences the behaving self must locomote in the direction prescribed by the character of each object.[1] I conclude that in this way "seemingly pure associations" are acquired. This does not mean, however, that such associations are acquired without motivation, but only that the motivation is the relatively "disinterested" one provided by a general exploratory need. Specific acts are not stamped in but new field relationships are learned.

Fig. 5 will indicate more clearly what this means in terms of the model. The diagram shows the assumed state of the need system, of an attached belief-value matrix, and of the behavior space upon the first presentation to the actor (let us assume a rat) of a simple *T*-maze. The behaving self of the rat is shown in the region of the bifurcation between the left-hand alley and the right-hand alley. A general exploratory need activates a belief-value exploratory matrix so that all alleys and other types of objects such as goal boxes are believed to have positive value for gratifying the exploration need and hence all instances of such objects will be perceived and valenced in the behavior space. Given, then, that the rat is in the presence of the two alleys, he will perceive and be ready to explore them both. Further, after he has loco-

---

[1] See below the discussion of the Bruner and Goodman experiment.

moted by releasing exploration down each alley he will also perceive the characters and contents of the goal boxes reached.

Turn now to Fig. 6. This shows two behavior spaces: one when the behaving self of the rat has locomoted to the left-hand goal box; and one when it has locomoted to the right-hand goal box. The causal arrows — the broken lines drawn from both behavior spaces back to the belief-value matrix — indicate that, as a result of perceiving each alley, locomoting down it, and then perceiving the resultant goal box and its contents, new beliefs tend to

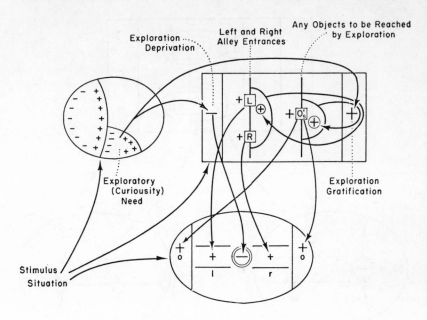

Fig. 5 RAT AT CHOICE - POINT; EXPLORATORY NEED

be produced in the belief-value matrix. These new beliefs are lassos issuing from each type of alley, involving a certain type of behavior, and arriving at a given type of goal box. This means that when, on a subsequent occasion the rat is presented with a left-hand turn or a right-hand turn, his belief-value matrix will contain beliefs about the further *types* of object he would arrive at by making such left- or right-hand turns; and his behavior space, at the moment of presentation of the two types of alley, will be *enlarged* so that he will then "perceive" not only these immediate turns but also their expected consequences of one kind of goal box on one side and another kind of goal box on the other side. Such learning is cognitive in nature, and there seems to be no *differential* "reinforcement" involved in it.

Let us turn now to the other type of empirical setup in which differential reinforcement may (without further analysis) seem to play a part.

b. The reward setup. The type of experimental setup designated by this term is the more conventional one. An actor, animal or human, is confronted with a number of possible alternative behaviors and is motivated by some specific need, such as hunger, thirst, desire for praise, or the like; one of these alternative behaviors leads to an appropriate goal for the specific need while the other alternative behaviors do not. The usually accepted theory to

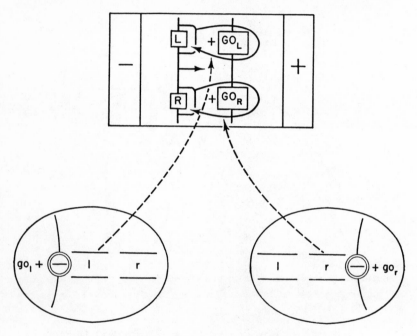

Fig. 6 BACK ACTION OF LOCOMOTION
ON CATEGORIZATIONS AND BELIEFS

explain learning in this kind of situation is the so-called reinforcement theory. Reinforcement theorists argue that learning is produced not by the gratification of a general exploratory or curiosity or placing need, for which all objects and relations are equally rewarding, but rather by the gratification of the specific need through the reaching of the specific goal object for that need. Thus, it is said, because the actor has behaved in a certain way in the presence of a given stimulus situation and has been led thereby to a goal object appropriate to the aroused specific need, the consequent reduction of this need (even though slight and relatively temporary) increases the tendency to perform this same response to the same stimulus on a subsequent occasion. As an empirical fact this, of course, is usually true. But in terms of our present analysis the important point is that the crucial behavior-space objects and directions of locomotion shall have been "noticed," i.e., shall have brought general exploratory-need gratification whichever response occurred. For I would contend that even with rats, to say nothing of men, there is already much evidence to show that the learning of what would appear to be merely a single response to a single stimulus may actually result in the ability to make wholly new but appropriate responses to a set of field relationships. See, for example, the studies of spatial learning in rats by Ritchie [19] and by Tolman, Ritchie, and Kalish [26–28], and by others [11] which indicate that rats, having learned one path on a maze to get to food, may be able to short-cut over a new path or to approach the food correctly from a totally different starting point. According to orthodox reinforcement theory, a stimulus-response connection is "stamped in" if any need reduction (relevant or irrelevant) takes place in close temporal contiguity after the response. According to the argument presented here, learning consists rather in the acquisition of perceptions of objects, directions, locations, and valences in the behavior space and eventually in the resultant acquisition of generalized categorizations, beliefs, and values in a superordinate belief-value matrix. And the latter kinds of learning take place as a result of the gratification of a merely "cognitive" exploratory need. However, this exploratory need will itself have in many instances been heightened by communication from some special specific need. But, in any event, it is the gratification of the cognitive exploratory need and not the gratification of the special need which determines the learning.

So much for learning; let us turn now to the second type of process through which behavior spaces and belief-value matrices may be enlarged or otherwise restructured: the so-called psychodynamic mechanisms.

The Psychodynamic Mechanisms

I shall limit myself here to a consideration of only four of these mechanisms. I should hope, however, that the treatment of these four will indicate the general pattern of approach which could be used successfully for the consideration of all the other mechanisms. The four I have chosen are: (a) identification, (b) the self-ideal, (c) repression, and (d) symbols and symbolic substitution. Before considering these individually, it should again be emphasized that any such mechanism will be conceived to involve, first, a restructuring of the behavior space relative to an initial, particular stimulus situation, and second, a resultant and relatively persistent change in one or more superordinate belief-value matrices.

a. Identification. Identification seems to arise out of initial, concrete behavior-space situations in which the behaving self contains a need-push for love and approval that impels it to locomote toward a region of behavior exemplified and approved by parent or other loved individual. As a result of such locomotions and the discovery of how to behave to obtain the love and approval of the parent, the given actor may develop a general belief that to behave "similarly" to the parent or other authority figure is a good way to get such love and approval.

Freud, in first introducing the concept of identification, assumed, as is well known, that the small boy identifies with the father (i.e., comes to behave

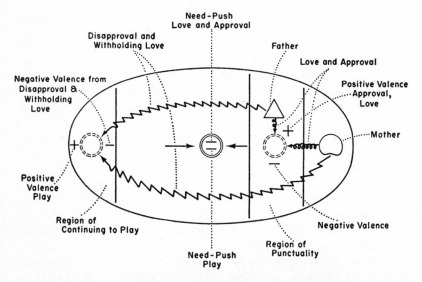

Fig. 7   BEHAVIOR SPACE IN IDENTIFICATION

as the father requires and in a manner similar to the father) to retain or regain not so much the love of the father as the love of the mother. That is, Freud believed that there was a really sexual sort of competition between the small boy and the father for the mother's love and that the boy came to believe that, if he behaved like the father, then the mother would love him as she did the father. Whether or not we accept all the implications of this Freudian analysis, it seems to be pretty much agreed that identification does involve at least two factors: (1) locomotion toward a region of love and approval from some alter or alters by ego's behaving in a prescribed way similar to that of the alter or alters; and (2) locomotion away from some other region of valenced activity because of the stronger need-push to get to the region of love and approval.

In Fig. 7 I have diagrammed the behavior space for the case of the small boy whose father is very strict about "punctuality." Look first at the symbols for the self at the left and right of the diagram and drawn in dashed lines. They are selves *toward which* the behaving self may locomote. They are shown in regions of the behavior space which ego perceives as potential goal regions. This introduction of self symbols into goal regions is to take care of the fact that, at least for human actors, goal regions and subgoal regions may contain not only other objects but also the actor's own self as potentially present and as acting upon, or being acted upon by, the other objects.[2] The valence charges deposited on these goal regions will, that is, often be attached primarily not to the other objects per se but rather to the self, as acting on the other objects or being acted upon by them. Thus, in this particular example, it is the self in the region of punctuality and therefore receiving love and approval from the mother (and presumably also from the father) which has the positive valence. The self in the region of being late, because continuing to play and therefore receiving disapproval and having love withheld, has the negative valence.

It is important to emphasize that the region of approval from the father and/or mother, the region of "punctuality," is also a region in which the father himself is said to be located. This highlights what is probably a crucial empirical problem in connection with the establishment of successful identification. If a father and mother preach punctuality but the father is himself unpunctual (i.e., is himself *not* in the region of punctuality), the boy's identification with the father is going to be relatively difficult. The boy's behaving self is pushed toward the region of the mother's love. He is told and he believes that to gain love he must *be like* the father. And he is also told to be punctual. But he discovers that the father is not himself punctual (i.e., is not in the region of punctuality). How, then, is the small boy to gain the mother's love: by obeying the mother's and father's prescription and locomoting toward the region of punctuality, which lies in one direction; or by becoming like the father and locomoting in an opposite direction toward the region of unpunctuality where the father actually is?

Furthermore, it is to be observed that, in locomoting toward the region of punctuality (assuming that it is not only prescribed but that the father himself is actually in it) the behaving self is at the same time locomoting away from a region which has a positive valence — the region of unpunctuality or "continuing to play." The behaving self of the small boy in locomoting toward the region of punctuality and identification is locomoting against a behavior in the opposite direction. That is, as was pointed out above, identification always involves the not-going to some other region or regions which in themselves have positive valence.

We have stated the essential features of identification, as described in

---

[2] "Objects" includes, of course, "other persons."

terms of the behavior space, to be (1) the locomoting toward a region of likeness to another or others in order to gain love or approval, and (2) the simultaneous locomoting away from some opposite region or regions which have their own positive valences. Whether or not good identification will be achieved will thus depend on the relative magnitudes of a number of factors, such as the clearness and unambiguity with which a single clear direction of locomotion to reach love and approval can be perceived, the strength of the need-push for such love and approval, and finally, the strengths of the opposing need-push or need-pushes.[3]

Finally, when complete identification has been achieved either with another individual or with a group,[4] ego perceives not only his "self" as a goal but also his behaving self as practically always in the region of the approved behaviors of the individual (or the group) with which he has identified. Behaviors which are approved and exhibited by the alter or alters have, in cases of strong identification, such powerful positive valences that they tend to win out over all others. An actor with strong identification may, in fact, come to sacrifice every other need, even life itself, because his behaving self is so strongly attracted by the positive valences of the "identification" region belonging both to him and the alter or alters with whom he has identified.

In Fig. 7 we depicted identification in terms of what happens in the behavior space. It is obvious, however, that identification involves not only changes in the behavior space but also resulting changes in the belief-value matrices. When ego accedes to alter's prescriptions on specific occasions in order to achieve love and approval, he not only perceives that love and approval as lying in the region of a given set of behaviors, also exemplified by alter, but he acquires an accompanying belief that these *kinds* of behaviors are in general the way to get to love and approval. Many of the problems involved in successful or unsuccessful identification undoubtedly arise in connection with the nature of the generalization gradients which ego develops with respect to such behaviors in his belief-value matrices.

Fig. 8 shows a belief-value matrix in identification. The generalization dimension represented at the left has arrayed along it types of activity which are to be "punctually" dropped. The generalization dimension depicted at the right has arrayed along it mother, father, and other individuals from whom acts of love and approval will, it is believed, result if such activities are

---

[3] It will be seen below that identification may sometimes be aided through the simultaneous operation of the mechanism of symbolic substitution which permits a "surreptitious" expression of a seemingly abandoned need-push.

[4] Space will not be taken to elaborate upon the problems of identification with a group. But such group identification seems to involve practically the same principles as identification with a single individual. The actor wants love and approval from the group, and to get them he has to behave in ways similar to those of the group. In so doing he has to locomote away from behaving in other ways which, because of other needs, also have for him positive valences.

dropped. Finally, there is the further belief that love and approval from mother, from father, and from others will lead in decreasing degrees to gratification of the need love and approval. The exact character of the identification achieved and represented in such a diagram will be indicated by what gets placed where along each of these generalization dimensions and by the shape and spread of the forked tail of each of the belief lassos.

b. The self-ideal. What I am here calling the self-ideal Freud discussed under the two separate heads of the superego and the ego-ideal. The superego according to his analysis consists, in my terms, of acquired negative values

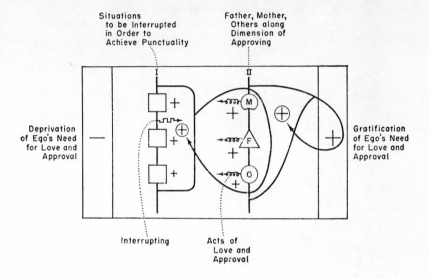

Fig. 8   BELIEF-VALUE MATRIX IN IDENTIFICATION

and valences for those types of behavior in which one should *not* engage; and the ego-ideal consists of acquired positive values and valences for those types of behavior in which one *should* engage. The two concepts are, however, I believe, best conceived as but obverse sides of one and the same process. The formation of a self-ideal is the final establishment of categorizations of the self (in belief-value matrix terms) and of perceptions of the self (in immediate behavior-space terms) as itself an alter which responds with love and approval to certain acts of the behaving self and also responds by withdrawing love and exhibiting disapproval to certain other acts of the behaving self.

Next, it is important to note that the establishment of such a self-ideal seems to grow out of identification. (This also was assumed by Freud.) But in a self-ideal mere identification as such has been gone beyond, in the sense that ego now perceives the positive goal region no longer as one in which the self merely behaves in ways similar to and approved by a "judging alter or alters" but as one in which the self behaves in ways similar to and approved by a "judging self." The proper diagram for the behavior space in the case of a self-ideal is shown by Fig. 9.

It would appear, however, that in order for such a judging, approving, or disapproving self to develop, there must also be, or have developed, self-love. For, only insofar as self-love, narcissism if you will, is present, will there be gratification as a result of the self's act of loving and approving itself. Only if the need from others has developed into a tertiary need for "love from self" will positive values and valences be attached to self-approval.

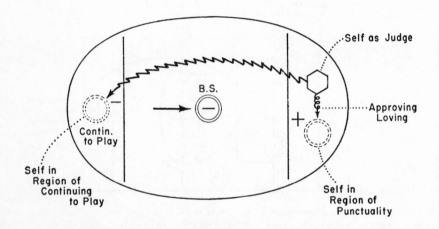

Fig. 9   BEHAVIOR SPACE – – SELF-IDEAL

A complete diagram for the self-ideal is, therefore, represented in Fig. 10. This diagram indicates that not only does a judging self become a particular perceived entity in particular behavior-spaces but also that the self as a *type of judge* will be located along a generalization dimension of judges (such as mother and father) in the belief-value matrix. Furthermore, the belief-value matrix is here shown to correspond to a sort of transition stage between mere identification and a true self-ideal. For it is indicated that the self-love of ego is still affected by the approval of these other judges. In the final stage of a self-ideal the self alone would be the sole and final judge.

If the above analysis is correct, then the important causal problems will consist in attempting to discover (1) what empirical conditions in early child-hood favor the development of strong identifications and (2) what conditions in early childhood favor the development of a requisite degree of self-love so that the individual will come to have as a goal not merely those types of behavior in which the self will be approved and loved by others but also those types of behavior in which the self will approve and love itself.

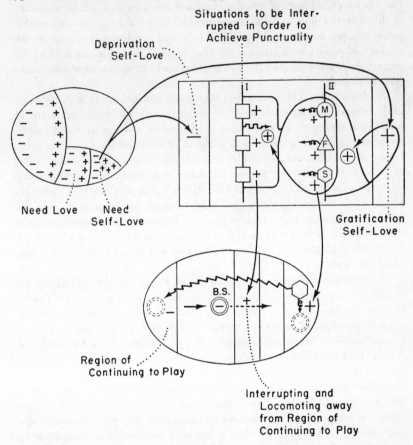

Fig. 10 NEED SYSTEM, MATRIX, AND BEHAVIOR SPACE
FOR SELF-IDEAL

Further, it would appear that, in extreme cases, a self-ideal may eventually accord positive values to behavior which only the self itself approves. Whereas the behaviors for which the self will love and approve itself will be at first primarily those which alters, with whom ego has identified, will love and approve; the self, eventually, if self-love is strong enough, may come to love and approve behaviors which are totally idiosyncratic. Hence, from a practical, social-welfare point of view the fact that ego has acquired a strong self-ideal may not necessarily mean that this self-ideal is, from the point of view of the society, good. The self-ideal may be that of a criminal or of an ego-maniac. But, obviously, all sorts of detailed empirical investigations will be necessary to discover just how socially nonacceptable, rather than socially acceptable ego-ideals, are acquired. The problem may well involve such factors as the strength of early identifications; the characters of those identified with; the magnitude of self-love; and the particular stage in development at which self-love developed.

c. *Repression.* This mechanism may go off simultaneously with instances of the others: thus, for example, in the above examples of identification and of a self-ideal repression may also tend to be involved. As was indicated before, the behaving self in locomoting to a region of identification locomotes away from a region of continuing to play and this latter region has a positive value of its own. But continuing to play also has a negative valence corresponding to disapproval and withholding of love. And it is this phenomenon of a region which is simultaneously both positively valenced and negatively valenced which, I shall assert, gives rise to *repression.* Repression is a blotting out from conscious awareness of a given region or regions of the behavior-space and a simultaneous blotting out of objects with plus and minus values from belief-value matrices.

As an example of repression I shall choose a case which bulks large in the literature — ego's repression of aggression against in-group members in order to retain the love and approval of such members. Fig. 11 represents the diagram for this kind of case. Look first at the behavior space. The behaving self is represented as between two regions. It may locomote toward a region, at the right, of identification with in-group members — a region in which the self and others in the in-group behave similarly and also approve the self and each other (the acts of approving the others have not been indicated); or it may locomote to a region, indicated at the left, labeled "play." The term "play" here represents, for purposes of illustration, *any* type of activity disapproved by the in-group. Further, it has been indicated that disapproval by in-group members is to be represented as a barrier in the behavior space on the way to play. Again, when any such barrier appears in the behavior space, aggression against that barrier will have positive valence. The total region, at the left, contains, then, both a positive valence on play and a positive valence on aggression against the barrier which is set up by the in-group members. It also contains two negative valences: one attached to disapproval for indulging in play and one attached to disapproval for indulging in aggression. But it is my hypothesis that *a region which has both positive and negative valences will tend to be blotted out from the conscious awareness in the behavior space.* This blotting out I have represented by stippling the region.

The next point to note is that such a perceptual blotting out, I believe, acts back (see dashed arrows) upon the corresponding belief-value matrices activated by the play and the aggression needs so that there is also a blotting out of the beliefs and resultant values for play and aggression in these governing matrices. The dashed arrows are to be conceived as transmitting the blotting out (represented by stippling) from the behavior space back to the belief-value matrices.

In other words, the actor in this situation neither consciously perceives nor consciously believes that he wants to play or that he wants to aggress

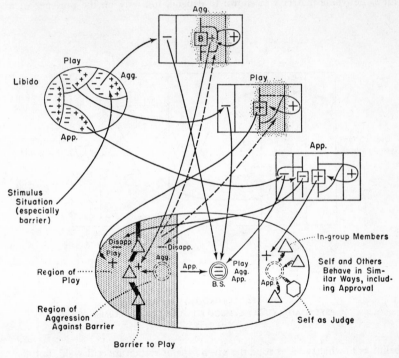

Fig. II A CASE OF REPRESSION

against in-group members for their blocking of such play. Nor does he consciously perceive or believe that he would be disapproved or punished for these behaviors. His behaving self is, however, still left with the need-pushes to locomote toward play and toward aggression as well as with the need-push to locomote toward approved in-group behavior. This leaves the behaving self in a restless condition. The two unreduced need-pushes will keep the behaving self restlessly locomoting. In fact, it is such repression — that is, such unresolved need-pushes — which, I believe, are the basis of much neurotic and maladaptive behavior. An apparent solution for such a neurotic state is, it appears, often brought about through the coöperation of still another mechanism — one which I would label symbolic substitution. To this we may now turn.

   d. Symbolism and symbolic substitution. In order to understand symbolic substitution, we must first consider simple psychoanalytical symbolism (in which substitution in the sense employed here need not as such be involved). For such a case of simple symbolism let us return to the example of restaurants and food. It will be recalled that the value depicted on a type of restaurant in the belief-value matrix was shown to depend, not only on the presence of a

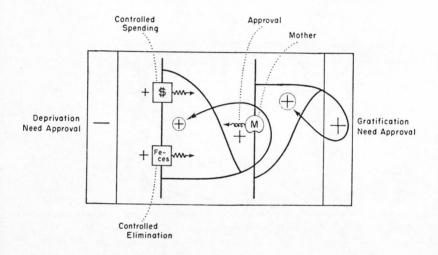

Fig. 12 CONTROLLED SPENDING
A PSYCHOANALYTICAL SYMBOL FOR CONTROLLED ELIMINATION

belief as to what types of food the given type of restaurant will yield, but also upon the belief as to how much money will have to be spent in such a type of restaurant. The effective positive value of the type of restaurant may be much reduced if the given actor has a high value for controlled spending and the given kind of restaurant costs much money. A common psychoanalytical suggestion as to why controlled spending should have a high positive value for a given individual is that money is for this individual a symbol for feces. Such an assumption (represented in Fig. 12) would be that the actor in question retains in his matrix the belief that controlled elimination is the way to get to mother's approval, which latter is cathected to gratification of his need for approval.[5] The crucial feature in this figure is the fact that it places money, the supposed symbol for feces, along the same generalization dimension as the feces themselves. That is, if controlled elimination of feces is believed to be good, then this belief would be assumed to *generalize* to the controlled spending of money. On such an assumption, a type of object and accompanying behavior are included along the generalization gradient of a belief, simply because they are *similar* to another type of object and its accompanying behavior which are already believed to lead to the given type of goal. It is a case of "overgeneralization." The symbolic object and behavior have come to be "believed in" as ways to reach the goal in question, not because they are really actually appropriate for so doing, but merely because they are similar to an original object and behavior which are, or were, appropriate.

But we shall see now that such psychoanalytical symbolism may be used in a further way to permit *symbolic substitution* in cases of repression. In the case of controlled spending as a symbol of controlled elimination, the controlled elimination itself is presumably not repressed. It also continues to occur. Hence the controlled spending does not take the place of — is not a substitute for — controlled elimination; the case, as we have said, is merely one of an inept overgeneralization. In our previous case of the repression of aggression against in-group members, it will appear now that aggression against the self and/or against out-group members may enter the picture as "symbolic substitutes" for aggression against the in-group.

This possibility is represented in Fig. 13. Look first at the belief-value matrix on the right. It will be seen that out-group members and the self have both become placed along the same generalization dimension as in-group members, because they are in many ways similar to, and hence may act as symbols of, in-group members. In other words, the original belief that by aggressing against in-group members ego will satisfy both his need play and his need aggression has been generalized to out-group members and to self so that ego now believes that aggression against out-group members, or against self, will also gratify need aggression and need play. The first of these resultant beliefs is veridical in the sense that such aggression against out-groups or self will actually gratify aggression. The other belief, that by aggression ego will gratify the play need, is nonveridical. Moreover, because it corresponds to a region in the behavior space which is blotted out from conscious awareness, it will also be blotted out in the belief-value matrix.

Look next at the behavior space. The regions for aggression against out-group members or against the self, since they have no negative valences resulting from disapproval, will not be blotted out and hence the behaving self will

[5] Whether or not this is a likely assumption must be left to the psychoanalysts. But, if this seems to the reader not too probable an example of symbolism, there are other examples that could be cited which the reader undobtedly would accept and the same principles would hold for them.

tend to locomote toward one or the other. In fact, the in-group may approve aggressions against the out-group or even, in some cultures, against the self. Hence these regions may have even stronger positive valences added to them. As a result, the behaving self will locomote toward aggression against one or the other, and the need-push aggression will be reduced. But the behaving self

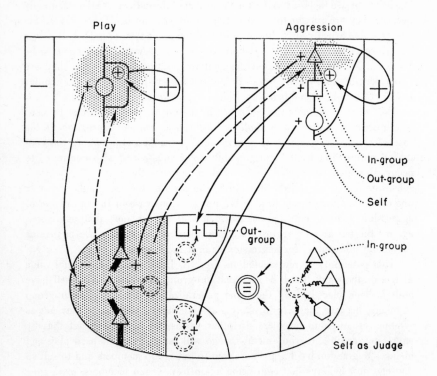

Fig. 13 SYMBOLIC SUBSTITUTION

will not locomote to the original play region and the need-push for play will remain unreduced. Hence such a substitute symbolic aggression, while adaptive in allowing release of aggression, is not successful in getting ego to the original positive goal. Furthermore, given the conditions of the actual world, it may lead ego to very bad subsequent situations such as retaliation from out-group members, or extreme sickness or injury in the cases in which he aggresses against himself.

4

Further Problems Connected

with the Model

We may turn now to several matters, briefly touched upon in preceding sections, but which need further elaboration. Specifically, let us consider in more detail: (1) the need system — especially the problem of tertiary needs and of functional autonomy; (2) further problems concerning matrices and their effects on the behavior space; (3) the problem of the discourse use of symbols; and (4) the problem of operational definitions.

THE NEED SYSTEM

As has already been indicated, the need system is to be thought of as a set of interconnecting compartments, each compartment corresponding to a differentiated need. The energy or tension in such compartments is conceived to be made up of positive and negative charges analogous to electromagnetic charges. These charges are supposed to be capable of spreading from one compartment to another through the dividing walls, which walls may be thought of as in the nature of semipermeable membranes. In considering the process of arousal of any specific need the following principles should now also be included: (1) Any independent physiological drive condition or stimulus which arouses a need will be assumed to do so by first increasing the total amount of charges in the libido compartment. (This compartment, it will be remembered, is conceived to be in contact with each of the specific need compartments.) (2) The arousal of a specific need will also be assumed to involve an increased permeability of the membrane dividing such a specific-need compartment from the libido compartment so that there will be an increased flow of charges from the libido into the specific need. (3) It will be assumed, further, that the arousal of a specific need may also cause an increase in the permeability of the membranes dividing this specific-need compartment from certain other specific-need compartments.[1] (4) Still further,

[1] It was suggested previously that in order to indicate diagrammatically such interactions between needs a hyperspace diagram would be necessary, so that each specific-need compartment could be depicted not only as in contact with the libido compartment but also in contact with each and every other need compartment.

such increased permeabilities of the membranes between pairs of specific compartments must be assumed to be either bidirectional or unidirectional. Thus, (*a*) if the permeability is bidirectional, an increase of charges, resulting from arousal in either one of a pair of two specific-need compartments will tend to flow into the other. That is, an increase in the magnitude of either need will tend to enhance the magnitude of the other. (*b*) If the increased permeability of the membrane between a pair of needs is unidirectional, it may mean either (i) that, when need *A* is aroused, need *B* will also tend to be aroused because of an increase in permeability in the direction from *A* to *B*, or (ii) that if need *A* is aroused, need *B* will tend to be lessened because of an increase in permeability in the direction *B* to *A*.

On the basis of the above assumptions I would attempt to integrate and to explain such already fairly well established empirical findings as the following:

First, the arousal of any specific need tends to be correlated with an observable increase in general energy. Example: a hungry rat also tends to be a lively and an active rat. (Explained by principles 1 and 2 above to the effect that, in the arousal of any specific need, charges first flow into the general libido compartment and then into the specific-need compartment.)

Second, if either one of certain pairs of needs is aroused, this will tend to increase the magnitude of the other need of the pair. Example: an increase in need dominance tends to give rise to an increase in need aggression; conversely, an increase in need aggression tends to give rise to an increase in need dominance. (Explained by principle 4*a* of a bidirectional increase in permeability of the membrane between the need compartments *A* and *B*.)

Third, when one of a given pair of needs is aroused, it may tend to increase the magnitude of the other need of the pair, but not vice versa. Example: if a basic viscerogenic need such as hunger is aroused, it will tend to increase the magnitude of, say, the aggression need, but not vice versa. (Explained by principle 4*b* (i) of a unidirectional increase in permeability from the hunger compartment into the aggression compartment, but not vice versa.)

Fourth, when one of a given pair of needs is aroused it may tend to decrease the magnitude of the other need of the pair, but not vice versa. Example: if a basic viscerogenic need, such as hunger, is aroused it will tend to decrease the magnitude of, say, the aesthetic need, but not vice versa. (Explained by principle 4*b* (ii) above of a unidirectional increase in permeability into the hunger compartment from the aesthetic compartment, but not vice versa.)

It may further be noted that with the aid of the above principles Maslow's striking and important hypothesis of a hierarchy of needs [16] could be explained. Maslow assumes that needs are to be arranged along some sort of continuum so that only when the basic "lower" needs are in a state of reasonable gratification can the "higher" ones develop any appreciable magnitudes. The viscerogenic hungers would be the outstanding basic needs lying at the bottom of the continuum whereas the intellectual, aesthetic, and the more "disinterested" types of social needs would lie at the top of the continuum. This assumption, translated into the above terms, would mean that when any need higher in the scale is aroused at the same time a "lower" need is also aroused, the permeabilities between the two compartments would be unidirectional in the sense that the arousal of the lower of the two needs would always tend to drain away the charges from the higher need. Only when the lower need is gratified would the higher need have a chance.

Another question about the need system which we have thus far avoided concerns a basic list of needs. I shall not attempt any final and precise answer to this question. I shall, however, assume, first, that there is a list of primary needs — i.e., a set of basic hungers and avoidances which man shares with his nearest kin the anthropoid apes — such needs as, say, hunger, thirst, sex, pain avoidance, aggression against obstacles, and a general exploratory, curiosity, or placing need. The final and precise statement of this list is yet to be agreed upon. I shall assume, secondly, that in addition there is a list of not as yet clearly differentiated *secondary* or socio-relational needs, such as affiliation (need for love and approval), dominance, dependence, submission, and the like.[2] I shall also assume that there is probably in addition some set of *tertiary* needs (which must definitely be assumed to be the product of learning) which are fairly universal in any given population. The tertiary needs will consist in wants to get to and from, to manipulate (as ways of getting to or from) certain relatively universal types of culturally provided goals; for example, *in our culture*: the want to get to wealth and away from poverty; the want to get to professional and business success and away from business failure; the want to get to a college or university degree and away from flunking out; the want to get to strolls in the park and away from the house or office; the want to get to a vacation in Miami and away from work; the want to play the violin; etc. It is, of course, such an assumption of acquired "tertiary" needs for culturally provided goals which is contained in Allport's doctrine of "functional autonomy" [1]. My point of view here, however, is perhaps somewhat different from Allport's. For I would grant, as Allport perhaps would not, that a complete analysis of both the conscious and the unconscious features of the given personalities might indicate that in cases of seemingly tertiary needs, the goals of these tertiary needs are not really final goals but mere means or subgoals connected by "beliefs" to more basic goals. However, these connecting beliefs may have

---

[2] The question as to whether these secondary needs are themselves to be considered innate, or as acquired early in life, must for the present be left open. I tend to believe that they are largely innate and can, for example, be studied reliably in chimpanzees, who are very like men but free from the teachings of any culture.

become so stable and unvarying in the given individual that, for the purpose of a given empirical study, an independent tertiary need can, pragmatically speaking, be assumed. The empirical criterion in such a case would be that, whenever the individual (or individuals) in question can be said for all *practical* purposes to persist to or from a certain type of culture object (wealth, academic success, etc.) *irrespective of any further consequences or lack of consequences,* then it is pragmatically useful and legitimate to assume an independent tertiary need.

But it is to be remembered that this assumption (like the assumption of all the other entities in the model) is no more than a pragmatic construct to be retained so long as, and only so long as, it proves helpful. Thus, we would be led into no dire consequences if we first assumed a separate, functionally autonomous, tertiary need which later, as a result of further empirical investigation, turned out to be better conceived as a mere means activity connected by the belief system to the goals of some more basic needs. Suppose, for example, that from studies of college sophomores we were first led to postulate a tertiary need (stronger in some individuals than in others) for "approval from college authorities." Suppose, that is, that one finds in the general area under investigation that such an assumed tertiary need has explanatory value. By this I would mean that for the students in question, "approval from college authorities" appears to be sought irrespective of any further consequences and enjoyed in consummatory fashion per se, and that ratings of the different intensities of this need in the different individual students was found to correlate sensibly with some other variable or variables. These initial conclusions would *not* be materially upset — although they might be further refined and amplified (i.e., some previous unexplained residual variance might be taken care of) — if, upon further investigation, it turned out that the goal "approval from authority" was more usefully conceived, not as an independent goal with its own final consummatory response, but as a subgoal connected by beliefs to some more ultimate goal such as that of being loved. If this proved to be the case, no basic feature of the previous findings would be upset. It would simply appear that by now examining variations in the more basic love need and in the connecting beliefs, some of the previously unexplained variance could be explained. The final conclusive test, however, in terms of our model, as to whether in the last analysis a tertiary need is or is not to be assumed will lie in the degree to which useful deductions can or cannot be made from the assumption of such a special need compartment connected to other needs by membranes of certain types of permeability.

Finally, if true tertiary needs really become formed, as they would according to the doctrine of functional autonomy, we would still be left with the empirical problem of establishing the laws and conditions under which the initial development of these functionally autonomous new needs takes place. This is a question which to date seems to have been but incompletely experimented upon. Is it, for example, the frequency and consistency with which a given type of means or subgoal has led to a given primary goal which causes the former to assume goal character? Or is it perhaps a lack of consistency of this sequence which (as has, in fact, been suggested by some experimenters) causes the means or subgoal to take over a functionally autonomous goal character and to be accompanied by the development of a new tertiary need of its own? These are questions which require further investigation.

Further Problems Concerning Matrices and Their Effects upon the Behavior Space

A first point to be emphasized under this heading is a fact already suggested, but not previously stressed, that the typed images for one and the same kind of objects may appear simultaneously in two or more matrices and the fact that the values given these images in the different matrices will be different. That is, the images may be ordered, or located, quite differently along the respective different generalization dimensions of the different matrices. Thus, for example, to return to our perhaps overworked example of foods and restaurants, it would appear that a given set of food images may be classified by the actor not only along the functionally defined generalization dimension of leading-to-hunger gratification, but also in a second matrix, along a functionally defined dimension of leading-to-palatability gratification.[3] This second matrix and the palatability need to which it is connected plays, no doubt, a dominant part in most middle-class, high-nutrition groups, whereas in a low-nutrition group the taste or palatability need may be conceived as drained through the increased permeability of the membrane into a strongly aroused hunger need. Or, again, restaurants may be arranged by the actor not only along the functional dimension of food-providing but also along such different functional dimensions as costing-money and prestige-providing.

Fig. 14 indicates a possible diagrammatic way in which such further complications of two or more matrices may be represented; it represents the orderings of three types of restaurants, X, Y, and Z, in three different matrices. The three matrices are conceived to be connected respectively to the three needs: (1) hunger and/or palatability need, here grouped together as simply a "good food" need; (2) a not-wanting-to-spend need; and (3) a prestige need. According, then, to this hypothetical example, X, Y, and Z are believed by the actor to be in the order named relative to providing "good food." As regards spending, X is rated as highly expensive, Y and Z as less expensive. Finally, in regard to prestige-producing values, X is believed by the actor to

[3] Sensations of palatability can be objectively — behavioristically — defined without resort to phenomenology by means of discrimination experiments. And so defined I have labeled them "discriminanda" [22].

be very high in leading to prestige gratification; whereas Y is believed to have low prestige-producing value, and Z, although cheap, is believed to have more prestige-producing value (for example, an artist's hangout) than Y, but still not as much prestige value as X.

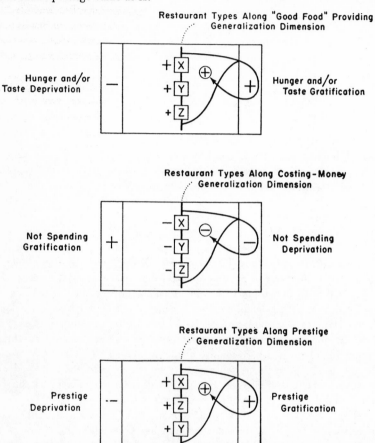

Fig. 14 THE SAME TYPES OF OBJECTS (TYPES OF RESTAURANTS) ORDERED DIFFERENTLY IN DIFFERENT MATRICES

That one of the three types of restaurant will be gone to in a particular case (if concrete instances of all three types are present in the environment and can be got at with equal ease) will be determined by some interactive effect on the behavior space of the values arising out of the three sets of positive and negative values. In the present simple example, it is probably accurate enough to assume that the interactive effects of these values will be additive and this will make a restaurant of the type X the most valenced and most likely to be locomoted to by the behaving self.

A second point in connection with matrices which deserves further elucidation is whether a given type of object is to be conceived as the final goal object in a special matrix attached directly to a special tertiary need of its own, or whether it is to be conceived as merely a means object on the way to

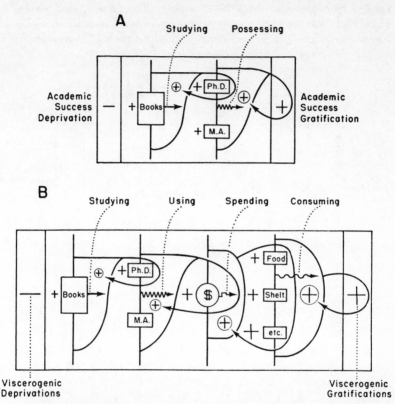

Fig. 15 ACADEMIC OR VISCEROGENIC GRATIFICATION ?

some more distant goal of a more basic need. The two alternatives are represented in Fig. 15, based on the example of working for academic degrees. In Fig. 15, A represents the assumption of a small belief-value matrix in which academic degrees are the finally cathected goals, and it is indicated that such a matrix is attached directly to a new tertiary, functionally autonomous, "need for academic success." On this assumption the absolute strength of the final gratification and deprivation values of such a matrix will be determined directly by the strength of the directly attached academic success need. That is, in diagram *A* it is assumed that there is an acquired need for academic success which, insofar as it is aroused, will determine directly the absolute magnitude of the gratification charge of this matrix, which in turn (given the generalizations and beliefs in the matrix) will determine the respective values for possessing professional degrees of Ph.D. or M.A. and for studying books as the way of obtaining such degrees. In diagram *B* of Fig. 15, on the other hand, I have presented the alternative possibility: namely, that possession of the Ph.D. and the M.A. does not in itself gratify a final need for academic success but is merely a means on the route to the goals of some more basic needs such as, say, the viscerogenic hungers.

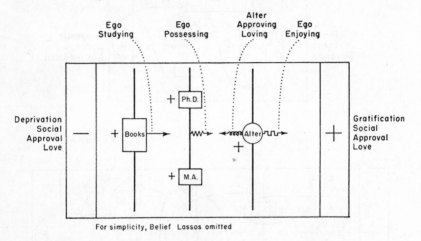

For simplicity, Belief Lassos omitted

Fig. 16   STUDYING TO OBTAIN LOVE AND APPROVAL

But perhaps a still more reasonable assumption would be that the obtaining of academic degrees is a means not so much to the gratification of the basic viscerogenic needs as to the gratification of the need for love and approval from an alter or alters. Fig. 16 suggests this possibility. Here the resulting values on the Ph.D. and M.A. degrees will be determined not by the viscerogenic needs but by the need for social love and approval. The significant new feature in Fig. 16 is that the final valued goal objects are the performances — overt or implicit acts of approval — represented by the corkscrew arrow issuing from the image of an alter or alters. It is these performances of the imaged alter, the "enjoyment" of which is believed by ego to lead to the gratification of the need for social love and approval.[4]

----

[4] These assumptions of a social love and approval need and of the goal as being the "approval response" of the alter or alters or even of a judging self have, of course, already been made above in our discussion of the development of identification and of the self-ideal.

A third example of a more complicated problem in connection with matrices is to be found in the well known Bruner and Goodman experiment [2]. In this experiment a group of children (who were separated into two subgroups of "poor children" and "rich children") were presented with coins: a penny, a nickel, a dime, a quarter, and a half-dollar. The children were asked to match the sizes of these coins by adjusting a diaphragm with a knob so as to make a patch of light shining through a ground glass screen appear the same size as the given coin. The children were also given the task of

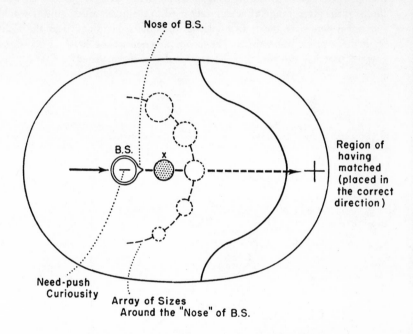

Fig 17 BEHAVIOR SPACE -- ESTIMATION OF SIZE

matching small circles of cardboard — one corresponding in size to each coin — in similar fashion. The results were briefly as follows: (1) In general, all children tended to overestimate the sizes of the coins as compared with the sizes of the corresponding equal-sized pieces of cardboard. (2) This over-estimation of the coins was greater, the greater the money value of the coins (the dime was for some reason an exception). (3) The poor children tended to overestimate the coins more than did the rich children.

Let me first indicate how such an act of estimating size is, as I see it, to be depicted in a behavior-space diagram (Fig. 17). In this figure, x is the perceived cardboard or coin to be matched. The act of adjusting the diaphragm until it appears equal to this object x is conceived as the "locomotion" of "placing" this object in the correct "size direction." The angular directions around the "nose" of the behaving self here represent thus not spatial directions but "size directions." The average size of the given set of cardboards, or coins, is represented as straight ahead of the behaving self's nose. Sizes larger than the average are represented as radiating above and sizes smaller than the average as radiating below the behaving self's nose. The extreme limits of the given range of actual sizes used in the given set of objects would fall somewhere near the right angle upwards and somewhere near the right angle downwards, respectively. The locomotion consists of "pushing" x in the correct direction and reaching the region of "having matched."

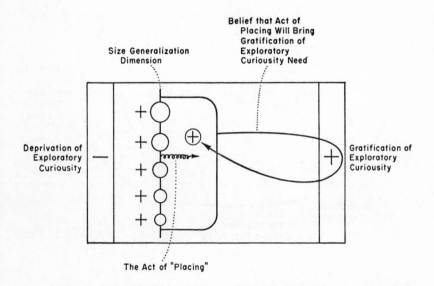

Fig. 18   BELIEF-VALUE MATRIX -- ESTIMATION OF SIZE

The next point to be noted is that in this size-matching task the positive valence to be reached by the act of matching will be the same irrespective of whether the given size is large or small. In other words, the positive values in the controlling matrix are to be conceived as equal for all sizes. To indicate just what is meant by this let me present now the diagram for the accompanying matrix (Fig. 18). It will be observed that in this matrix the different sizes are arranged along one generalization dimension. The belief as to the result of an "act" of "placing" (indicated by the corkscrew arrow) is assumed to have a flat generalization gradient in the sense that in such a matrix the resultant instrumental value from placing any one of these sizes will be the same. In other words, the same degree of gratification will, it is believed by ego, be received whatever the size of the particular object that is placed.

Finally, one further query about such a matrix. Is such a matrix to be conceived as attached directly to the independent curiosity, exploratory, or placing need? Or is it to be conceived, rather, as but a submatrix within a larger matrix, of which the ultimate goal is, to take the present example, to get "love" and "praise" from the experimenter? Personally, I am inclined to think that both types of causation were probably involved in this particular experiment, which used young children. However, I should certainly hold that with adults, and often also even with children or rats, a general exploratory, curiosity, or placing need has also to be postulated (see above). Further, this need, as already indicated, is assumed to be in contact with all the other needs, so that whenever a special need is aroused some of the tension from this special need will tend to flow into and arouse in some degree the pure exploratory or "cognitive placing" need. Hence even in this case the need of the children to get love and praise from the experimenter would pass over into and activate in some degree the pure exploratory or cognitive placing need.

But let us turn now to the purchasing power of the coins. For it would appear that a coin may also be locomoted toward for its purchasing power and that the valence for each coin will be greater, the greater its purchasing power. Fig. 19 presents a diagram which indicates this. There are a number of new assumptions introduced here. (1) It is assumed that the purchasing-power matrix and the cognitive matrix both produce an array of directions in the behavior space. (2) It is assumed further that these two sets of directions are "orthogonal" to one another. This has been indicated by centering the array of purchasing-power directions around a northerly axis and the array of size directions around an easterly axis. (3) It is assumed that the attempted locomotion of "placing" of the object according to size is distorted by a simultaneous locomotion of placing according to purchasing power. (4) It is assumed that this distortion in the direction of purchasing power is greater the greater the valence of the given coin, and also the poorer the children (i.e., the stronger the average valences for all the coins). In a word, the behaving self of the child locomotes in such a direction that the path which it takes, though supposedly a size-placing path, is in reality a compromise be-tween size placing and going toward the valence of the coin because of its money value.

Although the argument is complicated, the essential point is, I believe, clear: namely, that many "distortions" of perception may be conceived as distortions of discriminated directions of locomotion in the behavior space;

and further that such distortions of direction, when they occur, may be a result of the interference in the behavior space of a categorization of directions coming from one matrix upon the categorization of directions coming from another matrix.

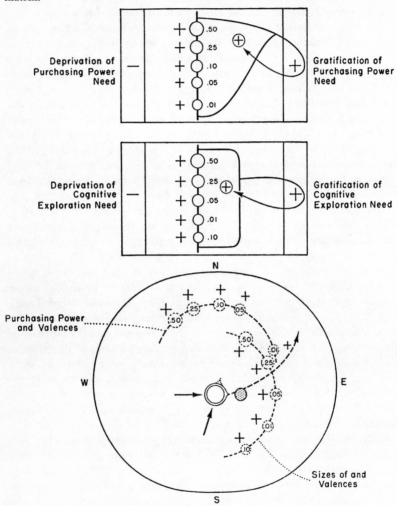

Fig. 19 ESTIMATION OF SIZE
AS AFFECTED BY PURCHASING POWER

Let us turn now to a consideration of still another problem concerning matrices — the use of language, or discourse, symbols.

THE DISCOURSE USE OF SYMBOLS AND SOCIAL
RELATIONSHIP UNITS

We have considered the nature of symbols in the psychoanalytical sense. There the symbol object was conceived to get placed along the same generalization dimension as the symbolized object and therefore to be behaved toward in the same way in which the symbolized object is behaved toward.

But now we must turn to symbols in the more ordinary, discourse or language, sense of the word. It is obvious that the "discourse" use of symbols is first of all a type of communicatory behavior. Furthermore, communicatory behavior obviously occurs only in the presence of an alter or alters and in the presence (but usually the "non-pointable to" presence) of either some concrete object or of some conceptual object. Ego then behaves so as to indicate to an alter or alters (or to himself in the temporary role of an alter) what the character of this concrete or conceptual object is.

How is this use of symbols taken care of by the model? Fig. 20 suggests a

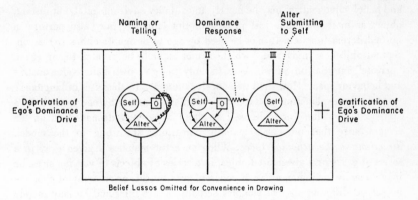

Belief Lassos Omitted for Convenience in Drawing

Fig. 20 BELIEF-VALUE MATRIX -- COMMUNICATORY BEHAVIOR

way in which it may be done. Note first that the entities placed along any generalization dimension are no longer, as in previous examples, single objects (nonhuman or human) relative to which ego has beliefs and values but are larger social-relationship objects containing the "typed" self,[5] and a typed alter, and other possible objects, labeled O. Further, these larger social-relationship units are defined not merely by self and alter and other objects but also by ego's differentiation of the communicatory and other interrelationships between these latter. Thus, in the social-relationship unit depicted on generalization dimension I, I have indicated the self as present to an alter and vice versa (double-headed arrow) and an object O is represented as present to

[5] The "self" as here depicted is ego's "universalized" image of himself.

self but not to alter (single-headed arrow). The curved corkscrew leading from O to alter represents the type of symbolic response (e.g., "naming") by which ego "believes" that the type of social-relationship unit depicted on generalization dimension II will be achieved. This relationship is depicted as one in which O is now present to alter as well as to self. The zigzag arrow indicates the type of dominance response by which ego believes that (now that O is present to alter as well as to self) self can dominate alter and the social-relationship unit of the type depicted on generalization dimension III is to be achieved. And, I have depicted on generalization dimension III a social-relationship unit in which alter is submitting to self. And, finally, this is believed by ego to lead directly to the gratification of his, ego's, need for dominance.

The above use of symbols is a type of behavior in which ego presents language symbols to an alter in default of being able to present the actual symbolized object. Often the object, which is in ego's behavior space and belief-value matrix and which ego wishes to bring into alter's behavior space and belief-value matrix, may be merely an ordinary environmental, but distant, object as in the example just presented. But language may also perform a quite different function. It may be used by ego to designate either (a) a conceptual object, a "universal," which cannot actually be pointed to, or (b) a "private" internal object which exists only in ego's own belief-value matrix and behavior space. How shall we conceive these two further uses of language?

(a) Our explanation of the use of language symbols by ego to indicate a "universal" to alter (or to himself as alter) apparently depends first on the circumstance that universals actually constitute, according to the model, *directions in the behavior space.* When an actor matches a given gray in a series of grays or a given sized object in a series of objects of varying sizes, he may do so by having an array of concrete gray objects or an array of concrete objects of different sizes as samples actually before him, and he may merely place the object to be matched on top of the most nearly similar sample in such an array. This is a simple response to the likeness of the two concrete objects. The actor may go a step further and simply arrange a series of test objects according to "grayness" or according to "size" with no chart or exemplar before him. He is then matching each object not to a concrete sample but to the "conceptualized" direction in the behavior space. All this can be done by an ego without the use of speech. When, however, the ego has learned the use of speech, he has learned a symbol which he can use to indicate a given variety of gray (or a given size), i.e., a given direction. In making use of this symbol, emitting this word, he is performing a new sort of locomotion in his behavior field. Instead of the behaving self merely placing the given object in the proper direction, the behaving self is also "conveying" this direction to an alter (or to self as alter).

(b) It appears, however, that there is a still more recondite use of language by human beings. They may use language not merely to convey objects and directions in their behavior space and the categorizations on their generalization dimensions, but they can also use language to convey their "conveyings." They can say not only: "This is yellow," "This is large," and so on; but they can also say: "I perceive this as yellow," or, "I believe this to be yellow." In other words, they can introspect or use verbal reports. They can talk *about* their behavior spaces or *about* their belief-value matrices. And this is a very crucial and important phenomenon. It means that the verbal reports of the actor can often be used in lieu of many complicated observations of actual behavior to discover both what an actor perceives and valences and what he conceives and values. Another crucial feature which, however, must be kept in mind in connection with such use of verbal reports is that, as has already been noted in our discussion of repression, significant parts of the behavior field or of the belief-value matrix may not be accompanied by conscious awareness — may not, that is, be available for such verbal report.[6]

An actual working out in terms of our model of the exact ways in which the causal determination of such verbal reports is to be conceived will not be attempted here. Suffice it to say that we do assume that by virtue of such "verbal reports" the constitution of an actor's belief-value matrix or of his behavior space can be to some degree correctly conveyed to another. Only, however, after the details of our assumptions concerning this process have actually been worked out in model terms, shall we be in a really good position to understand, better than we do now, the conditions under which such verbal reports (introspection) are or are not reliable indicators of the actual content of a matrix or of a behavior space.

Operational Definitions

By an operational definition of an intervening variable I shall mean, first, a statement about a standard defining experiment in which a certain measurable variation in some feature of the observed behavior will, by definition, be assumed to be a direct measure of corresponding variation in the magnitudes of a given intervening variable. Second, such a definition will involve an assumption about the linear or nonlinear nature of this mathematical function connecting the measured feature of the dependent behavior to the intervening variable. And, third, the specific constants in this form of mathematical function must also be known, or assumed, before such definitions will be final. And it must be admitted that at present our notions concerning such defining experiments and the precise forms of the mathematical functions connecting the intervening variables to the dependent behavior fall far short of the required precision. Our attempts, now, can be only partial and tentative. This does not, however, I believe, prevent our model from having considerable

---

[6] Conscious awareness means, I believe, in the last analysis, availability for verbal report.

theoretical and empirical usefulness, even at this time. For the model and the variables within it set a program for further empirical investigation, and prominent among such suggested new investigations would be the proposed defining experiments themselves. Furthermore, as the data from such experiments come in, not only will our store of empirical knowledge be increased but the model itself will thereby suffer corrections and revisions, or perhaps even final abandonment, and a new and better one will be arrived at. In the meantime, the model will have served its purpose in stimulating research and in leading to the discovery of ever more empirical facts.

Let us turn now to an indication of at least the sorts of defining experiments which can at this time be suggested for most of the intervening variables. To keep the task clearly before us, it will help to group the variables in the following outline.[7]

Variables to be Operationally Defined

Need Systems
- *a.* List of needs.
- *b.* Magnitude of a given need at a given moment.

Belief-Value Matrices
- *c.* The magnitude of the gratification and deprivation "values" of the given matrix at a given time.
- *d.* The shape of the cathexis belief attaching the various types of goal object (arrayed along a given generalization dimension) to the gratification end of a given matrix.
- *e.* The shape of the means-end belief attaching types of means object (arrayed along a given generalization dimension) to a given type of goal object or subgoal object.

Behavior Spaces
- *f.* Perceived qualities, distances, and directions in the behavior space.
- *g.* The strength of a need-push.
- *h.* The strength of a positive or negative valence.
- *i.* The strength and direction of a field force.
- *j.* The identification of a locomotion.

---

[7] It will be noted that I have omitted from the outline the individual difference variables, because, as indicated above, the main technique by which such variables have been arrived at to date — that of factor analysis — fails to integrate them in any way with such a "content" scheme as that of our model. Eventually, the manner in which individual difference variables will have to be handled to fit into our type of scheme will be in terms of individual differences in the magnitudes of the constants or parameters in the mathematical functions which are assumed to connect the intervening variables with each other and with the independent variables on the one hand, and with the dependent behavior on the other. But the task of developing the final forms of these equations and of measuring the variations in their constants and parameters for different individual lies, as has been suggested, a long way ahead.

This is a formidable array of items. All that can be attempted here will be very brief, schematic, and tentative suggestions as to the types of experiments or other empirical set-ups to be used for defining certain of these items.

a. List of needs. As has already been indicated, a need is to be defined as a readiness or tendency to persist toward and to perform a consummatory response relative to a certain more or less arbitrarily chosen "standard" goal object or situation and to avoid or go away from certain other objects or situations. Once the consummatory response to the standard goal object has been achieved, the given tendency to persist toward, and away from, ceases. Using this definition we would postulate, then, as many needs in a given actor as we can find standard objects or situations for which such tendencies to and from can be demonstrated.

At the present time psychologists seem to be fairly well agreed, in considering adult human beings, upon a list of common viscerogenic hungers, such as food hunger, palatability hunger, thirst, sex, temperature control, oxygen intake, rest and sleep, etc. — each of these to be defined and measured in terms of the strength of the propensities to go toward a "standard" food, a "standard" taste, a "standard" liquid, a "standard" sex object, a "standard" temperature, a "standard" degree of oxygen intake, a "standard" object to rest and sleep on. In such experiments, however, it would be necessary not only to undertake the measure of the strength of the given need by employing a well-chosen "standard" goal object but also by using a controlled, "standardized" test situation — one very familiar to the given actor so that the measurement of the strength of the given need will not be corrupted or diluted by any modifying simultaneous influence from some other need. Thus, for example, we would have to be sure in measuring the food-hunger need that our measures were not distorted by some hidden and unrealized simultaneous activity of, say, the thirst need or the fear need.

Second, it would appear in the cases of human beings (and, in fact, in the cases of all mammals) that there are also to be listed two other basic primary needs in addition to the viscerogenic hungers. These are fear and aggression. It is to be noted, however, that for both of these needs the standardized defining situation or object chosen for measuring will not be a standard variety of the to-be-got-to goal (i.e., safety in the case of fear and destroyed opposition in the case of aggression) but rather a standard variety of the situation to-be-got-from, (i.e., a standard type of pain or injury in the case of fear, and a standard type of blocking or obstruction in the case of aggression).[8]

Third, we have suggested in the preceding discussion that in human beings, and even in rats, there must also be assumed a general exploratory and curiosity, or "cognitive placing," need. The standard defining goal object for this

---

[8] We are using the term "aggression" somewhat differently from the way in which it was used in the earlier sections of this book.

need would be some sort of standard "new" object to be explored, examined, or matched. It will obviously require considerable experimentation and analysis to decide what to use as a standard "new" object for defining and measuring the basic strength of such a curiosity or exploratory drive. However, I believe that, in time, a concrete and satisfactory answer to this problem can be found.

Fourth, I would argue that there is probably also in man and in the higher apes a list of secondary innate social needs such as need gregariousness, need love, need approval, need dominance, need submission, and the like. The exact list of these is still to be determined. Again, whether or not we assume any one of these needs will be decided by whether we can agree upon a defining social goal situation, which can be made standard and used for measuring, for each of these needs.

Fifth, it has already been suggested that acquired, functionally autonomous, tertiary needs for culturally provided goals may also become established in human beings. Insofar as this assumption stands up after further empirical investigations, then we must also be able to set up defining standard goal objects or situations for each of these tertiary needs.

b. The magnitude of a given need at a given moment. It has just been indicated that for the measurement of the strength of a need at any time an agreed upon standard goal object for that need and an agreed upon standardized testing situation must be decided on. And it appears, further, that a measure of some quantitative aspect of the vigor of the behavior (e.g., frequency, intensity, force, consistency, latency, or the like) toward or away from the standard goal object in the standardized testing situation must also be agreed upon as constituting the measure of the strength of the given need.

The discovery of, and agreement upon, acceptable standard goal objects, acceptable standardized testing situations, and acceptable to-be-measured features of the behavior constitute the main task. The reaching of final agreement upon all these matters in connection with, say, the social needs seems to be a long way in the future. However, this has not prevented personality and social psychologists from making beginnings and from trying out quantitative measures (often ratings by an observer) of verbal or other responses of given subjects in either real or projective situations as indications of the strength of needs (see, for example, the original studies by Murray [17] and the later ones by Frenkel-Brunswik [4]).

An example of a relatively straightforward way of measuring the hunger and other viscerogenic needs in rats is the Columbia Obstruction Box [29]. By this method the number of crossings of an electric grill in a twenty-minute period to a standard food or other goal are counted and taken as a measure of the strength of the given need. As so measured, the strength of the hunger need, for example, is found to increase progressively over some forty-eight hours of food deprivation. After longer periods of starvation, it declines. This

I would take as indicating that at first the hunger need increases more or less linearly with the physiological hunger-drive condition, but with greater increases in the hunger-drive condition, other physiological factors intervene which lower the general libido need and because of this lowered libido the hunger need as such (not the hunger drive) declines. The electromagnetic charges in the hunger-need compartment tend, after greater periods of starvation, to be drained off into the libido compartment.

c. *The magnitude of the gratification and deprivation "values" of a matrix.* My assumption will be that, whereas the gratification values and deprivation values in any matrix vary proportionately (linearly) with the magnitudes of the need to which they are attached, their absolute magnitudes may be less than those of the total need. That is, any given need compartment may have attached to it numerous different matrices and the proportion of the total need strength which goes into a given matrix may be less than 1. For example, if the matrix aroused by virtue of the presented stimulus situation be that of restaurants and foods obtained in restaurants, the strength of the gratification and deprivation values for this matrix may be less (given one and the same actual hunger need) than the gratification and deprivation values of a matrix relative to home-cooked foods. This means, of course, that whereas the standardized testing situation for the pure hunger need must be one in which neither the peculiarities of restaurants nor of homes come into play (I am not sure what such a standardized situation might be), the defining situation for measuring the specific gratification and deprivation values of a given hunger matrix must be one which contains the specific types of means objects as well as types of goal objects constitutive of the given matrix.

d. *The shape of the cathexis belief attaching the various types of goal object (arrayed along a given generalization dimension) to the gratification end of a matrix.* It must be pointed out first that, by definition, the *most believed in* type of goal object placed on the final generalization dimension of a matrix will be said to have a belief strength of 1. Other goal objects arrayed along this same dimension will, according to the shape of the initial, generalization end of the belief lasso be less strongly "believed in." It is, then, the shape of this generalization fork which determines the degree to which the given type of goal object is believed to be good for reaching the given gratification end of a matrix. The empirical question which arises is how do we determine the shape of this forked tail. I suggest two empirical methods of attacking this problem.

The first method is to arouse the given need in our experimental subject and to discover, under the given conditions of need arousal, what will be the relative order of actual going to and performing the consummatory response upon the given selected array of goal objects in question. We may, for example, make the actor hungry and measure quantitatively how he actually selects from an array of different types of food in terms of going to and eating.

(This is the method of P. T. Young in his important studies [30] on hunger and appetite in rats.) Further, it is to be noted that it may turn out, when the test is made separately for different strengths of the hunger need, that the order of selected food types will be different for different strengths of the hunger need (i.e., for different magnitudes of positive value charge in the gratification end of the given matrix). In other words, the shape of the generalization end of the belief lasso may be different for different strengths of the hunger-gratification value. This is an interesting and important possibility which will need much further empirical study. Finally, it is to be noted that this method of testing the shape of the generalization end of a belief lasso is the only method which we can use with the lower animals. We have to make them actually hungry, thirsty, sexually aroused, or whatever, and then measure some quantitative feature of the relative order in which they will select from presented alternative types of goal object.

There is, however, a second method which can be used with human beings. We can use their verbal reports and we can obtain these stated preferences under conditions in which the corresponding need is not aroused, or not appreciably so. We can ask Mr. X what are his preferences relative to a list of types of food. And it may well turn out that we may get much the same answer whether or not his hunger need is aroused at the moment. That we can thus determine by verbal responses the shape of a food-gratification belief lasso indicates again the point made above; namely, that verbal reports of human beings must be assumed to be capable, with some degree of accuracy, of betraying directly the features of a belief-value matrix (however imperfect our conceptualization of the causal determination of verbal reports still remains).

e. The shape of the means-end belief attaching types of means objects (arrayed along a given generalization dimension) to a given type of goal object or subgoal object. Here, again, it would appear, in working with rats or other subhuman animals, that the only way we can arrive at the shape of a means-end belief — that is, the relative preferences with which certain types of objects will be selected as means to certain other types of objects as goals — will be through a long experimental procedure in which we first establish a type of goal object and then test out preferences for types of means objects over a long series of experiments in which many concrete instances of the goal objects and the means objects are used. In the case of men, however, the approach may differ. We can ask them about their beliefs when they are under conditions of no actual needs other than a social-approval need which leads to the readiness to "convey" information. For example, we ask them, when they are not hungry, to rate restaurants of types X, Y, and Z in terms of the degree to which they believe that these types of restaurants will lead to a good steak. And we shall probably find that their verbal ordering of these restaurant types when they are not hungry is very much the same as the ordering which would occur as a result of actual selection of restaurant types when they were hungry. And this means that verbal reports (with some validity) can indicate the characters of means-end beliefs in a belief-value matrix, even though the utilitarian need in question is not actually activated at the moment.

Before leaving this matter of the operational definition and measurement of cathexes and means-end beliefs, one more point, which has not perhaps been sufficiently emphasized, should be brought out. In the measuring of a belief relative to types of objects (if the measurement is carried out in non-verbal fashion) the measuring has to be done over a whole range of particular instances of each of the given types of object. If, for example, we are to conclude that a given actor believes strongly that Child's restaurants are better than ABC restaurants for leading to good flapjacks, we must try him out (or if possible a whole series of identical "him's" out) to see the consistency with which in Child's restaurants he will order flapjacks and in ABC restaurants he will order not flapjacks but, say, tea and buns. Similarly, in the case of rats, we will be able to say that a given population of rats (after a given training) has come to *believe* more strongly that right-hand alleys lead to food than that left-hand alleys lead to food, only if we try these rats on many pairs of right-hand and left-hand alleys. Only in this way will we know that it is right-handedness versus left-handedness as such, and not some peculiarity of a particular pair of alleys, that determines the selection of one turn or the other.

But let us turn now to the problem of the operational definition of features of the behavior space.

f. Perceived qualities, distances, and directions in the behavior space. In working with human subjects, the method usually resorted to for attempting to discover and define an actor's perceived qualities, distances, and directions is again verbal (introspective) reports. The subject says that he perceives such-and-such objects, qualities, or performances, and that these objects are placed in such-and-such ways relative to one another. As we have already seen, however, those features of the behavior space of which the actor is "consciously aware" (i.e., which he *can* verbally report) are not necessarily coextensive with the total behavior space which actually governs his locomotions and hence his actual behavior. It appears, therefore, that sometimes we must resort to other methods similar to those which we have to use with the lower animals.

The methods required for the lower animals all reduce essentially to experiments in which, by presenting the actor with successive pairs of stimuli (colors, shapes, tones, spatial directions, spatial distances, etc.), we eventually develop tables from which we can infer that if the given actor is presented with such-and-such actual physical qualities, distances, or directions in the stimulus situation, he will (other things being equal) be likely to perceive (contain in his behavior space of the moment) such-and-such objects in such-and-such directions and distances.

Thus from discrimination-box experiments with rats, we can now say, for example, that a rat will perceive only shades of gray and not chromatic colors; that he will perceive spatial length in the distances which he runs over, only if one length is at least 10 per cent longer than the other. Finally, as regards simple spatial direction, we are merely beginning to be able to say something (see experiments by Tolman, Ritchie, and Kalish [26–28]) about what sorts of orienting extra maze cues are necessary to enable rats to recognize a spatial short cut to food or to be able to choose the correct approach to a well-located food from some wholly new starting point on the other side of the maze. As for the problem of determining the probably perceived mechanical, social, aesthetic, etc., directions and distances of human beings without resort to verbal reports, hardly a start has been made.

g. *The strength of a given need-push.* I shall assume, very dogmatically, that a need-push in a given behavior space is measured directly by the strength of the deprivation value (or its equal the strength of the gratification value) in the controlling belief-value matrix. Thus, to return to our original example of restaurants and foods, I shall assume that the strength of the hunger need-push resulting from the activation of the restaurant-plus-food matrix is to be measured by the average magnitude of the eating or getting-to behaviors in consuming the most preferred restaurant food (under the given strength of the hunger need).

h. *The strength of a positive or negative valence.* The strength of the valence on the percept of, say, a given food will be a function of the general need-push for food activated by the given controlling matrix plus the degree of cathexis to the particular variety of food as determined by the shape of the generalization fork. In other words, whereas the need-push and the gratification value will be the same, and measured by putting the actor before an instance of the most preferred food, the valence for any given food may be less and can only be tested by putting the actor before an instance of this particular variety of food. Similarly, the strength of a negative valence will be measured by putting the actor before an instance of the special variety of — in the case of fear or aggression — a frightening or blocking object and measuring in some way the vigor of the actor's avoidance behavior in the presence of such object.

i. *The strength and direction of a field force.* The *strength* of a field force [9] is, I shall assume, directly proportional to the product of the need-push and the determining valence in question and inversely proportional to the square of the behavior-space distance between the region of the behaving self at the moment and the region of the corresponding valence. If, then, we know the magnitude of the need-push and the magnitude of the valence and

---

[9] The terms "field force" and "behavior force" are used interchangeably.

the magnitude of the perceived distance (not the actual physical distance) between the behaving self at the moment and the perceived location of the valence, we could compute (if we had the proper constant or constants) the strength of the resulting field force. Obviously, however, any such computations will require more precise measurements than we now have.

The *direction* of a behavior force is the direction as perceived by the actor between the region of the behaving self and the perceived region of a positively or negatively valenced distant object or region. The problem of direction in the behavior space is a complicated one. We are at the barest beginning, for example, in learning something about the nature and precision of the behavior-space directions of rats when compared with actual directions in physical space. Furthermore, as has already been indicated, the concept of direction in behavior space has been broadened by the present writer to cover every sort of discriminable differences — qualitative, mechanical, aesthetic, and other differences as well as spatial ones. That is, insofar as two objects are close together qualitatively, mechanically, aesthetically, or whatever, the more nearly they will be in the same "direction." Discriminable differences become, in terms of the behavior space, angular differences around the nose of the behaving self.

This whole concept of direction is, in short, as yet only sketchily developed. And certainly a great deal more analysis will have to be done to make it really workable and to allow for the complications which arise when both directions and distances are combined. Only when all this has been done, will we be able to handle such phenomena as short cuts and roundabouts not only with regard to space but also with regard to quality relations, aesthetic relations, mechanical relations, and the like.

j. The identification of a locomotion. In considering the operational identification of a locomotion it must be constantly emphasized that what is actually observed and measured is a behavior, or some quantitative aspect of a behavior, and not a locomotion. A locomotion is a purely hypothetical construct (an intervening variable). It is correlated with a behavior but is not the behavior itself. To take a simple example, assume that we observe a rat approaching a choice point in a maze, turning left and right a number of times when he reaches this point, and then finally proceeding down the one alley or the other. These would be behaviors. What, however, would be the corresponding locomotions of the rat's behaving self? The answer must be that only after we have been able to identify the probable behavior-space regions corresponding to the different objective features of the total stimulus situation would we really be able to identify the locomotions. A region in behavior space, it will be remembered, is to be defined as a set of potential behaviors, which the actor is ready to perform when in the presence of a given stimulus situation. And a locomotion was defined as a *selection* of one or more such behaviors out of this set of possible ones *as the way of passing to a next region.*

Only when we finally know enough to be able to say that an actor at this point had such-and-such behavior possibilities which he could release and that, out of all these, this one was selected and got him to such-and-such another set of possible behaviors, will we finally be able to identify his actual locomotions.

In the case of a human actor we would, of course, again resort to verbal reports, though with some uncertainty as to their ultimate reliability. We would ask him, "Where were you first; that is, what objects (behavior possibilities) were then before you? What behavior did you select and what new objects (behavior possibilities) were you then brought into the presence of?" And so on. After we had asked him these questions, we would also want him to report on such further complicated interrelationships as those concerning the roundabout routes and short cuts which he realized that he could have taken to arrive at one and the same final region. Obviously, it will take many experiments to pin all this down. Hence any final and complete definition of a rat's "locomotion" or a man's "locomotion" still lies far in the future.

To sum up, let us look once again at this matter of operational definitions as a whole. All such definitions reduce in the last analysis to assertions that in the attempt to think of precise ways of identifying and measuring each of the assumed intervening variables we shall be led, should our theoretical model have value, not only to clearer ideas about these hypothetical variables themselves but also to important empirical experiments. These experiments, whatever the truth of the model, will uncover new relationships between controlled, and measured, variations in independent variables, on the one hand, and resultant measured changes in final behavior, on the other.

Having now reviewed, as best we can, the parts and interrelations of our model, let us finally, in the next chapter, make an attempt to show its usefulness and applicability to some of the problems and concepts of the sociologist and the anthropologist as presented in other parts of this book.

5

Value Standards; Pattern Variables;

Social Roles; Personality

The four concepts of value standards, pattern variables, social roles, and personality have been selected for final consideration because they have figured prominently elsewhere in the book, and perhaps, more particularly, because they happen to be ones in which the present writer is personally interested and which he believes can be helpfully analyzed in terms of the model.

VALUE STANDARDS

Cultures have value standards — cognitive, appreciative, moral. These standards tend to be acquired by the actors living in these cultures. That is, an actor tends to differentiate between the true and the false, the beautiful and the ugly, the good and the bad, in ways prescribed by the culture. He adopts his standards from the culture. What now in terms of the model are such standards and how are they acquired?

It has already been argued that among the list of relatively basic needs present in both man and the lower animals is an exploratory or "cognitive placing" need.[1] This need leads to the development of belief-value matrices and of behavior spaces in which gratification is obtained from the mere *placing* of objects according to their qualities, directions, and distances. It will now be suggested that cognitive — or "understanding" — "value standards" are no more than such "placing matrices" as regards qualities and locations,[2] which the given culture tends to inculcate in its individual members.

However, before we analyze further this matter of the inculcation of culturally approved cognitive placing matrices, let us note that a similar situation

---

[1] See the discussion above of latent learning and of the Bruner and Goodman experiment.

[2] The term "location" is here used to cover all the spatial, mechanical, mathematical, logical, social, etc., directions and distances between objects or between objects and the behaving self.

seems to hold in relation to the other two types of value standard — the appreciative and the moral. I shall argue, in fact, that in addition to a purely cognitive placing need and resultant matrices, there are, or are developed, an appreciative (or aesthetic) placing need and matrices and a moral placing need and matrices. The appreciative placing need leads to matrices which categorize objects with respect to final resultant beliefs concerning their leading to immediate enjoyability — such beliefs as "this is pleasanter than that"; "this is nicer than that"; "this is more beautiful than that"; and so forth. The moral placing need leads to matrices which categorize objects (in this case primarily performances of self and others) according to resultant beliefs concerning their likelihood of receiving moral approval — such beliefs as: "this is good"; "this is bad"; "this is virtuous"; "this is sinful"; and so forth. Further, it will also be maintained that such appreciative and moral "placings," like the cognitive placings, are, as far as the resultant gratifications are concerned, equally rewarding whether the judgments (beliefs) in question assert the beauty or the ugliness, the virtuousness or the sinfulness, the truth or the falsity, of the given objects.

At this point, it may well be argued that all three of these placing needs are really subsumed under the first — that is, that all such placings are in the ultimate sense cognitive. To this, I would agree. They all "place." Thus, originally and genetically, placings according to the immediate employment properties of objects and placings according to the moral properties of objects, as well as placings according to the basic nature of objects, are probably all expressions of one and the same very general cognitive placing need. However, this original placing need soon becomes differentiated into the three subtypes: appreciative placing, moral placing, and cognitive placing. And it appears that these three subneeds may acquire quite different average magnitudes in different cultures, or in different individuals within one and the same culture. Thus, some cultures (or individuals) may be primarily cognitively oriented, others may be primarily aesthetically oriented, and still others morally oriented.[3]

Granted that cognitive, appreciative, and moral evaluations express three different placing needs, we must still consider the nature and meaning of "standards." For a culture not only tends to encourage cognitive, appreciative, and moral placings, it also tends to impose its rules or *standards* about just what is "so" or true, what is beautiful, and what is good. These standards, I would assert, consist merely in the fact that the basic ways of discriminating, generalizing, and believing which become incorporated into the placing matrices are imposed by the culture — learned from the culture. The precise

---

[3] It must be pointed out, as has been indicated several times before, that to date we have practically no good empirical techniques for the discovery of how such placing needs are acquired, or if they should have innate beginnings, how these beginnings are variously strengthened (or weakened) through learning.

empirical conditions which favor such learnings are still unknown. I shall, however, hazard the assumption that two main factors operate.

First, a culture has "names." It has, that is, symbolic ways of focusing the attention of its participants upon the particular discrimination and generalization units and beliefs that it favors. The result of such names is to point out to the actor repeatedly "what" he is to perceive and conceive, "how" he is to differentiate it from other "what's," and what further "what's" it will lead to. Hence, an actor growing up in a culture learns to "place" according to the standards of that culture, largely because language brings about a focusing upon and a frequency of presentation of such-and-such objects and relationships and no others.

Second, culture prescribes positive sanctions for discriminating and generalizing and believing according to its rules and negative sanctions for discriminating and generalizing and believing otherwise. As a result, any nonapproved discriminations, generalizations, or beliefs will tend to be repressed according to the principles of repression suggested earlier. It follows that the degree of acquisition of the value standards of the community will be affected strongly by the magnitude of the actor's need for social approval and hence his sensitivity to such sanctions. The stronger this need happens to be, the more likely the individual is to develop the "accepted" placing matrices.

Still another point is to be emphasized. It appears that value standards — i.e., cognitive, aesthetic, or moral discriminations, generalizations, and beliefs — do not necessarily bring about corresponding action. One may know the true, the beautiful, and the good without seeking them. Other practical, utilitarian needs such as the viscerogenic hungers may be too strong. Ordinarily, placing matrices indicate the layout and are then incorporated in other utilitarian matrices in which cognitive gratification, appreciative gratification, or moral gratification are not the main goals.[4]

In summary, cognitive, appreciative, or moral value standards are, according to this analysis, merely imposed ways of discriminating, generalizing, and believing, which become established in the placing matrices of given cultures or of given individuals. The culture or the subculture determines by "namings" and by social sanctions the precise units and the precise limits of such discriminations, generalizations, and beliefs which will tend to be accepted. However, it is also to be noted that even though an individual has been highly trained to "know" the true, the beautiful, and the good, this does

[4] The fact that an understanding matrix may later be incorporated in a utilitarian matrix was assumed in our discussion of the latent learning of rats. It was there implied that the discriminations, categorizations, and beliefs concerning maze alleys and the locations of food or water which the rats achieved as a result of a mere general exploratory (understanding) need, and which were laid down in an understanding placing matrix, could then be incorporated into a practical food-getting-to or water-getting-to matrix.

not necessarily mean that he will also want them. Actually to behave, an actor must not only have value *standards*, he must also have then-and-there activated values. His utilitarian as well as his placing needs must be aroused. But we will understand this better after we have considered the pattern variables.

PATTERN VARIABLES

The five pairs of pattern variables, presented in Chapter I of Part II, were listed as (*a*) affectivity *vs.* affective neutrality; (*b*) self-orientation *vs.* collectivity-orientation; (*c*) universalism *vs.* particularism; (*d*) ascription *vs.* achievement; and (*e*) diffuseness *vs.* specificity. Each pair will here be conceived to consist, not in a pair of alternate moral value standards, but in two opposing "moral placing" matrices, one or the other of which will tend to determine the behavior of the given individual, or the given culture, relative to a certain area of object relationships.

a. Affectivity vs. *affective neutrality*. When an object or situation presents an actor with an opportunity *either* for a relatively quick and easy gratification of a "lower" need *or* for a gratification of a relatively postponed, difficultly-to-be-arrived-at, and supposedly greater and "higher" [5] need, some individuals (or cultures) will "place" the postponed gratification as leading to moral gratification and the immediate gratification as leading to moral deprivation, whereas other cultures or individuals will "place" the two types of gratification in the reverse order. This means that in the moral placing matrix for the one culture or for the one individual, immediate gratifications are categorized as leading to final social disapproval; whereas in the moral placing matrix for the other culture, or individual, they will be categorized as leading to final social approval.

b. Self-orientation vs. *collectivity-orientation*. This alternative arises when an individual situation may be classified either as an opportunity for the gratification of ego's own relatively private ulitarian needs or as an opportunity for the gratification of the needs of a collectivity of which ego is a part. In the one case, ego's moral placing matrix will categorize final moral gratification (i.e., final social or self-approval) as resulting from ego's own private gratification, whereas in the other case, ego's moral placing matrix will categorize final social or self-approval as resulting from the gratification of the needs of the collectivity.

c. Universalism vs. *particularism*. In the case of "universalism" certain types of environmental objects and standards, for example, the relationships between patients and doctors, will be discriminated and categorized as situations in which the patient will choose (and behave to) a doctor (and vice

---

[5] See the brief remark on an earlier page concerning "higher" and "lower" needs in accordance with Maslow's theory [16].

versa) according to the generally accepted, universal standards of medicine. In the case of "particularism," on the other hand, the relationships between patients and doctors will be discriminated and categorized as ones of unique person-to-person relations such as those of friendship or kinship. This means, further, that in the moral placing matrix of the one culture the general relationship will be believed to lead to final moral gratification of ego, and the particular relationship to final moral deprivation of ego; whereas in the other culture the reverse will be true as far as such types of relationship are concerned.

d. Ascription vs. *achievement.* This contrast corresponds to two different categorizations by ego of both self and alters in a moral placing matrix: a categorization primarily in terms of their social statuses; or a categorization primarily in terms of their performances and achievements. Further, for one culture or individual the moral placing matrix says that to categorize according to status is proper, right, and virtuous (i.e., will meet with final social and self-approval); whereas the moral placing matrix of the other culture or individual says that to categorize human beings according to their behaviors or achievements is proper, right, and virtuous (i.e., will meet with final approval).

e. Diffuseness vs. *specificity.* In this pair of pattern variables, "diffuseness" corresponds to a moral placing matrix which makes no differentiation between the different "segmental" relations of an alter to ego and vice versa. If ego is involved in one sort of relationship with alter, he is categorized as also being involved in every other sort of relationship with alter. In the case of "specificity," differentiations between the different "segmental" relations of alter to ego, and vice versa, *are* made in the moral placing matrix. If alter is categorized as in one of these relationships to ego, he need not be categorized as also in the others. For example, in the case of diffuseness, if alter is classified as a sex object, he tends to be classified also and forthwith as guide, counselor, and friend. In the case of specificity, on the other hand, differentiations *are* made between the various potential roles of alter to ego; the fact that alter is classified in one of them does not as such lead to his classification in the others. Finally, the moral placing matrix of the one culture will thus contain the final belief that the diffuse categorization will lead to ego's moral gratification (i.e., to social- and self-approval); whereas the moral placing of the other culture will contain the belief that it is the specificity categorization which will lead to ego's moral gratification (i.e., to social- and self-approval).

In the above discussion of the pattern variables and in the preceding discussion of value standards certain assertions and implications have been made about placing matrices and their relationships to other matrices which perhaps can only be rendered completely intelligible with the help of a diagram. Let me present, then, by way of clarification a figure to represent one of the pattern-variable alternatives. I will choose the first pair — affectivity *vs.* affective neutrality. A diagram for any one of the other pairs would involve the same general principles.

Fig. 21 presents a concrete illustration of a moral placing matrix in the case of an individual, or a culture, for the case of affective neutrality. It also

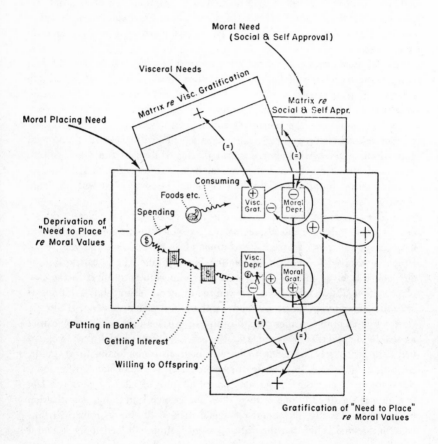

Fig. 21 AFFECTIVE NEUTRALITY

indicates two interacting utilitarian matrices. The placing matrix is shown as the horizontal one. The actor is conceived as being faced with money and the moral placing matrix shows two alternative sets of behavior and accompanying beliefs. One of these (represented as radiating slightly upward) envisages that money may be spent directly and lead to ego's own viscerogenic gratifications, which, however (given the general culture or the individual's private culture of "renunciation"), leads to the further belief that this will result in moral deprivation. The other set of behaviors and accompanying beliefs (represented as radiating slightly downward) envisages that money may be put in a bank to collect interest and then may be willed to offspring. This belief, given the culture of renunciation, leads to the further belief that this will lead to ego's own moral gratification. As far as the placing need is concerned, either of the belief chains will lead to the same final *placing* gratification.

We must assume in addition, however, in order to explain what will actually happen, the two "utilitarian" needs of (1) the viscerogenic hungers and (2) the moral (social- and self-approval) need. These two needs lead to further matrices, shown as cross-cutting the moral placing matrix, which indicate that if the social- and self-approval need is *very strong* (so that it heavily outweighs the viscerogenic hungers), then affective neutrality will have the greatest terminal positive value and ego will tend to locomote in his behavior space in the direction of saving his money and willing it to his offspring. If, however, the viscerogenic hungers are exceedingly strong, then, even though the moral placing matrix accepted by the culture and by the individual in question indicates that immediate viscerogenic satisfaction will lead to moral deprivation, the viscerogenic gratifications will have such strong positive values that ego will locomote toward them rather than toward saving. (Note: the double-headed arrows indicate that the gratification and deprivation values of the cross-cutting matrices are, for convenience of drawing, merely repeated inside the moral placing matrix.)

So much for a diagram of the matrix system for the pattern variable of affective neutrality; the matrix system for its antithesis of affectivity would be exactly the same, save that it would be the spending and immediate consummatory alternative which, in the moral placing matrix, would lead to final moral gratification and the other alternatives which would lead to moral deprivation. It is obvious that a pure gratification culture would produce practically no conflict. The viscerogenic hunger needs and the social- and self-approval needs would both lead to positive values.

Social Roles

Any social system is made up of mutually overlapping social structures or institutions. Each structure or institution (for example, the family) is constituted by a number of complementary social positions or, as Linton [14] calls them, social statuses. Thus, the institution of the family, as we know it in America today, is made up of the social status of a husband and father, the social status of a wife and mother, and the social status of each child (which will be different according to age, sex, and birth order). Further, the set of behaviors which ego is expected to perform by virtue of his position as father, mother, or child, is called a *social role*. A man in his role as father is expected to behave in certain ways; a woman in her role as mother in certain other ways; and each child according to age, sex, and birth order in still other ways. A role is thus a series of appropriate and *expected* ways of behaving relative to certain objects, by virtue of a given individual's status in a given social structure or institution.

Further, these expectations that individuals in given statuses will behave in such-and-such ways are called *role expectations*. This term has a double meaning. It applies not only to the expectations of the alters (in this example, the other members of the family and the public at large) that ego will behave in certain ways but it applies as well to the expectations of ego that if he behaves in these expected ways, the alters will meet his behavior with approval (or at any rate with lack of disapproval) and with other appropriate, complementary, meshing behaviors of their own. If ego does not so behave, the alters will meet his behavior with disapproval and with other behaviors of their own which do not mesh. Ego thus comes to expect these resultant approvals or disapprovals and these meshing or non-meshing complementary behaviors from the alters; and the alters come to expect the complementary behaviors from ego.

It is obvious that these concepts of social roles and role expectations are very close to the concept of the self-ideal presented in the section above on psychodynamic mechanisms. The only difference between the concept of a social role and the concept of a self-ideal seems to be that the concept of the social role is limited to a relatively prescribed set of stimulus situations, whereas the concept of the self-ideal concerns a relatively wide, more abstract, set of behaviors, such as courage, honesty, neatness, punctuality, and so on, which are demanded of ego in practically *all* types of social situation. Indeed, it would appear that the self-ideal probably develops out of the more limited social roles. Ego learns the expected behaviors in narrow role contexts and then generalizes them to all contexts. He thus builds up his general self-ideal. But there is a problem involved; the behavior which is expected by society in one role may turn out to be quite different from that which is expected and required in another role.

This brings us to the concept of role conflicts. The term "role conflicts" has been used to refer to this very fact that any ego is usually involved at different times, or even at the same time, in several different social structures or institutions and that the sorts of behaviors expected of him in these different social structures or institutions may be incompatible. For example, an adult male in our society will have to play the roles of father, lover, businessman, community leader, club member, helpful domestic, and tidy gardener (especially in California). And it appears that the types of behavior-space regions which he must locomote to and from in one such social role may be quite different from those which he must locomote to and from in others of these roles. The categorizations, beliefs, and values which he acquires in connection with one role may conflict seriously with the categorizations, beliefs, and values which he acquires in connection with other roles. The more complicated the society or the more fluid the institutions, the more likely such role conflicts become.

The actor may meet these conflicts by such mechanisms as repression and symbolic substitution, by a thoroughgoing neurosis or a psychosis, by discovering more general categorizations and beliefs, by establishing new needs which allow for the synthesis of such conflicting categorizations and beliefs and values, and/or by easy "compartmentalization," which prevents generalizations appropriate to the matrices required in one role from spreading over to those required in other roles.

The concept of role acceptance also has to be considered here. It concerns the conditions underlying an actor's original acquisition or acceptance of a role. Whereas many roles in our society (for example, that of a member of a family) cannot, generally speaking, be escaped, choices regarding the acceptance or adoption of certain types of role are encouraged. This is especially true in a society such as ours. For example, young people in our society are, in most cases, encouraged to select their own professional or work roles. What are the determining factors of such selections? The answer seems to be that the factors consist mainly in the histories and strengths of the successive positive and negative identifications which the child has made with father, mother, teachers, gang mates, or external prestige groups. The contents of these identifications and the order in which they occur seem to be the important factors. The youth aspires to a particular job, or other career, because he wants to be like his father or because he doesn't want to be like him; because he is trying to live up to some social ambition implanted by his mother; because he and his gang are protecting themselves against the ideals of teachers or parents; because of special school encouragements or school discouragements; and so forth. To put this in other terms, the factors that seem to determine ego's acceptance of any role, professional or other, would be all the previous multidinous relationships with alters which have developed ego's beliefs concerning the ways to obtain social approval and/or self-approval. And these beliefs are, in essence, that the way to obtain approval is by becoming like, or unlike, such-and-such other individuals. The tracing out of all the determining social experiences behind these beliefs in any concrete individual case, or in any characteristic group of cases, becomes, of course, a tremendously difficult empirical problem. An exciting first attack upon this problem, with special reference to the adoption of work or job aspirations by junior high school boys, has, however, already been made by Parsons, Stouffer, and Kluckhohn [18]. The problems of role acceptance, however complicated, are actually capable of empirical attack.

Let us turn now to our last concept, personality.

PERSONALITY

This topic, though of such tremendous importance for social science, can be touched upon only briefly here. In an earlier chapter, the significance of a personality as an on-going system was emphasized. What, in terms of the concepts of the present chapter, would be the necessary conditions for the non-disintegration, the on-goingness, of a personality system? The answer would be that all the "needs" and all the attached "belief-value matrices" which are relatively prominent in the make-up of a given personality must somehow coincide and fit together so that the actor possessing this personality will not be led into frequent conflict; will not, that is, be presented in his behavior space with regions that contain at one and the same time both a strong positive valence and a strong negative valence. This requires special types of coördination among the different belief-value matrices and their attached needs. In an earlier chapter the concepts of "integration" and "allocation" were advanced as useful analytical tools for the study of such types of coördination. Let us see how these concepts may be helpful.

First, let us consider integration. An integrated personality would be one whose belief-value matrices (i.e., whose view of the world) would add up to a set of relatively consistent ways of valuing any given group of objects. Probably, most important in achieving such an integrated personality would be the consistency of the actor's beliefs about parents and later about other authority figures. He should not be subject to too much strain of both love and hate for the same figures. And this would seem to require further that his moral placing matrix — his beliefs about how he is to achieve social- and self-approval — should not be too inconsistent with his beliefs about how he is to obtain his primary gratifications. The early authorities who helped, loved, and approved him must also have encouraged and not blocked too many of his simple primary needs. This sort of an integrated personality would be integrated because the parents and the culture would give approval for the sorts of activity also believed to be necessary and good for attaining gratification of the basic biological and social needs. The individual personality would tend to be integrated because the culture was integrated. Further, it must also be pointed out that a really integrated culture — producing really integrated personalities — would have to be integrated not only *internally*, as just suggested (that is, no conflicting moral and utilitarian values), but also *externally* (that is, no values, resulting from moral or utilitarian matrices, which were incompatible with the actually available, environmental conditions). One of the obvious examples of a lack of such "external" integration in our culture and a resulting difficulty in achieving personality integration is the emphasis put by us upon standards of material welfare which only a few can attain. This means the development of a type of self-ideal the achievement of which is constantly met by negative barriers in the behavior space. Conflict, repression, symbolic substitutions, and other tendencies toward disintegrations seem almost inevitable.

Let us turn now to allocation. Through allocation, as we use the concept here, a considerable measure of integration can be achieved in a culture, or in a personality, even though there are, in fact, a number of conflicting values. This is achieved by allocating the gratifications of the values to separate times and places. The culture and the personalities nurtured in the culture have learned to draw clear distinctions between acceptable and nonacceptable places and occasions for the gratification of specific needs. Thus, we have the traditional story of the New England dairyman and church warden who worshipped God and gave to the poor on Sundays and watered his milk on weekdays. Integration (i.e., lack of conflict) was achieved through allocated, *non-overgeneralized*, beliefs as to when and where this, that, or the other need is to be gratified. An on-going society and on-going personalities would, in a successfully allocative society, be brought about, on the one hand, by diminishing the original chances of overgeneralization and, on the other, by psychotherapy which would consist in the successful correction of such overgeneralizations when these overgeneralizations have occurred earlier in a given personality.

The above discussion of personality has been far too brief and far too abstract. It has not sufficiently included the specific concepts and problems of the personality psychologist. Further, it has not, as it should have, amplified the remarks, made in the earlier portions of this paper, about learning and the psychodynamic mechanisms. It should also have analyzed the ways in which the conscious and the unconscious portions of the belief-value matrices interact with one another and what happens when one or the other of these portions dominates. A further elaboration concerning the influence of sequences of roles should have been attempted; for it appears that any actor's final personality develops in large part through his being forced into such-and-such a series of successive roles. He acquires matrices (beliefs and values) appropriate to each successive role. His final personality depends, therefore, not only upon his innate, or early acquired, capacity and temperamental traits, which make some roles easier for him than others, but also upon the concrete nature of the roles, upon the order and the intensity with which they have been accepted by him, and upon the ways and the degrees to which they have or have not conflicted with one another.

A few final remarks: it must be reëmphasized that the study of personality, stated in terms of the present model, is a study of belief-value matrices — their integration or lack of integration — plus a study of need systems, the list of needs, the ways in which the individual needs do or do not enhance or depress one another, and their attachments to specific matrices. Further, it may be pointed out that although the "adjusted personality" in any given culture is perhaps usually the individual whose own belief-value matrix system is most consonant with the "modal matrix" [6] of the culture in general, this need not always be the case. For would it appear that there are types of unique individuals who deviate relatively widely from their culture and yet achieve an integration of their own — some sort of an inner consistency in their various need strengths and belief-value matrices which holds up even though these needs and matrices run counter to those of their fellows. Finally, it may be noted that there are so-called creative individuals who set new patterns, new value standards, for a society. Their need systems and belief-value matrix systems also differ from those of their society. But these creative individuals may or may not be internally well-integrated, well-allocated personalities. Many seem to be just the opposite. They are neither stable because they conform nor stable because they have an internal strength of their own. They are often highly unstable; and yet, in terms of the social system of which they are a part, they may make tremendous social innovations — sometimes good, sometimes bad.

To summarize, personality is to be defined in terms of innate and acquired need systems and in terms of belief-value matrices. Personalities may be integrated and likely to survive or not integrated and likely to break down. An integrated personality is one which does not have conflicting values or whose conflicting values are taken care of through allocation of their respective gratifications to socially acceptable times and places. The worth of a personality type, in terms of its contributions to the social system of which it is a part, cannot be evaluated directly in terms of its own degree of inner integration. Some nonintegrated, very unstable, but creative personality types may make great social contributions, some of which may add notably to the permanence and on-goingness of the given social system.

[6] See above for the meaning of this term.

6

Summary and Conclusions

An attempt will be made here to summarize more specifically the distinctive contributions of the model, as the present writer sees them, to psychology and to social science as a whole.

The average psychologist, immersed as he is in the details of empirical problems, perhaps centered around one narrow area or perhaps scattered over a wide range of areas, will ask what meaning such a model can have for him. My answer would be to point out, first, that the model indicates the loci within a single theoretical framework of all the different empirical problems with which psychologists concern themselves; and second, that the model also presents specific hypotheses concerning the functional, causal relationships involved in each of these empirical problems. The classical chapter headings of any general textbook in psychology run somewhat as follows: Sensation and Perception; Memory; Learning; Thinking; Motivation; Attitudes; Skills; Personality; Individual Differences. The point I should like to make is that the empirical problems designated by each of these chapter headings finds its own natural and, I believe, illuminating locus or loci in the model. Let us consider each of these usual chapters one at a time.

A chapter on *sensation and perception* would contain, first, statements of the detailed functional relations between types and intensities of delimited physical stimuli and resultant contents (discriminanda) in the behavior space. These statements are usually gathered together under the subheading *sensation*. But such a chapter would also contain considerations of the ways in which such details of discrimination will also be affected by the larger spatial and temporal stimulus contexts within which the given restricted stimuli are presented. Studies of this second type are those which were largely initiated by Gestalt psychology; such studies as those on figure and ground, completion of incomplete figures, *prägnanz*, distortion in simple forgetting, and the like.

Both of the above types of study would be located in the model by the arrow running directly from the independent variable of the stimulus situation to the intervening variable of the behavior space. In addition, however, a chapter on sensation and perception would include a study of all the further variations in the discrimination contents of the behavior space, which are brought about by variations in the beliefs and values in the superordinate belief-value matrices. It would include such studies as that by Bruner and Goodman on the effect of the money values of coins on the perception of their sizes, together with a host of other recently reported "new look" experiments — all of which indicate the tremendous effects on sensation and perception of the specific values in the belief-value matrices. All these "new look" studies would be located on our model by the causal arrows running from matrices to behavior spaces.

A chapter on *memory* (as I am using the term here) would consider primarily the independent effects of single past stimulus situations on present behavior spaces. The laws of memory as thus restricted would seem to be very much the same as those for immediate sensation. However, the term "memory" is often used to cover the problem of the extrapolation of a behavior space owing to the fact that the now presented stimuli have in the past been presented in temporal, spatial, and other conjunctions with such-and-such other stimuli. But in this sense the chapter on memory passes over into the chapter on learning, to which latter we may now turn.

A chapter on *learning*, as will be recalled from our previous discussions, will from the point of view of our model, have to deal with three main topics: (a) the establishment of new differentiations in the behavior space; (b) the establishment of new categorizations, new beliefs, and new values in belief-value matrices; and (c) the establishment of new acquired (tertiary) needs in the need system.

Let us consider each of these further. (a) The study of the establishment of new differentiations in the behavior space would be a study of the functional determination represented, in the model, by the arrow from the stimulus situation to the behavior space. These would be determinations over and above those considered in the chapter on sensation and perception. It would be a study also of an interaction effect between locomotion and the behavior space. (b) The study of learning as a change in more enduring and generalized differentiations, beliefs, and values in the matrix system would be a study of the laws represented in the model by the arrow running back from the behavior space to the belief-value matrix. This study would consist in further investigations of the facts already known — though in very inadequate detail — concerning permanency and generalizability of learned relations; facts that in former days were considered mainly under the heading of "transfer of training." (c) Finally, the study of the acquisition of new needs would be located on the model by the arrows leading back from a belief-value matrix to the need system. The laws and conditions of such learning are, however, as has aready been indicated, as yet practically unknown.

A chapter on *thinking* would concern itself with modifications of belief-value matrices, not as a result of concrete behaviors but as a result of some internal type of process. This points to a feature in connection with the model which we have up to now largely side-stepped. It arises out of the fact that human actors can apparently talk to themselves, or in some other not as yet clearly formulated way, modify the categorizations, generalizations, and beliefs in their belief-value matrices without overtly behaving — without, that is, actually coming in contact with any new stimulus features. Furthermore, the processes by which they do this cannot be observed by an outsider. An observer can tap the successive stages of the process by presenting simple objective tests every so often and discovering how the contents of the matrix have successively changed. But he cannot study the process itself which produces the changes except by asking for introspections. And the unsatisfactory and unreliable character of introspection, when it comes to reporting on thought processes, is notorious.

The process of thinking, then, seems to consist in some type of internal activity which enables an actor to bring into play the consequences of given potential types of behavior without, however, actually carrying out such behaviors. And as a result of these brought-into-play consequences, he modifies or reformulates or expands his behavior space and his belief-value matrix. Further, it is to be emphasized that these reformulations are not the ordinary ones which have, for the most part, been considered above as the result of actual behavior, but ones which result from purely sitting and thinking. Satisfactory psychological studies of this *process* are as yet, I would submit, almost nil. A real chapter on thinking has yet to be written.

A chapter on *motivation* would concern itself first with the relations between drives as independent physiological variables and the need system as a set of consequent behavior readinesses. It would, that is, be concerned with the arrow (see Fig. 2) running from the independent variable of drives to the intervening variables of the need system. The chapter would, secondly, also concern itself with the arrow running from the stimulus situation to the need system; that is, it would have to consider not only the arousal of needs as a result of physiological states but also as a result of presented stimuli. Third, this chapter would be concerned with the causal functions represented both by the arrows from the need system to the belief-value matrices and the arrows from the belief-value matrices back to the need system. That is, both the problem of the cathexis of a given matrix to a given need and the problem of how a change in a matrix may lead to a new need would have to be included. Still further, the chapter would be concerned with the problem of how values in a matrix act to produce valences in a behavior space as well as with the problem of how the deprivation value in a matrix produces a need-push in the behavior space. Finally, a chapter on motivation would concern the problem of the strengths of the resultant field forces in the behavior space as a result of the interaction of need-pushes, valences, and distances in the behavior space. In a word, it appears that the chapter would recapitulate from its own angle practically everything said in all the other chapters.

A chapter on *attitudes* would, from my point of view, be nothing more or less than a descriptive study of beliefs and resultant positive and/or negative values in belief-value matrices in specified populations of individuals. Indeed, attitude questionnaires, as was suggested earlier, would seem to be one of the main techniques for investigating belief-value matrices. Heretofore, of course, most attitude studies, resorting to questionnaires or to interviews, have been concerned with discovering merely the presence or absence of specific attitudes (belief-value matrices) in given populations for practical social or political purposes. In the sort of chapter on this topic which I would envisage, the emphasis would be rather on a study of the dynamic interrelations between different attitudes — different belief-value matrices. The ways in which one matrix can or cannot include another, the necessary relations of superordination between matrices, and the like — these would be studies which, from the point of view of our model, would be the most exciting.

A chapter on *sensory-motor skills* is for the most part yet to be written. In terms of the model a discussion of sensory-motor skills would be a discussion of how *locomotions* in the behavior space get translated into overt *behaviors*. It would also be a discussion of how the sensory-motor activities of the organism — the actual behaviors which he learns, or develops through mere maturation — come to react upon and become constitutive of regions of his behavior space. But, as I have said, such a chapter has as yet never really been attempted.

A chapter on *personality*, as would appear from the preceding section, would be concerned with the individual's need system and his belief-value matrices. But it would also be concerned, by tradition, with the nature of the psychodynamic mechanisms. Still further, it would have to consider individual differences. Thus, to a considerable degree, a chapter on personality, like a chapter on motivation, would be a chapter recapitulating, from its own point of view, practically the whole of psychology. This chapter would, that is, be concerned with psychology from the special angle of the resultant integration or non-integration, smoothness or non-smoothness, of the resultant functioning of the individual actor.

Finally, a chapter on *individual differences* would be concerned, as suggested above, with determining the values of the constants for different individuals in all the causal functions (represented in the model by arrows) considered in the other chapters. But this is a topic upon which I am not qualified to speak. The individual-difference psychologists, with their tests, their rating procedures, and their statistical techniques, have acquired an array of tremendously important facts, but these facts have still to be fitted into the structural concepts of such a model as ours. This remains a major task which, it is hoped, may be undertaken at some future time.

Let us turn now to the question of the significance of our model for social science as a whole.

FOR SOCIAL SCIENCE

The argument here will be brief. It has been indicated in the other sections of this book that the basic categories for the structural analysis of social systems, of culture systems, and of personality systems must be consonant with one another. For individual actors are but role-takers in collectivities; and both individuals and collectivities internalize culture patterns and respond to cultural accumulations; and, finally, individual actors respond to collectivities and collectivities respond to individual actors. The psychological model presented here is then, I would assert, no more than a restatement of the same conceptual categories developed in the other chapters of the book for social systems and culture systems, but colored somewhat by the special needs and interests of the psychologist. Psychology is in large part a study of the internalization of society and of culture within the individual human actor. Therefore, our psychological model has sought to ferret out and to classify the internal workings of the individual human actor by adopting the same kind of taxonomic principles used in the sociological and anthropological chapters of this book. And, although I have not always used the same words or retained all the same emphases, I have, I hope, remained true to the sense and to the spirit of these other social and cultural analyses.

Bibliography

1. Allport, G. W. *Personality, A Psychological Interpretation*. New York: Holt, 1937.

2. Bruner, J. S., and C. C. Goodman. "Value and Need as Organizing Factors in Perception," *Journ. Abnorm. and Soc. Psychol.*, XLII (1947), 33–44.

3. Brunswik, E. "Organismic Achievement and Environmental Probability," *Psychol. Rev.*, L (1943), 255–272.

4. Frenkel-Brunswik, E. "Motivation and Behavior," *Genet. Psychol. Monog.*, XXVI (1942), 121–264.

5. Guthrie, E. R. *The Psychology of Learning*. New York: Harper's, 1933.

6. Guthrie, E. P., and G. P. Horton. *Cats in a Puzzle Box*. New York: Rinehart, 1946.

7. Hebb, D. O. *Organization of Behavior*. New York: Wiley, 1949.

8. Hull, C. L. *Principles of Behavior*. New York: Appleton-Century, 1943.

9. Krech, D. "Notes toward a Psychological Theory," *Journ. Personal.*, XVIII (1949), 66–87.

10. ———. "Dynamic Systems, Psychological Fields, and Hypothetical Constructs," *Psychol. Rev.*, LVII (1950), 283–290.

11. Kendler, H. H., and W. P. Gasser. "Variables in Spatial Learning: I. Number of Reinforcements during Training," *Journ. Comp. and Physiol. Psychol.*, XLI (1948), 178–187.

12. Köhler, W. *Dynamics in Psychology*. New York: Liveright, 1940.

13. Lewin, Kurt. "The Conceptual Representation and the Measurement of Psychological Forces," *Contrib. Psychol. Theory*, I (1938), no. 4.

14. Linton, R. *The Cultural Background of Personality*. New York: Appleton-Century, 1945.

15. MacCorquodale, K., and P. E. Meehl. "On a Distinction between Hypothetical Constructs and Intervening Variables," *Psychol. Rev.*, LV (1948), 95–107.

16. Maslow, A. H. " 'Higher' and 'Lower' Needs," *Journ. Psychol.*, XV (1948), 433–436.

17. Murray, H. A. *Explorations in Personality*. New York: Oxford University Press, 1938.

18. Parsons, Talcott, S. A. Stouffer, and Florence Kluckhohn. Unpublished manuscript concerning Research Seminar on Social Structure, Harvard University.

19. Ritchie, B. F. "Studies in Spatial Learning: VI. Place Orientation and Direction Orientation," *Journ. Exp. Psychol.*, XXXVIII (1948), 659–669.

20. Sears, R. R. "Effects of Frustration and Anxiety on Fantasy Aggression." Address delivered at Sixtieth Anniversary Celebration, Clark University, April 1950.

21. Skinner, B. F. *The Behavior of Organisms: An Experimental Analysis.* New York: Appleton-Century, 1938.

22. Tolman, E. C. *Purposive Behavior in Animals and Men.* New York: Appleton-Century, 1932.

23. ————. "The Nature and Functioning of Wants," *Psychol. Rev.,* LVI (1949), 357–369.

24. ————. "The Psychology of Social Learning," *Journ. Soc. Issues,* V (1949), Supplement no. 3.

25. ————. "Interrelations between Perception and Personality: A Symposium, Part I, Discussion." *Journ. Personal.,* XVIII (1949), 48–50.

26. Tolman, E. C., B. F. Ritchie, and D. Kalish. "Studies in Spatial Learning: I. Orientation and the Short-Cut," *Journ. Exp. Psychol.,* XXXVI (1946), 13–24.

27. ————. "Studies in Spatial Learning: II. Place Learning versus Response Learning," *Journ. Exp. Psychol.,* XXXVI (1946), 221–229.

28. ————. "Studies in Spatial Learning: IV. The Transfer of Place Learning to Other Starting Paths," *Journ. Exp. Psychol.,* XXXVII (1947), 39–47.

29. Warden, C. J., *et al. Animal Motivation: Experimental Studies on the Albino Rat.* New York: Columbia University Press, 1931.

30. Young, P. T. "Food-seeking Drive, Affective Process, and Learning," *Psychol. Rev.,* L (1949), 98–121.

4

The Theory of Action and Its Application

1   GORDON W. ALLPORT

Prejudice: A Problem in Psychological
and Social Causation

The problem of prejudice may be viewed as one empirical focus in the wide region of social conflict and action. It should, therefore, provide a test case for the fruitfulness of the theory of action sketched in this volume.

Prejudice is manifestly a value-orientation. It can be, and should be, studied at the level of *personality system*, at the level of *social system*, and at the level of *cultural system*. Each approach, as the present essay will show, is conceptually independent in its handling of the numerous elements of action involved. But at the same time prejudice as a concrete phenomenon cannot be fully understood unless it is regarded as reflecting simultaneously all three forms of systematization. Thus a methodological paradox exists: prejudice (like other forms of social behavior) is many things; it is one thing. It may well be that the solution to this paradox lies, as the present volume suggests, in revising psychological theory — let us say — so that it corresponds in every essential feature with cultural and social theory. Certainly in the long run quarrelsome differences have no place in the scientific analysis of a single form of social action.

In the present essay I fear that I do not offer a point-for-point analysis of prejudice in terms of corresponding theories of action systems; nor do I attempt to fit the topic under a generalized statement of action theory. My approach is somewhat more timid. For several years I have struggled with the task of organizing the voluminous research and interpretation in the area of group conflict and prejudice. It would please me greatly if I could locate it all under a unified theory. While the direction taken by the present volume offers suggestions and encouragement, I fear that my own thinking has not progressed effectively beyond the comparatively pluralistic analysis that I offer in this essay. I have little to say concerning the eventual possibility of gathering the fragments under an embracing action theory. It may sometime be accomplished.

The form of this essay is accounted for in part by the occasion for which it was written. In September 1950 I delivered the Kurt Lewin Memorial Award Lecture to the Society for the Psychological Study of Social Issues. Group conflict and prejudice was one of the areas of investigation to which Lewin directed his genius (Lewin, 1948). It seemed appropriate, therefore, for me to survey the trends of recent research and to offer to a psychological audience such conceptualization and organization as I could. Since this self-set methodological assignment fits the scope of the present volume the lecture is printed here — as one example of the halting steps that social science is taking toward a more unified (or at least more broadminded) conceptualization of central problems of social behavior.

In recent years interest in group conflict and prejudice has spread like a flood both in social psychology and in adjacent social sciences. Publications are cascading from the presses. The outpouring within the past decade surely exceeds the output of all previous human history. Thousands of facts and scores of interpretations already lie before us. A unified theory is lacking. Why it is lacking and what we can do about the matter constitute the subject of this lecture.

Is Research on Prejudice Basic?

My approach to the problem differs from that of some of my colleagues. A few of them, distressed by the complexity and present disorganization of the field, are saying that the topic of prejudice is a scientific will-o'-the-wisp. They say it rests on nothing but a value judgment of liberal intellectuals. They say it is a sloppily descriptive concept; and that we would do better to give our attention to more basic research in terms of perception, cognitive reorganization, reinforcement, or the habit hierarchy. After all, prejudice, if it is not a mere value judgment, is a compound, and we would do better to explore ingredients than to consider the compound as an entity in itself.

While we should heed these criticisms, I for one do not find them particularly convincing. The fact that liberal intellectuals deplore prejudice does not in the slightest degree affect its veridicality as a mode of mental functioning. Psychopathologists regard paranoia or neurosis as undesirable; but paranoia and neurosis as syndromes nevertheless exist. School teachers regard certain mental sets as objectionable; the mental sets are there. Whatever our values may be prejudice is *a fact of mental organization* and *a mode of mental functioning*. It is our business to understand it.

Any definition of this attitudinal syndrome must contain two propositions: one, that the individual is affectively oriented toward an object of regard; and the other that this object of regard is overgeneralized. Most definitions observe these two conditions very well. Thus the *New Oxford Dictionary* calls prejudice "a feeling, favorable or unfavorable, toward any person or thing, prior to or not based on actual experience." There are, of course, *fav-*

orable prejudices — tendencies to accept objects or persons because of their membership in a class that is categorically approved. But for simplicity's sake we shall confine ourselves to *negative* prejudice and not at this time raise the question whether affiliative prejudices in all respects follow the same basic principles (cf. Allport, in Sorokin, 1950). We shall also confine ourselves to prejudice against people, though one can surely be prejudiced against colleges, cities, or cookery. There is no reason to suppose that prejudice against nonhuman objects differs in its essentials from prejudice against human beings. Developmentally, xenophobia is probably much like nosophobia.

But we shall limit ourselves to the negative attitudes toward human beings that are held because of their membership (or supposed membership) in a certain group. The prejudgment runs its course without due regard for individual differences. Misjudgment is also involved because no group as a whole has attributes that each member unvaryingly shares (Vickery and Opler, 1948). Thomistic psychology sums the matter up crisply. Prejudice against human beings is a form of "rash judgment," which, simply said, is a matter of "thinking ill of others without sufficient warrant."

Some of our hostile acts and repudiations are entirely realistic. This Negro, we may know from experience, is untrustworthy; that Britisher bores us. In such cases we think ill of others *with* sufficient warrant. But as soon as our ill-thinking becomes wholly or in part derivative — as soon as it borrows from the fallacious generalization that *all* Negroes are untrustworthy, or *all* Britishers bores — then prejudice is at work.

Three basic and universal psychological functions underlie the syndrome. Each in its way helps to account for the formation of fallacious overgeneralizations and for their impress upon specific judgments. The first is the familiar process of concept formation, which so easily goes to excessive lengths. Grouping, constellating, rubricizing leap far ahead of experience. They do so partly because of the impetus of culturally transmitted language. Aided by labels, we generalize concerning matters where our experience is limited — concerning chiropractors, vitamins, Eskimos. Every individual within the class is endowed with the handful of attributes by which the class as a whole is known. We have come to call the overgeneralized attribute, or constellation of attributes, by which the class is known a stereotype. Exceptions, as Walter Lippmann pointed out, are often pooh-poohed, forgotten, or otherwise not admitted to the category. It was prejudice that made the Oxford student remark that he dispised all Americans, but had never met one that he didn't like.

The second basic function concerns the generalization of feeling and emotion — sometimes referred to as *displacement, spread, irradiation,* or *diffusion.* A person who fears that he may lose his job is, first and foremost, an anxious *person.* We must expect this diffused organismic condition to affect his behavior generally. An individual severely frustrated at home but unable to master the situation becomes an angry and aggressive *person* whose impulses understandably enough may be discharged upon irrelevant targets. This diffusion of the affective life, as Tolman says, is all the greater "if the goal is perceptually blotted out by a type of negative barrier." If, for example, an individual does not understand his own problem — does not know, that is, what pathways are appropriate to his goals — he may transfer his anxiety to "similars, symbols, or associates." Discussing this matter in the Lewin Memorial Lecture of last year, Tolman (1949) describes, as an example, the manner in which sex repression may evade barriers of social disapproval by becoming charged with other libidinous energy, including aggression, and finally lead the individual to a socially permitted form of hostility toward out-groups. While, as Zawadski (1948) and Lindzey (1950) have shown, displacement cannot serve as an omnibus explanation of prejudice, still we shall not be able to understand our subject at all unless we concede that a person's distress may spread like a grease spot to "similars, symbols, or associates."

The third function is one that brings together the stereotype and the distress in a particular situation. It is the trick human beings have of rectifying their thought to conform to their feelings. This *rationalization*, though common enough, is an unrealistic and protective mental operation. It is true that mature and healthy minds often strive to rectify feelings to conform to the state of the objective evidence. But the very fact that some people do one thing and some another is further proof that the syndrome of prejudice is a special mode of mental functioning requiring direct study.

Any psychologist who admits these basic mechanisms of *categorization*, *displacement*, and *rationalization* to good standing ought to admit the product of their joint operation. Prejudice *is* something, and *does* something. It is not the invention of liberals. Its importance in society merely adds urgency to what is in any case a basic psychological problem.

As I have said, there is no single adequate theory of prejudice. The scapegoat theory, while partially valid, does not cover all the known facts. Explanations in terms of economic determinism, childhood insecurity, institutionalized aggression, or perceptual distortion, are all suggestive and demonstrably valid in part, but each by itself is incomplete. We are confronted here — as in many problems of interest to social psychology — with the phenomenon of multiple causation. In dealing with such problems it seems that the social psychologist must allow for six valid levels of causal analysis (see Fig. 1). He need not himself employ all six, but he must constantly be aware of their importance.

STIMULUS APPROACH

At the right of Figure 1 we see that investigations may center upon the nature of the stimulus object itself. This is a backward region of research.

Yet it has to do with the most basic of all issues in the field of prejudice: the nature of group differences.

If we were strictly logical, we would suspend further work upon prejudice until the objective nature of the relevant stimulus patterns were known. Thus if it should turn out to be true that all Negroes are dull, shiftless, aggressive, it would be folly to speak of prejudice when we reject Negro X for having these qualities. While we know that generalizations of this order of certainty are unlikely to be correct, it is important to learn just how false they are. After all, a stereotype and a negative attitude would be partially admissible if they had a high probability of according with facts. Until we know more about national, racial, ethnic character we shall not be able to distinguish between prejudice and what Zawadski calls "well-deserved repu-

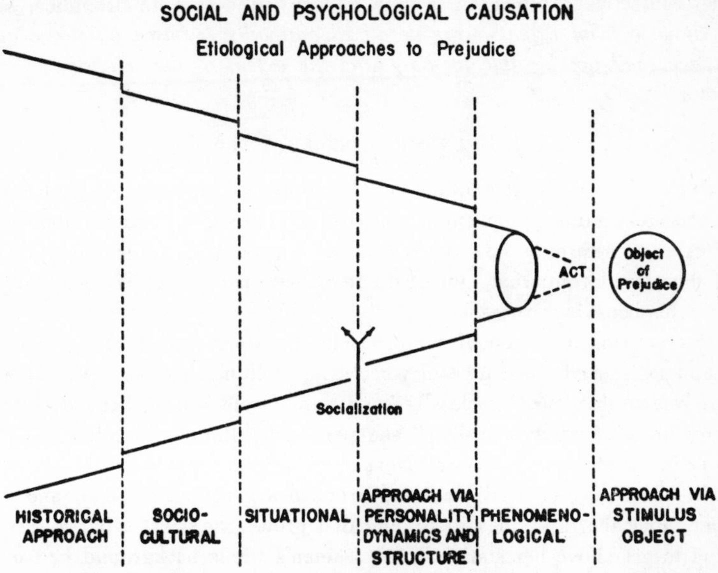

SOCIAL AND PSYCHOLOGICAL CAUSATION
Etiological Approaches to Prejudice

| HISTORICAL APPROACH | SOCIO-CULTURAL | SITUATIONAL | APPROACH VIA PERSONALITY DYNAMICS AND STRUCTURE | PHENOMENO-LOGICAL | APPROACH VIA STIMULUS OBJECT |

Fig. 1

tation." What percentage of Jews, as compared with gentiles, is aggressive, tax evading, or ostentatious? Does anyone know? If the percentage is high, then current judgments are semirealistic though they cannot safely be applied to a given individual; if low, then we shall have to invoke projection and agree with Ackerman and Jahoda (1950) that the Jew is little more than a "living inkblot." It goes without saying that if accusations against minority groups should turn out to be justified to an appreciable degree the problem would still remain whether the traits in question were the cause or the consequence of public prejudice. It would not be surprising if some members of minority groups developed certain defensive characteristics simply because people in the dominant group persistently refuse to treat them as individuals according to their personal merits.

The stimulus-approach will likewise teach us more than we know about the factor of visibility (Ichheiser, 1947). Unless members of a minority group can in some way be identified they cannot be victimized. What then are the psychological implications of skin color, ethnic names, customs, language, and — conceivably — odor? While some work has been done in this direction, there is much to learn.

A few years ago, under the impact of Gestalt theory, the concept of *illusion* was virtually lost to psychology. This is regrettable, for unless we know the objectively verifiable properties of the stimulus, how can we ever tell how much subjective rectification is taking place? And so with prejudice, *until we know to what extent our generalized antipathy is based on provocative fact, we shall not be able to determine the extent of the irrationality that remains.*

The Phenomenological Approach

But if the Gestalt revolution unduly minimized the stimulus it brought compensatory gains. The phenomenological level of analysis that it popularized invites us to determine how the individual is perceiving the stimulus object, and therefore, from what immediate regnancy (from what "causal integration") his behavior proceeds.

Once during a session of summer school a woman in my class came to me and with an alarmed tone of voice said, "I think there is a student with some Negro blood in this class" — and pointed out a dark brunette to me. To my non-committal "Really?" she persisted, "But you wouldn't want a nigger in the class, would you?" Next day she returned and firmly informed me, "I know she's colored because I dropped a paper on the floor and said to her, 'Pick that up.' She did so, and that proves she's just a darky servant trying to get above her station." The woman's whole background had over-sensitized her to a certain mode of seeing and behaving. In the forefront of her life she carried important hypotheses that selected her perceptions and sifted her actions.

In South Africa on a Public Service Examination candidates were instructed to "underline the percentage that you think Jews constitute of the whole population of South Africa: 1, 5, 10, 15, 20, 25, 30 per cent." When tabulated the modal estimate turned out to be 20 per cent. The true answer is just a little over 1 per cent (Malherbe, 1946). Here again we see how prejudice accentuates features within the phenomenal world.

In this connection the Chinese doctrine of immortality contains a revealing belief. The spirits of one's ancestors are presumed to grow smaller with each generation. Thus as one's memory and interest fail one's representation of outer reality shrinks.

A final example I borrow from the Deutsch-Collins (1949) research on integrated *versus* segregated biracial housing projects. The residential situations of two groups of white people cause them to perceive Negroes in different ways. The following tabulation (based on Deutsch-Collins, Table 18) shows the replies of white people to the question: "Are they (the Negro people in the project) pretty much the same as the white people who live here or are they different?"

Reply	Integrated housing units (%)	Segregated housing units (%)
"Same"	80	57
"Different"	14	22
"Don't know"	6	20

We note how residential contact affects the perception of sameness and difference. The same research contains even more subtle evidence that perceptions of people's qualities change through alterations in degree and kind of contact. When they mentioned the chief faults they thought Negro people had, white people living in segregated units tended to name aggressive traits: trouble-making, rowdy, dangerous. Those living in the closer association of integrated units mentioned predominantly an entirely different type of trait, namely, feelings of inferiority or oversensitiveness to prejudice. The shift here is from a fear-sustained perception to one sustained by a friendly, "mental hygiene" point of view. In this instance we note the transformation from what Newcomb (1947) calls "autistic hostility" to social reality.

Heider (1944) in his stimulating work on social perception has pointed out how our interpretations of causality are ordinarily anthropomorphic in character. We ascribe change wherever possible to *human* agencies. For example, in deteriorated residential districts we are far more likely to see the Negro who lives there as disfiguring the district than to perceive the district as disfiguring the Negro.

Memory, like perception, is selectively conditioned. Seeleman's study (1940) shows how people's power to recognize individual Negro faces varies inversely with their anti-Negro prejudice. In order to maintain our perceptual hypotheses (i.e., our stereotypes) intact we are forced to forget in a selective manner all the dignified, well-behaved Negroes, all the generous Jews, all the liberal-minded Catholics we have met. We think of them simply as Americans. Only when we encounter the expected pushing in a Negro, penny-pinching in a Jew, or narrow-mindedness in a Catholic, do we revive our favored hypotheses in our minds and proceed through our perceptions to confirm them. What has been called "motivated assimilation" in the process of rumor distortion is of this same order (Allport and Postman, 1947). Stories heard and told are tailored to preëxisting hypotheses. Rumors seem more often to conform to regnant hypotheses than to stimulus events.

I have illustrated the phenomenological approach to prejudice before I have defined it. Brought to prominence in recent years by Brunswik, Koffka, Krech and Crutchfield, Bruner and Postman, MacLeod, Heider and others, phenomenology deals with the individual's definition of the situation he finds himself in; that is, with his subjective reality. While this reality is in part a function of the stimulus situation, it is in varying degrees also a function of personal hypotheses within which are focused the needs and traits of the individual, the situational context of the moment, as well as cultural and historical influences (Bruner, 1950; Postman, 1950).

There is merit in this approach. Like a lens it directs the rays from remoter regions of causation upon the present need for adjustment. As Figure 1 suggests, it represents the convergence of many etiological factors, and defines the immediate regnancy that leads to specific acts of behavior. I have attempted in the diagram to represent in a crude manner the law that every act results from the final common path of convergent tendencies, from a "causal integration." The phenomenal field is a distillation of background forces and thus marks the final distribution of energy systems just prior to innervation.[1] Many of Lewin's topological diagrams depict these terminal vectorial arrangements within the phenomenal field that eventuate in overt behavior.

Let me add just one final example of the merits of this approach. Much investigation in social psychology is conducted through interviewing. Now it goes without saying that replies to questions will be determined by the way the respondent perceives the question asked. Morton has pointed out that to ask an individual, "Would you mind living next door to a Negro?" may not tap his deeper attitudes toward Negroes at all. The question might mean to him, "Do you want to risk lower status in the eyes of your friends and relatives?" Or, "Do you want to be cut off from your present neighbors?" Or, "Do you want to take an unnecessary chance that your daughter will fall in love with a Negro boy?" The precaution that we all take nowadays to pretest our questionnaires proceeds, whether we know it or not, from our recognition of the importance of phenomenological causation.

Valuable as this approach is, it obviously cannot serve as a complete conceptualization of prejudice. It deals only with the individual's definition of

---

[1] A serious issue arises when we ask whether the phenomenal field is, by definition, only the field of conscious meanings. If so, then we are compelled to say that the value of the phenomenological approach, though by no means destroyed, is limited. Any final common path, or "causal integration," may run its course, wholly or in part, with marginal consciousness, or even subliminally. My own view is that it is wise to consider the phenomenological approach as dealing with conscious meanings exclusively. To do so reveals an important level of causal analysis. At the same time it makes entirely clear the fact that phenomenology alone cannot solve all the etiological problems involved.

the presenting situation and does not tell what determines this definition. In etiological terms it represents only *proximate* (i.e., immediate) causation. The pivotal concepts in phenomenology such as "hypothesis," "cognitive map" (Tolman), and "life space" (Lewin) all imply that every factor required to formulate an event is operating in the field at the moment. Yet the *origin* of these factors, their peculiar *recurrence*, and their *functional significance* in the life of the individual can only be explained by pushing our causal analysis further.

PERSONALITY DYNAMICS AND STRUCTURE: THE FUNCTIONAL SIGNIFICANCE OF PREJUDICE

The greater part of the recent outpouring of research and theory has had to do with personality dynamics and structure.

Implicit in this approach, I should like first to point out, is a widespread acceptance of the concept of attitude. What we do with our measuring instruments, whether they be direct questionnaires (e.g., Adorno *et al.*, 1950; Allport and Kramer, 1946; Deri *et al.*, 1948), polls (cf. Kramer, 1949), or clever projective and trap devices (e.g., Razran, 1950; Gough, 1950) is to discover the range and intensity of prejudiced attitudes. The evidence for the high internal reliability of prejudice scales is conclusive (cf. Hartley, 1946), as is the evidence for their repeat reliability (cf. Dodd, 1935). In view of these facts it is surprising to note the various attempts that have been made in recent years to dislodge the concept of attitude. We may agree with Doob (1947) that attitudes should be tied to a sound learning theory and with Smith (1947–48) that attitudes should not be considered apart from their functional value in the context of the individual's life as a whole. But these, together with other recent critics, to my mind have succeeded not in eliminating the concept but in helpfully refining and establishing it.

Perhaps the chief progress that has been made in the psychology of attitudes during the past decade lies in the growing recognition that attitudes serve a purpose in the life-economy of the individual. The California farmer who is prejudiced against Japanese-Americans has a defineable attitude, but this attitude is not isolated in his life. Rather it may be for him a means of excusing his failures, maintaining his self-esteem, and enhancing his competitive position. While many studies of prejudice do run their course at the level of polling or measurement with only first-order breakdowns or simple accompanying correlations, those that have penetrated deeper disclose the stabilizing function that prejudice may play in personality. Investigations such as those of Escalona (1946), Ackerman and Jahoda (1950), Simmel (1946), Bettelheim and Janowitz (1950), and Adorno *et al.* (1950) show beyond doubt that prejudiced attitudes may serve as a psychological crutch for persons crippled in their encounters with life.

In such instances the dynamisms involved are those we have mentioned — categorization, displacement, and rationalization; they also include projection, reaction formation, and other sly tricks of ego defense. Summarizing the work in this area Theodore Newcomb concludes that "the personality factors most closely related to attitudes of prejudice are those which have to do with threat orientation" (1950, p. 588). From this point of view prejudice would seem to be largely a device for handling basic insecurity. Campbell's discovery (1947) that job dissatisfaction is associated with anti-Semitism is one of many lines of evidence supporting this proposition. So too Bixler's case (1948) of a domestic quarrel disrupting a truck driver's erstwhile friendly relations with a Negro companion. Much other evidence could be cited supporting this hypothesis.

Yet manifestly some people handle both outer and inner threats with complete equanimity. Although faced with a lowering standard of living, with downward mobility, for example, they do not necessarily react, as did many of the Chicago veterans, with acute prejudice. What we need to know, therefore, is the type of *character structure* that resorts to prejudice when threats are felt.

It is at this point that some of the most brilliant advances have recently been made. I refer first to an unpublished study by Nancy Carter Morse (1947). This investigator set herself the task of testing many hypotheses concerning anti-Semitism: that it varies with outer insecurity, with felt insecurity, with outer frustration, with self-frustration, with past experience, with "belief in essence" (e.g., "Jewishness"), and with different patterns of loyalty. She found that while several of these factors correlated with anti-Semitism they did so only in a contingent manner. Unless high "national involvement" were also present these etiological variables were not operative. Conversely, "national involvement" correlated with hostility against the Jews when everything else was held constant. The higher the degree of "patriotism," the higher the anti-Semitism. To my mind the significance of this study lies in its demonstration that prejudice is not merely a response to threat. It is also an element in a positive pattern of security. The bigot is first and foremost an institutionalist. He cannot tolerate uncertainty of membership. He fashions an island of safety and clings to it. The fact that the intercorrelation of prejudiced attitudes is known to be high (cf. Hartley, 1946) offers support for this interpretation. A person who is against one minority is in most cases against all other minorities. In short, *his mode of life is exclusionist.* He cannot welcome strangers or out-groups of any kind to his island.

For additional light on this syndrome we are in debt to the California investigators (Adorno *et al.*, 1950) and to others whose results provide support (cf. Allport, in *Scientific American*). Without attempting a final portrayal of the type of character structure in question, I list some of the findings concerning the "authoritarian personality." The type is also depicted by

Fromm (1947) who contrasts it with the "productive personality" and by Maslow (1943) who contrasts it with the "self-actualizing" personality (1949).

The authoritarian person has a general trait of extropunitiveness. Blame is seldom directed toward himself. He sees outer events, persons, circumstances as accountable for his failures.

His personal relations are characteristically regarded in terms of power and status rather than in terms of love and friendship.

Though he makes protestations of love and accord for his parents, deeper study shows that parent-child affection and trust were in fact lacking. Discipline and authority marked the relationship. Latent rebellion, firmly held in check, is therefore detectable.

Conventionalism and excessive institutionalism mark his life. Lacking a sense of inner security he seeks safety in well-defined in-groups — in church, sorority, or nation (cf. Morse, 1947).

Categorical thinking is prominent, especially a two-valued logic. What is not clearly good is *ipso facto* evil; a woman is "pure" or else "bad."

Insight into his own nature is lacking, although he is usually well satisfied with himself.

A rigidity marks the style of life. Preservative mental sets are found even in areas that have nothing apparently to do with prejudice (cf. Rokeach, 1948).

A need for certainty characterizes the thinking. Seldom does the person say, "I don't know." Roper (1946) finds that DK responses among anti-Semites are less than among tolerant people.

Such characters live in fear of punishment and retaliation. They are broadly suspicious. They agree with the proposition, "The world is a hazardous place where men are basically evil and dangerous" (Allport and Kramer, 1946).

Much of the world seems "ego alien" to them. They clutch at certainties. Even their Rorschach responses seem compulsively meticulous (Reichard, 1948). To maintain a precarious integration, they structure their island of safety rigidly lest confusion overwhelm them.

Often such individuals align themselves with authoritarian movements in order to codify and justify their own bigotry.

The agitator, the "prophet of deceit," may be looked upon as an individual in whom this syndrome is excessively marked and who possesses motivation and skill enough to become a leader in exclusionist and persecutory movements (Lowenthal and Guterman, 1949). Paranoid characteristics may be present in such individuals (Morlan, 1948).

It is important to note that this syndrome, originally established in adults, has been found to reach down into the middle years of childhood by Frenkel-Brunswik (1948) and Rokeach (1948), and even into the age of seven by

Kutner (1950). But we do not yet know for certain — through these studies strongly imply it — that early childhood training is responsible. Indications are that harsh and capricious discipline, affectional deprivation, feelings of rejection, may underlie the character structure thus formed. We dare not, however, rule out the possibility of a constitutional bent toward rigidity, though concerning this important matter we know absolutely nothing.

Adults — first encountering upsetting conditions in later years — may likewise adopt the safety-island method of adjustment and develop bigotry where apparently none existed before. There is important work to be done in establishing the conditions for latent bigotry that will develop only if and when suitable situational factors arise.

Most research on the dynamics and structure of personality in relation to prejudice utilizes extreme and contrasting groups. The subjects are chosen from those "high" and "low" in prejudice. Median subjects are usually discarded. This heuristic device leads to an overemphasis upon types. We study confirmed bigots and emerge with the concept of an "authoritarian" personality; or we focus on markedly tolerant people and emerge with the "productive," "mature," or "self-actualizing" personality. This procedure, though defensible, leads subtly to the depiction of "ideal types." We sharpen our findings, so that the whole complex subject falls a little too readily into a neat "schema of comprehensibility." This procedure tempts us to forget the many mixtures that occur in ordinary run-of-the-mill personalities.

While we are examining somewhat critically the methods employed in establishing the rigidity-prejudice correlation, we should mark the almost universal absence of a desirable control. It is not sufficient, for example, to determine that people high in prejudice are generally deficient in ability to change their mental set, but we must likewise prove that groups deficient in their ability to change their mental set are high in prejudice. Until we do so our parameters are not clearly established.

In framing our theories of dynamisms and character structure we should make room for the apparently serious conflict between biological and psychogenic motives that may enter into ethnic attitudes. In relations between white men and Negroes, for example, there is a considerable and growing amount of friendliness wherever cultivated and psychogenic interests are involved. Negro artists are in theaters, drawing rooms, sports arenas. Negro folk music is accepted as American folk music. At concerts, church, and in community activities we increasingly participate in a friendly fashion. In short, wherever there are mature areas of interest, association is readily handled. But where biological gratifications are in question, the authoritarian mode of adjustment seems more likely to assert itself. Two fiercely possessive needs — property and sex — appear to be the final bastions of conservatism. In a life where mature adjustments in these regions are not worked out, and where anxiety dwells, there seems to be a higher probability of rigid, exclusive, suspicious character formation. And in one and the same personality we find sentiments that are egalitarian up to a point, but that seem to turn turtle when miscegenation or occupational equality are mentioned. This suggested relation between "gut functions" and prejudice deserves further study.

CONFORMITY

Now we dare not assume that prejudiced attitudes are always psychological crutches employed by immature or crippled individuals. Many studies suggest that they may be peripheral to the personality, skin-deep as it were. On the basis of interviews with veterans, Bettelheim and Janowitz (1950; pp. 16, 26) classify attitudes toward Jews and Negroes as shown in the accompanying

ATTITUDES OF 150 RESPONDENTS TOWARD TWO MINORITY GROUPS
(In Per Cent)

Types of Attitude Expressed	Toward Jews	Toward Negroes
Intensely anti- (spontaneous)	4	16
Outspokenly anti- (when questioned)	27	49
Stereotyped	28	27
Tolerant	41	8
Total	100	100

Data from Bettelheim and Janowitz, *Dynamics of Prejudice*, pp. 16, 26.

table. One has the impression that the "stereotyped" cases (roughly one-quarter of each group), and perhaps some of the "outspoken" cases may be little more than cultural parrots, repeating idle chatter they have heard. These individuals do not live by their prejudice; its functional significance for them is low or else lacking. But, as I have observed, latent prejudice now expressed merely in stereotypes, may blaze with functional significance when conditions are ripe.

Again it is not that two distinct types are involved, but rather as Figure 2 suggests, a continuum of cases. At any given time a prejudiced individual presumably may be located at some point between a maximum degree of

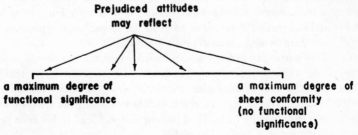

Fig. 2

ego-relevant functional significance, and a maximum degree of sheer (not ego-involved) conformity. It does not affect the continuum to argue that conformity itself has functional significance for the individual. We may grant that no person would adopt the folkways unless it served his purpose to do so. Yet there is a wide difference between, let us say, normal habits of cleanliness acquired from parents and culture and compulsive hand-washing. A similar difference obtains between bigotry that is simply stereotyped and bigotry that is saturated with need and necessity.

SOCIALIZATION

The topic of conformity leads to the problem of learning. As shown in Figure 1, the problem is properly located at the junction of the individual approach and the situational, for it is always through a concrete learning situation that the influences of a culture or subculture reach the person.

I shall say little about the acquisition of prejudice, not because facts and theories are lacking, but because the topic is inexhaustible. Let me mention only a few well-established findings.

(1) It takes considerable time for the young child to make the in-group and out-group distinctions prescribed by his culture. For example, to the simple question, "What are you?" only 10 per cent of four-year-olds reply in terms of racial, ethnic, or religious membership; whereas 75 per cent of nine-year-olds do so (Hartley, Rosenbaum, and Schwartz, 1948).

(2) Before the child can distinguish between various groups he often acquires power-words of violent opprobrium such as "nigger," "kike," "wop," whose affective significance he senses. Through these symbols he thus learns to reject a group even before he knows to what group they apply. Aggression may thus be prechanneled upon groups before the child has any experience with them (cf. Trager and Radke, 1947).

(3) In general, the role of firsthand knowledge of, or experience with, minority groups seems to be a negligible factor in the formation of prejudice in childhood. From the point of view of mental health it is regrettable that attitudes are not the generalized product of firsthand experience, but in the realm of ethnic attitudes, as in the case of most moral attitudes, they are taken over ready-made. Subsequent experience is ordinarily interpreted in a selective fashion so that it serves to confirm the secondhand hypotheses acquired from parents and associates (cf. Horowitz, 1936).

Now these particular findings bear primarily upon the *conformity* aspects of prejudice. While they are vastly important we should not forget that the ground work for an authoritarian *character structure* may also be laid through learning. Thus a rejected child, unable to identify securely with his parents, may be forced into a survival pattern that will lead in his later years to a rigid, out-group-hating mode of life.

Therefore, research on the acquisition of prejudice should deal equally with two basic problems which may well involve different *kinds* of learning: (1) the acquiring of content (i.e., of beliefs and categories) and (2) the acquiring of functional predispositions toward, or a need for, prejudice in the economy of the personal life (cf. Allport, 1950b).

THE SITUATIONAL APPROACH

The situational approach to the study of prejudice is the least easily defined. Broadly speaking, it seeks illumination from studying the confluence of outer forces that act upon the individual. Causation is seen as residing to a greater or lesser degree behind and beyond the individual. Now many psychologists, Lewin among them, might insist that it is the phenomenal field alone that matters. The person acts not on the basis of surrounding forces but on the basis of the subjective, causal integration he has fashioned. Reasonable as this argument sounds, the fact remains that we cannot know the phenomenal field directly. We infer it partly from the resultant act and partly from the outer situation.

Any field is a state of energy tension existing between two or more poles. Sometimes it is viewed as existing in space-time, sometimes as a dimension of thought. Often the two modes of existence are confused. What we think of as a phenomenological field sometimes turns out to be a space-time field. Even Lewin's classic investigations of the autocratic and democratic group atmosphere rest upon *outer* situational criteria and not directly upon the subject's perceptual structuring thereof. Valuable as the concept of phenomenal field is, we are forced to admit that in practice we often confuse what is phenomenal with what is situational. Take the common expression that we have adopted from Lewin: we speak of someone "going out of the field." Unless we were in fact viewing the field situationally we could not speak of an individual leaving it. For not even a Houdini could "go out of" his own phenomenal field.

An educator from South Africa told me the following incident. The pupils in a rural school were not making satisfactory progress in learning English, so the district supervisor of English instruction visited the school and asked the native teacher to give a demonstration to show how he taught. Thereupon the teacher did so, but only after speaking first to the children in the vernacular, "Come now, children, put away your things and let us spend an hour wrestling with the enemy's language." This is the situation in which the learning proceeded, or failed to proceed. We may *imagine* what structuring took place in the pupil's phenomenal field, but actually we can only know for certain the *outer* situation.

When one studies the relationship between unemployment and prejudice one is using the situational approach. So too when one investigates the effects of different types of contacts — residential, occupational, social, and wartime contacts in combat situations. A large number of important researches have dealt with this particular situational problem (e.g., Stouffer *et al.*, 1949; MacKenzie, 1948; Allport and Kramer, 1946; Deutsch and Collins, 1949; Deutscher and Chein, 1948). The generalization that emerges is to the effect that *only in situations where different groups meet on equal footing, enjoying equal status, does prejudice diminish; the effect is greatly enhanced if the groups holding such equal status engage in joint participation in a common task.*

Many if not most studies of the classroom employ the situational approach. Educators are nowadays insisting that a democratic atmosphere must mark relationships in the classroom if desirable intercultural attitudes are to be fostered (e.g., Kilpatrick and Van Til, 1947). Lewin has repeatedly made the point that the creator of group atmosphere is primarily the leader (or teacher) who inevitably serves as the "gatekeeper of the channel of communication" (1947).

A good example of the importance of the situation in the *expression* of prejudice is contained in the researches of Robinson and Rohde (1946) who found that Jewish-appearing interviewers, especially if introducing themselves with Jewish names, obtained far less open expression of anti-Semitism than did interviewers who seemed to the respondents to be non-Jewish. People of lower socio-economic levels were more restrained in their expression of prejudice to Jewish-appearing interviewers than were those of higher levels.

What I am here calling situational studies are, as these few examples show, diverse in type. Some situations are as enduring as family structure, others as transitory as a race riot. Some are as embracing as the impact of press and radio upon us, others as specialized as the fleeting anti-minority incidents in offices or tramways so cleverly studied by Citron, Chein, and Harding (1950).

Broadly speaking, in the concept of situation we are approaching a level of theory congenial to sociological investigators. Coutu (1949) has recently advised us to abandon the concept of attitude altogether and to speak exclusively of a tendency-in-a-situation. Prejudice would thus be defined as the range of situations in which an individual makes a negative or hostile response.

I feel that there is a desirable reciprocity between the individual theories of causation and the situational. They have a fortunate way of handling each other's exceptions. Thus if not all members of an agitator's audience fall for his line, of if not all dwellers in an area marked by Negro in-migration resent their arrival, we seek the explanation for the exceptions in terms of individual differences (in personality dynamics or structure). Conversely, if a given individual, noted for his tolerance, suddenly behaves out of character, explanation can be sought in terms of the situation. Take the case of the white woman living in an interracial project who was not merely content but actually enthusiastic about her experience there. Yet in spite of this warm and friendly attitude she decided to move away. The contradiction, it developed, was due to the fact that she had a twelve-year old daughter whom she expected "would just naturally fall in love with one of the fine young Negro lads in the project." The mother had no objection to the prospect herself, but she knew that the resulting situation would be fraught with trouble for her daughter. The mother's decision was contrary to her own attitudes; it was determined by a situational and cultural structure quite alien to her own nature (Deutsch, 1949).

We may state the point at issue a little more exactly. Few personalities are completely integrated and conflictless. Even the most consistent among us play many roles in the several groups of which we are members. But there are none the less bona fide psychophysical dispositions and habits within our own organisms to correspond to these roles. Sometimes one and sometimes another disposition or habit is evoked — according to the situation (cf. Myrdal, 1944).

This insistence upon the biophysical nature of conflict and of role behavior does not in the slightest degree weaken the situational approach to the study of prejudice. Quite the contrary, it grows more and more apparent that it is the varying situational *contexts* that set off varying action tendencies. Unless we admit the situation in our total analysis we shall never be able to deal adequately with the problem of consistency and inconsistency in individual behavior. Nor shall we discover those conditions (for example, equal-status contact) that are known to arouse tolerant, and to weaken intolerant, modes of response.

CULTURE AND SUBCULTURE

We come now to another level of causal theory favored by many. Prejudice, we are told, is lock-stitched with the folkways of a group, with its caste system, with its institutionalized outlets for aggression.

One of the strongest arguments in favor of the sociocultural approach is this: in every society on earth the children are thought to belong to the social and religious groups of their parents. By virtue of his kinship the child is expected, among other things, to take on the prejudices of his parents, and also to become the victim of whatever prejudice is directed against them. Thus prejudice is learned with all the authoritative support of the kinship system; it is germinal in the child's identifications, sometimes essential to his very survival.

This fact helps to explain why prejudice is not easily changed by non-family agencies — by school, church, or state. Although the official creed of

America is unexceptionably tolerant, prejudice flourishes. The explanation must lie in the fact that family influence outweighs official agencies in its impact upon youth. A little girl, who no doubt was receiving democratic training at school and church, burst into tears when the Negro family in her neighborhood moved away. "Now," she sobbed, "there is no one that we are better than."

We need this sociocultural emphasis upon the demand of individual and family for status. Psychologists, at least until the recent past, have talked more about hunger and sex than about self-esteem. Sociologists and anthropologists, by and large, are more properly aware of the basic importance of caste, power structure, and sanctions.

Another merit of the sociocultural approach lies in its insistence that there are "standard meanings" which in a rough way each member of a social group admits. It is only in recent years, thanks to the assistance of sociologists and anthropologists, that psychologists have begun to employ culturally established frames of reference as a starting point for an analysis of the social consciousness and behavior of the individual. It is by and large a wholesome thing to do.[2]

From the sociocultural approach come many important findings, among them the following:

> Only in a highly differentiated society where multiple secondary groups exist is there such a thing as group prejudice. A homogeneous society, such as the Navaho, may sanction hostility toward individual outcasts (witches) but not toward groups within the society (cf. Kluckhohn, 1944).
>
> Even a differentiated society does not generate acute intergroup hostility unless there is possible upward mobility within the social structure.
>
> The more numerous the members in an upwardly mobile minority group, the greater the prejudice against them.
>
> In times of rapid social change, and in times of calamity and war, prejudice mounts.
>
> Whenever a culture permits exploitative gains at the expense of a

[2] Wholesome though it is, there is a certain trap in this approach. To illustrate, I refer to an excellent recent textbook. Within the space of a few pages the author speaks of "shared meaning," "shared codes," "shared interests," "shared norms," "shared values," and "shared frame of reference." The trap lies in the Hegelian style of terminology. Just *where* is the norm or code that we "share"? Do we in fact "share" it, or have we in our minds only a personal and approximate version of the code? And is not the code itself merely an abstraction from many different (though comparable) codes that separate individuals have? The psychologist should not forget that every person is a unique unit and that his mental furnishing is his own — not "shared."

It seems appropriate enough for sociologists and anthropologists to speak of "shared values" and "shared codes," for by the nature of their profession their view of social conduct is normally "superorganic." But the psychologist has the inescapable duty to keep firmly in sight the unique and personal formations of meaning and evaluation in which all social norms are selectively rendered. While such formations may in many cases be *comparable* individual by individual, they are never actually *shared*.

minority group, prejudice is great. In our own society status-gains result
from social anti-Semitism (McWilliams, 1948), economic gains from exploitation of the Negro (Cox, 1948), sexual gains from intimidation of
the Negro male (Myrdal, 1944), and political gains from manipulated
anti-Semitism (Lowenthal and Guterman, 1949). Currently we see the
enormous political benefits that accrue to demagogues who fan the flames
of anti-Communist feeling.

To a truly extraordinary degree the prejudices of the dominant society
infect all subgroups within that society. Thus even in such a diverse culture area as America it is found that the order of preference for various
ethnic groups is nearly universal (cf. Newcomb, 1950, p. 581). So prevalent is this standard of judgment that members of certain minorities
even become infected with the prevailing scorn and dislike for themselves.

All legends that sustain and justify prejudice are part of the cultural
heritage. To take but one important consequence of this fact: every nation or clan has in its history the account of a "golden age." Modern
Greeks can judge their worth in terms of Greece's glorious antiquity.
Italians have their Renaissance. The Catholic Church once held all of
Christendom. Boston was once the hub of the universe. Thanks to this
golden-age legend — to its historical halo — nearly everyone on earth
can, with a bit of contriving, look down on nearly everyone else.

THE HISTORICAL APPROACH

This example leads us finally to our need for historical perspective. Without it all theories of prejudice seem foreshortened. One historian, in criticiz-
ing approaches made exclusively in terms of personality structure, writes,
"Such studies are enlightening only within narrow limits. For personality is
itself conditioned by social forces; in the last analysis, the search for understanding must reach into the broad social context within which personality
is shaped" (Handlin, 1949).

Take anti-Semitism — the most ancient known form of prejudice that is
still extant. Without the historical approach this phenomenon is almost unin-
telligible. For one thing, only history allows us to see how throughout the
ages Jews have been forced to occupy a position at the "fringe of stable
values" — as money-lenders, entertainers, entrepreneurs — in addition to (or
because of) their deviance in religious belief. The historical view helps us
likewise to understand why people at the fringe of stable values are regarded
as threatening agents by conservatives in every era; and why at certain
periods of time conditions have been ripe for persecution, pogroms, genocide.
Using the historical method, Massing (1949) has shown how the Nazi manipulations of anti-Semitism were a culmination of events in German social and
political life during the decades preceding Hitler's rise to power.

How could one comprehend the peculiar pattern of prejudice against the Negro in this country without a historical knowledge of slavery, emancipation, and carpetbagging? Historical patterns, even historical "accidents," form an essential ground work for research in prejudice. It may well be, as my colleague Jerome Bruner has remarked, that it is the historical process that establishes the Jew rather than the redhead as the object of prejudice. If perchance events had been such that the villainy of Frederick Barbarossa had been perpetuated over the centuries by other redheads, we might today have to cope with anti-rufutism.

It is not necessary to multiply instances. We have reason to regret the almost complete separation of psychology and history in our programs of teaching and research. While happy *rapprochements* are being effected between psychology and other social sciences, the gap between psychology and history is still wide.

One type of historical theory, economic determinism, should not be overlooked. Economic considerations enter not only in the broad sweep of history but focus our attention upon the exploitative elements in all cultures. Economic conditions likewise create situational fields to which the individual is forced to respond, sometimes in a prejudiced manner. And finally within personality structure itself, as I have pointed out, property demands, like sex, may determine the functional significance of prejudice in a given life. It would be as great an error to overlook economic considerations as to make them solely responsible for all group bias as Cox (1944) has done.

CONCLUSION

I have been using the topic of prejudice in order to adumbrate the problem of explanation and causation in social psychology.[3] Conceivably the time may come when all social science will employ a single set of descriptive dimensions and state its causal propositions at one and the same level of abstraction. Pioneer efforts in this direction are made in the present volume. But for the time being I believe the best we can do is to regard any social issue as accessible to several different but equally valid levels of analysis — analysis in terms of the stimulus object, the phenomenal field, the dynamics and structure of the individual life; the surrounding situation; the underlying cultural norms and laws of social structure and action; and the total relevant historical context. Not only prejudice but religious behavior, economic behavior, domestic behavior — almost any type of human conduct that is not exclusively reflex or biological can and should be viewed through this series

---

[3] Positivists will object to the frank and naïve use of "causation" throughout this paper. I make no apology. Methodologists who banish causation from the front door often admit it surreptitiously at the back. Or else they spin their logic too fine for the present needs of social science. To my mind social science at its present stage of development will be concerned with causation, or else it will be concerned with nothing of consequence.

of lenses. Causation may be proximate, or causation may be ultimate. Forces may be precipitating or underlying; they may be in the foreground or in the background. A social scientist is free to select his own level of approach, but he should be respectfully aware of the whole etiological sweep.

BIBLIOGRAPHY

Ackerman, N. W., and M. Jahoda. *Anti-Semitism and Emotional Disorder.* New York: Harper's, 1950.

Adorno, T. W., E. Frenkel-Brunswik, D. J. Levinson, R. N. Sanford. *The Authoritarian Personality.* New York: Harper's, 1950.

Allport, G. W. Review of M. Horkheimer and S. H. Flowerman (eds.), *Studies in Prejudice,* in *Scientific American,* Vol. 182 (1950), no. 6, pp. 56–58.

——— "A Psychological Approach to the Study of Love and Hate." Chapter 7 of P. A. Sorokin (ed.), *Explorations in Altruistic Love and Behavior.* Boston: Beacon Press, 1950.

——— and B. M. Kramer. "Some Roots of Prejudice," *Journ. Psychol.,* XXII (1946), 3–39.

——— and L. Postman. *The Psychology of Rumor.* New York: Holt, 1947.

Bettelheim, B., and M. Janowitz. *Dynamics of Prejudice: a Psychological and Sociological Study of Veterans.* New York: Harper's, 1950.

Bixler, R. H. "How G. S. Became a Scapegoater." *Journ. Abnorm. and Soc. Psychol.,* XLIII (1948), 230–232.

Bruner, J. S. "Perceiving and the Dynamics of Personality," in R. Blake and G. Ramsey (eds.), *Perception: an Approach to Personality.* New York: Ronald Press, 1950.

Campbell, A. A. "Factors Associated with Attitudes toward Jews," in T. M. Newcomb and E. L. Hartley (eds.), *Readings in Social Psychology.* New York: Holt, 1947.

Citron, A. F., I. Chein, and J. Harding. "Anti-Minority Remarks: A Problem for Action Research," *Journ. Abnorm. and Soc. Psychol.,* XLV (1950), 99–126.

Coutu, W. *Emergent Human Nature.* New York: Knopf, 1949.

Cox, O. C. *Caste, Class, and Race.* New York: Doubleday, 1948.

Deri, S., D. Dinnerstein, J. Harding, and A. D. Pepitone. "Techniques for the Diagnosis and Measurement of Intergroup Attitudes and Behavior," *Psychol. Bull.,* XLV (1948), 248–271.

Deutsch, M. "The Directions of Behavior: A Field-theoretical Approach to the Understanding of Inconsistencies." *Journ. Soc. Issues,* V (1949), no. 3, 43–51.

——— and M. E. Collins. "Intergroup Relations in Interracial Housing: A Study of the Socio-psychological Effects of Occupancy Pattern." Unpublished. New York University, Research Center for Human Relations 1949.

Deutscher, M., and I. Chein. "The Psychological Effect of Enforced Segregation — A Survey of Social Science Opinion," *Journ. Psychol.,* XXVI (1948), 259–287.

Dodd, S. "A Social Distance Test in the Near East," *Amer. Journ. Sociol.,* XLI (1935), 194–204.

Doob, L. "The Behavior of Attitudes," *Psychol. Rev.* LIV (1947), 135–156.

Escalona, S. K. "Overt Sympathy with the Enemy in Maladjusted Children," *Amer. Journ. Orthopsychiatry,* XVI (1946), 333–340.

Frenkel-Brunswik, E. "A Study of Prejudice in Children," *Human Relations*, I (1948), 295–306.

Fromm, E. *Man for Himself*. New York: Rinehart, 1947.

Gough, H. G. "Studies in Social Intolerance." *Journ. Soc. Psychol.* (in press).

Handlin, Oscar. "Prejudice and Capitalist Exploitation," *Commentary*, VI (1948), 79–85.

Hartley, E. L. *Problems in Prejudice*. New York: King's Crown Press, 1946.

—— M. Rosenbaum, and S. Schwartz. "Children's Perception of Ethnic Group Membership," *Journ. Psychol.*, XXVI (1948), 387–398.

Heider, F. "Social Perception and Phenomenal Causality," *Psychol. Rev.*, LI (1944), 358–374.

Horowitz, E. L. "The Development of Attitudes toward the Negro," *Archives of Psychol.*, 1936, No. 194.

Ichheiser, G. "Projection and the Mote-Beam Mechanism," *Journ. Abnorm. and Soc. Psychol.*, XLII (1947), 131–133.

Kilpatrick, W. H., and W. Van Til (eds.). *Intercultural Attitudes in the Making*. New York: Harper's, 1947.

Klineberg, O. (ed.). *Characteristics of the American Negro*. New York: Harper's, 1944.

Kluckhohn, Clyde. *Navaho Witchcraft*. Cambridge: Peabody Museum of American Archaeology and Ethnology, 1944.

Kramer, B. M. "Dimensions of Prejudice," *Journ. Psychol.*, XXVII (1949), 389–451.

Kutner, B. J. "Patterns of Mental Functioning Associated with Prejudice in Children." Unpublished thesis, Harvard University, 1950.

Lewin, Kurt. "Frontiers in Group Dynamics: II. Channels of Group Life; Social Planning and Action Research," *Human Relations*, I (1947), 143–153.

—— *Resolving Social Conflicts*. New York: Harper's, 1948.

Lindzey, G. E. "An Experimental Examination of the Scapegoat Theory of Prejudice," *Journ. Abnorm. and Soc. Psychol.*, XLII (1950), 296–309.

Lowenthal, L., and N. Guterman. *Prophets of Deceit*. New York: Harper's, 1949.

MacKenzie, B. K. "The Importance of Contact in Determining Attitudes toward Negroes," *Journ. Abnorm. and Soc. Psychol.*, (1948), 43, 417–441.

McWilliams, C. *A Mask for Privilege*. Boston: Little, Brown, 1948.

Malherbe, E. G. *Race Attitudes and Education*. Johannesburg, South Africa: Institute of Race Relations, 1946.

Maslow, A. H. "The Authoritarian Character Structure," *Journ. Soc. Psychol.*, XVIII (1943), 401–411.

—— "Self-actualizing People: A Study of Psychological Health," *Personality Symposium*, 1949, no. 1, pp. 11–34.

Massing, P. W. *Rehearsal for Destruction: A Study of Political Anti-Semitism in Imperial Germany*. New York: Harper's, 1949.

Morlan, G. K. "The Statistical Concept of Normal: A Criticism," *Journ. Gen. Psychol.*, XXXVIII (1948), 51–56.

Morse, N. C. "Anti-Semitism: A Study of Its Causal Factors and Other Associated Variables." Unpublished thesis, Syracuse University, 1947.

Myrdal, Gunnar. *An American Dilemma*. 2 vols. New York: Harper's, 1944.

Newcomb, T. M. "Autistic hostility and social reality," *Human Relations*, I (1947), 69–86.

———— *Social Psychology.* New York: Dryden Press, 1950.

Postman, L. "Perception and Social Behavior," in *Social Psychology at the Crossroads.* Norman: University of Oklahoma Press, 1950.

Razran, G. "Ethnic Dislikes and Stereotypes: A Laboratory Study," *Journ. Abnorm. and Soc. Psychol.,* XLV (1950), 7–27.

Reichard, S. "Rorschach Study of Prejudiced Personality," *Amer Journ. Orthopsychiatry,* XVIII (1948), 280–286.

Robinson, D., and S. Rohde. "Two Experiments with an Anti-Semitism Poll," *Journ. Abnorm. and Soc. Psychol.,* XLI (1946), 136–144.

Rokeach, M. "Generalized Mental Rigidity as a Factor in Ethnocentrism," *Journ. Abnorm. and Soc. Psychol.,* XLIII (1948), 259–278.

Roper, E. "United States Anti-Semites," *Fortune,* February, 1946, pp. 257 ff.

Seeleman, V. "The Influence of Attitude upon the Remembering of Pictorial Material," *Archives of Psychol.,* 1940. No. 258.

Simmel, E. (ed.). *Anti-Semitism: A Social Disease.* New York: International Universities Press, 1948.

Smith, M. B. "The Personal Setting of Public Opinion: A Study of Attitudes toward Russia. *Publ. Opin. Quart.,* Winter 1947–48, pp. 507–523.

Stouffer, S. A., E. A. Suchman, L. C. DeVinney, S. A. Star, R. M. Williams, Jr. *The American Soldier.* Vol. I. Princeton: Princeton University Press, 1949.

Tolman, E. C. "The Psychology of Social Learning," *Journ. Soc. Issues, Suppl. Series,* no. 3, 1949.

Trager, H. C., and M. Radke. "Early Childhood Airs Its Views," *Educational Leadership,* V (1947), 16–23.

Vickery, W. E., and M. E. Opler. "A Redefinition of Prejudice for Purposes of Social Science Research," *Human Relations,* I (1948), 419–428.

Zawadski, B. "Limitations of the Scapegoat Theory of Prejudice," *Journ. Abnorm. and Soc. Psychol.,* XLII (1948), 127–141.

2

CLYDE KLUCKHOHN AND OTHERS

Values and Value-Orientations in the Theory of Action[1]

An Exploration in Definition and Classification

Human life is — and has to be — a moral life precisely because it is a social life, and in the case of the human species coöperation and other necessities of social life are not taken care of automatically by instincts as with the social insects. In common-sense terms, morals are socially agreed upon values relating to conduct. To this degree morals — and all group values — are the products of social interaction as embodied in culture. From this point of view the examination which follows largely proceeds. On the other hand, there is a sense in which "conscience" may be said to be the last residuum of instinctive behavior in man — other than the relatively few hu-

[1] Various drafts of this paper have had the benefit of a critical reading by David Aberle, Chester I. Barnard, Munro Edmonson, Rose Goldsen, Florence Kluckhohn, Donald Michael, Donald Marquis, Robert Morison, Henry A. Murray, Thomas O'Dea, Talcott Parsons, John Peirce, John M. Roberts, Lauriston Sharp, Eliseo Vivas, E. Z. Vogt, John W. M. Whiting, and Robin Williams; their comments and criticisms have led to major revisions.

Grateful acknowledgment is made to the University of Nebraska and to the Division of Social Sciences, Rockefeller Foundation, for opportunities which have contributed to the writing of this paper. In April 1948, I was privileged to give the Montgomery Lectures at the University of Nebraska on the subject "An Anthropologist Looks at Values." Participation in the project, "A Comparative Study of Values in Five Cultures," supported by a grant from the Rockefeller Foundation, has greatly facilitated my research and thinking in this field. Finally, I am indebted to the "Summary of Discussions of the Cornell Value Study Group" (June 11, 1949). I am grateful to this group and to its chairman, Robin Williams, for permission to quote liberally from this valuable but unpublished memorandum.

It would be improper to claim single authorship for this paper, for I have borrowed ideas, sentences, and phrases from unpublished memoranda and oral communications from at least the following colleagues and students: David Aberle, Eleanor Hollenberg, William Lambert, David McClelland, Kaspar Naegele, Thomas O'Dea, John M. Roberts, Katherine Spencer, Arthur Vidich, E. Z. Vogt, and John W. M. Whiting. I have been benefitted by their help in the "Comparative Study of Values in Five Cultures" project. On the other hand, none of these individuals is to be blamed for any statement made herein; responsibility, though not originality, rests entirely with the senior author. Finally, I have incorporated with minor changes a few sentences from the chapter on values in Part II of this book.

man reflexes. At very least "conscience" certainly has a biological basis, though a broad and long-term one. Later in this essay the relations and distinctions between "values" and concepts such as "motivation," "drive," and "need," which have a strong biological reference, will be examined at some length. First we must make a detailed exploration of the concept "value." Since this will be oriented primarily by considerations of social science, it is probably inevitable that aesthetic values are inadequately dealt with. It is felt, as indicated below, that in a very broad and general way the same principles apply to aesthetic and expressive values as to moral and cognitive values. However, a conceptual analysis on the aesthetic side as full as that which follows on the ethical must be a separate task.

Charles Elton, the ecologist, has observed that it is not much use to observe and describe animals until you can name them. Data and reasoning can bring about more confusion than enlightenment unless they are firmly attached to referents which, if not universally accepted, are at least thoroughly understood. Indeed some philosophers today even define science as "the techniques for giving words precise meanings." A concept is a word which has been given a precise meaning. The term *value* urgently requires an attempt at precise definition of the conceptual territory covered and not covered before it can serve effectively as an analytical element in the theory of action. Moreover, as the Cornell value-study group has observed:

> The concept "value" supplies a point of convergence for the various specialized social sciences, and is a key concept for the integration with studies in the humanities. Value is potentially a bridging concept which can link together many diverse specialized studies — from the experimental psychology of perception to the analysis of political ideologies, from budget studies in economics to aesthetic theory and philosophy of language, from literature to race riots . . .
>
> Sophisticated use of value-theory can help to correct the wide-spread static-descriptive bias of the social sciences. (The pervasive emphasis, for example, upon static-equilibrium theories in economics; upon "social structure" in sociology: upon static "need-reduction" theories of personality in psychology.)

In addition to the varied and shifting connotations of *value* in ordinary speech, the word is a technical term in philosophy, economics, the arts, and, increasingly, in sociology, psychology, and anthropology. There can hardly be said to be an established consensus in any one of these fields. L. M. Fraser has shown that in economics there are three main senses, each with sub-variants.[2] In philosophy, there are numerous competing definitions.[3] One current of philosophical thought has distinguished the right (ethics) from

---

[2] *Economic Thought and Language* (London, 1937).

[3] The social scientist will find *Value Theory: A Coöperative Inquiry* (1949), edited by Ray Lepley, perhaps the most useful introduction to the current state of philosophical discussion.

the good (values). Charles Morris has recently defined the study of values as "the science of preferential behavior." Ralph Barton Perry's well-known definition is "any object of any interest." Reading the voluminous, and often vague and diffuse, literature on the subject in the various fields of learning, one finds values considered as attitudes, motivations, objects, measureable quantities, substantive areas of behavior, affect-laden customs or traditions, and relationships such as those between individuals, groups, objects, events. The only general agreement is that values somehow have to do with normative as opposed to existential propositions.

NORMATIVE AND EXISTENTIAL PROPOSITIONS

It is often said that all value judgments are selective and discriminative ways of responding. If this is accepted, there is nothing which cannot be — which has not been — "valued" by someone in some situation. The work of Adelbert Ames and Hadley Cantril, among others, has demonstrated the evaluative element in sheer perception. It is easy to magnify out of all proportion the distance from the indicative to the optative and imperative modes. Existential propositions often have nonempirical elements — for example, "There is a God." Charles Morris has shown that factual, wish, and appraisal sentences all have empirical, syntactical, and pragmatic or technic reference, but they differ in the degree to which various elements of reference are present.[4] There is a difference of emphasis, but the difference is seldom of an all-or-none character. A judgment that a person is destructive, greedy, jealous, envious is not too different from a physician's statement about a dysfunction of the heart or lungs. It can be argued that in both cases the underlying assumption is that of a lack of healthy fulfillment of naturally given potentialities.

In reaction against the prevalent intellectual folklore regarding the utter separateness of fact and value, some scholars have tried to merge the two categories. E. L. Thorndike, for example, in his 1935 presidential address to the American Association for the Advancement of Science, said:

Judgments of value are simply one sort of judgments of fact, distinguished from the rest by two characteristics: They concern consequences. These are consequences to the wants of sentient beings. Values, positive and negative, reside in the satisfaction or annoyance felt by animals, persons or deities. If the occurrence of X can have no influence on the satisfaction or discomfort of any one present or future, X has no value, is neither good nor bad, desirable nor undesirable. Values are functions of preferences. Judgments about values — statements that A is good, B is bad, C is right, D is useful — refer ultimately to satisfactions or annoyances in sentient creatures and depend

---

[4] *Signs, Language and Behavior* (1946). See also Charles L. Stevenson, *Ethics and Language* (1944), esp. chap. iii, which shows "how emotive and descriptive meanings are related, each modifying the other."

upon their preferences. Competent students judge the existence of things by observations of them: they judge the values of things by observations of their consequences.[5]

Reservations that are necessary concerning consequences as an operational test of values (at least as far as the more ultimate values are concerned) will be presented in the last section of this paper. With Thorndike's statement that the linkage between normative and existential propositions rests in the conception of the nature of things in relation to human interests we are in hearty agreement.

Ray Lepley, in a paper entitled "The Identity of Fact and Value," has argued that the separation of the two categories results solely from our conventional habits of thought:

The belief that valuative statements as expressive of means-end relations are inherently different from scientific propositions as denoting cause-effect relations has apparently risen, as has the view that valuative sentences are less verifiable than factual statements, from failure to see that the whole gamut of events and relations can be referred to by both forms of statement, and this failure has perhaps in turn risen from failure to escape wholly from what Dewey has deplored as the subjectivistic psychology. The habit of looking at personal and social events and relations from the inner, subjective viewpoint and referring to them in more valuative terms and of surveying non-human organic and especially inorganic events and relations and the outer, objective viewpoint and denoting them in more factual terms has given rise to the notions that means-end and cause-effect relations are inherently different, and that therefore factual and valuative propositions are inherently different because they respectively denote these two supposedly distinct kinds of relations.[6]

This much is certainly true: "The whole gamut of events and relations can be referred to by both forms of statement." Here is the source of much of our confusion. One can and does think both about values and about existence. And the two modes are often linked in the same proposition. "This is a value for me" is an existential proposition about me. When the scientist says, "This is valid," he is making an evaluation in terms of an existential standard, but he is not affectively neutral toward his utterance, for it is made partly in terms of his highest values: truth, validity, correctness.

There can be no doubt that an individual's or a group's conceptions of what is and of what ought to be are intimately connected. As McKeon says:

In the context of cultural expressions, ideas and ideals are not opposed to facts or derived from interests but are themselves facts. In that factual context the preferable and the possible are determined by what men want or think they want and by the social order which they plan or dream as means to attain it, not by what can be shown to be better for them on some grounds of practical or scientific argument and on some analysis of fact and prac-

---

[5] *Science*, January 3, 1936.
[6] *Philosophy of Science*, X (1943), 124–131.

ticability, or by what they can secure or think they can secure by negotiation with those possessed of related and opposed interests.[7]

Northrop is probably right in maintaining that primitive [8] concepts of nature and primitive postulates about nature underlie any value system. Values go back to a conception of nature, "verified" by facts which are in some sense independent of culture. However, the primitive concepts and primitive postulates are not independent of culture. We live in a world where the same sets of phenomena are being accounted for by different postulates and concepts. Different cultures are tied to different conceptualizations.

It can, however, be said that in all cultures "normal" individuals recognize some natural limitations upon what can be. To take an almost absurd but clear example: In their conceptions of a desirable state of affairs people do not postulate conditions under which the law of gravity ceases to operate, the threats and irritations of climatic variations disappear completely, or food and drink appear spontaneously ready for consumption.

Values are constrained within the framework of what is taken as given by nature. If the nature of human nature is conceived as intrinsically evil, men are not enjoined to behave like gods; though if human nature is believed to be perfectible, they may be. In other words, existential propositions also supply the clues for major values. The Navaho think of the natural order as potentially harmonious. It is therefore a prime value of Navaho ceremonialism to maintain, promote, or restore this potential harmony.[9]

George Lundberg has done a service in calling attention to the interdependence between normative and existential propositions, but he has strained unduly to dissolve the distinction completely. He writes:

The first step toward the recognition of the essential basic similarity of scientific and ethical statements will have been taken when we recognize that all "should" or "ought" statements, as well as scientific statements, represent *an expectation* which is, in effect, a prediction. This is true of such varied forms as "if the gasoline line and the ignition are both in order (etc.), then the engine ought to start"; or "he [under stated or implied circumstances] ought to be ashamed," (i.e., "if he were a 'decent,' 'civilized,' socially sensitive person, then he ought to be ashamed"). Sometimes the actual expectation may be very low and, in fact, may represent merely the individual's wishful thinking, that is, expectation according to the standards of an ideal or dream world; e.g., "People should not (ought not) gossip"; "We should love our enemies." (Incidentally, the latter statement involves a semantic confusion of its own in that, by definition, an enemy is someone not loved, i.e., if we loved our enemies we would no longer regard them as enemies.) *Expected behavior* of some kind (under whatever circumstances are assumed),

---

[7] Conflicts of Values in a Community of Cultures", *Journal of Philosophy*, XLVII (1950), 202.

[8] In, of course, the meaning of modern logic.

[9] See Clyde Kluckhohn, "The Philosophy of the Navaho Indians," in *Ideological Differences and World Order*, edited by F. S. C. Northrop (1949).

is implicit in all "ought" statements. Mankind often disappoints us; our predictions in this area are not, as yet, as accurate as those of the meteorologist. But this is merely saying that (a) the probability of the sequence "if . . . then" varies; that (b) the stipulated conditions or desiderata vary; and that (c) both may be misgauged in physical as well as in social affairs. Thus, all "ought" statements are essentially of the "if . . . then" type characteristic also of all scientific statements.

Why, then, do we have the deep-seated feeling regarding the difference between scientific and ethical statements? One, and perhaps the principal, reason is that certain implicit unspoken premises in ethical statements are usually overlooked, whereas in scientific statements these premises are always recognized. This fact, in turn, is related to a subtle and unrecognized assumption that, while scientific statements describe events of nature, ethical statements describe only personalistic judgments, wishes, or whims, whether of men or of gods. These latter are assumed not to be amenable to the methods found effective in predicting "natural" phenomena. Actually, as I have pointed out elsewhere, (*Can Science Save Us?* pp. 26–33, 97–103), the word "Values" refers to *valuating behavior* of some sort and as such can be studied scientifically like any other behavior. Most of our statistics on prices, salaries, occupations, migrations, consumption and, for that matter, all so-called "voluntary" or "choice" behavior whatsoever are studies of human "Values."

Consider, from this point of view, the following illustrations: (1) "If [specifying all the necessary and sufficient conditions], then we shall (with stated degree of probability) avoid another war." How does it differ from this statement: (2) "We ought to avoid another war"? Implicit in the "ought" form of this statement is the unspoken premise *"if we want to avoid all the undesirable consequences entailed in another war,* then we should (ought to) prevent another war." This proposition depends for its validity on (a) the accuracy of the estimated probability that another war would, in fact, entail the expected undesirable consequences, and (b) the reliability of the prediction that certain conditions prevent or produce war (the "if" clause of statement I) — both of them questions that can be approached by the same scientific methods as the first proposition. The reader is invited — and challenged — to produce a single "ought" statement which cannot be more fully expressed in the "if . . . then" form. At least one premise usually will be found unspoken, implicit, and taken for granted. That premise *implies a desideratum* which, it is assumed by the speaker of an "ought" statement, is a necessary and sufficient condition for the occurrence (or non-occurrence) of what it is asserted "ought" to happen.[10]

What Lundberg apparently fails to see is the somewhat arbitrary process of selection involved in his "unspoken" premises relating to the desirable. Values, as has been pointed out, are limited by nature and depart in some sense from nature, but are only to a limited extent given by nature. Existential propositions purport to describe nature and the necessary interconnections of natural prenomena. Values say, in effect: "This appears to be naturally possible. It does not exist or does not fully exist, but we want to move toward

[10] "Semantics and the Value Problem," *Social Forces*, XXVII (1948), 114–116. Cf. Max Weber, *The Methodology of the Social Sciences*, edited by Shils and Finch (1949), esp. pp. 50–55.

it, or, it already exists but we want to preserve and maintain it. Moreover, we aver that this is a proper or appropriate or justified want." Lundberg also equivocates in his use of "expected" between what is anticipated as a result of the operation of natural processes and what is demanded or hoped for in terms of humanly created standards. Finally, it should be noted that existential statements often reflect prior value judgments. In scientific discourse, at least, our propositions relate to matters we consider important.

"Nature" is one frame of reference; "action" is another frame of reference. In the former, one need only ask, "Is this the case (fact)?" In the latter, one must ask both this question and, "Ought this to be the case (value) in the conceptions of the subject(s) of the enquiry?" The two frames of reference, as has been shown, are intimately related. Perhaps one further statement is in order:

Because man inevitably builds up for himself an assumptive world in carrying out his purposive activities, the world he is related to, the world he sees, the world he is operating on, and the world that is operating on him is the result of a transactional process in which man himself plays an active role. Man carries out his activities in the midst of concrete events which themselves delimit the significances he must deal with.[11]

Existence and value are intimately related, interdependent, and yet — at least at the analytical level — conceptually distinct. It is a fact both of introspection and of observation that there are three fundamental types of experiencing: what is or is believed to be (existential); what I and/or others want (desire); what I and/or others ought to want (the desirable). Values are manifested in ideas, expressional symbols, and in the moral and aesthetic norms evident in behavioral regularities. Whether the cognitive or the cathectic factors have primacy in the manifestation of a value at a particular time, both are always present. Values synthesize cognitive and cathectic elements in orientations to an object world, most specifically a social object world — that it, a social relationship system. Values define the limits of permissible cost of an expressional gratification or an instrumental achievement by invoking the consequences of such action for other parts of the system and for the system as a whole.

DEFINITION OF VALUE FOR THE THEORY OF ACTION

No definition can hope to incorporate or synthesize all aspects of each conception established in the various fields of learning and yet remain serviceable. Selection or construction of a definition for our purposes must depend upon convenience (considering, of course, the problems at hand) and

---

[11] H. Cantril, A. Ames, Jr., A. H. Hastorf, and W. H. Ittelson, "Psychology and Scientific Research: III. The Transactional View in Psychological Research," *Science*, November 18, 1949.

upon meeting the special requirements of basic social science. Convenience demands doing as little violence as possible to whatever established core of meaning may exist in familiar usages in ordinary language and scholarly terminology. It also requires simplicity so far as this is consistent with precision.

Value implies a code or a standard which has some persistence through time, or, more broadly put, which organizes a system of action. Value, conveniently and in accordance with received usage, places things, acts, ways of behaving, goals of action on the approval-disapproval continuum. Furthermore, following Dewey, "the desirable" is to be contrasted with "the desired." Cathexis and valuation, though concretely interdependent in some respects, are distinguished in the world of experience and must therefore be distinguished conceptually. In all cultures people have wants for themselves and for a group which they blame themselves for wanting — or which at very least they do not feel or consider to be justifiable. Such cases represent negative valuation, to be sure, but the point here is the nonidentity of the desired and the desirable. The existence of the value element transforms the desired into the not-desired or into the ambivalently desired.[12]

A value is a conception, explicit or implicit, distinctive of an individual or characteristic of a group, of the desirable which influences the selection from available modes, means, and ends of action. A commentary on each term in this definition will be set forth below. It should be emphasized here, however, that affective ("desirable"), cognitive ("conception"), and conative ("selection") elements are all essential to this notion of *value*. This definition takes culture, group, and the individual's relation to culture and place in his group [13] as primary points of departure. Later a definition within the psychological frame of reference will be presented.

A *conception* identifies value as a logical construct comparable to culture or social structure.[14] That is, values are not directly observable any more

---

[12] Pragmatically speaking, values are also more or less stable ways of resolving ambivalence. That is, actors perhaps most often think about and refer to values when they are in doubt about alternative courses of conduct: when the long-run results of the possible selections of paths of behavior are not immediately obvious or scientifically demonstrable or when the pressures of personal motivation are strong on one side and social sanctions or practical expediency of some other kind strong on the other side.

[13] For example, a value is classified in a following section as "idiosyncratic" or "personal" only because the group is taken as the standard of reference and because values are taken as communicated and transmitted by symbolic means.

[14] In spite of the fact that *conception* is a noun this definition is thoroughly congruent with Lepley's "adjectival" position on *value*: "The underlying issue . . . is whether 'value' is a noun standing for something that is an entity in its own right or whether the word is adjectival, standing for a property or quality that belongs, under specifiable conditions, to a thing or person having existence independently of being valued. If the first view is adopted, then to say that a diamond, or a beloved person, or holding an official position, has or is a value, is to affirm that a connection somehow has been set up between two separate and unlike entities. If the second view is held, then it is held that a thing, in virtue of identifiable and describable events, has acquired a quality or property not

than culture is. Both values and culture are based upon what is said and done by individuals but represent inferences and abstractions from the immediate sense data. The statement, "people ought to help each other," is not a value in strict usage but rather one manifestation of a value. In its analytic meaning, the locus of value is neither in the organism nor in the immediately observable world; its locus is rather that of all scientific abstractions. Concretely, of course, any given value is in some sense "built into" the apperceptive mass or neural nets of the persons who hold that value — in the same way that a culture is "built into" its carriers. However, the social science abstraction "value" is not abstracted from neurological properties but from verbal and nonverbal behavioral events. These internalized symbolic systems do have a special status as regards methodology, requiring in part, at least at present, a *verstehen* rather than an *erklären* type of interpretation.

A value is not just a preference but is a preference which is felt and/or considered to be justified — "morally" or by reasoning or by aesthetic judgments, usually by two or all three of these. Even if a value remains implicit, behavior with reference to this *conception* indicates an undertone of the desirable — not just the desired. The desirable is what it is felt or thought proper to want. It is what an actor or group of actors desire — and *believe* they "ought" or "should" desire — for the individual or a plurality of individuals. This means that an element, though never an exclusive element, of the cognitive is always involved; and hence the word *conception* was deliberately included in the definition. The observer imputes to actor or actors ideas held in an implicit sense. Values are ideas formulating action commitments. These ideas are instigators of behavior "within" the individual but are not to be conceived as internal social "forces" in the classical sense of the word "force." Operationally, the observer notes certain kinds of patterned behavior. He cannot "explain" these regularities unless he subsumes certain aspects of the processes that determine concrete acts under the rubric "value."

The history of thought has always more or less clearly distinguished values from sentiments,[15] emotions, drives, and needs. To the extent that man is a species characterized by a propensity for rationalizing his acts verbally,

---

previously belonging to it. As a thing previously hard becomes soft when affected by heat, so, on this view, something previously indifferent takes on the quality of value when it is actively cared for in a way that protects or contributes to its continued existence. Upon this view, a value-quality loses the quasi-mystical character often ascribed to it, and is capable of identification and description in terms of conditions of origin and consequence, as are other natural events" (*Value*, p. 8).

[15] It is true that William McDougall defined "sentiment" as a combination of an affective disposition with a cognitive disposition, the centering of a system of emotions about the idea of some object. His "sentiments" run the gamut of specificity all the way from the "concrete particular" (e.g., love for a certain painting) through the "concrete general" (e.g., love for paintings) to the "abstract" (e.g., love for beauty). His notion of the "sentiment" is similar at many points to ours of a "personal value" (see "Organization of the Affective Life," *Acta Psychologica*, XI [1937], 233–346).

the consistent connection between values and notions of approval and dis-approval implies the potentiality for rational justification.[16] Values are eminently discussable, even though in the case of implicit values the discus-sion does not mention what the observer would call the value but rather cen-ters on approval or disapproval of concrete acts, with the value left as the tacit premise that is the least common denominator of the reaction to these acts. Finally, something which is "desirable" (not something merely "de-sired") means an emancipation from immediate physiological stresses and from the press of a specific, ephemeral situation. Such generalization and abstraction is referable only to the realm of concepts. While there are, of course, more general and more specific values, *conception* also implies refer-ence to a class of events which may encompass a variety of content and differ considerably in detail.[17]

The phrase *explicit or implicit* is necessary to our definition since it is an induction from experience that some of the deepest and most pervasive of personal and cultural values are only partially or occasionally verbalized and in some instances must be inferential constructs on the part of the ob-server to explain consistencies in behavior. An implicit value is, however, almost always potentially expressible in rational language by actor as well as by observer. On the other hand, the fact that everybody cannot readily verbalize such conceptions does not remove them from the realm of value. It may legitimately be asked, "Can a *conception* be *implicit*?" The answer is that "verbalizable" is not to be equated with "clearly and habitually ver-balized." The actor's values are often inchoate, incompletely or inadequately verbalized by him. But implicit values remain "conceptions" in the sense that they are abstract and generalized notions which can be put into words by the observer and then agreed to or dissented to by the actor. Verbalizability is a necessary test of value.

This is perhaps a way of saying that such matters as instinctual behavior and needs are below the level of abstraction and hence not part — directly — of the realm of value. Values must be susceptible of abstraction by the ob-server and formulable by the observer in such terms that the subject can under-

---

[16] To say, following certain contemporary usage, "Eating spinach is a value for Smith," because Smith likes spinach or prefers spinach to broccoli is to confuse the desired with the desirable. This practice both negates one of the few constant differentia of value (that of approval-disapproval) and makes the category value so broad as to be useless. It is much more convenient to separate "value" and "preference," restricting "preference" to those selections which are neutral (i.e., do not require justification or reference to sanctions) from the point of view of the individual and/or the culture. Of course, if Smith justified his preference for spinach in rational or pseudo-rational terms of vita-mins, mineral content, and the like, it then becomes by definition one of his values. If, however, he simply says "I just like spinach better than broccoli," it remains a mere preference.

[17] Cf. Perry's relational definition of values: "Value arises whenever interest is taken in something and does not inhere in an object as isolated entity."

stand and agree or disagree. The subjects on ordinary verbalization with respect to values will often be oblique or indirect, and implicit values will be manifested only in behavior and through verbalizations that do not directly state the pertinent values.

Values are clearly, for the most part, cultural products. Nevertheless, each group value is inevitably given a private interpretation and meaning by each individual, sometimes to the extent that the value becomes personally distinctive. Furthermore, the facts that values change and that new values are invented could not be accounted for, did we not posit idiosyncratic as well as group values. Moreover, as the Cornell value-study group has noted:

Some values are directly involved in the individual's existence as a "self." Values which manifest this quality appear to be especially important in many ways; they are powerful in the world. These values are registered or apprehended as part of the "self," as a psychological entity or system, no matter how diverse the structure or content of specific systems may be. (The quality in question is further suggested by alternative phrasings; such values act as components of super-ego or ego-ideal; they are constitutive of the person's sense of identity; if violated, there is guilt, shame, ego-deflation, intropunitive reaction.)

The word *desirable* is crucial and requires careful clarification. It places the category in accord with the core of the traditional meaning of value in all fields, with the partial exception of the economic. Value statements are, by our tradition, normative statements as contrasted with the existential propositions to which they are closely related. In the ethical sphere the *desirable* includes both the *ius* (strictly legal or cultic prescriptions) and the *fas* (general moral commandments) of the Roman jurists. The desirable, however, is not restricted to what is commonly designated as the "moral." It includes the aesthetic and those elements of the cognitive which reflect appraisal. The cue words are "right" or "wrong," "better" or "worse." It can be argued that these words are crude scalar dimensions just as Lundberg suggests that *ought* can be considered an implicit conditionality. Nevertheless it remains a fact that in all languages such words have strongly affective and conative tinges. Even the arts not only record values but are always in some sense implicit criticisms of society. The cue words are certainly used whenever it is felt that there is an incomplete matching between an existent state of affairs and what is possible in nature. "Things would be a lot simpler if people acted the way they 'ought' to." Perhaps there is an underlying assumption of least effort as the goal and hence desirable. At any rate there can be no question at all that when one talks of values one gets somehow into the realm of cathection.

The individual, as Henry A. Murray says, can cathect anything from an object to a philosophical idea. Since value always involves affect, cathexis and value are inevitably somehow interrelated. Sometimes the relationship is that the value is little more than a rationalization for a cathexis.[18] A probable example is the widespread conception among the working class that regular sexual intercourse is necessary for health — at least the health of the male. In other cases, cathexis in the strict sense and value in the strict sense pull against each other. Disvalued activities are cathected. People are strongly attracted to adulterous relationships. Conversely, a man goes to church on Sunday when (apart from the value element) he would strongly prefer to start his golf game early.

The reason that cathexis and value seldom coincide completely is that a cathexis is ordinarily a short-term and narrow response, whereas value implies a broader and long-term view. A cathexis is an impulse; a value or values restrain or canalize impulses in terms of wider and more perduring goals. A football player wants desperately to get drunk after his first big game, but this impulse conflicts with his values of personal achievement and loyalty to his teammates, coach, and university. In a society where livelihood depends upon the coöperation of members of the extended family, the group must attach strong sanctions to values which minimize friction among the relatives who live and work together.

More abstractly, we may say that the desired which is disvalued (i.e., cathected but not desirable) is that which is incompatible with the personality as a system or with the society or culture as systems. Values define the limits of permissible cost of impulse satisfaction in accord with the whole array of hierarchical enduring goals of the personality, the requirements of both personality and sociocultural system for order, the need for respecting the interests of others and of the group as a whole in social living. The focus of codes or standards is on the integration of a total action system, whether personal or sociocultural.

The influence of value upon selective behavior is, then, always related to the incompatibilities [19] and consequences, among which are those which follow upon rejection of other possible behaviors. In cultural systems the systemic element is coherence: the components of a cultural system must, up to a point, be either logically consistent or meaningfully congruous. Otherwise the culture carriers feel uncomfortably adrift in a capricious, chaotic world. In a personality system, behavior must be reasonably regular or predictable, or the individual will not get expectable and needed responses from

[18] For further consideration of cathexis, motivation, sentiment, and value see the last section below under "Psychology."

[19] It is perfectly true that both personalities and cultures can continue to function in the face of many internal incompatibilities. Integration is tendency rather than literal fact. We all live with more incompatibilities than our personality models would suggest were possible. Too many, however, are a threat to the preservation of the system as a system. Moreover, what appear superficially as incompatibilities are seen on closer examination to be functions of varying frames of reference. Compare the aged philosophical chestnut, "One can't step into the same river twice."

others because they will feel that they cannot "depend" on him. In other words, a social life and living in a social world both require standards "within" the individual and standards roughly agreed upon by individuals who live and work together. There can be no personal security and no stability of social organization unless random carelessness, irresponsibility, and purely impulsive behavior are restrained in terms of private and group codes. Inadequate behavior is selfish from the viewpoint of society and autistic from the viewpoint of personality. If one asks the question, "Why are there values?" the reply must be: "Because social life would be impossible without them; the functioning of the social system could not continue to achieve group goals; individuals could not get what they want and need from other individuals in personal and emotional terms, nor could they feel within themselves a requisite measure of order and unified purpose." Above all, values add an element of predictability to social life.

With many older people, as has often been remarked, the sharp contrast between wish and duty tends to become obliterated. Only in the exceptional personality, however, is the Confucian state reached in which "you want to do what you have to do and have to do what you want to do." Values and motivation are linked, but only rarely do they coincide completely. Values are only an element in motivation and in determining action; they invariably have implications for motivation because a standard is not a value unless internalized. Often, however, these implications are in the nature of interference with motivation conceived in immediate and purely personal terms. When there is commitment to a value — and there is no value without some commitment [20] — its actualization is in some sense and to some degree "wanted"; but it is wanted only to the extent that it is approved. Desirability and desiredness are both involved in the internal integration of the motivational system. But values canalize motivation. This is what has happened in the case of old people whose personalities are both well adjusted and internally harmonious.

The word *desirable*, then, brings out the fact that values, whether individual or cultural (and the line between these is elusive), always have an affective as well as a cognitive dimension. Values are never immediately altered by a mere logical demonstration of their invalidity. The combination of *conception* with *desirable* establishes the union of reason and feeling inherent in the word *value*. Both components must be included in any definition. If the rational element is omitted, we are left with something not very different from "attitude" or "sentiment." When the affective aspect is omitted, we have something resembling "ethics plus aesthetic and other taste canons." The elements of "wish" and "appraisal" are inextricably united in "value."

The word *influences* would have been rejected out of hand by most sectors

---

[20] Including, of course, repudiation in the case of negative values.

of the scientific world until quite recently. It was fashionable to regard ideas of any sort as mere epiphenomena, verbal rationalizations after the fact. Mechanists, behaviorists, and positivists [21] maintained, and natural science knowledge justified them in maintaining, that human beings responded only to particulars — not to universals such as ideas. This group agreed, though for different reasons, with the idealists and dualists that "scientifically verifiable knowledge of biological and other natural systems provides no meaning for purposes, for universals, or for human behavior which is a response to and specified as to its form by a temporally persistent normative social theory." [22]

However, the work during the past twenty years of Arturo Rosenblueth, Lorente de No, Norbert Wiener, Warren McCulloch, and other neurologists, physiologists, and mathematicians has demonstrated that not only can human beings reason deductively, but that, given the structural and physiological properties of their nervous systems, they must reason deductively, responding to general ideas as well as to particulate stimuli. The anthropologist Leslie White has been proven right in saying that symbolism is "that modification of the human organism which allows it to transform physiological drive into cultural values." In addition to the newly discovered neurological basis of the determinative force of ideas in human behavior, one might also on a cruder empirical level say simply, "Consider the history of Russia since the November Revolution." [23]

Selection is used in the definition as a more neutral word than *choice*.[24] There is no intention — or any necessity — to beg any metaphysical questions regarding "free will" or "determinism." However, it is proper to point out that for certain purposes the statements, "the actor can choose" and "the actor behaves in some respects as if he had the possibility of choice," are equivalent. From the viewpoint of the social scientist the propositions, "choice is real" and "choice is psychologically real," lead inevitably to about the same operations. In any case, the matter at issue here is clear-cut: as the observer sees behavior, the actor or actors have open in the observable world more

---

[21] A leading logical positivist, while denying the "objectivity" of value judgments has recently conceded their influence upon action (A. J. Ayer, "On the Analysis of Moral Judgments," *Horizon* [London], XX [1949], no. 117; see esp. pp. 175–176).

[22] F. S. C. Northrop, "Ideological Man in His Relation to Scientifically Known Natural Man," in *Ideological Differences and World Order* (Yale University Press, 1949), p. 413. This article also gives bibliographical references to the works of the writers referred to in the next paragraph.

[23] Of course, the fundamental question is that of frame of reference, not of ontology. More than one frame of reference is legitimately operative in the scientific world. In the social sciences selection ("choice") and evaluation are inherent in the frame of reference. The biological sciences are probably a meeting ground between the physical and social sciences in this respect.

[24] The union of "desirable" and "selection" in the definition signifies that *both* affective and conative elements are essential — neither has universal primacy.

than one mode, or means, or direction of action, each of which is "objectively" open.

The reality of "choice" in human action presents one major opportunity for the study of values. Values are operative when an individual selects one line of thought or action rather than another, insofar as this selection is influenced by generalized codes rather than determined simply by impulse or by a purely rational calculus of temporary expediency. Of course, in the long run, the person who disregards values is not behaving expediently, for he will be punished by others. Most selective behavior therefore involves either the values of the actor or those of others or both.

The social scientist must be concerned with the differing conceptions of "choice" from the viewpoints of the individual actor, a group of actors, and of the observer. Most situations can be met in a variety of ways. From the actor's point of view, his degree of awareness of these various possibilities will vary in different situations: in some cases he will make a conscious choice between alternatives for action; in others, an action will appear inevitable and the actor will not be aware that any selection is being made. From the viewpoint of the observer as scientist, "choice" becomes a process of selection from a range of possibilities, many (or even all) of which may not be obvious from a cultural point of view or from the viewpoint of any given individual. These three angles of vision may overlap or diverge in differing degrees.

Available, in our definition, is another way of saying that genuine selection is involved. It does not imply that the same amount of "effort" or "striving" is necessarily involved in one mode, means, or end as opposed to another. It implies merely that various alternatives are open in the external world seen by the observer. Nor is the question of "functional effectiveness" prejudged. So far as the satisfaction of the actor's need-dispositions are concerned, this cannot always be estimated in terms of the consequences of a "choice" as seen from the standpoint of an observer. It is clear that there is always an "economy of values," for no actor has the resources or time to make all possible "choices." But the effectiveness of a selection must be interpreted, in part, in accord with the intensity with which the actor feels the value — regardles of how little sense the "choice" makes according to an observer's rational calculus.

In any case, selection of modes, ends, and means of action is assumed to involve orientation to values. The relation between such selections and the objective limitations upon them (imposed by the biological nature of man, the particular environment, and the general properties of social and cultural systems within which men inevitably live) become problems for value research. For example, in the case of the comparative study of five cultures in the Ramah area, one could examine the alternatives that are open to all five societies in particular situations and the varying "choices" which have been made. There is a range of possibilities for dealing with drought (and other common environmental pressures), and each group has "selected" varying emphases in coping with this common problem — a selection which is determined in part by its particular value system as well as by such situational factors as technological equipment and capital.

Conceptions of the desirable are not limited to proximate or ultimate goals. Ways of acting are also valued; there is discrimination in approval-disapproval terms of the manner of carrying out an action, whether the act itself be conceived as a means or as an end. It is equally a fact of ordinary experience that, even when an objective is agreed upon, there is often violent disagreement about the "rightness" or "appropriateness" of the means to be selected. Of course, the distinction between *ends* and *means* is somewhat transitory, depending upon time perspective. What at one point in the history of the individual or the group appears as an end is later seen as a means to a more distant goal. Similarly, the discrimination between *modes* and *means* is sometimes blurred (empirically, not analytically). *Mode* refers to the style in which an instrument is used. For example, the English language is learned by some foreigners as a means of obtaining positions with our establishments abroad. But the language is spoken by some softly, by others loudly, by others with exaggerated precision of enunciation. These variations in the utilization of the instrument are attributable, in part, to the cultural or personal values of the learners.

In summary, then, any given act is seen as a compromise between motivation, situational conditions, available means, and the means and goals as interpreted in value terms. Motivation arises in part from biological and situational factors. Motivation and value are both influenced by the unique life history of the individual and by culture.

OPERATIONAL INDICES

Surely one of the broadest generalizations to be made by a natural historian observing the human species is that man is an evaluating animal. Always and everywhere men are saying, "This is good"; "that is bad"; "this is better than that"; "these are higher and those lower aspirations." Nor is this type of behavior limited by any means to the verbal. Indeed it might be said that the realm of value is that of "conduct," [25] not that of "behavior" at all. Approval is shown by many kinds of expressive behavior, by deeds of support and assistance. Acts regarded as "deviant," "abnormal," and "psychotic" provide clues to conduct valued by a group. Disapproval of the acts of others or of the particular actor is manifested on a vast continuum

---

[25] "Conduct" here means regularities of action-motivation which are explicitly related to or which imply *conceptions* of desirable and undesirable behavior.

from overt aggression, through persistent avoidance, to the subtle nuances of culturally standardized facial expressions.[26] Self-disapproval is indicated by defensive verbalizations, by motor reactions which in that culture express guilt or shame, by acts of atonement. No adults, except possibly some psychotics, behave with complete indifference toward standards which transcend the exigencies of the immediate situation or the biological and psychological needs of the actor at the moment. Even criminals, though they may repudiate many or most of the codes of their society, orient their behavior toward the codes of their own deviant groups and indeed (negatively) to the cultural standards. There is almost no escaping orientation to values.

The first area of action, then, which is relevant to the study of values is that where approval or disapproval is made explicit by word or deed. "Ought" or "should" statements and all statements of preference (where the preference is directly or indirectly shown to be regarded as justifiable in moral and/or rational, including aesthetic, terms) are constantly made in daily behavior. They are also embodied in the formal oral or written literature of the group, including laws, mythology, and standardized religious dogmas. Neither in the case of the individual nor in that of the groups are such "ought" or "should" statements random or varying erratically from event to event or from situation to situation. There is always some degree of patterned recurrence.

The observer should watch not only for approval and disapproval but for all acts which elicit strong emotional responses. What, in a given society, is considered worth-while to *die* for? What frightens people — particularly in contexts where the act is apparently interpreted as a threat to the security or stability of the system? What are considered proper subjects for bitter ridicule? What types of events seem to weld a plurality of individuals suddenly into a solidary group? Tacit approval-disapproval is constantly manifested in the form of gossip. Where gossip is most current is where that culture is most heavily laden with values. The discussability of values is one of their most essential properties, though the discussion may be oblique or disguised — not labeled as a consideration of values.

The second area relevant to the study of values is that of the differential effort exhibited toward the attainment of an end, access to a means, or acquisition of a mode of behavior. Brown will work hardest to get a scholarship in a college of engineering, Smith to get a chance to act in a summer theater.[27] Americans in general will strive hardest and undergo more deprivations for "success" in the occupational system, whereas members of other cultures will characteristically give their fullest energies only to preserving a received

---

[26] It is, of course, required by the definition that regularities of action or of motivation be referable to an expressed or underlying conception.

[27] These examples may imply only motivation but in such cases motivation is partly determined by value elements.

tradition or to types of self-fulfillment that do not make them a cynosure of the public eye.

The third area, that of "choice" situations, blends into the second. When two or more pathways are equally open, and an individual or a group shows a consistent directionality in its selections, we are surely in the realm of values, provided that this directionality can be shown to be involved in the approval-disapproval continuum. An example of an individual "choice" situation is the following: Three college graduates, from the same economic group, of equal I.Q., and all destined eventually for business, are offered by their fathers the choice of a new automobile, a year of travel, or a year of graduate study. Such "choice" points come up frequently in life histories. An example of a "choice" situation at the group level is: Five groups, each with a distinct culture, who carry on subsistence agriculture in the same ecological area in the Southwest, are faced with severe drought. Two groups react primarily with increased rational and technological activity, two with increased ceremonial activity, and one with passive acceptance. It should be profitable to observe members of two or more groups confronted with *any* objective crisis situation (war, epidemic, and the like). Under such circumstances the durability of values may come to light and hence the manner in which various challenges make or do not make for the suspension of values. Both individual and group crises (birth, death, illness, fire, theft) and conflict situations (marital, political, economic) throw values into relief.

Statements about the desirable or selections between possible paths of action on the basis of implicit conceptions of the desirable are crucial in the study of values. Neither of these, however, "are" values. They are rather manifestations of the value element in action. One measures heat by a thermometer, for example, but, if one is speaking precisely, one cannot say that a temperature of ninety degrees "is" heat. The concept of "force" in physical science is comparable. No one ever sees "a force"; only the manifestations of a force are observed directly.

OPERATIONS FOR THE STUDY OF VALUES [28]

It is interesting that it is precisely in the fields rejected by the behaviorists, positivists, and reductionists that perhaps the best social science techniques have been developed: the procedures of public-opinion polling and various

---

[28] Other remarks on operational methods will be found throughout this paper. It is impossible here to refer to all the literature on methodology for the study of values. Mention should be made, however, of George D. Birkhoff's *Aesthetic Measure* (Cambridge, Mass., 1933), an attempt to arrive at objective determination of universal aesthetic values, and of Ralph White's attempts at rigorous establishment of values by content analysis. See his "Value Analysis: A Quantitative Method for Describing Qualitative Data," *Journal of Social Psychology*, XIX (1944), 351–358. Rashevsky's mathematical approach to this problem is also noteworthy. See also S. C. Dodd, "How to Measure Values," *Research Studies of the State College of Washington*, XVIII (1950), 163–168.

projective instruments. The former are well suited to the establishment of explicit values and the latter to the discovery of implicit values.

There is, first of all, the establishment of regularities in "should" or "ought" statements by the usual procedures of sampling, formal and informal interviews, recording of normal conversations, analysis of the oral or written lore of the group.[29] One must discover the prescriptions of individuals and of groups about what behavior a person of given properties should manifest in more or less specified situations. The red herring, "This doesn't tell us what the values of the individual or the society 'really' are but gives us only speech reactions," should not be drawn across this argument. The fact of uniformities in code or standards is of signal importance, regardless of what the deviations in behavior may be. Acts, as has been said, are always compromises among motives, means, situations, and values. Sometimes what a person says about his values is truer from a long-term viewpoint than inferences drawn from his actions under special conditions. The fact that an individual will lie under the stress of unusual circumstances does not prove that truth is not a value which orients, as he claims, his ordinary behavior. As a matter of fact, people often lie by their acts and tell the truth with words. The whole conventional dichotomy is misleading because speech is a form of behavior.

It is true, of course, and important that the expression of group values is a way of remaining safe in most cultures. Surface conformity values are often not really learned in the sense of being internalized — rather they have been memorized and are used as outward and visible signs of acceptability. Sometimes the majority of a group may indeed conform only on the surface, deluding each other until a crisis situation exposes the superficiality or purely verbal character of certain values. However, the persistence of "verbal" values is itself a phenomenon requiring explanation. The point is that one dare not assume *ex hypothesi* that verbal behavior tells the observer less about the "true" values than other types of action. Both verbal and non-verbal acts must be carefully studied.

The uniformities in codes and standards can, with sufficient observation, be well established and the "real" values (those that influence overt nonverbal behavior) determined by noting trends in action. These will consist, in part, in motor events manifesting approval, disapproval, and self-disapproval — particularly when such acts are carried out at some cost to the actor in terms of the expediency of the immediate situation. In part, trends will be discovered by observing differential efforts made by various individuals and groups toward the same and different goals, instruments, and modes of be-

---

[29] The work of Charles Stevenson, B. L. Whorf, Dorothy Lee, H. B. Alexander, Charles Morris, and certain of the logical positivists provides highly sophisticated materials on the relations between values and language. Anthropologists, psychologists, and sociologists have as yet but little availed themselves of these resources.

having when other conditions are approximately the same. As Lundberg has pointed out:

> It is possible to infer the values of groups from the way in which they habitually spend their time, money, and energy. This means that values may be inferred from historic records of all times, from ancient documents to the latest census of manufactures, scales, and expenditures. In this category, also, falls the large literature on budgets of monetary expenditure.[30]

Hull has also developed the notion of energy disposal or striving as a measuring device for the study of values:

> The consumption of physiological energy in the pursuit of such goals or ends may accordingly be characterized as *work* or *striving*. Thus, generally speaking, that may be said to be valued which is striven for and, other things being equal, the maximum amount of work which an organism will execute to attain a given reinforcing state of affairs may be taken as an indication of the valuation of that state of affairs by the organism. Here, then, we have the basis, not only for an experimental science of value, but also for a theoretical science of value.[31]

In terms of our definition, Lundberg's and Hull's notion of energy disposal must be refined; "striving" is not enough unless it can be shown to be connected with one or more conceptions of the desirable.

The Cornell group's consideration of operations also presents some worthwhile suggestions:

> In our discussions, two main "operational tests" were suggested as means for identifying the presence of value-phenomena. First, on the personality side, it is suggested that *when a person violates* a value he will show evidences of "ego-diminution"[32] — subjectively felt as guilt, shame, self-depreciation, etc., and objectively manifest in observable ways, e.g., in drawing a smaller picture of himself. A variety of specific techniques are available for indexing reactions of this order. A parallel test for presence of values in a social group lies in the imposition of severe negative social sanctions in the case of threat to or violation of a value. Secondly, values may be indexed in various ways by analysis of *choices* — which constitute a specific kind of evidence as to "directions of interest."

Our group discussed the relative merits of studying values in circum-

[30] "Human Values — A Research Program," *Research Studies of the State College of Washington*, 1950. Lundberg's basic point is well taken, though a caveat must be entered against the culture-bound judgment inherent in the emphasis on "money." However LePlay has utilized budget studies and other economic data in what is, substantially, the study of values. Money is, of course, merely a cover for a very large system of needs and values which in our culture become expressed for market purposes in money. One may compare the objection to Veblen's economic theory, a theory founded upon the unstated cultural value premise that the ultimate objective of a society is to produce as many goods as possible and distribute them as well as possible.

[31] "Moral Values, Behaviorism, and the World Crisis," *Transactions of the New York Academy of Sciences*, VII (1945), 80–84.

[32] It might be suggested that "ego-magnification" is as worthy of observation as "ego-diminution."

stances of crises and threat as over against conditions of calm routine. Some of us prefer the one, and some the other; it seems that the only thing we can say is that both approaches are legitimate and fruitful, and that their respective advantages vary with the specific problem to be studied.

As to *sources of evidence* for research into values, a great many specific suggestions have been made, e.g., "content analysis" (explicit themes and implicit value-assumptions and implications) of communications, budget studies, interviewing parents as to their aspirations for their children, "disguised" choice-tests, and so on, indefinitely. Out of all these specifics, two suggestions seem especially noteworthy: (1) the need to pay attention to implicit materials as well as to explicit testimony; (2) the need to devise research techniques for recording values at the level and in the form in which they operate in actual behavior. For example, we need to know a great deal more about the relation between *asserted* values, at the level of explicit testimony, and *operating* values which are implicit in ongoing behavior.

Perhaps the most provocative idea which emerged from our discussions of research problems is the hypothesis that when one studies values directly, the values are changed by the process of study itself. This is a sort of "Heisenberg effect": the hypothesis is that one does not merely reveal, discover, or render explicit values which are themselves unchanged by the process of being revealed, discovered, or explicated. Thus the mere focusing of attention upon value-problems changes the problems. In so far as this hypothesis is correct, the values we discover are in part a function of the research approach. One research implication is the possibility of taking various groups of people, studying a certain value-problem by *different* methods for each group, and observing changes in behavior subsequent to the process of study.

The study of *choice-behavior* seems to offer the nearest approach to a research method uniquely adapted to the study of values.

"Real" values, then, can be discerned by careful analysis of selections made in "choice" situations, many of which occur in the usual run of living. But the investigation can be supplemented and refined by hypothetical selections, projective techniques, questionnaires, and simple experiments. The observation and investigation of behavior in crisis situations is particularly rewarding. In the comparison of values of groups, it should be particularly significant to examine those values that are clustered around recurrent human situations (such as the scapegoat problem) and those that crystallize about the invariant points of reference of all culture patterns and the functional prerequisites of social systems.[33]

To the extent to which the functional prerequisites are indeed "constants," they are also inevitable foci, on the sociocultural level, for value judgments. It should be noted, however, that any listing of "invariant points of reference" is done from the standpoint of a detached analyst. From the standpoint of the actor it is the meaningful congruence of the symbolically learned cultural values that counts. We must, in any case, ultimately go beyond such

---

[33] D. Aberle, A. Cohen, A. Davis, M. Levy, and F. Sutton, "The Functional Prerequisites of a Society," *Ethics*, LX (1950), 100–111.

lists and construct schemes that can be useful cross-culturally in describing the manner of solution of such constant problems and the way in which a given group creates, elaborates, or suppresses certain values and thus comes to sustain a unique value system. In the construction of such schemes, we must be aware of the dangers of elevating into general and scientific conceptual schemes our own culture's representations of the desirable. In some measure, the universe of value discourse of one individual or of one culture is probably never fully translatable into that of another. For that reason, it is all the more important to understand clearly the principles one uses for constructing schemes in terms of which to compare value systems. It is necessary to experiment with various conceptual schemes relative to the same value phenomena.

Experimentation is also necessary to test whether imputed implicit values are in fact held and whether an inferred hierarchy of values is really so ordered. In general, the conceptual model of the value system of an individual or a group, constructed with the aid of any or all of the methods sketched above, can be validated rigorously only by controlled tests of the assistance it gives in making successful predictions.

Value-Orientations

It is convenient to use the term *value-orientation* for those value notions which are (a) general, (b) organized, and (c) include definitely existential judgments. A value-orientation is a set of linked propositions embracing both value and existential elements.

Gregory Bateson has remarked that "the human individual is endlessly simplifying, organizing, and generalizing his own view of his own environment; he constantly imposes on this environment his own constructions and meanings; these constructions and meanings [are] characteristic of one culture, as over against another." [34] There is a "philosophy" behind the way of life of every individual and of every relatively homogeneous group at any given point in their histories. This gives, with varying degrees of explicitness or implicitness, some sense of coherence or unity to living both in cognitive and affective dimensions. Each personality gives to this "philosophy" an idiosyncratic coloring, and creative individuals will markedly reshape it. However, the main outlines of the fundamental values, existential assumptions, and basic abstractions have only exceptionally been created out of the stuff of unique biological heredity and peculiar life experience. The underlying principles arise out of, or are limited by, the givens of biological human nature and the universalities of social interaction. The specific formulation is ordinarily a cultural product. In the immediate sense, it is from the life-

---

[34] "Cultural Determinants of Personality," in *Personality and the Behavior Disorders*, edited by J. Hunt (1944), p. 723.

ways which constitute the designs for living of their community or tribe or region or socioeconomic class or nation or civilization that most individuals derive most of their "mental-feeling outlook."

If we return to the five groups in the Southwest faced with drought, we find a subtle problem. On the one hand, one can argue that the different reactions are based upon "is" rather than "ought" propositions. It is true that each response is related to each culture's conception of the workings of the physical universe. On the other hand, every conception includes both the conviction that human effort counts and that the course of events can be influenced by supernatural agencies. The relative weightings so far as action is concerned reflect value judgments concerning appropriateness.

It should be possible to construct in general terms the views of a given group regarding the structure of the universe, the relations of man to the universe (both natural and supernatural), and the relations of man to man. These views will represent the group's own definition of the ultimate meaning of human life (including its rationalization of frustration, disappointment, and calamity). Such a "definition of the life situation" for the group contains more than normative and aesthetic propositions; it contains also existential propositions about the nature of "what is." The relationship between existential and normative propositions may be thought of as two-way: on the one hand, the normative judgments must be based on the group's notion of what in fact exists; on the other hand, the group's conception of the universe (of "what is" and "what is natural or obvious") will presumably be based partly on prior normative orientations and on interests. What "must be done" is usually closely related to what is believed to be the "nature of things"; however, beliefs about "what is" are often disguised assumptions of "what ought to be." Moreover, the values of the group, when institutionalized and internalized, have for members of the group a practical kind of existential reality. The fact that one cannot fly through Harvard Square in an automobile is an existential proposition. That one cannot go through Harvard Square in an automobile at sixty-five miles per hour is a normative proposition, and one that will be enforced by police action. To the driver of the car, however, both of these have a great, though perhaps not equal, degree of "reality." Without entering into a discussion of ontology, it may be suggested that both define the "nature of things" for the driver of the car. With more fundamental norms, it should hold even more consistently that "what is right" is of equal importance with "what is" in defining the context of action. By institutionalization value *is* part of the situation.

This statement of a given group's definition of the meaning of life, a statement comprising both existential and normative postulates, will provide the student with the general *value-orientation* of the group concerned. This approach can be applied, for example, to a study of the Mormon system of religious thought. The theological tenets of the Church of Jesus Christ of

Latter-Day Saints define human life as a period in which man, through his experience in a mortal environment, advances toward greater mastery over gross matter. Learning and experience are the means through which this increasing mastery is developed. From these basic postulates, it was inferred that Mormon attitudes on a behavioral level would include a high evaluation of education and work. Investigation has amply supported this hypothesis. Another instance may be seen in the Mormon doctrines that man is not a depraved creature, but rather is of the same race as God and, moreover, was made that he might have joy. From this view of human nature it may be inferred that Mormons will place considerable emphasis upon the importance of recreation. Furthermore, from the fact that the basic Mormon view of life is a serious one, it follows that even joy and recreation will be approached as serious matters. That this is the case can be easily confirmed from the literature on Mormon social organization.[35]

Since value elements and existential premises are almost inextricably blended in the over-all picture of experience that characterizes an individual or a group, it seems well to call this over-all view a "value-orientation," symbolizing the fact that affective-cognitive (value) and strictly cognitive (orientation) elements are blended. More formally, a *value-orientation* may be defined as *a generalized and organized conception, influencing behavior, of nature, of man's place in it, of man's relation to man, and of the desirable and nondesirable as they may relate to man-environment and interhuman relations.* Such value-orientations may be held by individuals or, in the abstract-typical form, by groups. Like values, they vary on the continuum from the explicit to the implicit.

Florence Kluckhohn has noted that "all societies find a phraseology within a range of possible phraseologies of basic human problems." [36] The present concept is essentially the same, except (*a*) the term *value-orientation* (as opposed to simple *orientation*) calls explicit attention to the union of normative with existential assumptions; and (*b*) there is no limitation to "cultural" orientations; value-orientation is equally applicable to individuals and to groups. This is indeed an area where investigations of thematic principles in personalities and in cultures may usefully come together. Henry Murray speaks of the "unity thema" and "major and minor themas" of personality. Anthropologists speak of the "ethos" (i.e., unity thema) and the themes of cultures. The ideas of structure in the two cases are basically similar, and the overlap in content is considerable. To a greater or lesser extent, such patterns are thought to pervade the totality of a personality or the totality

---

[35] This paragraph, written by Thomas O'Dea, is taken from an unpublished memorandum without essential change. Appreciation is expressed to Mr. O'Dea for his permission to use this statement, which fits so well with the general argument of this paper.

[36] "Dominant and Substitute Profiles of Cultural Orientations: Their Significance for the Analysis of Social Stratification," *Social Forces*, XXVIII (1950), 376–393.

of a culture and, by their unique combination, to give personality or culture some degree of coherence, imbue it with distinctive character and outlook, and make individuals unique or make the carriers of a culture distinguishable from the representatives of other groups.

Evaluation, the individual's active behavior in terms of his value-orientations, is a more complex process than that behavior which is dominantly cathection or dominantly cognition. To paraphrase the General Statement of Part I: The cognitive-cathectic and evaluative orientations are connected by the "effort" of the actor. In accordance with a value standard and/or an expectation (based upon existential propositions), the actor through effort manipulates his own resources, including his body, his voice, et cetera, in order to facilitate the direct or indirect approximation to a certain valued goal object or state.

Value-orientation is a distinct modal aspect of any total action complex. The distinctive quality of each culture and the selective trends that characterize it rest fundamentally upon its system of value-orientations. As Bouglé has pointed out, it is primarily by the transmission of their values that cultures perpetuate themselves. It should be emphasized that cultural distinctiveness rests not merely — or even mainly — on value content but on the configurational nature of the value system, including emphases. Cultures differ, for example, in relative emphasis on degree of patterning of expressional, cognitive, and moral values.

Toward a Classification of Values and Value-Orientations

L. J. Henderson, the well-known biochemist, used to remark that in science any classification is better than no classification — even though, as Whitehead says, a classification is only a half-way house. Much of the confusion in discussion about values undoubtedly arises from the fact that one speaker has the general category in mind, another a particular limited type of value, still another a different specific type. We have not discovered any comprehensive classification of values. Golightly has distinguished essential and operational values; [37] C. I. Lewis intrinsic, extrinsic, inherent, and instrumental values. The Cornell group speaks of asserted and operating values. Perry has discriminated values according to modalities of interest: positive-negative, progressive-recurrent, potential-actual, and so on. There are various content classifications such as: hedonic, aesthetic, religious, economic, ethical, and logical. The best known of the content groupings is Spranger's (used in the Allport-Vernon test of values): theoretical, economic, aesthetic, social, political, and religious. The objection to these content classifications is that they are culture-bound. Ralph White has distinguished one hundred "general values" and twenty-five "political values," all with special references to Western culture.

[37] C. Golightly, "Social Science and Normative Ethics," *Journal of Philosophy*, XLIV (1948), 505–516.

It seems useful to make a tentative analysis of values in terms of "dimensions," as suggested in an unpublished memorandum by Professor John W. M. Whiting. The word *dimension* has here the fundamental meaning it has in mathematics, as defined in Webster's *Dictionary*: "The degree of manifoldness of a magnitude or aggregate as fixed by the number of coördinates necessary and sufficient to distinguish any one of its elements from all others." Certain of these dimensions (modality and content) have already been discussed above and will be listed here only for completeness of the grouping thus far arrived at.

Dimension of modality: Positive and negative values.

Dimension of content: Aesthetic,[38] cognitive, and moral values.[39]

Dimension of intent. The values relating to an approved or preferred style or manner in which an act is to be carried out or an object made can be termed *mode* values. These are similar to what have sometimes been called "expressive values." *Instrumental* values are those which actors and groups conceive as means to further ends. *Goal* values are "the aims and virtues which societies and individuals make for themselves." The distinction between these two types is comparable to that made by some authors between "operational" and "intrinsic" or "ultimate" values. The distinction between instrumental and goal values, however, is a slippery one, depending in part, as has been pointed out, on time perspective. It is also essential to discriminate explicitly and consistently between the viewpoints of actor and of observer. The relationship between instrumental and goal values is clearly one of complete interdependence, not of mere sequence. The utilization of certain means will, under specified conditions, inevitably defeat the ends sought.

Finally, it should be noted that the means-end dichotomy is not as clearcut in the category systems of all cultures as it is in Western culture. It may well be that by elevating this contrast into a general scheme we shall get comparative analyses of value systems that differ considerably from analyses based upon conceptualizations more congenial to the thinking characteristic of some non-Western cultures.

Dimension of generality. Some values are *specific* to certain situations or to certain content areas. Navaho Indians, for example, should not have ceremonials at the time of an eclipse of the moon. A particular type of the specific value is the *role* value — values appropriate only in certain roles. Navaho ceremonial practitioners ought not to have sexual relations with any person they have sung over. Other values are *thematic* — applying to a wide variety of situations and to diverse areas of culture content. Such a (negative) value in Navaho culture is fear of closure. The coils of a pot or basket must never

---

[38] "Expressional" may be preferable to "aesthetic."

[39] That the process of valuation is in crucial respects the same is indicated by the practice of speaking of "good" and "bad" ideas, pictures, music, and the like.

be brought end to end. A "spirit outlet" is always left in any design on silver or in a rug or sandpainting. A ceremonialist never teaches an apprentice quite the whole of his knowledge. A husband and wife or two intimate friends must invariably take care to "hold something back."

Dimension of intensity. The strength of value may be determined by observing the sanctions applied internally and externally and by measuring the degree of striving toward attaining or maintaining states, objects, or events. Repetition of behaviors judged to have been influenced by values is another measure of intensity. The method of paired comparisons is particularly applicable in determining the strength of a value. This does not necessarily imply a linear hierarchy. Some value systems tend to be circular, as McCulloch has suggested. Perhaps therefore, on semantic grounds, this dimension ought to be termed "incidence" rather than "intensity."

All cultures have their *categorical* values, their "musts" and "must nots," violations of which are attended by severe sanctions. Respect for the property of others is such a value in Western society. "Achievement," however, is a *preferential* value (though a strong one) in American culture. Those who "achieve" are rewarded materially and in prestige terms. There are convenient cultural rationalizations for those who fail to achieve, though all are urged to do so. In many cultures, though not in all, there are *utopian* values which influence the direction of behavior but which are considered beyond immediate attainment. Literal conformity to the conceptions of the desirable set forth in the Sermon on the Mount evokes amazement or suspicion of queerness, and nonconformity is unpunished. These are genuine values but of a different order from that of regard for human life (categorical value) or achievement (preferential value) in our culture. Of course, the utopian values of one historical epoch sometimes become the preferential or even categorical values of a later period.

Utopian values may also be regarded as a subclass of what may be termed *hypothetical* values — that is, values to which some "lip service" is given but whose influence upon action is relatively slight. The other subclass of hypothetical values are *traditionalistic* values. These are values of historic associations in the culture but which have lost most of their operative force because of changes in other aspects of the culture or in situation. One may instance the time-bound values relating to the aristocracy in contemporary England. In many formal and verbal respects the medieval conceptions are still manifested, but the value strength is primarily a historic residue. These values might also be called *passive* or *ritualistic* values; the feeling for content is largely gone; only the form persists.

Finally — and this extends into the realm of the organization of values — one can contrast *central* and *peripheral* values according to the number and variety of behaviors influenced and the extent to which a group or individual would be markedly different if the value disappeared.

In estimating the intensity of values and the conformity to them, one must be careful not to confuse variation with deviation. Most cultures have patterned choice ranges for those in different age, sex, class, occupational, and other groups. Personal values are ordinarily variants of group values, but the permitted range is often large — insofar as both intensity and sheer selection of values is concerned. Every culture permits, and must permit, a sizable range of alternatives.

From this point of view a meaningful classification along the dimension of intensity is suggested by recent work of Florence Kluckhohn. She suggests that all culture patterns may be grouped as *dominant, variant,* or *deviant.* This corresponds roughly to our statement that values deal with prescriptions, permissions, and prohibitions. Dominant values are those held by a majority of a group or by the most powerful elite. Conformance to dominant values brings the highest approval and reward. Adherence to variant values brings low-level approval, or at any rate, toleration rather than punishment. Deviant values, whether idiosyncratic or characteristic of a segmental or distributive minority, are disallowed by sanctions.[40]

Dimension of explicitness. This is, of course, a continuum without sharp breaks. In general, an *explicit* value is one which is stated verbally by actors, whereas an *implicit* value is one which is inferred by observers from recurrent trends in behavior, including verbal behavior. But a group value may be ordinarily implicit and yet have been stated one or more times by one or more individuals. An implicit value is a tacit conception which is inferred to underlie a behavioral sequence because the given train of events is interpretable only if this tacit conception is assumed to be one of the factors determining selective behavior. Such behavior sequences must involve acts in which "choice" is possible within the physical and biological dimensions of the environing situation and in which the "choices" made are not random but patterned. Such choices are presumed to be based upon unstated "ought" or "desirability" categories. The observer needs the concept of implicit value to give an organized interpretation of behavior, in particular to explain the continuity between symbolic elements of observed behavior. The *relevant* patterning is, of course, only that attributable to abstract standards of the aesthetically or morally desirable. The selection of steel rather than copper to build a bridge is primarily a decision based upon scientific or utilitarian grounds, not upon value grounds. However, the changing lengths of women's skirts in the same climate and where materials are about as available one year as the next reflect certain implicit values.

Dimension of extent. The spread of a value may range from a single individual to the whole of humanity. An *idiosyncratic* value is one held by

---

[40] The possibilities of this threefold classification for analysis of sociocultural process are far more intriguing and complex than can be indicated here. They will be developed in subsequent publications of F. Kluckhohn.

only one person in the group under consideration. This is, of course, one of the ways in which new group values evolve. New values come into being as a result of individual variability and new situations, though it should be added that new values are invariably created against a background of preëxisting values. A *personal* value is the private form of a group value or a universal value.[41] It is not entirely unique to one personality but has its own special shadings, emphases, and interpretations. Just as a social system may be said to have functional prerequisites, so any adult individual with a functioning consciousness is confronted by problems of meaning and integration.

Each people, it is true, has a distinctive set of values. However, no two individuals within the same society share identical values. Each individual adds a little here, subtracts a little there, makes this emphasis a bit stronger than most of his neighbors and makes that emphasis a little less strong. Moreover, every culture has to make some provision, however limited, for the variety of human temperaments that is the consequence of biological variability. Indeed, the group value system is an abstraction, a statement of central tendencies in a range of concrete variation. The abstraction is meaningful and useful, but one must never lose sight of the fact that it is an abstraction at a high level.

The convergence between personal values and *group* values will be found to vary; it will be greater on the part of representative or conforming individuals in relatively homogeneous cultures or subcultures. A value may be defined in psychological terms as that aspect of motivation which is determined by codes or standards as opposed to immediate situation. If the standards are those carefully abstracted to represent modalities more or less characteristic of some social unit, the value may be spoken of as a group value. If the reference is to the private form of a code that influences motivation in an individual, one speaks of a personal value. Gordon Allport has said that "shared value" constitutes a contradiction in terms. This is doubtless true at the very concrete level. But analytically, it is possible and useful to describe the central tendencies abstractly and to impute them to the group rather than the individual.[42]

[41] Clearly, personal values do not consist merely in conceptions of "what I ought to do." They include equally conceptions of what women ought to do, of what fathers ought to do, of what others who bear a specified relation to "me" ought to do to me under certain conditions.

[42] While values are by no means completely *culturally* relative, positive and negative affect, except in situations of extreme physiological need, can hardly be understood apart from group standards. In general, Geiger is right in saying: "Man finds his happiness in the activities the mores celebrate." Moreover, he continues, the transmutation of pleasure into value must be carried out by a group even though, in some instances, the group is expressing a universal rather than a culturally limited value. "Hedonic tones (not some substantialized Laetitia) are immediate experiences which have to be taken into account. They are not automatically *values*. Values, like truth, are names given to processes, to happenings, to choices men make" (*Value*, pp. 328–329).

Personal and idiosyncratic values, Parsons and Shils suggest, tend to be organized primarily around the individual's motivational problems, such as control of aggression, restrictions on gratification, self-permissiveness. Group values, on the other hand, are mainly organized around the problems of selection between types of normative patterns governing interpersonal relations, exploitation of the environment, and attitudes and behavior toward the supernatural. This is an arresting formulation, but it may be overschematic. Personal values would also seem to be organized about problems of interpersonal relations, attitudes toward the supernatural, and the like. There is a personal selection of limited cultural possibilities, which are, in turn, a selection from a limited number of universal possibilities.

A group value is distinctive of some plurality of individuals, whether this be a family, clique, association, tribe, nation, or civilization. Group values consist in socially sanctioned ends and socially approved modes and means. They are values which define the common elements in the situations in which the actors repeatedly find themselves, and they must make some kind of functional sense in terms of a group's special history, present social structure, and environmental situation.

The term *group value* is selected rather than *cultural value* for two reasons. First, the group may, at most, have only a subculture or be distinguished from a larger entity by only a few cultural properties.[43] Second, universal values are also cultural values in the sense that they are socially learned and transmitted.

Most of the values described in anthropological and sociological literature are purely cultural. Indeed they, like the phenomena of linguistics, are culture at its purest, because they involve the maximum element of convention, of arbitrary selection and emphasis. However, it seems increasingly clear and increasingly important that some values, perhaps entirely of a broad and general sort, transcend cultural differences, if one extricates the conceptual core from the superficial cultural trimmings. These *universal values*[44] have not yet been examined by social scientists in the same detailed way in which the gamut of cultural variability has been explored. We too often forget the extent of consensus concerning the satisfactions for individuals which any good social order ought to make possible or provide. Careful study of the public utterances of Robert Taft and Joseph Stalin will show that many of the things that they say they ultimately want for people are identical. As Lundberg has reminded us:

[43] For a discussion of the values of some subsystems of our society, see David Aberle, "Shared Values in Complex Societies," *American Sociological Review*, XV (1950), 495–502.

[44] Their universality is, of course, from the observer's point of view. The meaning of such universal values to the individual cultural carriers in each distant culture will vary in detail and must be determined in cultural context and in part — at least at present — by *Verstehung*.

There is general agreement by the masses of men on the large and broad goals of life as evidenced by man's behavior. Everywhere he tries to keep alive as best he knows how, he tries to enjoy association with his fellow creatures, and he tries to achieve communion with them and with his universe, including his own imaginative creations. The sharp differences of opinion arise about the *means*, the *costs*, and the *consequences* of different possible courses of action.[45]

Contrary to the statements of Ruth Benedict and other exponents of extreme cultural relativity, standards and values are not completely relative to the cultures from which they derive.[46] Some values are as much givens in human life as the fact that bodies of certain densities fall under specified conditions. These are founded, in part, upon the fundamental biological similarities of all human beings. They arise also out of the circumstance that human existence is invariably a social existence. No society has ever approved suffering as a good thing in itself. As a means to an end (purification or self-discipline), yes; as punishment — as a means to the ends of society, yes. But for itself — no. No culture fails to put a negative valuation upon killing, indiscriminate lying, and stealing within the in-group. There are important variations, to be sure, in the conception of the extent of the in-group and in the limits of toleration of lying and stealing under certain conditions. But the core notion of the desirable and nondesirable is constant across all cultures. Nor need we dispute the universality of the conception that rape or any achievement of sexuality by violent means is disapproved.[47] This is a fact of observation as much as the fact that different materials have different specific gravities.

Conceptions of "the mentally normal" have common elements — as well as some disparate ones — throughout all known cultures. The "normal" individual must have a certain measure of control over his impulse life. The person who threatens the lives of his neighbors without socially approved justification is always and everywhere treated either as insane or as a criminal. This is perhaps only a subcategory of a wider universal conception of the normal: no one is fit for social life unless his behavior is predictable within certain limits by his fellows. In all societies the individual whose actions are completely unpredictable is necessarily incarcerated (in jail or asylum) or executed.

Reciprocity is another value essential in all societies. Moreover, the fact that truth and beauty (however differently defined and expressed in detail) are universal, transcendental values is one of the givens of human life —

---

[45] *Can Science Save Us?* (1947), p. 99.

[46] Dewey also speaks of values as "definitely and completely sociocultural." For an empirical argument by a philosopher who shares the position of this paper, see F. C. Sharp, *Good Will and Ill Will* (1950), esp. p. 164.

[47] The occasional instance of ceremonial rape or of *ius primae noctis* is precisely the exception that proves the rule.

equally with birth and death. The very fact that all cultures have had their categorical imperatives that went beyond mere survival and immediate pleasure is one of vast significance. To the extent that such categorical imperatives are universal in distribution and identical or highly similar in content, they afford the basis for agreement among the peoples of the world.[48]

The word *universal* is preferable to *absolute* because whether or not a value is universal can be determined empirically. Some values may indeed be absolute because of the unchanging nature of man or the inevitable conditions of human life. On the other hand, such an adjective is dangerous because culture transcends nature in at least some respects and because propositions about values are subject to revision like all scientific judgments. New knowledge or radically changed circumstances of man's existence may alter universal values. At best, one might be justified in speaking of "conditional absolutes" or "moving absolutes" (in time).

To speak of "conditional absolutes" does not constitute that naïve identification of the "is" with the "ought" which has occasioned justified condemnation of certain work in social science. The suggestion here is rather that if, in spite of their tremendous variations in other respects, all cultures have converged on a few broad universals this fact is deeply meaningful. The question is at least raised whether — given the relatively unchanging biological nature of man and certain inevitables of life in a group — societies which failed to make these tenets part of their cultures simply did not survive. In other words, the existence of these universals reflects a series of categorical "oughts" only in the sense that these are necessary conditions — given by nature, invented by man only in their specific formulations — of adjustments and survival always and everywhere.

There are probably some personal values or value-orientations which tend toward universality in their distribution. At least we may say that in all or almost all societies of any size one can find one or more individuals having a bent for one of what Charles Morris has called Apollonian, Dionysian, Promethean, Buddhistic, and other "paths of life." To avoid confusion, these values corresponding to certian constitutional temperaments widely distributed over the world may be termed *temperamental values*.

Dimension of organization. The question of the extent to which personal or cultural values are hierarchically organized is a difficult one which can be finally settled only by vast empirical research. Certainly there is almost always a hierarchical notion to thinking about values: "more beautiful than," "better than," "more appropriate than." One essential quality of value is that of behaving discriminatingly; this inevitably means discriminating between values as well as "objective" situations. To speak of values is simply

[48] A number of psychoanalysts have been developing the psychological bases of a universal morality. See, for example, R. E. Money-Kyrle, "Towards a Common Aim," *British Journal of Medical Psychology*, XX (1944), 105–118.

to say that behavior is neither random nor solely instinctual or reflexive. Values determine trends toward consistency in behavior, whether on the individual or the group level. Without a hierarchy of values life becomes a sequence of reactions to stimuli that are related only in physical or biological terms. However, there is more to the organization of values than hierarchy. One value is tied to another logically and meaningfully, and it is this systematic and connected quality of values that makes them both interesting and difficult to deal with. At any rate, values do appear to occur in clusters rather than alone.

There also seem to be *priority* values. For the most part, the more general a value the higher its priority, because it contributes more to the coherent organization and functioning of the total system, whether a personality [49] or a culture. However, lacking extensive research, one must be cautious about invoking the image of a pyramid of values, a neat and systematic hierarchy. The extent to which an individual or a group has an affectively congruent or logically consistent "value policy" is a special problem for investigation.

This issue must not be prejudged on the basis of any one formal system of logic (such as the Aristotelian), or else exaggerated notions concerning the degree of harmony or of conflict within the system tend to arise. The elements of a value system have symbolic and historic connections in addition to their internal logical relations. One aspect of this problem is the manner in which the system distinguishes and emphasizes general versus specific values and handles conflicts between them. (We suspect that great internal differentiation can be both an opportunity for value conflict and a mode of resolving it.) The elaboration of the logic of the heart and of the head, and their mutual relation, probably varies from culture to culture. Consideration of this issue, theoretically and empirically, is imperative for a systematic analysis of *value systems* and their functioning.

Tentatively, we may distinguish *isolated* values (those which neither conflict nor demonstrably support other values) and *integrated* values (those which can be shown to be part of an interlocking — or possibly pyramiding — network.)

Group values seem to be organized into dominant and substitute profiles, as Florence Kluckhohn has pointed out for her "orientations." [50] This is one aspect of the range of variation tolerated in all cultures — on some matters. Another useful way of thinking about the organization of values is presented in the chapter on "Systems of Value-Orientation" in Part II of this book.

It should be noted — alike in the F. Kluckhohn, Parsons and Shils, and

---

[49] Crucial for the formation of personality and its organization are those priority values of the group which prescribe the ideal kind of personality (by sex and role) to which allegiance shall be given.

[50] "Dominant and Substitute Profiles of Cultural Orientations," *Social Forces*, XXVIII (1950), 376–393.

the present conceptual schemes — that these are all analyses from an observer's point of view and with a minimum of content. Valid analyses of this type can be based upon only the fullest kind of descriptions of cultures. The "feel of the culture" obtained from careful reading of classical ethnographies must not be sacrificed to overschematic and premature abstraction. The alternatives posed in pairs or triplets or in fourfold boxes are useful for comparative purposes,[51] but one cannot dispense with detailed description of events as actually observed or of value systems as they appear to culture carriers.

DIFFERENTIATION FROM RELATED CONCEPTS

In Anthropology. In the only complete, explicit definition of *value* I have discovered in anthropological literature, Ralph Linton says: "A value may be defined as any element, common to a series of situations, which is capable of evoking a covert response in the individual. An attitude may be defined as the covert response evoked by such an element." [52] Why the responses are limited to the "covert" is not specified. This definition is unsatisfactory also because it does not, apart from "common to a series of situations," differentiate *value* from any concept other than *attitude*.

In general, anthropologists use "value" vaguely, often as more or less synonymous with "strongly held belief," "moral code," "culturally defined aspirations," or even "sanctions." There is also a tendency, when one is talking about culture in general and at a high level of abstraction, to merge values and culture. It is true that the culture carrier who is thoroughly identified with his culture "values" all or most aspects of the culture in the sense that he is not affectively neutral to them. On the other hand, any culture consists only in part of conceptions of the desirable (and the nondesirable, for there are also negative values). It also includes the purely substantive and non-normative aspect of folklore, literature, and music; it includes technological and other skills.

An earlier, unpublished definition of *value* by the present writer was as follows: "A selective orientation toward experience, characteristic of an individual and/or of a group, which influences the choice between possible alternatives in behavior." This is unsatisfactory because, among other reasons, it failed to set values apart from the totality of culture. "Selective orientation toward experience characteristic of a group" would almost serve as a definition of culture. The essence of culture is its selectivity, its arbitrariness from the point of view of action alternatives equally open in the "objective" world and equally adequate in terms of the satisfaction of strictly biological or other survival needs. So far *culture* and *value* are very much alike. All cultural be-

---

[51] Also, to be sure, for internal dynamic analysis and in planning specifically pointed fieldwork.

[52] *The Cultural Background of Personality* (New York, 1945), pp. 111–112.

havior, like valuative behavior, involves an inhibition of the randomness of trial-and-error response. In cross-cultural comparisons, at least, any bit of cultural behavior is selective or preferential behavior. For instance, Americans in England usually continue to handle their knives and forks in the American, not the English, manner. Chinese women in this country often prefer dresses of Chinese type to those which they buy in our stores. One can think of countless other examples of culturally determined behavior which involves felt preferences *but not conceptions of the desirable* as these have been defined above. Value is more than mere preference; it is limited to those types of preferential behavior based upon conceptions of the desirable.

The relation of values to culture patterns, cultural premises, configurations, Opler's "themes," [53] Herskovits' "focus," [54] and to similar conceptions deserves comment. It should be noted, first of all, that these conceptions refer solely to structural aspects of sociocultural systems, whereas values refer alike to individuals, to cultures, and to panhuman phenomena which cut across all existing cultures. In the second place, many "themes" are in the almost purely cognitive realm, defining existential propositions only. Values do include those sanctioned or regulatory patterns prescribing culturally approved ways of doing things and culturally established goals; they also include the implicit cultural premises ("configurations") governing ends and means and the relation between them, insofar as conceptions of the desirable are involved. All cultures, however, include patterns and themes which are not felt by most culture carriers as justifiable. Prostitution, for example, is in certain cultures a recognized behavioral pattern but is not a value. The "success" theme in American culture is today questioned in value terms by many Americans.

There is unquestionably an overlap in these conceptions. But values constitute a more general category of the theory of action, themes and premises a more limited one. Some cultural premises, as we have said, are certainly values; others are almost exclusively cognitive or existential. The direction of the enquiry is different in any case. Themes, cultural premises, and the rest are structural concepts, primarily intended to map the culture in cogni-

---

[53] "A postulate or position, declared or implied, and usually controlling behavior or stimulating activity, which is tacitly approved or openly promoted in a society" ("Themes as Dynamic Forces in Culture," *American Journal of Sociology*, LI [1945], 198–205). This is very close to our definition of "cultural value."

[54] "Cultural focus designates the tendency of every culture to exhibit greater complexity, greater variation in the institutions of some of its aspects than in others. So striking is this tendency to develop certain phases of life, while others remain in the background, so to speak, that in the shorthand of the disciplines that study human societies these focal aspects are often used to characterize whole cultures" (*Man and His Works* [1948], p. 542). He elsewhere comments, "A people's dominant concern may be thought of as the focus of their culture: that area of activity or belief where the greatest awareness of form exists, the most discussion of values is heard, the widest difference in structure is to be discerned" ("The Processes of Cultural Change," in *The Science of Man in the World Crisis*, edited by Ralph Linton [1945], pp. 164–165).

tive terms for the outsider, to help depict the culture as a system. Values always look to action, in particular to the selections made by individual actors between different paths, each "objectively" open.

In Sociology. Sociology has consistently been more explicitly concerned with values than either anthropology or psychology. Hence it has developed related but distinct concepts to a much lesser extent. Durkheim, Weber, Sumner, and other classical sociologists all have treated the problems of value. Durkheim showed both that society was a moral phenomenon and that morality was a social phenomenon. He tended to maintain a positivistic ethic but also to deny the individual's independence in taking a position on values.[55] In general, he failed to segregate the value element in the concrete social structure. Sumner's concept of the mores overlaps with the notion of value as defined in this paper, but it is so little used today as a strictly technical term that a careful differentiation seems unnecessary.

Brief mention should be made of some of the more important recent sociological literature dealing with values. In *The Polish Peasant,* Thomas and Znaniecki propound their famous definition: "By a social value we understand any datum having an empirical content accessible to the members of some social group and a meaning with regard to which it is or may be an object of activity." This they contrast with *attitude:* ". . . a process of individual consciousness which determines real or possible activity of the individual in the social world." The contributions of Parsons, Mannheim, and Bouglé to the study of values are well known. Radhakanal Mukerjee has recently published *The Social Structure of Values* (1949), "a systematic attempt to present sociology from the viewpoint of valuation as the *primum mobile* in the social universe, the nexus of all human relations, groups, and institutions." Howard Becker has recently published *Through Values to Social Interpretation.*

In Psychology. Although there are a few famous examples to the contrary (notably the Allport-Vernon test and Wolfgang Köhler's *The Place of Value in a World of Facts*), psychologists have dealt with *values* — under this name — much less frequently than sociologists. There are, however, certain important psychological concepts, such as *attitude,* which cover some of the same territory and hence must be distinguished.

If one follows Allport's classic definition of *attitude* — "a mental and neural state of readiness, organized through experience, exerting a directive or dynamic influence upon the individual's response to all objects and situations with which it is related" — the principle differences from *value* are: (*a*) exclusive referability to the individual, and (*b*) absence of imputation of the "desirable." There would be a certain convenience if Woodruff's definition of attitudes as "momentary and temporary states of rediness to act" were

[55] See Talcott Parsons, *The Structure of Social Action,* esp. pp. 391 ff.

accepted, for then values and attitudes would be contrasted in the time dimension and the influence of values on attitudes could be more readily explored.[56]

If one approaches the explanation of behavior in a psychological framework, it is easy to confuse *value* with *motivation* and related concepts. David Aberle, in an unpublished memorandum, has wisely commented on my earlier "selective orientation" definition of value:

Whatever we mean by a value, the area of values is apparently difficult to circumscribe. The examples ordinarily used have a tendency to fall into one or another area that is already being successfully exploited under some other head. Descriptions of the values of an individual shade off into, or are readily absorbed by, such notions as motivations, conscious and unconscious; goals, goal-orientations; meanings, and the like. If we accept Kluckhohn's tentative definition, expedient behavior, "unconsciously self-destructive behavior," flight from the field, or collapse in the face of an overwhelming attack of anxiety are all instances of choices between alternative possibilities influenced by a selective orientation. Some of these behaviors we would, in ordinary parlance, wish to consider as value-influenced, and some we would consider more conveniently handled by other concepts, such as motivation.

The following definition by John W. M. Whiting, Eleanor Hollenberg, and William Lambert is also in a psychological frame of reference: "A value is the relationship between an individual or group and an event (i.e., any class of objects, actions or interactions) such that the individual or group strives to achieve, maintain or avoid that event." They go on to say that a value may be measured by "(a) an appraising statement, e.g., statements of choice or preference (questions of validity and reliability of both verbal report and behavioral observation must be taken into account), made by an informant; (b) an inference by an observer from the overt actions of the individual or group which imply choice or preference with respect to the event." Their memorandum continues:

It will be noted that this definition is similar to the Kluckhohn-Vogt definition of value insofar as striving to achieve, maintain or avoid an event is equivalent to *preference, choice* and *selection*. The definitions differ in that the Kluckhohn-Vogt definition makes value substantively either a *statement* (explicit value) or a *"tacit premise"* (implicit value), whereas the present definition reserves statements and tacit premises for operations of determining and measuring values. It will be noted that the substantive definition of the present statement is a *relationship* between an individual or group and an event.

With respect to the specifications for measurement, the present definition includes the method of paired comparisons under conditions of equal availability of events as specified by Kluckhohn and Vogt, but does not limit itself to that method alone. For example, it would permit us to use the ratings of judges with respect to appraising statements of informants without carrying out the operation of paired comparison.

It may, however, be useful for some purposes to have an alternative definition of value in psychological terms: *value may be defined as that aspect of motivation which is referable to standards, personal or cultural, that do not arise solely out of immediate tensions or immediate situation.* Motives, conscious or unconscious, provide instigation. The value component in motivation is a factor both in the instigation to action and in setting the direction of the act. The value element may be present alike in the tension of the actor and in the selection of a path of behavior. Selection, of course, is not merely a function of motives (including their value elements) but also of the habit strengths of the various alternatives. A given value may have a strength that is relatively independent of any particular motive, though it remains in some sense a function of the total motivational system. For example, a given value may be simultaneously reinforced by motives for achievement, social approval, security, and the like.

Finally, we must return briefly to the subject of cathexis. Murray and Morgan have defined *cathexis* as "the more or less enduring power of an entity to evoke relatively intense and frequent reactions, positive or negative, in a person." They also make a very useful clarification:

> The concept of cathexis and the concept of sentiment are merely two different ways of describing the same phenomenon; the first points to the persisting power of the object to stimulate the subject, whereas the second points to the disposition of the subject to be stimulated by the object. . . Cathexis is the more useful term when attention is to be focused on the object and its attributes, the nature of its *appeal* or its *repellence*, especially when the object has *demand-value* or *aversion-value* for a great number of people.[57]

Values and needs.[58] Dorothy Lee has recently called for "a re-examination of the premise which so many of us implicitly hold that culture is a group of patterned means for the satisfaction of a list of human needs." It will be worth while to quote at length from her argument:

> The concept of an inventory of basic needs rose to fill the vacuum created when the behaviorists banished the old list of instincts. . . Anthropologists borrowed the principle from psychology, without first testing it against ethnographic material, so that often, when the psychologist uses anthropological material, he gets his own back again in new form and receives no new insights. There are two assumptions involved here: (1) the premise that action occurs in answer to a need or a lack; and (2) the premise that there is a list. In recent years, anthropologists, influenced by the new psychology, have often substituted *drives* or *impulses* or *adjustive responses* for the old term *needs*, but the concept of the list remains with us. We hold this side by side with the conflicting conception of culture as a totality, of personality as organ-

---

[57] Murray and Morgan, pp. 22; 11.
[58] See also "Needs and the Organization of Behavior" in Chapter I, Part I.

ismic, as well as with adherence to psychosomatic principles. We deplore the presentation of culture as a list of traits, yet we are ready to define culture as an answer to a list of needs.

This definition of culture has proved a strain on us. When we found that the original list of basic needs or drives was inadequate, we, like the psychologists, tried to solve the difficulty by adding on a list of social and psychic needs; and, from here on, I use the term *need* in a broad sense, to cover the stimulus-response phrasing of behavior. When the list proved faulty, all we had to do was to add to the list. We have now such needs as that for novelty, for escape from reality, for security, for emotional response. We have primary needs, or drives, and secondary needs, and we have secondary needs playing the role of primary needs. The endless process of adding and correcting is not an adequate improvement; neither does the occasional substitution of a "totality of needs" for a "list of needs" get at the root of the trouble. Where so much elaboration and revision is necessary, I suspect that the original unit itself must be at fault; we must have a radical change. . .

If needs are inborn and discrete, we should find them as such in the earliest situations of an individual's life. Yet take the Tikopia or the Kwoma infant, held and suckled without demand in the mother's encircling arms. He knows no food apart from society, has no need for emotional response since his society is emotionally continuous with himself; he certainly feels no need for security. He participates in a total situation. Even in our own culture, the rare happy child has no need for emotional response or approval or security or escape from reality or novelty. If we say that the reason that he has no need for these things is that he does have them already, we would be begging the question. I believe, rather, that these terms or notions are irrelevant when satisfaction is viewed in terms of positive present value, and value itself as inherent in a total situation.

On the other hand, it is possible to see needs as arising out of the basic value of a culture. In our own culture, the value of individualism is axiomatically assumed. How else would it be possible for us to pluck twenty infants, newly severed from complete unity with their mothers, out of all social and emotional context, and classify them as twenty atoms on the basis of a similarity of age? On this assumption of individualism, a mother has need for individual self-expression. She has to have time for and by herself; and since she values individualism, the mother in our culture usually does have this need for private life. We must also believe that a newborn infant must become individuated, must be taught physical and emotional self-dependence; we assume, in fact, that he has a separate identity which he must be helped to recognize. We believe that he has distinct rights, and sociologists urge us to reconcile the needs of the child to those of the adults in the family, on the assumption, of course, that needs and ends are individual, not social. Now, in maintaining our individual integrity and passing on our value of individualism to the infant, we create needs for food, for security, for emotional response, phrasing these as distinct and separate. We force the infant to go hungry, and we see suckling as merely a matter of nutrition, so that we can then feel free to substitute a bottle for breast and a mechanical bottleholder for the mother's arms; thus we ensure privacy for the mother and teach the child self-dependence. We create needs in the infant by withholding affection and then presenting it as a series of approvals for an inventory of achievements or attributes. On the assumption that there is no emotional continuum, we withdraw ourselves, thus forcing the child to strive for emotional response and security. And thus, through habituation and teaching, the mother reproduces in the child her own needs, in this case the need for privacy which inevitably brings with it related needs. Now the child grows up needing time to himself, a room of his own, freedom of choice, freedom to plan his own life. He will brook no interference and no encroachment. He will spend his wealth installing private bathrooms in his house, buying a private car, a private yacht, private woods and a private beach, which he will then people with his privately chosen society. The need for privacy is an imperative one in our society, recognized by official bodies such as state welfare groups and the department of labor. And it is part of a system which stems from and expresses our basic value.

In other cultures, we find other systems, maintaining other values. The Arapesh, with their value of socialism, created a wide gap between ownership and possession, which they could then bridge with a multitude of human relations. They plant their trees in someone else's hamlet, they rear pigs owned by someone else, they eat yams planted by someone else. The Ontong-Javanese, for whom also the good is social, value the sharing of the details of everyday living. They have created a system, very confusing to an American student, whereby a man is a member of at least three ownership groups, determined along different principles, which are engaged cooperatively in productive activities; and of two large households, one determined along matrilineal lines, one along patrilineal lines. Thus, an Ontong-Javanese man spends part of the year with his wife's sisters and their families, sharing with them the intimate details of daily life, and the rest of the year on an outlying island, with his brothers and their families. The poor man is the man who has no share in an outlying island, who must eat and sleep only in a household composed of his immediate family and his mother's kin, when unmarried; and who must spend the whole year with his wife's kin, when married. He has the same amount and kind of food to eat as his wealthy neighbors, but not as many coconuts to give away; he has shelter as adequate as that of the wealthy, but not as much of the shared living which is the Ontong-Javanese good.

In speaking of these other cultures, I have not used the term *need*. I could have said, for example, that the Ontong-Javanese needs a large house, to include many maternally related families. But I think this would have been merely an exercise in analysis. On the other hand, when I spoke of our own culture, I was forced to do it in terms of needs, since I have been trained to categorize my own experience in these terms. But even here, these are not basic needs, but rather part of a system expressing our basic value; and were we able to break away from our substantive or formal basis of categorizing, I think we should find these to be aspects or stresses or functions, without independent existence. Culture is not, I think, "a response to the total needs of a society"; but rather a system which stems from and expresses something had, the basic values of the society.[59]

The Cornell group express themselves along similar lines:

Although values have this affective dimension, they are not identical with particular segmental "needs" of the organism; specific physiological depriva-

[59] "Are Basic Needs Ultimate?" *Journal of Abnormal and Social Psychology*, XLIII (1948), 43, 391–395.

tions and gratifications may be *relevant* to a great many values, but do not themselves constitute value-phenomena. . . To put it another way, "value" can only become actualized in the context of "need" but it is not thereby identified with need. (Some members of our group maintain that value might profitably be considered as "that which continues to be desired" after imperious segmental deprivations have been removed.)

At the level of highly generalized categories or dimensions of need, e.g., "security," "belongingness," etc., the same need may be met by widely different patterns of value; conversely, a generalized "value," e.g. religious salvation, patriotism, etc., may be the nexus of many specific needs.

Mrs. Lee shows a clear recognition of the necessity for conceptualizing the alternatives in behavior and puts a shrewd finger upon some real flaws in contemporary anthropological and psychological thinking. It is certainly true, for example, that how a language is learned is one thing and what difference it makes after learning is another. But while she rightly insists upon the importance of symbolic transmission by a culture (Sorokin's logico-meaningful) the situations which create needs (Sorokin's causal-functional) are equally significant.

Since a value is a complex proposition involving cognition, approval, selection, and affect, then the relationship between a value system and a need or goal system is necessarily complex. Values *both* rise from and create needs. A value serves several needs partially, inhibits others partially, half meets and half block still others.

Some needs arise from a group's desire for survival as a group. The need for integration is a requirement of the social system but is culturally transmitted and the specific means of meeting the need is culturally styled. Most peoples, for example, wear clothing not because of the rigors of the environment but to preserve group integration and, in some instances, to provide channels for the self-expression of individuals.

Other needs are culturally created without reference to underlying conditions of social life but are conditioned and limited by other aspects of the culture, including its relative over-all complexity. Why does an upper-middle-class New York woman set a table for a formal dinner party in a certain way, with flowers, fruit, special glasses, linens, and the like? She certainly feels a "need" to do so. But this fact requires a complicated explication. There must be a reference to the value system of upper-middle-class New Yorkers in 1950. This value system must have been internalized (a psychological rather than a cultural process). The total pattern is possible only given certain goods and services obtainable in a metropolitan area. If she belonged to another culture or if this culture were at a different time point, her "need" would be different in its specific manifestations, though the "deeper" need to conform and to maintain or elevate status might still be there. Her specific needs are both created and made possible of fulfillment by the culture in general. It is probable that in complex, literate societies the "secondary needs" are alike more burdensome and more inescapable. Also, her own presentation still contains too much of the older rampant cultural relativism. Most of the dilemmas she presents can be transcended in terms of the conceptual scheme presented earlier in this volume.

There is undoubtedly a close relation between needs and values, but it is important to note that the needs satisfied by orienting behavior in terms of a value is of an importantly different sort from that obtained from eating a good meal. As Dorothy Lee has observed:

There is no such contrast of passive absorption of values and rational choice of action: . . . the basis of choice is neither the passive inability to step out of one's ingrained social role, nor the calculating desire to avoid displeasing one's social contemporaries. It seems to me that from infancy each social being derives an active satisfaction from participating in the values of his society, and that this satisfaction lies at the basis both of acquiring social values and of acting according to them, choosing a course of action.[60]

There is also the caution expressed by Maslow:

Interests are determined by the gratification and frustration of needs. The current fashion is to treat attitudes, tastes, interests and indeed values of *any* kind as if they had no determinant other than associative learning, i.e. as if they were determined wholly by arbitrary extra-organismic forces. It is necessary to invoke also intrinsic requiredness.[61]

He goes on to point out that for the food-starved or water-starved person only food or water will ultimately serve. In other words, some choices do not involve value elements but solely need elements.

Values and goals. The concept *value* cuts across goals, drives, conditions, relative to an action sequence. *Value* looks not toward the sequential process but toward a component in all aspects of an action. The Cornell group again makes a clarifying statement: "Values are not the concrete goals of behavior, but rather are aspects of these goals. Values appear as the *criteria* against which goals are chosen, and as the *implications* which these goals have in the situation."

In brief, a goal represents a cathected objective with value elements interpreted as they apply in this concrete situation.

Values, drives, and learning. Values are presumably a learned element in behavior. They can well be regarded as components in need-dispositions ("acquired drives"). Most acquired or derived drives are dependent upon group values which the individual has somehow interiorized as part of him-

[60] Comment on Margaret Mead, "The Comparative Study of Culture," in *Science, Philosophy and Religion,* 2nd Symposium (1942), p. 77.

[61] "Some Theoretical Consequences of Basic Need-Gratification," *Journal of Personality,* XVI (1948), 402–416.

self. If he does not orient a high proportion of his behavior with at least some regard to these conceptions of the desirable, he neither respects himself nor is respected by others. Hull has remarked:

> Within the last twenty years the more important basic molar laws whereby organisms come to value, i.e. strive for, certain objects have gradually become fairly clear. In general, any act which is performed shortly before the reduction of a primary need, like that concerned with food, water, pain, optimal temperature, or sex, will be conditioned in such a way that when the organism is again in that situation or one resembling it, and suffers from that need or one resembling it, that act will tend to be evoked. This seems to be the basic molar law of conditioning or learning.

Reward and punishment as operative in the learning of values and in determining value strength must be accepted. However, it is necessary to avoid any *simpliste* reduction to primary drives or to a hedonic or utilitarian calculus.[62] The essential thing about values is their referability to standards more perduring than immediate or completely "selfish" or autistic motivations. One of the severest limitations of the classical theory of learning is its neglect of attachments and attitudes in favor of reward and punishments.

Values, utility, and consequences. Value should be distinguished from *utility* because of the arbitrariness and psychological character of *value. Utility* normally refers to a strictly rational calculus, often from the vantage point of the observer. Utility, in the direct and contemporaneous sense, is by no means always present in value judgments, in part because the aesthetic dimension is dominant in many value judgments.

In the long run "judgments of practice" in terms of consequences — or what are conceived as consequences — are doubtless one of the determinants of the survival strength of various values and influence their intensity at given time points. However, a value-choice is more often than not made in terms of psychologically felt compatibility, rather than by a primarily rational evaluation of probable consequences. The observer must be highly self-conscious of time perspective and generally wary about drawing inferences about what is advantageous or disadvantageous, beneficial or harmful in estimating the relation between values and consequences. Dewey is right in insisting that values are specially relevant to tensions and conflicting impulses. Values make their influence felt after desiring has occurred and when there is cognition and/or feeling about desirability. But he is only partly right in saying that the value "good" is fixed to whatever will solve the problem situation, if this be interpreted to mean the immediate or short-term problem situation.[63]

---

[62] Learning theory has also tended to overlook the "intrinsic appropriateness" of the Gestaltists. Cf. W. Koehler.

[63] Radcliffe-Brown has pointed out that some of his critics mistakenly thought that by "social value" he meant "utility" (*Taboo* [1939], p. 47). In the climate of British-

Values and functions. Function is always relative to a given basis of reference. In the case of values, the reference is to an action system — society or a subsystem thereof, or personality or a subsystem thereof. There is invariably a "moral" (i.e., total system) reference, whether the function be social or psychological. Hence the functions of values are largely, though not exclusively, at the latent or implicit level. A passage in Eliseo Vivas' recent book points out very effectively the danger in naïve functional or tension-reduction formulas:

> The self, or the integration of effective constellations which for the interest theory define it . . is only one, and an indeterminate, element in the achievement of the moral economy. Disruption of the economy does not result merely from frustration of surface interests or from manifest conflicts but from the manner — about which we are as yet almost entirely in the dark — in which the hidden factors of the self enter into the selection of values through the inhibition or encouragement of interests. The value of life as lived, which is distinct from the values acknowledged by the person or even those he espouses, seems to a very small extent to depend on cognitive preferences dictated by which Santayana and Perry call "reason." And even less does it seem to depend on whether a large or small number of interests decided on by the four notions of Perry are satisfied or not. The preferences operate below, as well as above, consciousness, and denial of interests is no less necessary than satisfactions to secure the tensions and tone without which life as it is lived loses its value. . . Tension and sometimes the anxiety generated by a conflict may be the essential factors in producing the tone and value.[64]

Values and sanctions. If conduct is to conform, even approximately, to standards, there must — for most of the behavior of most people — be sanctions, organized or diffuse. It may be guessed that the more organized and direct sanctions reinforce either group values that are newer in the culture or subculture or those which restrain imperious biological impulses, the free exercise of which endangers the security of individuals and the stability of society. Values of both of these types must be called constantly to the conscious attention, backed by the threat of direct and organized sanction on the part of at least some members of the group in which action takes place. The sanctions for implicit group values are either extremely diffuse or are mediated by the sanctions attached to explicit values subsumed under a more thematic implicit value.

Of course, anticipation of sanction is not precisely identical with asking,

---

American thought during the past century and a half "value" tends too insistently to imply "utility."

[64] *The Moral Life and the Ethical Life* (1950), p. 59. Vivas also in this book introduces the useful distinction between "espoused" and "recognized" values. Had this important book been available before the present chapter was put in "final form," many aspects of the chapter's content and organization would probably have been significantly different.

"What *ought* I to do?" Nevertheless sanctions and values are linked in the concrete motivational system of each individual actor. Also, they are involved in the determinism of selection: external as well as internal consequences follow upon choice. Sanctions and values are inextricably linked. It is from group values that rules are derived and sanctions justified. Why must one drive on the right side of the street and be punished for failing to do so? Because our culture puts a high value upon human life.

We do not yet understand very much about the steps through which a mere preference (on the part of an individual or a group) becomes a value (internally felt "oughtness") and then — in the case of literate societies — embodied as a law with formal sanctions.

Values and ideals. It appears to be in the nature of the human animal to strive after ideals as well as mere existence. To this extent, the realm of ideals and values is almost co-extensive. However, the concept of the ideal does not imply the property of "choice" or selection which is a differentia of value. Moreover, in popular speech at least, the "ideal" carries a connotation of the unattainable as opposed to the desirable-and-possible. In addition to the quasi-mystical connotation, there are metaphysical overtones from Plato and elsewhere which make the term dubious as a scientific concept. One might say that an ideal is an especially valued goal of an individual or a group. Thomas O'Dea suggests defining an ideal as "a constructed embodiment of values in a hypothetically concrete situation"; he gives as examples the scholar-gentleman in Confucian China, the independence of India, the building of Zion.

Values and beliefs. Values differ from ideas and beliefs by the feeling which attaches to values and by the commitment to action in situations involving possible alternatives. If you are committed to act on a belief, then there is a value element involved. The following crude schematization is suggestive: (1) This is real or possible (belief); [65] (2) this concerns me or us (interest); (3) this is good for me or us, this is better than something else that is possible (value). *Belief* refers primarily to the categories, "true" and "false"; "correct" and "incorrect." *Value* refers primarily to "good" and "bad"; "right" and "wrong."

Values and ideology. The term *ideology* is currently used in a number of somewhat distinct, though partially overlapping, senses. It always refers to a system of ideas, but the system is sometimes construed to be based on the special interests of some segmental or distributive minority within the society, sometimes upon a supernatural revelation, sometimes upon any nonempirical, nonscientific norm.[66] In general, *ideology* has today a somewhat pejorative

[65] In popular usage with respect to religion, *belief* is sometimes "the desirable" in the sense of the supernaturally commanded or approved.

[66] Lasswell and Kaplan (*Power and Society* [1950], p. 123) have recently given this definition: "The *ideology* is the political myth functioning to preserve the social struc-

sense which does not attach to *value*. *Ideology* is also distinguished by ex-plicitness, by systemic quality, and by overt emphasis on cognition (though there is clearly also an implication of commitment to these ideas). It might legitimately be argued that ideologies determine the choice between alterna-tive paths of action, which are equally compatible with the underlying values.

Nothing could be more evident than the fact that we have dealt with many topics inadequately and have failed to touch at all upon others. The source of values and the sources of sanctions for values have interesting aspects, both historical and functional. We have not even approached the problems of what kinds of value systems are correlated with various levels of technological and social development; of the compatibility and incom-patibility of various values. How values are learned, accepted, and diffused deserves a long monographic study. Murray and Morgan have well said:

Since there is only one acceptable method of testing the value of anything and that is by experience, there will never be a sound basis for a philosophy of life until the experiences of a vast number of different types of men and women have been accurately reported, assembled, and formulated in general terms. As things stand now only those who can write well enough to have their works published are in a position to make their experiences available to others. Since writers are not a representative sample of the population, it is necessary that records of experience be obtained from other classes of people.[67]

The assertion that "what is right is what is right for man's nature" needs a careful reëxamination in the light of existing anthropological, psychological, and sociological evidence. The above listing enumerates only a small part of the unfinished business in the field of values.

---

ture; the *utopia*, to supplant it." The Communist definition of *ideology* is, "The inte-grated total of 'scientifically' established ideas." Cf. K. A. Wittfogel, "How to Checkmate Stalin in Asia," *Commentary* (1950) pp. 334–341.

[67] Murray and Morgan, p. 8.

3   HENRY A. MURRAY

Toward a Classification of Interactions

In the domain of psychology few experiences have been more sobering, if not dismal, than the failures of the imagination, the confusions and dissensions, which have marked our collective efforts to explain the directionality of human behaviors. These defeats are most embarrassing, since no adequate theoretical system can be reared until a foundation of acceptable definitions and propositions relative to functional tendencies has been laid.

That muscle and/or words become temporally coördinated in such a way as to produce effects, momentary or enduring, is an observable and predictable fact of nature. Equally given and undeniable is the further fact that these achieved effects are commonly conducive to a man's physical and psychological well-being, his development and his survival. The problem, of course, is how to analyze and reconstruct, to interpret and predict, these directional proceedings.

In the field of biology, of animal action and learning, some radical differences of opinion are still unresolved, but the issues are straight-edged, and largely for this reason, progress is discernible. In the field of human action, on the other hand, the issues are fuzzy-edged and most of us are floundering in vagueness. We are still babblers, for the most part, in a Tower of Babel. In fact, one sibling in the social science family, the important subscience of interpersonal verbal behaviors, is only just beginning to focus its eyes, move its lips, and utter a few sounds which its parents fondly believe are publicly intelligible.

Where so many competent investigators are still fumbling, it is the part of prudence to proceed warily. Also, there are certain other considerations — say those of time and space — which likewise dictate caution in setting the scope of the endeavor. Therefore, my aim here will be merely that of helping to prepare for a theoretical foundation by disposing of a few interfering boulders of cognition and by submitting some boards for a frame into which propositional cement may someday be poured with confidence.

In this paper I shall attempt to elucidate the widely preached but narrowly practiced assumption that the social scientist's "real entity" (as Whitehead might say) is a temporal unit of interacting processes, the simplest being a short interpersonal proceeding, say the movements and words of the actor (the subject, S) and the reaction of the alter (the object, O). I submit that, in representing an interaction unit of this type, the object must be given the same conceptual status as the subject, that is, our model of the proceeding should include as much formulation of the object's thought and speech as of the subject's thought and speech. Also, I submit that on both sides of the equation the most crucial and indispensable of all the variables is that of directionality; that is, the need-aimed action of the subject and the need-aimed action of the object. In other words, we have to deal with the most troublesome of concepts, that denoted by such terms as conation, tendency, drive, propensity, motive, purpose, wish, desire, intention, impulse. This will constitute my chief conceptual focus, but it should be understood that whatever conclusions may be reached relative to this entity will apply to the object (chief constituent of the subject's situation) as well as to the subject (chief constituent of the object's situation).

The status of the entity, from the point of view of a logical positivist, is that of a nonobservable construct or intervening variable, which belongs, in Carnap's language, to the category of disposition concepts. It is a state, in short, that is characterized by the tendency to actions of a certain *kind*. (After a sufficient period of learning, these actions can be defined most significantly in terms of the *kind* of satisfying effect which they are likely to produce.) For the present, this is all we shall assume about the nature of this variable, which I shall call "need" or, more generally, "tendency."

One of the granite boulders of cognition, from my eccentric and unfashionable viewpoint, is the model of the culture-clear, conscience-free, maze-imprisoned, hunger-driven, cheese-seeking rat, which is forever engraved on the entablatures of our cortices. Greatly impressed, as we should be, by the strictly designed experiments and clear-cut findings of the animal psychologists, we have been disposed to accept one or another of their several formulations as the best paradigm of human conduct and thereby to accept, without so much as a scientific shrink, the audacious assumption of species equivalence. This decision of ours has resulted in a rigid circumscription and distortion of our view of behavioral phenomena, because knowledge of how a rat copes with its tasks is applicable to no more than a small portion of the event-manifold which constitutes the life history of a personality. It does not, for example, help us very much in understanding how a scientist copes with the task of constructing a theory of social action and of communicating it to his colleagues in such a way that it appeals to them as much as cheese appeals to a healthy rat. For several reasons, to be spelled out later, I believe that Maslow is right in characterizing the hunger drive as "atypical rather than typical."

The fact that the investigations of animal psychologists have been technically most satisfying should not produce "negative hallucinations" in respect to the many important kinds of human behavior which are susceptible to neither precise measurements, precise interpretations, nor precise predictions.

Since psychology is among the youngest and least sophisticated of the sciences, gnawing feelings of inferiority are almost universal (even normal) in our profession. As a result, many of us are harrassed by relentless and importunate cravings for scientific maturity, which incline us to leap over all the tedious stages of observation, description, and classification through which chemistry and all the biological and medical sciences have passed, and find short cuts to eminence via logical positivism and mathematical models. This zeal for uncriticizable statements and precisely verifiable measurements should certainly be encouraged, but not without the warning that in pursuing Certainty, the Absolute, one is likely to leave Man, the thinking reed, forsaken in the rear. Here, quite obviously, I am giving voice to a "prejudice" — that is, an unpopular opinion — which places me, however, in the company of Pratt, a clear thinker, who has suggested that psychology has not yet advanced to the state at which exact formalization of its theories is rewarding. As my friend Hanns Sachs used to say: "You can't make a leaf grow by stretching it." I am also prompted to quote Aristotle, not popular these days: "It is the part of an educated man to seek exactness in each class of subjects only so far as the nature of the subject admits."

Before settling on an animal paradigm as foundation for psychology, would it not be well to observe and collect records of a great variety of behaviors — especially interpersonal verbal behaviors — and attempt to classify them roughly? Despite shouts of "No!" this is my chief proposal for the present. But, before discussing it in greater detail, it seems advisable to set down some of the less commonly stated assumptions that are basic to the notions presented in this paper.

A Few Assumptions

1. *Proceedings of personality*. Personality is the governing organ of the body, an institution, which, from birth to death, is ceaselessly engaged in *transformative* functional operations. Its historic course may be viewed as a long succession of *proceedings* punctuated by periods of sleep, during which unconscious anabolic processes regenerate the stores of energies that have been expended in the catabolic processes of its waking life.

It is sometimes convenient to distinguish between internal and external proceedings. An *internal proceeding* is a temporal segment during which the personality, abstracted from its environment (as in sleep), is preoccupied with its inner life — daydreaming perhaps, or attempting to interpret and evaluate a past event, or to predict the future, or to settle some conflict, or to solve some intellectual problem, or to assess its own abilities, or (let us say finally) to select a goal and lay out a plan of strategies. Internal proceedings predominate during periods of solitude. They are usually more frequent and prolonged in scientists, artists, philosophers, religionists, and introverts generally. An *external proceeding*, on the other hand, is a stretch of time during which the processes of personality are engaged in dealing immediately and overtly with one or more things or persons of its environment — in observing or manipulating, in giving or taking, coöperating or competing, exchanging information or expressing values, persuading or yielding to persuasion, serving or being served, fighting or arriving at a peaceful settlement, and so forth.

The social scientist's unit of concrete reality is not an instantaneous thing, field, or structure, but an event, which I am calling a "proceeding." If necessary, the length of a proceeding can be precisely defined (say, the duration of a single interaction between two people), but, as a rule, it is more feasible to define it loosely. Any one of the small-group meetings which Bales and others have been observing so systematically might be taken as an example of a proceeding, the social psychologist's real entity. Ideally, the duration of a proceeding is determined by (1) the initiation and by (2) the completion of a dynamically significant pattern of behavior, exhibited, for example, by a rat running a maze and feeding to the point of satiation or by a pianist playing a sonata from start to finish.

In short, the temporal dimension is an integral part of all behaviors, and so, in order to discern the nature of any single sample of action, the psychologist must observe its course through a sufficient period of time. Instantaneous records (e.g., a photograph during the expression of an emotion) or observations regulated by the clock are incongruent with reality.

As I see it, then, proceedings are the things which we observe and try to represent with models and to explain, the things which we attempt to predict, the standards against which we test the adequacy of our formulations. Here the sociologist's task is much more complicated than the psychologist's, since he must conceptualize, very often, a complex system of concurrent (as well as consecutive) proceedings, a large event-manifold.

The widely recognized fact that reality is process has been reiterated here as a counterpoise to our inveterate cognitive disposition to "spatialize" everything (as Bergson put it), to conceive of instantaneous fields and structures, and to assume, in building our theories, that sameness (permanence, stability, consistency, survival) is more fundamental than change (growth and decay, creation and destruction, integration and disintegration).

2. *Fields.* Overt behavior can be understood only in relation to the sequence of instantaneous *fields* (a convenient abstraction) which constitute a proceeding. The field *at an instant* includes both the external situation and the internal state (e.g., energy level, emotion, abdominal pain, etc.). For Lewin, both the situation and the state are within the head of the subject, because for the subject there is no reality except the situation as he apperceives it. This, the subject's apperception of his environment, we may call the *beta situation.* The external situation as it actually exists (insofar as this can be determined by impartial inquiry) may be called the *alpha situation.* The distinction is important: it corresponds to that which can be made between a normal verifiable perception and an illusion or hallucination, and to the distinction between a normal verifiable apperception and a delusion. Since most of the psychologically crucial external proceedings are social interactions, the external situation for the subject (actor) — that is, his beta situation — commonly includes his apperceptions or beliefs in respect to the relevant beliefs and established sentiments of the object (alter) and his apperceptions in respect to the object's current feelings, thoughts, and purposes. The alpha situation — that is, the object's actual beliefs, sentiments, feelings, thoughts, and purposes — is often very different. The subject may be speaking on the basis of a gross misconception (delusion) of what is actually occurring in the object's mind. The discovery of these and other such factors involved in every interpersonal relationship is complicated and time-consuming, but in most cases it is no more difficult to arrive at some notion of the alpha situation, or what the object is feeling and thinking, than it is to arrive at some notion of the beta situation or what the subject believes the object is feeling and thinking.

3. *Interpersonal proceedings.* In analyzing and formulating an external proceeding it is as necessary to define the nature of the alpha situation — the attitudes and actions of the object — as it is to define the attitudes and actions of the subject. One person's experience of another person has a special quality, quite different from his perception of a piece of cheese, a machine, a mosquito, or even of a dog. It is marked by a recognition of mutuality, of more or less equality, accompanied by some appreciation of the feelings of the other person and some willingness to adjust to them. All this (and a lot more) makes interpersonal proceedings quite different from those in which a person is using some *thing* solely for his own gratification. This is another reason why the animal-in-maze model will not serve us.

According to the view that is being advanced here, an interpersonal proceeding is the psychologist's most significant type of real entity. The unit is not the subject's behavior, but the subject-object interaction. In the past I have called the subject's tendency "need" and the object's tendency "press" and the interaction of the two ($N \rightarrow P$, or $P \rightarrow N$) with its outcome (from the subject's standpoint) a "simple thema." Today, I am more doubtful of the aptness of this terminology. But, in any event, I believe that it is necessary to give subject and object equal status and to include them both in every real entity, or unit of interaction.

This principle should also be observed in formulating the various consistent components, or integrates, of the personality. Although the established dispositions reside in the brain, they cannot be described or explained without reference to the objects and situations which evoke them. In short, the environment is included in every adequate conceptualization of a personality.

4. *Serials.* Some actions can be sufficiently understood and appraised by witnessing one proceeding. Other kinds call for periodic observations. Most important here are the behaviors which are directed toward a distal goal (a goal which cannot be reached without months or years of effort) — receiving a Ph.D., building a large industry, being chosen Prime Minister, composing a symphony, educating a son. To arrive at a goal of this sort a man must plan and direct his energies through a long series of proceedings, each progressively related to the last and yet separated from it by an interval of time for recuperation and the satisfaction of other needs. Such a directionally organized intermittent succession of proceedings may be called a *serial*. Thus, a serial (such as a friendship, a marriage, a career in business) is a relatively long functional unit which can be formulated only roughly. One must obtain records of critical proceedings along its course and note such indices of development as changes of disposition, increase of knowledge, and of ability, quality of work accomplished, and so forth. No one proceeding in the serial can be understood without reference to those which have led up to it and without reference to the actor's aims and expectations, his time-schedule for the future.

Most people are in the midst of several on-going serials which occupy their minds whenever they are not forced by circumstance to attend to more pressing matters. Men who are intensely interested in constructing something — a house, a relationship, a political group, a scientific book — return eagerly every day to the next step or stage of their endeavor. Their behavior is so different from what is denoted by the old *S-R* formula (no stimulus, no response), that it calls for a differentiating word. I will suggest, then, that the term *proaction,* in contrast to *reaction,* be used to designate an action that is not initiated by the confronting external situation but spontaneously from within. An action of this sort is likely to be part of a serial program, one that is guided by some directional force (aim) which is subsidiary to a more distally oriented aim. As a rule, a proaction is not merely homeostatic, in the sense that it serves to restore the organism to a previously enjoyed equilibrium or state of well-being. If successful, it results in the addition or production of something — another bit of physical construction, let us say, or more money in the bank, or greater social cohesion, or another chapter of a novel, or the statement of a new theory. The integrates of serials, of plans, strategies, and intended proactions directed toward distal goals constitute a large portion of the ego system, the *establishment* of personality which inhibits impulses and renounces courses of action that interfere with progress along the elected paths of life.

5. *Subjective and objective facts for the formulation of a personality.* Since so many proceedings are incidents in some serial, they can seldom be understood without reference to certain crucial or typical earlier proceedings. If, for example, two people meet and converse with uncommon reserve and mutual suspicion, one has to obtain accounts of previous meetings in order to reveal the determinants of these attitudes.

In fact, it is difficult to interpret any interpersonal proceeding without knowledge of the history of both personalities and a knowledge of their current thoughts and feelings. Since we cannot observe the on-going (regnant) processes in the brain, these must be distinguished (whenever necessary) by introspection and reported to the psychologist (or communicated as they pass in the stream of consciousness). But since it has been proved that not all regnant processes have the attribute of consciousness, those that are not conscious must be inferred from what the subject says and does. The data, then, consist of *subjective facts* reported by the individual and of *objective facts* observed by the psychologist or by others.

The obtainable subjective facts are many and various. Besides the above-mentioned communications of current mental processes, the subject is capable of reporting with more or less accuracy: countless memories of past proceedings (internal and external); his failures and successes; estimates of his past and present valuations and attachments (attitudes and sentiments); his past and present memberships and commitments; his past and present fantasies, plans, hopes, and expectations; estimates of his major needs (motivations); traits, and abilities of significant figures (persons who have affected the course of his development); and a multiplicity of other impressions and self-assessments.

Instead of crippling himself by renouncing this source of invaluable information, limiting his data (as some scientists advise) to the behaviors which he himself can observe and faithfully record, the psychologist should discover and correct for all the determinants of error in the communication of memories, plans, valuations, self-estimates, and so forth.

The obtainable objective facts consist largely of observations of daily, uncontrolled proceedings, of lifelike (though somewhat artificial) situational tests, of laboratory reactions to standard stimuli, of so-called "projective" tests, and of tests of aptitude and ability. The observation and interpretation of these behaviors are liable to all the subjective distortions that can occur in the brain of a psychologist. So also are the objective facts reported by other observers (parents and acquaintances) of the subject's behavior.

Furnished with a sufficient supply of the above-listed kinds of data, the psychologist's mind attempts to distinguish the significant variables (establishments and processes) of the personality and to arrive at a conception of their interrelations. Thus, a man's "personality" is not a chronological sequence of behavioral facts, but, in actual practice, a *hypothetical formulation*, the object of which is to *explain* certain past proceedings and to *predict* the general character of cetrain kinds of future procedings.

OPINIONS UNFAVORABLE TO THE CLASSIFICATION OF TENDENCIES (NEEDS)

Before advancing to a survey of different types of actions, it seems advisable to examine some of the opinions or beliefs which in recent years have dissuaded psychologists from attempting to construct a comprehensive classification of behavioral tendencies. The following are noteworthy:

1. The opinion that the classification of tendencies is not desirable because every single tendency is, in truth, unique, and by classifying it one obliterates its particularity and so does violence to the facts.

The objection is a natural one, but if psychologists were to accept it as decisive, the science of human nature would come to a dead stop, since the observation of similarities and differences and the definition of classes are procedures essential to its life. The psychologist, as maker of science, generally disregards the uniqueness which, as a person, he most relishes, in order to further the long-range purposes of his profession.

Allport has been close to the facts in insisting on the uniqueness of every personality, but, in my opinion, he would be still closer to the facts if he insisted on the uniqueness of every proceeding in the career of a personality. One cannot represent a person as a combination of abstract traits without disregarding numerous critical events, traumas as well as signal achievements, moments of deterioration as well as seasons of creative development.

2. The related opinion that the classification of tendencies is impractical, if not impossible, because of the countless varieties of behaviors and the manifold combinations of tendencies which may be operating even in a single unit of interaction.

Many psychologists, I suspect, would concur with this judgment. If the definition of every variety of human action were easy, the task would have been accomplished long since, and our science would be firmly founded, as firmly, let us dream, as chemistry is founded on the periodic table of elements. The classification of needs is, in my experience, exacting, tedious, spirit-subduing toil, and only the most sanguine are capable of envisaging its completion in the near future. Yet, long as it may prove to be, the undertaking — to which so many psychologists are wittingly or unwittingly contributing — will eventually succeed.

To the casual eye the spectacle of social interactions is endlessly varied, but one has only to undertake a detailed motivational analysis of the behavior of some confiding friend or patient to discover that from multifarious starting places one arrives, time and time again, at one or another of a number of motives which do not necessitate further analysis. These motives are relatively few in number. They are ends which are desired for their own sake, ends in themselves. If, as Aristotle pointed out, men chose everything for the sake of something else, "the process would go on to infinity" and "desire would be empty and vain."

3. The opinion that there are only a very few — one, two, three, or more — *fundamental* tendencies which require definition.

Besides an overzealous or inappropriate adherence to the principle of parsimony, the following possible determinants of this opinion deserve mention:

a. A basic cognitive disposition to apperceive the events of nature as various manifestations of one force (monism), or of two opposing forces (dualism), or of a trinity or quaternary. It seems that some (if not all) minds are marked by a strong preference for one or more ideal configurations (such as a perfect circle, triangle, square) and that the tendency to project the preferred configuration into nature is scarcely resistible. Unhappily, events very seldom oblige us by flowing nicely into the molds that we have made for them.

b. The assumption that the only tendencies which require definition are those which are shared with lower organisms. Since mice do not babble spontaneously as children babble, and rats do not build religions and cathedrals, and dogs do not publish romantic novels, and pigeons do not conduct endless scientific discussions, we suspect that this assumption will be highlighted by future intellectuals as a conspicuous and typical superstition of the first half of the twentieth century, counterpoint to the medieval notion that the status of man's soul is next highest to the seraphim and cherubim.

c. The assumpion that only the viscerogenic tendencies (physiological needs) are innate and hence only these require definition; that all other tendencies are learned in childhood or later, having been instrumental in satisfying the physiological needs. The viscerogenic tendencies (thirst, hunger, sex, excretion, etc.) are certainly basic in the sense that survival depends on their fulfillment and all other tendencies require survival for their operation. But there are innate (not learned) tendencies, such as crying, and innate (not learned) dispositions, such as fear and anger, which, though instrumental to survival, are not, strictly speaking, viscerogenic. Also there are innate tendencies, such as the parental tendency, which are instrumental to the survival of the species but are not wholly viscerogenic. Furthermore, there are several kinds of activities — some of them spontaneously initiated, like the babbling and play of children, some of them situationally reactive, such as choosing a path of almost certain death in war ("dying for one's country"), or committing suicide out of desperation — which prove that the viscerogenic needs are not the *alpha* and *omega* of motivation. The principle of functional autonomy may be used to account for the relative independence of some of the "higher" needs, but even these seem to depend on the presence of innate potentialities.

According to Keith's very plausible "group theory" of evolution, various "social" dispositions should be included among the inherited constituents of man's perosnality. Their presence is explained by the fact that social dispositions are effective in maintaining a high degree of group solidarity, in peace and in war, and a high degree of solidarity has been one of the most potent determinants of group survival. In the struggle for existence groups which were less disposed to coöperate were more likely to be eliminated.

d. The assumption that the only tendencies which require definition are innate, and therefore basic, tendencies (prepotent reflexes) which can be distinguished at birth or shortly afterwards. One cannot hold to this belief without overlooking the fact that several innate tendencies (like the parental drive of animals) do not manifest themselves until a certain period of maturation has elapsed.

e. The common habit of disregarding tendencies which fall outside one's special sphere of interest, or which (like respiration and sleep) seldom require serious attention, since they are seldom frustrated, seldom influential in causing personal misery or social conflict. This very natural disposition leads the animal psychologist to confine his speculations to the few drives which are susceptible to experimental controls. Similarly, it leads the psychoanalyst to think mostly of sex, aggression, and anxiety, or the craving for superiority, since these are the commonest known determinants of neurotic illness.

f. The burning ambition to be considered "scientific" or, rather, the dread of being judged "unscientific," may underlie several of the above mentioned assumptions. This dread may confine a psychologist's field of vision to those phenomena which are wholly objective, relatively simple, and mechanically measurable, and thus black-out most of the activities, particularly the verbal activities, of human beings.

Whether or not one of the above-listed dispositions or some other disposition is influential, I believe that it is a mistake to limit ourselves to the definition of a very few tendencies. In the first place, if only a few tendencies are named and described, most actions must be left dynamically undifferentiated or wholly unconceptualized. For example, if all actions are attributed to one need — say, self-actualization (Goldstein) or libido (early Freud) — no action or no person is motivationally distinguishable from any other: drinking a glass of water, spitting blood, defecating, playing tennis, making love, educating a child, leading a regiment into battle, writing a scientific treatise are all one and the same. Adding a few more tendencies is not sufficient to dispel the amorphous generality of one's formulations and predictions.

If, as present evidence suggests, sex and aggression are the chief troublemakers in neurotic illness, therapists may, without serious embarrassment, forget the other cardinal sins — pride, envy, avarice, gluttony, and sloth — but psychoanalytic theorists have been assuming, implicitly or explicitly, that their system was adequate for the understanding of normal as well as abnormal behavior. This proposition should be tested. First, possibly by determining whether *all* the behavior that occurs at a psychoanalytic seminar, meeting, or congress can be explained by reference to sex and aggression.

As indicative of the fact that we require more than a few well-defined motives to account for human behavior, one has only to read a series of case histories and observe that their authors, in attempting to make dynamical sense out of the material, refer to a number of motives (such as the desire for upward mobility, wealth, prestige, self-esteem, authority, security, and so on) which, though acceptable to common sense, are not included in the author's scheme of concepts.

In the second place, if only a few tendencies are defined, generalizations about motivation will be based solely on the manifestations of these few, and consequently, they will be insufficiently general and not applicable to all tendencies. Furthermore, having arrived at a too specific concept of tendency, the psychologist will be encouraged to disregard or rule out the other kinds of tendencies he encounters, because they do not fit his formulation. Freud, for example, did not include among drives the tendency to get rid of pain or to avoid it (fear, anxiety, etc.) apparently because this negative withdrawing and inhibiting tendency is, in certain respects, different from the sex tendency, Freud's basic model.

The task of classifying all the directional forces manifested in the behavior of almost all men in almost all cultures is that of ascending one of the Himalayan peaks of psychology, a peak which up to date has defied all climbers. So formidable has this mountain proved to be, that few modern psychologists have been inclined to try it. The decision of the majority seems to be that it does not have to be climbed, or not at present, and that more progress can be made by going round it. If I were the rational master of myself I might agree with this nearly unanimous judgment, but unhappily I am the servant of a relentless compulsion to ascend this particular mountain, not audaciously to its very summit — *that* is out of sight — but to the next station, perhaps a thousand feet above our present elevation.

A comprehensive, coherent, and applicable classification of needs (need-aims, satisfying effects) will be valuable on two counts. First, it will provide the psychologist with the criteria, the signs and symptoms, which are required for the diagnosis of every directional force that is operating in any observed proceeding (social event). Second, it will supply him with as many models and concrete illustrations as he needs to arrive at an adequate definition of his key variable, the motivation construct. Our current definitions seem to have been constructed with a large fraction of the evidence excluded from the mind's field.

The succeeding section will be devoted to descriptions of different varieties of activity, different types and states of need-dispositions, which should be included in any preparatory survey of behavioral phenomena.

VARIETIES OF ACTIVITIES, ACTIONS, NEEDFUL STATES

1. *Activity needs.* Careful consideration of a wide variety of behavioral facts has persuaded me that it is necessary to distinguish between *activity needs* and *effect needs*. An activity need is a disposition to engage in a certain kind of activity for its own sake; activity, say, which is aesthetically appreciative or creative, or intellectually interpretative or creative, or socially cohesive or creative, or politically administrative or constructive, or physically manipulative or constructive. The satisfaction is contemporary with the activity itself (provided the processes are unobstructed) and it can be distinguished from the contentment that follows some achieved effect. For convenience, here, I am dividing activity needs into (*a*) *process needs* and (*b*) *mode needs*, despite a huge doubt as to whether the word "need" can properly be applied to spontaneous (unmotivated) mental processes.

a. Process needs (sheer function pleasure). Personality is not an organ that remains inert until stimulated from without. It is marked from first to last by a continuous flow of on-going activities. These unabatable processes are fundamental "givens," the most elementary characteristics of the life of the mind (brain). No external instigations are required for their production. They are spontaneous, involuntary, effortless, and random — random perceptions, random evaluations, random successions and combinations of images and symbols, random vocalizations and verbalizations, random gestures and movements. These undirected and hence uncoördinated pulsions, so prevalent in childhood, can be regarded as manifestations of surplus energies, or, as Murphy calls them, "tissue tensions." From infancy onward, these pulsions exhibit with increasing frequency some degree of directionality, though often without awareness of goal. As soon as an aimed need is aroused, these self-same processes become instruments of its fulfillment, coördinated and directed with a certain degree of force, persistence, and focality (definiteness of goal). As time goes on, stretches of voluntary, consciously planned, goal-directed, and practically effective actions occur with increasing frequency. But even in maturity speech is not invariably goal directed. Much of it consists of spontaneous expressions of ideas and sentiments, outpourings of emotion, not unlike the verbalizations of children described by Piaget, that run on without definite purpose and without much consideration of the feelings of others. This kind of thing is hard to distinguish from exhibitionism. As Lord Chesterfield has said: "All natural talk is a festival of ostentation; and by the laws of the game each accepts and fans the vanity of the other."

b. Mode needs. Needs which are satisfied by excellence of form (musical patterns, logical clarity and coherence, gracious social manners, executive efficiency as an art, verbal eloquence, beauty of physique and movement) are different from process needs insofar as they require *perfected* expressions, most of which can be achieved only by diligent application and discipline. The goal is to have them appear effortless, but to attain this ideal, constant practice, correction, and rehearsal are required. Mode needs are different from effect needs, because the experienced satisfaction is not linked with the effect of some consummatory act, but is present (to a varying degree) from the beginning to the end of the activity (e.g., listening to the performance of a symphony). The neglect of mode needs by American psychologists may be correlated with our ideology, our addiction to ceaseless hectic strivings for tangible results. As a man once said to me: "It was a dirty job but I got good clean money for it."

The fact that I am confining myself almost wholly in this paper to effect needs should not be construed as blindness to the significance of activity needs. On the contrary, I believe not only that activity needs are extremely common the world over, but that the satisfactions which psychologists usually associate with attained effects (tensionless states, satiations) are, in fact, more closely correlated with the activities which precede the attainment of these effects.

2. *Mental needs.* According to the nineteenth-century conception, the human mind is like an inanimate and impartial motion-picture film which accurately records the succession of physical events. It is a percept-registering or fact-registering organ, with the attributes of a scientific instrument. The introduction of the concept of tendency (animal drive) however, required that this notion of the mind be modified so as to embrace the function of *selection.* Out of the passing medley of physical patterns the brain picks out those which are pertinent to the reduction of hunger pangs and of sexual tensions. According to this view, the human mind is waiter and pimp to the body. That these are among its functions can hardly be denied, but if we attend to them exclusively, studying only those proceedings in which the governing organ yields to, or is pushed around by, this or that viscerogenic tension, we shall fail to observe that the mind has ways and interests of its own.

In its beginnings — in primitive men and in today's children — the human mind does not, like the animal mind, apply the bulk of its powers to the business of efficient physical manipulations and technical adjustments, but to the creation and expression of dramas: fantasies, stories, legends, and mythologies; comic and heroic plays, spectacles, and rituals. Fantasy invents another, better world and deems it present. Think of the millions who, in this "advanced," realistic, scientific era, spend such enjoyable hours day-dreaming at the movies? According to this view, it is not perception that is fundamental, but imagination. As Langer, among others, has shown so convincingly, the human mind is a *transforming* organ, its function being to make symbols (images and words) for things, and to combine and recombine these incessantly, and to express them in a variety of languages, discursive (referential) and expressive (emotive). The needs of the mind, though less prepotent than the viscerogenic needs, are much more important in the lives of intellectuals — scientists, artists, poets, philosophers, religionists — all of whom, positivists included, are more attached to their models, abstractions, and visions than they are to any facts.

3. *Creative needs.* Creativity is marked by spontaneous and involuntary eruptions of novel symbols and novel combinations of symbols (process need), and by great attention to form (mode need), and by hours of purposive thinking, with ceaseless reconstructions of emerging elements, rejections, and revisions (effect need). Thus, a creative need calls for all types of dynamic functioning, and if it is not too severely checked and frustrated by failures to solve its many problems, its activities are acocmpanied by the three chief types of satisfaction (process pleasure, mode pleasure, and effect pleasure, the latter accompanying the completion of each portion of the production).

Needs of this class are peculiar in having no clearly envisaged target or goal, the goal being something that has never existed (new machine or gadget, new social group, new political constitution, new dramatic epic, new scientific hypothesis or theory, new philosophy). Thus, the goal is something that must be constructed step by step. Besides this, it seems that some degree of creativity is required to adjust successfully to any novel situation. Fixation on certain ideas, rigidities of perspective, trite and banal proposals, are not apt to solve new problems or initiate courtships. They are manifestations of "trained incapacity," a state which, by preventing the attainment of new values, interferes with the development of personality.

4. *Negative needs.* Perhaps it is unnecessary to state that among our collection of needs we should include the "negative" dispositions to reject, to exclude, to expel, to withdraw or flee from, to avoid or hide from, or to defend oneself against, some noxious, contemptible, critical, censorious, injurious, or deadly object or situation, out of disgust, scorn, boredom, embarrassment, guilt, anxiety, or dread. Negative needs are likely to operate in an anticipatory fashion in order to avoid disagreeable or frightening situations, or, if possible, to prevent their occurrence (see next heading: proreactive need).

5. *Proactive, reactive, proreactive, reproactive needs.* A *proactive* need

has already been defined as one that becomes spontaneously kinetic (as the result, presumably, of some inner change of state), in contradistinction to a *reactive* need which is evoked by a certain kind of externally confronting situation. Proactive needs, such as those for physical activity, for food, for affectional relations, for knowledge, or for artistic composition arise (say, on waking) when no relevant instigations are perceptible. They inaugurate planning — images of activities to be enjoyed and goals to be reached and images of ways and means (strategies and tactics) — and, at once or later, direct the person's behavior toward the region where the plan may be turned into experience. Proactions, as a rule, are things which a person positively wants to do. Reactions, on the other hand, are more apt to be responses to situations which are unsought, unexpected, and dissatisfying.

A *proreactive* need is one which is ordinarily reactive and negative, but which, on the given occasion, has been evoked from within by anxiety-breeding images of an external situation (humiliation, danger) which might occur if some preventive measures are not taken.

A *reproactive* need is one which is ordinarily proactive but which, on the given occasion, has been evoked, not from within, but by an unexpected situation (sight of food, sudden appearance of an old friend).

"Proactive" might be used very loosely to describe people who act in the absence of outside instigations, zestful self-starters who initiate enterprises and lead off in conversations. Reactors are more apt to be followers than leaders, observers than performers. People who worry a great deal, whose peak of satisfaction is a clear conscience, are most likely to engage in pro-reactions.

6. *Generality and specificity: diffuse and focal needs.* A need is a *general* disposition which commonly becomes associated through "focalization," or "canalization," as Murphy would say, with a number of *specific* entities (a certain doll, or dog, or person, or group, or town, or theory, or work of art, or religion), and (through "generalization") with a number of *kinds* of *semispecific* entities (French wines, or horses, or women, or music, or novels, or philosophies).

These focalizations (specificities and semispecificities) rarely exhaust the possibilities of need activity. Unless the structure of the disposition has become rigid and fixated, it is always capable of becoming attached to a new object — new kind of food, new place, new acquaintance, new organization, new kind of art, new ideology. Indeed, the development of a personality can be partially represented by listing, in chronological order, the attachments it has acquired and perhaps outgrown in the course of its career; for example, a series of material objects, such as a rattle, toy truck, mechano set, bicycle, motorcycle, automobile, airplane; or a series of aesthetic forms, such as comics, dime novels, adventure stories, Dickens, Tolstoy, Shakespeare. Attachments (sentiments, attitudes), then, may be more or less enduring.

A permanent attachment to a nurturant person (e.g., mother fixation) dating from infancy is regarded by psychoanalysts as a sign of emotional immaturity. Equally indicative of retardation is its apparent opposite: lack of enduring attachments, that is, the inability to remain loyally committed to anybody or anything. Here we might speak of a *diffuse* need which is sensitive to a large number or variety of objects (e.g., free-floating sociability, free-floating anxiety, free-floating irritability) in contrast to a *focal* need which is enduringly centered on one object (e.g., satisfying marriage, specific phobia, canalized revenge).

An entity (material object, person, group, political policy, philosophy) to which one or more needs have become attached is said to have *cathexis* (power to excite). A *liked* entity which attracts the subject is said to have *positive* cathexis; whereas a *disliked* entity is said to have *negative* cathexis. An entity with negative cathexis (negatively cathected object) may evoke avoidant reactions, defensive reactions, or destructive reactions. Thus a *goal* object may be either a positively cathected (loved) person or a negatively cathected (hated) person whom the subject wants to subdue, injure, insult, or murder. Entities (places, animals, persons, topics of conversation) which the subject wishes to avoid (withdraw or flee from) may be called *noal* objects. The distribution in any personality of these different kinds of cathections (evaluations, sentiments, attitudes) is correlated with the relative potency of the three vectorial dispositions so well described by Horney: moving toward people (positive goal objects), moving against people (negative goal objects), and moving away from people (negative noal objects). A positive noal object might be a beloved person or a desired drug such as morphine or alcohol that the subject, for one reason or another, believes he should avoid or permanently renounce.

In a developing individual, positively cathected goals and goal objects are of two classes: (1) satisfying goals which have been experienced more or less regularly week after week and (2) goals which have not yet been attained, but which sway the imagination and orient the planning processes of the mind. In sanguine temperaments, visions of future goals (grass on the other side of the fence) are likely to be given higher values than goals which are attainable every day. This applies especially to the creative needs, the goals of which are always novel, never-yet-constructed entities.

We can affirm that goals of the above-defined first class are *learned*, but can we say this about the more greatly esteemed goals of the second class? Perhaps we can say that these are learned by "trial and error," in the imagination. Many of them, we know, become established through identification with some exemplar, in conformity with cultural expectations, and are therefore to be subsumed under the heading of social imitation. In any event, they are not innately given.

The fact that the word "learning" (when used by an American psychologist) refers almost always to the process of acquiring effective instrumental action patterns, might, I suppose, be cited as another illustration of how a prevailing ideology (e.g., the high valuation of technical skills; "How to Make Friends and Influence People") can influence the course of our supposedly chaste science.

More important than means-end learning, of course, is goal and goal-object learning; that is, the process whereby an individual comes to some conclusions as to the relative values of different possible goals and goal objects, or, looking at it from a developmental or educational standpoint, the process whereby he learns to enjoy (and so discovers for himself) the kinds of goals and goal objects which are worth striving for. Our knowledge of this latter process, however, is very meagre, since science has taught Western intellectuals to keep out of the domain of values, to cease thinking at the boundary between facts and sentiments, and consequently, to leave the determination of social goals to chance and the operation of blind forces. As R. W. Livingstone has said, ours is a "civilization of means without ends; rich in means beyond any other epoch, and almost beyond human needs; squandering and misusing them, because it has no overruling ideal." The truth, as I see it, is not that we moderns have no ends; we are pushing ourselves or being pushed toward a multiplicity of material, economic, political, and scientific ends, trying every conceivable short-cut and clawing and smearing each other without mercy in our efforts to get there first. The point is we have no common humanistic end. We have lost the vision of the good life, shared happiness.

7. *Role behaviors.* As Parsons and others have shown us, the concept of role is strategic to the integration of the two levels of theoretical analysis, psychological and sociological. To make this clear we might stretch this concept, for the moment, beyond its intended limits and say that every self-and-body, in order to develop, maintain, express, and reproduce itself, must perform a number of *individual* roles (functions) such as respiration, ingestion of food, construction of new tissue, excretion, defense against assault and disease, expression of emotions and sentiments, copulation, and so forth. Likewise, it can be said, that every group (social system), in order to develop, maintain, express, and reproduce itself, must perform a number of *social* roles, such as recruitment and training of new members, hierarchical organization of functions, elimination of incorrigible members, defense against attack by rival groups, expansion by reproduction (formation of similar groups in other parts of the world), and so forth. Also, both persons and social systems are devoted to the accomplishment of one or more further purposes, such as the manufacture and exchange of utilities, the acquisition and communication of knowledge, the creation and performance of plays, the correction of delinquents, the subjugation of enemies, and so forth. Finally, both persons and social systems (each taken as a consensus of in-

tentions) are desirous of improvement, of living up to their ideals, of deserving recognition and prestige. In the personality it is the governing ego system which assumes responsibility for the integration of *individual* roles and the actualization of plans. In the group it is the leader or government that assumes responsibility for the structuring of *social* roles and the carrying out of policies. The id of the personality is somewhat comparable to the disaffected low-status members of a social system, the "unwashed masses," including the "creative minority" (Toynbee), the radical reformers and fanatics, as well as the criminals and psychotics. Every structured ego "holds a lunatic in leash" (Santayana).

Thus, by extending the concept of role (social role) to include personal roles, a personality action system and a social action system can be represented as roughly homologous, at least in certain respects.

Furthermore — but I have not the time to demonstrate this — all social roles require the execution of one or more kinds of actions; that is, the habitual production of one or more kinds of effects, and these effects (goals) can be classified in the same manner as need-aims are classified. Indeed, the need-aim and the role-aim may exactly correspond. For example, a gifted actor with a need for artistic expression may be asked by a theater manager to play Hamlet (the very part which has long excited his ambition). Thus a man may *want* to do exactly what he is expected to do. But, so happy a congruence of "want" and "must" is, in the lives of most people, more of an ideal than an actual daily occurrence.

The chief reason for the frequent discrepancy between desire and obligation is the differentiation of society into subsystems, and the differentiation of subsystems into specialized and *temporally integrated* role functions, and, finally, the necessity of *committing* men to the *scheduled* performance of these functions. It is not so much that a man is obliged (expected) to do certain things, but that he is obliged (in order to integrate his actions with others) to do them at a *fixed time*. Consequently, it may happen that a man eats when he is not hungry, converses when he feels unsociable, administers justice when he has a hangover, makes a speech when his head is bereft of enlivening ideas, goes to the theater when he wants to sleep. Thus, in many, many cases, a need is not the initiator of action, but the hands of the clock. Spontaneity is lost, and will power (an unpermitted concept) must be constantly exerted to get through the days.

The point is that here every action is an instrumental one, not satisfying in itself. Instrumental to what? This varies from individual to individual: the need for sheer survival and hence the need for money, the need for upward mobility, or for fellowship, or for authority, or for prestige; but, more generally and more closely, the need for roleship (as I am calling it), that is, the need to become and to remain an accepted and respected, differentiated and integrated part of a congenial, functioning group, the collective purposes of which are congruent with the individual's ideals. So long as the individual feels this way about the group that he has joined, he will try to abide, as best he can, by its *schedule* of role functions.

8. *Miscellaneous distinctions.* It is hardly necesary to say that, although some needs are allowed free expression, others are habitually restrained or completely inhibited. The former are components of the *overt, manifest* personality (social self), whereas the latter are components of the *covert, latent,* personality (shadow self). Covert needs express themselves in dreams and fantasies, in various forms of projection, and in neurotic symptoms. The subject is usually conscious of the true goal of most of his overt needs, but he may be partly, or wholly, unconscious of the nature of several of his covert needs. The needs which are apt to be suppressed or repressed are those which are contrary to cultural standards: lust after some forbidden object and needs associated with avarice and miserliness, envy and jealousy, hate and anger, pride and vanity.

Needs may turn inward as well as outward, the subject's own body or self being the object of them. A man may encourage, adorn, inflate, console, belittle, curse, castrate, or kill himself.

9. *Gratuities.* It is important to note that needs are often satisfied without the subject's behaving. They are satisfied (as they are in infancy) by the actions of another person or by the course of events (as when a detested person dies of a coronary). Such providential effects may be called *gratuities*.

10. *Prepotency of needs.* Prepotent needs are those which become regnant with the greatest urgency if they are not satisfied. The need for oxygen can remain unsatisfied for no more than a few minutes. The need to get rid of pain or to jump away from danger is often most compelling. In a desert the need for water may take complete possession of cognition. Maslow has well described the focalizations and reëvaluations that occur in the mind of a hungry man, and how, after the viscerogenic need-aims are realized, other kinds of needs become prepotent, needs for interpersonal affiliations, needs for achievement (self-respect) and recognition (prestige, superiority), and earlier or later as the case may be, needs for creation and self-expression, for roleship and orientation toward the "higher" purposes of humanity. Individuals differ in respect to how much bodily or egocentric contentment they require before committing themselves to sociocentric aims. Those who are dedicated to the life of the imagination — especially religionists — are disposed to recommend, if not insist upon, restraints or renunciations of such physical enjoyments as those of lust, gluttony, and passivity (sloth).

DEBATED ISSUES AND POSSIBLE SOLUTIONS

1. *Attitudes, interests, values.* Social psychologists looking in at themselves and looking out at others concluded some time back that a great deal

of human thought and behavior is value-oriented. It seemed, for example, that the psychologist's own intellectual preoccupations, conversations, and activities could be largely explained by stating that he was *interested* in theories of personality and social behavior, *interested* in research, *interested* in educational procedures, *interested* in political policies, and so forth. These regions of thought and action were highly *valued*. He had a *positive attitude* toward them. More specifically, his attitude was positive toward *certain* concepts (e.g., traits), certain *kinds* of research (e.g., opinion polling), certain *kinds* of educational procedures (e.g., small research seminars), certain *kinds* of political policies (e.g., labor legislation), and so forth. "Attitude," as defined by Allport and others, became the social psychologist's key concept. A man's personality was conceived as a more or less integrated system of attitudes, each of which is a relatively permanent disposition to evalute some entity negatively or positively, and as a rule to support this evaluation with reasons, or arguments. The general or specific entity (object of the attitude) *was* a *value*, positive or negative, or *had* value (power to attract or repel).*

In the judgment of most social psychologists there is a big difference, or gap, between attitudes (vaguely defined as dynamical forces) and needs (or drives), probably because the latter are fixedly associated in their minds with hunger and sex. They are willing to concede that there are such "pushes from the rear" as hunger and sex, but these are said to be "segmental" and "lower." Attitudes, on the contrary, are consciously and rationally selected "pulls from the front." The principle of functional autonomy is usually invoked to sever whatever associations might have existed in the subject's past between needs and attitudes.

Assuming that this greatly telescoped account of the concept of attitude conforms roughly to the conventional notion, I submit that two modifications are required before it can be assigned an important place in a theoretical system. First, its scope must be extended to include all affect-invoking entities from feces to the Fallen Angel. There is no reason to limit the term to dispositions toward "higher" entities. We must be able to speak of attitudes toward the mother's breast, the mother herself, siblings, spinach, mechanical toys, play group, comics, fairly tales, and so forth. Second, the concept must be logically connected with directional activity, that is to say, with the concept of need. Knowledge that a certain person has, let us say, a positive attitude toward music does not tell us what he *does* about it, if anything. Perhaps he values music very highly (as checked on a questionaire), but is too busy to listen to it. Or, to take the opposite extreme, he may be a composer of

---

* Here it might be noted that "attitude" and "sentiment" are synonyms, both of them referring to a more or less lasting disposition in the personality; also that "value," in one sense, is synonymous with "cathexis" and "valence" and, in the other sense, with "cathected entity" and "object with valence." There is always a representation (image) of the valued, or cathected, entity *in* the personality.

music. If we are not told, the man does not become alive. We cannot guess how he spends his day or predict what he would do at a certain choice-point. Does he keep music alive in his head by humming it? Does he discuss music with other appreciators and defend the excellence of his favorite concertos? Does he play some instrument, privately for his own satisfaction, or publicly for the satisfaction of others? Is playing in an orchestra his professional role, his path to money and eminence? He may be a music critic, a writer of books on music, or a singing teacher. Or, is he merely an enjoyer of music as it comes over the radio? If a high evaluation of music is linked with one or more vectorial dispositions (such as reception, creation, expression), we can represent what a given appreciator *does* with music; we can picture many proceedings in his life. Otherwise, one has only a dangling abstraction.

Now, having pointed to the mote in the eye of the attitude construct, it is time for me to acknowledge the beam in the conception of need: not all needs have been defined as *dispositions operating in the service of a certain kind of value.* Language is always failing us, but perhaps the following words may indicate to an indulgent reader the kinds of values I have in mind: body (physical health), property (wealth), authority (power), affiliation (interpersonal affection), knowledge (science, history), beauty (art), ideology (philosophy, religion), and so forth. These are the six well-known Spranger values, with the addition of "physical health." Others will be added later. Here it is sufficient to suggest that the major tendencies be defined in relation to each class of values; for instance, *aggression* to defend body, to defend property, to defend position as leader, to defend the integrity of a relationship, to defend certain theories (truth), to defend the preëminence of certain works of art (beauty), to defend one's faith (religion), and so forth.

I hope that the concept of proactive, mental needs, outlined above, will disabuse social psychologists of the idea that needs operate solely in the service of the body. The human mind has imaginative interests peculiar to itself.

I suspect that at least one point of difference has not been resolved by these formulations. In contrast to the social psychologists, dynamic psychologists are disposed to believe that the seeds of attitudes (which are basically affective, rather than cognitive) are implanted in childhood and that their ramifying roots are in the inaccessible, unconscious earth of the personality. Furthermore, dynamic psychologists are apt to believe with Jonathan Edwards that a man may be able to do what he chooses, but he cannot choose what he chooses.

2. *Innateness of needs.* In the heyday of primitive behaviorism, the prime target for the revolutionists' machine guns and cap pistols was the despotic concept, instinct. In the ids of the Americans, this concept was somehow linked with the stereotype of the aloof and lofty Britisher, and with arm-

chair speculation, as well as with the noxious notion of constitutional determinism and its repellent offspring, racial superiority. McDougall's unpardoned error was to assume that in conjunction with certain dispositions, man inherits, as the lower animals inherit, certain modes of behavior: a pattern of flight in conjunction with fear, a pattern of combat in conjunction with anger, a pattern of nurturant behavior in conjunction with pity, and so forth.

Having shown that most instrumental acts are *learned* and that most goal objects (specific values) are *learned*, social scientists wasted no time in committing McDougall to limbo. His instinct theory was, to all appearances, killed and buried. But, in no time, it rose again, reshaped and disguised by a new name, "drive," and later, "need." This reincarnation of the irrepressible notion of directional force was welcomed by some as the herald of a new scientific era in psychology.

Today, all psychologists agree that some needs are inherited (say, the viscerogenic needs), but most of us are doubtful in respect to other kinds of needs. In my opinion, we do not have to solve this problem now, or in the near future. The task of classifying needs can proceed as if the question did not exist. The only required criterion is that of universality. The basic list of tendencies should be restricted to dispositions which are exhibited by almost all persons in almost all cultures, whether or not they have been proved innate. Here, the reader might be reminded again that "need" refers to an *internal* component (a necessary construct) and *not* to any specific action pattern or to any specifically valued entity.

Why not conceive of the inheritance of a number of *potential* dispositions, the activation and establishment of which depends on a variety of external (social, cultural) determinants? The near universality of the basic tendencies suggests that almost all societies and cultures provide, at least in some degree, the conditions which are necessary for their inauguration and perpetuation.

3. *Diagnosis of needs.* Some critics have objected to the need theory on the grounds that one cannot immediately tell them which need is being exhibited by a given person at a given time. But if anything should be clear it is that needs are not discernible facts. A need is an intervening variable, hidden in the head, the operation of which can only be inferred on the basis of certain symptoms. Hence, the task of identifying an active need is not that of labeling the kind of behavior that is observed, but of making a diagnosis. Sometimes the diagnosis is easy: the need is almost as obvious as the movements and the words. But, often, it is impossible to decide, even after hours of investigation, whether or not this or that disposition was operating during the observed event.

4. *Dissatisfaction, satisfaction.* One of the strangest, least interpretable symptoms of our time is the neglect by psychologists of the problem of happi-

ness, that inner state which Plato, Aristotle, and almost all succeeding thinkers of the first rank assumed to be "the highest of all goods achievable by action." Although the crucial role of dissatisfaction and of satisfaction is implicit in much that is said about motivation, activity, and reinforcement, psychologists are generally disposed to shun these terms as well as all their synonyms (displeasure-pleasure, discontent-content, sorrow-joy, and so forth) as if they were a horde of spirochetes capable of reducing us to a state of general paresis.

In many psychologists the phobia may be attributed to the fact that "satisfaction" is associated with a subjective state and animals cannot tell us in so many words whether they are satisfied or not. In other people the phobia seems to have been engendered through the association of satisfaction with hedonism (which suggests wine, women, and song to Puritans). McDougall's repudiation of the pain-pleasure principle was vibrant with moral indignation. Perhaps there are other, more subtle determinants. Perhaps we are wisely suppressing the very idea of happiness and do not wish to discuss it, because the state seems unattainable under present world conditions. Is this the case? Or is it that all of us are victims of a moral epidemic, that we have yielded to the *success compulsion* which, though depriving us of daily happiness, is a possession we are incapable of exorcising? The answer is too elusive for my clumsy grasp.

Be that as it may, satisfaction is an affective state which is likely to manifest itself *objectively* as well as subjectively. It is no more difficult to diagnose than anxiety or anger, and, in my opinion, should be thoroughly investigated, since it is the most refined sign that we have of whether need processes are being obstructed, advancing without friction, or attaining their aim, or after cessation of action, whether the effect produced did in fact appease the need.

It might be helpful to conceive of a physical variable (H) in the brain (possibly the thalamus) the concentration of which varies along a continuum, or scale, just as the hydrogen concentration of the blood varies along the acid-alkaline continuum. At the lowest end of the continuum H manifests itself *subjectively* as a feeling of extreme dissatisfaction (dejection, depression) and *objectively* by certain readily distinguishable postures, grimaces, gestures, and expressive sounds. At the highest end of the continuum we get extreme satisfaction (elation, joy) combined with its objective symptoms. At the middle of the continuum would be the zone of indifference. If we call H "hedone," and its continuum the "hedonic scale," we can say that every occurrence which moves H *down* the scale is *hedonically negative* and every occurrence which moves H *up* the scale is *hedonically positive*. With this terminological framework we can go on to study the kinds of events that are hedonically negative and the kinds that are hedonically positive.

There is not room here to discuss the pain-pleasure principle. All I can do is to reiterate the antique proposition (which research over the years has verified more often for me than any other psychological hypothesis or dictum) that the aim of all needs is hedonically positive (in the imagination). That is to say, the imaged goal of all activity is *believed* to be associated with more hedone (less dissatisfaction or more satisfaction) than the field in which the individual finds himself at the moment. This belief is no more than a prediction. The man may be mistaken. After attaining his goal the expected satisfaction may not occur, which only means that the discrimination of goals (values) is something that must be learned through experience.

This is not psychological hedonism in the sense that behavior can be understood as riddance of pain and pursuit of pleasure, because we are never dealing with pain *in general* or pleasure *in general*. The most that we can say is that behaviors tend to reduce or are calculated to reduce a certain *kind* of dissatisfaction (thirst, hunger pangs, sexual tensions, destitution, loneliness, inferiority feelings, disgust, and so forth), and that they tend to attain and to prolong a certain *kind* of satisfaction. In other words, a certain kind of dissatisfaction (e.g., fullness of the bladder) cannot be relieved by *any* kind of satisfaction (e.g., congenial discourse).

Need, then, is the fundamental variable and degree of satisfaction (hedone) the best indicator of its state or progress.

CRITERIA FOR THE CLASSIFICATION AND DISCRIMINATION OF NEEDS

The basic requirement for an acceptable classification of needs, or of anything else for that matter, is a set of reliable criteria by which each class may be distinguished from all other classes. In my judgment, reasonably reliable criteria have already been proposed by various authors, which, when defined more rigorously, should meet the demands of the majority of personologists.

Since psychologists have devoted themselves almost exclusively to the study of effect needs (as I have called them), I shall do likewise in this section, and confine myself to the criteria in terms of which dispositions of *this* type may be classified, or in terms of which they may be discriminated after they have been classified. I shall be dealing with *overt* needs; that is, needs which are not inhibited or repressed but are manifested objectively by motor and verbal actions.

1. *Kinds of initiating or reacting (inner) state.* This may be a pattern of sensations (e.g., thirst, hunger, lust), or a mild and scarcely definable tension or feeling (e.g., greed, envy, loneliness), or an intense emotion (e.g., fear, anger, love, pity). Since such internal states are not open to direct observation, they must be inferred from *objective signs* (e.g., characteristic expressions of apprehension, irritation, friendliness, mirth), or from *subjective reports* (e.g., "I feel very cold," "I dislike that arrangement of colors,"

"I feel humiliated"). This criterion, however, is not very reliable, because (1) there are many states of tension which have no clearly distinguishable objective manifestations, (2) some states are intrinsically vague, hard to discriminate introspectively, and hard to represent in words, and (3) the state may be unconscious, and the subject unable, therefore, to give a true account of it.

2. *Kind of initiating (external) situation.* The situational constituent that fixes the attention of the subject and excites activity can usually be discriminated *objectively* and diagnosed in terms of its meaning to most people of the same age, sex, status, and culture as the subject. I have called this the alpha situation. What the situation means to the subject, that is, how *he* interprets it, is the beta situation. The nature of the beta situation may be discovered sometimes by interrogation.

In most cases it is impossible to describe, formulate, and classify the situational processes in terms of their physical properties. These are almost infinite in variety and quantity. The physique of the alter, the clothes he is wearing, his facial expression, his gestures, the tempo of his speech, the structure of his sentences, the exact words he used, the ever-varying intonations of his voice — these can be recorded on a motion-picture film with sound track, but they cannot be represented symbolically as a changing pattern of shapes, lines, colors, textures, sounds, and odors. And, even if it were possible to construct models of the succession of such sense data, there would be little correlation, we can be certain, between these representations and the reactions of subjects. In the first place, a human being selects, consciously and unconsciously, out of the fast flow of perceptions those which seem relevant to his immediate well-being, to his intellectual or aesthetic concerns, to his serial goals. In the second place, almost simultaneously in most cases, the subject apperceives (interprets) and evaluates these selected impressions (decisively or tentatively) as a more or less meaningful unit. For example, he accepts them as signs of safety or of danger, of friendliness or of antagonism, of tolerance or of intolerance, of respect or of disrespect, and so forth. Furthermore, in arriving at his diagnosis of the object's proaction (the social situation) the subject invariably estimates it in relation to the moral, aesthetic, and intellectual standards to which a person of that age, sex, and status (relative to himself) is culturally expected to conform. A certain remark, for example, might be considered "bright" coming from a child but "stupid" in the mouth of an adult. Some gestures are considered "unbecoming" (effeminate) in a man, but "attractive" in a woman. Certain words are "offensive" if shouted by a subordinate, but "humorous" if uttered by a congenial peer. None of these subtleties can be discriminated and represented in terms of the physical properties of the alter's actions. They must be discerned and appraised, more or less intuitively, by a psychologist who is intimately acquainted with the society of which subject and object are members. This unavoidable task, or function, places the psychologist, sociologist, and cultural anthropologist outside the domain of positivistic science, since the latter is confined by definition to sense data, operationally defined.

Lewin tried to avoid this difficulty by affirming (1) that the nature of the beta situation can be inferred from the subject's behavior and (2) that the nature of the alpha situation (the situation as interpreted by representative and knowledgeable members of the given society) can be neglected. In my opinion, neither assumption is tenable, because (1) there is not, as far as we know, an invariable correlation between beta situation and behavior, and (2) if the nature of the alpha situation is not apperceived and its intensity appraised by the psychologist, it will be impossible for him to judge whether or not the subject is suffering from a delusion, whether or not his behavior falls within cultural expectations.

Granting that the psychologist's unit is a man-situation or subject-object interaction, it becomes necessary to classify object processes as well as subject processes. In the absence of such a classification, gross similarities and differences among proceedings cannot be defined, and without definitions of this sort science of human events is scarcely attainable. What we want to know is how people in general, or how people of a given type or category, respond to situations such as these: frustration, postponement of gratification, social rejection, injustice, despotic coercion, moral comdemnation, erotic advances, flattery, appeals for help, and so forth.

As I have suggested elsewhere, situations are susceptible of classification in terms of the different kinds of effects which they exert (or may exert) on the subject; that is, in terms of their significance to his well-being. In formulating an interpersonal proceeding, for example, the task would be that of defining the need-aim of the object (just as one would define the need-aim of the subject). The question is, what is the object doing to the subject, or intending to do, or capable of doing under certain circumstances? Is the subject being rejected or accepted, attacked or assisted? Are his tastes being criticized or praised? Is his behavior being blamed or commended? Is the object disagreeing or agreeing with his views, competing or coöperating with him? Such *press* (plural: *press*), as I have called them, may be roughly divided into *benefits* (satisfying press) and *harms* (dissatisfying press). Besides active harms, two additional classes of dissatisfying press deserve mention: *lacks* (absences of benefits, depriving situations, barren environments) and *barriers* (physical obstructions or social prohibitions — laws — which prevent the enjoyment of potential benefits, available, perhaps, to other people).

Many situations are not definable as press (which have already been exerted), but rather as signs of *potential press* — promises of benefits or threats of harm. In such cases, the subject will predict to himself or expect that the alter will respond with an agreeable or beneficial press if he is properly treated, or that he will exert a disagreeable or harmful press if the subject comes within reach of him or acts in a provocative manner.

To discriminate the press of the alter is not enough. We must know his relative age, sex, status, and so forth.

Distinguishing the kind of situation that confronts the subject is not only necessary to a definition of the thema of the proceeding, but is useful in limiting the number of probable need-aims in the subject, since there are only a few emotionally logical or culturally expected reactions to any given press (kind of situation). The unreliability of this criterion, however, is obvious. Personalities differ widely in respect to their *sensitivities* to, or *tolerance* of, similar situations. Some people are much more responsive than others to signs of physical danger, or of contempt, or of a friend's distress.

3. *Kind of initiating imaged situation which is accepted as a future possibility*. Many proactions and proreactions are instigated by images of possible future benefits to be enjoyed or of possible future harms to be forestalled or circumvented. The efficacy of such images is basic to the Christian drama of salvation: visions of eternal bliss in heaven as reward for virtuous conduct; visions of everlasting tortures as punishment of sin. The same holds, on the one hand, for soaring hopes of worldly success and fame ("last infirmity of noble mind"), and on the other hand, for a host of anxieties respecting ill health, economic insecurity, theft, social censure, hostility, loss of office, disgrace, defeat, and so forth. At times, indeed, it seems as if the majority of actions in complex societies were aimed at preventing or reducing pricks of conscience or apprehensions in regard to some potential future ill: going to the dentist, getting vaccine injections, taking out insurance, locking up valuables in a strong box, arranging one's things, performing an incessant round of duties and role obligations, working like mad to hold a job, to forestall criticism, or to prevent defeat at the hands of a rival. All self-corrective compulsions are behaviors of this type.

These proreactions are hedonically positive in so far as they serve to lower the level of dissatisfaction, but they are not apt to engender much elation.

The character of each of these initiating imaged situations can be ascertained by interogating the subject if he has insight and is honest. They are classifiable according to the same scheme that is used to discriminate perceived (external) situations.

By anticipatory behavior of the kind described here, man exhibits the "time-binding" (Korzybski) power and, in many cases, the constructive planning power which distinguish him from other animals. The temporal distance of the imaged situations may be used as a rough index of a subject's "time-perspective" (Lewin). Some people live in the present, endeavoring to extract maximum satisfaction from each experience; whereas others live a provisional existence, their inner eye fixed on some distal goal.

4. *Directionality of actones (movements and words).* Certain postural attitudes (e.g., clenching the fists), certain motor patterns (e.g., turning away), certain words or sentences (e.g., "Help!") are, in any given society, so commonly associated with the expression of a certain kind of disposition that the psychologist is probably more often right than wrong in inferring on these grounds the nature of the operating need, even though no final effect has been attained. In other words, it is sometimes possible to discern the *trend* of the movements or of the talk before any goal has been attained.

This criterion is reliable only when S uses common, effective, and direct modes of achieving his end. When his actions are unique, wholly inept, or indirect (e.g., a boy's attempting to catch pneumonia in order to punish his parents for treating him unjustly), their final aim is not clear. Equally equivocal, as a rule, are all preliminary instrumental acts (locomotions and manipulations), although it is not hard to guess what a person is going to do if we see him handling certain conventional *agency objects* (frying pan, broom, gun) or see him heading toward certain conventional goal places (restaurant, theater, library).

5. *Kind of aim (imaged goal, imaged effect).* The word "need" is often used, here and elsewhere, to denote an established general disposition to effect a certain *kind* of transformation of a certain *kind* of field (inner state and/or external situation). But more strictly speaking, "need" refers to a disposition which manifests itself in a particular place at a particular time by concrete and specific actions which, if competent, produce, sooner or later, a concrete and specific effect (goal). That is to say, a need, no matter how general, can be satisfied only by aiming at a *particular* target, or at a series of targets, *one at a time.* The particular target as the subject *imagines* it, the specific point in his "cognitive map" (Tolman) toward which all his mental processes and actions are oriented at a particular time will be called the *aim* of the need. "Aim" is synonymous with "imaged goal," "imaged effect." Since the effect has not yet been produced, the aim has no existence outside the mind. It is realistically or unrealistically imaginery. The aim might be to eat fish chowder at a certain restaurant, or to persuade a friend to join the Society for Living, or to write a play about the tribulations of an honest Congressman, or to carry out a series of experiments with turtles to prove that the human mind is aimless.

When a need is in a state of tension but lacks aim, images of possible goals, goal objects, goal places, and pathways will run through the mind until some cathected goal object is selected and its probable location (goal place) predicted. Thenceforth, the need (which might, perhaps, have been satisfied by anyone of a number of other goal objects) has a concrete aim. If this is lacking, it is impossible to orient and coördinate movements and words in such a way that the imagined effect is made actual. The subject is directed to his goal by a *plan*; that is, by a consecutive series of instrumentally related images. The pathway is clearly or vaguely seen *ahead of time* in the mind's eye. Unless such images are posited, means-end learning, I submit, cannot be explained, even in the rat. The difficulty of the task a human being sets for himself is called *level of aspiration*.

Information as to the subject's aim can usually be obtained by asking him: where are you going and for what purpose? or, why are you doing that? This is the best criterion that we have of the subject's need, if he is honest, and if but one need is operating. Very frequently, this is not the case: the aim is shared by several needs, some of which, being culturally shameful, are unconscious or, if conscious, likely to be denied. As Proust has put it, our imagination "substitutes for our actual primary motives, other secondary motives, less stark and therefore more decent."

6. *Kind of effect produced.* This criterion is crucial, because an effect need is defined in terms of the *kind of situational transformation* its processes produce. Unfortunately, it is not a very dependable criterion, for a number of reasons. (1) The subject may not have the capacity, the knowledge, the training, or the persistence to actualize his aim. Many conversations are un-acknowledged competitive situations in which each participant is frustrated by all, and all by each; no actions reach their mark. (2) The observed effect may not be the one intended. It may be an accident. (3) In social proceed-ings, the intended effect is apt to be some change in the mind of the alter. The subject wants to communicate a complicated idea to the alter, or he wants to impress him, or to show him the error of his ways, or to influence him in some subtle fashion. Who can tell for certain, in most cases, whether the goal has been achieved? The alter may be an accomplished disguiser of his feelings. (4) In proceedings which are parts of long *serials*, nothing final is accomplished, no closure reached, the enterprise is merely pushed along a step or two. (5) The subject's aim may not be a clear-cut effect, but rather a form of activity which lasts several hours (e.g., a drinking bout, or dance, or sexual courtship). (6) Finally, the psychologist has to deal here, as before, with both the alpha end-situation and the beta end-situation. According to cultural standards, the subject may have accomplished very little, or annoyed his associates, or said something shameful, and yet be unaware of it. The end-situation as *he* apperceived it (the beta end-situation) was fulfilling: he spoke well and pleased everyone.

7. *Kind of activity, effect, or situation with which hedone is associated.* This is the most sensitive index that we have of the class of need that is operat-ing or was operating, and by using both objective signs and subjective reports we can often approximate the correct diagnosis. It is not wholly reliable, of course, since satisfaction, like any other feeling or emotion, may be uncon-scious and barely show itself in facial expression or gesture.

Since this is a very long subject on which I have already touched, I shall conclude by recalling certain long-accepted facts of experience: hedone is relative. It is not associated with a fixed state, but rather with a transition between states. Also, positive hedone is closely associated with energy and zest, with the uninterrupted course of spontaneous thought and speech (process needs), with certain aesthetic patterns, with *expectations* of rewards, with reductions of tension, as well as with final achievements. The last type, as James pointed out, is correlated with the ratio of achievements over expectations.

The diagnosis of needs can be reasonably accurate if all the above-listed criteria are observed and weighed in the balance.

FINAL SUGGESTION

As indicated in the section on attitudes, I have come to believe (after identifying myself with Dr. Allport) that action tendencies must be linked with values, which means that both values and tendencies should be classified. Following Lewin and Erickson, I am calling the action tendencies *vectors*, each vector being defined as a *direction of transformation.* Every vector may be combined with every value, giving us a large but manageable number of *value-vectors,* each of which is a certain kind of need.

This scheme has worked so much better than any we have used so far that I am emboldened to give our present list of vectors and values, despite the fact that the words used do not convey the intended meaning. The best solution of the horrific terminological problem, I would guess, is to use letters, nonsense syllables, or special symbols (as in musical notation), but, as yet, nothing very practical has come to mind.

The vectors are these: (1) renunciation, (2) rejection, (3) acquisition, (4) construction, (5) maintenance, (6) expression, (7) bestowal, (8) retention, (9) elimination, (10) aggression, (11) defendance, (12) avoidance.

The values are these: (1) body [health], (2) property [usable objects, money], (3) knowledge [facts, theories], (4) beauty [sensory and dramatic patterns], (5) ideology [system of values], (6) affiliation [interpersonal relationship], (7) sex [with reproduction], (8) succorant object [child to be reared], (9) authority [power over others], (10) prestige [reputation], (11) leader [law-giver], (12) nurturant object [supporter], (13) roleship [functional place in group], (14) group [social system taken as a unit].

It would take a book to define these terms, illustrate each, explain their numerous relationships, and demonstrate the utility of the scheme. One illustration of how vectors and values are combined will bring this exposition to an abrupt halt. Take a value with which we are all concerned, knowledge (science), and link it with the action tendencies. A person may (1) *renounce* the intellectual life, the pursuit of scientific knowledge; or he may (2) *reject* certain inaccurate or irrelevant observations (e.g., rumors); or he may (3) *acquire* knowledge by exploration, observation, or reading; or he may (4) *construct* new theories and hypotheses; or he may (5) *maintain* and conserve by repetition what he has already acquired or constructed; or he may (6) *express* his ideas; or he may (7) *bestow* his knowledge on others, that is, teach; or he may (8) *retain* outworn ideas in a rigid fashion; or he may (9) *eliminate* facts and beliefs that have been shown to be erroneous; or he may (10) *attack* opposing views; or he may (11) *defend* his own theories against the attacks of others; or he may (12) *avoid* contacts which might lead to the weakening of his beliefs.

This is merely a thumbnail sketch of much work in progress.

BIBLIOGRAPHY

1. Allport, G. W. *Personality*. New York, 1937.
2. Aristotle. *Nicomachean Ethics*, trans. by W. D. Ross. Modern Library Edition. New York, 1947.
3. Bales, R. F. *Interaction Process Analysis*. Cambridge, Mass., 1950.
4. Carnap, R. "Logical Foundations of the Unity of Science," *Int. Enc. Unified Sci.*, Vol. I, no. 1, pp. 42–62.
5. Erikson, E. H. *Childhood and Society*. New York, 1950.
6. Goldstein, Kurt. *Human Nature in the Light of Psychopathology*. Cambridge, Mass., 1940.
7. Horney, Karen. *Our Inner Conflicts*. New York, 1945.
8. Keith, Sir Arthur. *A New Theory of Human Evolution*. London, 1948.
9. Langer, S. K. *Philosophy in a New Key*. Cambridge, Mass., 1942.
10. Lewin, Kurt. *A Dynamic Theory of Personality*, trans. by K. E. Zener and D. K. Adams. New York, 1935.
11. Livingstone, R. W. *The Future of Education*. Cambridge, England, 1941.
12. Maslow, A. H. "A Theory of Human Motivation," *Psychol. Rev.* L (1943), 370–396.
13. Murphy, Gardner. *Personality*. New York, 1947.
14. Piaget, Jean. *The Language and Thought of the Child*. New York, 1926.
15. Pratt, C. C. *The Logic of Modern Psychology*. New York, 1939.

4

ROBERT R. SEARS

Social Behavior and Personality

Development[1]

In recent years, a number of useful methods have been devised for measuring social behavior and the individual personality. The opinion poll, small group observational procedures, and attitude scales have contributed notably to the precision with which the action of groups can be measured and their future behavior predicted. Similarly, in the field of personality and motivation, such devices as the thematic apperception test, doll play, behavior unit or time sample observations, and standardized interviews have become more and more effective for providing objective and quantified statements about significant variables.

From a practical or applied standpoint, some of these methods have been enormously valuable. Market surveys, studies of morale in the military services, diagnostic analyses of disturbed children, and comparative studies of techniques of teaching have yielded findings that have much improved the quality of human output. In effect, the past decade has put in the hands of any competent technician procedures which permit the empirical discovery of facts and principles that hitherto had been the province of so-called men of wisdom. For many areas of human action intuitively skillful lucky guessing has given way to precise and replicable investigation. The result is a vigorously expanding body of empirical knowledge about the behavior of both individuals and groups.

One might feel encouraged, indeed, about this progress but for one thing — there is no systematic theoretical structure to integrate the empirical findings. By a *theory*, I mean a set of variables and the propositions that relate them to one another as antecedents and consequents. This involves such logical impedimenta as definitions, postulates, and theorems; the definitions of variables must be mutually exclusive; intervening variables must ultimately be reducible to operations; the reference events specified as the consequents in

[1] This is a modification, with some additions, of the author's Presidential Address delivered before the American Psychological Association at Chicago, September 3, 1951, and published in the *American Psychologist*, VI (September 1951).

theorems must be measured independently of the antecedents from which they are derived, and so on. The general procedure of theory construction is sufficiently standard that it needs no explication here.

The *findings* to be integrated are those that describe consistent relationships between behavior (or its products) and some other events. Essentially, these are the descriptive behavioral relationships that comprise the disciplines of individual and social psychology, sociology, and anthropology. Individual and group behavior are so inextricably intertwined, both as to cause and effect, that an adequate behavior theory must combine both in a single internally congruent system.

The chief advantages of a theory are two. First, it is economical in the sense that it permits many observed relationships to be subsumed under a single systematic proposition. For example, it has been found that severely punishing children's aggression at home reduces the amount of aggression, that reproving aggressive doll-play acts reduces these, that societies having severe negative attitudes toward children's aggression contain little in-group aggression, and that play groups with severely anti-aggressive leadership exhibit little quarreling. All these observed relationships can be summarized by the two propositions that punishment creates aggression-anxiety and that aggression-anxiety reduces aggression.[2] Another way of stating the economy point is that observed relationships have greater generality if the variables involved are part of a larger theory.

An appallingly small number of the relationships that have been discovered in social psychology can be generalized beyond the immediate situations in which the studies were made. With respect to attitude measurement, for example, one might well ask whether *any* general principles of an antecedent-consequent nature have been found. In personality study, descriptions of qualities are usually specific to the particular person examined. And an increasing number of investigations are casting grave doubts on the predictive value — the validity — of these descriptions.

The other virtue of a good theory is that it permits the use of multiple variables and their relating principles, in combination, for the prediction of events. For instance, it is common knowledge among teachers that a child who has been punished at breakfast is likely to be aggressive and uncoöperative in school. Frustration breeds aggression. But if one adds to this the principle of stimulus generalization, one can predict that children who are very severely punished at home will be nonaggressive in school.

There has been little opportunity in the behavior sciences as yet to gain the advantages of such compounding of propositions. Some efforts have been made to discover the personality characteristics of persons who behave in

---

[2] These particular findings could be conceptualized without the intervening variable of "aggression-anxiety," but this concept is needed for an adequate incorporation of several other findings into a theory of aggression.

specifiable ways in groups. The results have been minimal, probably because there is no systematic connection between personality variables and those describing social actions. Clinically one can often get a satisfying feeling that he "understands" a particular person's behavior, but *post hoc* understanding with *ad hoc* principles is no substitute for an internally coherent system of predictive laws.

The lack of such a system is not for want of hard work on the problem. Nor is there lack of brilliant achievement along the way. Neither social psychology nor personality study is new, and through the last half century there have appeared several reasonably elaborate theoretical formulations to systematize some of the facts in both fields. In social psychology there are those of William McDougall [8] and Floyd Allport [1]; in personality, those of G. V. Hamilton [4], Kurt Lewin [7], Gordon Allport [2], H. A. Murray [9], and the successive refiners of psychoanalytic theory. However, in the main, these systematizations have dealt with either individual or social behavior but not with both. What is needed at present is a single behavior science, with a theoretical structure that will account for the *actions* and the *changes of potentiality for actions* both of individuals and of groups.

ACTION

Every theory must have a subject matter. It must be a theory about something, obviously. A certain class of events must be selected for explication. These are the reference events, the consequents for which antecedents are discovered. The basic events to which behavior theory must have reference are *actions*. This follows from the very nature of our interest in man. It is his behavior, the things he does, the ends he accomplishes that concern us.

From a logical standpoint, a theory is of value to the extent that it orders a set of observations. There are many kinds of observations that can be and have been made of social and individual behavior. Some of these have involved inferred traits or needs; others have related to perceptions or to states of consciousness. By the criterion of logic, a theory that takes any of these phenomena as its basic reference events is acceptable.

But there is another criterion to be considered, the practical one. It is reasonable to ask what kind of events are important to us. On this score, action is clearly more significant than perception or traits. The clinician must make judgments about personality that will permit predictions of behavior. Will the patient attempt suicide? Will his performance at intellectual tasks continue to deteriorate? Will his level of social problem-solving improve under an anxiety-reduction therapy? Likewise, the teacher and the parent undertake methods of rearing a child with expectations that his actions will change in a particular direction. They want him to add more accurately, or paint more freely, or cry less violently when he is disappointed; even those changes commonly interpreted as perceptual, such as art or music appreciation, are evidenced in the form of choices as to where to go, what to look at, what to listen to.

The situation is even clearer with respect to social behavior. The social engineer is concerned with such questions as whether a certain parent-child relationship will establish habitually dependent behavior in the child, whether the eventual marriage of a courting couple will terminate in divorce or in the social facilitation of the labors of the two people, whether citizens will buy bonds or vote for a Congressman, whether a group will be shattered or solidified by external opposition — that is, whether there will be an increase or decrease in coöperative efforts and in-group aggression.

Aside from the fact that a behavior science rather than a *need* or *perceptual* science is of the greatest use to us, there is an evident practical advantage. Human beings deal with one another in terms of actions. The teacher has direct observation of the performance of her pupils. The parent or the husband or the foreman or the congressman can have only inferrential knowledge of the ideas or desires of those with whom he interacts. But he can describe the conditions that impinge on people and he can take note of the behavioral consequences. To put the argument briefly: actions are the events of most importance, and actions are most available to observation and measurement.

This is not to say that needs or motives, perceptions, traits, and other such internalized structures or processes are irrelevant. Any scientific system must contain both operational and intervening variables that are independent of the reference events forming the subject matter of the system. But the choosing of such variables must depend on their contribution to a theory that will predict actions. There is no virtue in a descriptive statement that a person or a class of persons possesses such-and-such a trait or need unless that statement is part of a larger one that concludes with a specification of a kind of action to be performed. To describe a person as having "high emotionality" or "low sensitivity" or "diffuse anxiety" is systematically acceptable only if other variables are added that will, together with these internal personal properties, specify what kind of behavior can be expected for him under some specific circumstances.

Monadic and Dyadic Units

Reference has already been made to the necessity of combining individual and social behavior into a single theoretical system. The reasons are obvious. In any social interaction, the interests, motives, habits, or other psychological properties of the acting individuals determine to some degree the kind of interaction that will occur. The shy youngster is likely to have less stimulating learning experiences with his teacher than is a bolder one; the traveler in a foreign land who knows the language forms different kinds of friendships than the traveler who uses an interpreter. Conversely, the social milieu, the interpersonal relationships, within which a person acts determine his psychological properties. A man in a subordinate role cannot act as a leader; a child reared as the younger of two develops differently from one reared as the elder of two. Whether the group's behavior is dealt with as antecedent and the individual's as consequent, or vice versa, the two kinds of events are interdependent.

To demand a combining theoretical framework is one thing, but to get it from a psychologist is quite another. In spite of their long prepossession with social influences on the individual, psychologists think monadically. That is, they choose the behavior of one person as their scientific subject matter. For them, the universe is composed of individuals. These individuals are acted upon by external events, to be sure, and in turn the external world is modified by the individuals' behaviors. But the universal laws sought by the psychologist almost always relate to a single body. They are monadic laws, and they are stated with reference to a monadic unit of behavior.

The main variables that compose such systems have been presented diagrammatically in many ways. Some are so well known that they represent, virtually, signatures for the theorists who devised them. There are Tolman's schematic sow-bug, Hull's behavior sequence, Lewin's field structure, and Miller and Dollard's learning paradigm. These diagrams differ considerably in the kinds of variables they incorporate. Some emphasize reward and reinforcement; others do not. Some are time-oriented; others are descriptive of a nontemporal force field. All specify antecedent stimulus conditions and consequent actions, but in very different ways and with quite different systematic constructs. But there is one thing in common among them — they are all monadic.

But if personality and social behavior are to be included in a single theory, the basic monadic unit of behavior must be expandable into a dyadic one. A dyadic unit is one that describes the combined actions of two or more persons.[3] A dyadic unit is essential if there is to be any conceptualization of the *relationships* between people, as in the parent-child, teacher-pupil, husband-wife, or leader-follower instances. To have a science of interactive events, one must have variables and units of action that refer to such events. While it is possible to systematize some observations about individuals by using monadic units, the fact is that a large proportion of the properties of a person that compose his personality are originally formed in dyadic situations and are measurable only by reference to dyadic situations or symbolic representations of them. Thus, even a monadic description of a person's action makes use of dyadic variables in the form of social stimuli.

---

[3] Although the prefix means "two," the term is used here simply as the minimal instance of multiplicity. Similar principles would hold whether the interactors were two or more.

This is exemplified in Fig. 1, a diagram of a monadic behavior sequence that, as will be seen, can be expanded into a dyadic sequence. One aspect of this figure deserves comment, the "environmental event." This concept refers to the changes produced in the environment by the instrumental activity; these are the changes necessary for the occurrence of the goal response. The

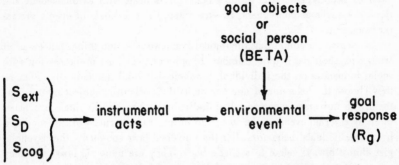

Fig. 1. THE MONADIC INSTIGATION-ACTION SEQUENCE

teacher trying to increase participatory activity in a class of children, for example, gets her reward when the youngsters spontaneously start a team game at recess. She makes her goal response — she has achieved her aim — when the environment changes, that is, when the children play a team game. Or a boy is seeking approbation from his father; he hits a three-bagger; his father grins with satisfaction. The grin is the boy's environmental event in his monadically conceived action sequence.

This concept achieves importance in the present context, because it is the necessary connecting link between a monadic and dyadic systematization of behavior. The framework for such a description is shown in Fig. 2. For con-

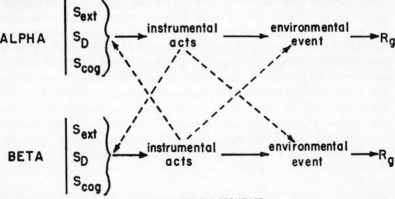

Fig. 2. THE DYADIC SEQUENCE

venience the two persons are labeled Alpha and Beta. A dyadic situation exists whenever the actions of Beta are, or produce, the environmental events for Alpha, and vice versa. The behavior of each person is essential to the other's successful completion of his goal-directed sequence of action. The drives of each are satisfied only when the motivated actions of the other are carried through to completion. The nurturant mother is satisfied by the fully loved child's expression of satiety, and the child is satisfied by the expressions of nurturance given by his mother.

It must be made clear in this connection that "environmental events" are *only those changes in environment produced by the behavior of the person*

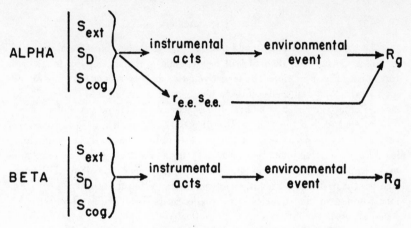

Fig. 3. THE DYADIC SEQUENCE WITH ANTICIPATORY RESPONSES
TO THE ENVIRONMENTAL EVENT

under consideration. The stroke of lightning that splits a log for the tired woodcutter is not in this category, nor is the food given the newborn infant by his mother, nor the empty taxi that providentially appears when the rain is hardest. These are certainly characteristics of the environment, manipulanda that govern in some ways the future behavior of Alpha, but they are not environmental events. They were not induced by any action of Alpha.

This is an important distinction. Unless the interaction of Alpha and Beta is based on something other than the fortuitously useful conjunction of their individual actions, there is no interdependence of each on the other. There is, in effect, no dyadic system, only a piling up of parallel monadic sequences.

The factor responsible for maintaining stability of the dyadic unit is exhibited in Fig. 3. It is the *expectancy* of the environmental event, diagrammed in a notation similiar to that used by Hull for the anticipatory goal response [6]. The existence of such anticipatory responses can be derived from the monadic principles of learning. Alpha's actions, whether instrumental or goal, that involve manipulation of the environmental events produced by Beta's behavior move forward in Alpha's sequence in the form of reduced or symbolic responses which, in turn, instigate response-produced cues. These are the *expectancies* of Beta's supportive behavior, and this is the mechanism by which a dyadic behavior unit can be derived from the combining of two or more monadic units.

The development of this part of the behavior theory is perhaps a task for sociologists. Cottrell [3] and Parsons [10] have given attention to the matter, and the next step appears to be the selection of appropriate variables.

DYNAMICS

The assertion has been made that any useful theory must be a theory of action. By definition, then, it will be dynamic — that is, having to do with force or energy in motion. The term *dynamic* has been so abused by psychologists during the last half century, however, that its meaning is no longer clear. Perhaps it never was. But with successive "dynamic psychologies" — those of Freud, Morton Prince, Woodworth, Lewin, and a host of contemporary theorists — the meaning has been more obfuscated than ever. Sometimes it refers to a motivational approach, sometimes to a developmental, sometimes to an emphasis on unconscious processes. Mostly, I suspect, it merely means that the theorist is revolting against what seem to him the stultifying structuralistic unhuman inadequacies of his predecessors. It boils down to a self-attributed accolade for virtue, a promise to deal with important characteristics of real live people rather than dry and dusty processes.

This is a waste of a good word. By no means all modern psychological systems are dynamic; some are trait-based and some are need-based. No one would deny that combinations of habit structures do exist and do provide a kind of integrated consistency in a person's behavior. Likewise, no one would attempt to order the events of human action without variables that relate to motivation, including those kinds that cannot be verbally reported by the person himself. But there is more to dynamics than motivation. There is *change*.

Changes in behavior are of two kinds. For a theory to be dynamic, both must be systematized, separately but congruently. One is on-going action and the other is learning. In Fig. 1 the sequence of events beginning with the instigators S_{ext}, S_D, and S_{cog}, and ending with the goal response R_g, is a single behavioral event. In other words, both the external factors and the internal ones (the potentialities of the person) that initiate action are indicated. The diagram describes such a predictive statement as this: that everything else being equal (i.e., nothing else contributing to the variance), a hungry man who sees a refrigerator, knows there is food in it, and knows how to get at it, will eat if the refrigerator door opens when he manipulates it. Principles that relate antecedent motivational factors to subsequent behavior are dealing with on-going action; they are statements about the resolution of field forces. "Frustration produces aggression" is an example, albeit one which is sometimes hard to swallow because in real life there are always so many other variables besides frustration that contribute to response variance.

Obviously, however, no predictive statement can be made about on-going action unless certain things are known about the person's *potentialities for action*. Action does not take place with an organism containing a psychological vacuum. The person has certain properties that determine what kind of behavior he will produce under any given set of circumstances. His motivation is weak or strong, he is frustrated or not in various goal-directed sequences, he has expectancies of the consequences of his behavior. Unless these various properties of the person are known, it is impossible to have any systematization of on-going action. And unless the *changes* in potentialities for action are systematically ordered, there is no possibility of constructing an on-going action theory that will enable one to predict beyond the termination of any single sequence of behavior.

In Fig. 1, the various potentialities for action are specified by S_D (motivation) and S_{cog} (cognitive structures). In large part these characteristics are a product of learning. The successful completion of a behavior sequence is a reinforcement, and this modifies the drives and habit structures of the person in certain lawful ways, these laws being part of the body of the laws of learning. In other words, there is a change in the person's potentialities for action. It is to be noted, therefore, that although Fig. 1 describes a single behavior sequence, there are two ways of ordering the events that compose it. Both refer to changes, to energy in motion. To be dynamic, a theory of behavior must encompass both.[4]

Personality as Antecedent

In this framework, personality is a description of those properties of a person that specify his potentialities for action. Such a description must include reference to motivation, expectations, habit structure, the nature of the instigators that activate instrumental behavior, and the kinds of environmental events that such actions will produce. Furthermore, all these factors must be described in terms of the dyadic aspects of the behavior that occurs. That is, the kinds of Betas who can serve as instigators for particular responses must be specified, and the environmental events that Beta creates for Alpha must

---

[4] The most elaborate theory of on-going action is that of Kurt Lewin [7], but his field theory has never been developed to care adequately for problems of personality development (learning). Similarly, the developmental theory of G. V. Hamilton [4] gave an excellent account of the changes in potentiality for response but did not cover so effectively the problems of on-going action.

be described not only as they fit into Alpha's activity but also as they fit into the whole motivational sequence of Beta.

This will give an adequate *description* of a personality, but it is not sufficient for a *theory* of personality. For this all these factors must be treated as part of an antecedent-consequent proposition. Sheer description of the properties of an object is of little value, either scientifically or practically, since the ultimate aim of any theory is to provide lawful predictions of those events that form the subject matter of the theory. This can be done only when "if x, then y" principles are added to description. Personality theory is adequate only if it predicts behavior.

In behavior science, personality must be treated as both antecedent and consequent. As antecedent, it is part of the total matrix that must be known in order to account for either individual or dyadic action. In recent years various approaches to personality have too much depended on assumptions of fixed traits and fixed needs. This has led to measurement procedures that do not include reference to the social stimulus conditions under which the traits or needs will be expressed. As Sanford has said, in connection with a study of leadership, there is no trait independent of the conditions that elicit it. Leadership is a quality in a person's behavior only if there are followers who react to him as a leader. Most behavior with which the personality psychologist is concerned is either directly dyadic or is in response to symbolic representation of the dyad. Therefore, any conceptualization of the person's properties must be done with consideration of the properties of the various Betas with whom Alpha is interactive.

A simple example of the measurement problem created by these considerations arose in connection with some data on aggressive behavior analyzed in the Harvard Laboratory of Human Development [5, 12]. Forty preschool children were the subjects. Two main measures of aggressiveness were secured. One was overt and socially directed aggression. This measure was obtained both by teachers' rating scales and by direct observation. The other was projective or fantasy aggression revealed in doll play. By a fixed trait or need assumption, one would expect these two measures to correspond somewhat. They did — somewhat! The correlation was $+ 0.13$!

But further analysis makes the meaning of this relationship clear. These children's mothers were interviewed concerning their methods of handling the youngsters' aggression at home. On the basis of this information it was possible to divide the children into three subgroups which had had different degrees of severity of punishment for aggression.

In Fig. 4 the frequency of both overt and fantasy aggression are shown for these three subgroups. It is to be noted that while the "mild" and "moderate" groups show a mean correspondence in amount of aggressive behavior of the two kinds, there is a radical disagreement in the "severe" punishment subgroup. These latter children, on the average, behaved rather nonaggressively in preschool, but in their doll-play fantasies there was an abundance of aggression. One could ask whether these children are very aggressive or very nonaggressive. Do they have strong need for aggression or weak?

Even if these questions could be sensibly answered, which they cannot, the answers would be of little help in predicting the future aggressive behavior

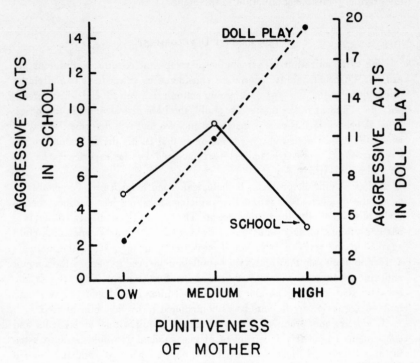

Fig. 4. RELATION OF INTERPERSONAL AND FANTASY AGGRESSION TO MATERNAL PUNITIVENESS

Interpersonal aggression is measured by frequency of aggressive acts occurring during four hours of observation in preschool; fantasy aggression is measured by mean frequency of aggressive acts occuring during two twenty-minute doll-play sessions. Punitiveness of mother is based on ratings of interview material concerning severity of mother's punishment of child's aggressive acts at home. Charted values are medians of the three groups, sizes of which are: Low = 7, Medium = 23, High = 10.

of these children. To accomplish the latter, which is our aim, there must be an analysis of the social stimulus conditions under which the future behavior is to be observed.

The minimum specification would concern whether the behavior would be observed in a nursery school or in a permissive doll play experiment. With a conceptualization of the dyadic variables involved, however, it is possible to make a statement that goes beyond the narrow confines of these two measuring situations. In this instance, the more general statements can be made that, first, the amount of aggression will be a negative function of severity of punishment; and second, with severity of punishment held constant, the amount of aggression will vary positively with dissimilarity of the dyadic situation to the original punishment situation in the home.

PERSONALITY DEVELOPMENT

The systematization of personality development requires a different approach. When personality factors are considered as antecedents to individual or group behavior, the laws of on-going action are involved. But when personality development is the matter for study, the laws of learning are the bases. What is needed in this case is a set of principles that will describe the way in which the child's potentialities for action — that is, his drives, habits, cognitive structures, and expectancies — are changed by the experiences he has throughout his life.

This is a difficult problem, both logically and empirically. Personality is partly the product of a lifetime of dyadic action which has modified the individual's potentiality for further action. The changed potentiality is therefore partly a product of his own actions. For example, in the data concerning child aggression and severity of maternal punishment for aggression, the mother's actions in punishing the child were doubtless influenced in part by the amount and kind of aggression exhibited toward her by the child. Thus, the dyadic behavior that served as an antecedent to the differential display of overt and fantasy aggression by the child was contributed to by the child himself.

Logically, and practically, a good theory requires that antecedents and consequents be entirely independent of one another. It would be most satisfactory if the child did not influence the mother's behavior, and if we could then say something about the effect of severity of punishment on later behavior. One solution to this problem appears to be a careful measurement of the child's contribution to the dyadic relationship and a partialling out of that influence in the comparison of antecedent mother behavior with consequent child behavior.

If this procedure does not prove feasible, as it may very well not, a developmental theory can still be constructed in which the antecedent variables are *specified changes* in the mother's contributions to the dyadic mother-child interaction. Such a theory would be more defensible logically, for it would be taking formal account of the dyadic nature of the learning situation. Empirically, however, it would be considerably more difficult. For the partialling-out method, naturalistic data are appropriate; natural variation in child-rearing methods, as this is found in any group of mothers, can be used as the antecedent. But if we are forced to use *specified changes* in maternal behavior as the antecedent, the research task will be complicated not only by the necessity of securing families in which such changes can be made, but by the long wait from early life, when the changes begin to be introduced, to later childhood, when the personality consequents are to be measured.

In any case, it is clear that an effective approach to the problems of the development of personality and of the influence of personality on the behavior of groups requires a theory that has the following properties: its basic reference events must be *actions*: it must combine congruently both *dyadic* and *monadic* events; it must account for both *on-going action* and *learning*; it must provide a description of personality couched in terms of *potentiality for action*; and it must provide principles of personality development in terms of *changes in potentiality for action*.

To spell out in detail the specific variables that must be defined for use in this theory is beyond the scope of the present paper. There are two general bodies of concepts and their relating principles, however, that appear promising. One of these is the set of definitions and postulates that compose the laws of learning. Whether the particular formulations used by Tolman, Hull, Guthrie, or Skinner are selected seems of little importance at the moment. Those of Hull and Tolman have certain a priori advantages, but the main point is the use of whatever laws of learning will best serve to account for changes in potentiality for action. The theoretical formulation of the research in our own laboratory stems from Hull through Miller and Dollard.

The second set of defined variables contains conceptualizations of those secondary motivational systems that arise universally as a product of the dyadic relationship between mother and child [11]. These include aggression, dependency, self-reliance, anxieties, competition, and status-seeking, as well as the various consequences of the training inherent in the socialization of the primary drives of hunger, sex, and elimination. The exact forms of behavior potentiality created in each of these motivational areas are different from child to child and from culture to culture. But the biological nature of man, coupled with his universal gregariousness, gives rise to various learning experiences that every child endures in one fashion or another.

BIBLIOGRAPHY

1. Allport, F. H. *Social Psychology*. Boston: Houghton, Mifflin, 1924.
2. Allport, G. W. *Personality: A Psychological Interpretation*. New York: Holt, 1937.
3. Cottrell, L. S. "The Analysis of Situational Fields in Social Psychology," *Amer. Sociol. Rev.*, VII (1942), 370–382.
4. Hamilton, G. V. *Objective Psychopathology*. St. Louis: C. V. Mosby, 1925.
5. Hollenberg, Eleanor, and Sperry, Margaret. "Some Antecedents of Aggression and Effects of Frustration in Doll Play," *Personality*, I (1951), 32–43.

6. Hull, C. L. "Goal Attraction and Directing Ideas Conceived as Habit Phenomena," *Psychol. Rev.*, XXXVIII (1931), 487–506.

7. Lewin, Kurt. *A Dynamic Theory of Personality*. New York: McGraw-Hill, 1935.

8. McDougall, William. *An Introduction to Social Psychology*. London: Methuen, 1908.

9. Murray, H. A. *Explorations in Personality*. New York: Oxford University Press, 1938.

10. Parsons, Talcott. *The Social System*. Glencoe, Illinois: The Free Press, 1951.

11. Sears, R. R. "Personality Development in Contemporary Culture," *Proc. Amer. Philos. Soc.*, XCII (1948), 363–370.

12. Sears, R. R. "Relation of Fantasy Aggression to Interpersonal Aggression," *Child Development*, XXI (1950), 5–6.

5   SAMUEL A. STOUFFER

An Empirical Study of Technical Problems
in Analysis of Role Obligations

The approach in this volume toward a system ot categories which may unify theories of culture, society, and personality is necessarily at a rather high level of abstraction. In its present tentative form and in the numerous further revisions which may be expected, the system will be appraised from at least two standpoints. One involves the correctness of the reasoning wherever logical inferences are made. The other involves the usefulness of the system, assuming that it passes muster logically. It is with the usefulness of such a theoretical scheme that the ensuing comments are concerned.

A theoretical system — for example, an elaborate mathematical model in economic theory — can be logically correct without necessarily being fertile in generating middle-range hypotheses capable of empirical verification. If such a theory organizes hitherto disconnected clusters of ideas into a single integrated system, it can be useful merely in providing a new context for evaluating the separate parts more critically at a theoretical level. But all of us would be quite disappointed if the type of thinking which has gone into this volume were to have only this as its end result.

As a minimum, it is hoped that the effort to tie together the significant ideas about culture, society, and personality will provide broad orientations which map, as it were, areas for suggested research, even if it does not directly generate specifically deducible, testable propositions at a middle-range level. This hope is based on the fact that the thinking of Professor Parsons and colleagues is decidedly not arm-chair thinking alone. The streams of influence which lie behind it represent decades of theory *and also* empirical research in the three disciplines of anthropology, sociology, and psychology. I have been impressed with the concern for empirical referents which the authors have constantly manifested during their work, even if this concern is not always visible in the resulting document.

One cannot yet say that the present approach to a system has matured enough to give assurance of its power to go further than signaling areas for further research. That is, it may be asking too much to expect now a large number of deductions of specific propositions as *necessary* logical consequences of the basic postulates. This would be ideal, of course. But we should not underestimate the possible value of the more modest objective, which is furthered by the anchoring of the basic postulates in experience and at the same time by the fact that these postulates are not *ad hoc*, but have logical interconnections.

The fact that big ideas of Darwin, Marx, or Freud do not generate by mathematical or logical deduction propositions in social science, like the ideas of Newton and Einstein in physics, is not an argument against the signaling value of abstract ideas in social science. Rather, these orientations encourage us to dig in one part of a field rather than another and are indispensable *because we cannot dig everywhere at once*. The theories will have been useful if the digging uncovers something, even if they did not tell us too explicitly what we might find.

At the same time, the history of social science, like the history of medicine, ought to warn us against an excess of optimism about the necessary usefulness of any new system of highly general orienting ideas. Many proposed systems have had little or no impact. Some — for example, ideas like those of Benjamin Rush in medicine — may have been positively harmful. Just as medicine has profited most from middle-range propositions, tested in empirical research though not deducible, as yet, from any single Newtonian formula, so it seems likely that social science now desperately needs middle-range testable propositions.

If the concepts central to the system of unified theory proposed in this volume are to be useful, even for suggesting if not deducing middle-range propositions, it would seem preferable that they be clear and unambiguous. The word *preferable* is used instead of the word *essential* — some of Freud's murkier concepts, for example, may prove to have been very useful. It would be as silly to demand immaculate precision in concepts at the present stage as it would be to demand correlations of 1.00 in all empirical research. Nevertheless, one suspects that there is a higher probability of a general theory having some impact on the vital task of setting up testable middle-range propositions if the concepts are capable of some kind of clear and, where possible, operational definition.

One of the significant ideas in the system outlined in this volume is the concept of role. (See, for example, the discussion of roles in the General Statement in Part I.) This is not a new concept, but its possible utility in unifying personality and societal theory has perhaps not before been seen so clearly. Attractive as the concept is, in the abstract, there has been as yet relatively little study of the technical problems involved in using it empirically.

The work of Professor Parsons and his colleagues has inspired the following modest pilot study, written in collaboration with Jackson Toby, which offers hope as to the possibility of operational definitions of certain types of role obligations and, at the same time, provides specific warnings as to the immensity and complexity of the task. The study was published in the *American Journal of Sociology*, March 1951. It is reproduced here with the *Journal's* permission, and with the hope that it will stimulate others to do such jobs better.

SAMUEL A. STOUFFER AND JACKSON TOBY

Role Conflict and Personality [1]

A convenient way to examine the informal social controls operating in a given institution is through the study of role conflict. In an earlier statistical analysis of an example of role conflict, stress was laid on the concept of variability and implications for the theory of role of different classes of variability.[2]

The present paper also is concerned with role conflict. But it seeks to provide a link between the study of social norms, with which the former paper was primarily concerned, and the study of personality. Specifically, when there is a lack of consensus in a group regarding the "proper thing to do" in a morally conflicting situation, is there a tendency for some individuals to have a predisposition or a personality bias toward one type of solution and for other individuals to have a predisposition toward another type of solution? If such a predisposition exists, there should be a tendency to carry over certain types of behavior from one role conflict to another with some consistency.

An especially common role conflict is that between one's institutionalized obligations of friendship and one's institutionalized obligations to a society.

[1] The research here reported was conducted with the assistance of the Laboratory of Social Relations, Harvard University. Special acknowledgment is due Paul F. Lazarsfeld, Talcott Parsons, and Gordon W. Allport. Professor Lazarsfeld proposed the applicability of a new form of latent distance structure and himself carried out the computations reported in the note appended to this paper. A pretest of the present study was the subject of a paper by the authors at the American Sociological Society in December 1949, at which the paper's discussion by Professor Leonard S. Cottrell contributed to the present formulation.
[2] Samuel A. Stouffer, "An Analysis of Conflicting Social Norms," *American Sociological Review*, XIV (December, 1949), 707–717.

The obligations of friendship in Western culture, to use the terminology of Talcott Parsons, are particularistic rather than universalistic, affectively toned rather than affectively neutral, and diffuse rather than specific.[3] A universalistic obligation is applicable to dealings with anybody (for example, obligation to fulfill a contract) ; a particularistic obligation is limited to persons who stand in some special relationship to one (for example, the obligation to help a relative or a close friend or neighbor). Diffuseness of particulartistic obligations provides flexibility in the definition of these roles. That is, the content of an individual's particularistic obligations (toward a friend, a brother, a grandchild) depends in part on the intimacy of the relationship itself. The greater the affection, the greater the sense of obligation. On the other hand, universalistic obligations are defined more rigidly, for they regulate behavior toward all human beings — regardless of affective involvement. Hence, in any specific situation involving conflict between duty to a friend and duty to society, we would expect that some individuals are more prone to regard the particularistic obligation as taking precedence than others, because there is variability from individual to individual in the intimacy of friendships. That is, respondents tend to project into the hypothetical situations *reference* friendships drawn from their own experience. A description of an institutionalized social norm must not only take into account, then, the beliefs and behavior of a modal member of the group but must also observe the individual variability in the perception of obligations. This variability — or "social slippage" — was a major concern in the earlier analysis of role conflict cited above.

In the present paper we shall deal with several situations involving conflicts between obligations to a friend and more general social obligations. If, as our conception of the intrinsic variability of particularistic obligations would lead us to expect, some people are more likely than others to choose in a variety of situations the particularistic horn of the dilemma rather than the universalistic, we should be able to devise a scale to measure such a tendency. With such a scale people should be ranked along a single dimension according to their probability of possessing the attribute or predisposition of choosing one type of solution rather than the other.

What we have to present here is only a crude beginning; indeed, only a classroom example. Yet it should prove instructive in a number of respects to those who may wish to carry on further research with needed refinements. Our data are based on a short pencil-and-paper questionnaire completed by 648 undergraduate students at Harvard and Radcliffe in February 1950. No claim is made for the representativeness of the sample, since almost all were members of a single course in Social Relations.

Four little stories were presented, as follows:

[3] See, e.g., Talcott Parsons, *Essays in Sociological Theory* (Glencoe, Illinois: The Free Press, 1949), chap. viii.

1. You are riding in a car driven by a close friend, and he hits a pedestrian. You know he was going at least 35 miles an hour in a 20-mile-an-hour speed zone. There are no other witnesses. His lawyer says that if you testify under oath that the speed was only 20 miles an hour, it may save him from serious consequences.

What right has your friend to expect you to protect him?

Check one:

☐ —— My friend has a definite right as a friend to expect me to testify to the lower figure.

☐ —— He has some right as a friend to expect me to testify to the lower figure.

☐ —— He has no right as a friend to expect me to testify to the lower figure.

What do you think you'd probably do in view of the obligations of a sworn witness and the obligation to your friend?

Check one:

☐ —— Testify that he was going 20 miles an hour.

☐ —— Not testify that he was going 20 miles an hour.

2. You are a New York drama critic. A close friend of yours has sunk all his savings in a new Broadway play. You really think the play is no good.

What right does your friend have to expect you to go easy on his play in your review?

Check one:

☐ —— He has a definite right as a friend to expect me to go easy on his play in my review.

☐ —— He has some right as a friend to expect me to do this for him.

☐ —— He has no right as a friend to expect me to do this for him.

Would you go easy on his play in your review in view of your obligations to your readers and your obligation to your friend?

Check one:

☐ —— Yes.

☐ —— No.

3. You are a doctor for an insurance company. You examine a close friend who needs more insurance. You find that he is in pretty good shape, but you are doubtful on one or two minor points which are difficult to diagnose.

What right does your friend have to expect you to shade the doubts in his favor?

Check one:

☐ —— My friend would have a definite right as a friend to expect me to shade the doubts in his favor.

☐ —— He would have some rights as a friend to expect me to shade the doubts in his favor.

☐ —— He would have no right as a friend to expect me to shade the doubts in his favor.

Would you shade the doubts in his favor in view of your obligations to the insurance company and your obligation to your friend?

Check one:

☐ —— Yes.
☐ —— No.

4. You have just come from a secret meeting of the board of directors of a company. You have a close friend who will be ruined unless he can get out of the market before the board's decision becomes known. You happen to be having dinner at that friend's home this same evening.

What right does your friend have to expect you to tip him off?

Check one:

☐ —— He has a definite right as a friend to expect me to tip him off.
☐ —— He has some right as a friend to expect me to tip him off.
☐ —— He has no right as a friend to expect me to tip him off.

Would you tip him off in view of your obligations to the company and your obligation to your friend?

Check one:

☐ —— Yes.
☐ —— No.

The problem is: do the answers to these questions indicate the existence of a unidimensional scale, along which respondents can be ordered according to the degree to which they are likely to possess a trait or bias toward the particularistic solution of a dilemma? For simplicity, we label for a given item the response, "My friend has a definite right . . . ," as particularistic; the response, "He has no right . . . ," as universalistic. If a person marks, "He has some right . . . ," we label the response particularistic if in the second part of the question he says he would favor the friend in action; and universalistic, if he says he would not favor the friend.

There was a considerable spread among the four items in the percentage giving particularistic responses:

Item	Per cent
1 (car accident)	26
2 (drama critic)	45
3 (insurance doctor)	51
4 (board of directors)	70

Such frequencies suggest the hypothesis of a distance or cumulative scale.

Following Louis Guttman's scalogram method, the responses to all the items were cross-tabulated and scale patterns arranged according to nearest scale type, as shown in Table 1. While the reproducibility (0.91) and the distribution of cutting points suggest the admissibility of the hypothesis that these items form a Guttman scale, the items are too few in number for us to speak with confidence, especially in the presence of two sets of rather numerous non-scale responses $(+ - + +$ and $- + - +)$. Rigor would require ten or more items to start with, in order to determine scalability, although we might in the end select fewer items for subsequent use.

The pure Guttman model can be viewed as the limiting case of a more general latent distance model which Paul F. Lazarsfeld has introduced.[4] It

Table 1

SCALOGRAM PATTERN FOR RESPONDENTS TO FOUR ITEMS ON ROLE CONFLICT

Scale type	Scale pattern 1 2 3 4	Particularistic response to item no. 1	2	3	4	Universalistic response to item no. 1	2	3	4	"Error"
5	+ + + +	66	66	66	66	..	..	..	..	0
	+ - + +	52	..	52	52	..	52	..	..	52
	+ + - +	15	15	..	15	..	..	15	..	15
	+ + + -	8	8	8	..	..	..	..	8	8
	+ - + -	5	..	5	..	..	5	..	5	10
	+ + - -	6	6	..	..	..	..	6	6	12
4	- + + +	..	95	95	95	95	..	..	..	0
	- + + -	..	16	16	..	16	..	..	16	16
3	- - + +	..	..	80	80	80	80	..	..	0
	- - + -	..	..	14	..	14	14	..	14	14
2	- - - +	..	..	..	71	71	71	71	..	0
	- + - +	..	66	..	66	66	..	66	..	66
	+ - - +	13	..	..	13	..	13	13	..	13
1	- + - -	..	21	..	..	21	..	21	21	21
	+ - - -	6	..	..	..	..	6	6	6	6
	- - - -	..	..	..	..	114	114	114	114	0
		171	293	336	458	477	355	312	190	233

Reproducibility $= 1 - [233/(4 \cdot 648)] = 0.91$

seems worth while, therefore, to examine the applicability to these data of the Lazarsfeld latent distance model, which postulates a latent continuum with as many ordered classes as there are items, plus one. The model assigns to each item a probability that a positive (e.g., particularistic) response to that item assigns the respondent to a particular segment of the hypothetical latent continuum.[5]

[4] Stouffer, Guttman, Suchman, Lazarsfeld, Star, and Clausen, *Measurement and Prediction*, Vol. IV of *Studies in Social Psychology in World War II* (Princeton University Press, 1950). Guttman's theory and procedures are described in Chapters 2 to 9, Lazarsfeld's in Chapters 10 and 11. Chapter 1 provides an introduction to both methods.

[5] Latent structure theory postulates that all the relationship between any two manifest items can be accounted for by the joint correlation of the items with the latent structure. In other words, within any segment of the latent structure the correlation between two manifest items is zero.

For reasons of space, the arithmetic in testing the applicability of the latent distance model to our data will not be exhibited here. However, a brief technical summary of the results appears at the end of this paper. Although the procedure used is still too new to have developed wholly satisfactory acceptance standards, the outcome was quite encouraging.

Actually, an additional precaution was taken. Experience with projective material has taught us to expect considerble differences when we ask, "What do you think about something?" from results if we ask, "What do you think somebody else would think about something?" Especially when we are seeking by crude question and answer procedures to learn something about social norms, it is very important to know what, if any, differences are produced by such shifts imposed on the point of view of the respondents. Hence, only a third of our 648 respondents were asked questions in the form exhibited above.

For a third of the subjects the stories were rewritten so that the friend of the respondent, not the respondent himself, faced the role conflict. To illustrate with the motor car example:

Your close friend is riding in a car which you are driving, and you hit a pedestrian. He knows that you were going at least 35 miles an hour in a 20-mile-an-hour zone. There are no other witnesses. Your lawyer says that if your friend testifies under oath that the speed was only 20 miles an hour it may save you from serious consequences.

What right do you have to expect him to protect you?

Check one:

☐ —— I have a definite right as a friend to expect him to testify to the lower figure.

☐ —— I have some right as a friend to expect him to testify to the lower figure.

☐ —— I have no right as a friend to expect him to testify to the lower figure.

What do you think he would probably do in view of his obligations as a sworn witness and his obligation as your friend?

Check one:

☐ —— Testify that you were going 20 miles an hour.

☐ —— Not testify that you were going 20 miles an hour.

For still another third of the respondents, a third version was presented. In this case neither the respondent nor his friend faced the dilemma, but two hypothetical people, Smith and Smith's friend, Johnson. Again to illustrate with the motor car example:

Smith is riding in a car driven by his close friend, Johnson, and Johnson hits a pedestrian. Smith knows that his friend was going at least 35 miles an hour in a 20-mile-an-hour speed zone. There are no other witnesses. Johnson's lawyer says that if Smith testifies under oath that the speed was only 20 miles an hour, it may save Johnson from serious consequences.

What right does Johnson have to expect Smith to protect him?

Check one:

☐ —— Johnson has a definite right as a friend to expect Smith to testify to the lower figure.

☐ —— He has some right as a friend to expect Smith to testify to the lower figure.

☐ —— He has no right as a friend to expect Smith to testify to the lower figure.

If Smith were an average person, what do you think he would probably do in view of his obligations as a sworn witness and his obligation to his friend?

Check one:

☐ —— Testify that Johnson was going 20 miles an hour.

☐ —— Not testify that Johnson was going 20 miles an hour.

The different forms of the questionnaires were interleaved and handed out at random. In testing for the goodness of fit of the latent distance scale, separate tests were applied to each of the three types of items. The model seemed to fit about equally well in all three cases, and the rank order assigned to particular scale patterns was very much the same, except for a few scale types containing a negligible number of cases. As would be expected, the rank-order groupings derived from the latent distance model is very close to the rank-order grouping obtained by scoring to nearest scale type in scalogram analysis.[6] For purposes of subsequent analysis the rank groupings for each of the three forms were constituted as in Table 1. The extent to which the three forms agreed with one another can be seen from Table 2. The principle discrepancies are due to differences in frequency of responses to Items 2 and 3 respectively, but the groupings in Table 2 do not differ from one form to another more than would be expected by chance, according to the chi-square test. Incidentally, it is of some interest to note that the reproducibility of each form is in the neighborhood of 0.90.

This is, of course, much too small a set of items about which to make any serious claims either to rigorous scalability or to generality, but the results encourage one to believe that we can develop good measures of individual predisposition to a bias in a particularistic or universalistic direction. We must note that a scale such as this is not an unequivocal measure of *particularism-universalism*. Since friendship obligations are diffuse and affectively

---

[6] In scoring to nearest scale type by scalogram procedure, the objective is to arrange the scale patterns to minimize "error." Thus $+ + - +$ is grouped with $+ + + +$, on the assumption that only the response to the third item is an error. If it were grouped with $- + + +$, we should have to assume two errors, in the first and third items, respectively. However, there are some items which might be grouped in different ways with the same amount of error. For example, $- + - +$ would be grouped with $- + + +$ if we assumed that the third item was an error, but would be grouped with $- - - +$ if we assumed that the second item was an error. Such doubtful cases are resolved by the latent distance analysis, which in the present example usually gave clear and consistent information.

toned as well as particularistic, and societal obligations are specific and affectively neutral as well as universalistic, we have scaled a predisposition for diffuse, affectively toned obligations over specific, affectively neutral obligations as well as a predisposition for particularistic over universalistic obligations. But this fusion of variables in our situations *does* seem to generate a

Table 2

SCALE PATTERN GROUPINGS SHOWN SEPARATELY FOR THREE FORMS
OF QUESTIONNAIRE

Scale type	Scale patterns 1 2 3 4	Form A: Ego faces dilemma	Form B: Ego's friend faces dilemma	Form C: Smith faces dilemma
5	+ + + +	20	20	26
	+ − + +	9	23	20
	+ + − +	6	4	5
	+ + + −	2	3	3
	+ − + −	2	3	0
	+ + − −	1	3	2
		40	56	56
4	− + + +	38	25	32
	− + + −	7	6	3
		45	31	35
3	− − + +	24	29	27
	− − + −	6	5	3
		30	34	30
2	− − − +	23	31	17
	− + − +	25	15	26
	+ − − +	4	4	5
		52	50	48
1	− + − −	6	6	9
	+ − − −	1	2	3
	− − − −	42	37	35
		49	45	47
		216	216	216
Reproducibility		0.92	0.91	0.90

unidimensional scale, the dimension involved being the degree of strength of a latent tendency to be loyal to a friend even at the cost of other principles. The rank groupings would represent ordered degrees of probability of taking the friend's side in a role conflict.[7]

Ideally, having assigned each of the 648 individuals to one of five scale types or rank groupings, we would like to see how these groupings relate to

[7] Of course, we shall eventually be interested in finding out whether a more abstract scale — for example, one of universalism-particularism alone — would stand up and, if it did, more about its genesis.

behavior in a new, nonverbal situation of role conflict. Such a design would be very costly and complicated but must be carried out sooner or later if we are to have full confidence that our scale is not an artifact — that it does not, for example, arise merely from differences in imaginative ability, a possibility which was suggested by Leonard S. Cottrell in his discussion of the first draft of this paper. As a simple but decidedly inferior procedure, we investigated the relationship between the scale and other verbal responses relative to role conflict. We selected some academic situations not too far removed from the experience of college students. The problem was to see whether respondents who were near the particularistic end of the scale, for example, tended to have a higher probability of giving particularistic responses in these academic situations than other respondents. (The scale itself involved no academic situations.)

Consider the following story:

You are employed by Professor X to mark examination books in his course. Your close friend makes somewhat under a passing grade. If you give him a special break you can boost him over the passing line. He needs the grade badly.

What right does your friend have to expect you to give him a special break?

Check one:

☐ —— He has a definite right as a friend to expect me to do this for him.
☐ —— He has some right as a friend to expect me to do this for him.
☐ —— He has no right as a friend to expect me to do this for him.

Would you give him this special break in view of your obligations to the university and your obligation to your friend?

Check one:

☐ —— Yes.
☐ —— No.

The same scoring system was used as in the scale items. Among those with Scale Type 1, only 7 per cent responded particularistically in this situation, but the percentage rose to 49 among those in Scale Type 5:

Scale type	Per cent
5	49
4	25
3	31
2	30
1	7

Another situation presented was the following, scored similarly to the others:

You are in charge of the reserve desk at a library. A certain reserve book is in heavy demand. A close friend is pressed for time and can only use the book at a certain hour. He has suggested that you hide the book for a while before his arrival so that he will be sure to get it. He needs it badly.

What right does your friend have to expect you to hide the book?

Check one:

☐ —— He has a definite right as a friend to expect me to hide the book for him.

☐ —— He has some right as a friend to expect me to do this for him.

☐ —— He has no right as a friend to expect me to do this for him.

Would you hide the book for him in view of your obligations to the library and your obligation to your friend?

Check one:

☐ —— Yes.

☐ —— No.

Variation in proportions responding particularistically was from 16 to 70 per cent:

Scale type	Per cent
5	70
4	55
3	58
2	46
1	16

The following story, almost identical with that used in the paper published in 1949 in the *American Sociological Review*, also was presented and scored according to the methods used in the present paper.

You are proctoring an examination in a middle-group course. *You are the only proctor in the room.* About half-way through the exam you see a fellow student, who is also your close friend, openly cheating. He is copying his answers from previously prepared crib notes. When he sees that you have seen the notes as you walked down the aisle and stopped near the seat, he whispers quietly to you, "O.K., I'm caught. That's all there is to it."

Under these circumstances, what right does he have to expect you not to turn him in?

Check one:

☐ —— He has a definite right as a friend to expect me not turn him in.

☐ —— He has some right as a friend to expect me not to turn him in.

☐ —— He has no right as a friend to expect me not to turn him in.

Under these circumstances, what would you probably do in view of your obligations as a proctor and your obligation to your friend?

Check one:

☐ —— Report him.

☐ —— Not report him.

Variation was from 6 to 50 per cent, in proportions responding particularistically:

Scale type	Per cent
5	50
4	35
3	28
2	25
1	6

These items, like the items included in the scale, were asked in three alternate forms. A respondent, for example, who had the Smith-Johnson form of the scale items also had a Smith-Johnson form of the new academic items. There was considerable variability in patterns of relationship, but the upward progression was present on all forms on each item, as is shown in Chart I.

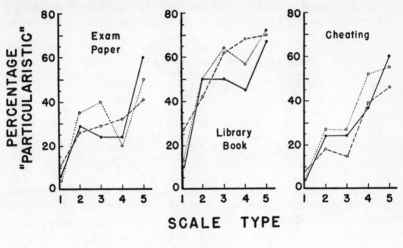

——— When respondent faces the dilemma
- - - - When respondent's friend faces the dilemma
·········· When "Smith" faces the dilemma

Chart I. SCALE SCORES AS RELATED TO THE PROPORTION "PARTICULARISTIC" IN CERTAIN ACADEMIC SITUATIONS

An important element of a friendship relationship is what Parsons calls an "other-orientation" rather than a self-orientation, such as is institutionalized in our society in a business transaction. Though other-orientation is institutionalized, it is probably not an absolute value. While the individual is supposed to subordinate his own interests to those of his friends under many circumstances, there are limits to the sacrifices which one may legitimately expect of a friend. These limits tend to be vague and undefined, perhaps so that they may vary with the intimacy of the friendship. This introduces another source of behavioral variability: the respondent's perception of the risk to himself by defying universalistic norms and coming to the friend's aid. It was of interest, therefore, to vary the cheating situation by asking the respondent to imagine an analogous setting with much greater risk to the proctor:

> Consider the same cheating situation as above, with an *additional* element. Suppose now *there is another proctor (an extremely conscientious fellow!) in the examination room with you* and that you would be running a fifty-fifty risk of personal exposure by him to the authorities for failing as proctor to turn in a cheater.

> The list to be checked was the same as before.

How the increase in risk reduced the particularistic responses is shown in Table 3.

We had hoped to make a further study of high and low risk to see how differences in predispositions might be related to other factors in this specific

Table 3
PERCENTAGE "PARTICULARISTIC" WHEN RISK VARIES

Scale type	In both situations	In low-risk situation only	In neither situation	Total
5	20	30	50	100
4	16	19	65	100
3	10	18	72	100
2	11	14	75	100
1	2	4	94	100

cheating situation, such as students' perceptions of the severity of penalties, of fellow students' attitudes, and of the cheater's own probable reactions. Questions were designed on these points, but they were not satisfactory. The main problem which emerged, however, and which negated much further intensive cross-tabulation, was the sizable differences in response depending on whether we asked the cheating question involving little risk to the proctor *before* or *after* the cheating question involving risk to the proctor. Actually, in a random half of the cases the little-risk situation was presented first; in the other half the higher risk situation was presented first.

For each form (ego as proctor, ego's friend as proctor, Smith as proctor) we have, then, two reports. There are six replications in all. Results are graphed in Chart II. The reader will observe that the form in which ego is proctor stands up well. We get about the same picture, irrespective of the order of presentation of the low-risk and high-risk situations, respectively. But the results are chaotic for the forms in which ego is the cheater or in which the actors are third persons.

The reasons for this result are not immediately obvious. Further trials and study are required before reaching a conclusion. One plausible suggestion is that a paper-and-pencil test like this requires a good deal of imagination on the part of a respondent and that the act of imagination is made easiest when ego himself is pictured as confronting the dilemma. By increasing the salience, one reduces the temptation for casual or careless checking. However,

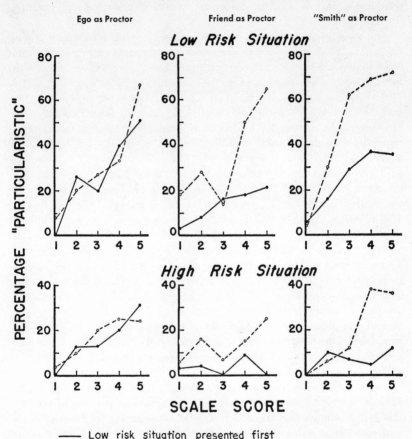

Chart II. SCALE SCORES AS RELATED TO THE PROPORTION "PARTICULARISTIC" IN THE CHEATING SITUATIONS — SHOWING VARIATIONS RELATED TO DIFFERENT FORMS OF QUESTIONNAIRES

this speculation is inadequate to explain why, on the two aberrant forms, the prior presentation of the high-risk situation produced a *higher* particularistic response to the two items than the prior presentation of the low-risk situation.

The systematic study of the extent to which identification, salience, ego defenses, and so forth, modify questionnaire responses is still in its infancy.

Hence, the superior results shown in Chart II on the form in which ego himself faced the dilemma should not tempt us to hasty conclusions. After all, as Table 2 shows, all three forms yielded about the same pattern of distribution of scale types, and as Chart I shows, all three scales showed about the same general relationship in the specific academic situations, including the cheating situation.[8]

Our study suggests that it is possible to classify people according to a predisposition to select one or the other horn of a dilemma in role conflict. As more studies are made — not only with pencil-and-paper tests, but also with role-playing in experimental and real-life situations and with other procedures — information exceedingly important to social science can be derived. We must anticipate the possibility, as Edward A. Suchman of Cornell has suggested in a letter to the writers, that tendencies of a respondent to adopt more stereotyped roles in hypothetical than in real life situations will complicate prediction.

Studies in this field will help sociologists in developing theories of institutionalization and social psychologists in developing theories of personality and, indeed, can serve as a crucial link between the two bodies of theory. The importance of such a link, employing such variables as particularism-universalism, affectivity–affective neutrality, specificity-diffuseness, self-orientation–collectivity-orientation, has been in the forefront of the thinking of Talcott Parsons and his associates, who have been working on a new schema looking toward unification of social science theory. The immensity of the technical task involved in making such concepts amenable to measurement in the years of patient work which lie ahead is at least suggested by the experience of our present study. Indeed, one of the most important values of this paper should be its service as a brake on the enthusiasm of those who may anticipate quick and easy progress in moving from highly abstract concepts in social science to empirical operations.

Such studies as ours can also be applied in practical research if sustained effort is devoted to technical developments. Leadership, for example, involves skill in the solution of role conflicts. Classic examples are the foreman in industry or the noncommissioned officer in the army. If such thoughtful observers as Chester I. Barnard are correct, skill in handling role conflicts is also an essential at the high executive levels.[9] Eventually, we may have role-playing situational tests, involving nonverbal as well as verbal behavior, which will be useful in the selection and training of leaders. The present study represents only a primitive effort to formulate some of the problems of definition and measurement.

[8] In the high-risk cheating situation (not shown in Chart I), when the two sequences of presentation are combined there is also relatively little difference among the three forms, all showing a definite correlation with the scale types.

[9] Chester I. Barnard, *The Functions of the Executive* (Cambridge: Harvard University Press, 1938) see especially chap. xvii.

Note on Lazarsfeld's Latent Distance Scale as Applied to Role
Conflict Data

In *Measurement and Prediction*, Chapter 11, pages 441–447, the reader
will find a numerical example of a latent distance analy̆is carried out in full,
on Research Branch data on psychoneurotic symptoms. That analysis used
only one computed parameter for each item. In the present example on role
conflict data, Lazarsfeld, who kindly made the analysis, introduced more
flexibility by computing two parameters for each item. The latent structure is
set up as follows:

Latent class	Item 1	Item 2	Item 3	Item 4
I	a_1	a_2	a_3	a_4
II	b_1	a_2	a_3	a_4
III	b_1	b_2	a_3	a_4
IV	b_1	b_2	b_3	a_4
V	b_1	b_2	b_3	b_4

Each value of a tends to be a large fraction and each value of b tends to be
small. (The example in Chapter 11 added the restriction that $a_i = 1 - b_i$. In
the perfect Guttman scale each $a = 1$ and each $b = 0$.) The algebra and arith-
metical routine involved will be presented by Lazarsfeld in a separate paper.
Final results, however, are shown here as Table 4, using as illustration, for
reasons of space, only the form in which ego faces the dilemma. In this table,
the scale patterns are ordered as in Table 2 and do not follow precisely the
rank order they would have in Lazarsfeld's schema. The most serious discrepancy between the ordering indicated by the Lazarsfeld model and by the
scalogram procedure of scoring to the nearest scale type is with respect to
pattern $+ - - +$ based on only four cases (see Table 4). The Lazarsfeld

Table 4

ILLUSTRATIVE RESULTS OF FITTING LATENT DISTANCE STRUCTURE

(Data for form in which ego faced role conflict)

Item 1 2 3 4	Per cent of each pattern in each latent class I	II	III	IV	V	Total	Totals Fitted	Actual
+ + + +	95.9	4.0	0.1	..	..	100	19.1	20
+ − + +	94.8	3.9	0.2	0.2	0.9	100	10.0	9
+ + − +	91.7	3.7	3.0	0.3	1.3	100	6.5	6
+ + + −	95.7	4.3	..	..	..	100	2.5	2
+ − + −	96.7	3.3	..	..	..	100	1.3	2
+ + − −	92.3	5.1	2.6	..	..	100	0.8	1
− + + +	0.9	95.6	3.0	0.3	0.2	100	39.9	38
− + + −	0.8	87.7	2.7	0.4	8.4	100	5.7	7
− − + +	0.9	88.9	2.7	4.8	2.7	100	22.2	24
− − + −	0.3	34.8	1.2	1.7	62.0	100	7.4	6
− − − +	0.3	25.3	19.9	34.7	19.8	100	25.4	23
− + − +	0.5	52.3	41.2	3.8	2.2	100	23.7	25
+ − − +	86.2	3.6	2.4	4.8	3.0	100	3.6	4
− + − −	0.3	23.1	18.4	1.6	56.6	100	6.9	6
+ − − −	33.9	1.8	..	1.8	62.5	100	1.2	1
− − − −	..	2.1	1.6	2.8	93.5	100	41.0	42

procedure would place this pattern within the top group. By scalogram procedure, to assign this pattern to the top group would be to imply that repondents made two "errors," in both Items 2 and 3, which, indeed, may have been the case. The present assignment implies only one error, on Item 1. The reader will note that two-error patterns $+ - + -$ and $+ + - -$, with two cases and one case respectively, which could have been assigned variously by scalogram methods, belong, by the Lazarsfeld model, just where they have been put.

The picture presented in Table 4 is analogous to the picture presented in *Measurement and Prediction*, Chapter 11, Table 13, but it must be remembered that it has involved a more flexible basic design.

The last two columns of Table 4 show good agreement between the fitted and actual totals. Approximately as good a fit was obtained with the other two forms of the questionnaire, and the rank ordering of the scale patterns on the basis of the percentage of a given pattern in each latent class is not markedly different. Much further study is needed of the latent distance model used here, especially with respect to reliability of small frequencies and, as has been mentioned earlier, to the testing of acceptance standards. The concept of a latent structure is theoretically quite appropriate to data of the type we are likely to assemble in subsequent investigations of role, and of informal social norms generally.

Index

Index

Aberle, David, 424
Abstraction, 161, 396
Achievement, 414
Ackerman, N. W., 369, 373
Acquisition of patterns of orientation, *see* Learning; Generalization
Action, behavior theory and, 53, 467, 477; and change, 472; child's potentiality for, 476; conceptualization of, 53; consummatory, 280; goals of, 53; institutionalized, 40; instrumental, expressive, and moral, 165, 166; maladaptive, 316; principles of, 31, 38; processes of, 6, 31; systems of, 5, 54, 78, 93; types of, 67–76; variables of, 42. *See also* Cultural Systems; Institutionalization; Orientation of Action; Personality; Social Systems
Action frame of reference, 4–8, 56, 76, 78
Actones, 461
Actor, 4, 31, 38, 54, 56, 99, 101; collectivity as, 4, 39, 56, 101; ego as, 191; individual, 4, 7, 38; malintegration of, 151; self-categorization of, 147, 151; status of, 40. *See also* Ego; Personality
Adjustment, mechanisms of, 19, 133, 137–142, 174, 237
Adorno, T. W. E., 373, 374
Affect, 398
Affectivity–affective neutrality, pattern variable: 77, 80, 94, 117, 131, 216; and moral placing matrices, 346; and obligations of friendship, 482
Affiliation, 321
Aggressiveness, 13, 141, 292, 317, 321, 335, 454, 466, 474, 477. *See also* Mechanisms, of adjustment, of integration
Allocative processes, 18, 108, 122, 352; and allocative foci, 75, 91, 92; evaluative standards relevant to, 206; allocation of facilities, 199–200, malintegration and, 152; and organization of social system, 205–218, 221; in personality system, 353; allocation of personnel, 205; regulation of, 207–208; allocation of rewards, 201–202; and social systems, 25, 148, 197–218
Allport, F. H., 467
Allport, G. W., 321, 373, 375, 380, 412, 416, 441, 453, 463, 467
Allport-Vernon Test of Values, 412
Alter, 15, 55, 56, 65, 87, 99, 100, 105; attitudes of, 106, 124; learning patterns from, 129; love, approval from, 326; reaction patterns of, 154; relations of, 209–218; and role expectations, 350; symbolic behavior in, 332
Alternatives of action, *see* Pattern variables
American culture, 186, 349, 414, 422, 426
Ames, Adelbert, 390
Analysis, 279; descriptive, 6, 43, 76; dynamic, 6, 43, 76, 93, 222, 243, 472
Anomie, 204
Anxiety, 477. *See also* Deprivation; Expectation; Fear; Pain
Ascription-achievement, pattern variable: 77, 82, 94, 117, 177, 207; and moral placing matrices, 347
Aspiration, level of, 462
Assimilation, 371
Authoritarian personality, 374, 376, 378
Autistic hostility, 371
Autistic motivation, 430
Attitudes, 358, 373, 380, 421, 423, 440, 453; and needs, 453, 463

Bales, R. F., 437
Barnard, Chester I., 494
Bateson, Gregory, 409
Becker, Howard, 423
Behavior, 8–16, 30. *See also* Action
Behavior space, 285, 296–299; and behaving self, 297; directions in, 332; identification in, 308–310; and introspection, 333; and need-push, 298; object in, 300, 307; operational definition of, 339–342; perception in, 296, 327, 339; region in, 299; repression in, 315; restructuring in, 301; self-ideal in, 312; symbolic substitution in, 317
Behaviorism, 454
Beliefs, means-end, 292, 307, 338; and values, 432
Belief-value matrix, 285, 290–296; and attitudes, 358; categorizations in, 290, 307, 311; changes in, 301; identification in, 310; introspection in, 330, 333; means-end beliefs, 292, 307, 338; modal for culture and individual, 294–295, 354; modifications in, 357; operational definition of, 337–339; and perception, 327; and personality integration, 352; placing, 343; repression and, 315, 353; self-ideal

HARPER TORCHBOOKS / The University Library

John R. Alden	THE AMERICAN REVOLUTION: 1775–1783. Illustrated. TB/3011
Ray A. Billington	THE FAR WESTERN FRONTIER: 1830–1860. Illustrated. TB/3012
J. Bronowski & Bruce Mazlish	THE WESTERN INTELLECTUAL TRADITION: From Leonardo to Hegel TB/3001
Edward P. Cheyney	THE DAWN OF A NEW ERA: 1250–1453. Illustrated. TB/3002
Carl J. Friedrich	THE AGE OF THE BAROQUE: 1610–1660. Illustrated. TB/3004
Myron P. Gilmore	THE WORLD OF HUMANISM: 1453–1517. Illustrated. TB/3003
Lawrence Henry Gipson	THE COMING OF THE [AMERICAN] REVOLUTION: 1763–1775. Illustrated. TB/3007
Wallace Notestein	THE ENGLISH PEOPLE ON THE EVE OF COLONIZATION: 1603–1630. Illustrated. TB/3006
Joseph A. Schumpeter	CAPITALISM, SOCIALISM AND DEMOCRACY. Third Edition. TB/3008
Frederick L. Nussbaum	THE TRIUMPH OF SCIENCE AND REASON: 1660–1685. Illustrated. TB/3009
Louis B. Wright	THE CULTURAL LIFE OF THE AMERICAN COLONIES: 1607–1763. Illustrated. TB/3005
Morton Dauwen Zabel, Ed.	LITERARY OPINION IN AMERICA. Third Edition, revised. Vol. I, TB/3013; Vol. II, TB/3014

HARPER TORCHBOOKS / The Academy Library

James Baird	ISHMAEL: The Art of Melville in the Contexts of Primitivism TB/1023
Herschel Baker	THE IMAGE OF MAN: A Study of the Idea of Human Dignity in Classical Antiquity, the Middle Ages, and the Renaissance TB/1047
Jacques Barzun	THE HOUSE OF INTELLECT TB/1051
W. J. Bate	FROM CLASSIC TO ROMANTIC: Premises of Taste in Eighteenth Century England TB/1036
Max Beloff	THE AGE OF ABSOLUTISM, 1660–1815 TB/1062
Jeremy Bentham	THE HANDBOOK OF POLITICAL FALLACIES. Intro. by Crane Brinton TB/1069
Henri Bergson	TIME AND FREE WILL: The Immediate Data of Consciousness TB/1021
H. J. Blackham	SIX EXISTENTIALIST THINKERS: Kierkegaard, Jaspers, Nietzsche, Marcel, Heidegger, Sartre TB/1002
Crane Brinton	ENGLISH POLITICAL THOUGHT IN THE NINETEENTH CENTURY TB/1071
Walter Bromberg	THE MIND OF MAN: A History of Psychotherapy and Psychoanalysis TB/1003
Abraham Cahan	THE RISE OF DAVID LEVINSKY. A novel. Intro. by John Higham TB/1028
Helen Cam	ENGLAND BEFORE ELIZABETH TB/1026
Joseph Charles	THE ORIGINS OF THE AMERICAN PARTY SYSTEM TB/1049
Thomas C. Cochran	THE AMERICAN BUSINESS SYSTEM: A Historical Perspective, 1900–1955 TB/1080
Thomas C. Cochran & William Miller	THE AGE OF ENTERPRISE: A Social History of Industrial America TB/1054
Norman Cohn	THE PURSUIT OF THE MILLENNIUM: Revolutionary Messianism in Medieval and Reformation Europe and its Bearing on Modern Totalitarian Movements TB/1037
G. G. Coulton	MEDIEVAL VILLAGE, MANOR, AND MONASTERY TB/1022
Wilfrid Desan	THE TRAGIC FINALE: The Philosophy of Jean-Paul Sartre TB/1030
Wilhelm Dilthey	PATTERN AND MEANING IN HISTORY: Thoughts on History and Society. Edited with Introduction by H. P. Rickman TB/1075
St. Clair Drake and Horace R. Cayton	BLACK METROPOLIS: A Study of Negro Life in a Northern City. Introduction by Richard Wright. Intro. to Torchbook edition by Everett C. Hughes. Revised and enlarged edition. Vol. I, TB/1086; Vol. II, TB/1087
Peter F. Drucker	THE NEW SOCIETY: The Anatomy of Industrial Order TB/1082
Cora Du Bois	THE PEOPLE OF ALOR: A Social-Psychological Study of an East Indian Island. Vol. I, illustrated, TB/1042; Vol. II, TB/1043
W. A. Dunning	RECONSTRUCTION, POLITICAL AND ECONOMIC: 1865–1877 TB/1073
George Eliot	DANIEL DERONDA. A novel. Introduction by F. R. Leavis TB/1039
W. K. Ferguson, et al.	THE RENAISSANCE: Six Essays by Wallace K. Ferguson, Robert S. Lopez, George Sarton, Roland H. Bainton, Leicester Bradner, Erwin Panofsky TB/1084
John N. Figgis	POLITICAL THOUGHT FROM GERSON TO GROTIUS: 1414–1625: Seven Studies. Introduction by Garrett Mattingly TB/1032
Editors of Fortune	AMERICA IN THE SIXTIES: The Economy and the Society. TB/1015
F. L. Ganshof	FEUDALISM TB/1058
G. P. Gooch	ENGLISH DEMOCRATIC IDEAS IN THE SEVENTEENTH CENTURY TB/1006
Albert Goodwin	THE FRENCH REVOLUTION TB/1064
Francis J. Grund	ARISTOCRACY IN AMERICA: A Study of Jacksonian Democracy. Introduction by George E. Probst TB/1001
W. K. C. Guthrie	THE GREEK PHILOSOPHERS: From Thales to Aristotle TB/1008
Marcus Lee Hansen	THE ATLANTIC MIGRATION: 1607–1860. Intro. by Oscar Handlin TB/1052
Alfred Harbage	AS THEY LIKED IT: A Study of Shakespeare's Moral Artistry TB/1035

John Higham, *Ed.*	THE RECONSTRUCTION OF AMERICAN HISTORY TB/1068
J. M. Hussey	THE BYZANTINE WORLD TB/1057
Dan N. Jacobs, *Ed.*	THE NEW COMMUNIST MANIFESTO *and Related Documents* TB/1078
Henry James	THE PRINCESS CASAMASSIMA. A novel. Intro. by Clinton Oliver TB/1005
Henry James	RODERICK HUDSON. A novel. Introduction by Leon Edel TB/1016
Henry James	THE TRAGIC MUSE. A novel. Introduction by Leon Edel TB/1017
William James	PSYCHOLOGY: *The Briefer Course.* Ed. with Intro. by G. Allport TB/1034
Arnold Kettle	AN INTRODUCTION TO THE ENGLISH NOVEL. *Vol. I, Defoe to George Eliot,* TB/1011; *Vol. II, Henry James to the Present,* TB/1012
Hans Kohn, *Ed.*	THE MIND OF MODERN RUSSIA: *Historical and Political Thought of Russia's Great Age* TB/1065
Samuel Noah Kramer	SUMERIAN MYTHOLOGY: *A Study of Spiritual and Literary Achievement in the Third Millennium B.C.* Illustrated TB/1055
Paul Oskar Kristeller	RENAISSANCE THOUGHT: *The Classic, Scholastic, and Humanist Strains* TB/1048
L. S. B. Leakey	ADAM'S ANCESTORS: *The Evolution of Man and His Culture.* TB/1019
Bernard Lewis	THE ARABS IN HISTORY TB/1029
Ferdinand Lot	THE END OF THE ANCIENT WORLD AND THE BEGINNINGS OF THE MIDDLE AGES. Introduction by Glanville Downey TB/1044
Arthur O. Lovejoy	THE GREAT CHAIN OF BEING: *A Study of the History of an Idea* TB/1009
Robert Lowie	PRIMITIVE SOCIETY. Introduction by Fred Eggan TB/1058
Niccolo Machiavelli	HISTORY OF FLORENCE AND OF THE AFFAIRS OF ITALY: *From Earliest Times to Death of Lorenzo the Magnificent.* Intro. by Felix Gilbert TB/1027
Paul Mantoux	THE INDUSTRIAL REVOLUTION IN THE EIGHTEENTH CENTURY. Preface by T. S. Ashton. Second Edition, revised TB/1079
J. P. Mayer	ALEXIS DE TOCQUEVILLE: *A Biographical Study in Political Science* TB/1014
John Stuart Mill	ON BENTHAM AND COLERIDGE. Introduction by F. R. Leavis TB/1070
William Miller, *Ed.*	MEN IN BUSINESS: *Essays on the Historical Role of the Entrepreneur* TB/1081
John B. Morrall	POLITICAL THOUGHT IN MEDIEVAL TIMES TB/1076
J. E. Neale	THE AGE OF CATHERINE DE MEDICI TB/1085
John U. Nef	CULTURAL FOUNDATIONS OF INDUSTRIAL CIVILIZATION TB/1024
Jose Ortega y Gasset	THE MODERN THEME. Introduction by Jose Ferrater Mora TB/1038
Erwin Panofsky	STUDIES IN ICONOLOGY: *Humanistic Themes in the Art of the Renaissance* TB/1077
J. H. Parry	THE ESTABLISHMENT OF THE EUROPEAN HEGEMONY: 1415-1715: *Trade and Exploration in the Age of the Renaissance* TB/1045
Talcott Parsons & Edward A. Shils, *Eds.*	TOWARD A GENERAL THEORY OF ACTION: *Theoretical Foundations for the Social Sciences* TB/1083
Robert Payne	HUBRIS: *A Study of Pride.* Foreword by Herbert Read TB/1031
Samuel Pepys	THE DIARY OF SAMUEL PEPYS: Selections edited by O. F. Morshead; Illustrated by Ernest Shepard TB/1007
Paul E. Pfuetze	SELF, SOCIETY, EXISTENCE: *Human Nature and Dialogue in the Thought of George Herbert Mead and Martin Buber* TB/1059
R. W. Postgate, *Ed.*	REVOLUTION FROM 1789 to 1906: *Selected Documents* TB/1063
George E. Probst, *Ed.*	THE HAPPY REPUBLIC: *A Reader in Tocqueville's America* TB/1060
Priscilla Robertson	REVOLUTIONS OF 1848: *A Social History* TB/1025
Ferdinand Schevill	THE MEDICI. Illustrated TB/1010
Bruno Snell	THE DISCOVERY OF THE MIND: *Greek Origins of European Thought* TB/1018
C. P. Snow	TIME OF HOPE. A novel TB/1040
Perrin Stryker	THE CHARACTER OF THE EXECUTIVE: *11 Studies in Managerial Qualities* TB/1041
N. N. Sukhanov	THE RUSSIAN REVOLUTION, 1917: *Eyewitness Account.* Edited and translated by Joel Carmichael. *Vol. I,* TB/1066; *Vol. II,* TB/1067
Percy Sykes	A HISTORY OF EXPLORATION. Introduction by John K. Wright TB/1046
Twelve Southerners	I'LL TAKE MY STAND. Introduction by Louis D. Rubin, Jr.; Biographical Essays by Virginia Rock. TB/1072
A. F. Tyler	FREEDOM'S FERMENT: *Phases of American Social History from the Revolution to the Outbreak of the Civil War* TB/1074
Dorothy Van Ghent	THE ENGLISH NOVEL: *Form and Function* TB/1050
J. M. Wallace-Hadrill	THE BARBARIAN WEST: *The Early Middle Ages,* A.D. 400-1000 TB/1061
W. H. Walsh	PHILOSOPHY OF HISTORY: *An Introduction* TB/1020
W. Lloyd Warner	SOCIAL CLASS IN AMERICA: *The Evaluation of Status* TB/1013
Alfred N. Whitehead	PROCESS AND REALITY: *An Essay in Cosmology* TB/1033
Louis B. Wright	CULTURE ON THE MOVING FRONTIER TB/1053

HARPER TORCHBOOKS / The Bollingen Library

Rachel Bespaloff	ON THE ILIAD. Introduction by Hermann Broch TB/2006
Joseph Campbell, *Ed.*	PAGAN AND CHRISTIAN MYSTERIES: *Papers from the Eranos Yearbooks.* Illustrated TB/2013

Elliott Coleman, *Ed.*	LECTURES IN CRITICISM: *By R. P. Blackmur, B. Croce, Henri Peyre, John Crowe Ransom, Herbert Read, and Allen Tate* TB/2003
C. G. Jung	PSYCHOLOGICAL REFLECTIONS. Edited by Jolande Jacobi TB/2001
C. G. Jung	SYMBOLS OF TRANSFORMATION: *An Analysis of the Prelude to a Case of Schizophrenia.* Illustrated. *Vol. I,* TB/2009; *Vol. II,* TB/2010
C. G. Jung & Carl Kerényi	ESSAYS ON A SCIENCE OF MYTHOLOGY: *The Myth of the Divine Child and the Divine Maiden.* Illustrated TB/2014
Erich Neumann	AMOR AND PSYCHE: *The Psychic Development of the Feminine: A Commentary on the Tale by Apuleius* TB/2012
Erich Neumann	THE ORIGINS AND HISTORY OF CONSCIOUSNESS. *Vol. I,* illustrated, TB/2007; *Vol. II,* TB/2008
St.-John Perse	SEAMARKS. Translated by Wallace Fowlie TB/2002
A. Piankoff	THE SHRINES OF TUT-ANKH-AMON. Edited by N. Rambova. Illustrated TB/2011
Jean Seznec	THE SURVIVAL OF THE PAGAN GODS: *The Mythological Tradition and Its Place in Renaissance Humanism and Art.* Illustrated TB/2004
Heinrich Zimmer	MYTHS AND SYMBOLS IN INDIAN ART AND CIVILIZATION. Illustrated TB/2005

HARPER TORCHBOOKS / The Cloister Library

W. F. Albright	THE BIBLICAL PERIOD FROM ABRAHAM TO EZRA TB/102
Tor Andrae	MOHAMMED: *The Man and His Faith* TB/62
Augustine/Przywara	AN AUGUSTINE SYNTHESIS TB/35
C. K. Barrett, *Ed.*	THE NEW TESTAMENT BACKGROUND: *Selected Documents* TB/86
Karl Barth	CHURCH DOGMATICS: *A Selection.* Edited by G. W. Bromiley, with Introduction by H. Gollwitzer TB/95
Karl Barth	DOGMATICS IN OUTLINE TB/56
Karl Barth	THE WORD OF GOD AND THE WORD OF MAN TB/13
Nicolas Berdyaev	THE BEGINNING AND THE END TB/14
Nicolas Berdyaev	THE DESTINY OF MAN TB/61
Anton T. Boisen	THE EXPLORATION OF THE INNER WORLD: *A Study of Mental Disorder and Religious Experience* TB/87
J. H. Breasted	DEVELOPMENT OF RELIGION AND THOUGHT IN ANCIENT EGYPT. Intro. by John Wilson TB/57
Martin Buber	ECLIPSE OF GOD: *The Relation Between Religion and Philosophy* TB/12
Martin Buber	MOSES: *The Revelation and the Covenant* TB/27
Martin Buber	THE PROPHETIC FAITH TB/73
Martin Buber	TWO TYPES OF FAITH: *The Interpenetration of Judaism and Christianity* TB/75
Rudolf Bultmann	HISTORY AND ESCHATOLOGY: *The Presence of Eternity* TB/91
R. Bultmann, et al.	KERYGMA AND MYTH: *A Theological Debate.* Ed. by H. W. Bartsch TB/80
Rudolf Bultmann & K. Kundsin	FORM CRITICISM: *Two Essays on New Testament Research.* Translated & edited by Frederick C. Grant TB/96
Jacob Burckhardt	THE CIVILIZATION OF THE RENAISSANCE IN ITALY. Illustrated Edition. Introduction by B. Nelson and C. Trinkaus. *Vol. I,* TB/40; *Vol. II,* TB/41
Edward Conze	BUDDHISM: *Its Essence and Development.* Foreword by Arthur Waley TB/58
Frederick Copleston	MEDIEVAL PHILOSOPHY TB/70
F. M. Cornford	FROM RELIGION TO PHILOSOPHY: *The Origins of Western Speculation* TB/20
H. G. Creel	CONFUCIUS AND THE CHINESE WAY TB/63
Adolf Deissmann	PAUL: *A Study in Social and Religious History* TB/15
C. H. Dodd	THE AUTHORITY OF THE BIBLE TB/43
Johannes Eckhart	MEISTER ECKHART: A Modern Translation TB/8
Mircea Eliade	COSMOS AND HISTORY: *The Myth of the Eternal Return* TB/50
Mircea Eliade	THE SACRED AND THE PROFANE: *The Significance of Religious Myth, Symbolism, and Ritual Within Life and Culture* TB/81
Morton S. Enslin	CHRISTIAN BEGINNINGS TB/5
Morton S. Enslin	THE LITERATURE OF THE CHRISTIAN MOVEMENT TB/6
G. P. Fedotov	THE RUSSIAN RELIGIOUS MIND: *Kievan Christianity, the 10th to the 13th Centuries* TB/70
Ludwig Feuerbach	THE ESSENCE OF CHRISTIANITY. Introduction by Karl Barth; Foreword by H. Richard Niebuhr TB/11
Harry E. Fosdick	A GUIDE TO UNDERSTANDING THE BIBLE TB/2
Henri Frankfort	ANCIENT EGYPTIAN RELIGION: *An Interpretation.* Illustrated TB/77
Sigmund Freud	ON CREATIVITY AND THE UNCONSCIOUS: *Papers on the Psychology of Art, Literature, Love, Religion.* Edited by Benjamin Nelson TB/45
Maurice Friedman	MARTIN BUBER: *The Life of Dialogue* TB/64
Edward Gibbon	THE TRIUMPH OF CHRISTENDOM IN THE ROMAN EMPIRE. [J. B. Bury Edition, illus., Chapters 15–20 of "The Decline and Fall"] TB/46

HARPER TORCHBOOKS / The Science Library